Acknowledgments

Thanks to Susan Limongelli for her work on this edition, and to the staff and students of The Princeton Review.

Special thanks to Adam Robinson, who conceived of and perfected the Joe Bloggs approach to standardized tests, and many other techniques in this book.

Contents

...So Much More Online!

More Information on Careers...

- Learn more about career books from The Princeton Review—*Guide to Your Career, 145 Things to be When You Grow Up, 120 Jobs That Won't Chain You to Your Desk, Best Entry Level Jobs*

- Career quiz and career search

More Information on College...

- Learn about more books on college from The Princeton Review— *The Complete Book of Colleges, The Best 377 Colleges, The Best 300 Professors, The Best Value Colleges*

- Detailed profiles for hundreds of colleges help you find the school that is right for you

- Dozens of Top 20 ranking lists including Quality of Professors, Worst Campus Food, Most Beautiful Campus, Party Schools, Diverse Student Population, and tons more

- Useful information about the admissions process

- Helpful information about financial aid and scholarships

- College Search combines your academic and extracurricular history with your school preferences to find the perfect college for you

princetonreview.com

Look For This Icon Throughout The Book

 More Great Books

Part I
Orientation

Chapter 1
Getting Started

This chapter will provide you with a description of exactly what is tested by the GED. It will also explain how to use this book to maximum effect while preparing for the test.

Listed below in the gray box on this page are just a few of the famous and successful people who took the GED and earned their equivalency certificate.

Perhaps you have something in common with them. People take the GED for many reasons. Some people are home schooled. Some people leave high school before they graduate. Some people have careers that do not enable them to attend a traditional high school.

Whatever their reasoning, you have something in common with all of the people on the list below. All of them had the desire to succeed.

You have the desire to succeed, too. How do we know? Well, for one thing, you bought this book, which means you've decided to take the GED. And taking the GED is one step toward making your life work the way you want it to.

Passing the GED can be an important step in your life because it shows other people *and* yourself that you have the follow-through to decide on a course of action and make it happen. It can be the starting place for admission to college, a promotion, or a pay raise. So, congratulations! You've made an important decision.

This book is here to help you make it happen.

WHAT IS THE GED?

The General Educational Development test is actually five small tests that you can take in one day or over a series of days. Many people call the GED the high school equivalency test because when you pass the test, you earn a certificate that most colleges and employers recognize as the equivalent of a high school diploma.

The questions on the test are all in multiple-choice format, except for one short essay that is part of your Language Arts, Writing test and a few short-answer problems on the Math test. The questions are supposed to measure your knowledge of some of the subjects taught in high school. However, the GED test writers don't expect you to remember specific details. For example, you will *not* be asked what year Columbus came to America or which planet is farthest away from the sun. If the GED test writers want to ask about Columbus, they will first provide you with a short reading passage about him, and then they will ask questions based on that passage. If the GED test writers want to ask about the planets, they will first give you a diagram of the solar system and then ask you questions based on that diagram.

That's a Lot of People!
In 2009, more than 780,000 candidates took some portion of the GED test battery.
(Source: American Council on Education [ACE])

Famous People Who Took the GED and Earned their Equivalency Certificate

Wally Amos
Walter Anderson
Augusten Burroughs
Senator Ben Nighthorse Campbell
Michael Chang
Bill Cosby
Eminem
Governor Jim Florio
Jerry Garcia
Michael J. Fox
Paris Hilton
D. L. Hughley
Bishop J. D. Jakes
Peter Jennings
Avril Lavigne
Fran Lebowitz
Governor Ruth Ann Minner
Danica Patrick
Mary Lou Retton
Chris Rock
Jessica Simpson
Britney Spears
Hilary Swank
Christian Slater
Dave Thomas
Mark Wahlberg
Tammy Wynette

If You Don't Understand Something

Don't worry if there is a word, phrase, or topic you don't immediately understand in this book. For example, in the next heading below, we mention "clauses" and "phrases." These terms, along with every term you need to know to pass the GED, will be explained very carefully in the chapters ahead.

The Five GED Tests

1. Language Arts, Writing

- Part One: *50 multiple-choice questions, 75 minutes*
- Part Two: *one essay, 45 minutes*

In the multiple-choice section of the test, each question will consist of a sentence. Most of the sentences will have something wrong with them, and you must choose the answer choice that fixes the sentence. The errors you'll have to spot include the following mistakes:

Sentence Structure (use of clauses and phrases)	30%
Usage (grammar)	30%
Mechanics (spelling, punctuation, and capitalization)	25%
Organization	15%

In Part Two, you'll be asked to write a short essay about a particular topic, such as "Crime never pays. Do you agree or disagree?"

2. Social Studies

- *50 multiple-choice questions, 70 minutes*

You will find a mixture of very short passages followed by a single question and longer passages followed by three or four questions. Sixty percent of the questions will be based on graphic materials—charts, diagrams, graphs, and cartoons. No outside knowledge is tested. The answer to each of the questions will be contained in the passage or diagram provided. The passages will be about these areas of social studies:

National History	25%
Government and Civics	25%
World History	15%
Economics	20%
Geography	15%

GED Spells \$\$\$!
More than 95 percent of employers in the United States consider GED graduates equivalent to traditional high school graduates in regard to hiring, salary, and opportunity.
(Source: ACE)

3. Science

- *50 multiple-choice questions, 80 minutes*

You will find a mixture of short passages followed by a single question and longer passages followed by up to five questions. About one-half of the questions will be based on charts and other graphic materials. The answers to the questions are almost always supplied in the passages or graphic materials. You need only a *general knowledge* of scientific principles. The questions will be about these general areas of science:

Life Science	45%
Physics and Chemistry	35%
Earth and Space	20%

4. Language Arts, Reading

- *40 multiple-choice questions, 65 minutes*

In this section, you will be given three fiction passages, each from a different time period. You will also see one excerpt from a play, one poem, and two of the following: a review of a performance, an article about popular culture, or a business-related topic. After each, you will be asked questions designed to test your reading comprehension and your ability to analyze and apply what you've just read. The passages will be divided into the following sections:

Literary	80%
(fiction, play, poem)	
Nonfiction	20%
(review, workplace document, popular culture)	

5. Mathematics

- *50 questions (80% multiple-choice, 20% short answer), 90 minutes*

The Math test comes in two parts, each with 25 questions. In the first half, you will be allowed to use a calculator. In the second half, you will not. The emphasis of both parts is on arithmetic problems you may be called on to do in your daily routine at home or at work.

Many of these will be word problems. About one-half of the questions will be based on diagrams or charts. Most of the questions will be multiple choice, but approximately ten questions will be short answer. The questions will be about these general areas of math:

Number Operations/Number Sense	20%–30%
Measurement/Geometry	20%–30%
Data Analysis/Probability/Statistics	20%–30%
Algebra/Functions/Patterns	20%–30%

Where Does the GED Come From?

The GED is written by a nonprofit company in Washington, D.C. called the American Council on Education (ACE). Unlike most testing companies that write a lot of different kinds of tests, ACE produces only one test. The GED was created during World War II. In 2005 alone, more than 650,000 people took the GED. Of those who took the test, about 62 percent passed.

What Does It Look Like?

If you want to see what the pages of a real GED look like, turn to the back of this book, where you will find two Princeton Review practice GED exams. These look like the real thing, down to the same typeface and pagination. Each section of the real GED comes in a separate booklet, and you are handed one booklet at a time.

How Tough Is the GED?

In some ways, passing the GED is harder than graduating high school. Every year, the people who write the GED try it out on a representative sample of graduating high school seniors across the country. About 30 percent of these high school seniors—and remember, these are people who are just about to get their high school diplomas—*fail* the GED. They get their diplomas anyway, which doesn't seem fair, but that's life. To pass your GED, you're going to need to be more on the ball than a lot of high school graduates.

Of course, in other ways, the GED is a lot easier than finishing high school. After all, the test in its entirety takes only seven hours and five minutes. It takes years to finish high school.

What Is a Passing Grade?

To pass the GED, you need to answer only about half of the questions on each of the five tests correctly. There are no points deducted for wrong answers. In 2009, 69 percent of test takers who completed the GED passed the exam.

How Is the GED Scored?

Each of the five GED tests is scored from 200 to 800. To pass the GED, you must get a score of at least 410 on each of the five tests, with an average score of at least 450. Individual states can decide to require a higher score, but at this point, no state has chosen to do this. To get the latest information on scoring requirements, visit the ACE website at **www.acenet.edu**.

Is There Any Reason to Get Better Than a Passing Grade on the GED?

Not really. Whether you get a perfect score or a barely passing score, you pass just the same. There are a few states and colleges that award scholarships for people with very high GED scores. In general, you should plan on studying hard enough to pass the GED, but there is no real reason to keep studying until you can get *every* question correct.

Do You Have to Take the Test All at Once?

Top Three Reasons for Taking the GED
(1) To become better educated (30%)
(2) To feel better about oneself (25%)
(3) To get a better job (15%)
(Source: New Brunswick poll of test takers)

Each state has its own rules about this. Some states require you to take the entire set of tests in one day. Other states are more flexible. In some states, you can take the individual tests one at a time, as you feel you're ready for them. In other states, you have to take the GED in its entirety over a two-day period. To find out the rules in your state, consult the list of state agencies' found on the official GED website at www.acenet.edu.

What Happens If You Pass Some of the Sections But Not Others?

In most states, you need to retake *only* the sections you didn't pass the first time. For example, if you passed Language Arts, Reading; Social Studies; and Language Arts, Writing, but didn't pass Mathematics and Science, you would have to take only the Math and Science tests over again. Some states encourage people to retake the entire test because only your best scores are kept. When you retake the test, you will be given a different version of it, with completely different questions.

How to Prepare for the GED

The review and test-taking skills we're going to show you in this book should help you ace the GED, but just reading this book is not enough. You have to practice actually taking the test.

Why? There are two reasons. First, you'll find that practice will increase your stamina, improve your test-taking skills, and cement the new knowledge you've acquired. Second, unless you take a practice test and score yourself, you won't know when you're ready to take the GED.

The Princeton Review Practice Exams

There are two practice exams located at the back of this book; each test contains approximately half of the questions that you'll see on the GED. We've also provided an answer sheet for you to use when taking the tests. After you've completed a test, you can use our scoring guides to find out where you stand in each of the categories.

We recommend that you take one of the practice tests now, before you begin studying. After all, it's possible that you're already ready. If you aren't (and most people find that they're not), the practice test will give you a pretty good idea of which areas you'll need to work on. Perhaps your reading skills are already top-notch, but your math needs real work, or vice versa.

After you've gone through the book, you'll want to take our second practice test to see if your scores are now high enough to pass.

In Fact, You May Want to Practice with More Than Just Two Tests

ACE, the company that writes the GED, puts out several half-length practice tests of their own. They are excellent, and we recommend that you try to get at least one. You can order official GED practice tests by calling 800-626-9433 (800 62 MY GED) or by going online to www.acenet.edu.

More Great Books
If you're planning to take the GED, practice is critical. The Princeton Review's *5 GED Practice Tests* gives you five full-length practice tests with detailed explanations to every question.

Is English the Only Language in Which the GED Is Given?
No. There are Spanish- and French-language versions of the GED. The English-language version of the test is also available on cassette, in a large-print edition, and in braille.
For more information, call (800) 62 MY GED.

How This Book Is Organized

In the chapters that follow, you will get a step-by-step introduction to the GED. We've devoted an entire section of this book to each of the individual GED tests. In these sections, you'll find a complete review of the skills necessary for that particular test as well as specific test-taking strategies.

However, there are some test-taking techniques that are so universal and so vital to every single section of the GED that we're going to begin with them. In Chapter 2, we'll give you some tips for the day you actually take the exam. In Chapter 3, we'll discuss guessing strategies and POE (Process of Elimination) which can quickly add points to your score. In Chapter 4, we'll show you how to read charts and graphs (which come up on three of the five tests). In Chapter 5, we'll talk about reading comprehension (which is important on all five tests).

What Is The Princeton Review?

How many college students received a GED instead of a high school diploma?
It's estimated that one out of every 20 college students received a GED.
(Source: Examtoolkits)

The Princeton Review is a test-preparation company based in New York City. It has offices in more than 50 cities across the United States and many branches in foreign countries. The Princeton Review's test-taking techniques and review strategies are unique and powerful. We developed them after studying all the real GED tests we could get our hands on.

A FINAL THOUGHT BEFORE YOU BEGIN

You may not have been in school for a while, and your study skills may be a little rusty, but don't get discouraged if you have trouble catching on to a rule of grammar or a math concept right away. All it takes to pass the GED is determination and some studying.

Chapter 2
Taking the GED

In this chapter, we'll talk about how to register for the GED and what to do on the day of the test.

The best way to prepare for a test is to know exactly what is on it. This book will provide you with just that information. We've taken each subject area, each question type, and each skill necessary for the GED and broken them down into easy-to-absorb segments, complete with drills for practice. After you've taken and scored your first practice test, work out a schedule for yourself based on how much you need to improve your score and in how many areas. Doing a little studying each day is much better than trying to cram it all into one week. Set reasonable goals for yourself and try to stick to them, but if work or other responsibilities get in the way, don't beat yourself up. Big things take time.

Registering for the GED

Need GED Information? Call 800 62 MY GED.

After you've gone through this book and gotten the score you need on one of our practice tests, it will be time to register to take the GED. If you're studying on your own, the best ways to register are to call the GED information number for your state and/or visit the website www.acenet.edu. These numbers are listed at the end of this chapter. You'll then be mailed an application packet and a schedule of test times. If you've been taking a preparation course, your teacher may take care of registration for you, but be sure to check if this is the case. The tests are offered all the time, but in some of the larger states, it may take a while for you to get a test date. In New York, for example, the wait is normally four to six weeks. If the first date you are offered is not convenient, don't hesitate to ask for another. In most states, it now costs money to take the GED—the fee could be as little as $10, but in some states it can run as high as $80.

Before You Take the GED

There are lots of drills in this book, so you will have some idea of how you're doing as you work your way through the various sections. But it's also really important that you take the practice tests at the back of this book and that you take them seriously. Many of the tips for taking the *real* GED can be applied to the practice tests as well. Even though you may feel funny about treating a practice test so seriously, doing so will help you be ready when you get to the real test. You may, for example, feel a little foolish bringing a snack with you to your own desk, but it is important that you practice *everything* just the way you plan to do it on the day of the GED.

When you take the real test, it should feel completely familiar. After all, you'll have seen all the question types already. You'll know the subject matter. You'll even know what the typeface on the test looks like. If you've practiced ahead of time, there will be no surprises.

Thus, the practice tests are your chance to get comfortable with the format, to practice the test-taking techniques we'll show you, and to increase your stamina. The GED always takes more out of you than you expect.

Scratch Paper

Considering that you are paying as much as $80 in some states to take the GED, you'd think that they would let you write in the test booklet, but they don't. Your test booklet is going to be used by several other test takers in the weeks ahead, and the people at ACE want to make sure that you don't give these future test takers the benefit of your wisdom. You're going to have to learn how to use scratch paper.

You may be asking, "What's so hard about using scratch paper?" But in fact, it takes some getting used to. Even when you're completing the drills that you will find throughout this book, get in the habit of doing your scratch work on a separate piece of paper. This is particularly important when you get to the Math section, where there are a lot of calculations to do. We recommend that you put the paper directly underneath each problem as you do it so that you have to copy as little information from the problem on to your scratch paper as possible.

It's also a good idea to label the work you do on your scratch paper so that you can come back to it if you need to. Remember, you aren't necessarily going to be doing the problems in exactly the order in which they are presented. You may begin a problem, do some preliminary calculations, decide to skip it for awhile, and then come back later after you've done all the problems you found easy. When you *do* come back, it will be a shame if you can't find the place on your scratch paper where you have done all the preliminary calculations and have to start all over again.

The Night Before the Test

You may be tempted to stay up all night trying to memorize mathematical formulas or the spellings of difficult words, but we think the best preparation you can do the night before the test is relax and get a good night's sleep. If you've prepared over a period of weeks or months, that will be much more important than knowing how to spell a last-minute word (the odds of that one word appearing on the GED are pretty slim) or memorizing the formula for the area of a triangle (which is printed, along with all the other formulas, on the first page of the Math test).

Remember, if you don't pass one or another section of the test, you are usually allowed to take *just that section* over again. No single performance is going to be crucial, so give yourself a break. Your final score on the GED will be a combination of your best performances on each of the five tests.

On the Day of the Test

Different states run their tests at different hours. If you are taking the test in the morning, make sure that you get up early enough to have a good breakfast, particularly if you are going to be taking the entire test in one day. After several hours of concentration, it is very easy to "hit the wall" when your blood sugar drops. Bring a snack with you—anything you like. Most state test examiners give breaks in between the sections of the test. So if you're taking more than one section of the GED in one day, you will have a chance to eat your snack, go to the bathroom, and walk around to get your circulation moving.

Good Test Snacks
- Apples
- Energy bars
- Raisins

What to Bring with You

Bring your GED registration if you received it in the mail. If you didn't get one, don't panic. Just call your local GED office (the same phone number you called to get a registration packet) to make sure it is expecting you. Dress casually. You are going to be spending a number of hours sitting at a desk and you want to be comfortable. Make sure you have several sharpened No. 2 pencils for the multiple-choice sections of the test and a blue or black ballpoint pen for the essay section. You will need to show two pieces of identification before you are allowed to take the test. A driver's license, social security card, birth certificate, green card, or passport are all acceptable. If you don't have two pieces of identification, be sure to discuss this with your local examiner before the actual test date.

Once the Test Starts

Tune out the rest of the world. If you're taking the test with other people, make sure that you're seated far enough away that you won't be distracted by rustling papers or coughing.

If you've reached a state of GED concentration, nothing that happens will bother you. GED concentration comes from having studied hard and having practiced taking the test a number of times. If you've done these things, then nothing should stop you. The hum from the air conditioner, the cough of the woman sitting behind you, the marching band that is practicing down the hall—you won't even hear them. When one section ends, put it behind you, even if you are disappointed with how you think it went. Most people in the middle of taking a GED are not good judges of how they are doing. Besides, if it did go badly, the next section will cover an entirely different topic and be graded separately. Even if you didn't pass one section, you can still pass all the others and have to take only the one section over again.

A Word on Cheating

Please don't let anyone copy your answers while you are taking the GED. All standardized tests use sophisticated methods to find out if anyone has cheated. Some test companies even have computers that compare the answers of people who take the test in the same room. If your answers are too similar to those of the person sitting next to you, you *both* might find yourselves in serious trouble.

Your Test Results

You will get your results in the mail no more than eight weeks after you take the test. In some states, the results may be available as early as the next day, except for the essay section, which takes a bit longer to score. Your score report will include the individual scores you received on each of the five tests and an overall score. If you need copies of your score report sent to colleges or an employer, you must request these copies from your state GED office. Some states charge a small fee for this service.

How many people have passed their GED?
Since the test began in 1942, over 17 million people have passed their GED. In 2008 alone, 493,000 people earned a GED.
(Source: ACE)

Mismarking Your Answer Sheet

If you've prepared for the GED, your score will most likely be pretty much what you expect. However, if you receive a score on one of the tests that is much lower than you've scored on practice tests, it is possible that you filled out your answer sheet incorrectly.

This is easy to do. Let's say you do the first three questions and then get stuck for awhile on question four. You decide to skip it and go on to question five. By the time you've figured out the answer to question five, you've forgotten that you skipped question four. You look for the next blank on your answer sheet, and from then on, every response you write down is going to be in the wrong place.

If you really feel that this has happened, you can request that your exam be hand-scored. The test examiner will look over your answer sheet. If the examiner sees that by moving over all your responses by one place, they are all suddenly right, then he/she is allowed to change the score. Of course, it would be much better if this didn't come up. By using the answer sheets that we provide with our practice tests, you can get used to the process of writing down your answers on a separate sheet of paper and keeping track of the questions you skip.

Whom to Contact

For information on registering to take the GED and for classes in your area, call 800-626-9433 (800 62 MY GED). To reach the individual state programs directly, go online to **www.acenet.edu/resources/GED/center_locator.cfm** where you can type in your ZIP code to find the nearest testing centers and programs.

Chapter 3
Guessing and POE

Use the multiple-choice format of the GED to your advantage. Learn how to boost your score by making educated guesses with the Process of Elimination.

Imagine the following situation for a moment: A man is buying a lottery ticket. He gives the woman at the counter a dollar and the little card that he's supposed to have filled in with the numbers he picked, but the card is blank. The lady behind the counter says, "Hey, you forgot to fill in the numbers," but the man says to her, "Well, I wasn't sure which numbers were going to win, so I left it blank."

You'd think the guy was crazy, right?

Well then, what about this situation? A man is taking the GED. He comes to a multiple-choice question he isn't sure about, so he leaves it blank. A lot of people would probably say that this was perfectly intelligent behavior, but let's just think about this for a minute. The odds against winning the lottery are about a billion to one, but none of us would ever dream of paying a dollar and then not picking numbers. Yet on the GED, where the odds on multiple-choice questions are never worse than one in five, we routinely leave questions blank.

Guess who's really crazy.

You Gotta Be in It to Win It

Some tests have guessing penalties to discourage random guessing, but there is no guessing penalty on the GED; the folks who score the GED never deduct points for wrong answers. Therefore, when you take the GED, there is one thing that *must* happen before you hand in your answer sheet. It is more important than the rules of capitalization or the distance formula, and even more important than bringing a snack with you to the test center.

You Must Answer Every Single Question on the GED!

There are 230 multiple-choice questions on the GED, not counting the essay or the 10 math short-answer problems. If you went into the test room, filled out your name, and then went to sleep for seven hours and five minutes, the number of questions you got correct would be 0, of course. However, if—before you went to sleep—you picked answer choice (3) 230 times, guess how many questions you would have gotten right. About 46! Not bad for a refreshing nap. Of course, we aren't suggesting that you use random guessing as your overall strategy, but guessing on the problems you don't have time to get to or the problems you aren't sure about can add important points to your score.

Ah, but there's guessing and then there's *guessing*.

How to Score Higher on the GED

Try the following question:

In what year did Texas become a state?

What? You don't know? Well, then, you'd better guess at random. (By the way, the GED will never ask such factual questions without providing a reading passage in which you could find the answer. We're just using this question to make a point.)

If you really don't know the answer to a GED question, of course, you should always guess. But before you choose an answer at random, take a look at the question the way you would see it on the GED—in multiple-choice format:

1. In what year did Texas become a state?

    (1)   one million years B.C.E.
    (2)   one billion years B.C.E.
    (3)   one trillion years B.C.E.
    (4)   one zillion years B.C.E.
    (5)   1836

All of a sudden, this problem doesn't seem so hard anymore, does it? You may not have known the right answer, but you certainly knew enough to eliminate the wrong answers.

POE

The Process of Elimination (referred to as POE, for short) will enable you to make your guesses really count. Wrong answers are often easier to spot than right answers. Sometimes they just sound weird. Other times, they are logically impossible. While you will rarely be able to eliminate *all* the incorrect answer choices on a GED question, it is often possible to eliminate two or three. And each time you eliminate an answer choice, your odds of guessing correctly get better.

Let's try another example.

1. What year was the U.S. Bill of Rights ratified?

    (1)   2003
    (2)   1984
    (3)   1791
    (4)   1789
    (5)   1492

More Great Books
If you're planning to take the GED, practice is critical. Boost your prep with The Princeton Review's *GED Basics,* a step-by-step review of all five tests plus tons of practice questions.

Eliminate the Crazy Answers
Q: What's the capital of Malawi?
 (1) Paris
 (2) Dukhan
 (3) New York
 (4) London
 (5) Lilongwe

Answer on page 20

This time you could probably eliminate only three of the answer choices—choices (1) and (2), because the Bill of Rights was written a long time ago, and (5), because although it was written a long time ago, the Bill of Rights was written long after Columbus arrived in America. However, that means you're down to a fifty-fifty guess, which is much better than random guessing.

Test-Taking Tip #1
Use POE to get rid of crazy answers.

You Can Increase Your Score by Guessing

POE is a tremendously powerful tool. We will refer to it in every single chapter of this book, and you will find that there are specific strategies to make use of it on each of the different tests.

The reason it is so powerful is that the people who write the test like to include answer choices that they know test takers are likely to pick.

Eliminate the Crazy Answers
A: The capital of Malawi is Lilongwe, but you didn't need to know that to eliminate choices (1), (3), and (4).

Let It Go. It's Not Worth It.

No one question is that important. If you read a question and you aren't immediately sure how to do it, put a small mark on your answer sheet next to the number of the problem and move on.

You haven't skipped the problem for all time. You're just putting it at the back of the line. If you have time, you'll come back to it later. If you don't have time, you'll fill in an answer at random before you hand in your answer sheet. But most people find that there is enough time to come back to the problems they've skipped. They also often find that sometimes a second look is all they need to realize what they missed when first looking at the problem.

Test-Taking Tip #2
If you haven't figured out an answer in a minute, skip the problem and come back to it later.

The GED's Big Weakness

Every standardized test has a weakness, and the GED is no exception. The problem with writing a test that has to be exactly equivalent to last year's version, and the one from the year before, and the one from the year before *that*, is that they become pretty predictable.

Every year, the GED has to test the same material in pretty much the same way. By analyzing the different GEDs, we've discovered which parts of grammar are actually tested and which parts are ignored. We know just what kind of algebra questions they are going to ask you and what kinds they won't. By going through the review in this book, you too will know just what is going to be on the GED.

Taking Charge

So much in life is outside of our control, and sometimes it's hard not to let ourselves get pushed around. The process of taking the GED can sometimes feel like that. They tell you when to show up. They tell you where to sit. They tell you when to begin and when to stop. They tell you not to write in the test booklet. They even tell you the *number* of the pencil that you must bring with you.

In the face of all this control, it's easy to think that there is nothing you can do to take charge, but in fact *nothing could be farther from the truth*.

The way you take charge is by preparing ahead of time, by learning the strategies and techniques we're going to show you in the chapters ahead. Learn what is actually going to be on the test. Be aggressive, and use POE (remember, that's Process of Elimination) to its best advantage.

And the most important way you can take charge is by keeping your sense of perspective. It's only a test. The GED doesn't measure your entire worth as a human being. It measures a few easily acquired skills, and if you don't know enough of them when you take the test the first time, then you can take the test again.

Chapter 4
Crazy Graphics

Graphics are a big part of the GED. In this chapter, we'll
show you how to improve your graphics-reading skills.

If you flip through any of the practice tests for the GED, you'll notice that every test contains its share of diagrams, graphs, tables, charts, and maps. Graphic materials, according to the people who write the exam, comprise about 60 percent of the Social Studies and Science tests and "even more" of the Mathematics test.

Obviously, it would be a good idea to get familiar with reading these charts and graphs and learning what kinds of questions the test writers ask about them. This chapter will teach you everything you need to know.

Question Types

Social studies and science questions can be broken down into four categories:

> Comprehension questions
> Application questions
> Analysis questions
> Evaluation questions

The GED test writers break down the math questions that can refer to graphs and charts into four categories:

> Number Operations
> Measurement/Geometry
> Data Analysis/Statistics
> Algebra/Functions

We have included sample questions from each type in the exercises that follow, but don't feel you have to learn to recognize each question by its type during the actual GED test. Frankly, we don't think it's worth the effort.

Difficult or Just Plain Boring?

Although many people have problems with graphics-based questions, it's hard to tell sometimes whether test takers are having problems reading GED graphics because the graphics are difficult or because the subject matter is so incredibly boring.

No matter how hard you try, it's difficult to get excited about "Nutrients Available in a Hen's Egg" or "World Oil Reserves."

CRAZY GRAPHICS!

In this chapter, we're going to concentrate on pure graphics-reading skills. You'll learn how to read bar graphs, charts, maps, pie graphs, and coordinate line graphs. However, to eliminate the boredom factor, we're going to stay away from dry subjects like "the percentage of electricity generated from nuclear energy" or "the density of gases." Later, in the parts of this book devoted to the specifics of social studies, science, and math, you will get a chance to apply the general graphics-reading skills you'll learn here. But for now, welcome to the wonderful world of Crazy Graphics.

The Bar Graph

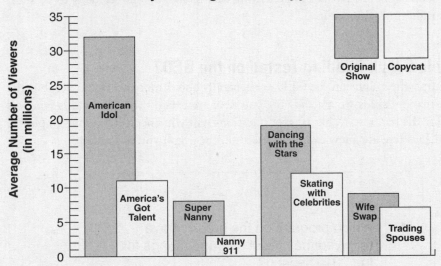

It's always tempting to jump straight into the graphic itself, but the first thing to look at in any graph or chart is the title. Force yourself to absorb what it is saying. In this case, the graph is comparing different reality TV programs in the year 2010. If you aren't quite sure what "Original vs. Copycat" means, let it go for a moment; we'll discover some clues in the graph itself.

The Vertical Axis and the Horizontal Axis

Look on the left side, along the vertical axis of the graph. What you see is a scale from 0 to 30 that measures how many millions of television viewers are watching these shows on average. Rising up from the horizontal axis across the bottom of the graph are bars that represent different reality TV programs. You probably recognize the names of many of these shows, but there's one more important detail to understand. You'll notice that some of the bars are gray while others are white.

Where You'll Find Graphs on the GED
- Social Studies test
- Science test
- Math test

The code at the top right of the graph explains that the gray bars represent "original" shows, while the white bars represent "copycat" shows. If you aren't sure exactly what that means, take a look at the first two bars: the first one, *American Idol* (the big hit for the Fox Network) is labeled an "original" show, while *America's Got Talent* (which was created by rival network NBC *after* it became clear how successful *American Idol* had become) is labeled a "copycat" show.

As you examine the graph, you'll probably notice that it is made up of *pairs* of bars: In each case, an original show is being compared to its copy.

Let's See How Your Graph Reading Is Progressing

Locate *Super Nanny* on the graph—it's the third bar over from the left. Now, draw your finger from the top of the *Super Nanny* bar over to the vertical axis on the left. How many viewers did *Super Nanny* have, on average? If you said 8 million, you're doing just fine. What about the copycat show *Nanny 911* that Fox rushed onto the air as soon as the media started predicting that *Super Nanny* was likely to be a hit? That's right: only 3 million.

How Is Graph Reading Tested on the GED?

Of course, the graphs on the GED are generally about more boring topics, but the graph-reading skills we are showing you here are exactly the same skills you will need for the real test. What type of questions will you encounter about graphs on the GED? Here are a few examples based on the graph you've just read.

---

1. Which program on the graph above received the lowest average ratings for the 2010 season?

    (1) *American Idol*
    (2) *Skating with Celebrities*
    (3) *Wife Swap*
    (4) *Nanny 911*
    (5) *Dancing with the Stars*

Here's How to Crack It

This type of question, which is considered a **comprehension** question, asks you to look up a piece of information on the graph. The length of each bar on this graph (as measured by the scale on the left) represents the number of viewers the program received, so in this problem, we are looking for the shortest bar. The correct answer is choice (4).

---

2. Which copycat program in the graph above got the highest ratings?

   (1)   *American Idol*
   (2)   *Survivor*
   (3)   *Skating with Celebrities*
   (4)   *Nanny 911*
   (5)   *Trading Spouses*

Here's How to Crack It

This **comprehension** question is a bit more difficult, because it isn't asking which program got the highest ratings, but which *copycat* program got the highest ratings. If you picked choice (1), you were reading a little too quickly. The correct answer here is the copycat program with the largest bar: *Skating with Celebrities*, which had 12 million viewers. This was choice (3).

You may have noticed that the program *Survivor* is not even on the graph, so you could have used POE to eliminate choice (2) right away.

3. How many fewer viewers watched *Skating with Celebrities* than watched *Dancing with the Stars*?

   (1)   19 million

   (2)   12 million

   (3)   7 million

   (4)   5 million

   (5)   2 million

Here's How to Crack It

This question asks you to figure out how many people watched *Dancing with the Stars* and how many people watched *Skating with Celebrities*, and figure out the difference between the two numbers. If you picked choice (1), then you figured out how many people watched *Dancing with the Stars* (19 million) and figured you must be done. If you picked choice (2), then you figured out how many people watched *Skating with Celebrities* (12 million) and figured you must be done. The correct answer was 19 million minus 12 million, which is 7 million. The correct answer to this **application** question was choice (3).

4. According to the graph above, which copycat TV program in 2010 got closest to achieving the same ratings as the original program it was based on?

   (1) *America's Got Talent*
   (2) *Nanny 911*
   (3) *Skating with Celebrities*
   (4) *Wife Swap*
   (5) *Trading Spouses*

Here's How to Crack It

This question asks you to figure out which of the copycat shows came closest to doing as well as the original show on which it was based. In other words, the test writers want you to look at the difference between each of the linked shows and pick the one with the least difference. This is considered an **analysis** question.

The difference between *American Idol* and *America's Got Talent* is huge—22 million viewers, so choice (1) can't be the right answer. The difference between *Super Nanny* and *Nanny 911* is much smaller: 5 million viewers. Let's hold on to choice (2) while we look at the other answers. The difference between *Dancing with the Stars* and *Skating with Celebrities* is 7 million viewers, so we can eliminate choice (3). You might have been tempted to pick choice (4) because the difference between *Wife Swap* and *Trading Spouses* is so small, but *Wife Swap* is not the copycat program; *Trading Spouses* is the copycat. The difference between them, 2 million viewers, is the smallest. Thus, *Trading Spouses* came the closest to achieving the same ratings as the original program it was based on, and the correct answer is choice (5).

5. Which of the statements below could best be supported by the graph?

(1) In 2010, copycat programs did better than the original programs they were based on.
(2) In 2010, copycat programs did not achieve the success of the original programs they were based on.
(3) In 2010, Americans watched less television than ever before.
(4) Reality programs are no longer as popular as dramas.
(5) In 2010, reality programs became more popular than dramas.

Here's How to Crack It

This type of question, called an **evaluation** question, appears only rarely on the GED. It asks you to choose a general statement that is *supported* by the graph. As you read through the possible answer choices, you should be on the lookout for an answer that comes pretty directly from the graph—not a statement that you happen to agree with, or a statement that goes further than the graph itself. For example, you might personally agree with choice (4) that reality programs are no longer as popular as dramas—but did you get that information from the graph? If not, then forget it. You might agree with (3) that Americans are watching less TV than they did before—but was that information found in the graph? Not a chance. Based on the graph, every single copycat program did worse than the original program it was based on. The correct answer here is choice (2).

The Chart

Comparison of Bottled Water and Tap Water			
	Bacterial contaminants (parts per million)	Mineral contaminants (parts per thousand)	Price in cents (per ounce)
Bottled Water	19	13	12
Tap Water	18	13	0

Just as you discovered with graphs, the first thing to look at in any chart is its title. In this case, the title says this chart will make a comparison. On the left side of the chart are the two things being compared: bottled water and tap water. Across the top of the chart are the three types of measurements that are going to be made: bacterial contaminants, mineral contaminants, and price. Now all that's left to do is see how the two kinds of water actually compare based on these measurements. Let's go to the questions.

1. Based on the information in the chart, which statement below is most accurate?

   (1) The lack of contaminants in the bottled water that was tested makes up for its additional cost.
   (2) The overall level of contaminants found in the bottled water that was tested is lower than it is in tap water.
   (3) Other dangerous contaminants in addition to bacterial and mineral contaminants can affect the price of water.
   (4) Bacterial contaminants are more dangerous than mineral contaminants.
   (5) The level of contaminants found in bottled water is almost the same as that found in tap water.

Here's How to Crack It

To answer this **analysis** question, we need to find out if the bottled water is actually better than the tap water. Of the bottled water and the tap water, which had the higher level of bacterial contaminants? If you said "bottled water, but only by a tiny fraction," you are doing just fine. Nineteen parts out of a million is not a lot. And of the two choices, bottled water or tap water, which had the higher levels of mineral contamination? That's right: they are exactly the same.

So let's look at the answer choices. Choice (1) says bottled water has *fewer* contaminants than tap water. Is that right? Nope, it actually contradicts the information in the chart. (And by the way, if you ever disagree with the information found in a GED chart—that is your right and privilege, but don't waste time choosing an answer that contradicts the chart's information—the test writers will just mark your answer "incorrect.") Choice (2) again says bottled water has *fewer* contaminants than tap water. That isn't actually true according to the information in the chart. Choice (3) says there are other types of contamination that aren't even mentioned here. While this might be true, it is outside the scope of the chart, and we're supposed to answer this question based on the information in the chart. Choice (4) says bacterial contaminants are more dangerous than mineral contaminants. This might be true, too, but it is not information we can get from the passage. Which leaves us with choice (5): the correct answer. According to the chart, bottled water and tap water have virtually identical levels of contaminants—and tap water is a lot cheaper.

2. Which professional would probably be most familiar with the information in the table above?

    (1) obstetrician
    (2) public health official
    (3) dentist
    (4) nuclear scientist
    (5) mental health official

Here's How to Crack It

It may not be clear to you right away which is the correct answer to this **application** question. But we bet you know some answers that are incorrect. Which choices can you eliminate? If you got rid of obstetrician (a doctor who looks after pregnant women), dentist, and nuclear scientist, you are doing very well indeed. And when you think about it, why would a mental health official be familiar with the amount of contaminants in water? The correct answer is a public health official, choice (2).

A More Complicated Chart

Talk Show Hosts and Household Liquids on the pH Scale

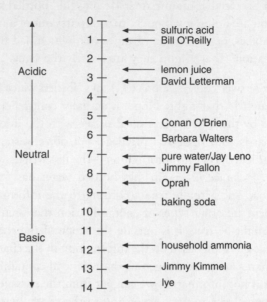

When an acid and a base are
mixed, they may neutralize each other

Chart Checklist
- Read the title.
- Study the details.
- Go for the questions you understand first.
- If there are two diagrams, concentrate on the *differences* between them.

As always, whenever you're confronted with any graphic material, you should start with the title. In this case, we are going to be looking at two different categories (talk show hosts and household liquids) as they appear on the pH scale. If you don't remember what the pH scale is, you are probably not alone. Don't panic. Maybe we can figure it out from the information in the chart. (By the way, the pH scale has appeared from time to time on the actual GED.)

You Don't Need to Know What Every Word Means Exactly

The pH scale, whatever that is, sits in the middle of the chart. On the left, you'll notice another line that tells us what the numbers on the scale mean: acidic, neutral, and basic. You may remember this from science classes in school, but if you don't, don't worry: We haven't looked at the whole chart yet. On the right side are various materials. The first is sulfuric acid. Well, that is certainly an acidic liquid. The next item is Bill O' Reilly—the crabby commentator from *Fox News* who is always complaining about something. He's pretty acidic, too, come to think of it.

Looking down at the bottom of the chart, we see lye, which is a basic liquid, and Jimmy Kimmel, who is pretty basic, too.

Apparently, the pH scale is a way to rank how acidic or basic something is.

Still Don't Understand the Chart? Don't Give Up—You May Be Able to Answer the Questions Anyway!

Often you will find that you can answer the questions even if you don't completely understand what is going on in the chart. After all, this *is* a multiple-choice test, so the correct answer will be always be right in front of you—all you have to do is find it. In addition, while some questions may ask you to analyze or apply information from the chart, other questions will simply ask you to find information from the chart. Let's look at some questions based on the chart on the previous page.

1.   What is the pH value for Bill O'Reilly?

   (1)   11
   (2)   8
   (3)   5
   (4)   3
   (5)   1

Here's How to Crack It

Who cares what a pH value is? You can answer this question without even knowing. In this **comprehension** question, all we have to do is look up Bill O'Reilly on the chart. What is his pH value? If you picked choice (5), you are doing just fine.

2.   Which talk show host is more basic than household ammonia?

   (1)   Jimmy Fallon
   (2)   Bill O'Reilly
   (3)   Jimmy Kimmel
   (4)   Oprah
   (5)   Jay Leno

Here's How to Crack It

Find household ammonia on the chart. Its pH value is between 11 and 12. Now that you've located the base liquid ammonia, you want to find a talk show host who is even more basic. The higher the baseness, the higher the pH value. Which talk show host has a higher pH value? The correct answer is choice (3), Jimmy Kimmel. This is considered a slightly more difficult **analysis** question.

3.   What is the pH value for Oprah?

    (1)   4
    (2)   5.5
    (3)   8.5
    (4)   11
    (5)   13

Here's How to Crack It

Like the first **comprehension** question, this is merely a matter of reading the chart. The correct answer is choice (3).

4.   Which talk show host would be the best substitute for lemon juice?

    (1)   David Letterman
    (2)   Conan O'Brien
    (3)   Oprah
    (4)   Jimmy Kimmel
    (5)   Barbara Walters

Here's How to Crack It

If you had just made tea and ran out of lemon, which talk show host should you squeeze into your cup? We need the host with the closest pH to lemon juice in order to answer this **application** question. Who is that? You guessed it: David Letterman, choice (1).

5. Which of the following substances could be expected to neutralize Bill O'Reilly?

(1) lemon juice
(2) sulfuric acid
(3) pure water
(4) Conan O'Brien
(5) baking soda

Here's How to Crack It

This is a somewhat tougher **application** question. Underneath the chart, the caption says that an acid can neutralize a base, and vice versa. To find the correct answer to this question, first we have to decide whether Bill O'Reilly is acidic or basic. According to the chart, he is acidic. Now, we need to find an answer choice that is basic enough to neutralize the acid. Only one of the five choices is a base: The correct answer is choice (5), baking soda.

The Map

It's All in the Details
GED map questions are usually based on small *details* of the map.

The United States Before the Earthquake Known As "The Big One"

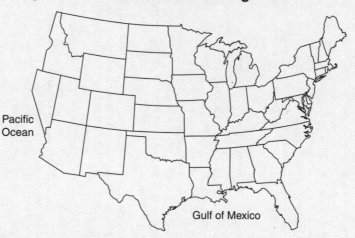

The United States After the Earthquake Known As "The Big One"

You may not have loved geography in school, but the geography on the GED is pretty easy stuff. You don't have to memorize the names of countries or know the names of rivers or large bodies of water. In fact, the maps themselves will almost always provide you with all the information you will need to answer the questions—provided you bring your common sense with you to the exam.

Always take a few moments to look over any map that appears on the GED, and pay special attention to the details. One map of Europe may show the borders of different countries. Another map of Europe may show industrial centers or population density. The GED questions will be based on the details of the maps.

An Ocean View in Idaho?

In this particular case, we have two maps of the United States, one before a hypothetical earthquake and one after. When the GED gives you two maps at the same time, the important thing is to concentrate on the differences between them. Examine the two maps carefully. What is missing on the second map? If you said "the names of all the states," you are right on target, but look further.

It turns out that a few other things are missing on the second map: among other things, the entire state of California, which has apparently fallen into the ocean.

Let's try some questions.

1. Which states will disappear completely after the earthquake known as "The Big One"?

   A. Washington
   B. Oregon
   C. California

   (1) A only
   (2) B only
   (3) C only
   (4) A and C only
   (5) A, B, and C

Here's How to Crack It

To tell which states are missing on the "after" map, we have to identify the states using the "before" map. A good place to start may be the states right above the Gulf of Mexico, since we can see their relative position on the two maps. Find the big state that's on the northwest corner of the Gulf of Mexico. That's Texas. Now identify all other states to the left of Texas. Is Washington still there? No, so cross off choices (2) and (3). Is Oregon still there? No, so cross off choice (4). Is California still there? No, so the answer must be choice (5). This is considered a reasonably difficult **analysis** question.

2. After "The Big One," which state will be the most northern state on the West Coast?

   (1) Florida
   (2) Washington
   (3) California
   (4) Idaho
   (5) New York

Here's How to Crack It

You've already identified the states on the "after" map, so this **analysis** question should be pretty easy. North is always at the top of any map. We want the West Coast of the United States, and west is always to the left. We can use POE to eliminate several answer choices right away—both Florida and New York are on the East Coast, so the answer couldn't be either choice (1) or choice (5). Washington *used* to be the most northern state on the West Coast, but it isn't there anymore, so the answer can't be choice (2). California isn't there anymore either, so the answer can't be choice (3). The correct answer to this question is choice (4).

3. Which state will have a new shape after the big earthquake?

   (1) Arizona
   (2) Nevada
   (3) California
   (4) Utah
   (5) Colorado

Here's How to Crack It

Look at the "after" map. Of the states on the West Coast that were affected by the earthquake, which has a new shape? Idaho looks the same. Utah looks the same. Arizona looks the same. Colorado looks the same. California is completely gone. The only state on the "after" map whose boundaries have changed is Nevada. The correct answer to this **analysis** question is choice (2).

4. According to the map of the United States after the earthquake, a construction company specializing in beachfront homes would be most likely to find new business in which of the following states?

   (1) California
   (2) New Mexico
   (3) Oklahoma
   (4) Arizona
   (5) Utah

Here's How to Crack It

In this **application** problem, you have to make a small leap of the imagination to realize that what the question is really asking is for you to identify a state that used to be inland but is now on the ocean. We can eliminate California because it is completely under water. New Mexico, Oklahoma, and Utah are still inland, just as before. Only Arizona is now located next to the ocean. The correct answer is choice (4).

The Pie Chart

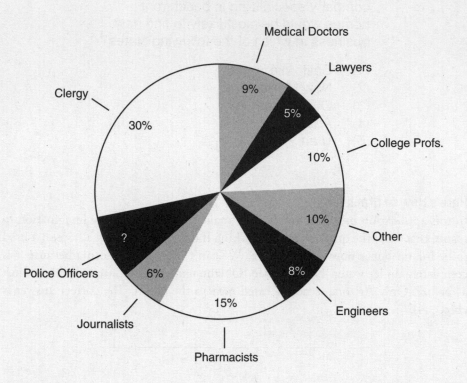

Most Honest Professions

The important thing to remember in a pie chart is that if you add together all the pieces of the pie, you should get a complete entity. Often the pieces of the pie are represented by fractions, in which case, the pieces of the pie should add up to one. Other times, the pieces of the pie are represented by percentages, in which case the pieces of the pie should add up to 100 percent.

In the case of the pie chart above, the pieces are represented by percentages. Let's look at some questions.

A pie chart must add up to 100 percent.

1. What percentage of the pie chart consists of pharmacists?

   (1)   6%
   (2)   7%
   (3)   15%
   (4)   19%
   (5)   28%

Here's How to Crack It

This is a simple **measurement** question. Find pharmacists on the pie chart. What percentage does it list? The correct answer is choice (3).

2. What percentage of people surveyed felt police officers were honest?

   (1)   7%
   (2)   15%
   (3)   25%
   (4)   34%
   (5)   52%

Here's How to Crack It

All the other categories on the pie chart have percentages listed inside them, but "police officers" does not. To find the answer, we have to do some addition. The sum of all the other categories plus the number we are looking for should add up to 100 percent.

Before we do this addition, however, let's get rid of any answer choices that don't make sense using POE. Just by looking at the chart, you can see that the police officers make up a small portion. How small? Well, look at the category right below the one we are interested in: "journalists," which is 6 percent of the entire pie. Obviously, "police officers" is not much bigger or smaller than that. Are there any answer choices that are obviously too big? Sure. Clearly, the answer can't be as large as 25 percent, 34 percent, or 52 percent. Cross off choices (3), (4), and (5).

Now, let's find the answer precisely:

$$
\begin{array}{r}
30\% \\
9\% \\
5\% \\
10\% \\
10\% \\
8\% \\
15\% \\
+\ 6\% \\
\hline
93\%
\end{array}
$$

So what percentage does "police officers" have to be to make the whole add up to 100 percent? The correct answer to this **number relationship** question is choice (1).

3. What percentage of people surveyed felt that car dealers were honest?

   (1)   10%
   (2)   12%
   (3)   20%
   (4)   22%
   (5)   Not enough information is given

Here's How to Crack It

When you first read this problem, you may have been tempted by answer choice (1). After all, "car dealers" is not one of the categories mentioned in the chart, so it may seem as if "car dealers" has to be the same thing as the category "other," and the answer should be 10 percent.

However, this **data analysis** question required you to think a little further. Was "car dealers" the only other profession that may be considered honest? What about nurses? What about elementary school teachers? What about…well you get the point. While "car dealers" is certainly *part* of the category "other," it is not necessarily the entire category. The answer to this question is choice (5), not enough information is given.

The Coordinate Graph

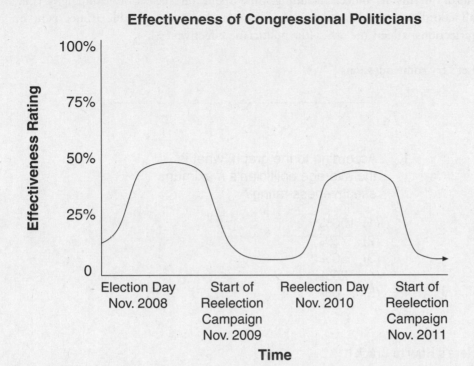

Effectiveness of Congressional Politicians

Like the graphs we saw earlier, a coordinate graph consists of a vertical axis and a horizontal axis, each of which represents a different variable. A coordinate graph illustrates how one variable affects another. For example, a coordinate graph may illustrate how a company's earnings are affected by the passage of time. Here are two examples:

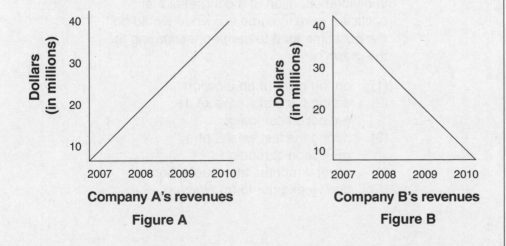

In figure A, you can see that company A's earnings are increasing over time. In figure B, you can see that company B's earnings are decreasing over time.

In the graph of the average politician, the vertical axis represents the politician's effectiveness, and the horizontal axis represents a time line of the politician's terms in office, including time spent on reelection campaigns. Like all coordinate graphs, this graph illustrates how one variable (time spent on reelections) affects the other (the politician's effectiveness).

Let's try some questions.

1. According to the graph, what is the average politician's maximum effectiveness rating?

    (1) 100%
    (2) 75%
    (3) 50%
    (4) 25%
    (5) 0%

Here's How to Crack It
This **comprehension** question asks you to read the graph and find the highest level that the average politician reaches. The correct answer is choice (3).

2. If a national crisis that required the undivided attention of a congressional politician were to come up, when would be the best time for it to happen, according to the graph?

    (1) on the night of an election
    (2) during the first weeks of a reelection campaign
    (3) during the last weeks of a reelection campaign
    (4) several months after reelection
    (5) one week prior to an election

Here's How to Crack It

It's important to remember that you are being asked to answer this question based on the information contained in the graph—not your outside knowledge of the subject. A politician would probably need all the effectiveness he or she could get during a crisis. Which answer choice describes a time, according to the graph, when the average politician has a relatively high effectiveness rating? If you picked choice (4) for this **analysis** question, you are right on the money.

○

Summary

○ Graphic materials make up about half of the Social Studies, Science, and Math tests. On the GED, you will find bar graphs, charts, maps, pie graphs, and coordinate line graphs.

○ Study the title of the chart or graph before studying its details.

○ Most line and bar graphs have a vertical and horizontal axis, each of which represents a different variable. A coordinate graph is an illustration of how one variable affects the other.

○ It is not necessary to understand every word or idea in a chart to get answers right. Look at the various parts of the chart as clues to a puzzle. Figure out as much of it as you can, and then attack the questions.

○ In a GED map, look for the details on which the map is concentrating. If there are two maps, concentrate on the differences between them.

○ A pie graph is a picture of a complete unit. If the pieces of the pie represent fractions, the entire pie must add up to one. If the pieces of the pie represent percentages, then the entire pie must add up to 100 percent.

○ Although we don't think it's worth trying to figure out which type of question you are answering *during* the GED, it is useful in preparing for the GED. The following are the main question types for social studies and science:

  • Some questions will ask you to look up a piece of information on the chart or graph. These **comprehension** questions are usually the easiest.

  • Other questions will ask you to compare two pieces of information on a chart or to apply a concept on a chart to another setting completely. These **application** questions are more difficult.

- Other questions will ask you to take the information in a chart or graph a step further and understand the reason *behind* that information. These **analysis** questions are generally difficult.
- A few questions will ask you to make predictions based on the graphic materials. These **evaluation** questions will never simply ask for your opinion.

Chapter 5
Crazy Reading

Reading comprehension is a big part of the GED. In this chapter, we'll show you how to improve your reading comprehension skills.

Many test takers have trouble with GED reading comprehension, but sometimes it's difficult to tell whether their problems are the result of incomprehension or just boredom. Both the social studies passages and science passages can be unbelievably dull. The passages in Language Arts, Reading are generally more fun, though even there some test takers find it difficult to relate to the cultures described in some of the passages.

In this chapter, we're going to use the same vocabulary, the same writing structures, the same transitions, and the same question types you will find on the GED, but we're going to stay away from the dreary subject matter so you can focus on our comprehension techniques. Later, in the Social Studies; Science; and Language Arts, Reading sections, you will learn to apply the skills you pick up in this chapter to the more prosaic passages chosen by the GED test writers. But for now, welcome to Crazy Reading.

A Dictionary and a Notebook

Have you ever noticed that people tend to use the same vocabulary over and over again when they speak? Most of us have a pretty small core of words that we use every day and a few big words for fancy occasions. It's kind of amazing how few words we need to get by. The average newspaper today is written so that it can be understood by someone with a vocabulary of only 1,000 words.

The GED test writers also have a core set of words that they use all the time, but their core set of words is different from ours. You are going to see these words throughout this book, in the sample questions we provide and in the practice tests at the back of the book. To do well on the reading comprehension sections of the GED, you are going to have to learn some of the GED's relatively small core vocabulary.

When we get to the sections on Social Studies; Science; and Language Arts, Reading, we'll give you some specialized vocabulary. However, if at any time during your review you see a word you don't know (in this book, in the official GED practice tests, in magazines, in newspapers, or anywhere else), get into the habit of looking it up in a dictionary and then writing down the word and the definition in a notebook.

For example, did you know the meaning of *prosaic*, a word we used in the second paragraph on this page? If not, make that the first word on your list. From time to time, as you study, you should quiz yourself on the words you've written down in your notebook.

Where You'll Find Reading Comprehension in the GED
- Social Studies test
- Science test
- Language Arts, Reading test

A Good Dictionary
The best kind of dictionary for GED preparation is small and portable. Take it with you everywhere. Or visit www.merriam-webster.com if you have web access.

Meaning from Context

At its most fundamental level, comprehension involves knowing the meaning of individual words, but what happens when we don't? If you were having a conversation with a friend and he or she used a word that you didn't know, what would you do?

Of course, one thing you could do is ask what the word means, but if your friend is in the middle of an interesting story, chances are you will probably do what most of us do: figure out the meaning of the word from the context of the sentence. Meaning from context is an extremely useful technique on the GED. Of course, in a perfect world, you would know the meaning of every word on the GED, but because that isn't very likely, it's good to have a backup plan.

Let's go back to the paragraph with the word *prosaic* in it (the second paragraph of this chapter). As you glance over the first and second paragraphs, ask yourself the following question:

How did the authors describe the GED science and social studies passages?

If you used words like *dull*, *boring*, or *uninteresting*, you are comprehending just fine—believe us, we know. (After all, in this case *we* were the authors, and we've certainly read enough GED passages to know what they're like.) So if the next sentence in the passage uses the word *prosaic* to refer to those *same* passages, what do you think *prosaic* means? You got it: dull, boring, and uninteresting.

Often, a hard vocabulary word will simply repeat something that has already been said in a much simpler way earlier in the passage. GED test writers tend to use synonyms to avoid repeating exactly the same word within a paragraph, which means that you can often figure out the meaning of a tough vocabulary word by looking at the context in which it is used.

Look at the following example:

1. When you compare the cognitive growth of people who play video games to the cognitive growth of people who don't, several observations can be made. Although mental growth seems to take place at identical rates, our studies indicate that people who play video games are much smarter and lead more fulfilling lives.

   —The National Organization for Video Gamers

More Great Books
The Princeton Review's *Essential GED* (flashcards) is chock-full of vocabulary and drills for Language Arts, Social Studies, Science, and Math.

You may not know initially what the word *cognitive* means. However, let's see if we can get it from the context. In this passage, each time *cognitive* was used, it was paired with the word *growth*. Was there any other word that was also paired with *growth*? Yes. In the second sentence, the author used the words *mental growth*. Could *cognitive* have something to do with *mental*? It seems like a good guess, in which case we can try using *mental growth* and *cognitive growth* interchangeably. To check this, read the rest of the paragraph. The passage goes on to say that people who play video games are much smarter than those who don't. This seems to back up our theory about the definition of cognitive. *Cognitive* in this case means the ability to understand or perceive.

As you read through this book and spot a word you don't know, take a moment before you look up the word to try to figure out its meaning from the context. Not only is this good practice for the real test, but it will also help you remember the word once you've looked it up.

Let's begin with the type of reading passage that contains the least amount of reading: the **classification** passage.

Classification Passages

A classification passage first defines five different categories in a sentence or two and then asks you to apply these categories to specific situations. For example, a passage may define five different kinds of government (perhaps including democracy and communism) and then describe a mythical country's government and ask you to classify it as one of the five types. To answer these questions, you are *applying* a classification to a new situation, so the GED test writers generally consider these questions to be **application** questions.

Classification passages can appear in the Social Studies test, the Science test, or both. When you spot one, take some time to read the classification types carefully. Try to figure out exactly how they differ from one another and how they're similar. If there are any vocabulary words you don't understand, see if you can get their meaning from the context. Then, once you've understood the categories, turn to the questions.

Read the following classification passage:

Questions 1 through 5 are based on the following information.

Five Types of Behavior That Are Very Common in Hollywood

(1) cannibalistic = describes an organism that eats others of its own species

(2) mimetic = describes an organism that acts or tries to look like another

(3) mutualistic = describes two or more organisms that live together for mutual benefit

(4) parasitic = describes an organism that lives in or on another, at whose expense it obtains nourishment and shelter

(5) saprophytic = describes an organism that lives on dead or decaying organic matter

Each of the following items describes a relationship that refers to one of the five categories defined above. For each item, choose the one category that best describes the relationship. Each of the categories above may be used more than once in the following set of items.

1.   Because the movie *Iron Man* was so successful, a sequel called *Iron Man 2* was made.

      This kind of behavior is called

      (1)   cannibalistic
      (2)   mimetic
      (3)   mutualistic
      (4)   parasitic
      (5)   saprophytic

Here's How to Crack It

If any of the words used in the passage gave you any trouble, first try to figure them out from the context of the rest of the passage, and then look them up and write them in your notebook. Of course, you don't have to bother looking up the categories themselves because the GED test writers will always define them for you. The passage is about different kinds of behavior in Hollywood.

Often it is easier to eliminate wrong answers than to find the correct answer. Let's use the Process of Elimination to narrow down our choices. You may have noticed that two of the categories are easy to think about together because they are both about death: cannibalistic and saprophytic. The situation in question 1 doesn't seem to concern death, but let's think about these two answers for just a moment to be sure. If the behavior were "cannibalistic," one *Iron Man* movie would in some way eat the other. That doesn't seem to be happening. Eliminate choice (1). If the behavior were saprophytic, one movie would be feeding off the dead flesh of the other. The only things dead in these movies are all the bad guys. Eliminate choice (5).

If the behavior were mimetic, one movie would be imitating the other. Wait a minute, that's *just* what's happening. A sequel generally blatantly rips off the first movie. This seems like it must be the right answer, but it always pays to look at all the possibilities.

Making a sequel doesn't seem to be mutualistic behavior exactly. Eliminate choice (3). Parasitic behavior implies that one movie is getting its nourishment or home from the other, which makes choice (4) seem *possible;* however, a parasitic relationship is at the expense of the organism that is doing the nourishing, and that doesn't seem to be the case here. Eliminate choice (4). The correct answer is choice (2).

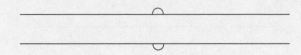

2. Angelina Jolie's personal manager gets 10% of all the money her client earns.

   This kind of behavior is called

   (1) cannibalistic
   (2) mimetic
   (3) mutualistic
   (4) parasitic
   (5) saprophytic

Here's How to Crack It

Which choices can we eliminate? Since no one is dead, we can rule out cannibalistic and saprophytic behavior. Is the manager imitating Jolie? No, so we can also eliminate mimetic behavior. The only possibilities left are choices (3) mutualistic and (4) parasitic. Because the manager is getting 10 percent of Jolie's salary, the manager *does* seem to fit the description of parasitic behavior: receiving nourishment at the expense of Jolie. The correct answer is choice (4).

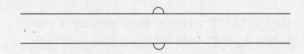

3. Universal and Disney agree not to compete to make the next George Clooney movie.

   This kind of behavior is called

   (1) cannibalistic
   (2) mimetic
   (3) mutualistic
   (4) parasitic
   (5) saprophytic

Here's How to Crack It

Again, no death here, so we can eliminate choices (1) and (5). Again, no one is imitating anyone else. Eliminate choice (2). All that is left is mutualistic and parasitic. In this situation, is one organism living off another? No. The correct answer is choice (3).

4. The family of Elvis agrees to license a small company to manufacture plastic cups with a picture of the dead star on them.

   This kind of behavior is called

   (1) cannibalistic
   (2) mimetic
   (3) mutualistic
   (4) parasitic
   (5) saprophytic

Here's How to Crack It

DEATH! Is it choice (1) or choice (5)? The family of Elvis is continuing to live off their famous relative even after he is long dead. The correct answer is choice (5).

The Process of Elimination

Even if you don't know the right answer, eliminating the wrong answers increases your odds of guessing the correct answer.

5. ICM, a talent agency, swallows up a rival talent agency with which it had been in competition.

   This kind of behavior is called

   (1) cannibalistic
   (2) mimetic
   (3) mutualistic
   (4) parasitic
   (5) saprophytic

Here's How to Crack It

One agency is swallowing up another, essentially feeding off the flesh of one of its own species. The correct answer is choice (1).

Putting It All Together: Classification Passages

You'll get plenty of chances to practice on classification passages in Part IV and Part V of this book. The key to doing well on these passages is using the Process of Elimination, as you've just seen. By eliminating wrong answers, you can often get the right answer, even when you aren't completely sure why the right answer is right. Another useful tool is to break down the categories into smaller groups, as we did in our sample passage by linking cannibalism and saprophysm. In this way, you can sometimes eliminate several answers at once.

The Structural Passage

Part of understanding any long reading passage is understanding its structure. The longer GED passages tend to be highly organized, and this is a good thing because it turns out that you can use the organization itself to give you clues about the passage. Let's suppose for a moment that a passage begins,

There are three kinds of democracy...

Guess what's going to happen in the rest of the passage? You got it: The author is going to describe three kinds of democracy. In fact, it's likely that the next paragraph is going to begin,

The first type of democracy...

and the paragraph after that is going to begin,

The second type of democracy...

and the paragraph after *that* is going to begin,

The third type of democracy...

This may seem like such an obvious structure that it would never be used on the GED, but in fact, this exact structure appears all the time.

Understanding Structure

Understanding structure helps you cut right to the heart of the passage and understand it faster. For example, the passage we've just been discussing is about three types of democracy. If the GED test writers ask you a question about one of those types, you would know the paragraph in which to look for the correct answer. If the GED test writer asks you to summarize the main idea of the passage, the structure itself would help answer this question: Describe three types of a popular form of government.

Reading Is Not Scored
You don't get any points for *reading*. You only get points for answering questions correctly.

Think of a GED reading passage as a house. The main idea of the passage is like the overall plan of the house; the main idea of each paragraph is like the plan of each room. Reading the passage is like walking through the house. As you walk, you don't want to waste time memorizing every detail of every room; you want to develop a general sense of the layout of the rooms and the structure of the house as a whole. If you tried to memorize every detail, you'd never get through the house. Later, if a GED question asks you what was sitting on the table beside the chair in the master bedroom, you won't know the answer off the top of your head, but you will know exactly where to look for it.

Spotting Organization Words

Certain words give away the organization of a passage. A "first of all" implies that there will be a "second of all" coming soon. Here are some commonly used organization words:

first → second → third

primarily → secondarily

one reason → another reason → finally

for one thing → for another thing

These words usually show up at the beginning of sentences, making them even easier to spot. Some other organization words are

therefore	as a result
thus	in conclusion
henceforth	finally
consequently	

These words imply that a conclusion has been reached. Often a sentence that begins with one of these words contains a summary of the main idea of the passage. Let's look at a passage on the next page.

There are several fundamental principles that can be used to explain much about the characteristic behavior of Lady Gaga.

One principle is that she will do anything for attention. You only have to look at her video "Bad Romance" to see that she doesn't seem to mind looking ridiculous as long as everyone is looking.

Another principle that explains Lady Gaga's behavior is that she will do anything to shock us. Like a small child who wants to go too far, Lady Gaga constantly reaches for new ways to be outrageous.

But the most important principle that explains Lady Gaga's behavior is that, in spite of the fact that she is always revealing herself in magazines, she will never actually reveal to us her true self.

1.   The purpose of the passage is to

   (1)   show how Lady Gaga will do anything to shock the public
   (2)   compare Lady Gaga to a small child
   (3)   compare Lady Gaga to other famous stars
   (4)   dispute the contention that Lady Gaga has published semi-nude pictures of herself in books and magazines
   (5)   describe some of the characteristic behavior of Lady Gaga

Here's How to Crack It

This **evaluation** question is essentially asking us for the main idea of the passage, and main idea questions often relate to the overall structure of the passage. What exactly was the structure here? The author announces that there are several principles that help explain Lady Gaga's behavior. The author then goes on to give us three principles and elaborate on each. As you were reading this passage, did you notice the key words that set up this structure (one principle…another principle… the most important principle)? Any correct answer to a main idea question is going to reflect that structure.

One or the Other
Try to eliminate the *wrong* answers, rather than find the right answer.

Let's look at the answer choices. Choice (1) mentions *one* of the three principles. Is this enough to be the main idea of the passage? Nope. Eliminate choice (1). Choice (2) does the same thing, focusing only on the *second* principle. The correct answer to this question will incorporate all three. Forget choice (2). Choice (3) is out of left field. The passage doesn't remotely do this. Nix choice (3). Choice (4) is all confused. The last paragraph makes it clear that Lady Gaga has appeared "revealed" in magazines, so the passage can't be disputing that contention, and even if it were, this is not what the entire passage is about. So much for choice (4). The correct answer is choice (5). Notice how this answer incorporates the structure of the passage. Its purpose was to give us three principles that would help us understand Lady Gaga.

Contrast Words

Certain words indicate that the author is about to contradict or disagree with what has just been said.

Some historians believe that Thomas Jefferson was the founder of our country. However…

What do you think the author is about to say now? That's right: The word *however* tells us that what was expressed in the first half of the sentence is now going to be contradicted in the second half.

However, other historians point to George Washington.

In English, there are a number of words that signal the arrival of a contrasting view.

but	despite
however	in spite of
on the contrary	rather
although	nevertheless
yet	instead
while	

Yin/Yang (Compare and Contrast) Passages

One of the GED's all-time favorite types of passages contrasts two opposing viewpoints—and certain words immediately give this away. See if you can supply the second half of the following sentences:

The traditional *view of the causes of global warming focuses on the burning of fossil fuel...*

(*Second half:* ...however, *the* new *view is that there is some other cause.*)

Until recently, *it was thought that the Mayan civilization was destroyed as a result of drought...*

(*Second half:* ...however, now *we believe that the Mayans were destroyed by disease.*)

The classical *model of laissez-faire capitalism does not even admit the possibility of government intervention...*

(*Second half:* ...but the rock-and-roll *version of laissez-faire capitalism says, "Let me just get my checkbook."*)

Before *1960, it was commonly assumed that the atom was the smallest particle in the universe...*

(*Second half:* ...however, after *1960, scientists began to suspect that there was something even smaller.*)

Whenever you spot a *yin* word, you should realize there is a *yang* on the way. Some other yin/yang words are

Yin	Yang
generally	(however, this time...)
the old view	(however, the new view...)
the widespread belief	(but the in-crowd believes...)
most scientists think	(but Doctor Spleegle thinks...)
on the one hand	(on the other hand...)

Let's look at an example:

_____

Do married women cheat on their husbands? The results of a study conducted several years ago by *Cosmopolitan* magazine suggest that they do, and in large numbers. According to the *Cosmopolitan* readers' survey, 39 percent of married women have had affairs.

However, a new survey, conducted by a scientific research group, says that extramarital affairs are actually conducted by only 26 percent of married women.

It is worth examining how the data was collected for both studies. The *Cosmopolitan* readers' survey was enclosed in an issue of the magazine. It was up to readers to decide whether to fill out and mail in the survey. The research group's study was conducted by means of a survey that was handed out and completed in doctors' waiting rooms.

Sponsors of the new study say that mail-in studies such as the one conducted by *Cosmopolitan* are not representative of the general population because results are predetermined first by the pool of readers who read *Cosmopolitan* and second by the group of people who actually mail in the completed form.

1. According to the passage, which of the following is true of the *Cosmopolitan* readers' survey?

    (1) It was conducted in doctors' waiting rooms.
    (2) It showed that 26 percent of married women have had an affair.
    (3) It was completed and then mailed in by readers of the magazine.
    (4) Its results are the same as the research group's.
    (5) Its results are very surprising.

Here's How to Crack It

Did you spot that this was a yin/yang passage? On the one hand, we have the *Cosmopolitan* study, and on the other hand, we have a *new* study. The passage is going to compare the two. Did you also notice the contrast word *however* that begins the paragraph about the new study? This word lets us know that the two surveys are going to be opposed to each other in some way. Spotting the structure of a passage is halfway to comprehension.

Frequently in yin/yang questions, the GED test writers will ask a question about the yin and then try to trick you by making several answer choices concerning the yang. For example, in this problem, choices (1) and (2) come straight out of the passage—but they are about the wrong survey. The question is asking us about the *Cosmopolitan* survey, and therefore we can eliminate any answer choices that are about the research group study. Choice (4) says that the results of the two studies are the same when in fact they are quite different. How do we know? Our first hint was that contrast word *however* in the second paragraph. Of course, as you read the passage, you also notice that the surveys produced different numbers and were conducted differently. How about choice (5)? Well, *we* may have found the results surprising, but this question begins, "According to the passage…," which means that our opinion doesn't count. Did the passage find the results surprising? We have no idea. The correct answer to this **comprehension** question is choice (3).

GED Pop Quiz
Q: What famous GED graduate played Mr. Huxtable on television?

Answer on page 64

2. Which of the following might have corrected the flaws in the *Cosmopolitan* survey that were pointed out by the sponsors of the new survey?

   (1)   offering a free subscription to readers who filled out the survey
   (2)   requiring each woman who filled out a survey to visit her doctor
   (3)   conducting the survey on a group of women selected at random
   (4)   increasing the number of women who read *Cosmopolitan*
   (5)   asking men the same questions

Here's How to Crack It

According to the sponsors of the new survey, what was wrong with the old survey was that it was not representative of the women of America. In other words, the readers of *Cosmopolitan* may not be a realistic cross section of the entire country. To fix this problem, we would need to widen the pool of survey takers. Which answer choice does this? Choice (1) might increase the number of readers who return the survey, but it would do little to widen the pool of survey takers because you had to be a *Cosmopolitan* reader to get a survey in the first place. Choice (2) is hoping that we will decide that anything about the new survey is better than the old survey and that because the new survey was conducted in doctors' waiting rooms, this will improve the old survey. Nice try. We can also eliminate choice (5). While it sounds very nonsexist, it doesn't address the problems pointed out by the survey takers, and after all, this *is* a survey about women. We are down to choices (3) and (4). Choice (4) seems tempting because if you increase the number of women reading *Cosmopolitan*, you might widen the pool of survey takers. But the best we can say is that this *might* happen. Expanding the number of women who read the magazine won't necessarily expand the types of women who read it. The correct answer to this **application** question is choice (3). By conducting the survey on women who were selected at random, they would have the best chance of getting a representative sample.

GED Pop Quiz
A: Bill Cosby

3. Which of the following conclusions is supported by the results of <u>both</u> studies?

    (1)   All women get married eventually.
    (2)   To be scientifically valid, a survey must never be conducted by mail.
    (3)   Some married women have affairs.
    (4)   The number of men having extramarital affairs is rising in the United States.
    (5)   The number of extramarital affairs is rising in the United States.

Here's How to Crack It

This **analysis** question asks you to find a similarity in a passage that is mostly about differences. The answer will probably not be stated directly in the passage, and as usual, we might as well let POE do some of the work for us. You've probably noticed by now that reading comprehension questions usually have several answer choices that are pretty silly. Let's get rid of those first.

Does either survey say all women get married eventually? No, so eliminate choice (1). Does either survey discuss the infidelity of men? No, so eliminate choice (4). Does either survey say anything to indicate that the number of affairs is rising? If anything, because the new survey has lower numbers, you might be led to think that the numbers are decreasing. Eliminate choice (5). Choice (2) might be a conclusion of the sponsors of the new survey, but certainly not the old one because they actually did conduct their survey by mail. The correct answer is choice (3), which you may have initially thought was too obvious. However, this was the one point on which both surveys agreed. *Some* married women are having affairs.

4. Which of the following would best summarize the passage's main point?

    (1) Married women *do* cheat and in large numbers.
    (2) Different methods of surveying lead to different assessments in the number of women who have had extramarital affairs.
    (3) The research group's survey was scientifically correct.
    (4) No one knows what percentage of married women are having affairs.
    (5) Reading women's magazines like *Cosmopolitan* can put ideas into married women's heads and make them commit adultery.

Here's How to Crack It

This **evaluation** question is essentially asking us for the main idea of the passage. Main ideas can often be found in the first sentence or the last sentence of the passage, but this is not etched in stone. Sometimes the main idea can be found in another part of the passage or even as part of the entire structure of the passage. You need to find the main idea for yourself each time a question like this comes up.

Answer choice (1) was designed for unwary test takers who are convinced that the main idea is always in the first sentence. Choice (1) was practically a direct quote from the first two sentences, but it was not the main idea of the passage. How did we know? The word *however* that began the second paragraph. When a second paragraph begins with a contrast word, you can bet that whatever was said in the first paragraph is about to be disputed. Choice (2) seems pretty good. Notice how it mirrors the yin/yang structure of the passage. Let's hold on to it and look at the other possibilities. Choice (3) might have tempted some people because the author seems to have preferred the second survey. However, was that the main idea of the passage? Not really. Choice (4) might have tempted some people who thought too much. When confronted with two surveys that have fairly divergent results, you might assume that no one really knows what the correct figure is. However, if you feel this way, it is *your* conclusion, not a conclusion that was stated in the passage. Choice (5) also goes far beyond what was said in the passage. If you were tempted by this answer, you should remember not to read too much into the passages. Choice (2) is the correct answer.

Where Do GED Reading Passages Come From?

We'll let the folks who write the GED speak for themselves.

> Among periodicals from which GED tests' stimulus material are drawn are *U.S. News & World Report, Newsweek, Time, Psychology Today, Discover, Science News, National Geographic, Popular Science,* and *American Health.*

How Bad Could It Be?

Well, here are just a few example topics:

- The conservation of our natural resources
- An excerpt from the play *I Remember Mama*
- The habits of jellyfish

Because very little specific knowledge in social studies or science is tested on the GED, a full-scale review of three years of science and history would not be as effective as practicing the techniques we've just shown you on actual GED reading passages. However, because practice materials are limited, you may want to go straight to the source and read articles from the magazines that the GED test writers draw on for passages.

Familiarity is a key concept in reading comprehension—familiarity with the subject matter and familiarity with writing style. If, over the next month or so, you get into the habit of reading at least one of these magazines a week, you will find that this type of reading matter will be much less intimidating when you get to the test center. Put it this way: Would you be nervous about a test if you knew the reading passages were all from *TV Guide*?

Summary

- The GED consists of five tests: Language Arts, Writing; Social Studies; Science; Language Arts, Reading; and Mathematics.

- The GED is scored from 200 to 800 points. In most states, you must get at least a 410 on each test, with an average score of 450 to pass.

- Passing the GED requires answering about half of the questions on each of the five tests correctly.

- To prepare for the GED, study this book and take practice exams from time to time as you prepare, to see how you are doing.

- To register for the GED, call 800 62 MY GED, or contact your state office (the numbers are at the end of Chapter 2).

- You can get a higher score by never leaving an answer blank and by learning to guess well using the Process of Elimination (POE).

- Graphs and charts are widely used on the GED. To do well on these questions, you must learn how to read bar graphs, charts, maps, pie charts, and coordinate graphs. A guide to understanding these types of graphic materials can be found in Chapter 4, "Crazy Graphics."

- Reading comprehension is a very important element of the GED. To do well on these passages, you must be able to understand classification passages, structural passages, and some of the words that help to signal a change within a passage: organizational words (like "first," "second," and "third"), contrast words (like "but" or "however") and yin/yang structures (like "on the one hand" and "on the other hand"). A guide to understanding these types of passages can be found in this chapter, "Crazy Reading."

Part II
How to Crack the Language Arts, Writing Test

Chapter 6
Language Arts, Writing Overview

Do you remember how different teachers' tests stressed different skills? If you got, say, Mr. Smith for English, you knew that his tests would have lots of spelling questions, whereas if you were assigned to Ms. Gonzales's English class, you knew that her tests would usually concentrate on grammar. So, as long as you knew what your teacher liked to test, you could study for just the questions he or she was going to ask you.

The GED Language Arts, Writing test is like any other test; if you know what the people who write it *think* is important, then you can score well without knowing every last rule of English.

Now we aren't saying that it isn't important to learn *all* the rules of spelling, grammar, and sentence structure. Writing and speaking well are incredibly important skills that you will be able to use your whole life.

However, if you don't know all the rules of English (and who does?), you may as well begin by learning about the rules that are tested on the GED. Your immediate objective is to pass this test, and it is pointless to concentrate on information you don't need right now. If you were to spend the next couple of weeks learning, for instance, about the future and conditional tenses, it would be good for your soul, but unfortunately, it wouldn't help your GED score at all. Only the present and the past tenses are tested on the GED.

It is only truthful to say that you don't need to know all the rules of English to do well on the GED. It turns out that the GED concentrates very heavily on a few rules—and in the next three chapters, we are going to teach you those rules.

Chapter 7 will cover the rules of sentence structure (which include topics like parallel construction and proper placement of clauses). Chapter 8 will cover the rules of usage (such as subject-verb agreement and tense). Chapter 9 will cover the rules of mechanics (such as spelling, capitalization, and punctuation) and organization.

What Is on the Test?

The Language Arts, Writing test is made up of questions that test your knowledge of the following topics:

Sentence Structure	(30% of the test—about 15 questions)
Usage	(30% of the test—about 15 questions)
Mechanics	(25% of the test—about 12 questions)
Organization	(15% of the test—about 8 questions)

In the next three chapters, we will teach you everything you need to know about these subjects.

What Does the Language Arts, Writing Test Look Like?

Here is a small example:

<u>Directions</u>: Choose the <u>one best answer</u> to each question.

<u>Questions 1 through 3</u> refer to the following voter registration pamphlet.

(1) When you turn eighteen, one are allowed to register to vote. (2) Some people believing that voting is a waste of time. (3) These people say that you have to stand on line for a long time. (4) They also say that one vote won't make a difference. (5) While it is true that no one vote will change an election, it is important that every person's voice is heard.

1. Sentence 1: **When you turn eighteen, one are allowed to register to vote.**

   Which correction should be made to sentence 1?

   (1)   change <u>turn</u> to <u>turns</u>
   (2)   remove the comma after <u>eighteen</u>
   (3)   replace <u>one</u> with <u>you</u>
   (4)   change <u>allowed</u> to <u>allowing</u>
   (5)   no correction is necessary

2. Sentence 2: **Some people <u>believing that voting</u> is a waste of time.**

Which of the following is the best way to write the underlined portion of this sentence? If you think the original is the best way, choose option (1).

(1) believing that voting
(2) believing that to vote
(3) believe that to voting
(4) believe that voting
(5) are believing that to vote

3. Sentences 3 and 4: **These people say that you have to stand on line for a long time. They also say that one vote won't make a difference.**

The most effective combination of sentences 3 and 4 would include which of the following groups of words?

(1) long time and that one vote
(2) time and making a difference
(3) make a difference, but you have to stand
(4) long time or also say
(5) These people won't make a difference.

4. Sentence 5: **While it is true that no one vote will change an election, it is important that every person's voice is heard.**

If you rewrote sentence 5 beginning with

<u>It is important that every person's voice be heard,</u>

the next words should be

(1) while true that no one vote
(2) unless it is true that no one
(3) because it is true that no one
(4) even if no one vote will change an election
(5) or no one vote will change an election

The Three Types of Language Arts, Writing Questions
1) Sentence Correction (finding an error)
2) Sentence Revision (revising an error)
3) Construction Shift (rearranging a sentence or sentences)

In each case, you are supposed to pick the answer choice that best answers the question. On the actual GED, there will be a number of passages like this one, only longer. The passages will have 200–300 words and will range from informational texts to "how to" texts to business communication. There will be a total of 50 questions, and you'll have up to 75 minutes to answer them.

Don't worry if you aren't sure right now what grammatical errors are being tested in the questions on the previous pages. We'll start our review of Language Arts, Writing very shortly. For now, let's concentrate on the question types. There are always three different types of questions on the Language Arts, Writing test.

Sentence Correction

Forty-five percent of the questions (about 22 out of 50) will look like question 1 from our example. This is called the sentence correction format. Here's that question again:

1. Sentence 1: **When you turn eighteen, one are allowed to register to vote.**

    Which correction should be made to sentence 1?

    (1) change <u>turn</u> to <u>turns</u>
    (2) remove the comma after <u>eighteen</u>
    (3) replace <u>one</u> with <u>you</u>
    (4) change <u>allowed</u> to <u>allowing</u>
    (5) no correction is necessary

In a sentence correction question, you have to decide which answer choice fixes the error in the sentence. Sometimes, as in this case, choice (5) will offer you the option of deciding that there is no error at all and the sentence is fine just as it is.

You'll notice that in a sentence correction question, each of the answer choices looks at a different part of the sentence. The answer choices are also arranged chronologically. That is, the first answer choice will be from the beginning of the sentence, the second and third will be from the middle of the sentence, and so on. (By the way, the correct answer to this question is choice (3), but don't worry if you got it wrong. We'll cover this type of error—pronoun reference—in Chapter 8.)

Sentence Revision

Thirty-five percent of the questions (about 17 out of 50) will look like question 2 from our example. This is called the sentence revision format. Here is that question again:

2. Sentence 2: **Some people <u>believing that voting</u> is a waste of time.**

   Which of the following is the best way to write the underlined portion of this sentence? If you think the original is the best way, choose option (1).

   (1) believing that voting
   (2) believing that to vote
   (3) believe that to voting
   (4) believe that voting
   (5) are believing that to vote

In a sentence revision question, you are again asked to fix the error in the sentence. However, this time you know exactly where in the sentence the error is supposed to be—the underlined portion. Each of the answer choices gives you a slightly different version of the same small group of words. If you believe there was *no* error, then you should choose choice (1), which, in a sentence revision question, always repeats the original sentence. (By the way, the correct answer to this question is choice (4), but don't worry if you got it wrong. We'll cover this type of error—sentence fragment—in Chapter 7.)

Construction Shift

Twenty percent of the questions (about 10 out of 50) will look like questions 3 and 4 from our example. These are two different versions of what is called the construction shift format. Here (you guessed it) is question 3 again:

3. Sentences 3 and 4: **These people say that you have to stand on line for a long time. They also say that one vote won't make a difference.**

   The most effective combination of sentences 3 and 4 would include which of the following groups of words?

   (1) long time and that one vote
   (2) time and making a difference
   (3) make a difference, but you have to stand
   (4) long time or also say
   (5) These people won't make a difference.

In this type of construction shift question, you are asked to recognize the answer choice that best bridges the two sentences into one. Many students find this type of question difficult but, fortunately, there are generally only about four of these questions per test. (By the way, the correct answer to this question is choice (1), but don't worry if you got it wrong. We'll cover this type of question in Chapter 7.)

4. Sentence 5: **While it is true that no one vote will change an election, it is important that every person's voice is heard.**

    If you rewrote sentence 5 beginning with

    It is important that every person's voice be heard,

    the next words should be

    (1) while true that no one vote
    (2) unless it is true that no one
    (3) because it is true that no one
    (4) even if no one vote will change an election
    (5) or no one vote will change an election

In this type of construction shift question, you are asked to recognize how the building blocks of a sentence can be rearranged. Many students find this kind of question difficult as well, but fortunately, there are only about six of these questions on each GED. (By the way, the correct answer to this question is choice (4).)

The nice thing about all construction shift questions is that they're really only testing one area of English: sentence structure. As soon as you see a construction shift question, you don't have to worry much about the rules of usage or mechanics.

The Language Arts, Writing Test

How Most People Approach the Language Arts, Writing Test

Most people read the sentence and hope that the mistake will happen to strike them. If it doesn't, they start to panic. As they stare and stare at the sentence, *all* the words start sounding incorrect. After all, English has so many rules, and there are so many things that can be wrong. Which one is it this time?

How *We* Approach the Language Arts, Writing Test

The Language Arts, Writing test is very predictable. Certain rules get tested all the time. Others never get tested. By knowing which rules the GED test writers like to concentrate on and in which types of questions, you can learn to spot the errors in these sentences. In the next three chapters, we will show you how to assemble a checklist of the GED's favorite errors. With a little practice, this will allow you to improve your score substantially. As you read each sentence, you'll simply go through your mental checklist looking for these mistakes. Believe us, they will be there.

But what happens if you don't spot the error as you read a particular sentence?

The Answer Choices Contain Valuable Clues   Even if you don't see the error as you read the question the first time, you shouldn't despair. There are five terrific clues waiting for you. If you're having trouble deciding if a passage has an error, it helps to look at the answer choices. These choices often provide insights into what is going on in the test writers' minds. To see what we mean, take a look at a slightly altered version of question 2.

2. Which of the following is the best way to write the underlined portion of this sentence? If you think the original is the best way, choose option (1).

(1)   believing that voting
(2)   believing that to vote
(3)   believe that to voting
(4)   believe that voting
(5)   are believing that to vote

Because we aren't letting you see the original sentence this time, you'll have to concentrate *only* on the answer choices. Look at them for a minute and see how they differ from one another. Did you notice that each choice begins with a different version of the verb *to believe*? In this question, the choices are simply giving you different ways of expressing the verb of the sentence.

So instead of wondering about capitalization, punctuation, or any of the other rules of English, you know immediately that this question is asking for the correct form of the verb *to believe*.

When Can You Work Backward from the Answer Choices?   Questions in the sentence revision format are particularly well suited for finding clues in the answer choices and using them to work backward to find the right answer. Why? Because in sentence revision questions (the ones in which part of the sentence is underlined), the answers give you several variations of the *same* part of the sentence.

Good Grammar Books
- *The Elements of Style,* by Strunk and White
- *Grammar Smart,* by The Staff of The Princeton Review

Can you use the answer choices as clues in a sentence correction question? Sure, but it's more complicated. To see what we mean, take a look at a slightly altered version of question 1.

1.   Which correction should be made to this sentence?

    (1)   change <u>turn</u> to <u>turns</u>
    (2)   remove the comma after <u>eighteen</u>
    (3)   replace <u>one</u> with <u>you</u>
    (4)   change <u>allowed</u> to <u>allowing</u>
    (5)   no correction is necessary

In sentence correction questions, each answer choice offers a completely different way to fix a completely different part of the sentence. In this question, choice (1) suggests that the verb may not agree with the subject of the sentence. Choice (2) suggests that the error may be one of punctuation. Choice (3) suggests this could be a pronoun error. Choice (4) changes the form of a verb. Choice (5) suggests there is no error. These answer choices do not provide us with *one* clue as to what is wrong with the original sentence—they give us *five* clues, which is much less helpful.

However, if necessary, you can still use the answer choices as clues in a sentence correction question. After all…

One of Them Has to Be Right   If you don't see the error as you read the original sentence in a sentence correction question, you can carefully try out each of the answer choices to see if it sounds right. Of course, it takes time and mental energy to take each answer choice seriously, one by one. That's why it is always better to use your checklist of GED errors to spot what is wrong as you read the sentence in the first place.

"Should I Read the Passage First?"   Each set of questions is preceded by a passage made up of all the sentences that are going to be tested (and maybe some that won't). Is it necessary to read the passage first? There are only two types of errors that require you to know the general context of a passage: verb tense questions and pronoun questions.

However, it is not necessary to read the passage before you start the questions, as long as you take a second to figure out what general tense the passage is in (present or past) and if there is a general pronoun in use throughout the passage ("you" or "we").

Take a moment now to look back at the sample passage we gave you a few pages ago. What tense is it in? If you said "the present tense," you are absolutely correct. What general pronoun is used? If you said "you," then you are batting two for two.

Before We Begin, Some Terminology

The GED is not going to ask you to identify parts of speech or diagram a sentence, but it will be helpful to your understanding of the next chapters if you know some basic definitions.

Here's a simple sentence:

Tom broke the vase.

This sentence is made up of two nouns, a verb, and an article.

- A **noun** is a word used to name a person, a place, a thing, or an idea.
- A **verb** is a word that expresses action.
- An **article** is a word that modifies or limits a noun.

A Warning

To forestall the objections of the expert grammarians out there, let us say at the outset that this discussion is not designed to be an all-inclusive discussion of English grammar and usage. You are reading this chapter to do well on the Language Arts, Writing section of the GED. Thus, if we seem to oversimplify a point or ignore an arcane exception to a rule, it's because we do not feel that any more detail is warranted when it comes to correctly answering a GED question.

In the sentence above, *Tom* and *vase* are both nouns. *The* is an article. *Broke* is a verb. *Tom* is the **subject** of the sentence because it is the person, place, or thing about which something is being said. *Vase* is the **object** of the sentence because it receives the action of the verb.

Here's a more complicated version of the same sentence:

Tom accidentally broke the big vase of flowers.

We've added an adverb, an adjective, and a prepositional phrase to the original sentence.

- An **adverb** is a word that modifies a verb.
- An **adjective** is a word that modifies a noun.
- A **preposition** is a word that notes the relation of a noun to an action or a thing.
- A **phrase** is a group of words that acts as a single part of speech. A phrase is missing a subject, a verb, or both. A **prepositional phrase** is a phrase beginning with a preposition.

In the sentence above, *accidentally* is an adverb modifying the verb *broke*. *Big* is an adjective modifying the noun *vase*. *Of* is a preposition because it shows a relationship between *vase* and *flowers*. *Of flowers* is a prepositional phrase that acts like an adjective by modifying *vase*.

Here's an even more complicated version of the same sentence:

As he ran across the room, Tom accidentally broke the big vase of flowers.

Now, we've added a secondary clause containing a pronoun to the original sentence.

- A **pronoun** is a word that takes the place of a noun.
- A **clause** is a group of words containing a subject and a verb.

"Tom accidentally broke the big vase of flowers" is considered the **independent clause** in this sentence because it contains the main idea of the sentence and could stand by itself. "As he ran across the room" is also a clause (it contains a subject and a verb), but because it is not a complete thought, it is called a **dependent clause.** This particular dependent clause is also known as an adverbial clause because it tells us something about the action that took place. *He* is a pronoun taking the place of *Tom.*

Now let's begin our sentence structure review.

Chapter 7
Sentence Structure

In this chapter, you'll learn to spot errors involving sentence fragments, run-ons, comma splices, conjunctions, and misplaced modifiers.

Good sentence structure is about putting clauses and phrases—the essential building blocks of sentences—together in logical ways. Before we talk about the *errors* of sentence structure, let's spend a moment talking about correct structure. Here is that example again:

> *As he ran across the room, Tom broke the vase.*

We said before that this sentence consists of two clauses. Each clause has a subject and a verb. The second clause ("Tom broke the vase") is considered the main clause and **independent** because it can stand alone. The first clause ("As he ran across the room") is called **dependent** because it can't.

You can easily change a dependent clause into an independent clause and vice versa. Often all it takes is a single word.

> *He ran across the room.*

By removing *As* from the dependent clause, we suddenly have a sentence that can stand on its own. By adding *As* to the second clause, we can instantly change it into a dependent clause.

> *As Tom broke the vase…*

If we stuck these two new clauses together now, the meaning of the sentence would be very different. Could we have kept the meaning more or less the same and still made the first clause independent? Sure. Try this:

> *Tom ran across the room, breaking the vase.*

Now the first half of the sentence contains the main independent clause. We had to change *he* to *Tom* so the reader would know who the sentence was talking about. We also had to change the second half of the sentence from a clause into a modifying phrase. While a clause has a subject and a verb, a phrase generally has no subject.

Putting the Pieces Together

Proficient writers use a mixture of dependent clauses, independent clauses, and phrases to add variety to their writing and to create emphasis. By combining these building blocks in different ways, writers show the reader which thoughts are most important and create a rhythm.

Here are the most often used structures:

- Independent clause (period) New independent clause (period)

> *Jane lit the campfire. Frank set up the tent.*

GED Pop Quiz
Q: Which late ABC News anchor earned a GED?

Answer on page 86

- Independent clause (comma) *and* independent clause (period)

  Jane lit the campfire, and Frank set up the tent.

- Independent clause (semicolon) independent clause (period)

  Jane lit the campfire; Frank set up the tent.

- Independent clause (comma) dependent clause (period)

  Jane lit the campfire, while Frank set up the tent.

- Dependent clause (comma) independent clause (period)

  As Jane lit the campfire, Frank set up the tent.

All of these sentences are correct. A writer may choose one over another to emphasize one thought over another. For example, in the last sentence, the writer is choosing to make "setting up the tent" the focus of the sentence. Perhaps the writer is setting the stage for the tent collapsing with Frank inside it.

- Phrase (comma) independent clause (period)

  Holding his flashlight in his teeth, Frank set up the tent.

- Independent clause (comma) phrase (period)

  Frank set up the tent, holding his flashlight in his teeth.

Both of these sentences are also correct. "Holding his flashlight in his teeth" is a phrase describing Frank.

There are five main types of errors in GED sentence structure:

1. Incomplete sentences
2. Comma splices and run-ons
3. Improper coordination and subordination
4. Misplaced modifiers
5. Parallel construction

All of these errors are the result of incorrect placement of the building blocks that make up sentences.

The Sentence Fragment Tip-Off
Sentences that don't contain an independent clause

Incomplete Sentences

A complete sentence must have a subject and a verb and stand alone. In other words, it must be, or contain, an **independent clause**. Remember the very first example we gave you?

> *Tom broke the vase.*

This is an independent clause, containing a subject (Tom) and a verb (broke). We can change it into a **dependent clause** by adding just one word.

> *When Tom broke the vase...*

Even though it still has a subject and a verb, this clause can no longer stand alone. It is now waiting for an independent clause to finish the sentence.

> *When Tom broke the vase, Sid ran to tell his Aunt Polly.*

You can turn many independent clauses into dependent clauses by adding one of these words to the beginning of it:

when	as
where	because
why	although
how	while
if	despite
that	who
what	

You may see these words referred to in grammar books as subordinating conjunctions or relative pronouns, but the names of these terms are not important.

By the same token, you can turn many dependent clauses into independent clauses by taking away the subordinating conjunction or relative pronoun.

The First Sentence Fragment Type

There are three kinds of sentence fragments (also known as incomplete sentences). The first is just a dependent clause waiting for a second half that isn't there. Here's an example:

Sentence 1: **As the two women ran for** the bus that was just about to pull away.

Which of the following is the best way to write the underlined portion of this sentence? If you think the original is the best way, choose option (1).

(1)   As the two women ran for
(2)   When the two women ran for
(3)   While the two women ran for
(4)   The two women ran for
(5)   The two women running for

Here's How to Crack It

The "sentence" in the example isn't a sentence at all; it is a dependent clause, beginning with one of those words we told you to be on the lookout for—*as*. We need to turn this dependent clause into an independent clause. Answer choice (1), as always, simply repeats the original sentence, so we know that's wrong. Answer choices (2) and (3) repeat the same error by using other words from the same list. Choice (5) is still not an independent clause, although for a different reason (we'll discuss this type of error in a moment). The only answer that makes the clause independent is choice (4).

The Second Sentence Fragment Type

In the second type of sentence fragment question, the GED test writers ask you to incorporate the sentence fragment into the complete sentence that comes immediately before or after the fragment. In the example that follows, notice that the underlining extends from the end of one sentence through the beginning of the next sentence and includes the punctuation as well.

Sentences 2 and 3: **Although you can clearly see the castle to the left as you drive up Route <u>Three. You</u> must make a right turn on Castle Lane to get there.**

Which of the following is the best way to write the underlined portion of these sentences? If you think the original is the best way, choose option (1).

(1) Three. You
(2) Three, you
(3) Three; you
(4) Three. One
(5) Three. But you

Here's How to Crack It

The underlined portion of this passage includes pieces of two sentences and the punctuation in between. We have to check both "sentences" to make sure that they are complete. Let's check the first "sentence" first. Can it stand on its own? No. It's a dependent clause beginning with one of the words on that list we gave you. Aha! This is the error. Could we have removed the *Although* at the beginning to create an independent clause? Sure, but in this case, that isn't an option because *Although* isn't underlined.

This time, the only way to fix the passage is to combine the dependent clause with the independent clause to form one big sentence. As we will discuss further in the punctuation review, you need a comma between a dependent and an independent clause. The only answer choice that contains a comma is choice (2). This must be the correct answer.

The Third Sentence Fragment Type

Let's go back one more time to that first example.

Tom broke the vase.

One of the GED's favorite ways to create a sentence fragment is to take an independent clause (like "Tom broke the vase") and change the verb into something that looks like a verb but isn't. Here's an example:

Tom breaking the vase.

At first glance, you might say, "This sentence still contains a verb." But even though *breaking* seems like a verb, it is actually something else. In English, it is possible to change a verb into either a noun or an adjective by adding an *-ing* to the end of it. Let's take the verb "to ski" and change it into a noun.

> *Skiing is Veronica's favorite outdoor activity.*

Now let's change the same verb into a kind of adjective.

> *Skiing down the hill, Veronica ran into a tree.*

In this sentence, *Skiing down the hill* is functioning as an adjective phrase, describing Veronica.

When a verb form is used as a noun, it is called a **gerund.** When a verb form is used as an adjective, it is called a **participle.** It isn't important to remember these names. All you ever have to do on the GED is recognize whether a sentence contains a *real* verb—not just a verb functioning as something else. Here's an example.

⎯⎯⎯⎯⎯⎯⎯ ◯ ⎯⎯⎯⎯⎯⎯⎯

Sentence 5: **Forgetting your driver's license resulting in a traffic ticket.**

Which correction should be made to sentence 5?

(1)   change the spelling of <u>forgetting</u> to <u>forgeting</u>
(2)   insert a comma after <u>license</u>
(3)   change <u>resulting</u> to <u>may result</u>
(4)   change <u>license</u> to <u>License</u>
(5)   replace <u>in</u> with <u>for</u>

Here's How to Crack It

Does this sentence contain a real verb? Let's look. There are two words that *seem* like they could be verbs: *forgetting* and *resulting.* Unfortunately, both have *-ing* at the end of them. In other words, this sentence is missing a verb.

Which of the answer choices changes one of the *-ing* words into a real verb? If you said choice (3), you were absolutely correct. "Forgetting your driver's license" is a phrase that is acting like a noun in this case, so the sentence should read:

> *Forgetting your driver's license may result in a traffic ticket.*

Here's why the other choices were wrong: The spelling of *forgetting* is correct, and this change won't help fix the verb problem in the sentence, so we can eliminate choice (1). Choice (2) adds a comma but still doesn't give the sentence a real verb. Choice (4) incorrectly capitalizes *license,* and choice (5) uses the wrong idiom after *result* and does not fix the verb problem.

How Do You Spot a Sentence Fragment?

That's easy. Check each sentence to make sure it contains an independent clause. If the question is referring to two sentences at the same time or asks you to combine two sentences, check to make sure that both contain independent clauses.

SENTENCE FRAGMENT DRILL

(Answers and explanations can be found in Part VIII.)

1. Sentences 1 and 2: **The bride and groom drove away in their <u>car. While the</u> children ran behind, shouting and laughing.**

   Which of the following is the best way to write the underlined portion of these sentences? If you think the original is the best way, choose option (1).

   (1)   car. While the
   (2)   car, while the
   (3)   car; while the
   (4)   car. As the
   (5)   car, or the

2. Sentence 3: **As the car was about to turn onto the main road, the engine breaking down.**

   Which correction should be made to sentence 3?

   (1)   replace <u>As</u> with <u>Because</u>
   (2)   change <u>to turn</u> to <u>turning</u>
   (3)   replace <u>engine</u> with <u>engin</u>
   (4)   insert a comma after <u>engine</u>
   (5)   change <u>breaking</u> to <u>broke</u>

3. Sentences 4 and 5: **When they telephoned a garage, the bride and groom were frustrated to find out that a tow truck could not get to them for two hours. Angry, too.**

   The most effective combination of sentences 4 and 5 would include which of the following groups of words?

   (1)   the bride and groom were frustrated but angry
   (2)   the bride and groom might be frustrated or angry
   (3)   the bride and groom were frustrated and angry
   (4)   the bride and groom were frustrated, angry
   (5)   the bride and groom were frustrated but not so angry

4. Sentence 6: **However, when the mechanics at the garage found out the couple were newlyweds, they sending the tow truck immediately.**

   Which correction should be made to sentence 6?

   (1)   replace <u>when</u> with <u>as</u>
   (2)   change <u>garage</u> to <u>Garage</u>
   (3)   insert a comma after <u>garage</u>
   (4)   change <u>found</u> to <u>find</u>
   (5)   change <u>sending</u> to <u>sent</u>

5.   Sentence 7: **While working on the <u>car, the mechanics</u> concentrated on their task and fixed the problem quickly.**

Which of the following is the best way to write the underlined portion of this sentence? If you think the original is the best way, choose option (1).

(1)   car, the mechanics
(2)   car the mechanics
(3)   car. The mechanics
(4)   car; the mechanics
(5)   car while the mechanics

Comma Splices and Run-Ons

In a **comma splice**, two independent clauses are jammed together into one sentence, usually with only a comma trying to hold them together.

>*Aunt Polly ran into the room, Tom was already gone.*

There are several ways to fix this sentence. The easiest way would be to break it up into two sentences.

>*Aunt Polly ran into the room. Tom was already gone.*

If there is a clear reason why one clause might be connected to the other (for example, if Tom has just broken Aunt Polly's vase), you can also fix it by putting a **conjunction** (such as "and" or "but") between the two thoughts.

>*Aunt Polly ran into the room, but Tom was already gone.*

If there is some connection between the two clauses but it is not really a case of cause and effect, you can break up the two thoughts with a semicolon instead of a period.

>*Aunt Polly arrived home several hours later; Tom was already gone.*

A **run-on sentence** is pretty much the same thing as a comma splice, without the comma.

>*Aunt Polly swept up the pieces of glass she was furious.*

Again, the easiest way to solve the problem is to break the sentence up into two new sentences.

>*Aunt Polly swept up the pieces of glass. She was furious.*

A run-on sentence is often much longer than our example, running on and on, and if you were to read it out loud, you might actually run out of breath and wonder whether perhaps it would have been better to have split it up into more than one sentence. (That last sentence, of course, was a run-on as well.)

How Do You Spot a Comma Splice or a Run-On?

That's easy. As you read each question, check to see if there is more than one independent clause in the sentence. As you know, there are several ways two independent clauses can be correctly combined together into one sentence (by using a conjunction or a semicolon, for example). However, if the two clauses do not seem to be closely related, then the best way to fix the sentence is probably to break it into two smaller ones.

Now that you know what to look for, you will often spot the error as you read the question itself. However, if you don't, the *answer choices* can often provide excellent clues. You should be on the lookout particularly for changes in punctuation. If one or more of the answer choices breaks up the sentence into two separate sentences, that is a good indication that the sentence contains a run-on. Always remember, however, that sometimes you can fix a run-on or comma splice by inserting a conjunction (such as *and* or *because*) if there is a clear relation between the two independent clauses.

Here's what they look like on the GED:

Sentence 1: **There is not much difference between the decision to enter politics and the decision to jump into a pit full of <u>rattlesnakes, in fact,</u> you might find a friendlier environment in the snake pit.**

Which of the following is the best way to write the underlined portion of these sentences? If you think the original is the best way, choose option (1).

(1)   rattlesnakes, in fact,
(2)   rattlesnakes in fact
(3)   rattlesnakes. In fact,
(4)   rattlesnakes in fact,
(5)   rattlesnakes, in fact

Here's How to Crack It

As soon as you see that one or more of the answer choices gives you the option of breaking the sentence up into two pieces, you should immediately consider whether there may be a comma splice or run-on problem. Are the two clauses surrounding the punctuation both independent? Yes! This is probably a comma splice error. Now, the question is how to fix it. Only one of the answer choices breaks the long sentence into two little ones. Answer choice (3) is probably correct. Remember, however, that there are other ways to fix a comma splice; to be certain, try out the other answer choices in the sentence. Perhaps one of them will use a conjunction to bridge the two clauses. Is that the case here? No. Therefore, the correct answer is choice (3).

Sentence 2: **The college's plans for expansion included a new science building and a new <u>dormitory if the funding drive</u> was successful there would be enough money for both.**

Which of the following is the best way to write the underlined portion of this sentence? If you think the original is the best way, choose option (1).

(1) dormitory if the funding drive
(2) dormitory, if the funding drive
(3) dormitory if the drive for funding
(4) dormitory. If the funding drive
(5) dormitories; if the funding drive

Here's How to Crack It

If you could start from scratch, there are lots of different ways you could express the thoughts in this passage. However, as always, you must find the way that the GED test writers intended to express them.

Again, the answer choices provide an immediate clue: In some, the sentence is broken up into two smaller sentences. Check to see if there are independent clauses on either side of the punctuation. Bingo—this is a run-on sentence. Which choices can we eliminate? Choices (1), (2), and (3) bite the dust. Both choices (4) and (5) successfully break up the two clauses. (Remember, a semicolon will often do the trick if the subject of the two clauses is related.)

Is there anything else wrong with either of them? Come to think of it, you can't say "*a* new dormitor*ies*." The correct answer is choice (4).

COMMA SPLICE AND RUN-ON DRILL
(Answers and explanations can be found in Part VIII.)

1. Sentence 1: **Old or frayed extension cords are <u>dangerous they can</u> short-circuit and cause a fire.**

    Which of the following is the best way to write the underlined portion of this sentence? If you think the original is the best way, choose option (1).

    (1) dangerous they can
    (2) dangerous. They can
    (3) dangerous they could
    (4) dangerous, they can
    (5) dangerous, however they can

2. Sentence 2: **New extension cords are safer they have a ground wire to prevent shocks.**

    Which correction should be made to sentence 2?

    (1) insert a comma after <u>safer</u>
    (2) insert <u>because</u> after <u>safer</u>
    (3) replace <u>they</u> with <u>you</u>
    (4) change <u>are</u> to <u>is</u>
    (5) change <u>shocks</u> to <u>shock</u>

3. Sentence 3: **For safety, every home should have a smoke <u>detector fire extinguishers</u> and escape ladders are useful, but they won't do any good if you don't know there is a fire.**

    Which of the following is the best way to write the underlined portion of this sentence? If you think the original is the best way, choose option (1).

    (1) detector fire extinguishers
    (2) detector, fire extinguishers
    (3) detector and fire extinguishers
    (4) detector. Fire extinguishers
    (5) detector; yet fire extinguishers

Improper Coordination and Subordination

Sometimes the best way to fix a sentence with two clauses in it is to break it into two smaller sentences as we just saw. However, if the two clauses are closely related, you can sometimes join them together into one sentence with the help of a conjunction (such as *and* or *when*). There are two kinds of conjunctions: coordinating and subordinating.

Coordinating Conjunctions

When two independent clauses are both talking about the same subject matter, you can often combine them into one sentence by putting one of the following words between them:

> *and, but, yet, or, nor, for, so*

These words are called **coordinating conjunctions**, although the GED will never ask you to name them. Let's look at an example. If you wanted to combine the following two sentences into one, how would you do it?

> *Tom could run.*
> *He couldn't hide.*

Try putting each of the words on the above list in between these two sentences to see which is best. If you decided that "but" or "yet" were the best choices in this case, you were absolutely correct.

> *Tom could run, but he couldn't hide.*

Each of the coordinating conjunctions implies a slightly different relation between the two clauses. *And* adds information. *But* or *yet* implies that the second clause is going to express an opposite or contrasting idea. *Or* shows a choice. *Nor* implies that neither choice is acceptable. *For* gives a reason or explanation for the first clause. *So* gives a result of the first clause.

You are probably already pretty good at choosing the correct conjunction. Here's a small drill just to make sure.

COORDINATING CONJUNCTION DRILL
(Answers can be found in Part VIII.)

Try combining the sentences below, using the coordinating conjunctions *and, but, yet, or, nor, for, so.*

1. Jane wanted to go dancing. Her date wanted to go to the movies.
2. We are going to the beach. We hope you will come, too.

The Bad Coordination Tip-Off
Two independent clauses that need to be split up into two sentences or linked by a better conjunction.

3. Derek was in the mood for a slice of pizza. He went to a pizza parlor.
4. Raoul could buy a blue shirt. He could buy a green shirt.
5. Kim is very happy. She just got a promotion.
6. Jessica can't swim. She can't scuba dive, either.

How Do You Spot Improper Coordination on the GED?

Well, that's easy, too. You're already checking each sentence to see if there is more than one independent clause (in case there is a run-on or comma splice). So if you do notice two independent clauses, you just have to decide whether it would be better to connect the two clauses with a conjunction or whether they are better split into two sentences. Fortunately, the GED test writers make this choice even easier by only giving you one of these options. On the GED, there is never more than one right answer. The answer choices will either give you several variations on a conjunction, or they will give you several variations on splitting up the sentence. They won't give you both. So all you have to do is check to see if the answers offer a choice of coordinating conjunctions. If they do, the error being tested is improper coordination.

Here's what they look like on the GED:

Sentence 1: **The weather report predicted snow, so the day turned out to be sunny and warm.**

What correction should be made to sentence 1?

(1) change <u>predicted</u> to <u>predicts</u>
(2) replace <u>so</u> with <u>but</u>
(3) change <u>turned</u> to <u>turns</u>
(4) replace <u>out</u> with <u>in</u>
(5) change <u>warm</u> to <u>warmly</u>

Here's How to Crack It

As you read the sentence, look for independent clauses. Remember, if there is no independent clause, this would be a sentence fragment. However, this time there are two: "The weather report predicted snow" and "the day turned out to be sunny and warm." Are these two thoughts related enough to be in the same sentence? Sure. And besides, if you look at the answer choices, you will notice that splitting the sentence into two smaller sentences was not one of the options. Is "so" the right conjunction to link them together? Now we're getting warmer. Let's look at the relation of the two independent clauses. The weather report said one thing, and then the weather did just the opposite. Which conjunctions indicate an opposite thought? If you said *but* or *yet,* you were right on the money. Look among the answer choices. Do any of them include *but* or *yet*? Yes! The answer is choice (2).

———————————○———————————

———————————○———————————

Sentences 2 and 3: **Video games help develop hand-eye coordination. Kids enjoy them, too.**

The most effective combination of sentences 2 and 3 would include which of the following groups of words?

Here's How to Crack It

This question type (construction shift) can be a little confusing at first, but you shouldn't be intimidated. It's still asking about the same information you've just learned.

Before we can combine the two sentences, we first have to see if they are sentences in the first place. To do this, all we need to decide is whether the two sentences in this question are independent clauses. Are they? You bet. As you know, probably the best way to combine two independent clauses is with a coordinating conjunction.

Without looking at the answer choices, see if you can combine the two sentences in your head. Write down your sentence below.

———————————————————————————————————

———————————————————————————————————

Okay, now look at the answer choices. You are looking for a group of words that resembles the sentence you just wrote. Of course, you may have to be a little flexible—the GED test writers might have written it slightly differently than you did.

(1) video games and kids
(2) coordination, and kids enjoy
(3) enjoy developing hand-eye
(4) help in developing
(5) coordination, nor do kids

In this particular case, we are looking for a group of words that uses a coordinating conjunction. There are only two: choices (2) and (5). Do you think the best way to join them should be with an *and* or a *nor*? If you said *and*, you just got this problem right. The correct answer is choice (2).

⎯⎯⎯⎯⎯⎯⎯⎯⎯◯⎯⎯⎯⎯⎯⎯⎯⎯⎯

Subordinating Conjunctions

When an independent clause needs to be joined to a dependent clause, you can often combine them into one sentence by putting one of the following words between them:

> *because, since, so that* (to indicate cause and effect)
> *although, though, even though* (to indicate contrast)
> *where, wherever* (to indicate place)
> *after, before, until, while, when, whenever* (to indicate time)
> *if, unless* (to indicate a condition or doubt)
> *as if, as though* (to indicate similarity)

These words are called **subordinating conjunctions,** although, again, the GED will never ask you to name them. Let's look at an example. If you wanted to combine the following two sentences into one, how would you do it?

> *Tom was in big trouble. He had broken Aunt Polly's favorite vase.*

Try putting each of the list words in between these two sentences to see which is best. If you decided that *because* or *since* were the best choices in this case, you were absolutely correct.

> *Tom was in big trouble because he had broken Aunt Polly's favorite vase.*

Each of the subordinating conjunctions implies a slightly different relation between the two clauses. In this case, we needed to show that the broken vase was the reason that Tom was in big trouble. Here's a drill to test your use of subordinating conjunctions.

SUBORDINATING CONJUNCTION DRILL
(Answers can be found in Part VIII.)

Fill in the blanks below, selecting from the following list of subordinating conjunctions: *because, since, so that, although, though, even though, where, wherever, after, before, until, while, when, whenever, if, unless, as if, as though.* Note that in some of these sentences, more than one conjunction will work.

1. _____ I go to school, I have to do my homework.
2. _____ I eat breakfast, I will wash the dishes.

3. _____ I eat broccoli, I get indigestion.
4. _____ You don't call me, I will call you.
5. _____ He is very tall, He is not as tall as John.
6. _____ You have come to work every day for a year, We are giving you a bonus.

How Do You Spot Improper Subordination on the GED?

You spot it the same way you spot improper coordination. If the problem gives you two separate sentences that need to be joined together, look among the answer choices for conjunctions. If the problem gives you one sentence with two clauses, look to see if they are separated with the correct conjunction.

Here's the way this might look on the GED:

Sentences 1 and 2: **The price of fuel oil is supposed to rise soon. Many people are filling up their tanks now.**

The most effective combination of sentences 1 and 2 would include which of the following groups of words?

(1) Although many people are filling
(2) Although the price of fuel oil is supposed to rise
(3) Because many people are filling
(4) Because the price of fuel oil is supposed to rise
(5) Although many tanks are being filled now

Here's How to Crack It

To combine two clauses into one sentence, we either need a semicolon in between (and there are no semicolons in any of the answer choices) or we need some kind of a conjunction. If you look at the answer choices, you will notice that this time we are being offered a choice of two subordinating conjunctions: *although* or *because*. Which conjunction makes sense this time? The word *although* implies that one clause is going to be contrasted with the other clause. Is the meaning of the sentence clear if we say that "although the price is rising soon, people are buying *now*"? Not really, so we can eliminate choices (1), (2), and (5).

The word *because* implies that the action in one clause is causing the action in the other. Is the meaning clear if we say that "because the price is rising soon, people are buying now"? Yes!

Choice (3) uses the right conjunction but gets the meaning backward. The correct answer is choice (4).

Subordinating Conjunctions Come Up Often in Construction Shift Questions

You may have noticed that in each sentence from the subordinating conjunction drill above, it didn't really matter which clause came first.

> *I have to do my homework before I go to school.*

The sentence above is just as correct as the one below:

> *Before I go to school, I have to do my homework.*

In most cases, it doesn't matter whether the dependent or the independent clause comes first. This means that sentences with subordinating conjunctions are ideal for the construction shift format. Let's look at an example.

Sentence 1: **Cats are the best pets to keep if you live in the city because they do not require walking.**

If you rewrote this sentence beginning with

Because they do not require walking,

the next words should be

(1) if you live
(2) cats are the best
(3) in the city
(4) keeping cats
(5) living in the city

Here's How to Crack It

This sentence has an independent clause ("Cats are the best pets to keep if you live in the city") followed by a dependent clause ("because they do not require walking"). The question is asking you to switch the order of the clauses.

What does the clause "Because they do not require walking" refer to? If you said *cats,* you're about to get this question correct. Which of the answer choices begins with *cats*? The right answer is choice (2).

The Wrong Conjunction?

Sometimes a question will simply ask you to realize that the original sentence is using the wrong conjunction.

Sentence 2: **This safe will protect valuables against fire so that the temperature in the room rises above 700 degrees.**

What correction should be made to sentence 2?

(1)   change <u>valuables</u> to <u>valubles</u>
(2)   replace <u>against</u> with <u>for</u>
(3)   replace <u>so that</u> with <u>unless</u>
(4)   insert a comma after <u>room</u>
(5)   change <u>degrees</u> to <u>Degrees</u>

Here's How to Crack It

Remember, when you're dealing with a sentence correction question, try not to look at the answer choices right away because they can be very confusing. Instead, let's begin, as usual, by looking for clauses. This sentence, like most of the ones we've seen so far, contains two clauses: an independent clause ("This safe will protect valuables against fire") and a dependent clause ("so that the temperature in the room rises above 700 degrees").

As always, we need to see if these two clauses are joined together properly. The conjunction "so that" is supposed to indicate *cause and effect*. Will the safe's fire protection *cause* the room to heat above 700 degrees? No. This is the wrong conjunction. Do any of the other answer choices give us an alternative conjunction? There's only one: choice (3), *unless*. If we substitute *unless* for *so that*, the meaning of the sentence becomes much clearer. The safe will protect its contents *unless* the temperature in the room goes above 700 degrees.

IMPROPER COORDINATION DRILL

(Answers and explanations can be found in Part VIII.)

1. Sentences 1 and 2: **The network television companies have lost viewers in the past few years. The ratings of some individual network programs are higher than ever before.**

   The most effective combination of sentences 1 and 2 would include which of the following groups of words?

   (1) the lost viewers are higher than ever before
   (2) some individual programs have lost viewers
   (3) few years, and the ratings
   (4) few years, although the ratings
   (5) few years, rating some individual programs

2. Sentence 3: **Unless it is too soon to say for certain, some networks believe that they will be able to recapture their lost viewers.**

   What correction should be made to sentence 3?

   (1) replace <u>Unless</u> with <u>Although</u>
   (2) remove the comma after <u>certain</u>
   (3) change <u>recapture</u> to <u>recapturing</u>
   (4) change <u>viewers</u> to <u>viewer's</u>
   (5) no correction is necessary

3. Sentence 4: **The networks will have a difficult time, but they may be able to succeed if they can give the public what it wants.**

If you rewrote sentence 4 beginning with

<u>Although the networks will have a difficult time</u>

The next words should be

(1) they can give the public
(2) they may be able to succeed
(3) the public will succeed
(4) what the public wants
(5) if they can get public success

Misplaced Modifiers

A modifying phrase needs to be near what it is modifying. If it gets too far away, it can get **misplaced**.

> *Sweeping up the pieces of glass, the missing key to the jewelry box was found by Aunt Polly.*

As written, this sentence gives the impression that the missing key was sweeping up the pieces of glass. When a sentence begins with a modifying phrase (a group of words without a subject), the noun being modified must follow the phrase. Who was sweeping up the pieces of glass? Aunt Polly, of course. The correct version of this sentence would be:

> *Sweeping up the pieces of glass, Aunt Polly found the missing key to the jewelry box.*

The following is a more subtle version of the same type of error:

> *Happy and excited, Aunt Polly's key opened the jewelry box for the first time in weeks.*

At first glance, it looks like the modifying phrase *happy and excited* is modifying Aunt Polly. However, what is the real subject of this sentence, as written? The key. *Aunt Polly's* is actually modifying the key. The correct version of this sentence would be:

> *Happy and excited, Aunt Polly was able to use her key to open the jewelry box for the first time in weeks.*

How Do You Spot Misplaced Modifiers?

Every time you see a sentence that contains a modifying phrase, check to make sure it modifies the correct noun. Modifying phrases often come at the very beginning of sentences.

Here's how a misplaced modifier might look on the GED:

Sentence 1: **Because there was no sunblock lotion left in the bottle, <u>which</u> had to drape towels over our shoulders.**

Which of the following is the best way to write the underlined portion of this sentence? If you think the original is the best way, choose option (1).

(1) which
(2) that
(3) one
(4) we
(5) it

Here's How to Crack It

A bottle can't drape towels over shoulders, so this is a misplaced modifier. There's also another problem: The first half of the sentence is a dependent clause (it begins with *because*). This means that neither half of the sentence can stand on its own. We need to make one of the groups of words in this sentence into an independent clause, and we don't have a lot of options because only one word in the entire sentence is underlined. Which choices create an independent clause in the second half of the sentence? If you said choices (3), (4), or (5), you are absolutely correct. So eliminate choices (1) and (2). Now, we want to be consistent. Let's look at answer choice (3). Does *one* go with the pronoun *our* used later in the sentence? No. If the sentence had read "one had to drape towels over one's shoulders," this would have been correct.

Because it doesn't, we can forget choice (3). Let's look at choice (4). Does *we* agree with *our*? Yes. This looks like the right answer, but let's just check choice (5). The pronoun *it* could only be referring to the bottle of sunblock lotion, which certainly can't drape towels. The correct answer is choice (4).

Parallel Construction

There are two major types of **parallel construction** errors tested on the GED. They both involve some kind of list. You may see a list of verbs.

> *When Tom finally came home, Aunt Polly kissed him, hugged him, and gives him his favorite dessert after dinner.*

The sentence above is wrong because all of the items on the list must be in the same tense. The first two verbs in the example above (*kissed* and *hugged*) are in the past tense, but the third verb (*gives*) is in the present tense. It is not "parallel" with the other two. The correct sentence should read:

> *When Tom finally came home, Aunt Polly kissed him, hugged him, and gave him his favorite dessert after dinner.*

You also may see a list of nouns.

> *Three explanations for Sid's locking himself in his room were a desire to be by himself, a need to prepare for his GED exam, and hating his brother Tom, who always got away with everything.*

The sentence above is wrong because while *a desire* and *a need* are both nouns, *hating* seems to be more verblike. Is there a more nounlike way to say the same thing? If you said *a hatred*, you were absolutely right. Here's the corrected version:

> *Three explanations for Sid's locking himself in his room were a desire to be by himself, a need to prepare for his GED exam, and a hatred for his brother Tom, who always got away with everything.*

The lists do not have to have three nouns or three verbs. Sometimes there may only be two; other times there may be four or more.

How Do You Spot Parallel Construction Problems?

That's easy. First, as you read each sentence, be on the lookout for a series of actions or nouns. Second, look for changes in verb tense or the way in which nouns are set up, among the answer choices. Let's look at two examples:

The Parallel Construction Tip-Off
A sentence with a series of actions or nouns

Sentence 1: **The two students studied for the exam by reading all the assigned books, making notes, and to quiz each other on important facts.**

Which correction should be made to sentence 1?

(1)   change <u>studied</u> to <u>studying</u>
(2)   change <u>reading</u> to <u>read</u>
(3)   remove the comma after <u>books</u>
(4)   change <u>and</u> to <u>or</u>
(5)   change <u>to quiz</u> to <u>quizzing</u>

Here's How to Crack It

As you read the sentence, did you notice the list of actions? The two students are preparing for the exam by

>   reading (all the assigned books)
>   making (notes)
>   and
>   to quiz (each other on important facts)

When there is a series of actions, each action is supposed to be expressed the same way. Which of the three actions is different from the other two? If you said *to quiz*, you're right. This is a parallel construction problem, and the way to fix it is to use the same form we found in the first two actions:

>   reading (all the assigned books)
>   making (notes)
>   and
>   *quizzing* (each other on important facts)

Looking at the answer choices, you will see that only one fixes this problem. The correct answer is choice (5).

Let's imagine, just for a moment, that you didn't spot the parallel construction error as you read the sentence the first time. Should you look at the answer choices for possible clues? As we said in the introduction to the Language Arts, Writing test, questions in the sentence revision format are excellent for working backward from the answer choices. However, this time, the question is in the sentence correction format. While you can still look at the answer choices for clues if you want to, this can be confusing because this format gives you five different kinds of errors from five different parts of the sentence. It takes time and mental energy to take each answer choice seriously and find out why it is incorrect.

Sentence 2: **Architects are responsible for <u>designing buildings and then to supervise</u> the construction.**

Which of the following is the best way to write the underlined portion of this sentence? If you think the original is the best way, choose option (1).

(1) designing buildings and then to supervise
(2) the design of buildings and then to supervise
(3) to design buildings and then supervising
(4) designing buildings and then supervising
(5) designing buildings and then the supervision

Here's How to Crack It

In this sentence, there is also a series of actions, but the series is easy to miss. Let's break down the sentence. Architects are responsible for

> designing (buildings)
> and then
> to supervise (the construction)

This time, there are only two actions, but the same parallel construction principles apply. We need to keep both actions in the same form.

If you didn't spot the parallel construction problem in this sentence, you could have taken advantage of the sentence revision format of this question and looked to the answer choices for clues. Each choice presents us with a different way to list two ideas. All we have to do is find the list that is parallel. Choice (1) simply repeats the original sentence, and we already know that isn't parallel. Choice (2) says architects are responsible for

> the design (of buildings)
> and then
> to supervise (the construction)

This isn't parallel because the first item on the list is a nounlike thing, while the second item on the list is a verblike thing. If it had said

> the design (of the buildings)
> and then
> the supervision of (the construction)

that would have been parallel, but it didn't say that. Choice (3) uses the incorrect idiom "responsible for to…" Choice (4) says architects are responsible for

> designing (buildings)
> and then
> supervising (the construction)

Bingo! Choice (4) lists two verblike things in the same form. This is the right answer. Choice (5) resembles choice (2) in that it mixes a nounlike thing with a verblike thing: Architects are responsible for

> designing (buildings)
> and then
> the supervision of (the construction)

In this case, the first item on the list is a verblike thing, while the second is a nounlike thing, so the sentence is not parallel.

PARALLEL CONSTRUCTION AND MISPLACED MODIFIER DRILL

(Answers and explanations can be found in Part VIII.)

1. Sentence 1: **The hardest things about vacations are getting the time off from work, saving the money to pay for them, and to decide on a great place to go.**

   Which correction should be made to sentence 1?

   (1) change <u>are</u> to <u>is</u>
   (2) remove the comma after <u>work</u>
   (3) change <u>to decide</u> to <u>deciding</u>
   (4) replace <u>great</u> with <u>good</u>
   (5) no correction is necessary

2. Sentence 2: **After picking the time and the place, <u>saving money is what most people forget to think about</u>.**

   Which of the following is the best way to write the underlined portion of this sentence? If you think the original is the best way, choose option (1).

   (1) saving money is what most people forget to think about
   (2) saving the money is what most people forget about thinking
   (3) the money is what most people forget to think about saving
   (4) most people forget thinking about saving the money
   (5) most people forget to think about saving money

SENTENCE STRUCTURE DRILL

Here's a drill that combines all the errors you've studied so far. Remember, occasionally the sentence will be fine just the way it is. Don't worry about timing yourself on this drill. Concentrate on using the summary we just gave you to find the problems in the sentences.

(Answers and explanations can be found in Part VIII.)

(A)

(1) Although most people believe that Shakespeare's plays were written by Shakespeare. (2) Some scholars believe they were actually written by someone else. (3) These scholars base their theory on educational records, old church documents, and analyzing Shakespeare's other known writing.

(B)

(4) When Shakespeare didn't write these famous English plays, who did? (5) Some scholars think the author of the plays must have been a member of the royal family, they say only royalty received the education necessary to produce these masterpieces. (6) Members of the royal family did receive fine educations. (7) However, there were many great writers from that time period who were not members of the royal family and who did not receive formal educations.

(C)

(8) Enormously popular at the time, other scholars believe the plays were written by someone who was a member of the working class. (9) If Shakespeare did not write the plays, the most likely candidate being another writer called Marlowe. (10) One important scholar examined Marlowe's writing. (11) She discovered that it contained many similarities to the plays attributed to Shakespeare. (12) Her examination was thorough, but she forgot to look at the works of other writers from the same time period. (13) Many writers from that time period used similar writing styles, only Shakespeare had true genius.

1. Sentences 1 and 2: **Although most people believe that Shakespeare's plays were written by <u>Shakespeare. Some</u> scholars believe they were actually written by someone else.**

   Which of the following is the best way to write the underlined portion of this sentence? If you think the original is the best way, choose option (1).

   (1) Shakespeare. Some
   (2) Shakespeare; some
   (3) Shakespeare, some
   (4) Shakespeare and some
   (5) Shakespeare but some

2. Sentence 3: **These scholars base their theory on educational records, old church documents, and analyzing Shakespeare's other known writing.**

   Which correction should be made to sentence 3?

   (1) change the spelling of <u>educational</u> to <u>edjucational</u>
   (2) remove the comma after <u>records</u>
   (3) change <u>documents</u> to <u>document</u>
   (4) remove <u>analyzing</u>
   (5) Change <u>Shakespeare's</u> to <u>shakespeare's</u>

3. Sentence 4: **When Shakespeare didn't write these famous English plays, who did?**

   Which correction should be made to sentence 4?

   (1) replace <u>When</u> with <u>If</u>
   (2) change <u>English</u> to <u>english</u>
   (3) change <u>plays</u> to <u>play</u>
   (4) remove the comma after <u>plays</u>
   (5) change <u>who</u> to <u>whose</u>

4. Sentence 5: **Some scholars think the author of the plays must have been a member of the <u>royal family, they say</u> only royalty received the education necessary to produce these masterpieces.**

   Which of the following is the best way to write the underlined portion of this sentence? If you think the original is the best way, choose option (1).

   (1) royal family, they say
   (2) royal family. They say
   (3) royal family, then they say
   (4) royal family, however, they say
   (5) royal family, but say

5. Sentences 6 and 7: **Members of the royal family did receive fine educations. However, there were many great writers from that time period who were not members of the royal family and who did not receive formal educations.**

   The most effective combination of sentences 6 and 7 would include which of the following groups of words?

   (1) great writers did receive fine educations
   (2) the royal family did not receive formal educations
   (3) fine educations, or there was
   (4) fine educations, and there were
   (5) fine educations, but there were

6. Sentence 8: **Enormously popular at the time, <u>other scholars believe the plays were</u> written by someone who was a member of the working class.**

Which of the following is the best way to write the underlined portion of this sentence? If you think the original is the best way, choose option (1).

(1) other scholars believe the plays were
(2) other scholars believing the plays to be
(3) believing, as the scholars do, that the plays were
(4) the plays are believed by other scholars to have been
(5) the plays are believed by other scholars to be

7. Sentence 9: **If Shakespeare did not write the plays, the most likely candidate being another writer called Marlowe.**

Which correction should be made to sentence 9?

(1) change <u>plays</u> to <u>Plays</u>
(2) remove the comma after <u>plays</u>
(3) change the spelling of <u>likely</u> to <u>likley</u>
(4) change <u>being</u> to <u>is</u>
(5) replace <u>another</u> with <u>other</u>

8. Sentences 10 and 11: **One important scholar examined Marlowe's writing. She discovered that it contained many similarities to the plays attributed to Shakespeare.**

If you rewrote sentences 10 and 11 beginning with

<u>After examining Marlowe's writing,</u>

the next words should be

(1) one important scholar discovered that it
(2) the plays attributed to Shakespeare
(3) it discovered that the plays
(4) she discovered that it contained
(5) many similarities were contained

9. Sentence 12: **Her examination was thorough, but she forgot to look at the works of other writers from the same time period.**

What correction should be made to sentence 12?

(1) replace <u>thorough</u> with <u>through</u>
(2) replace <u>but</u> with <u>or</u>
(3) change <u>forgot</u> to <u>forgetting</u>
(4) insert a comma after <u>writers</u>
(5) no correction is necessary

10. Sentence 13: **Many writers from that time period used similar <u>writing styles, only Shakespeare had</u> true genius.**

Which of the following is the best way to write the underlined portion of this sentence? If you think the original is the best way, choose option (1).

(1) writing styles, only Shakespeare had
(2) writing styles, but only Shakespeare had
(3) writing styles and only Shakespeare had
(4) writing styles only Shakespeare had
(5) writing styles, if only Shakespeare had

SENTENCE STRUCTURE: PUTTING IT ALL TOGETHER

You've now seen all the ways the GED will test your knowledge of sentence structure. Let's review what you are going to be looking for as you read each question in the Language Arts, Writing test.

- Every sentence must have an independent clause. Does this one? To check, make sure there is a subject and a real verb (-*ing* words all by themselves don't count). If the sentence doesn't contain a real verb, look for one in the answer choices.

- If a sentence has two independent clauses, they must be linked by either a semicolon (;) or a coordinating conjunction (*and, but, yet, or, nor, for, so*). Are they? If not, one of the answer choices will probably contain a conjunction.

- If a sentence has one independent clause and one dependent clause, the dependent clause must begin with a subordinate conjunction (*because, before, although, when, where,* etc.). If you don't find the conjunction in the original sentence, you will find it in one of the answer choices.

- If the question asks you to combine two sentences, you will need a coordinating conjunction or a semicolon (to combine two independent clauses) or a subordinating conjunction (to combine an independent clause with a dependent clause).

- If the sentence contains a series of actions or a list of things, the items must all be expressed in the same way.

- If the sentence begins with a modifying phrase, the noun that comes right after must be what the phrase is describing.

Chapter 8
Usage

In this chapter, you'll learn how to spot errors involving subject-verb agreement, pronouns, and tense.

Now that you've seen how the larger parts of a sentence—clauses and phrases—are combined to form GED questions, it's time to look at the *smaller* parts of a sentence and see how the GED tests them.

The GED concentrates on three types of usage questions:

1. Subject-verb agreement
2. Pronoun reference
3. Verb tense agreement

Subject-Verb Agreement

The verb of a sentence must always agree with its subject. Let's look at an example.

>   *My computer play chess better than I do.*

Does that sound right to you? Let's check it out. The subject of this sentence is *computer,* which is singular. The verb of the sentence is *play,* which is in the plural form. In this case, the subject and the verb don't agree. Here's a corrected version of the same sentence:

>   *My computer **plays** chess better than I do.*

The GED likes to test whether you can spot subject-verb agreement problems. Sometimes they are as simple as that last example. Here's how one of these would look on the GED:

Last week, your complaints <u>was received</u> via e-mail and sent to the appropriate department.

Which of the following is the best way to write the underlined portion of this sentence? If you think the original is the best way, choose option (1).

(1)   was received
(2)   will be received
(3)   received
(4)   being received
(5)   were received

Here's How to Crack It

As always, you want to begin by making sure that the sentence is a real sentence, not just a fragment. A real sentence has an independent clause with a subject and a verb. What is the subject of this sentence? If you said *complaints*, you are absolutely correct. What is the verb? *Was*. Does the verb agree with the subject? No. *Complaints* is plural and needs a plural verb: *were*. Which of the answer choices offers the verb *were*? The correct answer is choice (5).

Subject (#@*&^%) Verb

The GED test writers often make subject-verb questions more difficult by putting other words, phrases, or dependent clauses in between the subject and the verb so that by the time you get to the main verb of the sentence, you have forgotten if the subject was singular or plural. Here's an example:

> *My computer, which is really just a bunch of silicon chips, play chess better than I do.*

The adjective clause *which is really just a bunch of silicon chips* is describing the *computer*, but it isn't part of the subject or the verb of the independent clause of the sentence. Try putting parentheses around the words describing the computer so you can see the independent clause more clearly. It should look like this:

> *My computer (which is really just a bunch of silicon chips) play chess better than I do.*

The GED test writers are hoping that by the time you've read the adjective clause that ends with the plural *silicon chips,* you will think that the sentence needs a plural verb. However, if you ignore the words in between, the subject of the sentence is still *my computer* and the verb is still *play*. Here's the sentence the way it should be written:

> *My computer, which is really just a bunch of silicon chips, **plays** chess better than I do.*

Let's see how a question like this would look on the GED.

Agreement Quiz
Q: In the sentence below, does the subject agree with the verb?

The tree with the maple-shaped leaves were cut down.

Answer on page 120

Sentence 1: **One of the best ways to enjoy apples are to bake a delicious apple pie.**

Which correction should be made to sentence 1?

(1) insert a comma after <u>ways</u>
(2) change <u>enjoy</u> to <u>enjoying</u>
(3) change <u>are</u> to <u>is</u>
(4) change the spelling of <u>delicious</u> to <u>delishus</u>
(5) change <u>pie</u> to <u>pies</u>

Here's How to Crack It

To make sure this is a complete sentence, we need to find a subject and a verb. What is the subject of this sentence? You may be a little surprised to learn that the subject of this sentence is simply *One*.

The rest of the words describing *one* (*of the best ways* and *to enjoy apples*) are prepositional phrases modifying *one*. These words are not part of the subject of the sentence; they simply help to describe it. Again, let's put parentheses around the prepositional phrases between the subject and the verb.

One (of the best ways to enjoy apples) are to bake a delicious apple pie.

The subject of the sentence is *one,* and the verb is *are.* This is a complete sentence, but do the subject and the verb agree? No way. The subject is singular, but the verb is plural. Which of the answer choices changes the verb to singular? The correct answer is choice (3).

No Way!
A: The subject *tree* requires the verb *was*.

Subject-Verb Agreement in Two-Clause Sentences

As you know, some sentences contain more than one clause. In these sentences, each clause has its *own* subject and its *own* verb, which must agree with each other.

I get mad at my computer because it play better than me.

In this sentence, the independent clause ("I get mad at my computer") is fine, but the dependent clause ("because it play better than me") has a subject-verb agreement problem. The subject of this clause is the singular *it*, which does not agree with the plural *play*. The correct version of this sentence should read:

*I get mad at my computer because it **plays** better than me.*

Compound Subjects

Sometimes the GED test writers will give you a sentence with a **compound subject.**

> *My sister and my brother beats me at chess.*

If the subject of a sentence is made up of two nouns with *and* in between, then the verb must be plural.

> *My sister and my brother **beat** me at chess.*

However, if the subject of a sentence is made up of two nouns with *or* or *nor* in between, then the verb must agree with the part of the subject closest to it.

My uncle or my nieces watch the chess games.
(*Watch* agrees with *nieces*.)
My nieces or my uncle watches the chess games.
(*Watches* agrees with *uncle*.)
Neither my uncle nor my nieces watch the chess games.
(*Watch* agrees with *nieces*.)

Inverted Structures: Verb-Subject

Every once in a while, you will see a sentence in which the verb comes before the subject. Here is an example of a correctly **inverted structure:**

> *In the room with the chessboard sits my whole family.*

This is perfectly acceptable English, although it can be a little confusing when you are trying to find the subject and the verb of the sentence. In fact, the subject of this sentence is *family.* Let's look at the same sentence in its more normal form.

> *My whole family sits in the room with the chessboard.*

Now it's easier to see, isn't it? The subject of the sentence (*family*) agrees with the verb (*sits*).

How Do You Spot Subject-Verb Agreement Problems?

Well, you're already looking at each GED sentence to identify its clauses. As you do this, take a few seconds to see if the verb of each clause agrees with its subject. If it doesn't, you've spotted a subject-verb problem. Then just look for an answer choice that fixes the verb.

SUBJECT-VERB AGREEMENT DRILL

(Answers and explanations can be found in Part VIII.)

1. Sentence 1: **A collector of gourmet recipes do not necessarily ever cook any of the recipes she has collected.**

   Which correction should be made to sentence 1?

   (1) change the spelling of <u>recipes</u> to <u>resipies</u>
   (2) change <u>do</u> to <u>does</u>
   (3) change the spelling of <u>necessarily</u> to <u>necesarily</u>
   (4) insert a comma after <u>ever</u>
   (5) no correction is necessary

2. Sentence 2: **A magazine recipe or a newspaper recipe <u>is</u> not exotic enough for a true collector.**

   Which of the following is the best way to write the underlined portion of this sentence? If you think the original is the best way, choose option (1).

   (1) is
   (2) are
   (3) were
   (4) being
   (5) be

3. Sentence 3: **A true collector is interested only in a handwritten recipe <u>that have been passed</u> down from generation to generation.**

   Which of the following is the best way to write the underlined portion of this sentence? If you think the original is the best way, choose option (1).

   (1) that have been passed
   (2) that, being passed
   (3) that has been passed
   (4) having been passed
   (5) having passed

Pronoun Reference

A pronoun takes the place of a noun that has previously been mentioned either in the same sentence or in an earlier sentence. The pronoun must always agree with that noun. The GED test writers have several favorite **pronoun errors.** Here's one of them:

Phil and John played chess, and he won.

As you read the sentence, look for pronouns. Did you find one? If you didn't, don't worry: We're going to give you a complete list of all the pronouns later in this chapter. For now, take our word for it that there is one pronoun in this sentence, and it's *he.*

The pronoun *he* is supposed to replace a noun, but can you tell which one? In this sentence, we aren't sure whether it was Phil or John who won. The pronoun is ambiguous. To clear up our confusion, we must get rid of the pronoun and replace it with the name of the person who actually won the game.

Phil and John played chess, and John won.

On the GED, it would look like this:

Sentence 1: **Germs can infect a small cut, but <u>it</u> can be avoided by using an antiseptic lotion.**

Which of the following is the best way to write the underlined portion of this sentence? If you think the original is the best way, choose option (1).

(1) it
(2) they
(3) the infection
(4) the cut
(5) them

Here's How to Crack It

There's only one word underlined in the entire sentence, and it is a pronoun. What you have to do is decide if it is crystal clear—not just to you but also to a grammatically uptight GED test writer—exactly to what the pronoun *it* is referring.

Could *it* refer to germs? No, because germs are plural and *it* is singular. Could *it* refer to the cut? Not really, because you can't avoid a cut by putting lotion on it. In other words, it is *not* clear what the pronoun refers to, and that means we'll have to replace the pronoun with whatever it is that *can be avoided*. Let's look at the answer choices.

Choice (1) simply repeats the original mistake, so get rid of that one. Choice (2) uses the pronoun *they*. At first glance, this seems possible, because now the pronoun clearly must modify the plural *germs*. However, you really can't avoid germs; you can avoid getting *an infection* from germs. Aha! Choice (3) gives us the words *an infection*. This is precisely what can be avoided by using an antiseptic lotion. Just to be sure, let's look at the other choices. Choice (4) implies that you can avoid a cut by using antiseptic lotion. That doesn't make any sense. Choice (5) uses the wrong form of an ambiguous pronoun. The correct answer was choice (3).

Using the Wrong Pronoun

More often, the GED tests pronouns that are actually wrong, not just ambiguous.

> *Phil was so angry that he took the chess pieces and threw it across the room.*

There's a pronoun in this sentence (*it*), but does this pronoun agree with the noun it is supposed to be referring to? No. Obviously, the sentence is trying to say that Phil threw the *chess pieces* across the room. However, *chess pieces* is plural. To make the pronoun agree with its noun, the sentence should read:

> *Phil was so angry that he took the chess pieces and threw **them** across the room.*

Here's how this type of error would be tested on the GED:

Sentence 2: **When a company is formed, they must be registered with the local government.**

Which correction should be made to sentence 2?

(1) remove the comma after <u>formed</u>
(2) replace <u>they</u> with <u>it</u>
(3) change <u>be</u> to <u>being</u>
(4) change <u>registered</u> to <u>register</u>
(5) change the spelling of <u>government</u> to <u>goverment</u>

The Pronoun Error Tip-Offs
- Doesn't agree with the noun to which it refers
- Doesn't refer to a noun at all

Here's How to Crack It

After you check for sentence structure and subject-verb agreement, look for any pronouns. There is one pronoun in this sentence: *they*. To what does this pronoun refer? If you said *company*, you were exactly right. However, is *company* singular or plural?

In informal English, we use *they* all the time when we refer to a company, for example, or the government or another country. "They went bankrupt." "They should all be thrown out of office." "They declared war on us." However, in GED English, this is incorrect. A country, a government, a company—all of these things are singular.

So, in this sentence, we need a singular pronoun. The only possible answer is choice (2).

When you spot a pronoun in a sentence, you must match it up with a noun. Here is a list of nouns that sound plural but are generally singular.

> **Some Nouns That Are Generally Singular**
> The Netherlands (the name of any city, state, or country)
> the government
> the company
> Tom or John (any two singular nouns connected by *or*)
> the family
> the audience
> politics
> measles
> the number
> the amount

Pronoun Shift

The last kind of pronoun error that comes up on the GED is a needless shift from one pronoun to another, either within a sentence or during the course of an entire paragraph. Here's an example of a shift within one sentence:

> *You can always tell a lot about a person when one watches him play a game of chess.*

This sentence begins with one pronoun (*you*) but then switches for no good reason to another pronoun (*one*). Pronouns have to stay consistent throughout a sentence. This should read:

> *You can always tell a lot about a person when you watch him play a game of chess.*

However, it would also have been correct (if a little "highfalutin") to say:

> *One can always tell a lot about a person when one watches him play a game of chess.*

The main idea here is that pronouns must stay consistent with one another.

The Toughest Pronoun Error to Find: Consistency Throughout the Passage

There are only two kinds of errors on the GED that ever require you to read the passage: **pronoun shift** and **verb tense**. Once or twice per passage, the GED test writers will ask a question that requires you to look beyond the sentence or sentences in the question.

As we said in the introduction to the Language Arts, Writing section, if you don't feel like dealing with these, you can just ignore them; don't worry, you will still be able to pass the test even if you skip these completely. However, take a moment now to see if you can spot the error in the sentence below. Who knows? You may be good at this.

Here's part of a Language Arts, Writing paragraph. Note that you need to read the first sentence to decide whether the pronoun in the third sentence is correct.

———————◯———————

<u>Question 1</u> refers to the following paragraph.

(1) As we get older, we begin to wonder about the meaning of life. (2) Is everything that happens accidental? (3) Are you simply at the mercy of chance encounters, or can fate be controlled?

1. Sentence 3: **Are you simply at the mercy of chance encounters, or can fate be controlled?**

    Which correction should be made to sentence 3?

    (1) replace <u>you</u> with <u>we</u>
    (2) remove the comma after <u>encounters</u>
    (3) change <u>fate</u> to <u>Fate</u>
    (4) change the spelling of <u>controlled</u> to <u>controled</u>
    (5) no correction is necessary

Here's How to Crack It

As always, you should begin by checking for sentence structure: Is there an independent clause? In fact, there are two, joined correctly by a coordinating conjunction. Let's move on to usage then: Is there a subject-verb error? No. Is there a pronoun in the sentence to check? Yes, the pronoun *you*.

Let's see if the pronoun is being used correctly in the sentence. Yes, it is—but because we know that the GED sometimes tests pronoun shifts from the entire paragraph, we should take a few seconds to see if *you* agrees with the rest of the passage. Does it? No way. In the first sentence, the author uses *we*. Which of the answer choices replaces *you* with *we*? The correct answer is choice (1).

How Do You Spot a Pronoun Error?

That's easy. Look for pronouns. Here's a list of common pronouns. (You don't need to memorize these—just be able to recognize them.)

Single	Plural	Can Be Singular or Plural
I, me	we, us	none
he, him	they, them	any
she, her	both	you
it	some	who
each	these	which
another	those	what
either		theirs
neither		
one		
other		
such		
mine		
yours		
his, hers		
ours		
this		
that		

Every single time you spot a pronoun, you should immediately ask yourself the following three questions:

1. Is it completely clear, not just to me but also to a meticulous GED test writer, to whom or what the pronoun is referring?
2. Does the pronoun agree in number with the noun to which it is referring?
3. Does the pronoun agree with other pronouns in the sentence or in the passage as a whole?

PRONOUN DRILL

(Answers and explanations can be found in Part VIII.)

Questions 1 through 3 refer to the following paragraph.

(1) When you get your first job, the salary seems so huge that you don't think you could ever spend them all. (2) However, when the first paycheck comes, with tax, Social Security, and health insurance withheld, we are shocked to discover that there is almost nothing left. (3) You may have no money, but your best friend won't kid you about them because she won't have any money either.

1. Sentence 1: **When you get your first job, the salary seems so huge that you don't think you could ever spend <u>them</u> all.**

    Which of the following is the best way to write the underlined portion of this sentence? If you think the original is the best way, choose option (1).

    (1) them
    (2) they
    (3) it
    (4) of them
    (5) of it

2. Sentence 2: **However, when the first paycheck comes, with tax, social security, and health insurance withheld, we are shocked to discover that there is almost nothing left.**

    Which correction should be made to sentence 2?

    (1) change <u>comes</u> to <u>come</u>
    (2) remove the comma after <u>tax</u>
    (3) replace <u>we</u> with <u>you</u>
    (4) change the spelling of <u>discover</u> to <u>diskover</u>
    (5) no correction is necessary

3.   Sentence 3: **You may have no money, but your best friend won't kid you about <u>them</u> because she won't have any money either.**

Which of the following is the best way to write the underlined portion of this sentence? If you think the original is the best way, choose option (1).

(1)   them
(2)   themselves
(3)   one's poverty
(4)   your poverty
(5)   their poverty

Tense Errors

On the GED, the rules about tense are a lot like the rules about parallel construction. There are two main rules.

Rule One

In general, if a sentence starts out in one tense, it should probably stay there. Let's look at an example:

> *When he was younger, John studied every morning and plays chess every afternoon.*

The clause *when he was younger* puts the entire sentence firmly in the past. Thus, the two verbs that follow should be in the past tense as well. The sentence should read:

> *When he was younger, John studied every morning and **played** chess every afternoon.*

Here's how this would look on the GED:

To open the program, double-click on the icon and <u>selected</u> a font.

Which of the following is the best way to write the underlined portion of this sentence? If you think the original is the best way, choose option (1).

(1)   selected
(2)   select
(3)   selecting
(4)   have selected
(5)   are selecting

Here's How to Crack It

Only one word is underlined here, and it happens to be a verb. If you look at the answer choices (always a good idea when you are dealing with a sentence revision question), you will notice that the choices all give you different versions of the same verb.

To find out which one is best, look at the rest of the sentence. In what tense did this sentence begin? If you said the present tense, you were right on the money. Because most GED sentences and passages stay in the same tense throughout, the best answer is one that stays in the same tense. The correct answer is choice (2).

Rule Two

If a passage starts out in one tense, it should generally stay there. As we've said before, the only time you need the context of the entire passage when you're answering a question is on a pronoun or tense problem. There will be at least one (but no more than two) of these per passage. Here's an example:

---

(1) When people go camping, they always take too many things with them. (2) Some people brought three changes of clothes for a two-day trip.

Sentence 2: **Some people <u>brought</u> three changes of clothes for a two-day trip.**

Which of the following is the best way to write the underlined portion of this sentence? If you think the original is the best way, choose option (1).

(1)　brought
(2)　bringing
(3)　were bringing
(4)　bring
(5)　to bring

The Tense Error Tip-Offs
Changes of tense in the entire passage or within a sentence

Here's How to Crack It

The only word underlined in the sentence is the verb *brought*. Grammatically speaking, this is correct, so the only possible error is that this verb does not agree with the other verbs in the passage. If we look at the first sentence, we notice that the verbs are in the present tense. Therefore, we need the present tense of *brought*, which is *bring*. The answer is choice (4).

Only two tenses come up on the GED.

Tense	Example
present	He *plays* chess three times a day.
past	When he was younger, he *played* chess three times a day.

That's it. Of course there *are* other tenses in English, but the GED chooses not to test them. Just for your information, here are the other most common tenses:

Tense	Example
present perfect	He *has played* chess three times a day for the last several years.
past perfect	He *had played* chess three times a day until Phil threw away all the chess pieces.
future	He *will play* chess again, starting tomorrow.

It isn't important that you know these tenses for the multiple-choice section of the Language Arts, Writing test, but they can be very useful in writing, and their use may help you increase your score in the essay section of the test.

However, for the multiple-choice test, there are only two tenses: present and past. In general, a sentence that begins in one tense should stay in the same tense. The only exception to this rule is when one action in a sentence clearly precedes another.

The dinosaurs are extinct now, but they were once present on the earth in large numbers.

In this case, the sentence is clearly referring to two different time periods: "now," which requires the present tense, and a period long ago, which requires the past tense.

How Do You Spot Tense Errors?

That's easy. Look for changes in verb tense in the *answer choices*. If one of the answer choices changes the tense of a verb, you should look first to see if the verb agrees with any other verbs in that sentence and second to see if the verb agrees with other verbs in the rest of the passage.

TENSE DRILL

(Answers and explanations can be found in Part VIII.)

<u>Questions 1 through 3</u> refer to the following paragraph.

(1) Here in the United States, we have one of the highest standards of living in the world, and yet we paid less in taxes than many other nations. (2) We all know that nobody liked to pay taxes. (3) On the other hand, nobody wants to see services cut, either.

1. Sentence 1: **Here in the United States, we have one of the highest standards of living in the world, and yet we <u>paid less in taxes than many other nations.</u>**

    Which of the following is the best way to write the underlined portion of this sentence? If you think the original is the best way, choose option (1).

    (1) paid
    (2) is paying
    (3) paying
    (4) pay
    (5) could pay

2. Sentence 2: **We all know that nobody liked to pay taxes.**

    Which correction should be made to sentence 2?

    (1) replace <u>We</u> with <u>You</u>
    (2) change <u>know</u> to <u>knew</u>
    (3) replace <u>that</u> with <u>which</u>
    (4) change <u>liked</u> to <u>likes</u>
    (5) no correction is necessary

3. Sentence 3: **On the other hand, nobody wants to see services cut, either.**

    Which correction should be made to sentence 3?

    (1) replace <u>On</u> with <u>In</u>
    (2) remove the comma after <u>hand</u>
    (3) replace <u>nobody</u> with <u>somebody</u>
    (4) change <u>wants</u> to <u>wanted</u>
    (5) no correction is necessary

USAGE DRILL

Here's a drill that combines all the errors you've studied in this chapter. Remember, every once in a while, the sentence will be fine just the way it is. Don't worry about timing yourself on this drill. Concentrate on using the summary we just gave you to find the problems in the sentences.

(Answers and explanations can be found in Part VIII.)

(A)

(1) People who live in the country often wonders what it would be like to live in the city. (2) Some believed that there will be gangsters shooting one another on every block. (3) Others think that crime and violence is less prevalent than television news programs would like you to believe.

(B)

(4) Some tourists visit big cities like Los Angeles or New York hoping to sight famous movie stars, but they don't happen very often. (5) No one ever says that life in the city is boring. (6) You can see live plays every night and ate late at night, long after restaurants are closed in the country. (7) One can also go to great concerts and the opera.

(C)

(8) There are some things you should know before you arrived. (9) The taxi, like the old horse-drawn carriage of the past, are the quickest way to get around the city. (10) However, if there is a lot of traffic, many cities have subways that travels underground.

---

1. Sentence 1: **People who live in the country often <u>wonders</u> what it would be like to live in the city.**

   Which of the following is the best way to write the underlined portion of this sentence? If you think the original is the best way, choose option (1).

   (1) wonders
   (2) is wondering
   (3) wonder
   (4) wondering
   (5) can wonders

2. Sentence 2: **Some <u>believed</u> that there will be gangsters shooting one another on every block.**

   Which of the following is the best way to write the underlined portion of this sentence? If you think the original is the best way, choose option (1).

   (1) believed
   (2) believe
   (3) believing
   (4) are believed
   (5) still believed

3. Sentence 3: **Others think that crime and violence is less prevalent than television news programs would like you to believe.**

   Which correction should be made to sentence 3?

   (1) replace <u>that</u> with <u>of</u>
   (2) change <u>is</u> to <u>are</u>
   (3) change the spelling of <u>prevalent</u> to <u>prevelent</u>
   (4) replace <u>than</u> with <u>like</u>
   (5) replace <u>you</u> with <u>one</u>

4. Sentence 4: **Some tourists visit big cities like Los Angeles or New York hoping to sight famous movie stars, but they don't happen very often.**

   Which correction should be made to sentence 4?

   (1) change <u>visit</u> to <u>visits</u>
   (2) insert a comma after <u>cities</u>
   (3) replace <u>sight</u> with <u>cite</u>
   (4) replace <u>they</u> with <u>these sightings</u>
   (5) no correction is necessary

5. Sentence 5: **No one ever says that life in the city is boring.**

   Which correction should be made to sentence 5?

   (1) replace <u>one</u> with <u>you</u>
   (2) change <u>says</u> to <u>say</u>
   (3) replace <u>life</u> with <u>live</u>
   (4) change <u>is</u> to <u>was</u>
   (5) no correction is necessary

6. Sentence 6: **You can see live plays every night <u>and ate late at night</u>, long after restaurants are closed in the country.**

   Which of the following is the best way to write the underlined portion of this sentence? If you think the original is the best way, choose option (1).

   (1) and ate late at night
   (2) but ate at late night
   (3) and, at night, ate late
   (4) and eat late at night
   (5) and eats at late night

7. Sentence 7: **One can also go to great concerts and the opera.**

   Which correction should be made to sentence 7?

   (1) replace <u>One</u> with <u>You</u>
   (2) change <u>can</u> to <u>could</u>
   (3) change the spelling of <u>great</u> to <u>grate</u>
   (4) insert a comma after <u>and</u>
   (5) no correction is necessary

8. Sentence 8: **There are some things you should know before you arrived.**

   Which correction should be made to sentence 8?

   (1) replace <u>there</u> with <u>their</u>
   (2) change <u>are</u> to <u>is</u>
   (3) replace <u>know</u> with <u>no</u>
   (4) insert a comma after <u>know</u>
   (5) change <u>arrived</u> to <u>arrive</u>

9. Sentence 9: **The taxi, like the old horse-drawn carriage of the past, <u>are the quickest way to get</u> around the city.**

Which of the following is the best way to write the underlined portion of this sentence? If you think the original is the best way, choose option (1).

(1) are the quickest way to get
(2) are the quickest ways of getting
(3) is the quickest way to get
(4) are the quick way of getting
(5) is the quickest ways to get

10. Sentence 10: **However, if there is a lot of traffic, many cities have subways that travels underground.**

Which correction should be made to sentence 10?

(1) remove the comma after <u>However</u>
(2) change <u>is</u> to <u>are</u>
(3) change <u>cities</u> to <u>city's</u>
(4) change <u>travels</u> to <u>travel</u>
(5) no correction is necessary

USAGE: PUTTING IT ALL TOGETHER

You've now seen all the ways that the GED will test your knowledge of word usage. Let's review what you are going to be looking for as you read each question in the Language Arts, Writing test.

o   In each clause of a sentence, the verb must agree with the subject. Does it? To check, find the subject and verb of each clause. (It may help to cover up any extraneous words, phrases, or clauses that are in between the subject and the verb.) If you find a subject that doesn't agree with the verb, look for an answer that fixes the problem in the answer choices. In sentence revision questions, the answer choices will offer *several* different versions of the same verb.

o   A pronoun takes the place of a noun, but in order to do so correctly, first, it must be clear to what or whom the pronoun is referring, and second, the pronoun must agree with the noun. As you read each sentence, look for pronouns. As soon as you've spotted one, check to see if it is used correctly. Again, in sentence revision questions, the answer choices will help clue you in by offering *several* different pronouns from which to choose.

o   On the GED, there are only two tenses: present and past. In general, the verbs within a sentence should stay in the same tense. The passages as a whole should also stay in the same tense. To spot tense problems, look at the answer choices for different forms of the verb.

o   On the Language Arts, Writing test, the only time it is necessary to look at the passage in front of the questions (to answer questions correctly) is when the questions concern pronouns or tense. These are the only questions that test your understanding of the context of the passage.

Chapter 9
Mechanics and Organization

In this chapter, you'll learn how to spot errors involving punctuation, capitalization, spelling, and organization.

Now that you know about sentence structure and the rules of usage, let's look at the last two categories tested on the Language Arts, Writing test: mechanics and organization. There are three parts to mechanics on the GED:

- Punctuation
- Capitalization
- Spelling (including possessives, contractions, and soundalikes)

While it may seem that the rules of mechanics are less important to proper writing than, say, sentence structure or usage, they still account for 25 percent of the subject matter on the Language Arts, Writing multiple-choice test. Think of it this way: The smaller details of writing can make a big impression. Poor spelling, improper capitalization, a comma in the wrong place—any of these can undermine even the most thoughtfully written passage.

Fortunately, it turns out that the GED really only touches the surface of English mechanics, and you won't need to know very much to do well on the test.

Punctuation

Punctuation is designed to help make a sentence's structure clear to the reader. Punctuation marks imitate the natural pauses that we insert into a sentence when we read it aloud, including the momentary hesitation of a comma, the upward lilt of a question mark, and the full stop of a period.

On the GED, however, only one type of punctuation is ever tested: **the comma.** It's not that you won't see periods and question marks. These appear in the passages and the questions all the time—but they're always correct just the way they are. Thus, the only type of punctuation that is ever wrong on the test is the comma. If you've gone through our sentence structure chapter, you've already learned most of the rules you'll need.

> **Which Punctuation Marks Are Wrong?**
> Generally speaking on the GED, look no further than the comma. While you'll see periods and question marks, the only punctuation mark that is ever incorrect is the comma.

The Rules of Commas

Rule One Whenever two independent clauses are joined together in one sentence with a coordinating conjunction (such as *and* or *but*), insert a comma between the two clauses.

> *Rita finished her GED review last week, but Jeff is still reviewing.*

Rule Two   Whenever a dependent clause (beginning with a subordinating conjunction such as *because, while, after, although*, etc.) comes before an independent clause, insert a comma between the two clauses.

> *Because she was already done, Rita had time to help Jeff.*

However, if the dependent clause comes *after* the independent clause, you do not need to add the comma. Let's take the same example we just used and turn it around.

> *Rita had time to help Jeff because she was already done.*

Rule Three   Whenever a sentence is introduced by an introductory phrase, separate the phrase from the rest of the sentence by a comma.

> *According to Rita, Jeff is an excellent student.*

> *Studying quickly, Jeff made lots of progress.*

Rule Four   When a phrase in the middle of a sentence adds parenthetical information, separate it from the rest of the sentence by putting commas on both sides of it.

> *Rita, who wants to become a high school teacher, was happy to help.*

> *Jeff, of course, was thrilled.*

Rule Five   Whenever a sentence lists a series of three or more nouns or three or more actions, insert a comma between each element in the series.

> *Jeff needed help with his science, math, and English.*

> *Jeff studied, memorized, and practiced.*

You don't need to put a comma *before* the series or *after* it. For example, it would be incorrect to write:

> *Jeff needed help with, his science, math, and English.*

You also don't need to put a comma between two items in a series. The following is incorrect:

> *Jeff studied, and memorized the vocabulary words.*

The Punctuation Error
Tip-Off
General bad structure plus
changes in punctuation in
answer choices

How Do You Spot Punctuation Errors?

The whole purpose of punctuation is to make sentence structure clear to the reader. Therefore, because you are already on the lookout for sentence structure errors, you are already well on your way toward spotting punctuation errors on the GED.

As you check a sentence to see if it has more than one independent clause, check to see if there is a comma between the two clauses. While you are checking a sentence with a series of items to see if they are parallel, look for commas between each item as well. If a sentence begins with an introductory clause or phrase, make sure there is a comma separating it from the independent clause that follows.

As always, if a question is in the sentence revision format, you will be able to spot the type of error by looking at the answer choices. Commas inserted in different locations are a good sign that the error is one of punctuation.

PUNCTUATION DRILL

(Answers and explanations can be found in Part VIII.)

<u>Questions 1 through 4</u> refer to the following paragraph.

(1) Obviously, although many people try to climb Mount Everest few people succeed. (2) The well-prepared climber must bring rope food, water, and warm clothing. (3) For many days any persons attempting the climb will be completely on their own. (4) For beginning climbers, that is any climbers who have not already scaled several major mountains, Mount Everest seems too difficult to tackle.

1. Sentence 1: **Obviously, although many people <u>try to climb Mount Everest</u> few people succeed.**

   Which of the following is the best way to write the underlined portion of this sentence? If you think the original is the best way, choose option (1).

   (1) try to climb Mount Everest
   (2) try to climb Mount Everest,
   (3) try climbing, Mount Everest
   (4) trying to climb Mount Everest
   (5) attempt Mount Everest

2. Sentence 2: **The well-prepared climber must bring rope food, water, and warm clothing.**

   Which correction should be made to sentence 2?

   (1) change <u>bring</u> to <u>brought</u>
   (2) insert a comma after <u>bring</u>
   (3) insert a comma after <u>rope</u>
   (4) replace <u>and</u> with <u>or</u>
   (5) change the spelling of <u>clothing</u> to <u>clothin</u>

3. Sentence 3: **For many <u>days any</u> persons attempting the climb will be completely on their own.**

   Which of the following is the best way to write the underlined portion of this sentence? If you think the original is the best way, choose option (1).

   (1) days any
   (2) days and any
   (3) days however any
   (4) days but any
   (5) days, any

4. Sentence 4: **For beginning climbers, that is any climbers who have not already scaled several major mountains, Mount Everest seems too difficult to tackle.**

   Which correction should be made to sentence 4?

   (1) insert a comma after <u>is</u>
   (2) change the spelling of <u>several</u> to <u>sevaral</u>
   (3) change <u>Mount Everest</u> to <u>mount everest</u>
   (4) change <u>seems</u> to <u>seem</u>
   (5) no correction is necessary

Capitalization

Proper capitalization helps clarify the meaning of sentences. By capitalizing the first word of a sentence, we emphasize that a new thought is beginning. By capitalizing proper names, we stress the uniqueness of the person, place, or thing we are describing.

On the GED, capitalization errors concerning the first word of a sentence are never tested. Instead, the GED test writers concentrate on four rules.

The Rules of Capitalization

Rule One   Capitalize the name of any specific person, place, or thing. This will hold true as long as the noun used is the name of a particular person, place, or thing. For example:

Capitalize

> I think Fred Jones is my neighbor.
> Spain is a beautiful country.
> The National Organization for Women has many members.
> I hear that Washington State gets a lot of rain.

Do not capitalize

> I think the guy across the street is my neighbor.
> The country next to France is very beautiful.
> The organization has many members.
> The states in the northwest part of the country get a lot of rain.

As you can see, while a specific noun must be capitalized, a nonspecific noun or group of nonspecific nouns is not.

Rule Two   Capitalize the adjective form of any nouns capitalized under rule one:

> The Spanish countryside is very beautiful.
> The January snowfall is often very heavy.

Rule Three   Capitalize a person's title as long as the title is being used in connection with the name of the person.

Capitalize

> I would like to speak to Doctor Kevorkian right away.
> Will Senator Smith be at the vote today?

Do not capitalize

> I would like to speak to the doctor right away.
> Will the senator be at the vote today?

GED Pop Quiz

Q: Which famous Olympic gymnast was a GED graduate?

Answer on page 146

Rule Four   Capitalize the *specific* names of national holidays, days of the week, and months. Do not capitalize seasons or personal holidays such as birthdays or anniversaries.

Capitalize

> I will see you on Christmas Day.
> This year, Christmas takes place on a Tuesday.
> It is usually very cold in January.

Do not capitalize

> I will see you in the winter.
> I don't know the day of the week on which the holiday occurs.
> The first month of the year is usually very cold.
> My birthday is today.

Common Mistakes

There are not many capitalization errors on the GED, but when they do come up, they tend to concern words that many students are unsure of. The best way to prepare for capitalization questions on the GED is to study the rules above. The key is to decide whether a word is the specific name of a person, place, or thing or whether it is being used instead in a more generic sense.

> *The Chrysler Company will have a big profit this year.*

> *The company will have a big profit this year.*

Pay particular attention to specific months (February, August, etc.), days of the week (Tuesday, Wednesday, etc.), and school topics (French, history, science, English, etc.). As you probably noticed from the last example, only school topics that involve a language are capitalized.

How to Spot Capitalization Errors

Capitalization errors on the GED are divided between sentences in which a word that is *not* capitalized needs to be capitalized and sentences in which a word that is *already* capitalized needs instead to be in the lowercase.

As you read a sentence, keep capitalization in the back of your mind, but remember that there are very few capitalization errors on the GED—so you don't need to drive yourself crazy examining every word with a microscope.

The Capitalization Error Tip-Off
There are very few of these, so the only time you have to worry about it is if you see changes in capitalization in the answer choices.

The only words you will ever have to examine for capitalization problems are the ones you find in the *answer choices*. Here is a set of answer choices without the original sentence. Which of these words do we need to check for proper capitalization?

(1)   remove the comma after <u>this</u>
(2)   change <u>were</u> to <u>was</u>
(3)   change the spelling of <u>tomorrow</u> to <u>tomorow</u>
(4)   insert a comma after <u>books</u>
(5)   no correction is necessary

GED Pop Quiz
A: Mary Lou Retton

We don't have to check any! In this question, capitalization is not even an option. The only time you have to consider capitalization is when it shows up in the answer choices. Here's another set of answer choices. Do we need to check the capitalization? If so, which words must we check?

(1)   change <u>Countries</u> to <u>countries</u>
(2)   change <u>have</u> to <u>has</u>
(3)   remove the comma after <u>authorities</u>
(4)   replace <u>that</u> with <u>which</u>
(5)   change <u>are</u> to <u>is</u>

This time, the only possible capitalization problem concerns the word *Countries*.

CAPITALIZATION DRILL
(Answers and explanations can be found in Part VIII.)

Questions 1 through 4 refer to the following paragraph.

(1) One of the most annoying things that can happen is when a relative calls you on friday to tell you that he is coming to spend the weekend. (2) Even presidents and congressmen are not exempt from this problem. (3) Last Fall, Congressman Brown from Kentucky had seven relatives arrive for Easter, with no warning at all. (4) The worst thing about the unexpected visitors was that they happened to arrive in the middle of dinner on the congressman's Birthday.

1. Sentence 1: **One of the most annoying things that can happen is when a relative calls you on friday to tell you that he is coming to spend the weekend.**

   Which correction should be made to sentence 1?

   (1) insert a comma after <u>happen</u>
   (2) change <u>is</u> to <u>are</u>
   (3) change <u>friday</u> to <u>Friday</u>
   (4) change <u>weekend</u> to <u>Weekend</u>
   (5) no correction is necessary

2. Sentence 2: **Even presidents and congressmen are not exempt from this problem.**

   Which correction should be made to sentence 2?

   (1) change <u>presidents</u> to <u>Presidents</u>
   (2) replace <u>and</u> with <u>or</u>
   (3) change <u>congressmen</u> to <u>Congressmen</u>
   (4) insert a comma after <u>exempt</u>
   (5) no correction is necessary

3. Sentence 3: **Last Fall, Congressman Brown from Kentucky had seven relatives arrive for Easter, with no warning at all.**

   Which correction should be made to sentence 3?

   (1) change <u>Fall</u> to <u>fall</u>
   (2) change <u>Congressman</u> to <u>congressman</u>
   (3) change <u>Kentucky</u> to <u>kentucky</u>
   (4) change <u>arrive</u> to <u>arrives</u>
   (5) change <u>Easter</u> to <u>easter</u>

4. Sentence 4: **The worst thing about the unexpected visitors was that they happened to arrive in the middle of dinner on the congressman's Birthday.**

   Which correction should be made to sentence 4?

   (1) change <u>was</u> to <u>were</u>
   (2) replace <u>in</u> with <u>on</u>
   (3) insert a comma after <u>arrive</u>
   (4) change <u>Birthday</u> to <u>birthday</u>
   (5) no correction is necessary

Spelling

Unfortunately, English words are often not spelled the way they sound, and this means that improving your spelling in any meaningful way takes time—time spent reading articles and books, time spent memorizing words, and time spent writing essays and letters.

While improving your spelling in general is a worthwhile long-term project, it does not take that long to learn some of the most commonly misspelled words that come up on the GED. That's because the GED tests only three rules of spelling.

The Rules of Spelling

Rule One—Possessives   To make a singular noun possessive, simply add *'s* to the word.

> *Jane's car is parked outside.*

To make a plural noun that already ends in an *s* possessive, simply add an apostrophe to the end of the word.

> *The three boys' bicycles were in the garage.*

If the word is one of the rare plural nouns that doesn't end in *s*, then add *'s*.

> *The firemen's truck was double-parked.*

When you use a pronoun, the possessive forms of pronouns don't need apostrophes.

me	→	my, mine
you	→	your, yours
he	→	his
she	→	her, hers
it	→	its
they	→	their, theirs

Spelling Flash Card

Q: Which of the following is spelled correctly?
- librarys
- holidays
- studys

Answer on page 150

Rule Two—Contractions   In English, we frequently use shortcuts to express what we are trying to say. Rather than write

>   *I cannot do that.*

we often write

>   *I can't do that.*

On the GED, the only time contractions can be confusing is when you aren't sure whether a word is truly a contraction or just a possessive pronoun. Look at the three sentences below and decide which choices are correct.

>   *(Its, It's) time for me to go to work.*

>   *(Your, You're) not ready.*

>   *(Their, They're) coming to work with me.*

The GED test writers love to try to confuse you with these three commonly confused sets of words, but there is an easy way to decide which word is correct. In each example, you should ask yourself whether the word could be replaced by the two words that a contraction stands for.

Let's look at those sentences again. To decide if we need a contraction, try substituting the un-contracted form of the word in each sentence. If it makes sense, then the contraction is correct.

>   ***It is** time for me to go to work.*

>   ***You are** not ready.*

>   ***They are** coming to work with me.*

Did these sentences make sense? Yes! This means that the contractions were correct in all three sentences. Let's try another.

>   *You're car is blocking the driveway.*

To see if this sentence is correct, let's replace the contraction *you're* with the two words it really stands for: *you are.*

>   *You are car is blocking the driveway.*

Does that make sense? No way. This time, we need the possessive pronoun. Here's how this sentence should look:

>   *Your car is blocking the driveway.*

Rule Three—Look Out for Soundalikes   On the GED, you will sometimes run across sentences that offer a choice of two *correctly* spelled words. These words, called **homophones,** sound very similar but mean two entirely different things. In this case, what is being tested is not your spelling, but your understanding of the definition of these words. Here is a list of some of the pairs of soundalikes that appear on the GED. If you are unsure of the meaning of any of these words, look them up in the dictionary, make flash cards, and have a friend quiz you until you know them.

Spelling Flash Card

A: *Holidays* is correct because the *y* is preceded by a vowel. The other two should be spelled *libraries* and *studies*.

accept/except	no/know
advice/advise	peace/piece
affect/effect	personal/personnel
board/bored	principal/principle
brake/break	quiet/quite
capital/capitol	role/roll
chose/choose	sight/site
coarse/course	there/their/they're
council/counsel	through/thorough
desert/dessert	to/two/too
loose/lose	weak/week
new/knew	weather/whether

How to Spot Spelling Errors

It's easy to get paranoid and start suspecting that every word in each sentence is misspelled. Relax. First of all, there are an average of only eight spelling questions on the GED anyway, and you can get many of them wrong and still pass the test. Second of all, you don't have to worry about spelling at all unless it is an option in one of the answer choices.

Remember, this is a multiple-choice test, and there can be only one correct answer.

If none of the answer choices change the spelling of a word in a sentence, then there cannot possibly be a spelling mistake in that sentence.

Spelling errors mostly appear in questions in the sentence correction format. Here are the answer choices to a typical question in this format:

(1) insert a comma after <u>appears</u>
(2) change the spelling of <u>your</u> to <u>you're</u>
(3) replace <u>something</u> with <u>someone</u>
(4) replace <u>that</u> with <u>and</u>
(5) no correction is necessary

Did we have to worry about spelling in this question? Yes. There is potentially *one* contraction to check: *your* versus *you're*. We don't even have to think about the spelling of any other word in this sentence.

The only other things to look out for are soundalikes. Here is another set of answer choices. Do we have to be concerned about spelling in this case?

(1) change <u>offices</u> to <u>office</u>
(2) remove the comma after <u>entertainment</u>
(3) replace <u>new</u> with <u>knew</u>
(4) change <u>match</u> to <u>matches</u>
(5) change <u>is</u> to <u>was</u>

Obviously, there is no spelling mistake in this sentence, but there is a potential soundalike problem. If this were a real question, we would have to check the sentence to see which word—*new* or *knew*—was correct.

Spelling Flash Card

Q: Which of the following is used incorrectly?

- You're place or mine?
- Their apartment is a mess.
- It's time to leave.

Answer on page 152

SPELLING DRILL

(Answers and explanations can be found in Part VIII.)

1. Sentence 1: **Small companies offer a new employee more responsibility, and there health benefits are generous.**

    Which correction should be made to sentence 1?

    (1) change <u>companies</u> to <u>Companies</u>
    (2) remove the comma after <u>responsibility</u>
    (3) replace <u>there</u> with <u>their</u>
    (4) change <u>are</u> to <u>is</u>
    (5) no correction is necessary

2. Sentence 2: **If your thinking about getting a job, the best place to look is the classified section of a local newspaper.**

    Which correction should be made to sentence 2?

    (1) replace <u>your</u> with <u>you're</u>
    (2) remove the comma after <u>job</u>
    (3) change <u>place</u> to <u>places</u>
    (4) insert a comma after <u>look</u>
    (5) no correction is necessary

3. Sentence 3: **Lets be frank; only small companies advertise in local newspapers.**

    Which correction should be made to sentence 3?

    (1) replace <u>Lets</u> with <u>Let's</u>
    (2) change <u>frank</u> to <u>Frank</u>
    (3) change the spelling of <u>companies</u> to <u>company's</u>
    (4) change the spelling of <u>in</u> to <u>inn</u>
    (5) insert comma after <u>advertise</u>

MECHANICS DRILL

In this drill, you will find only the errors of mechanics that have been covered in this chapter.

(Answers and explanations can be found in Part VIII.)

(A)

(1) Accept for dentists' offices, the place people dislike the most is airport waiting rooms. (2) They hate the noise the boredom, and the crowds. (3) Its always difficult to get there in the first place.

(B)

(4) For example, last Thanksgiving it took passengers two hours to get to the airport from downtown Chicago. (5) Once they finally got there they were told that all flights were delayed for several hours because of bad weather. (6) If anyone left without breakfast, there was plenty of time for a bowl of serial. (7) The passengers tried to call their relatives but the phone lines were jammed. (8) Even the president of a large company had to wait in the long lines, and she decided she was not going to travel again until the Spring.

(C)

(9) Finally, the airport was officially closed for the day because of heavy fog. (10) Everyones luggage had to be found, and then the passengers faced the difficult trip back to Chicago.

1. Sentence 1: **Accept for dentists' offices, the place people dislike the most is airport waiting rooms.**

    Which of the following is the best way to write the underlined portion of this sentence? If you think the original is the best way, choose option (1).

    (1)   Accept for dentists' offices
    (2)   Accept for dentist's offices
    (3)   Except for dentists' offices
    (4)   Except for dentists' office
    (5)   Accept for the offices' of dentists

2. Sentence 2: **They hate the noise the boredom, and the crowds.**

    Which correction should be made to sentence 2?

    (1)   replace They with We
    (2)   insert a comma after noise
    (3)   remove the word the before boredom
    (4)   remove the comma after boredom
    (5)   replace and with or

3. Sentence 3: **Its always difficult to get there in the first place.**

Which of the following is the best way to write the underlined portion of this sentence? If you think the original is the best way, choose option (1).

(1) Its always difficult to get
(2) It's always difficult for getting
(3) It's always difficult to get
(4) Its always difficult for getting
(5) Its difficult always to get

4. Sentence 4: **For example, last Thanksgiving it took passengers two hours to get to the airport from downtown Chicago.**

Which correction should be made to sentence 4?

(1) remove the comma after example
(2) change Thanksgiving to thanksgiving
(3) replace it with they
(4) change to get to for getting
(5) no correction is necessary

5. Sentence 5: **Once they finally got there they were told that all flights were delayed for several hours because of bad weather.**

Which correction should be made to sentence 5?

(1) replace there with their
(2) insert a comma after there
(3) change were to are
(4) insert a comma after hours
(5) replace weather with whether

6. Sentence 6: **If anyone left without breakfast, there was plenty of time for a bowl of serial.**

Which correction should be made to sentence 6?

(1) change breakfast to Breakfast
(2) replace there with their
(3) change was to is
(4) replace serial with cereal
(5) no correction is necessary

7. Sentence 7: **The passengers tried to call their relatives but the phone lines were jammed.**

   Which correction should be made to sentence 7?

   (1) change <u>passengers</u> to <u>passenger's</u>
   (2) replace <u>their</u> with <u>they're</u>
   (3) insert a comma after <u>relatives</u>
   (4) replace <u>but</u> with <u>and</u>
   (5) change <u>were</u> to <u>are</u>

8. Sentence 8: **Even the president of a large company had to wait in the long lines, and she decided she was not going to travel again until the Spring.**

   Which correction should be made to sentence 8?

   (1) change <u>president</u> to <u>President</u>
   (2) change the spelling of <u>had</u> to <u>has</u>
   (3) remove the comma after <u>lines</u>
   (4) change <u>decided</u> to <u>decides</u>
   (5) change <u>Spring</u> to <u>spring</u>

9. Sentence 9: **<u>Finally, the airport was officially closed</u> for the day because of heavy fog.**

   Which of the following is the best way to write the underlined portion of this sentence? If you think the original is the best way, choose option (1).

   (1) Finally, the airport was officially closed
   (2) Finally the airport was officially closed
   (3) Finally the airport is, officially, closed
   (4) The airport was, finally officially closed
   (5) The airport is officially closed finally

10. Sentence 10: **<u>Everyones luggage had</u> to be found, and then the passengers faced the difficult trip back to Chicago.**

    Which of the following is the best way to write the underlined portion of this sentence? If you think the original is the best way, choose option (1).

    (1) Everyones luggage had
    (2) Everyones' luggage had
    (3) Everyone's luggage had
    (4) Everyone's luggage has
    (5) Everyones luggage has

Organization

While the rest of the Language Arts, Writing test is about what happens *inside* sentences, organization questions are about how you put whole sentences together. If you've already read our chapter on Crazy Reading, you're well on your way to being prepared for these questions because they are really all about structure.

In organization questions, you will be asked to rearrange the sentences within a paragraph or to rearrange entire paragraphs of a reading passage, to make the idea of the passage clear.

Organizing Sentences

Let's begin with a simple example. Read the following four sentences and rearrange them so that they make sense as a paragraph.

---

(1) First, you must have a high school diploma or equivalent. (2) Finally, you must send your school transcripts to the office of admissions by October 15th. (3) You must complete an admission application. (4) To apply for entry to The Green Technical Institute, there are three basic requirements.

Here's How to Crack It

At first glance, you might think sentence 1 should begin the paragraph because it starts with the word *first*. But keep reading. Do you see a sentence that seems to summarize and set up the other sentences? If you said sentence 4, then you're exactly right. Sentence 4 should go first in this paragraph. It's called the topic sentence because it introduces the topic of the entire paragraph. In this case, it tells us that there are three requirements for admission to this school.

Now, which of the remaining sentences should follow? If you said sentence 1, then you're right again. Because there are three requirements, it makes sense that the author would list the three requirements in order. The sentence that begins with *first* is the logical next sentence. Which sentence should go last? Well, when three things get listed, the last one often begins with a *finally*. Here is the paragraph correctly rearranged.

(4) To apply for entry to The Green Technical Institute, there are three basic requirements. (1) First, you must have a high school diploma or equivalent. (3) You must complete an admission application. (2) Finally, you must send your school transcripts to the office of admissions by October 15th.

How to Spot Sentence Organization

The key to sentence organization is to find the topic sentence of the paragraph. In a well-written paragraph, the topic sentence is often the first sentence. It states the main idea of the paragraph and sets up the sentences that follow. The GED tests your ability to spot topic sentences in two ways: by asking you to reorganize a paragraph, as you did just a moment ago, or by asking you to pick a topic sentence for a paragraph that is missing one.

SENTENCE DRILL

(Answers and explanations can be found in Part VIII.)

Read the paragraph below and answer the questions that follow.

(1) Unlike hardcover books, you can easily put them in a purse or pocket. (2) They are cheaper and easier to find in stores. (3) Furthermore, paperbacks are more easily biodegradable and thus better for the environment.

1. Which sentence below would be most effective if inserted at the beginning of the paragraph above?

    (1) Hardcover books have many disadvantages.
    (2) Paperback books have many advantages.
    (3) Some things don't fit easily into the purse or pocket.
    (4) Paperback books have many disadvantages.
    (5) Reading can be fun.

2. What would most likely be the first sentence of a paragraph that followed this one?

    (1) However, hardcover books have advantages, too.
    (2) Purses are too bulky these days.
    (3) The environment is not in as great danger as people say.
    (4) Stores sell many products.
    (5) One writer that I like a lot is Shakespeare.

Organizing Paragraphs

Organizing paragraphs is a lot like organizing the sentences *within* a paragraph, in that what's important is spotting topic sentences. Take a look at the following three-paragraph example, in which all but the topic sentences have been left out:

(A)

However, the George Washington Bridge is the city's most underrated. Blah blah blah Blah blah. Blah Blah blah blah Blah blah blah Blah blah blah Blah blah blah Blah blah blah.

(B)

New York's oldest bridge, the Brooklyn Bridge, is perhaps the city's most famous. Blah blah blah Blah blah. Blah Blah blah blah Blah blah blah Blah blah blah Blah blah blah Blah blah blah.

(C)

Some of the finest bridges in the world were built in New York City. Blah blah blah Blah blah. Blah Blah blah blah Blah blah blah Blah blah blah Blah blah blah Blah blah blah.

Here's How to Crack It

To figure out the order of several paragraphs, all you have to do is look at the topic sentence of each. In the example above, of course, you can't read anything else because the rest of the paragraphs are missing. But you'll find that topic sentences are generally all you'll need. Just as a paragraph has a topic sentence, a passage generally has a topic paragraph, which sets out in general terms what the passage will be about. Usually this paragraph is the first one in the passage, but there are exceptions.

In the passage above, paragraph A tells us about a particular bridge. Paragraph B tells us about another bridge. Paragraph C, however, gives us a general statement that seems to tell us what the passage is about. Which do you think should start the passage? If you guessed paragraph C, you are absolutely correct.

How to Spot Paragraph Organization

Look for topic sentences. Don't even bother to read the rest of the paragraphs right away. All you want is an overview of what the passage is about. This will help you understand the entire passage and help you reorder the paragraphs if need be. You can read the rest of the passage only if necessary—for example, when you are asked a more specific question that involves reordering sentences *within* a paragraph.

As you read topic sentences, look for the same organization words we discussed in Chapter 5, "Crazy Reading."

first → second → third   thus
primarily → secondarily   henceforth
one reason → another reason → finally consequently
for one thing → for another thing as a result
therefore   in conclusion, finally

These words help give away the organization of a passage. Also keep your eyes peeled for contrast words like:

but   while
however   despite
on the contrary   in spite of
although   rather
yet   nevertheless, instead

Contrast words signal a big change, and they can often be found at the beginning of paragraphs.

ORGANIZING PARAGRAPHS DRILL
(Answers can be found in Part VIII.)

3.   In the passage below, reorder the paragraphs.

(A)

The next step is to sift through everything you've written and organize it by topic. You will probably revise your resume many times before you're finished, but it will all be worthwhile when you finally look at the finished product.

(B)

However, the intimidation does not have to be permanent. With a little work, you can learn how to overcome your resume fears. The first step is to write down a complete record of your education, work experience, and activities—but not as a polished document. You just want to get everything down on paper.

(C)

Writing a resume can be a difficult experience. Confronting a blank page and your own lack of experience is intimidating for everyone, especially for first timers.

ORGANIZATION LETTER DRILL

Read the passage below, and answer the questions that follow.

(Answers and explanations can be found in Part VIII.)

June 12, 2011
Richard Gonzales
Computer Services Inc.
45 Wilshire Boulevard
Los Angeles, CA 90231

Dear Mr. Gonzales:

(A)

(1) I have been employed as an office manager for the past five years, at two different firms, Silicon Services and Mercer Textiles, both companies with about 30 employees. (2) Before entering the office environment, I worked for two years as a cook where I learned to keep an even disposition. (3) My responsibilities as office manager at both companies included managing support staff, ordering supplies, and interfacing with building maintenance and security. (4) At Silicon Services, I was also in charge of coordinating computer technical support for all staff workstations. (5) In addition, at Mercer Textiles, I set up a new tracking system to keep track of office inventory, which is still being used three years later.

(B)

(6) I am writing in regard to the advertisement you placed in the *Daily Gazette* this Thursday for an office manager. (7) I would very much like to apply for the position.

(C)

(8) I am good with people and very organized. (9) My coworkers know that I am fair but firm when it comes to keeping down costs. (10) The fact that I am bilingual has also come in handy—particularly at Mercer Textiles, where half the staff spoke Spanish. (11) I am a motivated person and can help to get others motivated as well.

(D)

(12) I hope that you will take a look at my resume, which I have attached to this letter. Please feel free to call me with any questions you may have or to contact any of my references. (13) I hope we speak soon in person. (14) You can reach me at (213) 555-2424 or at Nsilver@email.com.

Sincerely,
Nancy Silver

4. Which of the following revisions would most improve this letter?

    (1) Move paragraph B to the beginning of the letter.
    (2) Move paragraph A to the end of the letter.
    (3) Place paragraph C before paragraph B.
    (4) Place paragraph D before paragraph C.
    (5) Remove paragraph D from the letter entirely.

5. Which sentence below would be most effective if inserted at the beginning of paragraph C?

    (1) It's really hard to explain my abilities.
    (2) Although I have had some problems with authority in the past, I believe that I have licked the problem.
    (3) I feel that my experience matches the qualities you said you were looking for in your advertisement.
    (4) If anything, I think I am overqualified for this job.
    (5) One of my friends told me about this job.

6. Which of the following revisions would improve paragraph A?

    (1) Move sentence 2 to the end of paragraph A.
    (2) Move sentence 2 to the end of paragraph B.
    (3) Move sentence 2 to the beginning of paragraph A.
    (4) Remove sentence 3.
    (5) No revision is necessary.

MECHANICS & ORGANIZATION: PUTTING IT ALL TOGETHER

You've now seen all the ways that the GED will test your knowledge of mechanics. Let's review what you are going to be looking for as you read each question in the Language Arts, Writing test.

- The only punctuation that is really tested on the GED is the comma. As you check each sentence for its structure, take a second to make sure its punctuation is correct as well.

  - A comma is needed between two independent clauses or after a dependent clause that leads into an independent clause.
  - A comma also goes between an introductory phrase and an independent clause.
  - A comma is also needed on either side of a parenthetical phrase.
  - Commas must be inserted between each item in a series of three or more actions or nouns.

- The GED never tests the capitalization of the first word of a sentence. There is no need to check capitalization of each word in a sentence. Instead, check the capitalization of words in the *answer choices*. Use the following rules:

  - Capitalize the name of any specific person, place, or thing.
  - Capitalize the adjective form of any specific person, place, or thing.
  - Capitalize the title of a person as long as the title is being used in connection with the name of the person.
  - Capitalize the *specific* names of national holidays, days of the week, and months but *not* the names of seasons or personal holidays.

- There are only three rules of spelling tested on the GED:

  - To indicate possession, add *'s* for singular nouns (and plural nouns that don't end in *s*).
  - Be careful to distinguish between a contraction and a possessive pronoun.
  - Look out for soundalikes—see the list on page 150.

- Organization questions involve either moving, removing, or inserting a new sentence into a paragraph—or moving around whole paragraphs. Either way, the key is to look for the structural words we've shown you here and in Chapter 5, "Crazy Reading," to help you find topic sentences.

Part II Summary

The multiple-choice portion of the Language Arts, Writing test consists of 50 questions that test your grammar, spelling, punctuation, and capitalization skills. But the good news is that the GED tests only very specific rules of English, which can be readily mastered.

- You can fix sentence fragments (incomplete sentences) by changing dependent clauses into independent clauses that contain subjects and verbs.

- You can fix comma splices by turning long run-on sentences into two separate sentences. Or you can fix them by linking related clauses together with a conjunction such as *and* or *but* or with a subordinating conjunction such as *because* or *although*.

- You can generally fix misplaced modifiers by making it crystal clear that the modifying phrase refers to the noun it is supposed to be modifying.

- Parallel construction involves spotting a list of verbs or nouns. Each item on the list must be in the same form.

- Verbs must agree with their subjects. GED test writers will sometimes put modifying phrases between the subject and the verb to try to confuse you—but if you check to make sure the subject and the verb agree, you won't be fooled.

o   Whenever you spot a pronoun, you should check to see (1) if it agrees with the noun it refers to and (2) if it is consistent with the other pronouns being used in the piece; a needless shift in a passage from one type of pronoun to another often signals an error.

o   If a sentence starts in one tense, then the rest of the sentence should stay in that tense. If an entire passage starts in one tense, the rest of the passage should stay in that tense. Only two tenses show up on the GED: the present and the past.

o   On the GED, the only type of punctuation you have to understand is the use of commas. To ace the punctuation on the Writing test, study the five comma rules in Chapter 9.

o   The rules of capitalization in English are complex, but GED capitalization is based on four rules covered in Chapter 9.

o   Spelling errors on the GED tend to involve possessives, contractions, and soundalikes (words that sound similar but which are spelled differently, such as *accept* and *except).* The best way to prepare for these words is to review the rules and memorize the lists contained in Chapter 9.

Part III
How to Crack the Language Arts, Essay Test

Chapter 10
Language Arts,
Essay Overview

When you get your GED score report in the mail about eight weeks after you take the exam, you will notice that even though you took two writing-related tests (part one, the multiple-choice test we've just described in the last three chapters, and part two, the essay test we'll describe here), you will receive only one score. This is because the results from the two tests are combined. The essay counts for 35 to 40 percent of your total Language Arts, Writing score.

You may think there is really no way to prepare for the essay section of the GED (other than by practicing writing over a long period of time). After all, you won't find out the topic of the essay until you get there, and there is no way to plan your essay in advance.

Breaking It Down
Around 40 percent of your total writing skills score is based on your essay.

Oh Yes, You *Can* Plan Your Essay in Advance!

In fact, there are some very specific ways to prepare for the GED essay. Like the multiple-choice portion of this test, the essay test is completely predictable. The essay topics have to conform to a rigid set of rules designed to ensure that all topics are of the same difficulty and test the same set of skills. While it is impossible to predict the *exact* essay topic you will see on your GED, it is very easy to predict the general characteristics of the topic. We will describe these characteristics to you in the next chapter.

It's also easy to predict the *responses* to the essay topics that will receive the highest grades. The essay portion of the GED is the only part of the test that can't be scored by computer. The people who create the GED have a huge problem—they have to read more than 700,000 essays every year. It takes a lot of readers to do that, and it's difficult to make sure that all the readers are grading according to the exact same scale. To ensure that all the essays are scored the same way, the people who write the GED came up with a method of scoring GED essays known as the holistic method. This method is rigidly enforced. Essay readers are trained to look for very specific criteria in your essay—and we will tell you those criteria later in this chapter.

Who Are the Essay Graders Anyway?
They're English teachers. To become a GED essay grader, you have to have a college degree in English and some experience in teaching English at the high school level or higher. In addition, you have to have gone through a training session and passed some kind of an essay-grading test.

A few of the graders are college teachers, but most are current or former high school teachers.

How Are the Essays Graded?

Two different graders will read your essay. Each assigns it a grade from 1 (not too good) to 4 (you're our kind of people). If the two grades are within one point of each other, they are averaged to determine your essay score. If the two grades are more than one point apart, a *third* grader reads your essay and decides your essay score. This is to ensure that no one reader can overly influence the scoring process.

How Much Time Do They Get to Grade Each Essay?

Two minutes, tops. Essays are graded in eight-hour marathon sessions (nine to five, with an hour off for lunch). According to an ACE spokesperson, a good essay reader can do 25 to 35 per hour, which averages out to about two minutes each.

Obviously, these overwhelmed graders do not have time for an in-depth reading of your essay. They probably aren't going to notice how carefully you thought out your ideas or how clever your analysis was. Under pressure to meet their quota, they are simply going to read your essays with a checklist. As soon as they have found the items on their checklist, they are on to the next essay.

By the time your reader gets to your essay, she will probably already have seen more than 100 others—and no matter how ingenious you were in coming up with original thoughts, many of those essays will almost certainly have used some of the same ideas.

Our point is that GED essay readers are not necessarily going to be impressed by imagination or intelligence. For one thing, they really don't have time to notice qualities like these. For another thing, imagination and intelligence are, unfortunately, not on their checklist. The essay readers have to follow strict GED guidelines. If they don't, they get canned.

So what's on their checklist?

Organization and Support

The two most important things essay readers are told to look for are (1) the organization of the essay and (2) the specific examples that you give in support of your main point. These examples can be personal observations from your own experience or examples from literature.

Good organization and good examples backing up your argument are vital for scoring well on the GED essay. Also important, of course, is your ability to effectively use "the rules of Standard Written English"—spelling, grammar, and so on.

So given what we know about the GED essay, the way it is graded, and who grades it, how can you plan your essay in advance?

Creating a Template

When a builder builds a house, one of the first things he does is construct a frame. The frame supports the entire house. After the frame is completed, he can nail the walls and windows to the frame. In the next chapter, we're going to show you how to build the frame for the perfect GED essay. Of course, you won't know the exact topic of the essay until you get there (just as the builder may not know what color his client is going to paint the living room), but you will have an all-purpose frame on which to construct a great essay no matter what the topic is.

We call this frame the **template.**

A builder can also prebuild certain parts of the house, so they can just be nailed into place when he is ready for them. Just as a window maker can construct the windows of a house in his workshop weeks before he arrives to install them, you can prebuild certain elements of your essay.

We call all this **preconstruction.**

Chapter 11
The Template

You can prepare in advance for writing your GED essay. We will show you how with a ready-made template.

Writing a GED essay requires a series of steps.

> **Step One:** Read the topic. We'll show you several sample essay topics on the next page. You'll see that they are all, in some ways, very similar.
>
> **Step Two:** Decide what your main thesis or idea is going to be. Are you going to agree or disagree with the topic statement, or will it be a little of both?
>
> **Step Three:** Come up with a bunch of supporting ideas or examples from your personal experience or from literature. It helps to write these down on a piece of scratch paper. These supporting statements are supposed to help persuade the reader that your main thesis is correct.
>
> **Step Four:** Look over your supporting ideas, and throw out the weakest ones. There should be three to five left over.
>
> **Step Five:** Write the essay using all the preconstruction and template tools you'll learn in this chapter and the next one.
>
> **Step Six:** Read over the essay, and do some editing. The GED readers will not take away points for small additions written in the margin or cross-outs to correct spelling or grammar mistakes.

How Much Time?

The entire process of planning, writing, and editing an essay of about 250 words is not supposed to take longer than 45 minutes. This will be more than enough time if you learn how to plan your essay by doing the practice exercises in this book. Many test takers worry about writing an essay that is too long or too short. Don't worry; in the next chapter, we'll show you a quick way to make sure that your essay is about the right size. Besides, the GED essay readers don't actually count the number of words in your essay, and they won't take off any points if yours is a little bit short or a little bit long.

How Important Is Handwriting?

Legible Is Good Enough
It doesn't have to be neat. It just has to be legible.

The GED essay readers are supposed to ignore handwriting completely. However, they wouldn't be human if they didn't subconsciously give a sigh of relief when they pick up essays with neat penmanship. If your handwriting is so tiny or messy that your essay is illegible, then the readers may not be able to see that your essay's organization and support are actually superb. As you do the exercises in this chapter, practice writing each sentence neatly (with a ballpoint pen—no pencils are allowed on the essay).

What Are the Topics Like?

There are only three formats for the essay topics that come up on the GED. We're going to show you examples of each. You'll see these same examples again throughout this chapter as we take you from the planning stage to the writing stage to the editing stage of your essay. At the end of Chapter 12, you'll even find sample essays written on each of these topics for you to grade using the holistic method.

The First Format: Heads or Tails?

Some GED topics begin by giving two opposing views on a particular issue and then asking you with which view you agree.

Topic One   Some people argue that the United States should not interfere in other countries' internal affairs, but others say that it is our country's moral responsibility to come to the aid of starving people. Which view do you take?

Write an essay of about 250 words on this topic and support it with specific examples from your own experience or your observations of others.

The Second Format: Heads! But Do You Agree?

However, the vast majority of GED topics begin by taking a position on *one* side of some issue. You are then asked whether you agree or disagree with the statement. We're going to show you four examples of this format because it is so popular.

Topic Two   Every year, Americans seem to read fewer and fewer books. Unless the situation is changed, the art of reading may be lost forever, and with it, a vital part of our culture.

Do you agree or disagree with this statement? Write an essay of about 250 words presenting your view and supporting it with specific examples from your own experience or your observations of others.

Topic Three   The budget for the average Hollywood movie keeps getting higher and higher. Movies today cost too much to make.

Do you agree or disagree with this statement? Write an essay of about 250 words presenting your view and supporting it with specific examples from your own experience or your observations of others.

Topic Four   Government bureaucracy wastes taxpayers' money. To cut this needless spending, we must overhaul the entire system.

Do you agree or disagree with this statement? Write an essay of about 250 words presenting your view and supporting it with specific examples from your own experience or your observations of others.

Topic Five "Youth is wasted on the young."

Do you agree or disagree with this statement? Write an essay of about 250 words presenting your view and supporting it with specific examples from your own experience or your observations of others.

The Third Format: Why Tails?

Finally, a few GED essay topics ask you to come up with a single example of a phenomenon described in the question. In this rarer format, your supporting arguments must explain why your example is apt.

Topic Six In our society today, there are many professions that can make a difference in improving the quality of our lives.

Identify a profession that you believe to be particularly helpful to humankind. Write a composition of about 250 words explaining why you feel this profession is helpful. Provide reasons and examples to support your view.

What's the Right Answer?

There's no one right or wrong answer to any of these topics, and you won't get penalized for saying something with which the essay reader disagrees. Remember, the readers can only grade you based on the criteria on their checklists, and the two most important items on those lists are the twin mantras of the GED essay: organization and support.

Making the Grade
GED essay graders are required to grade for organization and supporting evidence.

Good Organization: Constructing a Template

As we said earlier, constructing a frame is one of the most important steps in building a house. By constructing a frame for your essay in advance and by practicing with that frame until you are completely comfortable with it, you will have a ready-made organizational structure for *any* topic the GED test writers come up with.

After that, it's just a matter of filling in the blanks.

In Chapter 12, we'll show you how to construct your *own* essay template, but let's begin by practicing with some of ours.

The First Template

Paragraph One

> *The issue of*_____
> *is a controversial one. On the one hand,*_____.
> *On the other hand,* _____.
> *However, in the final analysis, I believe that* _____.

Paragraph Two

One reason for my belief is that _____.

Paragraph Three

Another reason is _____.

Paragraph Four

Perhaps the best reason is _____.

Paragraph Five

For all these reasons, I therefore believe that _____.

Let's see how the first sample topic fits into this organizational structure.

Topic One   Some people argue that the United States should not interfere in other countries' internal affairs, but others say that it is our country's moral responsibility to come to the aid of starving people. Which view do you take?

Write an essay of about 250 words on this topic and support it with specific examples from your own experience or your observations of others.

How would this topic fit into the first paragraph of our template? Take a look.

> *The issue of* the United States' involvement in the internal affairs of foreign countries *is a controversial one. On the one hand,* as a civilized nation, surely we have some responsibility to prevent mass starvation such as we saw in the recent situation in Darfur. *On the other hand,* it seems only fair that one country should agree not to butt in on an internal situation in another country. *However, in the final analysis, I believe that* our responsibilities as human beings are more important than being polite.

If we were writing the rest of this essay, we would now start giving supporting examples and reasons for our position, but for now, let's concentrate on the first paragraph. Could we have used this template to take the other side of the argument? Sure. Here's how that would look:

> *The issue of* the United States' involvement in the internal affairs of foreign countries *is a controversial one. On the one hand,* it seems only fair that one country should agree not to butt in on an internal situation in another country.

> *On the other hand,* as a civilized nation, surely we have some responsibility to prevent mass starvation such as we saw in the recent situation in Darfur. *However, in the final analysis, I believe that* by stepping into the affairs of foreign countries, even for good reasons, we end up doing more harm than good.

Okay, It Works with That Topic, but Will It Work with Another?

Of course. Let's try the same template with Topic Two.

Topic Two   Every year, Americans seem to read fewer and fewer books. Unless the situation is changed, the art of reading may be lost forever, and with it, a vital part of our culture.

Do you agree or disagree with this statement? Write an essay of about 250 words presenting your view and supporting it with specific examples from your own experience or your observations of others.

> *The issue of* dwindling readership in America *is a controversial one. On the one hand,* you could argue that books are simply being replaced by newer and better technologies, such as television and computer software. *On the other hand,* you could argue that the cultural impact of books can never be replaced by new technologies. *However, in the final analysis, I believe that* even if books become as obsolete as the steam engine, their cultural legacy will not be lost.

As you can see, this template will fit practically *any* situation. To prove it, let's try it out on one of the great philosophical arguments of our time.

Tastes Great/Less Filling

Topic Seven   Some people say they like diet soda because it tastes great. Other people say it's less filling. Which view do you take?

Write an essay of about 250 words on this topic and support it with specific examples from your own experience or your observations of others.

> *The issue of* whether diet soda is so popular because of its taste or because of its lack of calories *is a controversial one. On the one hand,* diet soda does have a pleasingly mild taste. *On the other hand,* diet soda also offers a sharply reduced number of calories. *However, in the final analysis, I believe that* diet soda is so popular because it is less filling.

Now You Try It

Read the following topic carefully. Decide which side of the argument you want to be on, then fill in the blanks of the first paragraph of this template. You may want to use a pencil during practice so that you can erase if you want to, but remember that you must use a pen on the real exam.

You may have noticed in the previous examples that to make this template work most effectively, the first "on the one hand" should introduce the argument that you are ultimately going to support. The "on the other hand" should be the argument you are *not* going to support. The sentence beginning "however, in the final analysis" will return to the point of view that you believe in.

Topic Three   The budget for the average Hollywood movie keeps getting higher and higher. Movies today cost too much to make.

Do you agree or disagree with this statement? Write an essay of about 250 words presenting your view and supporting it with specific examples from your own experience or your observations of others.

ESSAY TEMPLATE DRILL

The issue of _____
is a controversial one. On the one hand, _____
_____.
On the other hand, _____
_____.

However, in the final analysis, I believe that _____
_____
_____
_____.

If you were completing the entire essay, now you would write paragraphs giving support to your belief, but for now, let's concentrate on that first paragraph. Here's one way Topic Three could have gone:

> **The issue of** the exploding costs of making Hollywood feature films **is a controversial one. On the one hand,** with costs routinely approaching the $20 million mark, it is hard to justify these budgets. **On the other hand,** it has been argued that the artistic freedom of the directors should not be limited by concerns over cost cutting. **However, in the final analysis, I believe that** there is no reason why Hollywood cannot make great films for less money.

Are There Other Templates?

There are many ways to organize a GED essay. We'll show you how to create your own personalized template in the next chapter, but let's look at another one of ours first.

The Second Template

How to Fill Up Space
Rephrase the question
in your essay.

Paragraph One   *I both agree and disagree with the statement that* "[just quote the statement word for word]."

Paragraph Two   *On the one hand,* [list the reasons why you agree].

Paragraph Three   *On the other hand,* [list the reasons why you don't agree].

How would Topic Two have fit into this template? Let's look at the first paragraph.

> *I both agree and disagree with the statement that* "the art of reading may be lost forever, and with it, a vital part of our culture."

Hey look, we've already written 26 words!

In some ways, the organization of this template is simpler than the first one we showed you. All that's necessary for the essay writer to do in the first paragraph is copy the statement from the essay topic word for word. This makes for a short first paragraph, but that's okay. The second and third paragraphs are organized to look *first* at the reasons why you agree and *then* at the reasons why you disagree.

Two possible variations on this template are:

Paragraph One   *I agree with the statement that* "[just quote the statement word for word]."

Paragraph One   *I disagree with the statement that* "[just quote the statement word for word]."

In either of these variations, you would now proceed to give all your arguments in support of your opening paragraph. Even though these two templates may seem the simplest of all, there is a potential danger in simplicity. Because you are graded in part on your organization, an essay with such simplistic organization may actually bring down your score.

So Will These Templates Work for Every Topic?

The templates we've shown you so far will work with virtually no alteration on every topic format—except one. Take a look at Topic Six.

Topic Six   In our society today, there are many professions that can make a difference in improving the quality of our lives.

Identify a profession that you believe to be particularly helpful to humankind. Write a composition of about 250 words explaining why you feel this profession is helpful. Provide reasons and examples to support your view.

Hmmm...

Unfortunately, this time the topic has no opinion for you to agree or disagree with. In this type of essay question, you will be asked to come up with your own opinion from scratch. While this topic format seems to occur less frequently on the GED than the others, you still want to have a strategy to deal with it. Is there a template for this kind of topic?

Of course. Generally, questions like these ask you to "identify" something—an invention, an idea, an event—and then describe why it is good or bad.

The Third Template

Paragraph One   *Although there are many _____ that are _____ [good/ bad], I think the [best/worst] of all is _____.*

Paragraph Two   *[Describe the problems that (whatever it is) might be able to solve.]*

Paragraph Three   *[Explain how (whatever it is) can actually solve those problems.]*

Let's see how sample Topic Six fits into this organizational structure.

> *Although there are many professions that are beneficial to humankind, I think the profession that is the most beneficial of all is that of politician.*

After this first paragraph, the writer could now describe the problems that politicians might be able to solve. Then, in the third paragraph, the writer could describe *how* the politicians might solve these problems. In the next chapter, you'll get to see this sample essay in its entirety.

Supporting Your Main Idea

We've shown you how templates can be used to help organize your GED essay. However, organization is not the only important item on the essay reader's checklist. You will also be graded on how you support your main idea.

The Key to Good Support: Brainstorming

Let's go back to our six-step plan for writing the GED essay. You have already completed the first two steps: reading the topic and deciding what your main thesis or idea is going to be. Now it is time for Step Three: coming up with supporting ideas or examples. As we said in the beginning, it helps to write these down on scratch paper. Go crazy. Write down all the arguments you can think of that support your main idea. After you're done, you'll pick the strongest arguments to use in your essay. These supporting statements will persuade the reader that your main thesis is correct.

Use Your Scratch Paper
Always use your scratch paper to plan your essay and brainstorm.

Here's an example of what some brainstorming may produce in the way of support for Topic One:

Main Idea   America should continue to aid people who are starving around the world.

Support

1. The governments of some countries don't always care about their starving citizens. If we don't help, no one will.
2. It's good public relations—the people we help may be grateful.
3. Maybe someday *we* will need help.
4. Each person we keep alive is a potential consumer—he or she may eventually be able to buy American-made products, which will help our economy.
5. I remember once, when I was a child, my father got laid off, and there were some nights when we went to bed hungry. It was the worst feeling in the world, and I hate the idea that anyone should ever have to go through that.
6. It's just the right thing to do. There is a higher law of decency that we can't ignore.

After you've finished brainstorming, look over your supporting ideas and throw out the weakest ones. There should be three to five ideas left over. Plan the order in which you want to present these ideas. You should start with one of your strongest ideas and end with *the* strongest idea.

BRAINSTORMING DRILL

Each of the following is the first sentence of a GED essay. In the space that follows, list three to five specific reasons or examples to back up that first sentence. Don't write the essay—just list your reasons or examples.

1. I disagree that there are too many books published.

    _____
    _____
    _____
    _____
    _____
    _____

2. I agree that movies cost too much to make.

    _____
    _____
    _____
    _____
    _____
    _____

3. While I agree that there is some waste of taxpayer money, I do not believe that the system has to be overhauled.

    _____
    _____
    _____
    _____
    _____
    _____

Getting Specific

The GED readers look for supporting ideas or examples that are, in their words, "specific and illustrative." What do they mean by *specific*? Suppose you asked your friend about a movie she saw yesterday, and she said,

> *It was really cool.*

Well, you'd know that she liked it, and that's good, but you wouldn't know much about the movie. Was it a comedy? An action adventure? Did it make her cry?

The GED readers don't want to know that the movie was cool. They want to know that you liked a movie because

> *It traced the development of two childhood friends as they grew up and grew apart.*

or because

> *It combined the physical comedy of* The Three Stooges *with the action adventure of* Raiders of the Lost Ark.

You want to make each example as precise and compelling as possible. After you have brainstormed a few supporting ideas, spend a couple of moments on each

Don't Be Vague
Example of a BAD statement: It's unfair how some people pay lots of taxes and others get away with much less.

Be Specific
Example of a GOOD statement: People who can afford tax shelters and fancy accountants often find ways to pay *less* in taxes than people who are poor.

one, making it as specific as possible. For example, let's say we are working on Topic One and we are supporting the idea that the United States should stay out of other countries' business.

Too vague: When the United States sent troops to Vietnam, things didn't work out too well.

(*How* didn't they work out? What were the results?)

More specific: Look at the result when the United States sent troops to Vietnam. After more than a decade of fighting in support of a dubious political regime, American casualties numbered in the tens of thousands, and we may never know how many Vietnamese lost their lives.

SPECIFICS DRILL
(Answers and explanations can be found in Part VIII.)

Take each of the following vague and wimpy supporting arguments and make it more specific and compelling.

1. Starvation is a really bad thing.
   _____

2. Nobody reads anymore—they do other things instead.
   _____

3. Big Hollywood movies sometimes waste a lot of money.
   _____

4. One way to cut government spending is to fire a lot of people.
   _____

5. Old people don't have any fun anymore.
   _____

6. Nurses help people.
   _____

Create Your Own Template
Don't use our template word for word. Come up with your own variation.

Customizing Your Own Template
Now that you have the basics of organizing an essay and supporting your thesis with specific ideas, let's move on to the next chapter where you can create your *own* template and learn how to avoid making the grammar and spelling mistakes that can cost you points.

Chapter 12
Constructing Your Own Template

This chapter will show you ways to customize your essay template to make it your own and how to edit your essay during the test.

In the last chapter, you saw a few examples of GED essay templates designed by The Princeton Review. We hope you have learned a lot from them, but when you take the real GED, it is important that you bring your *own* template, based on your own preferences and your own personality. Of course, yours may have some similarities to ours, but it should not mimic ours exactly—for one thing, because it's pretty likely that the folks who write the GED have read this book, and they may take a dim view of anyone who blatantly copies one of our templates word for word.

Much more important, however, by doing the exercises that follow and by creating your *own* version of the GED template, you will become a stronger writer, and good writing is one of the most important skills you can acquire.

In Chapter 5, "Crazy Reading," we showed you how the GED test writers use certain structural tools to organize the reading comprehension passages. By spotting the structural words in a passage, you saw that you can cut right to the heart of a passage and understand it faster. In this chapter, you'll see how to use the same words to create an organizational framework for your own essay.

CONTRAST

Contrasting Viewpoints Within a Sentence

One of the most effective tools of writing is to contrast opposing views. You may not have realized this, but you probably contrast opposing views all the time in your daily conversations.

> *She wanted to go to the movies, but I didn't feel like it.*

The word *but* tells us that what was expressed in the first half of the sentence ("She wanted to go to the movies") is going to be contradicted in the second half (*I didn't feel like it*). In English, there are a number of words that signal the arrival of a contrasting view:

but	despite
however	in spite of
on the contrary	rather
although	nevertheless
yet	instead
while	

By using these words, you can instantly give your writing the appearance of depth. The idea is to set up your main idea by first introducing its opposite.

Let's say you are writing an essay based on Topic Two (Americans read fewer and fewer books), and you want to express a relatively simple idea:

I like books.

You can make this idea much richer by first offering another point of view.

While most people like going to the movies, I prefer reading books.

Most people like going to the movies, but I prefer reading books.

Let's say you are writing an essay based on Topic Five (youth is wasted on the young), and you want to express a particular thought.

People enjoy life more when they are older and wiser.

Again, you can make this idea much richer by first offering another point of view.

Although some people believe that the best time in your life is when you are young, I believe that people enjoy life more when they are older and wiser.

CONTRAST DRILL
(Answers and explanations can be found in Part VIII.)

In each of the following sentences, write a new sentence that introduces the main thought by first stating its opposite.

1. I believe great movies can be made more cheaply.
2. Some government spending is wasteful.
3. Lawyers can sometimes save you money.
4. Some people believe that there is alien life on other planets.

Contrasting Paragraphs
Contrast words can be used to signal the opposing viewpoints of entire paragraphs. Suppose you saw an essay that began:

Many people believe that youth is wasted on the young. They point out that young people never seem to enjoy, or even think about, the great gifts they have been given but will not always have: physical dexterity, good hearing, good vision.

However...

What do you think is going to happen in the second paragraph? That's right; the author is now going to disagree with the "many people" of the first paragraph.

Setting up one paragraph in opposition to another lets the reader know right away what's going on. The organization of the essay is immediately evident. You may remember that we used this device in the second template we showed you in Chapter 11. Take a look below to see what it looked like.

Paragraph One

> *I both agree and disagree with the statement that* "[just quote the statement word for word]."

Paragraph Two

> *On the one hand,* [list the reasons why you agree].

Paragraph Three

> *On the other hand,* [list the reasons why you don't agree].

When two entire paragraphs contradict each other, there are some useful *pairs* of words that help to make this clear.

> on the one hand → on the other hand
> the traditional view → the new view

CREATING STRUCTURE

Certain organizational tricks of wording in an essay create a sense in the reader that everything is under control, that the author knows what he or she is doing. The GED essay readers will be very impressed if you use these words.

For example, if you have three points to make in a paragraph, it helps to point this out ahead of time:

> *There are three reasons why I believe that Keanu Reeves is not really breathing. First...*

The reader now knows exactly what is going to happen. You are going to make three points, and you are going to signal each point by numbering it.

> *First, his mouth never moves. Second, his facial expression never changes, and third, even when he dances, he never breaks a sweat.*

There are a number of words that help indicate structure. We're going to outline them for you here and then give you some exercises to practice using them in sentences.

Structure Words

There are words that tell the reader that the author is about to **support** the main idea with examples or illustrations.

> for example   for instance
> to illustrate   because

Other words help to **organize** a series of ideas or examples.

> first, second, third
> for one thing → for another thing

Some words indicate you are going to **add** yet another example or argument in support of your main idea.

> furthermore   just as
> in addition   also
> similarly   moreover

The following words indicate that the idea you are about to **bring up** is important, special, or surprising in some way:

> surely   indeed
> truly   as a matter of fact
> undoubtedly   in fact
> clearly   most important
> certainly

Use Structure Words
Using structure words gives the appearance of good organization.

The following words indicate to the reader that you are about to reach a **conclusion**:

> therefore   hence
> in summary   in conclusion
> consequently   in short

How to Use Structure Words in Your Essay

The words we've just shown you can create instant organization in a paragraph. Used appropriately, they help to suggest to the GED reader that you are not only a writer who knows what he or she is doing—but also the kind of writer who deserves a high score.

Let's see how these words can be used in an essay to organize it better and give it some pizzazz. Here's a paragraph consisting of a main point and two supporting arguments:

> *I believe he is wrong. He doesn't know the facts. He isn't thinking clearly.*

Watch how a few structure words can improve this paragraph and make it clearer at the same time.

> *I believe he is wrong. **For one thing**, he doesn't know the facts. **For another**, he isn't thinking clearly.*

> *I believe he is wrong. **Clearly**, he doesn't know the facts. **Moreover**, he isn't thinking clearly.*

> *I believe he is wrong **because first**, he doesn't know the facts, and **second**, he isn't thinking clearly.*

> ***Certainly**, he doesn't know the facts. He isn't thinking clearly, **either**. **Consequently**, I believe he is wrong.*

STRUCTURE DRILL

(Answers and explanations can be found in Part VIII.)

The following paragraphs contain two or three sentences each. Use the structure words from the past few pages to organize these paragraphs. (Obviously, there are several different ways to organize each one. Try more than one option for each paragraph.)

1. I think there are many ways for a movie company to save money. The actors could agree to take smaller salaries.
2. Pest exterminator is the most important profession. Without exterminators, we would be inundated with mice and roaches.
3. Government bureaucracy serves important purposes. It employs thousands of Americans. It helps run the country.
4. Some types of book sales are actually increasing. "How to" books are selling very well. Self-help books are selling better than ever.
5. Doctors help humankind a lot. They heal the sick. They sometimes discover cures for diseases.

RHYTHM

Many people think good writing is a mysterious talent that you either have or don't have, like good rhythm. In fact, good writing has a kind of rhythm to it, but there is nothing mysterious about it. Good writing is a matter of mixing up the different kinds of raw materials that you have available to you—phrases and dependent and independent clauses—to build sentences that don't all sound the same.

Short Sentences, Long Sentences

If you've read Chapters 7 and 8 of this book, you already know all about phrases and clauses. If you've started with this section, don't worry. You don't have to know the formal names of these raw materials to be able to use them effectively. Here's an example of a passage in which all the sentences sound alike:

> *Movies cost too much. Everyone agrees about that. Studios need to cut costs. No one is sure exactly how to do it. I have two simple solutions. They can cut costs by paying stars less. They can also cut costs by reducing overhead.*

Why did all the sentences sound alike? Well, for one thing, they were all about the same length. Good writing uses a mixture of short and long sentences for variety. For another thing, the sentences were all made up of independent clauses with the same exact setup: subject, verb, and sometimes object. There were no dependent clauses, almost no phrases, no structure words, and frankly, no variety at all. Here's the same passage, but this time we varied the sentence length by combining some clauses and by using conjunctions. We also threw in some structure words.

Don't Fall into a Rut
Always alternate short and long sentences. In good writing, the sentences shouldn't all sound alike.

Everyone agrees that movies cost too much. Clearly, studios need to cut costs, but no one is sure exactly how to do it. I have two simple solutions: They can cut costs by paying stars less and by reducing overhead.

VARYING SENTENCE LENGTH DRILL
(Answers and explanations can be found in Part VIII.)

If there are two sentences in a passage, try to combine them into one using conjunctions (*and, but, or, for, nor, because, although, if, when, as, while*). If there is only one sentence, try to separate it into two sentences.

1. My friends think becoming a police officer is a waste of time. I think it is one of the most valuable things a person could do.
2. The police save lives, stop crime, and arrest criminals, while they also interact with the community.
3. Young kids sometimes have bad attitudes. They don't have very stable home lives.
4. A police officer can show these kids that it is possible to grow up to be somebody and make a difference, and a police officer can also make sure these kids don't get bullied by other kids.

PRECONSTRUCTION

On Vocabulary
While you won't know the specific topic of your GED essay until you see it in the examination room, there is a lot you can do in advance to prepare. One effective way to show your GED essay grader that you deserve a high grade is to use—and correctly spell—several words that he or she thinks are pretty difficult.

VOCABULARY AND SPELLING DRILL
1. Is it better to grow up with a large family or a small family? Write a 100-word essay on this subject that includes the following 10 words, correctly spelled, in any order you like:

controversy	dilemma
whether	essential
view	examine
answer	truly
because	therefore

Here's one way this essay could have been written:

*Every family has **controversy**, but I guess the question is **whether** a big family is a healthier environment for a child to grow up in than a small family. The **answer** to that question depends on your point of **view because** most people who grow up in a large family wish they had grown up in a small family and vice versa. The **dilemma** for parents with lots of kids is how to give their children the **essential** love and individual attention they need. Parents must **therefore examine** whether they are **truly** providing for their children by having more.*

2. The car and the airplane were at one time brand-new methods of transportation.

What do you think will be the *next* new method of mass transportation? Explain your reasoning in a 100-word essay using those same 10 words again, correctly spelled, in any order:

controversy	dilemma
whether	essential
view	examine
answer	truly
because	therefore

3. The media shapes public opinion. In this country today, it is a simple case of "out of [the media's] sight, out of [the public's] mind."

Do you agree or disagree with the statement? Write a 100-word essay on this subject that includes the following 10 words, correctly spelled, in any order you like:

although	neither
explanation	prefer
likely	probably
instead	reason
necessary	consequently

4. The education system in America works very well. Those people who say we need to revamp it entirely are wrong.

Do you agree or disagree? Explain your reasoning in a 100-word essay using those same 10 words from the previous essay again, correctly spelled, in any order:

although	neither
explanation	prefer
likely	probably
instead	reason
necessary	consequently

Impress the Graders
Use the words from the GED's list of frequently misspelled words (of course, you must be very careful that you spell them correctly).

If you did the previous exercises, you now have 20 impressive GED structure words, correctly spelled, at your command. As you refine the template or templates that you will bring with you to the actual exam, you should make sure that you know how to spell every word in your templates as well.

The Artsy Book Reference

Another way to impress the essay reader is to use a classic book as a supporting example in your essay. Remember who the essay readers are: English teachers. They wouldn't be English teachers if they didn't have a soft spot in their hearts for someone who can quote from *Beowulf*.

What book should you pick? Obviously it should be a book that you have actually read and liked. We do not advise picking a book if you've only seen the movie. Hollywood has a habit of changing the endings. For what it's worth, here is a list of "classic" writers that the folks who make the GED use in their Language Arts, Writing test:

> Mark Twain, Toni Morrison, Ernest Hemingway,
> F. Scott Fitzgerald, William Faulkner, Ralph Waldo Emerson,
> Gabriel García Márquez, Henry David Thoreau, John Steinbeck,
> Langston Hughes, Thomas Wolfe, Maya Angelou,
> Eugene O'Neill, Tennessee Williams, Robert Frost,
> Carl Sandburg, Katherine Anne Porter, Edith Wharton,
> Stephen Crane, G. K. Chesterton, and D. H. Lawrence

Good Authors to Mention
Mark Twain
Edith Wharton
Ernest Hemingway

You might think that it would be impossible to pick a book to use as an example for an essay before you even know the topic of the essay, but it's actually pretty easy. Just to give you an idea of how it's done, let's pick a book most people have read: *Tom Sawyer* by Mark Twain.

Now let's take each of the topics we used in the last drill and see how we could work in a reference to *Tom Sawyer*.

1. Is it better to grow up with a large family or a small family?

    In the case of Mark Twain's characters Tom Sawyer and Huck Finn, we can see that a good small family environment was not everything. While Tom grew up in a small family setting with his aunt Polly, he still seems more devious and mischievous than Huck.

2. The car and the airplane were at one time brand-new methods of transportation. What do you think will be the next new method of mass transportation?

I only have to remember how Mark Twain's characters Tom Sawyer and Huck Finn looked in awe at the steam-driven riverboats on the Mississippi to realize that we will always think that we have seen the ultimate creation of man, only to be surprised a few years later by something even more magnificent.

3. The media shapes public opinion. In this country today, it is a simple case of "out of [the media's] sight, out of [the public's] mind." Do you agree or disagree with this statement?

However, to say that this situation is new is ridiculous. All we have to do is remember Mark Twain's Tom Sawyer to realize that nothing has changed. Tom and Huck get into endless trouble by imitating pirates, made famous from popular stories of the time.

4. The education system in America works very well. Those people who say we need to revamp it entirely are wrong. Do you agree or disagree?

Children have always stared out the window of their schoolroom as mournfully as Huck Finn in Mark Twain's Tom Sawyer and wondered if it was ever going to be three o'clock.

You get the idea.

EDITING FOR STRUCTURE, USAGE, AND MECHANICS

Once you've written your essay, you should read it over and check it for all the grammar, spelling, and punctuation errors we taught you to recognize in Part II of this book. If you skipped Part II, you may want to go back and read those chapters before you proceed with this chapter.

Any errors you find in the essay should be corrected as neatly as possible. Don't be afraid to cross out an unnecessary word or to add a word or phrase if it helps clarify the meaning. The GED essay readers are not allowed to deduct points for cross-outs or corrections. To see how your editing skills are shaping up, here is a full-length essay based on one of the topics we showed you in the last chapter.

Not-So-Good Authors to Mention
John Grisham
J. K. Rowling
Dr. Phil

EDITING DRILL
(Answers and explanations can be found in Part VIII.)

Read the following essay carefully and correct any mistakes of grammar, punctuation, or spelling that you find.

Essay Final Check
- Grammar
- Spelling
- Length

Altho there are many professions that are beneficial to humankind, I think the profession that is the most beneficial of all is to be a politician.

The world today is in the midst of making very important changes. In russia, the russian people must decides what kind of government they will live under. In the United States we must curb the deficit and decide how to fund a health care system for everyone. And all countries must decide how to tackle the esential problems of polution and conservation.

Who will have the most say in each of these important changes? I think it will be the politicians, in Russia, it will be up to the men and women in politics transforming the country into a democratic, free market economy, where everyone has enough to eat, and the chance to become whoever he or she wants to be, without fear of being arrested or imprisoned for political views. In the United States it will be our Congressmen and Senators who has the power to bring spending under control and find a way to have affordable health care. And it will be up to the politicians of the world to come to terms with the threats to the ozone layer, the forests, and the endangered species.

Putting It All Together

We've shown you what the GED readers are looking for. We've shown you how to use a ready-made framework to write an essay that will melt their hearts and how to use preconstruction to bring correct sentence structure, pointed vocabulary words, correct spelling, and cable-ready literary references into the examination room with you. Now it's time to try writing some essays on your own.

Before you begin, construct a trial template or two on a piece of scratch paper. Feel free to adapt the templates we showed you in Chapter 11, but it is important that you put your own stamp on the process and that the essay shows aspects of your own personality. Even though they have only two minutes, the GED essay readers will be able to tell if you're being yourself. After you've finished the first essay, read it over, and see if you want to make changes to your template. Then write another essay and repeat the honing process.

It would be great if you could take some time for these exercises. Don't try to write all the essays in one day, and don't be frustrated if you feel like an essay is not going well. Any professional writer will tell you that the process of reading over and rewriting is at least as important as the process of writing itself.

How Much Is Enough?

Test takers always worry about the length of their essays. Is it too short? Is it too long? As we said earlier, the readers are not going to count the exact number of words, nor will they take off points as long as the essay's length is in the ballpark. A good indication that your essay is long enough is if you have filled between one and a half and two of the pages the test proctor will provide for you. This works out to about 40 lines, depending on the size of your handwriting.

Dividing Up Your Time

In Chapter 11, we outlined six steps in writing your essay. How long should each step take?

Step One:	Read the topic.	*1 minute*
Step Two:	Decide what your main thesis or idea is going to be.	*2 minutes*
Step Three:	Come up with a bunch of supporting ideas or examples.	*5 minutes*
Step Four:	Look over your supporting ideas, and throw out the weakest ones.	*2 minutes*
Step Five:	Write the essay.	*25 minutes*
Step Six:	Read over the essay, and do some editing.	*10 minutes*

These are not rigid guidelines, of course. If one step in the process takes more or less time, that's fine. The important thing is that you do some careful planning before you begin writing and save enough time to be able to read over and edit what you've written when you're done.

THE ESSAY DRILL

Topic One   Some people argue that the United States should not interfere in other countries' internal affairs, but others say that it is our country's moral responsibility to come to the aid of starving people. Which view do you take?

Write an essay of about 250 words on this topic and support it with specific examples from your own experience or your observations of others.

Topic Two   Every year, Americans seem to read fewer and fewer books. Unless the situation is changed, the art of reading may be lost forever, and with it, a vital part of our culture.

Do you agree or disagree with this statement? Write an essay of about 250 words presenting your view and supporting it with specific examples from your own experience or your observations of others.

Topic Three   The budget for the average Hollywood movie keeps getting higher and higher. Movies today cost too much to make.

Do you agree or disagree with this statement? Write an essay of about 250 words presenting your view and supporting it with specific examples from your own experience or your observations of others.

Topic Four   Government bureaucracy wastes taxpayers' money. To cut this needless spending, we must overhaul the entire system.

Do you agree or disagree with this statement? Write an essay of about 250 words presenting your view and supporting it with specific examples from your own experience or your observations of others.

Topic Five   "Youth is wasted on the young."

Do you agree or disagree with this statement? Write an essay of about 250 words presenting your view and supporting it with specific examples from your own experience or your observations of others.

Topic Six   In our society today, there are many professions that can make a difference in improving the quality of our lives.

Identify a profession that you believe to be particularly helpful to humankind. Write a composition of about 250 words explaining why you feel this profession is helpful. Provide reasons and examples to support your view.

Scoring the Essay

A helpful way to see how your essay-writing skills are progressing is to try scoring several sample GED essays yourself. This way, you'll be able to compare your own essays with the sample essays and compare the grades you awarded the samples to the grades they received from our Princeton Review readers.

Try grading the following three essays, all written on Topic 3.

You'll find the grades Princeton Review essay readers assigned to these papers on page 201.

Essay A

> The issue of the exploding costs of making Hollywood feature films is a controversial one. On the one hand, with average costs approaching the $50 million mark, it's hard to justify these budgets. On the other hand, people argue that the artistic freedom of the directors should not be limited by concerns over cost cutting. However, in the final analysis, I believe there is no reason why Hollywood can't make great films for less money.
>
> Maybe keeping costs under tight control can sometimes prevent a director from doing what she really wants with a film, but the big Hollywood budgets mean that thousands of young aspiring directors don't get to make any films at all. One movie that costs $100 million means that four directors like Spike Lee or Woody Allen don't get to make their $25 million movies. And young, unknown directors, who only need a few hundred thousand dollars, are just laughed at by studios who can only think about the big score.
>
> The ironic thing is that every year, in spite of how difficult it is to find backing, unknowns somehow manage to make great movies for very little money. Sometimes these films earn more profits than the big-budget Hollywood movies.
>
> Movie studios have to learn that making a lot of little movies will make just as much money as making a few big movies. And if one of the little movies doesn't make back its $1 million, it isn't as big a deal as when one of the big movies doesn't make back its $100 million.

Essay B

I both agree and disagree with the statement that "Movies today cost too much to make."

On the one hand, to make real quality movies costs a lot of money. What if *Avatar* or *The Matrix* couldn't have used all those special effects? Those movies would have been pretty bad. And maybe it's a lot to pay Brad Pitt millions of dollars, but he deserves to get paid, too, doesn't he? His award-winning performances help society to understand life better. New technology always costs more at first. I think that even if right now movies are too expensive, they could get cheaper, after the new technology gets cheaper, too.

On the other hand, some movies cost way too much. They should have figured out that *Battlefield Earth* was terrible, and pulled the plug. I saw that film and wanted my money back. There should be some way so that the studios only spend lots of money on good movies. Of course, I guess it's hard to tell what movies are good in advance. A better way would be to only give big money to directors who's made good movies before. Another thing they could do is go back to the system they used to have, where all the stars and cameramen and directors are under contract to the studio. That way, it pays the studio to make as many movies as possible, and they all cost less.

Essay C

I agree. Movies cost too much. I read where one film cost a hundred million dollars. That is discusting. If movies cost less to make then they'd cost less to see too. We could all use a break.

I also think that the movies on television cost too much too. Like, every week, there is a movie of the week, and these cost lots of money. It can't be that hard to make these movies, because Robert Townsend did it for real cheap, and so did the guy who made *Sex, Lies, and videotape.* So it IS possible, and these people in Hollywood got to realize they're wasting too much money.

Also, the actors should work for less. They don't need so much. Actors love to act. They'd do it for free. My friend who is an actress says she would be in a movie for free in a second. So the movie companys just have to be tough, and say, you want to be in my movie, you work for what I tell you. Then they wouldn't cost so much.

(Grades: Essay A received a 4, Essay B received a 3, and Essay C received a 2.)

Part III Summary

○ There are six steps to writing a GED essay.
  - Read the topic.
  - Decide what your main thesis or idea is going to be.
  - Come up with a bunch of supporting ideas or examples. It helps to write these down.
  - Throw out the weakest ones.
  - Write the essay, using preconstruction and template tools.
  - Read over the essay, and do some editing.

○ You have 45 minutes to write an essay of about 250 words.

○ There are three possible formats:
  - Two views are presented, and you are asked to pick one and support it.
  - A single view is presented, and you are asked if you agree or disagree.
  - You are asked to come up with a single example of a phenomenon described in the question and then explain your choice.

○ One of the key items the readers look for is organization. You can best organize your essay by using a template—a framework that gives the essay form.

○ Another key item the readers look for is support. The best support, as far as they are concerned, is specific and compelling.

○ It is important to develop your own templates, using your own words, rather than just copying one of ours word for word.

o   To develop an effective template, you need to understand some tricks of writing:

- Use contrast words (such as *however, but, on the other hand*) to create drama and add class to your essay.
- Use structure words (such as *first, second, because, hence*) to help organize your essay.
- Use vocabulary words from the GED master list. Some of these words are also structure words and will help organize your essay.
- Consider bringing up an artsy book, perhaps from the list of authors on page 194, as an example in your essay.

o   Plan your essay carefully. Before you start writing, first set down your supporting ideas on a piece of scratch paper and decide on the order in which you will present them. Be sure to leave time to read over the essay and make corrections.

o   Developing your own template takes some time. The best way to get better at GED essay writing is to practice by writing essays on each of the six topics we provided.

Part IV
How to Crack the Social Studies Test

Chapter 13
Social Studies
Overview

If you look in some of the other GED study guides out there, you may get the impression that you will have to memorize a huge number of facts for the GED Social Studies test. In fact, the Social Studies test does not require *any* specific knowledge of history, economics, or geography (or any of the other social studies topics). Every question will be based on a brief passage, and the information you need to answer the question will almost always be contained in that passage. Thus, the Social Studies test is mostly just a reading comprehension test. In this section, we will show you how to build on the techniques you saw in Chapter 5, "Crazy Reading."

What Do the Questions and Passages Look Like?

In the Social Studies test, you will have 70 minutes to answer 50 multiple-choice questions. Each passage will be followed by one to six questions based on that passage. About half the questions will be in groups of four to six questions based on a single passage, called an item set. The other half of the questions will be stand-alone items. Here's an example of an item set:

Questions 1 through 3 refer to the following paragraphs.

The United States has always been a haven for immigrants seeking a better life. From its earliest days, our country has been populated by people fleeing oppression or poverty in their native countries. Recently, some critics have charged that the United States has closed the door on immigration.

However, a look at the record will show that these critics are mistaken. The number of residents of the United States for whom English is a second language increased by more than a third in the 1980s after a wave of immigration from Latin America, Asia, and Europe. Today, there are almost 33 million people living in the United States who speak English as a second language. The majority of these are the 17 million people who have arrived from Latin America in the past 20 years.

Although the United States does have some restrictions on the numbers of immigrants who are allowed to enter the country per year, it is still the most generous country in the world in welcoming immigrants and providing them with hope for a new beginning.

Dear Princeton Review,
There are very few social studies facts in my head. Should I be worried?

Sincerely,
Worried in Walla Walla

1. Which of the following observations about recent migration to the United States is supported by the article?

   (1) Restrictions on immigration have stopped the flow of immigrants to the United States.
   (2) Immigrants to the United States come from only one country.
   (3) Many of the immigrants who arrived during the 1980s speak Spanish as their first language.
   (4) Immigrants come to the United States for the oppression they find here.
   (5) The decision to immigrate has not helped the standard of living of the people who have come to the United States.

2. Which of the following is an example of immigration?

   (1) A Dutch family visits France for two weeks to see the Louvre museum.
   (2) A Costa Rican citizen who has been working abroad for several years returns to Costa Rica.
   (3) A U.S. citizen moves from Texas to New York.
   (4) A Chinese couple moves permanently from China to Canada.
   (5) An Australian family stays in Australia.

GED Social Studies Fact #1
The Social Studies test is just a reading test.

3. Which of the following statements is the most likely explanation for the large numbers of people who have recently migrated to the United States?

(1) There is a better standard of living and more freedom in the United States than in the countries from which they came.
(2) There are fewer employment opportunities in the United States.
(3) The standard of living is higher in most other countries than it is in the United States.
(4) The countries from which they were fleeing offered too much political freedom.
(5) The United States has a policy of forbidding all immigration.

Here is an example of a stand-alone item:

4. Because of concerns about the environment, the government is thinking about regulating the United States' steel industry.

Which of the following might be an action the government could take to accomplish its goal?

(1) Force large steel companies to break up into smaller, more competitive companies.
(2) Increase subsidies to stimulate an increase in production.
(3) Create tariffs on steel imported from other countries.
(4) Tax the steel-makers' competitors in other industries.
(5) Mandate the elimination of carbon emissions from steel plants.

Dear Worried in Walla Walla,
No. All the social studies facts you need will be in the passage.

Sincerely,
The Princeton Review

As we mentioned in Chapter 5, "Crazy Reading," you don't have to recognize the question types to answer them correctly during the exam. However, it's useful to see exactly how they are used. Let's review the four question types again.

Question Types

Comprehension Questions

A comprehension question asks you to find a particular piece of information from the passage itself and then recognize that piece of information, slightly restated, among the answer choices. Occasionally, comprehension questions will ask you to go just a bit further to identify a logical implication of that information.

Take a look at the first question from the item set on pages 209 and 210.

Comprehension Questions
These questions ask you to recognize information in a slightly altered form.

1. Which of the following observations about recent migration to the United States is supported by the article?

    (1) Restrictions on immigration have stopped the flow of immigrants to the United States.
    (2) Immigrants to the United States come from only one country.
    (3) Many of the immigrants who arrived during the 1980s speak Spanish as their first language.
    (4) Immigrants come to the United States for the oppression they find here.
    (5) The decision to immigrate has not helped the standard of living of the people who have come to the United States.

Here's How to Crack It

This is a comprehension question designed to see if you understood what you read. Let's use POE to go through the answer choices and eliminate those that contradict the passage itself. According to the passage, some critics say that the United States has "closed the door on immigration," so you might have been tempted by choice (1)—unless you noticed the contrast word that began the next paragraph:

However, *a look at the record will show that these critics are mistaken.*

This contrast word helped to reveal the structure of the passage: The second paragraph is obviously going to contradict the view of those critics. Eliminate choice (1). Choice (2) states that immigrants to the United States came from only one country, but the passage says they came from Latin America, Asia, and Europe. So much for choice (2). Choice (3) states that many recent immigrants speak Spanish. While the passage does not declare this directly, it *does* say that many new immigrants came from Latin America. What's the dominant language in Latin America? You guessed it! Spanish. The correct answer to this question is choice (3). Let's take a quick look at the other answers, just to make sure. Choice (4) maintains that immigrants came to the United States because it had *worse* conditions than their original countries (which is directly contradicted by the passage), and choice (5) goes much further and discusses how the new immigrants have done since they arrived in the United States (which is not mentioned directly in the passage). Choice (3) restates information from the passage in slightly altered form—which is just what to expect from a comprehension question.

Application Questions

Application Questions
These questions ask you to apply a concept from one situation to another situation.

To answer an application question, you must first understand the meaning of a concept described in the passage and then apply that concept to an entirely different situation. Question 2 from the item set on pages 209 and 210 is a good example:

---

2. Which of the following is an example of immigration?

    (1) A Dutch family visits France for two weeks to see the Louvre museum.
    (2) A Costa Rican citizen who has been working abroad for several years returns to Costa Rica.
    (3) A U.S. citizen moves from Texas to New York.
    (4) A Chinese couple moves permanently from China to Canada.
    (5) An Australian family stays in Australia.

Here's How to Crack It

To answer this question, we must first understand the meaning of *immigration* and then apply that meaning to the examples that make up the answer choices. While you may not have been sure of the exact meaning of *immigration*, you can probably make a guess based on the context of the rest of the passage. After referring to immigrants in the first sentence, the author writes of people who come to America "fleeing oppression or poverty in their native countries." So obviously, immigration involves leaving your former country for another in the hope that your life there will be better.

Now we have to take this definition and *apply* it to the question. Which of the answer choices describes an act of immigration? In choice (1), the Dutch family is clearly just visiting France. From what we can infer from the passage, immigration seems to be more permanent. In choice (2), a Costa Rican is returning home to the country of his birth. This does not seem to be immigration either. In choice (3), a U.S. citizen moves from one part of the United States to another. Again, this does not seem to be immigration in its strictest sense. In choice (4), a Chinese couple moves permanently to another country. This seems like the correct answer, but let's look at choice (5) just in case. No, in choice (5), no one is moving anywhere. We have correctly applied the definition; the correct answer is choice (4).

————————◯————————

Analysis Questions

An analysis question asks you to break down information from the passage into more specific categories and explore the relationship of those categories. For example, in question 3 from the item set on pages 209 and 210, we are asked to provide an explanation for behavior described in the passage.

————————◯————————

3. Which of the following statements is the most likely explanation for the large numbers of people who have recently migrated to the United States?

   (1) There is a better standard of living and more freedom in the United States than in the countries from which they came.
   (2) There are fewer employment opportunities in the United States.
   (3) The standard of living is higher in most other countries than it is in the United States.
   (4) The countries from which they were fleeing offered too much political freedom.
   (5) The United States has a policy of forbidding all immigration.

The Four Types of Social Studies Questions on the GED
Comprehension—20%
Application—20%
Analysis—40%
Evaluation—20%

Here's How to Crack It

The passage itself told us in the first sentence why immigrants have *traditionally* come to the United States:

"The United States has always been a haven for immigrants seeking a better life. From its earliest days, our country has been populated by people fleeing oppression or poverty in their native countries."

While the passage does not directly go into the motivations of the newest wave of immigrants, it implies in the last sentence that they have similar motives:

"…it is still the most generous country in the world in welcoming immigrants and providing them with hope for a new beginning."

The question asks us to connect the motivations of the older immigrants (which were directly stated) to those of the new immigrants (which were not). Choice (1) does exactly this, saying that the new immigrants are looking for a better standard of living and more political freedom—the two aspirations that have motivated immigrants to the United States for the past 300 years. Choices (2) and (5) are directly contradicted in the passage. Choices (3) and (4) do not seem likely given what was said in the passage. The correct answer to this analysis question is choice (1).

Analysis Questions
These questions ask you to explore the relationship of implied categories within the passage.

Evaluation Questions

To answer an evaluation question, you must make a judgment or prediction about the information provided in the passage—sometimes by applying outside knowledge or information that you bring with you to the test. This is the most difficult type of question. Question 4, the stand-alone item from pages 209 and 210, is an example of an evaluation question.

4. Because of concerns about the environment, the government is thinking about regulating the United States' steel industry.

Which of the following might be an action the government could take to accomplish its goal?

(1) Force large steel companies to break up into smaller, more competitive companies.
(2) Increase subsidies to stimulate an increase in production.
(3) Create tariffs on steel imported from other countries.
(4) Tax the steel-makers' competitors in other industries.
(5) Mandate the elimination of carbon emissions from steel plants.

Here's How to Crack It

We are asked to make a prediction as to how the government might accomplish a goal set out in the passage. Why does the government want to regulate the steel industry? Because of environmental concerns. Which of the possible actions described in the answer choices would have an impact on the environment? Choice (1) seems pretty irrelevant. Choices (2), (3), and (4) might actually make the environment worse by increasing the amount of steel produced in the United States. Choice (5) is the only answer that would help improve the environment. Thus, the only possible prediction or judgment that we can make in this evaluation question is choice (5).

Evaluation Questions
These questions ask you to make a prediction based on the passage.

Graphic Material Questions

The Social Studies test will also include comprehension, application, analysis, and application questions based on graphic materials. If you've already read Chapter 4, "Crazy Graphics," you're well on your way toward acing these questions. But there are two types of graphics that appear on the Social Studies test that we didn't cover in Chapter 4, "Crazy Graphics": cartoons and photos.

The GED Cartoon

The test writers want to see if you can figure out the point behind these mostly political cartoons. Sometimes the cartoons will be fairly recent; other times they may be more than 200 years old. Here's an example from somewhere in between:

<u>Question 1</u> refers to the following cartoon.

THE CROWNING ACHIEVEMENT

THIS LATEST SUBMARINE VICTIM MAY BE THE LAST

1. This American World War I cartoon was published in 1916, before the United States entered the war. The U.S. ship has just been torpedoed by a German submarine. What is the sinking ship in the cartoon meant to imply?

    (1) Many people from this ship would end up in the hospital.
    (2) The United States' patience with Germany was about to run out.
    (3) The ship was carrying illegal war supplies and was a legitimate war target.
    (4) The United States should be more patient.
    (5) In wartime, even innocent people can get hurt by mistakes.

Here's How to Crack It

Read this comprehension question carefully, and then study all information in the cartoon itself, including any words contained as a caption or inside the drawing itself. We know from the question that a U.S. ship has been torpedoed by a German submarine in the early days of World War I, before the United States entered the war. Even if you don't know much about World War I, you can imagine how the people of the United States probably felt about one of their ships being torpedoed: pretty mad.

The cartoonist has labeled the ship the *U.S. Patience*, and it's about to sink. What is the cartoonist implying by this? If you picked choice (2), you are doing just fine. The cartoonist was implying that the patience of the United States was about to run out in the face of Germany's sinking one of its ships—and, in fact, less than a year later, the United States did enter the war and helped to defeat Germany.

If you were tempted by choice (1), you probably confused *patience* (the quality of enduring without complaint) with *patients* (people being treated in a hospital). Choices (3) and (4) made new assumptions without any basis in information supplied in the cartoon or the question. Choice (5) certainly could have been true, but made no use of the important information contained in the drawing itself: the labeling of the ship as the *U.S. Patience*.

The GED Photo

In introducing photographs into the GED Social Studies test, ACE says test takers must "dig deeper, examining details, key subjects, and background features," as well as written information such as captions and information contained in the question itself. As with GED cartoon questions, the key to GED photo questions is to understand the point behind the photos and the relationship of the photo to any text that goes with it. Here's an example:

<u>Question 1</u> refers to the photo below.

Photofest Archive

1. This early 1920s photograph of a silent movie being shot in Hollywood shows that many of the same methods used in today's movies were already in use back then. Which of the following would NOT have been present on the film set shown in this photograph?

    (1) actors
    (2) movie cameras
    (3) lights
    (4) a dialect coach
    (5) a set designer

Read this evaluation question carefully, and then study all information in the photo itself. We know from the question that this is a behind-the-scenes photograph on the set of a silent movie. Which of the answer choices would NOT have been necessary back then? If you picked choice (4), you're absolutely right. This was a SILENT movie—there would be no need for a dialect coach because the audience was not going to hear the actors. All the other choices were vital elements of movie-making, then and now.

The Practical Document Excerpt

In this section, there will also be at least one excerpt from what the test writers call a "practical" document, such as a manual, a voter's guide, a tax form, an almanac, an atlas, a website, or a statistical report. The excerpts may be either textual or graphical in nature, but the questions asked about them are of the same types we've already shown you. Below is an example of one of these practical document text excerpts.

GENERAL BALLOT: BOND PROPOSITION NO. 1

( ) Yes

( ) No

"Shall the government of Smithville, Texas, be authorized to issue and sell the bonds of the County in the amount of $1,430,000 for the purpose of the construction of a new road spur to link route 101A and route 267 and to levy taxes, without limit as to rate or amount, upon all taxable property within the County annually sufficient to pay the interest on the bonds as it accrues?"

Arguments For   The new road paid for by the bonds will decrease congestion and improve safety on County roadways.

Arguments Against   Smithville may be entering a period of recession and may be burdened by increased indebtedness. Passage of these bonds could increase taxes per household by an average of $17 annually by 2007. In addition, increased traffic will likely produce more air pollution.

---

1. Which of the following statements related to the bond proposition is supported by the information above?

   (1) The money that would be raised by this bond sale would go to paying off Smithville's general debts.
   (2) The money raised by this bond sale would be spent to help eliminate air pollution.
   (3) The money raised by this bond sale would have the effect of relieving traffic congestion and will address safety concerns.
   (4) The money raised by this bond sale would go directly toward reducing taxes in Smithville.
   (5) The money raised by this bond sale would reduce the effects of a recession.

Here's How to Crack It

The proposition voters are being asked to vote on is whether the town should sell bonds to finance a new road. The advantages and disadvantages of both the road itself and the effect of the bond sale are laid out. This comprehension question asks us to recognize information stated in the excerpt. Choice (1) states that the money raised by the bond sale would be used to pay off Smithville's general debts. While the excerpt mentions Smithville's debts, the money being raised by the sale is clearly to be spent on the road, not on paying off those debts, so we can eliminate choice (1). And although pollution is mentioned as a possible consequence of building the new road, the money being voted for in this proposition is to finance the road, not reduce the pollution that might come after it is built, so we can eliminate choice (2). Choice (3) correctly states the reasoning behind the bond sale: to relieve crowding on the road and improve safety. Let's hold on to this and keep reading. Choice (4) incorrectly says the money is to reduce taxes. In fact, the bond sale is to fund the road and will have the side effect of raising taxes. Choice (5) is also backward: According to the passage, the bond sale may, in fact, spur more recession. The correct answer is choice (3).

The Practical Document Graphic Excerpt

Practical documents can also come in graphical format. If you've already read through Chapter 4, "Crazy Graphics," you should have no trouble handling these. Here's an example:

Tax Table		
Asset Protection Allowance (line O)		
Age of Older Parent in Household	Two-Parent Family	One-Parent Family
39 or younger	$36,600	$23,000
40–44	$40,900	$25,800
45–49	$46,700	$28,700
50–54	$53,200	$32,000
55–59	$61,500	$36,400
60–64	$71,600	$41,700
65 or older	$78,900	$45,500

2. According to the tax table above, if you are a single parent, aged 52, with two children, what is your asset protection allowance?

   (1) $53,200
   (2) $32,000
   (3) $28,700
   (4) $25,800
   (5) $23,000

Here's How to Crack It

To get this measurement question, look on the chart for a single parent, aged 52, with two children. In the left column, find the correct age. Now, you're down to two choices, (1) $53,200 and (2) $32,000. Which is correct? If you said choice (2), you're doing just fine. "Single parent" is the same as one-parent family. There didn't seem to be any place on the chart for the number of children, so that piece of information turned out to be irrelevant.

The Practical Document Form Excerpt

The third type of practical document is a form. Let's try one.

Questions 1 and 2 refer to the following business document.

Mutual Mortgage Company Mortgage Application

Section A—Personal Information:

Name	Social Security Number
Telephone	Date of Birth
Current Address	City/State/ZIP code
Current Employer	Current Salary

Section B—New Home Information:

Purchase Price of New Home	Amount of Down Payment (to be made by applicant)
Mortgage Amount Requested	Type of mortgage requested (fixed or variable rate)
Address of New Home	City/State/ZIP code

Section C—Reference Information:

Bank Accounts (please list all current accounts	Loans or Mortgages Outstanding
Have you ever held a mortgage before?	(If yes, list Mortgage Company and loan # here)
Driver's License (including state)	Marital Status/dependents

1. What is the general financial purpose of this document?

    (1) To show that a person is qualified for a job opening
    (2) To show how to sell a home
    (3) To show that a person is eligible to borrow money to buy a home
    (4) To show that a person is eligible for a credit card
    (5) To transfer funds from a savings account to a checking account

Here's How to Crack it

The title of this form is "Mutual Mortgage Company Mortgage Application." You may know that a mortgage is a loan by a bank or financial institution to a customer who is buying a home. If you didn't know that, you might have gotten some clues by reading the form. For example, in section B, the form asks for the "purchase price of the new home" and refers to the "down payment."

If you selected choice (3) you are doing just fine—but as always, it helps to use POE (Process of Elimination) to get rid of incorrect answers and zero in on the correct answer. Choice (1) would be the correct answer if this form had been a job application—but it's a mortgage application, so we can eliminate it. Choice (2) might seem tempting, because it concerns a home—but this form is for someone buying a house, not selling a house, so we can eliminate it. The application is for a mortgage, not a credit card, so we can eliminate choice (4). And while the form does ask about bank accounts, there is no mention of transferring funds between them, so we can eliminate choice (5). The correct answer is choice (3).

Let's do another question based on the same form.

2. Which piece of information required on the form above would most likely NOT affect the decision of the Mutual Mortgage Company?

    (1) Current salary
    (2) Outstanding loans
    (3) Amount of down payment
    (4) Purchase price of the new home
    (5) Current address

Here's How to Crack It

If you were a bank deciding whether to loan someone money for a house, which information would be important to you? Certainly an applicant's salary would be important. So would the amount of money that person already owed to other banks. And so would the amount of money he/she had saved for a down payment. Of course, how much the house cost would also be very important. These are choices (1) through (4). Since the question is asking for which information on the form would NOT affect the bank's decision, the best answer is choice (5). If you were thinking, "But the current address might say a lot about a person," you were thinking a little too much; that distinction is too subtle for the GED test writers.

What Topics Are Covered on the Social Studies Test?

Here are the topics as they are described by the people who write the test:

History (U.S. or Canada)	25%
World History	15%
Civics and Government	25%
Economics	20%
Geography	15%

This is a pretty vague list. Just trying to acquaint yourself with all the topics covered in high school economics classes alone would take a long time. Fortunately, we will be able to give you much more exact information in the two chapters that follow.

Our Approach

While no particular knowledge of the facts of history, economics, or political science is necessary to do well on this test (you can virtually always find the correct answers contained in the passages), some *general* knowledge of these subjects and the specialized vocabulary that comes with them can be extremely helpful, if only because it will give you confidence. It's no fun answering questions about a topic you haven't heard about before.

We're going to discuss the topics that come up most often on the GED Social Studies test. Don't try to memorize them. The idea is simply to get familiar with the subject matter and to practice answering GED social studies questions.

Words to Look For

As you read each social studies question, you should be on the lookout for certain key words:

fact, opinion, inference, conclusion

If you spot one of these words, chances are the question just got a little easier. Here's why: The GED test writers want to see if you know the very specific differences between these terms. And once you understand these differences, it is often possible at least to eliminate several of the INCORRECT answer choices.

Here are the definitions you'll need:

> **fact**— information already contained in the passage or chart
> **conclusion**—a judgment or decision based on the facts of the passage. Sometimes a conclusion is stated inside the passage itself; sometimes you'll have to supply your own. (Another way the test writers may frame a conclusion question is to ask, "Which of the following statements **is best supported** by the passage?")
> **opinion**—an interpretation of the facts of the passage or chart, which goes further than a conclusion would warrant
> **inference**—something the author hints at without stating directly

Now, let's try a sample passage:

Questions 1 and 2 refer to the following information.

> At the Mariotta Machine Works in Illinois, three separate plans to increase productivity were introduced over the past three years. Each time a plan was introduced, productivity increased but then fell back by the end of the year, leaving company managers baffled.

Innovation	Productivity: Jan.–June	Productivity: July–Dec.
New quota system (2008)	+10%	−9%
Incentive bonus system (2009)	+12%	−13%
Strategic management system (2010)	+15%	−15%

But in the opinion of the company accountant, the managers completely failed to understand what was really going on: a little-known phenomenon known as the Hawthorne effect. According to the Hawthorne effect, when you introduce an innovation, productivity goes up simply because the innovation is new. Managers try harder because they are dealing with a new system. Workers try harder because they are trying out something new as a team. Then, as the innovation becomes routine, results slide back to pre-innovation levels.

1. Which of the following is a fact outlined in the passage or chart above?

   (1) The productivity increases for all three years were because of the Hawthorne effect.
   (2) The productivity level at the machine works ended up almost exactly the same after three years.
   (3) The company managers failed to understand the reasons behind the eventual productivity decreases.
   (4) Productivity decreased 10 percent in 2008.
   (5) Productivity increased 12 percent in the first half of 2009.

Here's How to Crack It

The question is asking for a **fact**, so we are looking for something that was directly stated in the passage or chart. Any answer choice that goes further than a statement of fact is going too far and can be eliminated. Choice (1) goes much further than a simple fact: It actually seems more like a **conclusion** summarizing the effect of the entire passage. Throw it away. Choice (2) also goes much further, essentially putting together information in the passage to make an **inference** that is never said out loud. We can eliminate this choice as well. And choice (3) offers up the accountant's **opinion** of the company managers. In this question, we want no opinions, just facts. Choice (4) is a statement of fact, but it gets the fact wrong; productivity actually *increased* in 2008. Choice (5) is a statement of fact and turns out to be the correct answer. Note how spotting these key words in the question allowed you to quickly put all the answer choices in perspective.

Here's another question based on the same passage:

---

2. Which of the following is an opinion expressed in or implied by the passage?

(1) The productivity increases for all three years were because of the Hawthorne effect.

(2) The productivity level at the machine works ended up almost exactly the same after three years.

(3) The company managers failed to understand the reasons behind the eventual productivity decreases.

(4) Productivity decreased 10 percent in the first half of 2008.

(5) Productivity increased 12 percent in the first half of 2009.

Here's How to Crack It
This time we are looking for an opinion expressed in the passage. Do you know what the answer is? That's right, it's choice (3), the only *interpretation* of the facts in the passage. Choice (1) was a **conclusion.** Choice (2) was an **inference.** Choices (4) and (5) were **facts,** right or wrong.

FACTS, CONCLUSIONS, OPINIONS, AND INFERENCES DRILL

Read the passage below, and then decide which of the statements that follow is a fact, a conclusion, an opinion, or an inference.

(Answers and explanations can be found in Part VIII.)

In congressional elections, studies have shown that incumbents are much more likely to win a race than newcomers. The Griswald study showed that incumbents have a 53 percent greater chance of winning the election. The Duke study showed that newcomers are three times less likely to be elected in their first election. The Council on Legislative Reform believes this is unfair and says that new laws are necessary to even out the playing field.

(1) There are usually many more incumbents returning to office each legislative session than there are newcomers.

(2) Incumbents have a greater chance of winning an election than have newcomers.

(3) The Griswald study shows that incumbent congressmen and congresswomen have a 53 percent greater chance of winning an election.

(4) Current laws favor the incumbent and should be changed.

(5) The Duke study shows that newcomers in congressional elections are three times less likely to be elected in their first election.

Chapter 14
Social Studies,
Part One

In this chapter, we'll go over some of the topics covered on the Social Studies test, including political systems, types of government, historical documents, supply and demand, economics, and markets.

While it is impossible to predict *exactly* what is going to be on the GED Social Studies test that you take, we can be pretty sure that it will include certain topics that come up on the test all the time. And while it isn't necessary to bring any specific outside social studies knowledge to the test, some general understanding of the processes of social studies can be very useful.

In this chapter, we'll cover some of the GED test writers' favorite social studies topics. After each review, we'll give you some helpful vocabulary words to think about, and we'll ask some GED-type questions based on that particular area.

Learning how to think about the GED social studies questions is probably more important than learning facts, so at the end of each review, there will also be a short drill for you to try on your own.

Here are the topics we'll cover in this chapter:

- Political systems
- The U.S. government
- The documents on which the U.S. government is based
- Economics
- Supply and demand
- Markets

POLITICAL SYSTEMS

There are several different kinds of political systems in use today. Under a **monarchy,** a country is ruled by a king or queen. Power passes from one member of the royal family to the next and from one generation to the next. **Constitutional monarchies,** such as Great Britain and Denmark, retain a monarch even though the country has elected representatives who actually run the government. Under a **dictatorship,** a country is ruled absolutely by a single leader, who is neither elected nor accountable to the people he or she leads. Examples of modern dictatorships include the regime of Adolf Hitler in Germany and that of Mu'ammar al-Gadhafi in Libya. An **oligarchy** is a government that is controlled by a small group of leaders who have not been elected by the citizens of their country. Russia and other former communist countries used to be considered oligarchies. A **representative democracy** is a system of government in which the leaders of the country are chosen by the citizens of the country in regularly scheduled elections. The United States is a representative democracy. A **pure democracy** is a system of government in which the citizens vote directly on how they want their country to run. Because it would be almost impossible to consult each citizen of a country on every decision, no one presently uses this system on a large scale.

Vocabulary

> **absolute monarch**—a king or queen who rules without any elected body's supervision
>
> **junta**—a group of persons who rule after overthrowing a government

Let's try a stand-alone problem.

Question 1 is based on the following interpretation of an oligarchy.

> In an oligarchy, a country is ruled by a small nonelected group of individuals who make all political decisions and some social decisions for the country's citizens.

1. It can be inferred that which of the following would be the biggest drawback of an oligarchy to the citizens?

    (1) Because there are so few leaders, the leaders may become overworked.
    (2) Without the ceremonial presence of a king or queen, order will be impossible to maintain.
    (3) Without accountability to the citizens, the rulers may make decisions that are against the best interests of the country.
    (4) Because their decisions may be unpopular, the rulers must spend a lot of money on security and crowd control.
    (5) The cost of reelection campaigns would prevent needed repairs to the country's infrastructure.

Here's How to Crack It

This analysis question is asking you to identify something that is wrong with an oligarchy. But before you start thinking about your answer, did you notice the word *inferred* in the question itself? This lets us know right away that we are looking for something that is not directly stated in the passage but that is supported by the information in the passage. Choice (1) represents a possible drawback to the *leaders* of the oligarchy, but not to the general population. Let's keep reading. Choice (2) implies that the only way to maintain order is to have a monarch. Because the United States and other countries have functioned reasonably well without a king or queen for hundreds of years, this doesn't seem likely. Choice (3) states a very serious drawback of an oligarchy: Absolute rulers often get carried away and make decisions based on their own best interests, not those of the people they rule. Let's hold on to this one and check the last two choices. Choice (4) describes, again, something that is a problem only if you are one of the ruling class, so we can eliminate it. Because there are no reelections in an oligarchy, there can be no reelection campaigns, which means that choice (5) is not a possible drawback. The correct answer is choice (3).

POLITICAL SYSTEMS DRILL

(Answers and explanations can be found in Part VIII.)

<u>Questions 1 through 4</u> refer to the following information.

Five types of political systems are classified below.

direct democracy—a system in which all important decisions are voted on by eligible citizens

representative democracy—a system in which citizens elect representatives who make the important decisions

oligarchy—a system in which a small group of people (who have not been elected by citizens) controls the government

constitutional monarchy—a system in which a king or queen is the ceremonial head of state, but the decision making is carried out by representatives elected by the citizens

dictatorship—a system in which one man or woman controls all decision making without accountability to the country's citizens

Each of the following statements describes a political system. Choose the classification from the types described above that most resembles this system.

1. A glee club gets together to decide on the songs that will be sung at its spring concert.

    (1) direct democracy
    (2) representative democracy
    (3) oligarchy
    (4) constitutional monarchy
    (5) dictatorship

GED Government Quiz

Q: Which part of Congress has 100 members?

Answer on page 234

2. A junta of military officers seizes power and declares that it will rule the country as a committee "until the end of the emergency."

    (1) direct democracy
    (2) representative democracy
    (3) oligarchy
    (4) constitutional monarchy
    (5) dictatorship

3. An elected president suddenly dissolves the country's congress and declares that he is now "president for life."

    (1) direct democracy
    (2) representative democracy
    (3) oligarchy
    (4) constitutional monarchy
    (5) dictatorship

4. Each district in a county holds elections of school board members who will speak for their district at a national convention.

    (1) direct democracy
    (2) representative democracy
    (3) oligarchy
    (4) constitutional monarchy
    (5) dictatorship

THE U.S. GOVERNMENT

In the U.S. Constitution, the country's founders created a government that embodied the idea of checks and balances. The **legislative** branch of the government (called the U.S. **Congress**) is charged with making laws. It has two parts: the **Senate** (there are two senators from every state) and the **House of Representatives** (the number of representatives per state varies with the population of each state). The **executive** branch of the government consists of the president of the United States, his (or her) staff at the White House, and all the departments and agencies that enforce the laws enacted by the legislative branch. The **judicial** branch of the government consists of the U.S. courts, which decide on the constitutionality of the laws proposed by the executive and legislative branches. The highest court in the land is the U.S. **Supreme Court**. Federal judges are appointed to the court for life.

Each branch of the government is designed to check the power of the others, ensuring that no one branch becomes too powerful. For example, if a president feels that a law proposed by Congress is wrong, the president can veto that law. If Congress still feels the law is correct, it can vote to override that veto. But if the Supreme Court feels that the law is contrary to the principles of the Constitution, it can declare the law unconstitutional.

Vocabulary

veto—the power to prevent the carrying out of measures enacted by the legislature

impeach—to challenge a public official in a public hearing

separation of powers—the system of checks and balances that keeps any one of the parts of the U.S. government from controlling the others

federalism—the system that permits the sharing of power between federal and state governments

constituent—a voter who is represented by a particular lawmaker

GED Government Quiz
A: The Senate

Let's try a question:

—————————————◯—————————————

When a member of Congress sits down to decide how to vote on a particular law, the lawmaker must consider two things that may outweigh the question of how he or she feels about the law personally. An elected official must first ask how this law will affect the people he or she represents. Second, the lawmaker must think ahead. If the president plans to veto the law, is there enough support to override the veto (which requires at least a two-thirds majority of both the Senate and the House of Representatives), or can the bill simply be amended to make it acceptable to everyone?

Which of the following would illustrate a potential reason for a member of Congress to vote against a law?

(1)   The law would lower taxes for the member's constituents.
(2)   Both the Congress and the president find the law acceptable in its present form.
(3)   The law requires no amendments.
(4)   The law will result in loss of jobs and revenue for the member's constituents.
(5)   The member of Congress personally approves of the law.

Here's How to Crack It

As you read, you may have noticed the structure words that helped organize the passage. According to the author, a member of Congress must consider *two* things when deciding how to vote on a new law: (A) how it will affect the people who he or she represents and (B) what will potentially happen if the law is vetoed. So when the question asks us which of the choices is a potential reason to vote against a bill, the correct answer must concern one of the two considerations just mentioned in the passage.

Let's look at our options. Choice (1) would *help* the citizens represented by the member of Congress by lowering their taxes, so this would not be a good reason to vote against the bill. Choices (2) and (3) eliminate anxiety a lawmaker may have about the second consideration: that the bill will be vetoed or need amendments. Again, this is not a reason to vote against a bill. Choice (4) is the correct answer. A bill that puts constituents out of work is a bill that a lawmaker may want to reconsider. Choice (5) ignores the first line of the passage, which says there are other considerations that may be more important than the member's personal belief. The correct answer to this evaluation question is choice (4).

U.S. GOVERNMENT DRILL

(Answers and explanations can be found in Part VIII.)

Questions 1 through 2 refer to the following information.

GED Government Quiz

Q: Which former
U.S. governor was a
GED graduate?

Answer on page 238

After the House of Representatives votes to impeach the president, the Senate has the power to convict the president. In such a case, the chief justice of the Supreme Court must preside over the proceedings, and the Senate must, after deliberating, vote to convict by a two-thirds majority.

1. Convicting the president of the United States involves

   (1) a majority decision by a legislative body, monitored by the head of the judicial branch of government
   (2) a majority decision by a judicial body, monitored by the head of the legislative branch of government
   (3) a minority decision by the executive branch of government, monitored by both the legislative and judicial branches of government
   (4) a general election by eligible voters
   (5) the president himself agreeing to step down

2. In 1868, the seventeenth president, Andrew Johnson, was called before an impeachment hearing in the Senate because he fired the secretary of war without notifying Congress. He was acquitted by one vote. Andrew Johnson was not convicted because

   (1) no one liked the secretary of war
   (2) the vote to convict failed to achieve a two-thirds majority
   (3) the House of Representatives voted to acquit the president
   (4) he was pardoned by the vice president
   (5) the chief justice ruled that he was innocent

THE DOCUMENTS THAT STARTED IT ALL

Angered at Britain's refusal to grant them the rights of British citizens, the people of the 13 colonies decided to revolt. The Declaration of Independence was written by Thomas Jefferson in 1776. It said, in part,

We hold these truths to be self-evident, that all men are created equal, that they are endowed by their Creator with certain inalienable Rights, that among these are Life, Liberty, and the Pursuit of Happiness...

It went on to list the colonists' grievances against the king of England. The declaration was adopted on July 4, 1776.

During the war with England that followed (called the **Revolutionary War** or the **War of Independence**), the colonists ruled themselves through an organization called the **Continental Congress**. However, after England was defeated, the former colonists wrote the **U.S. Constitution** in 1787, which created principles of government that are still in use today. The Constitution was designed to compromise between the need for autonomy of the individual states and the need for a strong central government. It began

We, the people of the United States...

The U.S. Constitution listed the powers of the states and the powers of the federal government and set up the system of government that we have described above. Worried that the rights of individuals were not sufficiently protected, the founding fathers wrote the first ten amendments to the Constitution in 1791. These have come to be known as the **Bill of Rights.** These rights include freedom of speech, the right to bear arms, the right to a trial by jury, protection against illegal search and seizure, and protection against cruel and unusual punishment.

Since that time, there have been a total of 26 amendments to the Constitution.

Vocabulary

> **amendment**—a change to the laws set forth in the Constitution
> **Continental Congress**—the governing body of the American colonists while they were fighting the War of Independence against the British
> **universal suffrage**—the right of all adult citizens of a country to vote in elections regardless of gender or race

Let's try the following problem:

Question 1 refers to the following excerpt from the Declaration of Independence.

> ...Prudence, indeed, will dictate that governments long established should not be changed for light and transient causes; and accordingly all experience hath shown, that mankind are more disposed to suffer, while evils are sufferable, than to right themselves by abolishing the forms to which they are accustomed. But when a long train of abuses and usurpations, pursuing invariably the same object, evinces a design to reduce them under absolute despotism, it is their right, it is their duty, to throw off such government, and to provide new guards for their future security.

1. Which statement about the excerpt above best summarizes its conclusion?

   (1) Under no circumstances should a people overthrow the government.
   (2) The citizens of a country should overthrow their government the first time it does something they don't like.
   (3) Citizens should only overthrow a government if it has consistently abused their rights.
   (4) Mankind should learn to suffer the abuses of bad government.
   (5) If a government is overthrown, security guards must be hired.

Here's How to Crack It

This comprehension question asks us to understand a document that was written at a time when people spoke a slightly different kind of English. However, if you are having trouble understanding the passage, don't lose hope. For one thing, you may have noticed the word *conclusion* in the question. We are looking for a judgment or decision based on the facts of the passage. You know the general purpose of the Declaration of Independence. Maybe that will be enough to find the right answer. Let's go straight to the answer choices. Choice (1) would be a pretty strange answer to this question because the Declaration of Independence announced the overthrow of a government. Eliminate choice (1). If choice (2) were correct, there would be a revolution every five minutes. This one just doesn't make sense. Choice (3), however, is more reasonable: If things get really bad, then the people have the right to revolt. Let's hold on to this one. It is a nice restatement of the passage's conclusion. If choice (4) were true, there should never be a revolution, and this passage would never have been written, so the answer can't be choice (4). Choice (5) mixes together several words from the last line of the passage, but gets the meaning wrong. The "guards" referred to by the founding fathers were new laws that would protect the rights of the citizens. The correct answer is choice (3).

U.S. DOCUMENTS DRILL

(Answers and explanations can be found in Part VIII.)

<u>Questions 1 through 3</u> refer to the following information about some of the amendments to the Constitution.

18th Amendment (ratified in 1919)—made it illegal to manufacture or sell alcoholic beverages in the United States

19th Amendment (ratified in 1920)—gave women the right to vote

20th Amendment (ratified in 1933)—set new terms for elected officers

21st Amendment (ratified in 1933)—repealed the 18th Amendment

22nd Amendment (ratified in 1951)—limited the number of terms that a president could serve to two

1. Which of the amendments above is no longer in force?

    (1)   18th Amendment
    (2)   19th Amendment
    (3)   20th Amendment
    (4)   21st Amendment
    (5)   22nd Amendment

2. Which of the amendments above was responsible for an increase in the number of eligible voters?

   (1) 18th Amendment
   (2) 19th Amendment
   (3) 20th Amendment
   (4) 21st Amendment
   (5) 22nd Amendment

3. If the 22nd Amendment had been in force, which president would have served fewer years in office?

   (1) Gerald Ford, who, after being named vice president, became president in 1974 when Richard Nixon resigned, and who then lost the bid for election in 1976
   (2) George Washington, the country's first president, who won a second term as president in 1792
   (3) Theodore Roosevelt, who as vice president became president after McKinley died in 1901; in 1904, he was elected president for four more years
   (4) Franklin Delano Roosevelt, who was elected president four consecutive times
   (5) William Henry Harrison, who caught pneumonia during his inauguration and died 31 days later

ECONOMICS

Economics is not just the study of money—it's the study of how a society meets its needs through the production and distribution of goods and services.

How successful a country is in meeting its needs is a function of many interconnected things such as:

Natural resources: Every country has some natural resources. Some have oil or valuable metal deposits in their lands, others have rich farmland, and others have miles of coastline that can be used for fishing or shipbuilding.

The labor pool: Are the country's workers highly skilled or uneducated? Are there enough workers to meet the needs of production, or are there too many, leaving some unemployed?

The industrial base: Does a country have the technical know-how, the factories, and the ability to raise money to acquire new knowledge and new factories?

Types of Economies

The concept of pure capitalism was first described in 1776 by a Scottish economist named Adam Smith, in a book called *The Wealth of Nations*. Smith advocated a laissez-faire (from the French "to let alone") economic system in which the government does not interfere with the free market at all, allowing the interplay of supply and demand to determine prices. In later years, other economists, such as John Maynard Keynes, argued that in the real world, governments must use a combination of tax and spending programs to stabilize a capitalist-based economy.

Some countries have installed economies based on **central planning**—in other words, government ownership of a country's resources and government control of its economic activities. **Communism**, as it was practiced in the former Soviet Union, is an example of such an economy. All the means of production in the Soviet Union were owned by the state, which decided what would be produced and when. **Socialism** is also an example of an economy based at least in part on central planning. In a socialist country, many of the largest industries (such as the transportation industry or the steel industry) are owned and operated by the government, as is a comprehensive system of public welfare.

The United States, like most countries today, practices a modified version of capitalism, sometimes called a **mixed economy**. The government regulates some aspects of business (for example, the Food and Drug Administration makes sure that products sold in our stores will not poison us) and offers some social welfare systems, but the majority of economic decisions are made by private individuals and companies.

Vocabulary

nationalize—to convert an industry from private ownership to state ownership

free-market economy—an economy in which prices are determined in the marketplace, rather than being fixed by the government

Let's try a problem.

A country with a large population but no mineral deposits, no coastline, no industrial base, and no land suitable for farmland could be said to be rich in which of the following ways?

(1) The country will need a large defense budget.
(2) The country will have to import much of its food.
(3) The country can mine for gold and silver.
(4) The country has no natural harbor.
(5) The country has a large labor pool.

Here's How to Crack It

This analysis question is presenting us with a hypothetical country that apparently has no natural resources. Nevertheless, the question says that the country has some kind of riches. Choices (1), (2), (3), and (4) don't make sense. The need to spend money on defense is not a blessing, nor is the need to import food from abroad, nor the lack of a good harbor. And because the country has no mineral deposits, it would be silly to mine for them. The only answer that makes sense is choice (5). A country with a large population has a ready source of cheap labor. These days, industrialized countries are rushing to build factories in such countries to take advantage of low labor costs.

ECONOMICS DRILL

(Answers and explanations can be found in Part VIII.)

Questions 1 and 2 refer to the following passage.

The socialist system is based on the principle that government has a responsibility to provide certain basic necessities to its citizens, such as free education, free medical care, and a cheap system of public transportation.

Yet many countries governed by socialist political parties have also embraced some of the principles of capitalism, including private ownership of some businesses, and allow prices to be set by the market.

1. A socialist country is dedicated to the values of

    (1)   personal gain
    (2)   social welfare
    (3)   expensive private medical centers
    (4)   independent bus companies running in competition for passengers
    (5)   private schools that charge tuition for gifted students

2. Which of the following would be an example of a socialist country that also uses some of the attributes of capitalism?

    (1)   a country in which government officials make all key decisions about how goods are produced, priced, and distributed
    (2)   a country in which all resources are the property of the state
    (3)   a country in which key industries are owned by the state, but many other industries are owned by individuals or stockholders
    (4)   a country in which all marketplace decisions are determined by the laws of supply and demand and all property is privately owned
    (5)   a country run by a small group of powerful business owners

Questions 3 and 4 refer to the graph below.

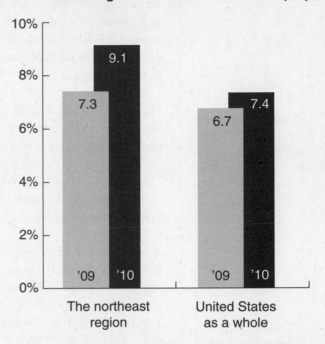

Percentage of the Labor Force Unemployed

The northeast region: '09 = 7.3, '10 = 9.1
United States as a whole: '09 = 6.7, '10 = 7.4

3. According to the graph, the difference in the employment rate in the northeast region from 2009 to 2010 represented a change of what percent?

    (1)   16.4%
    (2)   10.9%
    (3)   7.2%
    (4)   3.1%
    (5)   1.8%

4. An evaluation of the graph above would show that the overall <u>economy</u> of the United States in 2010 probably performed

    (1)   worse than it did in 2009
    (2)   worse than it did in the northeast region
    (3)   better than the economies of other nations
    (4)   better than it did in 2009
    (5)   at the same level as it did in 2009

Supply and Demand

In a capitalist economy, prices are determined by supply and demand. **Supply** is the amount of goods and services available at a particular time. **Demand** is the consumers' need for those goods and services. For example, a sneaker company might produce 200,000 pairs of sneakers. This is its supply. The public might end up buying 150,000 pairs. This is the demand for this particular product. If supply and demand are equal, then the price will remain the same. However, if there is more supply than demand, then prices fall. For example, because there was a surplus of 50,000 pairs of sneakers that were not sold, the company is going to have to reduce its price to make the public want to buy them.

However, if there is more demand than supply, then prices rise. For example, if these sneakers become very popular, then there will be a shortage, and the sneaker company may charge more for the sneakers because they are scarce.

These forces work on a global scale, which is why the prices of oil, gold, and shares of stock in different companies go up and down every day in reaction to the supply and demand of the market.

If an economy is functioning properly, there is an ever-increasing demand for goods and services that is met by an ever-increasing supply. However, if there is too much demand and not enough supply, then **inflation** can result. Inflation is a general rise in prices. A little inflation is to be expected, but too much can start a spiraling effect in which prices rise so rapidly that a country's currency loses it value. During the 1930s in Germany, it was not uncommon to see people bringing wheelbarrows full of money to the store to pay for their groceries.

When there is too little demand and too much supply, then **deflation** can result. Most of the countries of the world experienced deflation during the Great Depression.

Simple Economics
If supply is greater than demand, prices fall. If demand is greater than supply, prices rise.

Vocabulary

recession—a period during which employment and economic activity decline

depression—a longer period of drastic declines in the economy and employment

import—to buy goods from another country and bring them back to your own country for consumption

export—to sell goods to another country for consumption in that country

Let's try a problem.

Recent political instability in the Middle East has shown that the United States cannot depend entirely on Middle Eastern countries as its primary source of imported oil. If we are not to be dependent on the stability of this region, we must develop other sources of oil.

Which of the following statements can be inferred from the passage above?

(1) The United States does not produce enough oil to meet its own demand.
(2) Political instability always leads to war.
(3) The United States will replace oil with nuclear power.
(4) The other sources of oil will be Mexico and Canada.
(5) The United States exports oil to the Middle East.

Here's How to Crack It

Test takers often feel that the answer to GED social studies questions must involve higher thinking or specific knowledge of a subject. However, finding the correct answer to a GED question often has much more to do with using common sense. Did you notice the word *inferred* in the question? We are looking for something the author hints at without stating directly. The answer to this analysis question is supposed to come, indirectly, from the passage itself. But when you examine the answer choices, you will notice that several of them seem to go much further than the passage does. Look at choice (2). Does the passage state that political instability always leads to war? This is going much further than the passage itself. Forget choice (2). Look at choice (3). Does the passage say that oil will be replaced by some other form of energy? No, it only says we need to look for new sources of oil. So much for choice (3). Look at choice (4). Does the passage tell us *where* the United States should look for its new sources of oil? Nope. Eliminate (4). Look at choice (5). Given the fact that the United States is dependent on Middle Eastern oil, is it likely that the United States is *exporting* oil to the Middle East? No way. Forget choice (5).

You might have initially ignored choice (1) because it seems so obvious. If the United States is depending on oil from other countries, then clearly it does not produce all the oil it needs. The correct answer is choice (1).

SUPPLY AND DEMAND DRILL
(Answers and explanations can be found in Part VIII.)

1. Which of the following would most likely happen if the oil-producing nations ceased production of oil for a one-year period?

   (1) The price of oil in the United States would rise.
   (2) The price of oil in Europe would fall.
   (3) Middle Eastern countries would go broke.
   (4) Car production in Japan would halt completely.
   (5) The price of other types of fuels would fall.

2. New technology produces a type of computer that makes an older brand of computer obsolete.

   Which of the following will most likely result from this new development?

   (1) Production of software for the old computer will increase.
   (2) The demand for the new computers will decrease.
   (3) The supply of new computers will decrease.
   (4) Production of the old computer will increase.
   (5) The price of the old computers will decrease.

3. In the trickle-down theory of economics, it is held that if the rich are not heavily taxed, they will invest their money, which will make the economy grow. Wealth will eventually "trickle down" to the poor in the form of new jobs and opportunities.

An economist who believes in trickle-down economics would say that the best way to improve the economy would be to

(1) increase taxes on the rich in order to fund social welfare programs
(2) create a new tax on the rich to prevent the economy from growing too fast
(3) decrease the tax on investment profits in order to stimulate further investment
(4) create a socialist economic system
(5) distribute the wealth of the nation equally among all citizens

Markets

If one company controls an entire industry or becomes the only company to make a certain product, that company is said to have a monopoly. In the United States, this is illegal. If the government believes that one company is gaining control of an industry, it will institute an **antitrust** court action to force that company to let other companies into the field. An example of this was the antitrust action that forced AT&T to break up into smaller independent telephone companies. The case against Microsoft was another antitrust action.

Because all countries lack some natural resources, each country trades certain goods and services in exchange for other goods and services that it needs. This is known as **international trade.** If a country buys more goods from foreign countries than it sells, it has a **balance of payments deficit.** If it sells more than it buys, it has a **balance of payments surplus.**

Balance of Payments Quiz

Q: The United States buys more goods from Japan than it sells to Japan. Does it have a balance of payments deficit or a surplus?

Answer on page 248

Vocabulary

antitrust laws—laws designed to prevent the formation of monopolies

GNP—the gross national product, the total value of the nation's production

Let's try a problem.

A monopoly exists when one company or organization controls the sale of a good or service. In a socialist country, the government itself holds some monopolies in the form of state-run industries for which the government sets production levels and prices. This is to ensure that

(1) prices are determined in a free market
(2) the good or service will be available at a low price to all its citizens
(3) business is not regulated by the government
(4) there is always a demand for the state-produced products
(5) there will be a shortage of essential goods and services, thus driving up prices

Here's How to Crack It

Many social studies questions encompass more than one social studies topic. This is a case in point. The question asks you to decide the purpose behind state-run monopolies in socialist countries. Let's use POE to get rid of some answer choices. Choice (1) is wrong because according to the passage, a socialist country does not have an entirely free market: The government itself sets prices. Choice (3) is wrong because in a socialist country, some business obviously is regulated by the government. Choice (4) is wrong because the government cannot directly control demand for a product merely by controlling supply. Choice (5) is wrong because no government wants a shortage of essential goods and services—its citizens might not have enough to eat. The correct answer to this analysis question must be choice (2).

MARKETS DRILL

(Answers and explanations can be found in Part VIII.)

Questions 1 and 2 refer to the following graph.

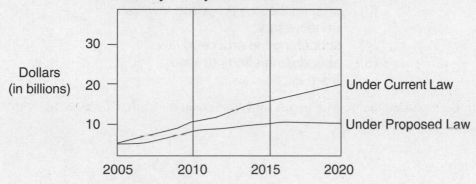

The U.S. Balance of Payments Deficit with Country X Projected to the Year 2020

1. Which of the following statements describes the most likely consequence of the proposed law?

    (1) an increase in the deficit
    (2) an increase in trade between the two countries
    (3) a decline in production in the United States
    (4) increased friendship between the two countries
    (5) a decline in the deficit

2. U.S. businessmen who wish to lower the balance of payments deficit with country X would most likely have used the information in this graph to justify

    (1) calling for increased trade with country X
    (2) breaking off all diplomatic relations with country X
    (3) arguing that the proposed law was unnecessary
    (4) supporting the proposed law
    (5) abandoning efforts to lower the deficit

In the next chapter, we will discuss some additional topics that are more likely to contain charts and graphs.

Chapter 15
Social Studies,
Part Two

In this chapter, we'll cover geography, maps, immigration, civil rights, conservation and the environment, education, and our guide to world history.

We'll continue with the topics that come up most on the GED Social Studies test, with a special focus on graphic materials. Here are the topics we'll be covering:

- Geography
- Globes and maps
- Immigration
- The civil rights movement
- Conservation and the environment
- Education
- History

Geography

Geography is the study of the physical features of the earth and the ways in which these features affect the people who live on the earth. When most people think about geography, they think only of surface terrain, but the study of geography also includes the natural resources underneath the surface of the earth and the climates of atmosphere above the various regions of the world.

Globes

A globe is a three-dimensional representation of the earth. On the GED, you may see two-dimensional drawings of a globe such as the one below:

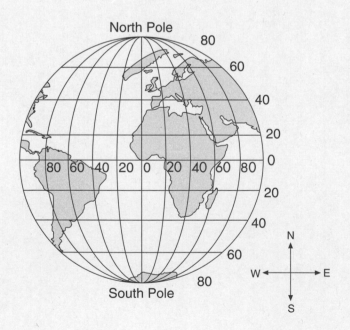

In this figure, you can see about half the earth's surface. You are looking at Africa in the middle of the globe. Above Africa, you can see most of Europe. At the bottom left of the globe, you can see most of South America. The line running horizontally across the center of the globe is called the **equator**. This line, like all the lines on this map, is imaginary. If you go to the equator, you will not, of course, find a red line drawn all the way around the globe. The part of the earth above the equator is called the **Northern Hemisphere**. The part below is called the **Southern Hemisphere**. The horizontal lines above and below the equator are called lines of **latitude**. Any point on the equator has a latitude of 0 degrees. A point 20 degrees above the equator would be called 20 degrees north. The vertical lines running along the globe are called lines of **longitude**. A longitude of 0 degrees describes an imaginary line that runs right through Greenwich, England, dividing the globe into the **Eastern and Western Hemispheres**. Using a combination of latitude and longitude, you can locate the position of any point on the earth.

Let's try a question.

Question 1 refers to the following diagram of the globe.

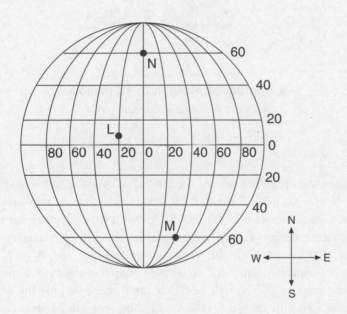

Map Lines
horizontal lines = latitude
vertical lines = longitude

It can be inferred from the diagram above that which of the following statements is most likely to be true?

(1) Point M is warmer than point L.
(2) Point N is warmer than point M.
(3) Point N is warmer than point L.
(4) Point L is warmer than point N.
(5) Point M is warmer than point N.

Here's How to Crack It

The nearer the equator, the warmer the average temperature. Which point is nearest the equator? If you said point L, you are absolutely right. The correct answer to this analysis question is choice (4).

Maps

A map is a drawing of a smaller part of the globe. Below, you can see one of the GED's favorites: a map of the United States.

Hey, Look!
Directly east of this sentence you'll find a map of the United States.

■ population more than 10 million
(Source: U.S. Bureau of Census)

Where?
Directly north of this sentence you'll find a sentence saying, "Directly east of this sentence…"

This map shows the different states of the United States. You saw one very similar to it in our "Crazy Graphics" chapter. However, note that on this map, you are also given some additional information. States with a population more than 10 million are shaded. Almost certainly, this information will be necessary to answer the question that comes with this map. As we said in the "Crazy Graphics" chapter, the information you need to answer map questions is almost always located on the map itself. You will find that some maps include information on the population living in the area, others will show climate patterns, and others will give topographical information, such as how far the land is above sea level.

As with almost all maps, north is at the top of the page, which means that south is at the bottom, west is toward the left, and east is toward the right. Let's look at the question that went with this map:

According to the map above, the biggest concentration of states with large populations can be found in which region of the United States?

(1)   the central region
(2)   the southwestern region
(3)   the southeastern region
(4)   the northwestern region
(5)   the northeastern region

Here's How to Crack It

Where are most of the high-population states? That's right, the top right-hand corner of the United States. Which region is that? If you're stuck, consult the paragraph right above the question. The correct answer to this comprehension question is choice (5).

Vocabulary

North Pole—the northernmost point on the globe

South Pole—the southernmost point on the globe

arid—dry, desertlike climatic conditions

rain forest—a tropical forest with rainfall of at least 100 inches per year

tundra—northern treeless Arctic region

taiga—a northern region still warm enough to sustain coniferous forests

MAP AND GLOBE DRILL

(Answers and explanations can be found in Part VIII.)

Questions 1 and 2 refer to the map below.

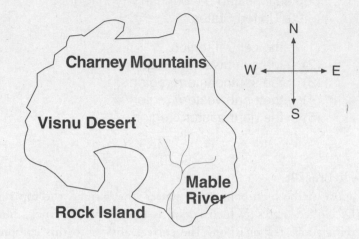

1. The map suggests that the best location for farming on Rock Island might be in which region of the island?

   (1) the northwest region
   (2) the southeast region
   (3) the western region
   (4) the northeast region
   (5) the central region

2. If there is another island, called Crab Island, located ten miles to the east of Rock Island, the overall weather on Crab Island is likely to be most different from Rock Island in which way?

   (1) Crab Island will be warmer.
   (2) Rock Island will shelter Crab Island from eastern storms.
   (3) Rock Island will have more rain.
   (4) Crab Island will have more sun.
   (5) There should be no appreciable difference in weather for the two islands.

Questions 3 and 4 refer to the globe below.

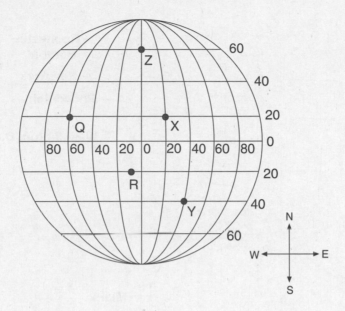

3. Which point on the globe is located at approximately 40 degrees south latitude, 40 degrees east longitude?

    (1) Q
    (2) R
    (3) X
    (4) Y
    (5) Z

4. If the South Pole is located at 90 degrees south latitude, what is the latitude of the North Pole?

    (1) 90 degrees north latitude
    (2) 80 degrees north latitude
    (3) 80 degrees south latitude
    (4) also 90 degrees south latitude
    (5) 0 degrees latitude

Question 5 refers to the following map.

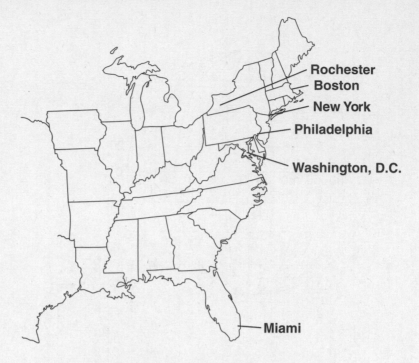

5. High-pressure systems generally approach the Philadelphia area from the northwest. Based on the map above, if a weatherperson in Philadelphia wants to predict the temperature tomorrow, she should call which city?

(1) Miami
(2) Washington, D.C.
(3) Rochester
(4) New York
(5) Boston

Immigration

Throughout history, humankind has migrated from one area to another in search of trade, food, adventure, and freedom. The early settlers came to America to escape persecution in Europe. These were the first of a long line of **immigrants** who found a new beginning in our country. The United States is sometimes called a **melting pot** because of the rich brew of different cultures that has helped form the American culture.

Vocabulary

refugee—someone fleeing from one country to another out of fear or necessity

immigrate—to enter a new country

emigrate—to leave your own country

IMMIGRATION DRILL

(Answers and explanations can be found in Part VIII.)

Questions 1 and 2 refer to the following passage.

Much of the history of immigration in the nineteenth and early twentieth centuries focuses on the migration of people from Europe who came through Ellis Island in New York. However, there was another large migration that came from an entirely different direction: the East. A large number of Asians (we will probably never know exactly how many) came to California to help build the railroads that ultimately united the different regions of North America into one country. These men, ill-paid, ill-treated, and now largely forgotten, helped realize the dream known at the time as "manifest destiny"—the creation of a country that stretched from one ocean to the other.

1. Which of the following gives the most likely explanation for why the Asians migrated to California in the nineteenth and early twentieth centuries?

    (1) They were looking for opportunities to work and earn money.
    (2) They liked the warm climate.
    (3) They were already experts at building railroads.
    (4) They wanted to see the world.
    (5) They were on their way to seek employment in Europe.

2. Which of the following best explains why the building of railroad lines was so important to the creation of the United States?

    (1) It provided high-paying jobs to the U.S. citizens.
    (2) It made other countries envious.
    (3) A large, spread-out country needs fast transportation.
    (4) Without the railroad, there was no way to reach California.
    (5) Every country should have a railway.

The Civil Rights Movement

One group of immigrants came to this continent against their will. Beginning in the early 1600s, Africans were brought to America as slaves. In spite of the Civil War (fought largely over the North's resolve to free the slaves), the **Emancipation Proclamation** signed by Abraham Lincoln, amendments to the Constitution, and various other laws, the civil rights of African Americans were too often more theoretical than real in the 1950s. The phrase *separate but equal* was a way to excuse **segregated**, inferior schools. "Jim Crow" laws excluded many blacks from voting in elections.

The civil rights movement began to gather steam in the 1950s as black leaders began to rally support for nonviolent protest. In 1954, the *Brown vs. Board of Education* Supreme Court decision made it illegal to segregate schools. In 1957, the first of a string of civil rights bills was passed by Congress—this one to protect the right of African American citizens to vote. There were sit-ins across the South and rallies in Washington, and from time to time, the anger spilled over and resulted in riots. Americans lost two of their most brilliant leaders in the 1960s when both Martin Luther King Jr. and Malcolm X were killed by assassins.

Civil rights legislation continued under the presidencies of Kennedy and Johnson, notably the Civil Rights Act of 1964, which banned discrimination based on "race, color, religion, or national origin"; the Voting Rights Act of 1965, which protected voting rights; and the Civil Rights Act of 1968, which banned discrimination in housing.

After decades of calm, race riots erupted in 1992 in Los Angeles after a jury acquitted four white police officers in the videotaped beating of Rodney King. But these decades also saw a number of historic events: the appointment of the second African-American Supreme Court Justice, Clarence Thomas (Thurgood Marshall was the first); the appointment of the first African-American Secretary of State, Colin Powell, in 2001; the appointment of the first female African-American Secretary of State, Condoleezza Rice, in 2006; and, in 2008, the election of Barack Obama, the first African-American President of the United States.

Vocabulary

"one person one vote"—a principle that allows fair apportionment of seats in state legislatures

discrimination—the unjust treatment of one group of people by another

Let's look at this question.

In 1957, President Eisenhower sent federal troops into Arkansas to protect nine black students as they entered a previously all-white high school in Little Rock. Which of the following was being upheld by the president's action?

(1) the 1954 Supreme Court ruling, making school segregation unconstitutional

(2) the 19th Amendment, giving women the right to vote

(3) the Taft-Hartley Labor Act, curbing strikes

(4) the 24th Amendment, barring poll taxes

(5) the 15th Amendment, stating that the right to vote shall not be withheld because of race

Here's How to Crack It

The key here is that these were students trying to go to what had been an all-white school. This is obviously not about voting rights, which means we can immediately eliminate choices (2), (4), and (5). Choice (3) has nothing to do with the question. Choice (1) was a ruling directly concerning desegregation. The correct answer is choice (1).

CIVIL RIGHTS DRILL

(Answers and explanations can be found in Part VIII.)

Questions 1 and 2 refer to the following passage.

In the United States, laws have been passed that prohibit discrimination in housing. Neither renters nor prospective homeowners can be barred from an apartment or a house because of race or gender. The regulations allow landlords or sellers of homes to determine prospective renters' abilities to pay based on credit reports, assets in the bank, and past reliability. However, no one can be refused housing for any other reason.

Unfortunately, in practice, this has sometimes been difficult to enforce because discriminatory landlords have simply said that prospective tenants did not pass their credit checks. However, compliance has risen over the past 20 years after several successful prosecutions of landlords who have tried to abuse the law.

1. Under the regulations, which of the following could be used by a landlord as a basis for turning down a renter?

   (1) ethnic group
   (2) the renter's sex
   (3) past credit history
   (4) the records of a family member
   (5) the renter's religious affiliation

2. Support for the passage of these regulations most likely came from

   (1) associations of landlords
   (2) civil rights groups
   (3) credit bureaus
   (4) church groups
   (5) associations of lawyers

Conservation and the Environment

Only recently have the earth's inhabitants realized that their planet is not an inexhaustible resource. As populations have increased and man-made products, such as nuclear waste and Freon, have leaked into the earth and the atmosphere, there has come a new awareness that without responsible behavior, we could make our planet literally uninhabitable.

Scientists are worried about a hole in the **ozone layer,** a protective part of the earth's atmosphere that prevents harmful rays from the sun from getting through to the surface of the earth. Scientists believe the hole is caused by pollutants released by cars, aerosol spray cans, and air conditioners. Scientists also worry about a phenomenon called **global warming.** They theorize that as the hole in the ozone layer gets bigger, the overall temperature of the earth could get hotter, melting the polar ice caps and changing the **ecology** of the entire earth. **Nuclear waste disposal** is another vexing problem. It takes thousands of years for radioactive material to become harmless. Nuclear waste has routinely been buried or dumped in the oceans—sometimes in thin steel drums that will eventually corrode. The increasing population that has caused these environmental dangers has also driven many species of animals and fish to the brink of **extinction.**

To try to solve all these problems, many countries have begun efforts to **conserve** our natural resources and to curb pollution. **Endangered species** are now protected by law. The governments of many countries regulate industrial and automotive **emissions.** And scientists are studying ways to make our **pollutants** less deadly and to develop alternative forms of energy.

Vocabulary

> **scarcity**—the principle that there is not enough of certain natural resources that cannot be synthesized by man
>
> **depletion**—the reduction of a natural resource

Let's try a question.

In 1986, an accident at a nuclear power plant in Chernobyl, a town near Kiev in the former Soviet Union, released a cloud of radiation that spread over several European nations. Some European nations destroyed milk from cows that had been exposed to the radioactive cloud. It can be inferred that which of the following is the most likely reason for this destruction?

(1) People in these countries had developed a new dairy product that they liked better.

(2) It was a protest against the nuclear policies of the Soviet Union.

(3) The milk would have turned sour soon anyway.

(4) It was feared that the contaminated cow's milk would harm children who drank it.

(5) The milk was too rich for the taste of these countries.

Here's How to Crack It

Did you notice the word *inferred* in the question? This means we are looking for an answer that has been hinted at by the author, but has not been stated directly. Radioactive material is poisonous to human beings. People exposed to it can die of radiation sickness immediately or develop cancer years later. Choices (1), (3), and (5) did not address the serious health concern that an accident such as Chernobyl would cause in a nation. It is difficult to see why Europeans would choose to throw away milk as a sign of their displeasure with the Soviet Union. The best answer is choice (4).

CONSERVATION AND THE ENVIRONMENT DRILL

(Answers and explanations can be found in Part VIII.)

Questions 1 and 2 refer to the information below.

Endangered Species in the United States

Species endangered: 409

Endangered species being aided by government-approved recovery plans: 301

Species threatened: 130

Threatened species being aided by government-approved recovery plans: 76

Note: Six U.S. species are listed twice on this chart; Grizzly bear, leopard, gray wolf, bald eagle, piping plover, and roseate tern are listed as both endangered and threatened.

(Source: U.S. Department of the Interior)

1. According to the information above, which of the following statements about the endangered species is true?

    (1) There are fewer endangered species than threatened species.
    (2) The government is ensuring that all endangered species will be saved.
    (3) There are other non-approved plans to save endangered species.
    (4) The government is making efforts to save many species from extinction.
    (5) It is useless to try to save a species from extinction.

2. If the animals that were listed twice above were only listed as endangered species, how many threatened species would there be?

    (1) 70
    (2) 124
    (3) 295
    (4) 320
    (5) 403

Education

Before the Industrial Revolution, most people received what little education they got from their parents at home. As parents went to work outside the home, the need for elementary schools emerged. Until the twentieth century, most people never got as far as high school. Today, more than 70 percent of U.S. citizens eventually get their high school diploma.

The need for increasing levels of education comes from the rapid technological advances in the workplace, which require workers to have more skills. Studies indicate that, on average, high school graduates out-earn non–high school graduates by a large margin.

Vocabulary

literacy—the ability to read and write

EDUCATION DRILL

(Answers and explanations can be found in Part VIII.)

Questions 1 through 3 refer to the chart below.

Elementary and Secondary School Statistics

State	Pupils Per Teacher	$ Spent Per Student
Vermont	12.3	$7,984
West Virginia	13.8	$7,176
Michigan	15.2	$7,199
California	21.0	$6,045
Utah	22.0	$4,478

Source: U.S. Department of Education

1. If pupil-teacher ratio were the only factor in the quality of education, which state would have the best educational system?

    (1) Vermont
    (2) West Virginia
    (3) Michigan
    (4) California
    (5) Utah

2. If expenditure per student were the only factor in the quality of education, which state would have the worst educational system?

    (1) Vermont
    (2) West Virginia
    (3) Michigan
    (4) California
    (5) Utah

3. If the best criteria to judge an educational system is a combination of pupil-teacher ratio and the expenditure per student, which of the states listed above has the best educational system?

    (1) Vermont
    (2) West Virginia
    (3) Michigan
    (4) California
    (5) Utah

The GED's Version of World History

The world is a large place and has been around for a long time—but you wouldn't think so if you talked to the GED test writers. History, as far as *they* are concerned, centers on a few hundred years and one or two geographic locations—notably North America; sometimes it expands to include Europe.

Here is all the history you need to know for the GED:

- **B.C. to 1492**—America is inhabited by Native Americans, like the Sioux and the Cheyenne. Farther south, the Mayas, the Aztecs, and the Incas have empires in Central and South America. There are several theories about the first settlers in America—one theory says people traveled across a land bridge that used to connect Russia with what is now Alaska and then moved down to the rest of America.
- **1492**—Columbus "discovers" America.
- **1492–1776**—Various European countries (including England, France, and Spain) try to get control of North America to colonize it.
- **1776**—The American colonies proclaim their independence from England. The big movers and shakers are Benjamin Franklin, Thomas Jefferson, John Adams, and George Washington. After the Revolutionary War is won in 1781, the 13 colonies begin discussions for what will become the U.S. Constitution. It is ratified in 1789.
- **1789–1865**—The United States adds to its territories, buying some lands and gaining others through annexation and war. The Native Americans are gradually pushed off their land onto reservations. City populations explode as the Industrial Revolution gains force.
- **1860–1865**—The election of Abraham Lincoln on an antislavery ticket causes southern states to secede from the Union. This begins the Civil War. During the war, Lincoln issues the Emancipation Proclamation, freeing the slaves in the seceding states.
- **1867–1877**—In the Reconstruction period, the northern states ratify the 13th, 14th, and 15th Amendments, extending Civil Rights and voting privileges to African Americans.
- **1877–1914**—The Industrial Revolution continues. Large industrial empires are born in the United States, including railroad and shipbuilding companies.
- **1914–1918**—World War I begins in Europe. The United States enters the war in 1917 on the side of the Allies. Germany loses the war.
- **1918–1929**—During the "Roaring Twenties," laissez-faire economic growth continues without any safeguards to protect investors.
- **1929–1939**—The stock market crash of 1929 begins a ten-year depression. Franklin Delano Roosevelt is elected president and promises to try to bring the country back to prosperity. His New Deal policies bring more regulation to the business world, and his social programs employ hundreds of thousands.
- **1939–1945**—Germany, falling under control of the Nazi party, is persuaded by a new leader, Adolf Hitler, to expand by invading other countries. This begins World War II. The United States enters the war directly after Japan (an ally of Germany) bombs Pearl Harbor.

Local History
The GED is interested almost exclusively in North American history.

- **1945–1953**—The United States enjoys a period of economic prosperity, although political tensions between the United States and Communist Russia increase. The period begins what is known as "the Cold War," during which both sides start a nuclear arms race. From 1950 to 1953, the United States takes part in the Korean War in an attempt to prevent Korea from becoming a communist state.
- **1954–1963**—The Civil Rights movement begins. School segregation is ruled unconstitutional by the Supreme Court. Martin Luther King Jr. becomes a national figure and delivers his "I have a dream" speech.
- **1963–1973**—The United States gradually gets entangled in the Vietnam war. Several popular political figures are assassinated, including John F. Kennedy; Martin Luther King Jr.; Robert F. Kennedy; and Malcolm X. The Civil Rights movement continues to gain ground nonetheless. The Watergate scandal forces President Nixon to resign and brings American confidence in its political system to a low point.
- **1973–1990s**—Nuclear armaments around the world begin to be dismantled as the Cold War wanes. The USSR is disbanded, and many of the Eastern Bloc (formerly communist) countries begin to move toward capitalism. A new awareness of the environment leads to the ecology movement, and new technologies begin what would be called the Information Age.
- **1990–2010**—The September 11th attack on New York's World Trade Center in 2001 leads the United States to declare a "war on terrorism" resulting in the invasion of Afghanistan and Iraq. Several large natural disasters (including Hurricane Katrina) help propel global warming to the forefront of public debate. Both China and India come into their own as economic forces to be reckoned with, just as a credit and housing crisis in the United States leads to the bankruptcy of major banks and other financial institutions, resulting in a global recession.

Let's try a passage.

---○---

Questions 1 and 2 refer to the interpretation below.

World War I was called "the war to end all wars," and so it is staggering to ponder that only 20 years later, a dictator who had claimed power in Germany would set in motion yet another war, even more massive in scale.

There were several reasons that World War II was inevitable. First, Germany, like the rest of Europe, had been in the grip of a great depression. Adolf Hitler was able to reduce unemployment through public works programs, armament production, the creation of a large and well-trained army, and the ruthless suppression of all dissent. However, to keep his country economically healthy, Hitler felt he had to expand. He began by annexing the Saar in 1935, the Rhineland in 1936, and Austria in 1938.

Second, the nonaggression pact between the Soviet Union and Germany gave Hitler the opportunity to attack Poland without fear of communist reprisals.

Third, there was a major miscalculation on the part of Hitler, who believed that the other European nations would not defend Poland. However, although they had tolerated the first annexations, England and France had promised to defend Poland, and so they declared war in 1939.

1. What was meant by the quote, "the war to end all wars"?

    (1) It was the most important war ever fought.
    (2) All the countries involved agreed they would soon fight another war.
    (3) It was a minor war with few casualties.
    (4) The war was fought by many countries from all over the world.
    (5) The destruction and loss of life was so severe that no one thought they would ever have the stomach for war again.

Here's How to Crack It

Did you notice the structure of this passage? After beginning with a quote about the *first* World War, the main idea of the passage actually came at the beginning of the second paragraph: There were several reasons for the *second* World War. In fact, the author gave us three reasons. Did you notice the "first…second…third"?

Question 1 is a comprehension question, asking us for the meaning of the quote that began the passage. Let's use POE to eliminate answers. Choice (1) goes much further than the passage itself. We know it was an important war, but was it *the* most important? It's hard to say. Choice (2) seems to get the meaning of the quote backward. If it were a war to end all wars, why would they be agreeing to fight again soon? If it had been a minor war, as choice (3) indicates, they wouldn't have called it a world war. Choice (4) seems to be true, but was it the reason for the quote? Let's hold on to it and look at choice (5). Aha! If World War I was a devastating experience, that would be a pretty good reason never to want to fight a war again. The correct answer is choice (5).

2. In the writer's opinion, which of the following was a cause of World War II?

   (1) Hitler annexed the Saar in 1935.
   (2) In the economic situation at that time, Germany felt it must expand.
   (3) Russia retaliated when Germany invaded Poland.
   (4) The English and the French were long-standing enemies.
   (5) Hitler annexed the Rhineland in 1936.

Here's How to Crack It

This analysis question asks us about the writer's opinion, so we can immediately rule out mere facts. Choice (1) merely states one of the facts of the passage, so cross it out. The same is true of choice (5), so get rid of that as well. Choice (2) seems like a good paraphrase of the first reason given in the passage. Let's hold on to it and look further. Choice (3) gets one of the facts of the passage wrong—Russia did not retaliate because they had a nonaggression pact with Germany. If you chose answer choice (4), you might have been thinking of an earlier time. Years before, England and France had been enemies, but by the 1930s, they were allies. The correct answer is choice (2).

HISTORY DRILL

(Answers and explanations can be found in Part VIII.)

Questions 1 through 4 refer to the acts, laws, and decisions described below.

Missouri Compromise (1820)—allowed slavery in Missouri but not anywhere else west of the Mississippi and north of the 36° 30′ line of latitude

Kansas-Nebraska Act (1854)—went against earlier rulings by allowing settlers in western states to decide by vote if they wished to allow slavery

Dred Scott decision (1857)—The Supreme Court held that a slave did not become free when taken into a free state.

Homestead Act (1862)—Congress granted free family farms to homesteaders.

Emancipation Proclamation (1863)—The president freed all slaves in areas still in rebellion.

1. Which of the following would have had the greatest effect on a slave who had escaped to a free state in 1860?

   (1) Missouri Compromise
   (2) Kansas-Nebraska Act
   (3) Dred Scott decision
   (4) Homestead Act
   (5) Emancipation Proclamation

2. Which of the following effectively overturned the Missouri Compromise?

   (1) Missouri Compromise
   (2) Kansas-Nebraska Act
   (3) Dred Scott decision
   (4) Homestead Act
   (5) Emancipation Proclamation

3. Which of the following may have helped settlers afford to move to western states?

(1) Missouri Compromise
(2) Kansas-Nebraska Act
(3) Dred Scott decision
(4) Homestead Act
(5) Emancipation Proclamation

4. Which of the following effectively nullified the Kansas-Nebraska Act and the Dred Scott decision?

(1) Missouri Compromise
(2) Kansas-Nebraska Act
(3) Dred Scott decision
(4) Homestead Act
(5) Emancipation Proclamation

PRACTICAL DOCUMENT REVIEW

Finally, before we send you on to our chapters about the GED Science test, take a few moments to try two last questions based on a Social Studies practical document:

Practical Document Drill

(Answers and explanations can be found in Part VIII.)

Lakeville Municipal Employment Application

Position Applied for	[for office use only]

Name	Social Security Number
Telephone	E-mail address
Current Address	City/State/ZIP code

Last Employer	Position/Years with the company
Address	City/State/ZIP code
Supervisor's Name	Supervisor's Telephone
Previous Salary	Full time/Part time
Name of High School	Did you graduate?
Personal Reference	Reference's Telephone Number

1. What is the general function of this document?

   (1) to determine whether a person is qualified for a job
   (2) to determine if a person is eligible for unemployment benefits
   (3) to show that a person is qualified to attend college
   (4) to show that a person has no criminal history
   (5) to compare previous employment to current employment

2. Based on the form above, all of the following could be factors in the company's decision to hire the applicant EXCEPT

   (1) previous experience
   (2) previous salary
   (3) education
   (4) age
   (5) personal reference

Part IV Summary

○ The Social Studies test consists of 50 multiple-choice questions based on short passages, graphs, and charts, but the good news is that any specific knowledge you will need to answer a question will be contained within the passage, graph, or chart on which the question is based.

○ Some questions may be based on a photograph or cartoon. To understand these questions, first tackle the photograph or cartoon, looking for the point that is being made in any accompanying caption. Bear in mind that important information may be contained in the question itself.

○ Several questions will be based on an excerpt from a practical document such as a manual, tax form, voter's guide, almanac, or statistical report. The best training for these questions is to do the practice tests at the back of this book.

○ The topics covered on the social studies test include history, civics and government, economics, and geography.

○ While this test does not require you to know specific facts of history, economics, or political science, some general knowledge of these subjects can be very helpful. For this reason, we suggest you read through Chapters 14 and 15 to familiarize yourself with these topics.

Part V
How to Crack the Science Test

Chapter 16
Science Overview

Like the GED Social Studies test, the GED Science test requires no specific knowledge of the subject. You will *not* need to memorize the periodic table or know the composition of a cell or the difference between a bacteria and a fungus. Every question will be based on a brief passage, and the information you need to answer the question will almost always be contained in that passage. Thus, the Science test is also mostly just a reading comprehension test. In this section, we will show you how to apply to the GED Science test the techniques you first saw in "Crazy Reading" and "Crazy Graphics."

What Do the Passages and Questions Look Like?

On the Science test of the GED, you will have 80 minutes to answer 50 multiple-choice questions. Each passage will be followed by one to five questions based on that passage. Here's an example:

Questions 1 through 4 refer to the following information.

> Biologists have long known that some types of electromagnetic radiation, such as X rays and gamma rays, can be dangerous to human beings.
>
> However, until now, no one has ever suggested that microwave radiation might also be harmful. In preliminary test-tube laboratory results, a scientist has found elevated growth rates in cancer cells exposed to low doses of microwaves.
>
> These results are only preliminary because, first, there has been no controlled study of the effects of microwaves on human beings. Second, this study was of short duration, raising the possibility that the dangers of long-term exposure have not yet been assessed.
>
> Although federal guidelines for how much electromagnetic energy can be allowed to enter the work and home environment have been made more stringent since they were first implemented in 1982, the recent study poses troubling questions about the safety of microwaves.

1. According to the information presented, the cancer cells' increased growth in the laboratory experiment is most probably because of

    (1) the sterile conditions of the laboratory
    (2) the cancer cells' natural reproductive cycle
    (3) a short-term growth spurt that may mean nothing
    (4) exposure to microwaves
    (5) a mistake in laboratory procedures

2. A scientist who wanted to make a study of the effect of microwaves on human beings might select which of the following groups of people?

    (1) lab technicians who are exposed to X rays
    (2) children in a day-care center
    (3) families who frequently use their microwave ovens
    (4) workers in a factory with fluorescent lighting
    (5) cement-mixer operators

3. Which of the following is the most likely explanation for the fact that there have been no long-term studies of the effects of microwaves on human beings?

    (1) Scientists were prevented by federal guidelines.
    (2) Until relatively recently, human beings had not been exposed to microwaves in large numbers.
    (3) The microwave technologies industry prevented these studies from being done.
    (4) Scientists believe only short-term studies are valid.
    (5) Cancer cells are killed by microwaves.

4. Which of the following, if it turned out to be true, would lend most weight to the scientists' initial findings?

A. A study of human beings exposed to microwaves reveals higher cancer levels.

B. A long-term study of cancer cells exposed to microwaves in the laboratory shows the same patterns of growth found in the short-term study.

C. A study of human beings who were not exposed to microwaves indicates increased cancer levels.

(1) A only
(2) B only
(3) C only
(4) A and B only
(5) A, B, and C

The same four types of questions that make up the Social Studies test are used on the Science test: comprehension questions, application questions, analysis questions, and evaluation questions. Most of the questions you will see will be application or analysis questions. Let's see how science fits into these formats.

Question Types

Comprehension Questions

A comprehension question, as you know, asks you to find a particular piece of information from the passage and then recognize that piece of information, slightly restated, in the answer choices. Comprehension questions may ask you to go just a bit further to identify a logical implication of that information. Question 1, from the passage on page 280, is a comprehension question.

1. According to the information presented, the cancer cells' increased growth in the laboratory experiment is most probably because of

   (1) the sterile conditions of the laboratory
   (2) the cancer cells' natural reproductive cycle
   (3) a short-term growth spurt that may mean nothing
   (4) exposure to microwaves
   (5) a mistake in laboratory procedures

Here's How to Crack It

Before you begin the questions from any passage, you should always make sure that you understand the *structure* of the passage. For example, someone in a hurry might have read the first paragraph of *this* passage and gotten the impression that it was going to be about the danger of gamma rays and X rays. However, if you looked past the first paragraph, you would realize that this was sort of a yin/yang passage. It began by talking about the kind of rays scientists have "long known" to be dangerous and then segued in the second paragraph to another type of ray that may, it turns out *now*, be dangerous as well. The passage describes a laboratory study, gives two reasons that the results are only preliminary, and then summarizes.

In question 1, we are asked a comprehension question about the *laboratory study*. Do you know where in the passage to look for this information? That's right: paragraph two. Read through the paragraph again quickly, and then start eliminating answers.

Choice (1) says that the cancer cells' increased growth is because of sterile laboratory conditions. Because all labs are supposed to be sterile to prevent contamination of specimens, this doesn't seem like a good reason for the cells to grow faster than normal. Eliminate it. Choice (2) says the growth is because of ordinary cell reproduction. This might be possible except for two things: One, the question says, "According to the information presented…" According to the information presented, the growth is because of exposure to microwaves. Two, ordinary reproduction wouldn't explain growth that was faster than normal. Eliminate (2). Choice (3) sounds reasonable, but again, this was not a reason presented in the passage. Choice (4) is exactly what we might have expected: The results of the study showed that microwaves led to increased growth in cancer cells. Choice (5) blames the growth on a mistake in the laboratory. Again, this is possible, but not a reason "according to the information presented." The correct answer is choice (4).

Application Questions

To answer an application question, you must understand the meaning of a concept described in the passage and then apply that concept in a different context.

---

2. A scientist who wanted to make a study of the effect of microwaves on human beings might select which of the following groups of people?

   (1) lab technicians who are exposed to X rays
   (2) children in a day-care center
   (3) families who frequently use their microwave ovens
   (4) workers in a factory with fluorescent lighting
   (5) cement-mixer operators

Here's How to Crack It

One of the reasons the results of the laboratory study are only preliminary is that the study looked only at cells in a test tube. There has been no study of the effects of microwaves on *people*. Question 2 asks us to construct just such a people-oriented study. What kind of people would we want to observe? Let's look at the possible answers. Choice (1) gives us X-ray technicians, but we already know X rays are dangerous. What we're interested in this time are microwaves. Eliminate it. Choices (2) and (5) have nothing to do with *any* kind of waves that we know of. Perhaps (2) is a trap for people who are not exactly sure what microwaves are and who figure that they may have a greater effect on "micropeople." (By the way, if you aren't sure what microwaves are, don't give up. There's an excellent clue coming up in just a second.)

If you're not 100 percent sure what microwaves are, choice (3) gives you a great hint: the energy waves used to cook food in microwave ovens. This is a bit like finding the meaning of a word from the context of the passage—except that this time, we found the meaning of the word from the context of a question. If microwaves are used in microwave ovens, then it may make sense to study people who use their microwave oven all the time. Let's hold on to this one. Choice (4) offers us people exposed to fluorescent lighting. This doesn't seem to have anything to do with microwaves. Fluorescent light, as you may know, is from the visible light spectrum. Microwaves are invisible. Eliminate choice (4). The correct answer to this question is choice (3).

Analysis Questions

An analysis question asks you to break down information from the passage into more specific categories and then explore the relationship of those categories.

---

3. Which of the following is the most likely explanation for the fact that there have been no long-term studies of the effects of microwaves on human beings?

   (1) Scientists were prevented by federal guidelines.
   (2) Until relatively recently, human beings had not been exposed to microwaves in large numbers.
   (3) The microwave technologies industry prevented these studies from being done.
   (4) Scientists believe only short-term studies are valid.
   (5) Cancer cells are killed by microwaves.

Here's How to Crack It
Why haven't scientists already studied the dangers of microwaves? That is the question that is asked here. To answer it, we will have an easier time using POE than trying to reason it out for ourselves. We might come up with good answers, but they won't necessarily be the same answers the GED test writers thought up. It's much easier to find *their* answer, especially because it has to be one of the five choices they've provided for us.

Choice (1) doesn't make much sense. The government provides guidelines to prevent dangerous products from getting into the workplace, not to prevent studies to determine if they're dangerous. Strike choice (1). Choice (2) seems possible. There would have been no reason to study the effect of microwaves on people if microwaves were rarely used around people. Microwave ovens and cellular telephones (which also use microwave technology) are relatively recent inventions. Let's hold on to choice (2). Choice (3) represents the conspiracy theory of microwaves: It's all a plot by the manufacturers. It would make a great "movie of the week," but the GED test writers don't usually show this much imagination. Strike choice (3). Choice (4) seems unlikely because the author is himself proposing long-term studies, and the author is clearly a scientist. If choice (5) were correct, then the cells in the original study would have been killed rather than growing abnormally quickly, so it can't be right. This means the correct answer was choice (2) after all.

Evaluation Questions

To answer an evaluation question, you must make a judgment or prediction about the information provided in the passage, sometimes by applying some knowledge or information you bring with you to the test.

4. Which of the following, if it turned out to be true, would lend most weight to the scientists' initial findings?

   A. A study of human beings exposed to microwaves reveals higher cancer levels.

   B. A long-term study of cancer cells exposed to microwaves in the laboratory shows the same patterns of growth found in the short-term study.

   C. A study of human beings who were not exposed to microwaves indicates increased cancer levels.

   (1)   A only
   (2)   B only
   (3)   C only
   (4)   A and B only
   (5)   A, B, and C

Here's How to Crack It

One of the most useful things you can know for the Science test of the GED is the **scientific method.** We will cover it in the review that begins in the next chapter, but for now, you should know that evaluation questions often ask you to bring some knowledge of the scientific method to bear on the question—and that is certainly the case here.

Given what the passage said about the preliminary nature of the study and what needs to be done next, which of the answer choices would help to prove the initial findings? The passage gave two reasons why the findings were only preliminary. First, the study was only at the test-tube stage. No studies involving people have been done yet. Second, it was only a short-term study. To know for sure if microwaves cause increased growth in cancer cells, a long-term study is needed.

Let's look at the three possibilities. Statement A addresses the first reason presented in the passage (no study as yet on human beings) and provides us with a study that supports the initial findings with new findings on human subjects. Statement B addresses the second reason presented in the passage (no long-term study as yet) by providing us with a long-term study of cancer cells exposed to microwaves. Statement C, however, presents us with a study of people who have *not* been exposed to microwaves but who have increased levels of cancer cells anyway. Would this study lend weight to the initial results described in the passage? No way. If anything, it would discredit them. The correct answer is choice (4).

What Topics Are Covered on the Science Test?

Here are the topics as they are described by the people who write the test:

Life Science	45%
Physics and Chemistry	35%
Earth and Space	20%

This is a pretty vague list. Just trying to acquaint yourself with all the topics covered in high school biology classes alone would take a long time. Fortunately, we will be able to give you much more exact information in the two chapters that follow.

Our Approach

While no particular knowledge of the facts of biology, earth science, physics, or chemistry is necessary to do well on this test (you can virtually always find the correct answers contained in the passages), some *general* knowledge of these subjects and the specialized vocabulary that comes with them can be extremely helpful. This is even more true for the Science test, in which the terminology is sometimes much harder than it is for the Social Studies test. In addition, we find that it's very important to have a grounding in the scientific method, which we'll talk about in the next chapter.

We're going to discuss the topics that come up most often on the GED Science test. Please don't try to memorize them. The idea is simply to get familiar with the subject matter and get practice answering GED science questions. However, if you find yourself getting curious about a particular topic, do yourself a favor by going to the library and reading some more about that topic. Some of this stuff is pretty fascinating.

Chapter 17
Life Science

In this chapter, we'll go over some of the topics covered on the Science test—including the scientific method, biology of cells, plant life, natural selection, the food chain, and fossils.

Sometimes science teachers can be long on knowledge and short on teaching skills. You may have had one of these teachers, in which case you are probably convinced that science is tough and deadly dull. In fact, science can be fun if you learn to look in the right places. The GED test writers say that they frequently get their topics and ideas from *Discover, Science News, National Geographic, Popular Science,* and *American Health.* If you want some added confidence for the GED Science test, you may consider reading one of these magazines from time to time as you prepare for the GED. It will help you get into a "science head," and besides, you may be astonished at how interesting you'll find these magazines. Of course, it isn't necessary to know any specific facts about science to do well on the GED test, but as we have said, *general* knowledge can be extremely useful—and more important, feeling comfortable with a subject gives you an important psychological advantage.

While it is impossible to predict *exactly* what is going to be on the GED Science test that you take, we can be pretty sure it will include certain topics that come up on the test all the time. In this chapter, we'll cover some of the GED test writers' favorite life science topics. After each review, we'll give you some helpful vocabulary words to think about, and we'll ask some GED-type questions based on that particular area.

Here are the topics we'll cover in this chapter:

- The scientific method
- Biology of cells
- Plants
- Natural selection
- The food chain
- Fossils

The Scientific Method

How did scientists learn anything about biology, the solar system, or the movement of continents in the first place? In each case, a scientist first came up with a hypothesis to explain an event that was not yet understood. A hypothesis is simply a possible explanation of an event or a phenomenon. Once she has her hypothesis, the scientist performs experiments to see whether the hypothesis is correct. These experiments must be carefully designed to make sure that the information they provide is accurate and that each experiment tests only one phenomenon at a time. For example, if you were testing whether aspirin alleviates headaches, you would have to make sure that the test subjects took only aspirin—nothing else. A good scientist would properly wonder whether it might be the water the subjects took to swallow the aspirin that actually alleviated the headache.

Often, an experiment will be repeated many times to make sure that the same results occur. Sometimes the scientist will use what is called a **control group.** A control group is a group of test subjects that are not subjected to the phenomenon being tested. For example, a scientist who is studying the effect of microwaves on cancer cells (like the man in the passage you just read in the last chapter) may also study a second group of cancer cells that are *not* exposed to microwaves. This is called the control group. The scientist will watch both groups closely. After all, how will he know if the cells exposed to microwaves behave abnormally if he doesn't know what normal is?

Only after other scientists have conducted the same experiments and gotten the same results is a hypothesis accepted as fact. And even then, scientists continue to re-examine their own thinking and the thinking of their predecessors. Sometimes accepted facts turn out to be wrong.

On the GED Science test, you will occasionally be asked to evaluate the accuracy of information or the relevance of a method. These can be the most complicated questions on the test—and they almost always involve your thinking through the question based on the scientific method. Let's look at an example.

An experiment was conducted to determine whether drinking a small amount of an alcoholic beverage every day can reduce the chance of heart attack. The scientists gave a group of 400 first-heart-attack survivors who were already in a health and fitness program one drink per day for two years. The scientists found that the people in their study had a much smaller chance of having a second heart attack than the national average of first-heart-attack survivors. They therefore concluded that drinking alcohol in small amounts lowers your risk of a heart attack.

Which of the following is the main flaw of this study?

(1) The number of people examined in the study was too small.

(2) The results of the study may be because of the health regimen the subjects were on, not the alcohol.

(3) Experiments should be performed on laboratory animals, not people.

(4) Many people believe drinking in moderation is good for you.

(5) The scientists were themselves heart-attack survivors.

The Scientific Method Quiz

Q: If you were testing the effectiveness of a cream that's supposed to grow hair on bald men's heads, which of the following would be a good control group?

(1) a group of bald women

(2) a group of men with full heads of hair who are also given the cream *x*

(3) a group of bald men who are given a harmless cream that has no effect

Answer on page 292

Here's How to Crack It

As soon as you see the word *experiment*, you can be pretty sure that this passage will concern the scientific method. Not every evaluation question is about an experiment or the scientific method, of course, but clearly this one is. We're asked to find a flaw in the way the study was conducted. Let's use POE to get rid of some answer choices first. Choice (1) would be a good answer if the number of people in the survey was small. An inadequate sample size could be a major flaw in a scientific survey, but a sample size of 400 seems large enough to be meaningful. Choice (3) is unrealistic. Even if laboratory testing is preferable to using human subjects, there is just no way to avoid that completely. Put it this way: You can't recommend a new form of treatment or a new drug for mass human consumption without first testing it out on a few human test subjects. Choice (4) basically agrees with the results of the survey, so it doesn't seem likely that this is the fatal flaw.

Choices (2) and (5) both seem to deserve some serious consideration. Choice (2) points out that, for better or for worse, this survey observes not just a single variable (alcohol consumption) but several variables at the same time (not just alcohol consumption but also a health and fitness regimen). As we said above, it is much better to measure a single variable at a time; otherwise, you won't know which of the variables is really responsible. Choice (5) hints that the scientists may be biased because they are heart-attack survivors themselves. However, this doesn't seem as big a potential flaw as choice (2), which is the correct answer to this question.

If you were torn between these two, it might help to remember that when the GED test writers select a passage about an experiment, they like to see how much you know about the scientific method. Typical flaws of experiments include relying on a sample size that is too small, failing to include a control group, and allowing your sample to be tainted by other possible causes of the phenomenon you're trying to explain (this is what happened in our case).

The Scientific Method Quiz

A: The best control group would be bald men using a harmless cream that has no effect.

Vocabulary

control group—the group of people not being subjected to a phenomenon in a study

hypothesis—a possible explanation of an event or phenomenon

sample size—the number of subjects in a study

variable—an element that changes in a study

SCIENTIFIC METHOD DRILL

(Answers and explanations can be found in Part VIII.)

<u>Questions 1 and 2</u> refer to the following passage.

The fossilized remains of a bird have been found in volcanic rock at Pompeii, site of a large volcanic eruption in the year 79 A.D. Scientists studying the bird believe it to be part of a species that is now extinct.

1. Which of the following statements is the best conclusion based on the data provided?

   (1) The volcanic eruption at Pompeii was responsible for the extinction of this species.
   (2) The bird did not live in Pompeii, but was on its way south for the winter.
   (3) No one survived the volcanic eruption at Pompeii.
   (4) Most of the casualties from the eruption were birds.
   (5) The bird was most probably from the same period as the volcanic eruption.

2. To test their hypothesis that this bird is from a particular extinct species, the scientists could do which of the following?

   (1) Compare the fossilized remains of this bird with the fossilized remains of other species killed in the eruption.
   (2) Search for live specimens of the extinct species.
   (3) Compare the fossilized remains of this bird with the fossilized remains of birds known to be from that species.
   (4) Test the composition of the volcanic rock found around the fossil.
   (5) Keep digging in the immediate area, hoping to find more fossilized remains.

The Biology of Cells

All living organisms are made up of cells. Some organisms, such as an amoeba, consist of a single cell, while other organisms, such as a human, are composed of millions of different cells. All cells have a **nucleus** containing the essential genetic information of that organism. This information is made up of DNA and is contained in structures called **chromosomes**. Cells receive nourishment by **diffusion.** For example, in the human body, the food we eat is broken down and then transported in a watery solution throughout the body. The nutrients needed by the individual cells diffuse through the permeable outer membrane of the cell, where they are converted to energy.

Most cells reproduce all by themselves in a process that is called **mitosis,** in which a cell splits into two new ones, each an exact copy of the original cell. Reproductive cells in animals divide by a different process called **meiosis,** in which the new cells contain only half the chromosomes of the original cell. Thus, when the sperm of a male unites with the egg of a female, together they make up the correct number of chromosomes.

Single-cell organisms can be as complex in structure as the plantlike algae and the animal-like amoeba or as relatively simple in structure as **bacteria** and **viruses.** If a microbial organism can cause disease, it is called a **pathogen.** Many bacteria and viruses are considered pathogens, although some kinds of bacteria can be helpful to humans. For example, certain kinds of bacteria in the small intestine help us digest food.

Let's see how the GED test writers might construct a question based on single-cell organisms.

When a cell undergoes mitosis, the cell makes an exact replica of itself. If a cell that has 46 chromosomes undergoes mitosis, how many chromosomes will there be in each newly formed cell?

(1)　23

(2)　46

(3)　47

(4)　92

(5)　138

Cell Division Quiz

Q: If a cell divides into two cells, which process would ensure that each of the new cells had the same number of chromosomes as the original?

(1) mitosis
(2) meiosis

Answer on page 297

Here's How to Crack It

As you can see, it wasn't necessary to know about mitosis ahead of time to answer this question. The question itself gives you all the information you need. Each new cell in mitosis is a carbon copy of the original. So, if the original had 46 chromosomes? That's right: Each copy will have 46 as well. The correct answer is choice (2).

Vocabulary

cytoplasm—fluid inside cells

permeable membrane—a barrier that lets certain molecules through it

CELLS DRILL

(Answers and explanations can be found in Part VIII.)

Questions 1 through 3 refer to the following information.

The bacterium that causes tuberculosis was for many years susceptible to drug therapy. However, recently new drug-resistant strains of tuberculosis have emerged, as the bacterium has mutated. Today, before a tuberculosis patient can be treated, it is first necessary to find out which strain of bacterium is causing the disease and then find a drug that will kill that particular strain.

Fortunately, according to the journal *Science*, a new technique has been discovered to aid in this process. By inserting *luciferase*, the enzyme that makes fireflies glow in the dark, into tuberculosis cells taken from the patient, scientists are able to make the tuberculosis cells themselves glow in the dark.

Scientists can then try out different drugs on the cells. An effective drug will make the cells stop glowing. This new test is much faster than older tests, which required up to five weeks.

1. If, after the injection of a drug into a tuberculosis cell as described above, the cell keeps on glowing, which of the following is most likely the case?

    (1) A higher dosage of the drug is needed.
    (2) The tuberculosis cell has been destroyed.
    (3) The patient is recovering.
    (4) The cell is resistant to that particular drug.
    (5) The scientist has performed the experiment incorrectly.

2. What is likely to be the most important reason to save time on a tuberculosis test?

   (1) The patient can begin effective drug therapy that much sooner.
   (2) The scientists can perform twice as many tests and thus have more time for other experiments.
   (3) The enzyme luciferase lasts almost indefinitely.
   (4) Other types of bacteria have shown themselves less able to mutate.
   (5) More than half of tuberculosis patients recover.

3. It can be inferred that, until recently, the new luciferase technique

   (1) was available, but too expensive for general use
   (2) was unnecessary because the tuberculosis virus responded to standard treatment
   (3) was regarded as unsafe and reactionary
   (4) took longer than conventional procedures
   (5) was considered too cruel to fireflies

Plants

Most plants are made up of many cells. Plants make their own food through a fascinating process called **photosynthesis.** Plant cells contain a chemical called **chlorophyll,** which gives plants their green color. When a plant's leaves absorb sunlight, the chlorophyll in the leaves converts the sunlight into energy. Meanwhile, the roots of the plant have been drawing water from the ground all the way up into the leaves. The plant uses the energy it has just converted to split the water (H_2O) into its two components—hydrogen and oxygen. The hydrogen is used by the plant, along with carbon dioxide from the air, to create sugar and starches for its own nutrition. The oxygen is released into the atmosphere—incidentally making it possible for humans to go on breathing.

The growth process of plants is dependent on the seasons. Some plants last only one growing season and die during the winter. To carry on the species, these plants produce **seeds,** which lie fallow during the winter months and then **germinate** in the spring. Other plants, called **perennials,** live for many years. The upper shoots of a perennial wither and die during the winter, but the roots live through the winter and produce new shoots in the spring.

Cell Division Quiz
A: In mitosis, a cell divides into two identical cells, each with the same number of chromosomes as the original cell.

Trees are also a kind of plant whose stalks have become woody. Trees survive the winter because their trunks protect them from the cold. If you were to cut down a tree and look at a horizontal cross section inside, you would find many circular rings. This is because in the spring and summer, the tree grows more rapidly, producing wider pores. During the winter, the growth is slower, producing denser wood. By counting the rings of a tree, you can tell how old it is.

Let's look at a classification passage based on plant life:

Questions 1 through 4 are based on the following information.

When plants respond to an environmental stimulus by growing in a particular way, that response is called a tropism. There are five kinds of tropism:

phototropism—a response in which plants turn toward the light

geotropism—a response in which roots grow toward the earth and the shoots and flowers grow toward the sky

thigmotropism—a response in which plants curl around any object they touch

hydrotropism—a response in which plants' roots grow toward a source of water

chemotropism—a positive attraction of roots toward the presence of certain chemicals

Each of the following items describes a relationship that refers to one of the five categories defined above. For each item, choose the one category that best describes the relationship. Each of the categories above may be used more than once in the following set of items.

1. A seed is planted upside down so that its root end faces up and its shoot end faces down, but after germination, the seed's root grows downward, and the shoot grows upward.

    Which of the following processes is described above?

    (1) phototropism
    (2) geotropism
    (3) thigmotropism
    (4) hydrotropism
    (5) chemotropism

Here's How to Crack It

As we've said before, the best way to approach a classification passage is to try to divide the different categories into a couple of easy-to-manage groups. In this case, let's divide the categories into things that affect the leaves and stem of the plant and things that affect the roots of the plant.

Phototropism and thigmotropism concern the leaves and stem. Hydrotropism and chemotropism concern the roots. Geotropism is a little bit of both.

What is affected in question 1? If you said a little bit of both, you are absolutely correct. The roots are growing downward, and the shoots are growing upward. This is an example of geotropism, and the correct answer to this application question is choice (2).

2. Poison ivy, if left unattended, will grow up trees and wrap itself around their lower branches until the trees are, in effect, strangled by the vines.

Which of the following processes is described above?

(1) phototropism
(2) geotropism
(3) thigmotropism
(4) hydrotropism
(5) chemotropism

Here's How to Crack It

This question is about the *vines* of a plant growing *up* trees. Obviously, in this case, we're concerned only with the *top* half of the plant, so we can eliminate choices (2), (4), and (5). Now, are they growing up trees because they are attracted to the sunlight or because they like to curl around objects? In this case, it seems more likely that it is because they like to wrap around the lower branches. The correct answer to this application problem is choice (3).

3. A house plant that bends toward the window is turned around 180 degrees. Six months later it again bends toward the window.

Which of the following processes is described above?

(1) phototropism
(2) geotropism
(3) thigmotropism
(4) hydrotropism
(5) chemotropism

Here's How to Crack It

This question is not about the roots but about the visible part of the plant above the soil. We have only two possibilities: phototropism and thigmotropism. Because the question does not mention curling and does mention that the plant bends toward the window, the correct answer to this application question is choice (1). By the way, the GED test writers sometimes use the same category twice, so don't rule out a category just because you've already picked it once.

4. A tree located more than 30 feet from a stream is found to have roots running underground all the way up to the stream itself.

Which of the following processes is described above?

(1) phototropism
(2) geotropism
(3) thigmotropism
(4) hydrotropism
(5) chemotropism

Here's How to Crack It

This question is about roots alone, so we are down to only two possibilities: hydrotropism and chemotropism. Are these roots heading toward water or toward chemicals? As far as we can tell, the roots are headed toward a stream of water. You might argue, "Well, maybe there are chemicals in the water," but this is just a little too subtle for the GED. The correct answer is choice (4).

Vocabulary

stomates—the microscopic openings through which gases diffuse into and out of leaves during photosynthesis

pistil—female reproductive organs of a flower

stamen—male reproductive organs of a flower

PLANTS DRILL

(Answers and explanations can be found in Part VIII.)

<u>Questions 1 and 2</u> refer to the following statement.

Each ring inside the trunk of a tree represents the annual growth of the tree. In ideal growing conditions, a ring may be larger because the tree was able to grow more during that time.

1. From this information, which of the following cross sections of trees represents the <u>oldest</u> tree?

(1)

(2)

(3)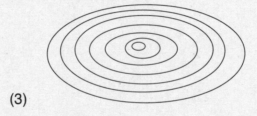

(4)

(5)

2. In the cross section of the tree below, which ring represents a year in which there were better-than-normal growing conditions?

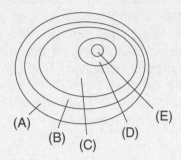

(1)   A
(2)   B
(3)   C
(4)   D
(5)   E

Natural Selection

It was Charles Darwin who first published the **theory of evolution.** This theory holds that species change slowly in response to factors in their environment. For example, if Earth's climate started to get colder, dogs that happened to have thicker, warmer fur would tend to survive better than members of their species with thinner fur. The surviving dogs would pass on the thicker fur gene to their puppies, and so this trait would gradually become a dominant characteristic of their species. This process in which traits that help an organism survive gradually triumph over traits that don't is called **natural selection.**

Darwin theorized that all species on Earth descended from one or two very simple organisms that gradually evolved into different kinds of more complex organisms. Thus, according to Darwin, human beings are thought to have evolved from simple sea creatures that gradually changed over millions of years into a common ape-like ancestor that in turn gradually evolved into Homo sapiens.

Today, animals are divided into two categories: invertebrates and vertebrates. **Invertebrates** do not have a backbone—they include worms, jellyfish, and insects. **Vertebrates** *do* have a backbone and include most of the animals you know, including fish, birds, and mammals. **Mammals** are animals that nurse their young. The whale is the largest mammal. Homo sapiens (otherwise known as human beings) are also mammals.

Let's look at a question:

In natural selection, the conditions of nature slowly force changes in a species through evolution, as species with needed traits survive and those without die off. A poultry breeder wants to produce chickens that grow faster and have more meat on them. To do this, the breeder selects chickens that have these characteristics and breeds them together.

Which of the following best describes what the breeder is doing?

(1) decreasing the meat on the chickens
(2) making sure that the chickens develop genetically less desirable traits
(3) decreasing the growth rate of the chickens
(4) using the principles of natural selection to encourage certain desirable traits in his chickens
(5) creating chickens with impaired immune systems that will be unable to survive disease

Here's How to Crack It

Let's get rid of the obviously wrong choices first. The breeder's intention is to produce chickens that grow faster and have more meat. Thus both choices (1) and (3) are obviously incorrect. Choice (2) also seems to go against the breeder's intentions—he doesn't want genetically *less* desirable traits. In fact, choice (5) wouldn't make much sense for a breeder of chickens, either, would it? If the chickens he raises can't survive disease, he will soon go out of business. The correct answer is choice (4). By mimicking the process of natural selection, the breeder can create chickens that will make him more money.

Vocabulary

survival of the fittest—another name for natural selection
adaptation—short-term changes in a species
evolution—long-term changes in a species

Survival of the Fittest Quiz

Q: Which of the following is an example of natural selection?
(1) A frog survives by hiding under a rock.
(2) Over thousands of years, a frog species gradually changes color to mimic the color of the rocks it likes to sit on.

Answer on page 306

NATURAL SELECTION DRILL

(Answers and explanations can be found in Part VIII.)

<u>Questions 1 through 3</u> refer to the following passage.

Scientists have speculated for years about the extinction of the dinosaurs. Various hypotheses have been presented to account for the disappearance of these huge creatures. One theory holds that a large asteroid collided with Earth. The impact raised a cloud of dust that prevented sunlight from reaching the planet's surface for many years. Temperatures fell rapidly, and without sunlight, much of the plant life on the planet's surface disappeared. Without warmth or food, the dinosaurs became extinct.

1. If the preceding information is true, which of the following is the most likely explanation for the fact that there is still life on Earth today?

    (1) Some forms of life were able to survive in spite of the lack of sunlight.
    (2) The dinosaurs went into hibernation.
    (3) Sunlight is unnecessary for the survival of plant forms.
    (4) There was no food at all on the planet's surface during these years.
    (5) Research indicates that life arrived from another planet.

2. If there had been time for the process of evolution to save the dinosaurs, which traits would have been most helpful for a dinosaur to survive during this time?

A. the ability to eat plant life

B. the ability to stand extremely low temperatures

C. darker pigmentation to prevent sunburn

(1) A only
(2) B only
(3) C only
(4) A and C only
(5) A, B, and C

3. Which of the following is a small-scale example of the climatic changes proposed by the theory described above?

(1) A piece of a Russian spacecraft falls out of orbit and crashes to Earth in a barren section of South America.
(2) A volcanic eruption raises a cloud of volcanic ash that lowers temperatures underneath it by two degrees.
(3) The tern, an endangered species of bird, becomes extinct because of pollution and overcrowding.
(4) It rains steadily for a month, causing local flooding and forcing the army corps of engineers to build up the banks of a local river.
(5) There is an unusually mild winter, which leads to bumper crops in the farm belts.

The Food Chain

A **food chain** is the passing of energy from one organism to another. The first step on a food chain is when a green plant absorbs the energy from the sun and converts it to chemical energy through photosynthesis. An animal then eats the plant, converting the energy contained by the plant into energy that can be stored by the animal in its cells. This is the second step. A bigger animal then eats the first animal and stores the energy from it in its cells. And so on. Eventually, at the end of the food chain is a fungus or bacterium that breaks down decaying organic matter.

A **food web** is a slightly more complicated chart that takes into account the fact that there is often more than one animal vying for a particular kind of food.

Try a question.

Question 1 is based on the following food chain.

Grasses → Grasshopper → Frog → Raccoon

The producers at the beginning of the food chain above convert the sun's energy into food. Then consumers eat the producers, transferring the grasses' energy to themselves. Other consumers then eat the consumers for their energy.

Which of the following is another example of a producer?

(1) a mosquito
(2) a tree
(3) a bear
(4) a whale
(5) a fungus

Here's How to Crack It

The passage says that the producer takes the sun's energy and converts it to food. You knew that from the material we gave you, but notice that you could have figured it out from the question itself. What kind of organism can convert sunlight to chemical energy? Only plants. Therefore, we need another plant—something with leaves that is capable of photosynthesis. There is only one answer choice that has leaves. The correct answer is choice (2).

Vocabulary

producers—green plants and algae that take the sun's energy and convert it into chemical energy

consumers—animals that eat the producers and/or sometimes each other

decomposers—saprophytic organisms like bacteria that break down organic matter into its basic ingredients and begin the life process all over again

FOOD CHAIN DRILL

(Answers and explanations can be found in Part VIII.)

Questions 1 through 3 refer to the food web below.

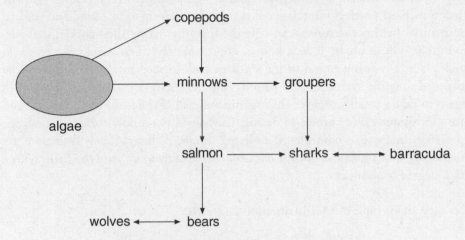

1. Which of the following organisms in the food web above are eaten by both land and sea creatures?

    (1) minnows
    (2) wolves
    (3) salmon
    (4) groupers
    (5) algae

2. The absence of which of the following members of the food web above would most devastate the rest of the web?

    (1) minnows
    (2) wolves
    (3) salmon
    (4) groupers
    (5) algae

3. As shown in the food web above, which are the only two fish that may eat each other?

    (1) minnows and groupers
    (2) salmon and sharks
    (3) groupers and salmon
    (4) sharks and barracudas
    (5) wolves and bears

GED Pop Quiz

Q: Which famous fast food hamburger mogul graduated high school with a GED?

Answer on page 310

Fossils

Much of what we know about both animal and plant life in ancient times comes from studying fossils—the preserved direct or indirect remains of ancient life. Millions of years ago, a tiny insect might have gotten caught in the mud of a riverbank. Eventually, if conditions were right, that riverbank became sedimentary rock, and although the organic matter of the insect decayed long ago, the rock preserved a perfect impression of that insect, waiting to be found and studied by man. Sometimes scientists can date the fossil by dating the material that surrounds it. For example, if it is known approximately when a volcanic eruption took place, any fossils found in the volcanic rock formed by the eruption can be assumed to come from the same period. Another method of discovering a fossil's age is to take a small sample of the organic material of the fossil (if any exists) and use a technique called **carbon-14 dating**. Carbon-14 is a mildly radioactive isotope of carbon that occurs naturally in all living things. It decays slowly over time. By measuring how much the isotope has decayed, scientists can date the fossil with a high degree of accuracy.

Let's try an example of a GED question on fossils:

Archaeologists have discovered the fossils of ancient sea creatures deep in the Sahara desert. Which of the following is the most likely explanation for the presence of the remains of saltwater fish in the middle of a land mass?

(1) The fish were carried into the desert by traders.

(2) Ancient fish could propel themselves for short distances over land.

(3) A huge storm swept material from the beaches of the African continent and deposited it thousands of miles inland.

(4) Part of the land that now makes up the Sahara desert was once underwater.

(5) The fish were carried into the desert by animals.

Here's How to Crack It

Just as you can sometimes discover important facts about fossils from their surrounding material, so too can you sometimes find out important facts about the surrounding material from the fossils it contains. In this case, while it is interesting to speculate about how the remains of fish could have been *carried* thousands of miles into the desert by people, by themselves, by the wind, or by animals, the simplest explanation is probably the best one, even if it is startling: At one time, part of the Sahara desert was underwater. The correct answer is choice (4).

FOSSILS DRILL

(Answers and explanations can be found in Part VIII.)

<u>Questions 1 and 2</u> refer to the following view of rock layers.

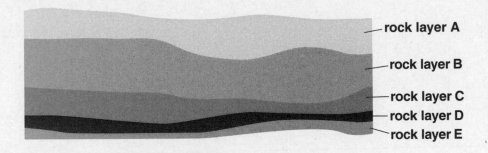

1. If organic material in rock layer D is carbon-14 dated and found to come from 4,000 years ago, which rock layer is likely to contain fossils that are even older than this?

    (1) layer A
    (2) layer B
    (3) layer C
    (4) layer D
    (5) layer E

2. If rock layer B contains the fossilized remains of shellfish, it can be hypothesized that

    (1) this piece of land was at one time in or near water
    (2) there are always fossilized shellfish found in rock deposits
    (3) all the other rock layers should also contain fossilized shellfish
    (4) there will be no land-animal fossils to be found at this site
    (5) fishermen lived nearby

Chapter 18
Physical and Earth Sciences

In this chapter, we'll cover the changing earth, glaciers, the ice age, oceans, astronomy and the solar system, the physics of solids, liquids and gases, and the physical laws.

A study of any *one* of the physical sciences could take several hundred pages, but fortunately the GED test writers don't delve very deeply into any of the subjects that make up the physical sciences—for the very good reason that they've already decided to ask nearly half of their questions about life sciences. This means that the remaining questions must be spread between three different topics: earth and space science, chemistry, and physics. In this chapter, we're going to show you the physical science topics that come up most on the GED Science test. Here are the topics we'll cover in this chapter:

- The changing earth
- Glaciers, erosion, and the ice ages
- Oceans, tides, and the moon
- Astronomy and the solar system
- Solids, liquids, and gases
- Physical laws

The Changing Earth

Although it generally feels pretty solid underfoot, the earth is undergoing constant change. We have discovered that the continents—that's right, entire *continents*—are actually moving slowly on the face of the earth. This is called **continental drift.** Looking at the map below, you will notice that if you pushed the continent of Africa up against the continent of South America, you would have an almost perfect fit.

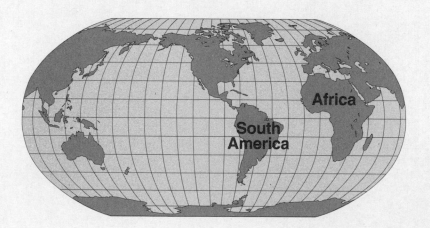

Scientists theorize that at one time, the two continents may have been joined together. Nowadays, it is believed that the earth's crust is composed of several large pieces—called **tectonic plates**—that move slowly over the mantle of the earth. When these plates rub against one another, the friction between them causes **earthquakes.** The places where the plates rub together are called **fault lines.**

The inner portions of the earth are under enormous pressure and are very hot. Sometimes, when the pressure becomes too great, it forces hot molten rock to the surface of the earth. This is called a **volcanic eruption.**

So far, scientists have had little luck predicting earthquakes and volcanic eruptions, although one interesting avenue for exploration may be the fact that animals often seem to know when an earthquake is coming.

The earth is composed of several layers. The outer layer is called the **crust.** The next layer down is called the **mantle.** The center of the earth is called the **core.** The crust of the earth (the only part we generally ever get to see) is composed of several different kinds of rock. **Igneous** rock is formed from cooled **magma;** magma is rock from the mantle that is so hot it has turned to liquid. **Sedimentary** rock is made up of sediment from the earth—such as sand—that has been hardened by compression. **Metamorphic** rock is made up of either of the other two types of rock, but it has been subjected to either a great deal of pressure or heat way below the surface of the earth.

Let's look at how the GED test writers might ask a question about the changing earth.

Scientists have found fossils of identical species of animals on the west coast of Africa and the east coast of South America. These species, from exactly the same time period, are not thought to have existed anywhere else on Earth.

Which of the following statements is best supported by the information above?

(1)   The fossils from South America floated across the ocean to Africa.
(2)   The climates of the two regions must have been very different.
(3)   The species happened to develop in two different places at the same time.
(4)   The continents of Africa and South America may at one time have been joined together.
(5)   The fossils should be kept as far away from one another as possible.

Here's How to Crack It

Whenever different fossils are spotted in identical rock strata, we can assume that the fossils have things in common. At the same time, when *identical* fossils are spotted in apparently *different* rock strata, it may turn out that this rock strata is not so different after all. Let's use POE on the answer choices. Choice (1) is unlikely because fossils are usually embedded in rock and rock seldom floats. Choice (2) doesn't make sense because identical species would need similar climates to survive. Choice (3) is a possibility. Choice (4) also seems possible. Let's hold onto both of them. Choice (5) is a little ridiculous. What would happen if the two fossils got together? Would they fight?

We are down to choices (3) and (4). How do you decide which is correct? One way to decide is to look at the other information in the passage. Why, of all places, did the GED test writers pick the east coast of South America and the west coast of Africa? Could this question have to do with continental drift? Well, that is exactly what choice (4) implies. The correct answer is choice (4).

Vocabulary

Richter scale—a scale used to measure the magnitude of earthquakes
epicenter—the place where an earthquake originates
dormant—a volcano that is inactive at the moment
strata—layers of rock

THE CHANGING EARTH DRILL
(Answers and explanations can be found in Part VIII.)

Questions 1 through 3 refer to the map below.

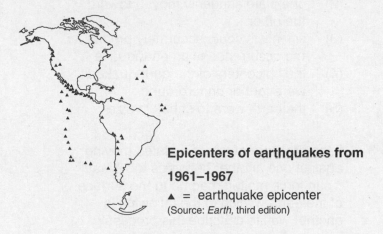

Epicenters of earthquakes from 1961–1967

▲ = earthquake epicenter
(Source: *Earth,* third edition)

Scientists have found that earthquake activity is usually the result of friction between tectonic plates of the earth. There has been a great deal of earthquake activity along the western coast of North and South America, as shown on the map above.

1. From the information presented above, which of the following statements can be concluded?

    (1) The places marked on the map are the only places on the earth where earthquakes occur.
    (2) Two tectonic plates are rubbing together along the west coast of the Americas.
    (3) Two tectonic plates are rubbing together along the east coast of the Americas.
    (4) There will be fewer earthquakes in the future.
    (5) Canada reports more earthquakes than the United States does.

2. The San Andreas Fault is located on the west coast of the United States in California. There would be no more earthquakes along this fault if

   (1) there were no further friction between the two tectonic plates
   (2) one plate suddenly moved toward the other
   (3) scientists could accurately predict the occurrence of an earthquake
   (4) the epicenters of the earthquakes were farther underground
   (5) the earth were to shrink in size

3. If the pressure of tectonic plates moving against one another becomes too great, it can force molten magma to the surface of the earth. Which of the following is another way to describe this process?

   (1) glacier formation
   (2) mountain formation
   (3) volcanic eruption
   (4) tidal wave
   (5) climatic low pressure

Glaciers, Erosion, and the Ice Ages

Glaciers are giant pieces of ice that are many miles long. The glaciers in Greenland and Antarctica are nearly as big as continents. Glaciers begin as deposits of snow that gradually change to ice. They move very slowly by the process of gravity. At one time, these glaciers covered large parts of the earth. Over the course of time, the glaciers have advanced and retreated several times, for reasons that are still not yet entirely understood. These movements have caused large fluctuations in sea level, covering many shallow areas of land with water for long periods of time.

The advance of the glaciers led to periods called the ice ages. (During one of these, the Pleistocene age, ice covered much of North America.) As a glacier advances, it **erodes** the soil and bedrock in front of it, dragging large quantities of debris along with it. Other processes can also cause erosion. For example, a river gradually erodes the banks on either side of it. Even the wind can erode topsoil.

Let's try a GED-type question based on this material.

Glaciers Quiz

Q: If the glaciers suddenly melted, what would happen to the sea levels?

Answer on page 322

Most people think of erosion as a bad thing. When the soil on a farm is eroded by the wind or when a beach is eroded by wave action, this is indeed a bad thing. However, some types of erosion can be useful.

Which of the following would be an example of useful erosion?

(1)   Rainfall washes away valuable nutrients in the soil.
(2)   A riverbed undermines the foundations of a house built along its banks.
(3)   Lava from a volcanic eruption blocks the entrance to a valley.
(4)   A glacier's erosion creates a natural aquifer of glacial sand and gravel that holds abundant water supplies.
(5)   Weathering of a mountain causes rock slides.

Here's How to Crack It

The key word is *useful*. As we look at the answer choices, be on the lookout for something positive. Is choice (1) positive? If valuable nutrients are washed away, it will be harder to raise crops. Eliminate it. Is choice (2) positive? If the foundations of the house are undermined, the house may fall down. Forget choice (2). It's difficult to find anything positive about a volcanic eruption, so let's eliminate choice (3). In choice (4), even the vocabulary seems to be positive. There is a *natural* aquifer and *abundant* water supplies. These are good things. Useful things. However, choice (5) presents us with a rock slide. The correct answer is choice (4).

Vocabulary

weathering—the process by which rock is broken down into small pieces

iceberg—a small piece of a glacier that breaks off and drifts in the ocean, mostly submerged

GLACIERS, EROSION, AND THE ICE AGES DRILL

(Answers and explanations can be found in Part VIII.)

1. Long ago, glaciers covered much of the surface of the earth. This ice age occurred when the temperature of the earth fell dramatically for reasons not yet understood. Nor do we know why the temperatures increased again, bringing an end to the ice age.

   Based on the information above, which of the following is most likely true?

   (1) Glaciers begin melting when the temperature of the earth rises above freezing.
   (2) Glaciers are only found near the equator.
   (3) When glaciers melt, the level of water in the oceans goes down.
   (4) Glaciers are affected by the gravitational pull of the moon.
   (5) Glaciers move only at night.

2. Glaciers are formed over time as snow gradually turns to ice. Which of the following can be concluded about glaciers?

   (1) When they move, glaciers move rapidly.
   (2) Glaciers are composed of salt water.
   (3) Glaciers occur only in valleys.
   (4) Glaciers will never again cover the earth.
   (5) Glaciers are composed of freshwater.

Oceans, Tides, and the Moon

More than two-thirds of Earth's surface is covered by water. The oceans on Earth are affected by the gravity of the moon. The moon pulls the water in the ocean toward it, creating **tides**. High tide, which occurs twice a day, is when the moon has its maximum gravitational pull.

Underneath the oceans are huge mountain ranges, and scientists suspect there are many species of fish and single-cell organisms that have yet to be discovered.

Let's look at a question.

The gravity of the moon causes Earth's oceans to bulge in the direction of the moon. The action of tides is most easily viewed in shallow coastal waters. This is because

(1) there is no tidal action in the oceans
(2) the rise and fall of the tides is easier to observe relative to a stationary piece of land
(3) the moon appears only over land
(4) the moon's orbit is erratic
(5) storms can interrupt the tidal flows

Here's How to Crack It

Why would it be better to view the actions of tides along the coast? Could it be because there *are* no tides in the ocean? If tides are caused by the moon's gravity pulling at Earth's oceans, why would this only happen near the coast? Eliminate choice (1). Choice (2) seems pretty good. What happens in the middle of the ocean would be hard to measure. However, anyone standing at the edge of the ocean can notice if the water gets higher and then lower. Just to be sure, let's look at the other answers. Choice (3) defies all reason. Because the moon orbits Earth, it can be seen from any point on Earth at various times—and more important, its gravitational pull should also be observable at different times all over Earth. Even if choices (4) and (5) were true, it is difficult to see why they would make it difficult to see the action of tides from anywhere but coastal waters. The correct answer is choice (2).

OCEANS, TIDES, AND THE MOON DRILL
(Answers and explanations can be found in Part VIII.)

1. At a certain beach on the coast of Florida, there are about $12\frac{1}{2}$ hours between one high tide and the next. If you prefer to swim at high tide, and the last high tide occurred at 4:00 A.M., when should you plan on going swimming next?

   (1) 5:00 A.M.
   (2) 10:15 A.M.
   (3) 12 noon
   (4) 4:30 P.M.
   (5) 7:00 P.M.

2. The moon's gravitational field causes the action of the tides. Which of the following would most probably occur if the moon's gravitational force was weaker?

   (1) Earth would stop spinning on its axis.
   (2) The action of the tides would become more pronounced.
   (3) Tidal action would become less severe.
   (4) The moon would be full all year long.
   (5) Crops and livestock would be affected.

Astronomy and the Solar System

No one knows for sure how the universe originated. Some scientists hypothesize that there was a huge explosion, known as the **big bang.** This theory helps to explain the fact that the entire universe seems to be expanding away from one central point, which is consistent with the aftereffects of a huge explosion.

All the matter of the universe gradually began to combine into small clumps because of the effect of gravity, according to the big bang theory. These clumps of matter and gases became **galaxies** and **stars.**

The sun is one of these stars. It is about 100 times the size of Earth and is composed of superheated gases, at a temperature of about 6,000 degrees centigrade (10,800 degrees F). Surrounding it are eight **planets**, some of which have moons as well. The planets, starting closest to the sun, are Mercury, Venus, Earth, Mars, Jupiter, Saturn, Uranus, and Neptune. Pluto, which used to be called the ninth planet, is now considered a dwarf planet. The planets **orbit** the sun at different rates and at different distances from the sun.

Each of the planets has two main types of movement—its orbit around the sun and its rotation on its **axis.** One complete orbit around the sun constitutes a year. One complete spin on a planet's axis constitutes one day. As you know, it takes 365 days for Earth to orbit the sun and 24 hours for it to spin around once on its axis.

Let's try a question based on the solar system.

Astronomy Quiz

Q: Earth orbits the sun. What large body orbits Earth?

Answer on page 326

Shutter Stock

The photograph above shows Earth as seen from space.

Earth's axis is tilted in such a way that for half the year, the Northern Hemisphere is closest to the sun, and for the other half of the year, the Southern Hemisphere is closest to the sun. This most likely accounts for

(1)   deterioration of the ozone layer
(2)   earthquakes and volcanic eruptions
(3)   the action of tides
(4)   the changing seasons
(5)   the formation of metamorphic rock

Here's How to Crack It

This question is somewhat difficult because several answer choices may seem pretty tempting if you don't have some outside knowledge. If you know nothing about science, it may seem possible that the tilt to Earth's axis has something to do with deterioration of the ozone layer, earthquakes, tidal movements, and rock formation.

Of course, because we've already covered all these subjects, you probably didn't find it all that difficult. However, because it is impossible to cover every topic that may conceivably appear on the GED, let's think about how we could have gotten the answer even if we had no outside knowledge. The GED does not generally test complicated ideas, so try to think simply and pay attention to the information they give you. The question mentions the Northern and the Southern Hemispheres taking turns being closer to the sun. When you are closer to the sun, what happens? That's right: It gets warmer. Looking at the answer choices, which one has something to do with it getting warmer and colder? You got it. The correct answer is choice (4).

Vocabulary

solar system—a group of planets that orbit a star
galaxy—a group of stars; our galaxy is called the Milky Way
asteroid—a very small planet

THE SOLAR SYSTEM DRILL

(Answers and explanations can be found in Part VIII.)

<u>Questions 1 and 2</u> refer to the following chart of the solar system.

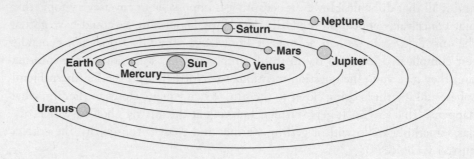

1. Which of the following planets has the lowest surface temperature?

    (1)   Mercury
    (2)   Venus
    (3)   Earth
    (4)   Mars
    (5)   Jupiter

2. A year is the length of time it takes for a planet to complete one entire orbit around the sun. If each of the planets revolved around the sun at exactly the same speed, which of the planets would have the shortest year?

    (1)   Mercury
    (2)   Venus
    (3)   Earth
    (4)   Mars
    (5)   Jupiter

Solids, Liquids, and Gases

Chemistry is the study of matter. All matter is made up of **molecules,** tiny invisible pieces of matter. However, even molecules are not the smallest particles in the world. Molecules are made up of **atoms,** which are in turn composed of **protons** and **neutrons** (at the atom's center, which is known as the **nucleus**) and **electrons** that circle the nucleus.

Certain types of atoms break down slowly over time. The nuclei of these atoms gradually decay over thousands of years and give off charged particles of energy. The particles that are discharged are called radioactive, and because they are coming from the nucleus of an atom, the process is called **nuclear radiation.** Some radioactive elements are highly dangerous—uranium comes to mind—but other elements are essentially harmless.

Matter exists in one of three states. When its temperature is low, matter exists in a **solid** state, with its molecules closely joined, barely moving. As the temperature increases, the molecules begin to move more freely, and the matter changes into a **liquid.** If the matter is heated even further, the molecules will break away from one another to form a **gas.** The point at which a solid turns into a liquid is called its **melting point.** The temperature at which a liquid turns into a solid is called its **freezing point.** Each element in nature changes from a solid into a liquid and from a liquid into a gas at different temperatures. Ice turns to a liquid (water) when the temperature is above 32 degrees Fahrenheit. Iron, however, does not turn into a liquid unless the temperature is much hotter.

Solids keep their own shape. Liquids will flow into any container but still have chemical bonds that hold the liquid together. Gases have no shape and will disperse unless they are contained. By increasing the temperature, in most cases you increase the volume of a substance. One exception is water, which actually increases slightly in volume *when frozen.*

An **element** is a substance that occurs in nature. For example, hydrogen and oxygen are elements. When two elements are mixed together, the result is called a **mixture.** However, if you mix the two elements and they bond together through a chemical interaction, then the new product formed is called a **compound.** For example, water (H_2O) is a compound. Many compounds can be classified either as an acid or a base. Acids, such as lemon juice, taste sour. Bases neutralize acids. An example of a base is baking soda.

When a substance such as salt is **dissolved** in water or another liquid, the result is called a **solution.** You can keep adding more of the substance until the solution reaches its **saturation point.** A higher temperature will often increase the saturation point. Let's look at a chemistry question:

Matter Quiz
Q: What happens if you freeze a pipe full of water?

Answer on page 328

When water reaches a certain temperature, it becomes a gas. Salt, however, requires a much higher temperature to do the same. A solution of salt and water is placed in a pot and boiled until all the liquid has evaporated. Which of the following describes what has happened to the salt?

(1) It evaporated with the water.
(2) It combined chemically with the water and disappeared.
(3) It is still in the bottom of the pot.
(4) It evaporated before the water.
(5) It changed to a liquid.

Here's How to Crack It

The problem tells us that the temperature it takes to change salt into a gas is much higher than the temperature it takes to change water into a gas. Thus, if we boil a solution of the two, it stands to reason that the water should change to a gas a long time before the salt does. Which answers can we eliminate? Choice (4) is impossible given what we know. Choice (1) is also pretty impossible. If choice (5) were correct, then because the question tells us that all the liquid has evaporated, the salt must have evaporated, too, and we know that shouldn't have happened. Choice (2) is a little troubling because you may not know if such a thing is possible. However, remember that the GED does not get too complicated. The correct answer is choice (3). Don't believe us? Give it a try, but we recommend that you use an old pot.

Matter Quiz

A: The pipe might break because when water freezes, it increases slightly in size.

Vocabulary

pH value—a scale to measure the baseness or acidity of a compound
evaporation—the process by which a liquid becomes a gas
half life—the amount of time it takes half of a radioactive element to decay

SOLIDS, LIQUIDS, AND GASES DRILL

(Answers and explanations can be found in Part VIII.)

1. A pressurized container measuring 3 feet by 2 feet by 2 feet is to be filled with a gas. If it is important to get as much of the substance into the container as possible, which of the following ideas would be most useful?

    (1) Store the substance in bright sunlight.
    (2) Cool the container to give the substance as little volume as possible.
    (3) Mix the substance with water before storing it.
    (4) Leave the container open to keep the pressure low.
    (5) Insert dye into the gas so any leaks can be discovered.

2. Adding salt to a pot of boiling water temporarily stops the water from boiling. Which of the following is the best explanation for this occurrence?

    (1) The salt raises the boiling point of the water.
    (2) Salt prevents water from ever boiling.
    (3) Salt neutralizes the water.
    (4) Water neutralizes the salt.
    (5) Salt water is easier to float in than freshwater.

3. In measuring the baseness or acidity of a compound, the pH scale is used. On a scale of 0 to 14, pure water is exactly a 7. Stomach acid is a 1. Which of the following might be the pH value of the base compound baking soda?

    (1) 2.3
    (2) 3.5
    (3) 5.0
    (4) 7.0
    (5) 9.2

Physical Laws

Physics studies the *behavior* of matter. One of the basic physical laws that affects all matter is the law of **gravity**. Gravity is the force that attracts any two objects toward each other. The strength of the gravitational pull depends on the masses of the two objects and the distance between them. Earth's gravitational force keeps the moon orbiting around it, just as the sun's gravitational pull keeps Earth and the other planets orbiting around it. Earth's gravitational force also keeps your feet anchored firmly to the ground.

A scientist named Sir Isaac Newton, working in the early 1700s, came up with some additional physical laws.

- **The First Law**—This law states that an object will remain at rest or continue moving at the same speed and in the same direction forever, unless some outside force intervenes. This is also called the law of **inertia.** According to Newton, if you threw a ball, it would continue forever, except that the forces of gravity and air resistance interfere.
- **The Second Law**—If an object accelerates because another force propels it, it will accelerate in proportion to that force. In other words, that ball will only be propelled as hard as you throw it in the first place.
- **The Third Law**—For every action, there is an equal but opposite reaction. This law is difficult to illustrate by throwing a ball. The best example of this is the recoil you feel if you fire a gun.

Let's try a question.

Gravitation is the force that attracts two objects toward each other in space. There are two factors in gravitation: the mass of the two objects and the distance between them. If a stationary spacecraft were exactly equidistant between two asteroids that maintained a constant distance between them, what would determine whether the craft drifted toward one asteroid instead of the other?

(1) The craft would be blown toward one of the asteroids by the wind.

(2) A thinner atmosphere on one asteroid would attract the craft.

(3) The craft would be attracted by the gravitational force of the asteroid with the greatest mass.

(4) The craft would be attracted to the asteroid with the greatest volume.

(5) The craft's own inertia would prevent it from moving.

Here's How to Crack It

Many students are intimidated by physics, so take a moment to realize that, as always, the question itself provides you with the information you need. In this case, it tells you the two forces that determine gravity: mass and distance between the two objects. Because the spacecraft is equidistant between the two objects, distance is no longer a factor. Therefore, mass is the important consideration. Which of the answer choices addresses mass? The correct answer is choice (3).

PHYSICAL LAWS DRILL

(Answers and explanations can be found in Part VIII.)

Questions 1 and 2 refer to the following information.

> A man pushes against a rock for 20 minutes to move it out of his driveway, but the rock never budges.

1. A physicist might describe the force that prevented the rock from moving as which of the following?

   (1) weight
   (2) mass
   (3) electricity
   (4) inertia
   (5) diffusion

2. According to a physicist, *work* is defined as the force it takes to actually move an object. Using this definition, how much work did the man do?

   (1) none
   (2) more than was necessary
   (3) enough work to get the job done
   (4) 20 minutes' worth
   (5) enough to tire him out

Part V Summary

○ The Science test consists of 50 multiple-choice questions based on short passages, graphs, and charts, but the good news is that any specific knowledge you need to answer a question will be contained within the passage, graph, or chart on which the question is based.

○ The test covers **life sciences** (which includes the scientific method, the biology of cells, plants, natural selection, the food chain, and fossils); **physical sciences** (which include solids, liquids and gases, chemistry, and physical laws); and Earth and space science (which includes the changing earth, glaciers, oceans, astronomy, and the solar system).

○ While no specific knowledge is required, it is very helpful to have a general understanding of science. For that reason, we suggest you read Chapters 17 and 18 to familiarize yourself with scientific terms and the general topics.

○ It can also be very helpful to spend a little time reading articles from some of the science magazines that the GED test writers say they use when they write questions: *Discover*, *Science News*, *National Geographic*, and *Popular Science*. Over time, these articles will help you get used to the kind of scientific writing that you will find on the test.

Part VI
How to Crack the Language Arts, Reading Test

Chapter 19
Language Arts,
Reading Overview

Most people find that the Language Arts, Reading test is the best part of the GED. The excerpts not only tend to be interesting, with real human drama, but also are frequently written by some of our finest authors. The general nonfiction articles tend to be about subjects of common interest to most people, the business documents are generally realistic and clear, and even the poems are not too difficult to understand.

Language Arts, Reading
The answer to every question in the Language Arts, Reading test can always be found in the passages.

Like the Social Studies and Science sections of the test, this is still just reading comprehension. In fact, in some ways, it is much more purely a reading comprehension test than the others are. There are no distracting charts, no quasi-math questions, no specialized scientific vocabulary. In this section, we will show you how to build on the techniques you learned in Chapter 5, "Crazy Reading."

What Topics Are Covered in the Language Arts, Reading Test?

In the Language Arts, Reading section of the GED, you will have 65 minutes to answer 40 multiple-choice questions based on several passages. Each passage will be followed by two to eight questions based on that passage.

The general subject matter breaks down like this:

Literary text (fiction, drama, poetry)	80%
Nonfiction text (review, workplace document, popular culture)	20%

Literary texts can include excerpts from novels, short stories, plays, and poems. Here is a partial list of writers who are often used by the GED test writers:

Joyce Carol Oates, Toni Morrison, Maya Angelou, Robert Stone, John le Carré, John Irving, Ken Kesey, Mary Gordon, Betty Friedan, James Baldwin, Gail Godwin, Mary McCarthy, Ralph Ellison, William Golding, Studs Terkel, Mark Twain, Gabriel García Márquez, Ernest Hemingway, F. Scott Fitzgerald, William Faulkner, Ralph Waldo Emerson, Henry David Thoreau, John Steinbeck, Thomas Wolfe, Eugene O'Neill, Tennessee Williams, Robert Frost, Carl Sandburg, Katherine Anne Porter, Edith Wharton, Stephen Crane, G. K. Chesterton, and D. H. Lawrence

Don't worry! We aren't suggesting you go out and read all the works of all these people. At least not right away. However, if you have some time, probably the single best way to improve your score on this section of the test would be for you to do some reading—and this is a great list from which to start.

The nonfiction passages consist of writing about literature and the arts and business-related subjects. Reviews of books, movies, television programs, dance programs, art, and music are selected by the GED test writers from popular magazines. Business-related documents, such as excerpts from a company training manual, are adapted from real documents.

What Do the Questions and Passages Look Like?

The passages on the Language Arts, Reading test are generally longer than they are in any other section of the GED. However, they are also a lot more interesting. Here's an example:

Pearl opened her eyes when Ezra turned a page of his magazine. "Ezra," she said. She felt him grow still. He had this habit—he had always had it—of becoming
(5) totally motionless when people spoke to him. It was endearing but also in some ways a strain, for then whatever she said to him ("I feel a draft," or "the paper boy is late again") was bound to disappoint him,
(10) wasn't it? How could she live up to Ezra's expectations? She plucked at her quilt. "If I could just have some water," she told him.

He poured it from the pitcher on the bureau. She heard no ice cubes clinking;
(15) they must have melted. Yet it seemed just minutes ago that he'd brought in a whole new supply. He raised her head, rested it on his shoulder, and tipped the glass to her lips. Yes, lukewarm—not that she minded.
(20) She drank gratefully, keeping her eyes closed. His shoulder felt steady and comforting. He laid her back down on the pillow.

"Dr. Vincent's coming at ten," he told her.

(25) "What time is it now?"

"Eight-thirty."

"Eight-thirty in the morning?"

GED Pop Quiz
Q: Which longtime editor of a popular Sunday magazine is a GED graduate?

Answer on page 338

"Yes."

"Have you been here all night?" she asked.

(30) "I slept a little."

"Sleep now. I won't be needing you."

"Well, maybe after the doctor comes."

(35) It was important to Pearl that she deceive the doctor. She didn't want to go to the hospital. Her illness was pneumonia, she was almost certain; she guessed it from a past experience. She recognized the way it settled into her back. If Dr. Vincent found out he would take her out of (40) her own bed, her own house, and send her off to Union Memorial, tent her over with plastic. "Maybe you should cancel the doctor altogether," she told Ezra. "I'm very much improved, I believe."

Anne Tyler, DINNER AT THE HOMESICK RESTAURANT, 1982. (Abridged)

1. Where is Pearl in the passage above?

   (1) She is in the hospital.
   (2) She is staying with Ezra at his house.
   (3) She is at home.
   (4) She is on a European vacation.
   (5) She is at a health clinic.

2. Pearl has spent the night

   (1) talking to Ezra
   (2) making plans to go to the hospital
   (3) talking on the telephone
   (4) sleeping in her bed
   (5) doing crossword puzzles

3. If Ezra knew that Pearl had pneumonia, he would most probably

   (1) agree to let her stay where she is
   (2) insist that she go to the hospital
   (3) make sure she got more rest
   (4) lie to the doctor about it
   (5) ask for a second opinion

4. How does the author reveal the passage
    of time in the second paragraph?

    (1) The ice cubes have melted.
    (2) The sun has come up.
    (3) Ezra has arrived.
    (4) Pearl closes her eyes.
    (5) The water is cold.

There are four types of questions asked on the Language Arts, Reading test: comprehension questions (20 percent), synthesis questions (30 to 35 percent), analysis questions (30 to 35 percent), and application questions (15 percent). As we mentioned in Chapter 5, "Crazy Reading," you don't have to recognize the question types to answer them correctly during the exam. However, it's useful to see exactly how they are used.

Question Types

Comprehension Questions

A comprehension question asks you to find a particular piece of information from the passage itself and then recognize that piece of information, slightly restated, among the answer choices.

Take a look at the first question from the passage set on the previous page.

---

1. Where is Pearl in the passage above?

    (1) She is in the hospital.
    (2) She is staying with Ezra at his
         house.
    (3) She is at home.
    (4) She is on a European vacation.
    (5) She is at a health clinic.

Here's How to Crack It
When you first started reading the passage, you may have leapt to the conclusion that she was in the hospital already. However, there is one key place in the passage where we find out exactly where she is: Look at the last paragraph. Here, directly stated, is her intention to try to *avoid* going to the hospital (meaning she isn't there now) and her intention to stay in "her own bed, her own house." The only possible answer is choice (3).

GED Pop Quiz

Q: Which high school dropout went on to star in the movie *Saturday Night Fever*?

Answer on page 340

Synthesis Questions

Some comprehension questions in the Language Arts, Reading test will ask you to go just a bit further than a regular comprehension question to identify a logical implication of that information.

Take a look at the second question.

───────○───────

2. Pearl has spent the night

    (1)   talking to Ezra
    (2)   making plans to go to the hospital
    (3)   talking on the telephone
    (4)   sleeping in her bed
    (5)   doing crossword puzzles

Here's How to Crack It

At no time in this passage is the answer to this question stated *directly*. However, there are a series of clues. First, she opens her eyes at the beginning. Second, the ice cubes that Ezra had brought "it seemed just minutes ago" were already melted. And third, she doesn't know whether it is day or night. What has she been doing? That's right: getting some z's. The correct answer is choice (4).

───────○───────

Application Questions

To answer an application question, you must first understand information and ideas described in the passage and then apply that information to a different situation. Question 3 from the item set above is a good example.

───────○───────

3. If Ezra knew that Pearl had pneumonia, he would most probably

    (1)   agree to let her stay where she is
    (2)   insist that she go to the hospital
    (3)   make sure she got more rest
    (4)   lie to the doctor about it
    (5)   ask for a second opinion

Here's How to Crack It

If Ezra knew she had pneumonia, what would he do about it? This is a hypothetical question. To answer it, we must think about what we know of Ezra. He stayed with Pearl all night. When she drank some water, he propped her up with his own shoulder. And he refused to go to sleep until after he'd heard what the doctor had to say. Given all this, what do you think he would do if he knew she had pneumonia? The correct answer is choice (2).

Analysis Questions

On the Language Arts, Reading test, analysis questions are a bit different from the ones on the Social Studies and Science tests. Analysis questions on this test ask you to examine the techniques used by the writer to produce an effect. For example, in question 4 from the item set above, we are asked to identify the method in which information is presented to us in the second paragraph.

---

4. How does the author reveal the passage of time in the second paragraph?

   (1) The ice cubes have melted.
   (2) The sun has come up.
   (3) Ezra has arrived.
   (4) Pearl closes her eyes.
   (5) The water is cold.

Here's How to Crack It

Go back to the second paragraph, and read it again. How do we know from *this* paragraph that time has gone by? Let's go through the answer choices and do a little elimination. Choice (1) seems very possible. If she feels that Ezra brought ice only a few minutes ago and yet the ice has melted, that implies that she has missed some time. Let's hold on to that one. The second paragraph doesn't mention that the sun has come up. Later in the passage, he tells her it is already morning, but he hasn't by the second paragraph. Eliminate choice (2). Choice (3) is wrong because Ezra has been here all night. Eliminate (3). Pearl does close her eyes in this passage, but only while she is drinking. It's hard to see the passage of time in a sip of water, so choice (4) bites the dust. Choice (5) directly contradicts the passage: The water is not cold—it is now lukewarm. The correct answer must be choice (1).

Our Approach

In the chapters that follow, we will discuss each type of passage that turns up on the GED Language Arts, Reading test. After a description of a passage type, we'll take you through a sample of that type, complete with questions, and then give you another to try on your own.

Chapter 20
Fiction and Drama

In this chapter, you'll learn everything you need to know to help you answer questions based on excerpts from novels and plays.

Excerpts from novels and plays are two types of passages that come up on the Language Arts, Reading test. These are categorized as fiction and drama, respectively.

Fiction

In fiction, a writer uses a combination of plot, characters, and description to tell an imaginary story. If the writer does his or her job properly, the imaginary world created in the fiction becomes real to the reader. GED test takers generally find popular fiction to be easier than classical fiction because the language is more contemporary, and the same principles apply to both. To answer GED questions about fiction of either type, there are several questions to ask yourself *first* while you're reading the passages:

Who's Talking?

A story can be told in the first person (an "I" character who is an integral part of the story) or in the third person (an omniscient narrator who tells the story without getting involved in the action). If the story is told in the first person, it is important to decide on the point of view of this person. Does she have an ax to grind? Is he a reliable narrator, or do we have to take what he says with a grain of salt?

What's Going On?

In most fiction passages, there will be some action or movement—what we generally think of as "plot." What happens during this passage? Is there a moment of revelation for one of the characters? Is there a choice being offered to someone? Is a decision made? In fiction passages, the answers to these questions usually qualify as the main idea of the passage.

What Is the Mood?

Some passages are somber, while others are funny. Is this one addressing heavy, important issues—such as war or social injustice—or is it about something more lightweight—such as going to a prom or having a spat with your sister? On the GED, questions about mood tend to be analysis questions.

Who Are the Main Characters?

Identify for yourself the major characters in a fiction passage. There will only be two or three. It isn't that there are *no* works of fiction with more than two or three main characters, but the GED test writers aren't going to pick one of these to put on the test—they're too complicated to keep straight.

How does the author describe the main characters? How do other characters react to them? Understanding the characters will take you a long way toward understanding the passage as a whole.

Where Does the Action Take Place?

The setting can be irrelevant or completely crucial to a story, and it will be up to you to distinguish which it is. A tip-off that setting will be important might be large sections of the passage devoted to descriptions and details.

Putting It All Together

Let's try a fiction passage. Read it once, and then ask yourself the questions we've just discussed above. Don't be afraid to write down your answers this first time. Then attack the questions. Note that this is a classical passage—the idiom is a bit old-fashioned, and some expressions may be new to you. Remember what we said in "Crazy Reading" about finding meaning from context. In this part of the test, context is even easier to use because you are not just limited to the context of ideas— you can look at the context of *feelings* as well. If you understand the emotion a character is going through, you may well understand exactly what he or she is saying, even if you don't understand all the words he or she is saying.

WAS AUNT POLLY RIGHT TO BE SUSPICIOUS?

While Tom was eating his supper,
and stealing sugar as opportunity offered,
Aunt Polly asked him questions that were
full of guile, and very deep—for she wanted
(5) to trap him into damaging revealments.
Like many other simple-hearted souls, it
was her pet vanity to believe she was
endowed with a talent for dark and
mysterious diplomacy, and she loved to
(10) contemplate her most transparent devices
as marvels of low cunning. Said she:

"Tom, it was middling warm in
school, warn't it?"

"Yes'm."

(15) "Powerful warm, warn't it?"

"Yes'm."

"Didn't you want to go in
a-swimming, Tom?"

A bit of a scare shot through
(20) Tom—a touch of uncomfortable suspicion.
He searched Aunt Polly's face, but it told
him nothing. So he said:

"No'm—well, not very much."

(25) The old lady reached out her hand and felt Tom's shirt, and said:

"But you ain't too warm now, though." And it flattered her to reflect that she had discovered that the shirt was dry without anybody knowing that (30) that was what she had in her mind. But in spite of her, Tom knew where the wind lay, now. So he forestalled what might be the next move:

"Some of us pumped on our (35) heads—mine's damp yet. See?"

Aunt Polly was vexed to think she had overlooked that bit of circumstantial evidence, and missed a trick. Then she had a new inspiration:

(40) "Tom, you didn't have to undo your shirt-collar where I sewed it, to pump on your head, did you? Unbutton your jacket!"

The trouble vanished out of Tom's (45) face. He opened his jacket. His shirt-collar was securely sewed.

"Bother! Well, go 'long with you. I'd made sure you'd played hooky and been a'swimming. But I forgive ye, Tom. (50) I reckon you're a kind of a singed cat, as the saying is—better'n you look. *This* time."

She was half sorry her sagacity had miscarried, and half glad that Tom (55) had stumbled in to obedient conduct for once.

But Sidney said:

"Well now, if I didn't think you sewed his collar with white thread, but (60) it's black."

"Why, I did sew it with white! Tom!"

But Tom did not wait for the rest.

As he went out at the door he said:

"Siddy, I'll lick you for that."

Mark Twain, TOM SAWYER, 1876. (Abridged)

1. Why did Aunt Polly want to know if Tom's shirt was dry?

   (1) She suspected he had gone swimming.
   (2) She wanted to see if it needed laundering.
   (3) She wanted to see if he had spilled part of his supper on the shirt.
   (4) She hoped to see if it had rained earlier.
   (5) She wanted to compare it to Sidney's shirt.

Here's How to Crack It

This is a synthesis question. Aunt Polly is convinced that Tom played hooky from school and went swimming. We get this not so much from her feeling his shirt as from the tone of her interrogation: "Powerful warm, warn't it?" As the passage says, "she wanted to trap him into damaging revealments." The correct answer is choice (1). None of the other choices has anything to do with Aunt Polly's mission: to discover Tom's transgression.

2. How did Tom explain his damp hair?

   (1) He said that he had gotten sweaty from playing outside.
   (2) He said that he went swimming.
   (3) He said that he put his head under the water pump.
   (4) He said Sidney wet it.
   (5) He couldn't explain it.

Here's How to Crack It

Context could be very important to this synthesis question. We know *where* in the passage to find out about damp hair, but the expression Tom uses, "Some of us pumped on our heads…" is probably unfamiliar to you. Even so, if they pumped on their heads and his hair is still wet, it's a pretty good bet that you know what happened. The correct answer is choice (3).

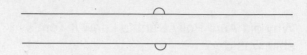

3. Why does the author say that "The trouble vanished out of Tom's face" in lines 44–45?

   (1) Tom had done nothing wrong.
   (2) Tom had planned ahead and was prepared for Aunt Polly's thread test.
   (3) Tom had already finished all his chores and was looking forward to going to sleep.
   (4) Tom was looking forward to dessert.
   (5) Tom was very worried.

Here's How to Crack It

Aunt Polly's interrogation is pretty transparent to Tom. When she brings up the shirt collar that she carefully sewed shut on his neck that morning, he is way ahead of her—obviously he took it off and then sewed it back on himself. The correct answer to this synthesis question is choice (2).

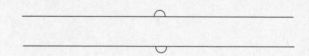

4. Sidney's feelings for Tom could be described as

   (1) supportive
   (2) loyal
   (3) proud
   (4) indifferent
   (5) unfriendly

Here's How to Crack It

You probably noticed that Sidney told on Tom by reminding Aunt Polly that she sewed Tom's collar with a different color thread. What kind of feelings would provoke this? The correct answer is choice (5).

———————◯———————

———————◯———————

5. When Tom and Sidney meet later, what do you think will happen?

   (1) They will have a good laugh.
   (2) They will make fun of Aunt Polly.
   (3) They will go swimming together.
   (4) Tom will try to beat up Sidney.
   (5) Sidney will try to beat up Tom.

Here's How to Crack It

This application question asks you to decide from the context of this scene what will happen in a future scene. This might have been difficult if there had been no hint, but Tom's last words to Sid are a distinct threat: "Siddy, I'll lick you for that." By the way, in those days, *licking* someone meant beating someone up. The correct answer must be choice (4).

———————◯———————

FICTION DRILL
(Answers and explanations can be found in Part VIII.)

WHO IS MR. SMILEY?

"Oh it's you, is it? Come in."

She led Smiley into a large room.
In a far chair a man was reading *The
Daily Telegraph*, holding it in front of his
(5) face so that Smiley only saw the bald
head, and the dressing-gown, and the
short crossed legs ending in leather
bedroom slippers; but somehow he knew
at once that Mr. Pelling was the kind of
(10) small man who would only ever marry
tall women. The room carried everything
he could need in order to survive
alone: his television, his bed, his gas
fire, a table to eat at, and an easel for
(15) painting by numbers. On the wall hung
an over-colored portrait photograph of
a very beautiful girl, with an inscription
scribbled diagonally across one corner
in the way that film stars wish love to
(20) the unglamorous. Smiley recognized
it as Elizabeth; he had seen a lot of
photographs already.

"Mr. Oates, meet Nunc," she said,
and all but curtsied.

(25) *The Daily Telegraph* came down
with the slowness of a garrison flag,
revealing an aggressive, glittering little
face with thick brows and managerial
spectacles.

(30) "Yes. Well, just who are you
precisely?" said Mr. Pelling. "Are you
Secret Service or aren't you? Don't
shilly-shally, out with it and be done. I
don't hold with snooping, you see. What's
(35) that?" he demanded.

"His card," said Mrs. Pelling,
offering it. "Green in hue."

"Oh, we're exchanging notes, are
we? I need a card too then, Cess, don't
(40) I? Better get some printed, my dear. Slip
down to Smith's, will you?"

"Do you like tea?" Mrs. Pelling
asked, peering down at Smiley with her
head on one side.

(45) "What are you giving him tea for?"
Mr. Pelling demanded, watching her plug
in the kettle. "He doesn't need tea. He's
not a guest. He's not even intelligence. I
didn't ask him. Stay the week," he said to
(50) Smiley. "Move in if you like. Have her bed.
'Bullion Universal Security Advisors,' my
aunt Fanny."

"He wants to talk about Lizzie,
darling," said Mrs. Pelling, setting a tray for
(55) her husband. "Now be a father for a
change."

"Fat lot of good her bed would do
you, mind," said Mr. Pelling taking up his
Telegraph again.

(60) "For those kind words," said Mrs.
Pelling, and gave a laugh. It consisted
of two notes like a bird-call and was not
meant to be funny. A disjointed silence
followed.

(65)   Mrs. Pelling handed Smiley a cup of tea. Accepting it, he addressed himself to the back of Mr. Pelling's newspaper. "Sir, your daughter Elizabeth is being considered for an important appointment with a major

(70) overseas corporation. My organization has been asked in confidence—as a normal but very necessary formality these days— to approach friends and relations in this country and obtain character references."

(75)   "That's us, dear," Mrs. Pelling explained, in case her husband hadn't understood.

John le Carré, THE HONOURABLE SCHOOLBOY, 1977. (Abridged)

1. Which of the following describes Smiley's relations with the beautiful Elizabeth?

   (1)   At one time they were friends.
   (2)   They have never met.
   (3)   They are working together.
   (4)   He is a friend of her parents.
   (5)   He is in love with her.

2. From his interjection, "'Bullion Universal Security Advisors,' my aunt Fanny," it is clear that Mr. Pelling

   (1)   doesn't believe the company exists
   (2)   believes the company is genuine
   (3)   is very impressed by the company
   (4)   doesn't like Smiley's card
   (5)   has decided to accept Smiley

3. The description of Mr. Pelling in lines 3–11 is effective because it shows

   (1)   his intelligence
   (2)   his strength
   (3)   his sense of humor
   (4)   his weaknesses
   (5)   his profession

Drama

Drama exists in the interplay between plot and character. The big difference between drama and fiction is that in drama there is little or no description. All plot and character traits must therefore be picked up through the dialogue alone. Even more important for drama, a play often begins at the very moment of crisis or epiphany of its characters—the moment when the characters will be most severely tried. Many of the same questions you asked yourself about fiction apply to drama as well.

What's Going On?

In most plays, the action revolves around that pivotal moment when a crisis comes to a head. Will a decision be made? Can the characters resolve their conflict?

What Is the Mood?

Some plays are somber, while others are funny. The mood of an excerpt from a play is the general feeling you get from reading the excerpt. This does not mean that the *tone* of the dialogue can't be funny or lighthearted. The juxtaposition of tone and mood can also give a drama power.

Who Are the Main Characters?

Again, the GED test writers aren't going to pick a play with a million characters—they'll stick to two or three. Identify who they are. How does their dialogue differentiate them? How do other characters react to them?

Where Does the Action Take Place?

The setting can be irrelevant or completely crucial to a story, and it will be up to you to distinguish which it is. A tip-off that setting will be important may be that large sections of the passage are devoted to descriptions and details.

Putting It All Together

Let's try a drama passage. Read it once, ask yourself the questions we've just discussed, and then attack the questions. Note that this is an excerpt from a popular play—the idiom will not be as challenging as it would be in a classical piece, but you may *still* encounter a word or two you don't know. See if you can find the meaning from context, and remember to look it up later and practice it at home.

WHAT HAPPENED TO OUISA AND FLAN?

A couple runs on stage, in nightdress, very agitated. FLANDERS KITTREDGE is 44. OUISA KITTREDGE is 43. They are very attractive. They speak

(5)   to us.

OUISA: Tell them!

FLAN: I am shaking.

OUISA: You have to do *something*!

FLAN: It's awful.

(10)   OUISA: Is anything gone?

FLAN: How can I look? I'm shaking.

OUISA (to us): Did he take anything?

FLAN: Would you concentrate on yourself?

(15)   OUISA: I want to know if anything's gone.

FLAN (to us): We came in the room.

OUISA: I went in first. You didn't see what I saw.

FLAN: Calm down.

(20)   OUISA: We could have been killed.

FLAN: The silver Victorian inkwell.

OUISA: How can you think of *things*? We could have been murdered.

(25)   (An actor appears for a moment holding up an ornate Victorian inkwell capped by a silver beaver.)

FLAN: There's the inkwell. Silver beaver. Why?

OUISA: Slashed—our throats slashed.

(30)   (Another actor appears for a moment holding up a framed portrait of a dog, say, a pug.)

FLAN: And there's the watercolor. Our dog.

(35) **OUISA:** Go to bed at night happy and then murdered. Would we have woken up?

FLAN: Now I lay me down to sleep—the most terrifying words—just think of it—

(40) **OUISA:** I pray the Lord my soul to keep—

FLAN: The nightmare part—If I should die before I wake—

OUISA: If I should die—I pray the Lord my soul to take—

(45) **FLAN AND OUISA:** Oh.

OUISA: It's awful.

FLAN AND OUISA: We're alive.

John Guare, SIX DEGREES OF SEPARATION, 1990. (Abridged)

1. Why does Flan mention the silver Victorian inkwell?

   (1) He is concerned that it has not been polished.
   (2) He wants Ouisa to see it.
   (3) He wants to show it to the audience.
   (4) He thinks it may have been stolen.
   (5) He is afraid that it is not actually made of silver.

Here's How to Crack It

It seems clear that this couple believe they have been robbed. "Did he take anything?" asks Ouisa. From the way they exclaim, first for their own safety and then for some of their possessions, this has been a traumatic night. Human behavior, as any playwright will tell you, is best observed during a crisis. The fact that Flan asks about the inkwell out of all his possible possessions is revealing on several levels. But don't start thinking too deeply. This is the GED, and the test writers are looking for a basic answer: He thinks it may have been stolen. The correct answer to this synthesis question is choice (4).

2. Why does the author have the actors talk
    to the audience directly?

    (1) to achieve a formal, somber style
    (2) to make the audience identify with
         the emotions of the characters
    (3) to prevent the audience from
         realizing that this is only a play
    (4) to exclude the audience from the
         action on the stage
    (5) to disguise the weaknesses of the
         play

Here's How to Crack It

You don't see a play every day in which the actors talk directly to the audience. If
the author makes that choice here, it's for a reason. Let's use the Process of Elimination to figure out the right answer. By addressing the playgoer, the playwright
certainly does *not* create a formal style. In fact, this style is deliberately informal.
Cross off choice (1). Choice (2) seems pretty good. By talking directly, as if to a
friend, the characters in the play seem more real to the audience, and the audience
feels included. Let's hold on to that one. Speaking of inclusion, we can therefore
eliminate choice (4) because of the word *exclude*. As for choice (3), it would be
pretty hard to get an audience to forget that they are watching a play. Finally, it
would take more than being addressed personally to make an audience forgive a
play's weaknesses. The correct answer to this analysis question is choice (2).

3. According to the excerpt, what time of day
    is it when this dialogue takes place?

    (1) night
    (2) morning
    (3) afternoon
    (4) early evening
    (5) lunchtime

Here's How to Crack It

This is a direct synthesis question. When they run on stage, the stage directions
say that they are *in nightdress*. The correct answer is choice (1).

4.   The characters in this excerpt tell their story

   (1)   as if they were talking to friends
   (2)   without emotion
   (3)   without repetition
   (4)   as if they don't trust each other
   (5)   as if they are bored

Here's How to Crack It

Let's use POE. Are they without emotion? No way. They are incredibly emotional. Do they avoid repetition? Nope, they keep repeating themselves and each other all through the scene. Do they act like they don't trust each other? Not at all. Are they bored? They've just been frightened out of their wits. The correct answer to this synthesis question is choice (1).

5.   It can be inferred from the passage that the characters in the excerpt

   (1)   are somewhat poor
   (2)   remain calm in every situation
   (3)   are moderately well off
   (4)   are cat lovers
   (5)   have never met before

Here's How to Crack It

It can be inferred often means that this is a synthesis question. Are they poor? Well, they can afford an antique silver inkwell. Are they calm? They are practically hysterical. Are they cat lovers? Well, they have a painting of their dog. Are they strangers? No, obviously they are quite familiar with each other. The correct answer is choice (3).

DRAMA DRILL
(Answers and explanations can be found in Part VIII.)

IS THIS YOUR AVERAGE BIRTHDAY PARTY?

MARGARET: Brick, honey, aren't you going to give Big Daddy his birthday present? (Passing by him, she snatches his liquor glass
(5)   from him. She picks up a fancily wrapped package.) Here it is, Big Daddy, this is from Brick!

BIG MAMA: This is the biggest birthday Big Daddy's ever had, a hundred
(10)   presents and bushels of telegrams from—

MAE (at same time): What is it, Brick?

BIG MAMA: The fun of presents is not knowing what they are till you open
(15)   the package. Open your present, Big Daddy.

MAE: I bet 500 to 50 that Brick don't know what it is.

BIG DADDY: Open it you'self. I want to
(20)   ask Brick somethin'! Come here, Brick.

MARGARET: Big Daddy's callin' you, Brick. (She is opening the package.)

BRICK: Tell Big Daddy I'm crippled.

BIG DADDY: I see you're crippled. I want
(25)   to know how you got crippled.

MARGARET (making diversionary tactics): Oh, look, oh, look, why, it's a cashmere robe! (She holds the robe up for all to see.)

(30) **MAE:** You sound surprised, Maggie.

MARGARET: I never saw one before.

MAE: That's funny—Hah!

MARGARET (turning on her fiercely, with a brilliant smile): Why is
(35)   it funny? All my family ever had was family—and luxuries such as cashmere robes still surprise me!

BIG DADDY (ominously): Quiet!

MAE (heedless in her fury): I don't see
(40)   how you could be so surprised when you bought it yourself at Loewenstein's in Memphis last Saturday. You know how I know?

BIG DADDY: I said, Quiet!

(45) **MAE:** —I know because the salesgirl that sold it to you waited on me and said, Oh, Mrs. Pollitt, your sister-in-law just bought a cashmere robe for your husband's father!

(50) **MARGARET:** Sister Woman! Your talents are wasted as a housewife and mother, you really ought to be with the FBI or—

BIG DADDY: QUIET!

(Reverend Tooker's reflexes are slower
(55)   than the others'. He finishes a sentence after the bellow.)

REVEREND TOOKER (to Doc Baugh): The Stork and the Reaper are running neck and neck! (He starts
(60)   to laugh gaily when he notices the silence and Big Daddy's glare. His laugh dies falsely.)

BIG DADDY: Preacher, I hope I'm not butting in on more talk about
(65)   memorial stained-glass windows,

am I, Preacher? (Reverend Tooker laughs feebly, then coughs dryly in the embarrassed silence.) Preacher?

Tennessee Williams, CAT ON A HOT TIN ROOF, 1955. (Abridged)

1. According to the passage, whose birthday is it?

    (1) Big Mama's
    (2) Margaret's
    (3) Brick's
    (4) Big Daddy's
    (5) Mae's

2. According to lines 35–37, Margaret is

    (1) from a poor background
    (2) an orphan
    (3) allergic to cashmere
    (4) a good friend of Mae
    (5) pleased to receive a robe

3. Mae laughs at Margaret in line 32 because

    (1) she got Big Daddy the same robe
    (2) she doesn't believe that Brick bought the present
    (3) she thinks Margaret is a nice person
    (4) she thinks the robe is the wrong color for Big Daddy
    (5) she laughs at everyone

4. According to the excerpt, Big Daddy is probably the kind of person who

    (1) enjoys listening to others
    (2) tries to reach a consensus
    (3) is used to getting his way
    (4) would rather be wrong than hurt someone's feelings
    (5) hates to embarrass anyone

5. Why is the argument between Margaret and Mae an effective dramatic device?

    (1) Because by the end of the excerpt, we realize they actually like each other.
    (2) It shows that they are both vying for the attention of Big Mama.
    (3) It shows that no one pays any attention.
    (4) It points out undercurrents of rivalry in the family.
    (5) It establishes Brick's role as a peacemaker in the family.

Chapter 21
Nonfiction and Poetry

In this chapter, you'll learn everything you need to know to help you answer questions based on business-related documents, nonfiction articles, and poems.

Nonfiction

Nonfiction passages can include popular and classical authors, although you are more likely to see popular nonfiction passages on the GED. One of the passages will be a business-related document, such as an excerpt from an employee handbook or training manual. If you have already gone through our sections on the Social Studies test and the Science test, then you are already something of an expert on nonfiction reading. Structure, organization words, contrast words, and yin/yang passages are relatively commonplace here as well. But best of all, the passages in this section are more interesting than those in the Science and Social Studies tests. We can practically guarantee that you won't fall asleep during this part of the GED.

Because these passages are much more opinionated than the nonfiction you've seen in other sections of the test, there are a few new questions to ask yourself.

What Is the Main Idea?

Most nonfiction—and certainly *all* of the nonfiction you will find in this section of the GED—has an idea to get across. Sometimes this main idea will be stated outright; other times it will only be hinted at. Your main job in reading an excerpt from a nonfiction passage is to figure out what that main idea is.

Some questions may actually ask you for the main idea, but even when they don't, you will find it tremendously useful to know the main point even when answering more peripheral questions.

How Does the Author Support the Main Idea?

Almost as useful as the main idea itself is how the author supports the main idea. Are there specific examples? Moral arguments?

What Is the Author's Point of View?

Is the author *for* or *against* whatever is being discussed, or hasn't he made up his mind? What is the tone of the piece? The tone can range from friendly neutrality to vicious sarcasm. Irony comes up all the time.

Putting It All Together

Bearing all this in mind, read the following passage. Feel free to summarize main points for yourself on scratch paper, and then try the questions.

WHY DID THIS WOMAN STOP READING *GOURMET* MAGAZINE?

I'm not sure you can make a
generalization on this basis, which is the
basis of twice, but here goes: Whenever
I get married, I start buying *Gourmet*
(5)   magazine. I think of it as my own
personal bride's disease.

The first time I started buying it was in
1967, when everyone my age in New York City
spent hours talking about things like where to
(10)   buy the best pistachio nuts. Someone recently
told me that his marriage broke up during that
period on account of veal Orloff, and I knew
exactly what he meant. Hostesses were always
making dinners that made you feel guilty,
(15)   meals that took days to prepare and contained
endless numbers of courses requiring endless
numbers of plates resulting in an endless
series of guests rising to help clear. Every time
the conversation veered away from the food,
(20)   the hostess looked hurt.

I got very involved in this stuff. Once
I served a six-course Chinese dinner to
twelve people, none of whom I still speak to,
although not because of the dinner. I also
(25)   specialized in little Greek appetizers that
involved a great deal of playing with rice,
and I once produced something known as
the Brazilian national dish. Then, one night
at a dinner party, a man I know looked up
(30)   from his chocolate mousse and said, "Is this
Julia's?" and I knew it was time to get off.

I can date that moment almost
precisely—it was in December 1972—
because that's when I stopped buying
(35)   *Gourmet* the first time around. And I can
date that last *Gourmet* precisely because
I have never thrown out a copy of the
magazine. At the end of each month, I
place it on the top of the kitchen bookshelf,
(40)   and there it lies, undisturbed, forever.

Nora Ephron, SCRIBBLE, SCRIBBLE, 1975. (Abridged)

1. From the excerpt it seems clear that the author

    (1)   has never married
    (2)   has been married once
    (3)   has been married more than once
    (4)   is not yet old enough to get married
    (5)   has no plans to marry again

Here's How to Crack It

The author's tone in this passage is chatty, and the main idea is not directly stated. Do you have a sense about how she feels about her subject? Put it this way: Is this essay a love poem to *Gourmet* magazine? No. She is gently making fun of it and the behavior of people who buy it. This particular question is a comprehension question. The author states that she starts buying *Gourmet* magazine whenever she gets married. In the first line, she says that this generalization "is on the basis of twice." Therefore, we can conclude that she has been married twice, and the correct answer is choice (3).

2. According to the essay, how does the author now feel about "meals that took days to prepare"?

    (1)   They were the most memorable of her life.
    (2)   They cost her all her friends.
    (3)   In retrospect, they were a little silly.
    (4)   They required surprisingly little cleaning up afterward.
    (5)   They provided a backdrop for conversations about other subjects.

Here's How to Crack It

In the second paragraph, she talks about getting *very involved* and then coming to her senses over a chocolate mousse: "I knew it was time to get off." Which answer choice comes closest to expressing this sentiment? The correct answer to this synthesis question is choice (3).

3. Why is "veal Orloff" an effective example?

   (1) It is the author's favorite dish.
   (2) It illustrates the kind of complicated, overblown meals that people were making at the time the author is writing about.
   (3) Veal is a type of meat that is enjoyed by most people.
   (4) It sounds like a simple, everyday dish that anyone could make.
   (5) It sounds delicious.

Here's How to Crack It

Let's use POE to get rid of the clunkers here. The author never says veal Orloff is her favorite dish, nor that most people enjoy veal, nor that this dish is simple. The theme of the second paragraph is that these dishes are incredibly elaborate. So eliminate choices (1), (3), and (4). Choice (5) is possible, but choice (2) is so much better. The author uses a fancy-sounding name to make us realize the typically excessive meals people were making at that time. The correct answer to this analysis question is choice (2).

4. According to the author, how frequently does she look at back issues of *Gourmet* magazine?

   (1) all the time
   (2) only when she gets married
   (3) during holidays
   (4) only when she gets divorced
   (5) never

Here's How to Crack It

A back issue is any issue that is not the current one. Because she tells us she puts them on top of the kitchen shelf and there they lie "undisturbed, forever," the correct answer to this comprehension question is choice (5).

5. Given the author's feelings, she would most likely view another magazine devoted to food and recipes as

   (1) a welcome addition to the magazine world
   (2) a better alternative to *Gourmet*
   (3) a new excuse to buy a food magazine
   (4) an unnecessary purchase
   (5) a new excuse to get married

Here's How to Crack It

This question asks us to take what we know about the author's attitudes and imagine how she would react in another situation. It is an application question. Because she is gently making fun of one food magazine and its readers, it seems unlikely that she would be ecstatic about reading *another* one. The correct answer is choice (4).

The Business Passage

One of the nonfiction passages in the Language Arts, Reading test will be a business-related document. Here is an example to give you an idea:

BOOKMART INC. EMPLOYEE CODE OF CONDUCT

Employees of Bookmart Inc. are expected to conduct themselves appropriately with fellow employees while in the workplace. Although it is

(5) understood that sometimes coworkers can develop a mutual attraction, it is the policy of Bookmart to condone such relationships *only* when neither party is in a supervisory capacity over the other.

(10) Sexual Harrassment

It will be considered harrassment and grounds for instant dismissal if an employee in a supervisory capacity makes any kind of overtures, welcome

(15) or unwelcome, to any employee under

(20)   that person's supervision. It will also be
considered harrassment and grounds
for dismissal if an individual or group of
individuals engages in conversation of a
lewd or base nature for the purpose of
giving discomfort to another individual or
group of individuals.

Sensitivity Training

(25)   All employees will be required to
attend mandatory workshops twice a year
on proper professional decorum between
coworkers. There will be no exceptions
to this requirement.

Avoid Even the Appearance of
(30)   Impropriety

(35)   While the company respects
the privacy of all its employees, it is
important that employees understand and
respect the reputation and obligations
of the company. Employees are asked
to avoid even the appearance of
wrong-doing by refraining from any
conversations of a "risqué" or sexually
frank nature with coworkers.

1. Based on this excerpt, what would
the company's policy be about a vice-
president of marketing asking out a worker
who reports directly to him?

Such behavior would be considered

(1) unacceptable
(2) practical
(3) reasonable
(4) normal
(5) understandable

Here's How to Crack It

The passage makes clear in both the first and second paragraphs that it is against company policy for an employee to get involved with a worker who is under his or her supervision. So, how would the company feel about a vice-president who asked out someone who reports directly to him? In other words, a person who is under his direct supervision? The correct answer to this synthesis question is choice (1).

———————○———————

2. Based on this excerpt, what would be the consequences if an employee made continued lewd comments to a fellow worker for the purpose of causing discomfort?

   The employee would be

   (1) reprimanded
   (2) fired
   (3) forced to attend sensitivity training
   (4) promoted
   (5) fined

Here's How to Crack It

The answer to this comprehension question can be found at the end of the second paragraph: "It will also be considered harassment and grounds for dismissal if an individual or group of individuals engages in conversation of a lewd or base nature for the purpose of giving discomfort to another individual or group of individuals." The expression *grounds for dismissal* means that the company will fire that person. The correct answer is choice (2).

———————○———————

NONFICTION DRILL

(Answers and explanations can be found in Part VIII.)

HOW DOES THIS WRITER FEEL ABOUT THE FUNERAL INDUSTRY?

Oh death, where is thy sting?
O grave, where is thy victory? Where,
indeed. Many a badly stung survivor faced
with the aftermath of some relative's funeral
(5) has ruefully concluded that the victory
has been won hands down by a funeral
establishment—in disastrously unequal
battle.

Much has been written of late about
(10) the affluent society in which we live, and
much fun poked at some of the irrational
"status symbols" set out like golden snares
to trap the unwary consumer at every turn.
Until recently, little has been said about the
(15) most irrational and weirdest of the lot, lying
in ambush for all of us at the end of the
road—the modern American funeral.

If the dismal Traders (as an
eighteenth-century English writer calls
(20) them) have traditionally been cast in
a comic role in literature, a universally
recognized symbol of humor from
Shakespeare to Dickens to Evelyn Waugh,
they have successfully turned the tables
(25) in recent years to perpetrate a huge,
macabre and expensive practical joke on
the American public. It is not consciously
conceived of as a joke, of course; on
the contrary, it is hedged with admirably
(30) contrived rationalizations.

Gradually, almost imperceptibly, over
the years, the funeral men have constructed
their own grotesque cloud-cuckoo-land
where the trappings of Gracious Living are
(35) transformed, as in a nightmare, into the
trappings of Gracious Dying. The same
familiar Madison Avenue language has
seeped into the funeral industry.

So that this too, too solid flesh might
(40) not melt, we are offered "solid copper—a
quality casket which offers superb value to
the client seeking long-lasting protection,"
or the "colonial Classic Beauty—18-gauge
lead-coated steel, seamless top, lap-jointed
(45) welded body construction." Some caskets
are equipped with foam rubber, some with
inner-spring mattresses. One company
actually offers "the revolutionary Perfect
Posture bed."

Jessica Mitford, THE AMERICAN WAY OF DEATH, 1963.

1. Why does the author use the quote, "Oh death, where is thy sting?"

   (1) to introduce the subject of death
   (2) as a quick way to get people's attention
   (3) to suggest that the sting of death can also affect the living who have to pay for the funeral
   (4) to illustrate that funeral directors are caring members of a sensitive profession
   (5) to say that death does not have any effect on the author at all

2. According to the passage, the "dismal Traders" mentioned in line 18 are

    (1) undertakers
    (2) shopkeepers
    (3) writers like Shakespeare and Dickens
    (4) practical jokers
    (5) stock and bond salesmen

3. To sell their new products, funeral directors are using

    (1) giveaways
    (2) incentive plans
    (3) the language of advertising
    (4) two-for-one specials
    (5) young spokespersons

4. The author's tone could best be described as

    (1) nostalgic
    (2) ironic
    (3) happy
    (4) indifferent
    (5) lyrical

5. If the author were to plan her funeral in advance, which of the following would she most likely try to do?

    (1) buy an expensive casket with a Perfect Posture mattress inside
    (2) invite all her friends
    (3) buy a plot overlooking a river
    (4) prepay her funeral so that it could be as elaborate as possible
    (5) leave instructions for a simple, inexpensive funeral

Poetry

GED test takers are often intimidated by the poems that show up on the Language Arts, Reading test. However, while you may find these passages the most difficult to read, they generally are the subject of the *easiest* questions. You won't have to delve deep beneath the surface of a poem to answer a GED question; and while some of the selected poems are quite complex, you won't have to understand all their intricacies.

The First Step

The first step to poetry reading is so simple that when you hear it you won't think it's as valuable as it really is: Read the poems *twice*. See what we mean? You probably aren't impressed, but it really works. The first time, don't try to grasp every word. Just read slowly. Don't even think about it much. Then immediately read it again. It's amazing how much you start to get the second time.

Literal Meaning Versus Figurative Meaning

Only after you've read a poem twice should you even *think* about analyzing it. Start with the most literal reading you can think of. If it is a poem about a flower, just think about the poem as being about a flower. Then maybe you can branch out to the figurative meaning of the poem (if there is one) and think about it being a metaphor for the transitory nature of all life, or whatever.

Mood

Even if you aren't sure precisely what a poem is about, you may have some sense of the mood. Just knowing that a poem is upbeat may be enough to eliminate several of the answer choices, so never just give up. Find out what you can, and then go for it.

Here is an example:

WHAT DOES THE JAR DO TO THIS LANDSCAPE?

Anecdote of the Jar

I placed a jar in Tennessee,
And round it was, upon a hill.
It made the slovenly wilderness
Surround that hill.

(5) The wilderness rose up to it,
And sprawled around, no longer wild.
The jar was round upon the ground
And tall and of a port in air.

It took dominion everywhere.
(10) The jar was gray and bare.
It did not give of bird or bush,
Like nothing else in Tennessee.

Wallace Stevens, "Anecdote of the Jar," from THE PALM AT THE END OF THE MIND, 1967.

---

1. When the author set the jar down in the wilderness, the jar

    (1)   seemed to take on characteristics of the wilderness around it
    (2)   fell over and broke
    (3)   seemed to lose its color
    (4)   seemed to bring order and civilization to the wilderness
    (5)   reminded the author of other jars from his youth

Here's How to Crack It

Read the poem twice. Don't think too much about it; just read it. There are two elements in this poem: the wilderness and the jar. Which one is affecting the other? If you thought the wilderness was affecting the jar, you'd pick choice (1), but in fact, in this poem, it is the jar that's affecting the wilderness. As soon as he placed the jar on the ground, the wilderness around it was *no longer wild*. The correct answer to this question is choice (4).

---

2. Which of the following most resembles the scene described in the poem?

   (1)   an island in the middle of an ocean
   (2)   an oasis in the middle of the desert
   (3)   a tree in the middle of the forest
   (4)   a bank in the middle of a street
   (5)   a house in the middle of a grassy
         plain

Here's How to Crack It

This application question asks us to analyze the elements in the poem and then recognize similar elements in one of the answer choices. Remember, we said there were two elements: the wilderness and the jar. One is made by nature, one by man. The wilderness surrounds the man-made object, yet it is the man-made object that tames the wilderness.

Take a look at the answer choices. Which of them gives us a man-made object surrounded by nature? If you said choice (5), you are correct.

POETRY DRILL

(Answers and explanations can be found in Part VIII.)

WHY DID HE TAKE THE SECOND ROAD?

The Road Not Taken

Two roads diverged in a yellow wood,
And sorry I could not travel both
And be one traveler, long I stood
And looked down one as far as I could
(5) To where it bent in the undergrowth;

Then took the other, as just as fair,
And having perhaps the better claim,
Because it was grassy and wanted wear;
Though as for that the passing there
(10) Had worn them really about the same,

And both that morning equally lay
In leaves no step had trodden black.
Oh, I kept the first for another day!
Yet knowing how way leads on to way,
(15) I doubted if I should ever come back.

I shall be telling this with a sigh
Somewhere ages and ages hence:
Two roads diverged in a wood, and I—
I took the one less traveled by.
(20) And that has made all the difference.

Robert Frost, "The Road Not Taken," from THE POETRY OF ROBERT
FROST, edited by Edward Connery Lathem, 1916.

1. Why does the author say that, "I shall be telling this with a sigh / Somewhere ages and ages hence"?

    (1) When he is older, he will not believe that he even hesitated before taking the second path.
    (2) He will be too old to remember the incident at all.
    (3) He will go back and travel the first road.
    (4) He will wonder what was down the path he didn't travel.
    (5) He will be filled with relief that he didn't choose the wrong path.

2. What does the author mean by the line, "Because it was grassy and wanted wear"?

    (1) It was a good spot to lie down.
    (2) It was a well-traveled road.
    (3) It was less traveled than the other.
    (4) It needed mowing.
    (5) It led in the direction in which he had started out.

3. The speaker in this poem is most likely

    (1) a young child
    (2) a teenager
    (3) a middle-aged man
    (4) an old man
    (5) a ghost

4. If the poet had taken the first road, his life would most likely have been

    (1) better
    (2) the same
    (3) worse
    (4) different
    (5) more unusual

Part VI Summary

○ The Language Arts, Reading test consists of 40 multiple-choice questions based on excerpts from literary texts or business topics.

○ 75 percent of this test will be based on literary texts (novels, short stories, plays and poems). The other 25 percent will be based on nonfiction texts (articles about literature or business topics).

○ For fiction and dramatic passages, the questions you should ask yourself as you read are: Who's talking? What's going on? What is the mood of the passage? Who are the main characters? Where does the action take place?

○ For nonfiction passages, the questions you should ask yourself as you read are: What is the main point of the passage? How does the author support the main idea? What is the author's point of view?

○ One passage on the test will be a business-related document, such as a manual, application, or memo.

○ Some test takers are intimidated by poems—but the questions asked about the poems tend to be relatively easy. The single best strategy with poems (which are relatively short) is to read them twice.

Part VII
How to Crack the Math Test

Chapter 22
Math Overview

A review of basic math terminology and definitions including the number line, positive and negative numbers, digits, rounding off, multiplying and dividing, using the order of operations, fractions, decimals, and percents.

If the GED Math test covered all the math topics they teach in high school, it would be a pretty tough test. Fortunately, it doesn't, and it isn't. The GED test writers concentrate on a few areas very heavily, which means that by reading the chapters that follow and doing the exercises we provide, you should be able to score very well—even if you've always hated math.

What's on the Test

The GED Math test contains 50 questions to be answered in 90 minutes, which gives you more than a minute and a half for each question if you try to figure out every question. The areas covered in the GED Math test are as follows:

Number Operations/Number Sense	20–30%
Measurement/Geometry	20–30%
Data Analysis/Probability/Statistics	20–30%
Algebra/Functions/Patterns	20–30%

What Isn't on the Test

The test does *not* cover most of the normal high school algebra curriculum; there is also nothing about calculus or even precalculus. No logs, no proofs, no advanced graphing. To make things even easier, the Math test begins with an entire page of formulas, so that in case you don't remember how to find the area of a triangle, for example, you can always just look it up.

Can You Use a Calculator?

The 50-question GED Math test is broken up into two parts of 25 questions each. In the first part, you *will* be allowed to use a calculator. In the second part, you will *not* be allowed to use a calculator.

The Calculator Section

You may think that the first section (in which you can use a calculator) would be easier than the second, but there's one hitch: You can't bring your OWN calculator. You must use the one they will provide at the test center, the Casio FX-260 Solar, shown below.

Like any new calculator, this one takes some getting used to. It is *vital* that you become familiar with this particular model ahead of time. The testing centers are supposed to show a video on how the calculator works before the test begins, but we still strongly recommend that you buy (or borrow) this specific calculator and practice with it for several weeks before the test. It is available in many stores, or you can buy it from the company that makes the GED by calling (800) 531–5015. It is available in most office supply stores or online for about $10.

The Weirdness of Calculators

There are three functions on the Casio FX-260 that can be pretty confusing. The first involves using negative numbers. (And, by the way, if you aren't sure what negative numbers are, don't worry. We'll cover them in the next chapter.) To enter a negative number, you first have to enter the number, then hit the "change sign" key located directly above the "7" key. The display now shows the negative number.

The second confusing feature of the FX-260 involves parentheses. (And, again, if you aren't sure how to use parentheses in math, don't worry. We'll cover them in the next chapter.) Parentheses in math usually mean an implied multiplication that you can't actually see on the page. You must remember to multiply to get the right answer. Here's an example: To enter the expression $3(2 + 5)$, you would enter 3, then the multiplication key, then the left parentheses key, then 2, then the plus key, then the 5 key, then the right parentheses key. To complete the problem, press the "equals" key.

The third confusing feature of the FX-260 involves square roots. (We'll cover them, too, in a later chapter.) There is no dedicated square root key on this calculator—the key for square roots is also the key for squaring. To find the square root of a number, first enter the number (let's say 9), and then locate the square root symbol, which is in smaller letters on the key that says "x^2." If you just pressed this key, it would square the number (9 times 9, or 81), but that's not what we want to do in this case. To find the square root of 9, first enter 9, then press the "shift" key (located at top left), then press the "x^2" key. This will access the second function of the key and give you the square root (in this case, 3).

You can see why we are telling you to get the calculator in advance and become familiar with it.

Will All the Math Questions Be Multiple Choice?

Eighty percent of the Math test is multiple choice. But both Part One and Part Two of the Math test will include a few short-answer questions in which you must mark your answer into a grid on the answer sheet. Here is a simple example of what one of these questions might look like:

1. What is 15 + 0.3 + 6?

The answer to this very simple number operations problem is 21.3. To mark your answer on the grid, write your answer across the top of the grid, including any decimal points. Then bubble in the correct numbers underneath. Here is how a correctly bubbled answer would look:

Now, the Good News

In Chapter 3, we introduced you to the concept of POE, and we've referred to it often in the chapters that have followed. Well, on the GED Math test, you will find that you can elevate POE to an art form. In fact, there will be many problems on the Math test that you can solve *without doing any traditional math at all*. We'll show you our most powerful POE technique (Backsolving) in Chapter 25, but for now let's begin with a slightly less advanced, but just as useful, POE technique.

Ballparking

In school, you may once have encountered a short-answer problem on a math test that looked like this:

> This month, 1,500 new members joined a particular health club. The club's goal for this month was 2,000 new members. What percentage of the club's goal was achieved?

If you weren't sure how to solve this short-answer problem during that test, you were pretty much out of luck. It certainly wouldn't have made sense to guess, would it? For example, if you had closed your eyes and picked a number at random ("…uh, 14!"), the chances that you would happen to pick the right answer would have been pretty slim. (By the way, if you aren't sure how to do this problem right now, don't worry. We'll cover percentage problems in Chapter 23.)

But most of the problems on the GED test are NOT in the short-answer format. Most GED questions are in the multiple-choice format. Here's how that question would look on the GED:

> This month, 1,500 new members joined a particular health club. The club's goal for this month was 2,000 new members. What percentage of the club's goal was achieved?
>
> (1) 75%
>
> (2) 82%
>
> (3) 112%
>
> (4) 133.33%
>
> (5) 150%

You may be saying, "Big deal. Same problem." But, in fact, this is not the same problem at all. If you happened to spot this question on the real GED and still didn't know how to do it (which, by the way, isn't too likely because we're going to show you how to nail every single percentage problem on the test), you would have an enormous advantage because you no longer have to guess completely at random. In the multiple-choice format, there are only five possibilities, and *one* of them has to be right. Just by guessing among the five answer choices, you have a 20 percent chance of answering the question correctly.

Now, the Very Good News

Guessing at random among the five answer choices will give you a 20 percent chance of getting the question right, but we can do better than that. If each of the answer choices were equally reasonable, random guessing would make sense. Fortunately, it turns out that many answers on multiple-choice GED math questions aren't reasonable at all. In fact, some of them are pretty crazy.

Let's just think about that problem above. The health club's goal was 2,000 new memberships, but they actually got only 1,500 new memberships. Did they reach their goal? No way. Putting this in the language of percentages, let's restate the question: Did they reach 100 percent of their goal? The answer is still no.

Out of the Ballpark

Obviously, the correct answer to this problem must be *less* than 100 percent. Even if you are unsure about how to calculate the exact percentage, there are several answer choices that are simply way out of the ballpark. Look at choice (5), 150%. This answer implies that not only did the club meet its goal, it exceeded it as well. Forget choice (5). Look at choice (4), 133.33%. Again, this is just crazy. The correct answer must be less than 100%. Look at choice (3), 112%. This answer is still way out of the ballpark.

We have eliminated three answer choices. This means the correct answer to this question is either choice (1) or choice (2). All of a sudden, your odds of getting this question correct are much better. You now have a fifty-fifty chance of being right. Pick one. If you picked choice (1), you just got the question correct.

You'll find that once you start looking at GED multiple-choice problems in this way, you'll spot many opportunities to ballpark. This is because the GED test writers construct their incorrect answer choices not to be reasonable but to anticipate common errors that test takers make when they're in a hurry. Let's look at another problem:

Use Common Sense
When you take the GED, don't check your common sense at the door. In fact, by taking a step back from a problem, you can often eliminate at least one or two answer choices.

Eric buys a coat from a mail-order catalog. The coat costs $140, plus an $8 shipping charge and a $2 handling fee. If there is a 10% sales tax on the entire amount, what would be the <u>total</u> cost of buying the coat?

(1) $15

(2) $135

(3) $150

(4) $160

(5) $165

Like many problems on the GED Math test, this requires several steps. First, let's add up what we have so far:

the coat	$140
shipping	$8
handling	+ $2
	$150

We are already up to $150, and we haven't even added in the tax yet. Do you see any answer choices we can cross out? If you said choices (1), (2), and (3), you are right on the money. The correct answer *must* be greater than $150, which means there are only two possibilities left: choices (4) and (5).

Why did the GED test writers choose three answers that didn't make sense? Because they wanted to include some answers that many test takers are likely to pick by mistake. For example, let's say that you were doing this problem, and you got to the point we have already reached: You added up the numbers and got $150. If you were in a hurry (and who isn't during the GED?), you might look at the answer choices, see choice (3), $150, figure that you must be done, and pencil in choice (3) on your answer sheet. The GED test writers felt it was important that you have that opportunity.

Or let's say that you realized there was another step to this problem: In order to find the true total cost of the coat, you have to add the 10 percent tax. To compute this tax, you find 10 percent of $150, which turns out to be $15. (By the way, don't worry if you weren't sure how to find 10 percent of 150. We'll show you how in Chapter 23.) Well, it turns out that $15 is one of the answer choices, too, so if you were not quite as cool and collected as you would like to be (and who is during the GED?), you might just pick answer choice (1), not realizing that you have to add this to the $150 to get the true total.

Partial Answers

To find the correct answer to this question—choice (5), $165—requires you to do three separate calculations. First, add up the cost of the coat and the postage and handling. Second, calculate the tax. Third, add the tax to the previous total. If a test taker chose choice (3), $150, or choice (1), $15, it was not because he made a mistake in his calculations. The answer to step one of this problem is $150. The answer to step two is $15. However, both of these numbers are only *partial* answers to the question.

On the GED, you will frequently find partial answers lurking in wait for you. To avoid getting taken in by one of these, you have to read the problem very carefully the first time and then read it again just as carefully right before you mark down your answer.

How Do You Use Partial Answers?

Because the test writers employ partial answers so often on the GED Math test, you can actually use the partial answers as clues to help you find the final answer. For example, working on a two-step problem, you may find that the answer to the first step of the problem is also one of the answer choices. This is a good sign. It means you are on the right track. If the answer to your first step is *close* to one of the answer choices, but just a little off, you might try redoing the calculation to see if you made a mistake.

How Do You Use Ballparking?

Okay, let's say you know exactly how to do a problem. Should you bother to ballpark it first? Definitely. Taking the GED does funny things to people. You might be the greatest mathematician in the world ordinarily, but by the time you get to the Math portion of the GED, your brain may be so fried from the other four tests that you just aren't thinking completely straight. Or you may be rushing to finish a question and make a mistake that you would never normally make.

Ballparking as a Reality Check

Ballparking is a way to bring reality into the test room. You can prevent lots of careless errors by stepping back from a math problem and saying,

> *Wait a minute. Before I even start multiplying or dividing, which answers don't make sense?*

Once you've gotten rid of the crazy answer choices, *then* you can start solving the problem. And if your calculations happen to lead you, mistakenly, to one of those crazy partial answer choices—well, you'll know you just made a mistake, and you'll be able to figure out what went wrong.

Can You Ballpark If the Question Is Short-Answer?

Ballparking can still be a great reality check even when you have to come up with your answer from scratch. While you will not be able to eliminate answer choices the way you can with multiple-choice questions, you will still be able to stop yourself from making careless errors by knowing ahead of time approximately what your answer should look like.

What If You Have No Idea How to Do the Problem?

Then ballparking is even more important. As we said in Chapter 3, there's no guessing penalty on the GED. It is in your interest to fill in every blank on your answer sheet. But there's guessing and then there's *guessing*. If you can eliminate several of the answer choices because they are simply out of the ballpark, your odds of getting the problem correct go way up.

For example, take the two problems we've shown you so far in this chapter. In both cases, we were able to eliminate three of the five choices by ballparking. Thus, in each problem, we were down to a fifty-fifty guess. Let's assume for a moment that you didn't know how to do either problem. What would be the results if you were to guess on both of them? The odds say you're going to get one of them wrong. That's a shame, but after all, there's no guessing penalty, and more to the point, you didn't know how to do the question anyway, so you're no worse off than you were before.

However, the odds also say that you're going to get the other one *right*! And that's not bad, considering you had no idea how to do that question either.

The Very, Very Good News

About one-half of the test questions on the GED refer to "graphic material": drawings of geometric figures, graphs, and charts. If you've read Chapter 4, "Crazy Graphics," you've already learned a lot about charts and graphs. But that isn't the very, very good news. It's much better than that.

The Diagrams Are Drawn Roughly to Scale!

Whenever you see a diagram on the Math test of the GED, you have the single most efficient way to ballpark that you could possibly imagine: You can just *measure* the diagrams. We know it's bizarre, but it's true.

Here's a typical multiple-choice geometry problem:

Question 1 refers to the following diagram.

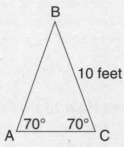

If angle A and angle C both equal 70°,
then what is the length of side AB?

(1)   3 feet

(2)   7 feet

(3)   9 feet

(4)   10 feet

(5)   15 feet

Don't worry if you don't remember the geometric principle involved in solving this problem (the properties of an isosceles triangle). We'll review geometry in Chapter 26.

The question is, how long is side AB? Let's find out. Simply take any straight edge you can find, and carefully measure side BC, which the diagram says is 10 feet long. Remember, it's illegal to mark your test booklet, so be careful during the real GED not to let your pencil touch the test booklet. However, you can always make marks on your scratch paper. Measure off side BC, and mark down its length against your piece of scratch paper. Now all you have to do is compare that length to side AB. If it's a lot bigger, you can get rid of any choices less than 10. If it's a lot smaller, you can get rid of any choices greater than 10.

If you measured our diagram correctly, you probably noticed that side AB appears to be exactly the same size as side BC. So is the correct answer choice (4)? Well, in fact it is. However, because the GED drawings are only drawn *roughly* to scale, you wouldn't know for sure that the answer is exactly 10 feet unless you knew the geometric reasoning behind the problem. Going by the diagram alone, you could only have gotten the answer down to choices (3), 9 feet, and (4), 10 feet. Between these two, it would have been too close to call. However, you could be pretty certain that the answer was *not* choices (1), (2), or (5).

The diagrams seem to be most closely drawn when they illustrate standard geometric shapes, such as circles, number lines, and triangles. When there is a diagram of a garden or a pie chart, the illustrators seem to feel they don't have to be as careful.

Can You Measure Diagrams If the Question Is Short-Answer?

Because the diagrams on the GED are only roughly drawn to scale, the odds of getting exactly the right answer on a short-answer question by measuring are pretty small. However, just as ballparking helps to prevent making careless errors in the few short-answer questions that come up on the GED, measuring diagrams will help prevent your gridding in an answer that makes no sense.

The Red Herring

On every GED Math test, there will be several problems that give you more information than you actually need. We call this extra information the "red herring." Here's an example:

Sounds Fishy to Me
A "red herring" is an expression in which a clue or piece or information is intended to be misleading or distracting from the actual question. Distractor answers are common on standardized tests like the GED.

This year, $\frac{3}{4}$ of the employees at Acme made contributions to a voluntary retirement fund. Last year, only $\frac{2}{3}$ of the employees contributed. If there are now 2,100 employees, how many contributed to the voluntary retirement fund this year?

(1)   525

(2) 1,400

(3) 1,575

(4) 1,800

(5) 2,245

The most important part of any GED math problem is the last line, which is where the test writers tell you what they really want. In this case, they want the number of employees who contributed to their retirement fund *this* year. In this problem, the only year we care about is *this* year. To answer the question, we have to find out from the problem what fraction of the total employees contributed this year, and then multiply that fraction times the total number of employees. (By the way, if you aren't sure how to find a fractional part of a number, don't worry. We'll show you how in Chapter 23.)

Looking at the problem, do we see any information that is not about this year? Well, as a matter of fact, we do. The second sentence, "Last year, only $\frac{2}{3}$ of the employees contributed," has nothing to do with what the question asks us. The GED test writers threw that sentence in to see if it would trick us. It was a red herring.

To answer this question, we need to take $\frac{3}{4}$ of 2,100. The correct answer is choice (3), 1,575. Incidentally, did you notice that there is one answer choice that is out of the ballpark? There were only 2,100 employees total. So how could 2,245 of those employees have contributed to their retirement funds? Choice (5) is crazy.

Taking the GED Math Test

When you turn the page to begin the Math test, you will probably begin with Question 1, then do Question 2, and then do Question 3, and so on. This is a fine strategy as long as you are prepared to be flexible. Every year, we hear stories from test takers who got stuck on some early problem—let's say it was Question 3. They just couldn't get it. They read it and read it again. They tried solving it one way and then another. But some people have orderly minds, and *darn it*, they aren't going to go on to Question 4 until they get Question 3. After 10 minutes, when they finally give up and go on to number 4, they are thoroughly rattled, jittery, and very angry at themselves for wasting so much time.

The lesson here?

Don't Get Stubborn

There are always going to be problems that, for whatever reason, you just can't get. It might be a mental block, or maybe you never learned a particular type of problem, or maybe the question was simply written so poorly that it is impossible to understand. No matter how easy you think the problem ought to be, don't be mulish. Even if you can't do the very *first* problem, there are 49 others waiting for you, and you will find that many of them are pretty easy.

First Pass, Second Pass

Of course, it isn't necessary to solve every problem to do very well, and in fact, you will see that by skipping the problems you don't know how to do, you can actually increase your score. How does this work?

The Passes
First pass: Do the ones you can get right away.
Second pass: Go back over the ones you skipped.

We recommend that you take the GED Math test in two passes. On your first pass, you'll begin at the beginning and do every problem that comes easily to you. If you read a question and know just what to do, then it is a first-pass problem. However, if you read a problem and have no idea of how to solve it, then you should put a little mark next to the number on your answer sheet and move on. You have not skipped this problem forever. You are merely saving it for later, after you've locked in all the easy points. As you read each new problem, what you want to ask yourself is...

"Do I Want to Do It *Now*?"

If the answer is *yes*, then go ahead. But if the answer is, "I'm not sure," skip it immediately and go on to the next one.

Do you remember that terrible feeling when the teacher said, "Sorry, time's up," and you knew that if you had only had two more minutes, you'd have been able to solve that last question? Well, if you take our advice, this will never happen again. By the end of the exam, you will already have done all the problems you *know* you can do, and you'll be working on ones you weren't sure of anyway.

When you finish your first pass, go back to the beginning, and consult your answer sheet to see which problems you skipped. Now you can take a second look. Sometimes, when you read the problem again, you'll immediately see what was unclear to you the first time, and you'll know just what to do. Other times you may not be sure, but you'll be able to eliminate several answer choices by ballparking. And sometimes, of course, you will just say, "Yuck!" and skip the problem forever.

No Writing in the Test Booklet

You've had to put up with this instruction in each of the other GED sections, but the no-writing-in-the-test-booklet rule seems particularly unfair on the Math test. It's so helpful to be able to write in the margins right next to the problem, and this is particularly true if you start a problem, decide to skip it, and then come back to it later. How will you know which scratch paper went with which problem?

Oh, well. Because you can't write in the test booklet, you'll have to learn to get comfortable with using scratch paper. Don't put this off until the actual GED.

It takes a while to adapt, and you don't want to be learning during the real test. Our diagnostic exams should provide plenty of practice.

To counter both the problems we've just mentioned, we recommend (A) that you put your scratch paper directly below the question you're working on so that you can do your calculations as close to the actual problem as possible; and (B) that you label your scratch work with the problem numbers so that, if necessary, you can find them again when you come back for a second pass.

> **Don't You Dare Skip That Problem!**
> When we said "skip" in that last paragraph, what we *meant* was "don't spend any time figuring it out." Remember, you should never *ever* leave a multiple-choice problem blank when the time comes to hand in your answer sheet. Right before you finish the Math test, make sure that you have answered every single multiple-choice question.

Chapter 23
Basic Arithmetic

A review of basic math terminology and definitions including the number line, positive and negative numbers, digits, rounding off, multiplying and dividing, using the order of operations, fractions, decimals, and percents.

The arithmetic on the GED is not necessarily the arithmetic you learned in school. The folks who write the test are striving to make GED math more relevant to real life. Consequently, you won't find any questions on the more theoretical aspects of arithmetic—properties of integers, for example. Nor will there be any questions about prime numbers, imaginary numbers, or any of the other terms that generally go under the name "axioms and fundamentals." Instead, the test focuses on practical math. Several of the questions will be word problems that try to evoke situations you might find in everyday life.

In this chapter, we're going to show you all the basic arithmetic topics that come up on the GED. With each topic, we'll first show you the concept behind the topic, then illustrate it with GED-type examples, and finally give you a small drill so you can practice the concept on your own. At the end of the entire chapter, there will be a big drill in GED format, including all the concepts we've shown you. The purpose of this is to give you some practice recognizing the different types of questions when they are all mixed together—as they are on the real GED. In the next chapter, we'll cover *applied* arithmetic topics in just the same way.

Here are the basic arithmetic concepts that appear on the GED:

- The number line
- Rounding off
- Multiplying positive and negative numbers
- Order of operations
- Associative and distributive properties
- Fractions
- Decimals
- Percents
- Ratios and proportions

The Number Line
The number line is a two-dimensional way of looking at positive and (sometimes) negative numbers in relation to one another.

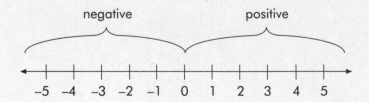

Positive numbers are to the right of zero on the number line above. Negative numbers are to the left of zero on the number line above. Zero itself is neither negative nor positive.

Note that positive numbers get bigger as they move away from zero. Negative numbers get smaller. For example, –3 is smaller than –1. A number line can extend infinitely to the left or right, but the number lines on the GED generally look like the example on the previous page, with a fairly small number of position points. Let's try identifying some points on the number line.

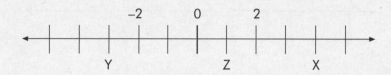

Find point X on the number line. What number does point X represent? If you said 4, you were absolutely right. How about points Y and Z? If you said –3 and 1, you were right again. Here's how a number line problem would look on the GED:

Question 1 refers to the following number line.

1. Which letter on the number line above represents the number –2?

    (1)   A

    (2)   D

    (3)   E

    (4)   F

    (5)   G

Here's How to Crack It
Generally, the only thing that's difficult in a number line problem is orienting yourself. The best place to begin is to find 0. Did you find it? Now locate –2. Which letter corresponds to –2? The correct answer is choice (2).

Here's a slightly more difficult number line problem:

Question 2 refers to the following diagram.

A   B   C   D

2.   On the number line above, AB = BC = CD.
If AD = 12, then what is the length of AB?

(1)   4

(2)   5

(3)   6

(4)   8

(5)   10

Here's How to Crack It

In this problem, there is no way to orient yourself because neither the diagram nor the problem identifies a specific point on the number line. Instead, this problem is concerned with the *lengths* of segments on the line. On the GED, lengths are always positive, never negative. In this case, the only actual length you are given is AD, which equals 12. Let's look at the other information in the problem. If AB = BC = CD, then these segments break up AD into three equal parts. Because the whole is 12, what is the length of a single part? You're right: The length of AD is 4, and the answer is choice (1).

Sometimes number line problems will ask you about the midpoint of a line segment. A **midpoint** is simply the place halfway between either end of the line segment. A GED problem might look like this:

Question 3 refers to the following diagram.

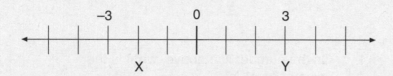

3. If point X on the line above represents −2 and point Y on the line represents 3, then the midpoint of segment XY would be between which two numbers?

    (1) −2 and −1
    (2) −1 and 0
    (3) 0 and 1
    (4) 1 and 2
    (5) 2 and 3

Here's How to Crack It

This time, there are concrete numbers marked on the number line, so take a second to get oriented. Now, the midpoint of XY is the point exactly halfway between point X and point Y. Count how many spaces there are between X and Y. Did you get 5? Good. What is half of 5? Of course, the answer is $2\frac{1}{2}$. So all you have to do is count over $2\frac{1}{2}$ to the right of point X or $2\frac{1}{2}$ to the left of point Y. In either case, the midpoint is between 0 and 1, and the correct answer is choice (3).

NUMBER LINE DRILL

(Answers and explanations can be found in Part VIII.)

Questions 1 through 3 refer to the diagram below.

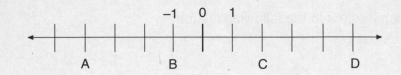

1. On the number line above, what is the value of point A?

    (1)   −4
    (2)   −3
    (3)   −1
    (4)   3
    (5)   4

2. On the number line above, the midpoint of line segment CD is between which two points?

    (1)   0 and 1
    (2)   1 and 2
    (3)   2 and 3
    (4)   3 and 4
    (5)   4 and 5

3. If a new point E was to be added to the number line exactly halfway between points A and D, where would it be located?

    (1)   between points −3 and −2
    (2)   at point 0
    (3)   between points 0 and 1
    (4)   at point 2
    (5)   between points 3 and 4

Positive and Negative Numbers

Let's look at that number line one last time.

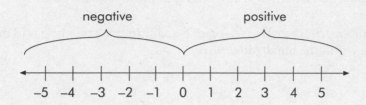

Lots of people have trouble adding and subtracting negative numbers. There is a very easy way to do this, using the number line. When you add two *positive* numbers, you are actually counting over to the right on a number line. For example, let's add 2 + 3. To find two on the number line, count over two places to the right of zero. That's 2. Now let's add three, by counting over three more places to the right. Thus, 2 + 3 = 5.

Okay, okay, we know that's pretty simple. But the great thing is that it's just as simple to add or subtract negative numbers. Let's add a positive number and a negative number: 5 + (−3). Find 5 on the number line by counting over five places to the right from zero. Now, to add −3, count over three places to the *left*. Where are you? That's right,

$$5 + (−3) = 2$$

By the way, adding a negative number is exactly the same thing as subtracting a positive number. Thus, the addition problem above could also have been written this way:

$$5 − 3 = 2$$

Now, let's add two negative numbers: (−2) + (−1). First, find −2 by counting over two places to the left of zero on the number line. Now, to add −1, count over one more place to the left.

$$(−2) + (−1) = −3$$

Again, we could have written this as

$$(−2) − 1 = −3$$

To make a number negative on your Casio FX-260, first enter the number, then hit the "change sign" key.

Digits

All numbers are made up of digits. In the number 6,342, there are four digits: 6, 3, 4, and 2. In this case, the 2 is in the ones' place. The 4 is in the tens' place, the 3 is in the hundreds' place, and the 6 is in the thousands' place.

In the number 0.57, there are two digits: 5 and 7. In this case, the 5 is in the tenths' place. The 7 is in the hundredths' place.

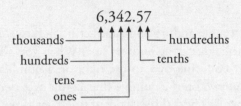

Rounding Off to the Nearest Whatever

The GED test writers sometimes ask you to round off a number. The problem might read, "To the nearest thousand, how many…" or "What number to the nearest tenth…"

Whether you round to the nearest thousand or the nearest tenth, the process is exactly the same. Let's begin by rounding to the nearest dollar. If you have up to $1.49, then to the nearest dollar you have $1. If you have $1.50 or more, then to the nearest dollar you have $2.

Exactly the same principles hold true when you round any type of number.

To the nearest

10	up to and including 14 is 10
	15 or more is 20
100	up to and including 149 is 100
	150 or more is 200
1,000	up to and including 1,499 is 1,000
	1,500 or more is 2,000

To the nearest

10th	up to and including 0.14 is 0.1
	0.15 or more is 0.2
100th	up to and including 0.014 is 0.01
	0.015 or more is 0.02

Here's how this might look on the GED:

The median salary of a surgeon was recently reported to be $233,800 per year. What would this figure be to the nearest thousand?

(1) 200,000

(2) 230,000

(3) 233,000

(4) 234,000

(5) 240,000

Here's How to Crack It

Which is the thousands' place? If you aren't sure, try saying the number out loud: "Two hundred thirty-three *thousand* eight hundred dollars." So we have 233 thousand plus 800 more. Now the only decision to make is whether the 800 is halfway or more to the next thousand. Is it? Sure. The correct answer is choice (4).

ROUNDING OFF DRILL

(Answers can be found in Part VIII.)

1. To the nearest thousand, what is 3,400?

2. To the nearest tenth, what is 3.46?

3. To the nearest hundred, what is 565?

4. What is $432.70 to the nearest dollar?

5. What is 4.80 to the nearest hundredth?

Digit Quiz

Q: Which of these numbers has more digits?
(1)   37.5
(2)   342

Answer on page 401

Multiplying Positive and Negative Numbers

Multiplication is actually just the process of adding a number several times. For example, to multiply 4 by 3, you are actually just adding 4 three separate times

$$4 \times 3 = 4 + 4 + 4 = 12$$

or adding 3 four separate times

$$3 \times 4 = 3 + 3 + 3 + 3 = 12.$$

To multiply 5 by 2, you are actually just adding 5 two separate times

$$5 \times 2 = 5 + 5 = 10$$

or adding 2 five separate times

$$2 \times 5 = 2 + 2 + 2 + 2 + 2 = 10.$$

Of course, it's a lot quicker to use the multiplication (times) tables. We just wanted to remind you of the theory behind multiplication. If your times tables are a little rusty, don't worry. You're going to get lots of opportunity to practice over the next three chapters.

There are three rules regarding the multiplication of positive and negative numbers.

positive $\times$ **positive = positive**	$2 \times 3 = 6$
positive $\times$ **negative = negative**	$2 \times -3 = -6$
negative $\times$ **negative = positive**	$-2 \times -3 = 6$

Dividing Positive and Negative Numbers

Division is actually the opposite of multiplication. If we multiply 2 by 3, we get 6. If we divide 6 by 2, we are actually asking what number times 2 = 6?

$6 \div 2 = 3$. You can also write this as $\dfrac{6}{2}$ or $2\overline{)6}$.

The same three rules of multiplication apply to the division of positive and negative numbers.

positive ÷ positive = positive	$6 \div 2 = 3$
positive ÷ negative = negative	$6 \div -2 = -3$
negative ÷ negative = positive	$-6 \div -2 = 3$

ADDING, SUBTRACTING, MULTIPLYING, AND DIVIDING POSITIVE AND NEGATIVE NUMBERS DRILL

Do these problems first on your own. Then, on a separate piece of paper, do them again using your calculator.

(Answers and explanations can be found in Part VIII.)

1. $5 + (-3) =$

2. $(-4) + (-7) =$

3. $(6 \times 3) =$

4. $(-2)(6) =$

5. $(-3) - (2) + (6) =$

6. $10 \div 2 =$

7. $(-5)(-2) =$

8. $-21 \div -7 =$

9. $12 \div -3 =$

10. $-12 \div 3 =$

That Wacky Zero!

Any number $\times 0 = 0$

Any number $\div 0 =$ undefined

Order of Operations

In a problem that involves several different operations, the operations must be performed in a particular order. There's an easy way to remember the order of operations:

Please Excuse My Dear Aunt Sally

First, you do operations enclosed in Parentheses; then you take care of Exponents; then you Multiply, Divide, Add, and Subtract. We're going to save exponents for the next chapter, but let's try out PEMDAS with a couple of problems.

$$\left((-5)+4\right)\left(\frac{8}{2}\right)+4=$$

How about this one?

$$(3)+\left(\frac{8}{2}\right)(4-5)+1=$$

If you did these in the correct order, you should have gotten the same answer both times: 0.

Using Your Calculator on Order of Operations

PEMDAS Quiz

Q: $3(7-[5-3])=$?

Answer on page 404

During Part One of the Math test, the Casio FX-260 calculator you will be given in the testing room automatically knows the order of operations. As long as you enter the equation correctly, it will give you the correct answer every time. But entering the equation correctly can be painstaking work. For example, in the operation above, you would enter 3, hit the "plus" key, then the "left parentheses" key, then 8, then the "division" key followed by the 2, then the "right parentheses" key, then the "multiplication" key, then the "left parentheses" key, then the 4 followed by the "minus" key, then the 5, then the "right parentheses" key, then the "plus" key, then the 1 key, and finally the "equals" key.

Many students find that they can do this faster on paper.

Associative and Distributive Properties

The Associative Property: When you add a string of numbers, you can add them in any order you like. The same thing is true when you are multiplying a string of numbers.

$$4 + 5 + 8 \text{ is the same as } 8 + 5 + 4.$$

$$6 \times 7 \times 9 \text{ is the same as } 9 \times 7 \times 6.$$

The Distributive Property: The GED test writers will sometimes use an equation that can be written in two different ways. They do this to see if you know about this equation and if you can spot when it is in your interest to change the equation into its other form.

The distributive property states that

$$a(b + c) = ab + ac \text{ and } a(b - c) = ab - ac$$

Example: $3(4 + 2) = 3(4) + 3(2) = 18$
Example: $3(4 - 2) = 3(4) - 3(2) = 6$

If a problem gives you information in "factored" format—$a(b + c)$—you should distribute it immediately. If the information is given in distributed form—$ab + ab$—you should factor it. Take the following example:

$$\frac{1}{2}(5) + \frac{1}{2}(3) =$$

Finding $\frac{1}{2}$ of 5 and $\frac{1}{2}$ of 3 is a bit troublesome because the answers do not work out to be whole numbers. It isn't that you can't find half of an odd number if you have to (or at least you *will* be able to, after our review of fractions later in this chapter), but why do more work than necessary?

Look at what would happen if we changed this distributed equation into its factored form instead:

$$\frac{1}{2}(5 + 3) =$$

Isn't that a lot easier? One half of 8 equals 4. Always be on the lookout for chances to do less work on the GED. It's a long, tiring test, and you need to conserve your strength. Now, try this one.

If $3X + 3Y = 21$, then what is the value of $X + Y$?

(1)   3

(2)   5

(3)   6

(4)   7

(5)   not enough information is given

Parentheses often involve multiplication. To enter 2(5 + 3), first enter 2, then the "multiplication" key, then "left parentheses," then 5 "plus" 3, then "right parentheses."

Here's How to Crack It

Everyone's first impulse on a problem like this is to pick choice (5), not enough information is given. After all, there are two different variables (X and Y), so unless we know what both variables are, how can we figure out the problem?

The answer is the distributive property. You may not have noticed that the equation in the problem above was in one of the formats we were just looking at: $ab + ac$, otherwise known as the distributive form. Therefore, before we give up hope, let's try putting the equation into its mirror-image format: $a(b + c)$, otherwise known as its factored form.

$$3X + 3Y = 3(X + Y) = 21$$

Hmm. We want to know what $(X + Y)$ equals. Well, three *times* $(X + Y)$ equals 21. Three times what number equals 21? That's right, 7, and the correct answer to this question is choice (4).

ORDER OF OPERATIONS AND ASSOCIATIVE AND DISTRIBUTIVE PROPERTIES DRILL

Do these problems first on your own. Then on a separate piece of paper, do them again using your calculator.

(Answers can be found in Part VIII.)

1. $5(3 - 4) + 2 =$

2. $7 \times 2 \times 3 =$

3. $3(3 - 1 - 2) + 6(2 - 4) =$

4. $8[4(3 - 5)] =$

5. $\dfrac{1}{4}(3) + \dfrac{1}{4}(9) =$

Fractions

A fraction is one part of a whole. Take a look at the pie below:

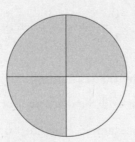

This pie has been divided into four equal pieces. Three of the four pieces are shaded. If we wanted to express the part of the pie that is shaded, we would say that $\dfrac{3}{4}$ of the pie is shaded. If we wanted to express the part of the pie that is not shaded, we would say that $\dfrac{1}{4}$ of the pie is not shaded.

A fraction is always a part over a whole.

$$\frac{1}{2} \quad \frac{\text{part}}{\text{whole}}$$

In the fraction $\frac{1}{2}$, we have one part out of a total of two equal parts.

In the fraction $\frac{3}{7}$, we have three parts out of a total of seven equal parts.

Another way to think of a fraction is as just another kind of division. The expression $\frac{1}{2}$ means 1 divided by 2. The fraction $\frac{x}{y}$ is nothing more than x divided by y. A fraction is made up of a numerator and a denominator. The numerator is on top; the denominator is on the bottom.

$$\frac{1}{2} \quad \frac{\text{numerator}}{\text{denominator}}$$

Reducing Fractions

Every fraction can be expressed in many different ways:

$$\frac{1}{2} = \frac{2}{4} = \frac{3}{6} = \frac{4}{8} \dots \text{etc.}$$

Each of these fractions means the same thing. To reduce a fraction with large numbers, see if the numerator and the denominator share a number that divides evenly into both of them. For example, both the numerator and the denominator of $\frac{2}{4}$ can be divided by 2, which reduces the fraction to $\frac{1}{2}$. With larger fractions, it may save time to find the largest number that will divide into both numbers, but this isn't crucial. Whatever number you think of first will be just fine. Let's take the fraction $\frac{6}{8}$. Is there a common factor? Yes, 2 divides evenly into both 6 and 8.

$$\frac{6}{8} = \frac{\cancel{2} \times 3}{\cancel{2} \times 4} = \frac{3}{4}$$

Get used to reducing all fractions (if they can be reduced) before you do any work with them. It saves a lot of time and prevents errors that crop up when you try to work with big numbers.

REDUCING FRACTIONS DRILL

(Answers and explanations can be found in Part VIII.)

1. $\dfrac{4}{6}$

2. $\dfrac{9}{12}$

3. $\dfrac{10}{20}$

4. $\dfrac{10}{8}$

5. $\dfrac{4}{9}$

How to Grid In Fractions

On the grid below, you'll notice three slash-marks on the second row down from the top. Any of these can be used to create a fraction. So, for example, the fraction $\dfrac{2}{7}$ could be written as:

Comparing Fractions

Sometimes a problem will involve deciding which of two fractions is bigger.

Which is bigger, $\frac{2}{5}$ or $\frac{4}{5}$? Think of these as parts of a pie. Which is bigger, two parts out of five, or four parts out of five? The fraction $\frac{4}{5}$ is clearly bigger. In this case, it was easy to tell because they both had the same whole, the same denominator.

It's more complicated when the fractions have different denominators. Which is bigger, $\frac{2}{3}$ or $\frac{3}{7}$? To decide, we need to find a common whole, or denominator. You can change the denominator of a fraction by multiplying it by another number. To keep the entire fraction the same, however, you must also multiply the numerator by the same number.

Let's change the denominator of $\frac{2}{3}$ into the number 21. To get 3 to equal 21, we have to multiply it by 7. Of course, anything you do to the denominator, you have to do to the numerator, so we also have to multiply the numerator by 7.

$$\frac{2 \times 7}{3 \times 7} = \frac{14}{21}$$

The fraction $\frac{14}{21}$ still has the same value as $\frac{2}{3}$ (it would reduce to $\frac{2}{3}$) because we multiplied the fraction by $\frac{7}{7}$, or one.

Let's change the denominator of $\frac{3}{7}$ into 21 as well.

$$\frac{3 \times 3}{7 \times 3} = \frac{9}{21}$$

The fraction $\frac{9}{21}$ still has the same value as $\frac{3}{7}$ (it would reduce to $\frac{3}{7}$) because we multiplied the fraction by $\frac{3}{3}$, or one.

Now we can compare the two fractions. Which is bigger, $\frac{14}{21}$ or $\frac{9}{21}$? Clearly $\frac{14}{21}$ (or $\frac{2}{3}$) is bigger than $\frac{9}{21}$ (or $\frac{3}{7}$). Why did we decide on 21 as our common denominator? The easiest way to get a common denominator is to multiply the denominators of the two fractions you wish to compare: $7 \times 3 = 21$.

Let's do it again. Which is bigger, $\frac{2}{3}$ or $\frac{3}{5}$?

This time, the easiest common denominator is 15.

$$\frac{2}{3} \qquad\qquad \frac{3}{5}$$

$$\frac{2}{3} \times \frac{5}{5} = \frac{10}{15} \qquad \frac{3}{5} \times \frac{3}{3} = \frac{9}{15}$$

So $\frac{2}{3}$ is bigger than $\frac{3}{5}$.

Using Your Calculator on Fraction Problems

We have found that a calculator is only of limited use on fraction problems. It can make comparing fractions very easy: Simply divide the numerator by the denominator of each fraction and pick the biggest number. But especially in multiple-choice questions—where the answers are in fraction form as well—it often takes longer to solve than doing it on paper. This is particularly true once you learn a great new time-saving technique we call "the Bowtie."

The Bowtie

Here is how to use the Bowtie. Let's compare the last two fractions again. First, we get the common denominator by multiplying the two denominators together:

$$\frac{2}{3} \longrightarrow \frac{3}{5} = \frac{}{15}$$

Fraction Quiz

Q: Which is bigger,

$\frac{8}{9}$ or $\frac{7}{8}$?

Answer on page 410

Then, we get the new numerators by multiplying using the bowtie-shaped pattern shown below:

$$\text{⑩}\frac{2}{3}\times\frac{3}{5}\text{⑨} = \frac{\quad}{15}$$

Finally, compare the fractions. Once again, we see that $\frac{10}{15}$ (or $\frac{2}{3}$) is bigger than $\frac{9}{15}$ (or $\frac{3}{5}$).

Adding and Subtracting Fractions

Now that we've reviewed finding a common denominator, adding and subtracting fractions is simple. Let's use the Bowtie to add $\frac{2}{5}$ and $\frac{1}{4}$.

$$\text{⑧}\frac{2}{5}\times\frac{1}{4}\text{⑤} = \frac{8+5}{20} = \frac{13}{20}$$

Let's use the Bowtie to subtract $\frac{2}{3}$ from $\frac{5}{6}$.

$$\text{⑮}\frac{5}{6}\times\frac{2}{3}\text{⑫} = \frac{15-12}{18} = \frac{3}{18} = \frac{1}{6}$$

ADDING AND SUBTRACTING FRACTIONS DRILL

(Answers and explanations can be found in Part VIII.)

1. Which is bigger, $\dfrac{4}{5}$ or $\dfrac{4}{7}$?

2. $\dfrac{4}{5} + \dfrac{4}{7} = ?$

3. $\dfrac{2}{3} - \dfrac{2}{9} = ?$

4. $\dfrac{1}{3} + \dfrac{1}{6} + \dfrac{1}{18} = ?$

5. $\dfrac{5}{15} - \dfrac{1}{3} = ?$

Multiplying Fractions

To multiply fractions, line them up and multiply straight across.

$$\frac{5}{6} \times \frac{4}{5} = \frac{20}{30} = \frac{2}{3}$$

Was there anything we could have canceled or reduced *before* we multiplied? You betcha. We could cancel the 5 on top and the 5 on the bottom. What's left is $\dfrac{4}{6}$, which reduces to $\dfrac{2}{3}$.

Sometimes people think they can cancel or reduce in the same fashion *across an equal sign*. For example:

$$\frac{\cancel{5}x}{6} = \frac{4}{\cancel{5}} \quad \text{No!}$$

You *cannot* cancel the 5's in this case or reduce the $\dfrac{4}{6}$. When there is an equal sign, you have to cross-multiply, which yields $25x = 24$, so x in this case would equal $\dfrac{24}{25}$.

Dividing Fractions

To divide one fraction by another, just invert the second fraction and multiply.

$$\frac{2}{3} \div \frac{3}{4} \text{ is the same thing as } \frac{2}{3} \times \frac{4}{3} = \frac{8}{9}.$$

You may see this same operation written like this:

$$\frac{\dfrac{2}{3}}{\dfrac{3}{4}}$$

Again, just invert and multiply. Try the next example.

$$\frac{6}{\dfrac{2}{3}}$$

Think of 6 as $\dfrac{6}{1}$, and so we do the same thing.

$$\frac{6}{1} \times \frac{3}{2} = \frac{18}{2} = 9$$

Converting to Fractions

A normal number, such as 8, can always be expressed as a fraction by making that number the numerator and one the denominator: $8 = \dfrac{8}{1}$.

Sometimes the GED gives you numbers that are mixtures of normal numbers and fractions, for example, $3\dfrac{1}{2}$. These numbers are called compound fractions. It is often easier to work with these numbers by converting them completely into fractions. Here's how you do it: Because the fraction is expressed in halves, let's convert the normal number into halves as well: $3 = \dfrac{6}{2}$. Now just add the $\dfrac{1}{2}$ to the $\dfrac{6}{2}$. You get $\dfrac{7}{2}$.

MULTIPLYING, DIVIDING, AND CONVERTING FRACTIONS DRILL

(Answers and explanations can be found in Part VIII.)

1. $\dfrac{4}{5} \times \dfrac{3}{4} =$

2. $\dfrac{9}{10} \div \dfrac{3}{10} =$

3. $\dfrac{\frac{2}{9}}{\frac{12}{10}} =$

4. $\dfrac{2}{3} \times \dfrac{3}{4} \times \dfrac{4}{5} =$

5. $1\dfrac{1}{3} \times \dfrac{3}{8} =$

Now let's try some fraction problems in the GED format:

If $\dfrac{1}{2}$ of a group of students say their favorite leisure activity is swimming, and $\dfrac{1}{3}$ of the group say their favorite leisure activity is tennis, what fraction of the group prefer neither swimming nor tennis?

(1) $\dfrac{1}{8}$

(2) $\dfrac{1}{6}$

(3) $\dfrac{1}{2}$

(4) $\dfrac{5}{6}$

(5) $\dfrac{11}{12}$

Here's How to Crack It

Test takers are often intimidated by word problems, but you should realize that beneath all those words there lies a simple math problem.

Before you even read it, there should be one thing you notice right away: There are fractions in the problem. That can only mean one thing. This is a fraction problem.

On the GED, the only things you are ever asked to do with fractions is add them, subtract them, multiply them, divide them, or compare them—and you've just learned how to do all those things, if you didn't know them already.

Let's read the problem. Half of the students like swimming. One-third like playing tennis. Basically, the question is, who's left? After we take away the students who like swimming and tennis, what fraction of the students remains?

Before you do any work at all, let's see if we can *ballpark* a little. If we add $\frac{1}{2}$ and $\frac{1}{3}$ together, that's quite a lot. There can't be too much of the whole left over. So do any of the answer choices strike you as unlikely? Choices (4) and (5) are clearly out of the ballpark. Let's eliminate both of them and now actually solve the problem.

First, let's use the Bowtie to add up the parts of the whole that we know about.

$$\frac{1}{2} \diagtimes \frac{1}{3} = \frac{3+2}{6} = \frac{5}{6}$$

So $\frac{5}{6}$ of the students like either swimming or tennis. Now the big question: What part of the whole remains? That's right, the answer is $\frac{1}{6}$, and the correct answer is choice (2). Note that choice (4), $\frac{5}{6}$, was a *partial* answer. It was there for people who were in a hurry and thought they were done when they finished adding $\frac{1}{2}$ and $\frac{1}{3}$. However, if you read the question carefully and ballparked this problem first, there was no way you were going to fall for that trap. You already knew it was a crazy answer.

Here's another example:

It takes $1\frac{1}{4}$ hours for a factory worker to assemble one television set. How many television sets can be assembled in $17\frac{1}{2}$ hours?

(1)   4

(2)   7

(3)   10

(4)   12

(5)   14

Here's How to Crack It

Again, at first glance, you may feel intimidated by all the words in this problem, but don't let it fool you. This one's easy.

First, let's *ballpark* a little. Each set takes a bit more than one hour. There are a bit more than 17 hours total. Roughly speaking, how many sets do you think could be produced in 17 hours? Could the answer be as little as 4? No way. Eliminate choice (1). Could the answer be as little as 7 or 10? These answers still seem too small. Probably the correct answer is either choice (4) or choice (5).

If this was as far as you could get, you are already down to a fifty-fifty guess, and that's very good.

But let's see if we can actually solve the problem exactly. As we said earlier, whenever you see compound fractions, you probably should change them into normal fractions before you do any calculations.

$$1\frac{1}{4} = \frac{4}{4} + \frac{1}{4} = \frac{5}{4}$$

$$17\frac{1}{2} = \frac{34}{2} + \frac{1}{2} = \frac{35}{2}$$

It takes $\frac{5}{4}$ of an hour to make one TV. How many sets can you make in $\frac{35}{2}$ hours? We want to know how many $\frac{5}{4}$s go into $\frac{35}{2}$, and that just means division.

$$\frac{35}{2} \div \frac{5}{4} = \frac{35}{2} \times \frac{4}{5}$$

Let's do some canceling.

$$\frac{\cancel{35}}{2} \times \frac{4}{\cancel{5}} = \frac{7}{\cancel{2}} \times \frac{\cancel{4}}{1} = \frac{7}{1} \times \frac{2}{1} = 14$$

The correct answer is 14, choice (5).

FRACTION WORD PROBLEM DRILL
(Answers and explanations can be found in Part VIII.)

1. In the town of Arkville, a total of 80 people came in to be tested for Lyme disease. Half of them were found to have the disease. Of those who did not have the disease when first tested, one quarter later developed it. What fraction of the original 80 people got Lyme disease?

    (1) $\frac{1}{4}$

    (2) $\frac{1}{2}$

    (3) $\frac{5}{8}$

    (4) $\frac{3}{4}$

    (5) $\frac{7}{8}$

2. A pie company baked 100 pies in July. In August, the company increased production by $\frac{1}{10}$. If, in September, the pie company again increased production by $\frac{1}{10}$, how many pies did the company bake in September?

(1) 102

(2) 110

(3) 112

(4) 120

(5) 121

3. According to a company survey, $\frac{1}{3}$ of the workers take public transportation to get to work, $\frac{2}{5}$ drive cars to work, and the remainder walk to work. What fraction of the workers walk to work?

(1) $\frac{1}{5}$

(2) $\frac{4}{15}$

(3) $\frac{1}{3}$

(4) $\frac{1}{2}$

(5) $\frac{2}{3}$

Decimals

Fractions can also be expressed as decimals and vice versa. You probably know the decimal equivalent of certain fractions by heart (for example, $\frac{1}{2} = 0.5$), but you may not know how to convert a fraction into a decimal.

As we said earlier, one way to think of a fraction is just as a division problem.

$$\frac{1}{2} = 1 \div 2 = 2\overline{)1.0}^{.5}$$

$$\frac{3}{4} = 3 \div 4 = 4\overline{)3.00}^{.75}$$

You can also convert any decimal into a fraction. The first digit to the right of the decimal is the tenths' place. The second decimal is the hundredths' place. For example:

$$0.5 = \frac{5}{10} = \frac{1}{2}$$

$$0.75 = \frac{75}{100} = \frac{3}{4}$$

Adding and Subtracting Decimals

Calculating with decimals, unlike calculating with fractions, is almost always faster on the calculator. However, because you won't have the calculator during the second half of the test, it makes sense to practice these both ways. To add or subtract decimals, all you have to do is line up the decimal places and then add or subtract, just as you would any two normal numbers.

$$
\begin{array}{r} 2.5 \\ + 9.3 \\ \hline 11.8 \end{array}
\qquad
\begin{array}{r} 10.3 \\ - 6.4 \\ \hline 3.9 \end{array}
\qquad
\begin{array}{r} 1.423 \\ + 2.620 \\ \hline 4.043 \end{array}
\qquad
\begin{array}{r} 3.92 \\ + 2.61 \\ \hline 6.53 \end{array}
$$

If you're adding or subtracting one number that has fewer digits than another, it helps to add zeros to fill out the decimal places. For example, to subtract 3.26 from 8.4, adding a zero to 8.4 makes the problem easier to see:

$$
\begin{array}{r} 8.40 \\ - 3.26 \\ \hline 5.14 \end{array}
$$

Multiplying Decimals

The best way to multiply decimals is to ignore the decimal points entirely until after you've done the multiplication. For example, let's multiply 4.3 by 0.5. We'll start by multiplying 43 times 5:

$$
\begin{array}{r}
43 \\
\times\ 5 \\
\hline
215
\end{array}
$$

Now count the total number of digits to the right of the decimal points in the two original numbers you were multiplying. In this case, there were a total of two digits to the right of the decimal points. Therefore, this is how many digits there should be to the right of the decimal point in your final product. The answer is 2.15. Let's do another.

$$
\begin{array}{r}
5.6 \\
\times 0.03 \\
\hline
\end{array}
\qquad
\begin{array}{r}
56 \\
\times 0.3 \\
\hline
168
\end{array}
$$

There are a total of three digits to the right of the decimal points in the original numbers, so after multiplying, we place the decimal so that there are three digits to the right in the answer as well. The answer in this case is 0.168.

Dividing Decimals

The best way to divide decimals is first to convert the number you are dividing *by* (in math terminology, the **divisor**) into a whole number. You do this simply by moving the decimal point as many places as necessary. This works as long as you remember to move the decimal point in the number that you are *dividing* (in math terminology, the **dividend**) the same number of spaces.

For example, to divide 12 by 0.6, set it up the way you would an ordinary division problem:

$$
0.6\overline{)12}
$$

To make .6 (the divisor) a whole number, you simply move the decimal point over one place to the right. You must also move the decimal one place to the right in the dividend. Now the operation looks like this:

$$6\overline{)120} \qquad 6\overline{)\overset{20}{120}}$$

DECIMALS DRILL

Do these problems first on your own. Then, on a separate piece of paper, do them again using your calculator.

(Answers and explanations can be found in Part VIII.)

1. $1.34 + 5.72 =$

2. $7.6 - 3.24 =$

3. $3.4 \times 2.41 =$

4. $6.4 \div 0.002 =$

5. $32 \div 0.8 =$

Percents

Percents are a popular type of question on the GED. Count on seeing up to eight percentage problems on your test. This is good news because without too much trouble, you can learn to get all eight right.

A percent is really just a fraction whose denominator happens to be 100.

$$25\% = \frac{25}{100} \qquad 50\% = \frac{50}{100} \qquad 32\% = \frac{32}{100}$$

Like any fraction, a percentage can be converted to a decimal and vice versa. Percentage/decimal conversion is even easier than converting a normal fraction because both percentages and decimals are almost invariably *already* being expressed in hundredths.

$$25\% = \frac{25}{100} = 0.25 \qquad 0.50 = \frac{50}{100} = 50\%$$

To convert a regular fraction into a percent, you can first convert the fraction to a decimal, which, as we just said, is very close to a percentage already. Here are a few examples:

$$\frac{2}{5} = 5\overline{)2.0} \,\, ^{0.4} = 0.4 = 0.40 = 40\%$$

$$\frac{12}{20} = 20\overline{)12.0} \,\, ^{0.6} = 0.6 = 0.60 = 60\%$$

$$\frac{2}{3} = 3\overline{)2.000} \,\, ^{0.666} = 0.666666\ldots = 66\frac{2}{3}\%$$
$$\begin{array}{r} 18 \\ \hline 20 \\ 18 \\ \hline 20 \end{array}$$

In that last example, you'll notice that no matter how many places you carry that division to, you will always get a remainder. The fraction $\frac{2}{3}$ produces a decimal that goes on forever. However, if we are going to round to the nearest percent, then it's 67%.

There are some fractions, decimals, and percentages that come up so often that it's worth memorizing them.

Fraction	Decimal	Percent
$\frac{1}{5}$	= 0.2	= 20%
$\frac{1}{4}$	= 0.25	= 25%
$\frac{1}{3}$	= 0.333...	= $33\frac{1}{3}$ %
$\frac{1}{2}$	= 0.5	= 50%
$\frac{2}{3}$	= 0.666...	= $66\frac{2}{3}$ %

Most percent problems on the GED ask you to find a percentage of a larger number. For example:

> If 10% of the 3,400 people who enter a sweepstakes won a prize, how many people did <u>not</u> win a prize?
>
> (1)   34
>
> (2)   68
>
> (3)   340
>
> (4) 3,060
>
> (5) 3,366

We'll come back to this problem in a minute. But first, we want to show you…

Old-Fashioned Percents

Here's the way you probably learned percents: A percentage is just a fraction with 100 in the denominator, and the word *of* always means *multiply* in math. So when the GED asks you to find 20 percent of 400, it can be written this way:

$$\frac{20}{100} \times \frac{400}{1} = ?$$

Now you could do some canceling.

$$\frac{20}{\cancel{100}_{1}} \times \frac{\cancel{400}^{4}}{1} = 80$$

While this method will get you the right answer, it can be a long and tedious process when the numbers don't work out as nicely as the ones we chose for this example. But don't worry because you are about to learn a more efficient way to approach these problems.

The Princeton Review Percents

We have a fast, foolproof method for finding percents. This method involves almost no written calculation at all. You can thank us later.

To find 20 percent of a number, multiply the number by 0.20. To find 35 percent of a number, multiply the number by 0.35. To find 5 percent of a number, multiply the number by 0.05.

Ballparking Percent Quiz
Q: Roughly speaking, what's 10 percent of 305?

Answer on page 424

To find 10 percent of any number, all you have to do is move the decimal point of that number over one place to the left.

> 10% of 4 = 0.4
> 10% of 30 = 3
> 10% of 520 = 52
> 10% of 21 = 2.1

Now, here's the great part. Ten percent of 30 = 3, right? So how much is 20% of 30? That's easy. It's twice as much as 10 percent, or 6. Here are a few examples:

> What is 20% of 520?
> 10% of 520 = 52, so 20% of 520 = 2 × 52 = 104.

> What is 20% of 4?
> 10% of 4 = .4, so 20% of 4 = 2 × 0.4 = 0.8.

> What is 30% of 600?
> 10% of 600 = 60, so 30% of 600 = 3 × 60 = 180.

> What is 40% of 500?
> 10% of 500 = 50, so 40% of 500 = 4 × 50 = 200.

This takes care of a lot of GED problems right here, but there are some GED problems that will ask you to find amounts like 15 percent or 27 percent. How do you do this?

To find 1 percent of any number, all you have to do is move the decimal point of that number over *two* places to the left.

> 1% of 4 = 0.04
> 1% of 30 = 0.3
> 1% of 520 = 5.2
> 1% of 21 = 0.21

In just the same way that we found 20 percent by doubling 10 percent, we can now find 2 percent by doubling 1 percent.

> What is 2% of 500?
> 1% of 500 = 5, so 2% of 500 = 2 × 5 = 10.

> What is 3% of 60?
> 1% of 60 = 0.6, so 3% of 60 = 3 × 0.6 = 1.8.

Now, here's the *really* great part. We can combine these two techniques to find any percentage the folks who write the GED can invent.

Let's find 23% of 600.

Ballparking Percent Quiz

A: Roughly speaking, 10 percent of 305 is about 30.

Well, 10% of 600 = 60.
So 20% of 600 = 2 × 60 = 120.
And 1% of 600 = 6, so 3% of 600 = 18.

So what is 23% of 600?
20% of 600 = 120
3% of 600 = 18
120 + 18 = 138

Most students find that with a little practice they can do this process in their heads or with minimal scratch work. Which is faster: using this method or using a calculator? Why don't you try it both ways on the following drill?

PERCENTAGES DRILL
Do these problems on your own. Then, on another piece of paper, do them again using your calculator.

(Answers and explanations can be found in Part VIII.)

1.   Find 10% of 80.

2.   Find 20% of 30.

3.   Find 40% of 700.

4.   Find 1% of 70.

5.   Find 6% of 200.

6.   Find 23% of 500.

7.   Find 15% of 200.

8.   What is 35% of 60?

9.   What is 50% of 40?

10. What is 25% of 80?

(Hint: On the last two problems, remember that 50% = $\frac{1}{2}$ and 25% = $\frac{1}{4}$.)

Outta Here!
In the following question, find the answers that are out of the ballpark.

Q: Barry Bonds hits three home runs of lengths 375 feet, 380 feet, and 400 feet. What was the average length of his home runs?

(1) 385 feet
(2) 405 feet
(3) 420 feet
(4) 1,155 feet

Answer on page 426

Percent Word Problems

Now, let's go back to the first percentage problem we showed you.

——————————◯——————————

If 10% of the 3,400 people who enter a sweepstakes won a prize, how many people did <u>not</u> win a prize?

(1)   34

(2)   68

(3)   340

(4) 3,060

(5) 3,366

Here's How to Crack It

The first thing we see is "10% of 3,400." At this point, figuring out 10 percent of anything should be second nature to you. Of course, 10 percent of 3,400 is 340. But are we done?

Reread the last line of the question. It asks us how many people did *not* win a prize. We need to take one more step. The total number of people who entered the sweepstakes was 3,400. We now know that 340 of them won a prize. So how many people didn't? All we have to do is subtract the winners from the entire group. What we're left with is the number of losers: 3,400 − 340 = 3,060. The correct answer is choice (4).

——————————◯——————————

If you were really thinking, you could have saved yourself a step by realizing that if 10 percent won, then 90 percent didn't. You could simply have multiplied 340 (10 percent) by 9 to get 3,060 in one step.

Could we have ballparked this problem? Sure. A careful reading of the question would have told us that the number of people we were looking for was the number who did not win. Because only 10 percent won, we were looking for a large percentage of the people who entered. Which answers didn't make sense? Choices (1) and (2) were ridiculously small. Choice (3) was a partial answer for those who forgot that they were looking for the losers, not the winners. It was easy to pick choice (3) from a math standpoint, but impossible to pick if you were ballparking.

Here's another example:

Outta Here!

A: Choice (4), 1,155, is WAY out of the ballpark—it's the sum of all three numbers in the question. So are choices (2) and (3) because the average length can't be bigger than any of the numbers being averaged. The correct answer is choice (1).

A DVD player is on sale for 20% off its normal price of $400. If the sales tax is 5%, what is the cost of the DVD player?

(1) $300
(2) $320
(3) $336
(4) $350
(5) $420

Here's How to Crack It

This question requires two separate operations. First, let's find the sale price of the DVD player.

What is 20% of 400?

10% of 400 = 40
20% of 400 = 2 × 40 = 80

So if the DVD player has been marked down by $80, the sale price is $320. Notice that in case you were in too much of a hurry and thought you were already done, $320 was included among the answer choices as a partial answer.

Now let's find the sales tax.

What is 5% of $320?

10% of 320 = 32

$5\% \text{ of } 320 = \frac{1}{2} \times 32 = 16$

So what's the final price?

$$
\begin{array}{r}
\$320 \\
+ \ \$16 \\
\hline
\$336
\end{array}
$$

The correct answer is choice (3).

Backward Percents

Sometimes the test writers will ask you a percentage problem backward.

If a mailing of 15,000 letters resulted in 3,000 responses, what was the percentage of responses to the mailing?

(1)   10%

(2)   20%

(3)   30%

(4)   40%

(5)   50%

Here's How to Crack It

Your old teacher from high school, a gleam in her eye, would be telling you to set up an equation—but there's a much simpler way. Let's use POE to get rid of wrong answers.

Start with choice (5), 50%. Let's say, just for a moment, that the correct answer is, in fact, 50 percent. This would mean that 50 percent of the 15,000 letters is 3,000. Does that sound right? No way! In fact, 50 percent of 15,000 is half—7,500—which is a lot more than the 3,000 they are supposed to have received.

Let's try another answer. How about choice (3), 30%? What is 30 percent of 15,000? Ten percent of 15,000 is 1,500, so 30 percent of 15,000 = 3 × 1,500 = 4,500. This is still too big. We want a response of 3,000.

Let's try choice (2), 20%. What is 20 percent of 15,000? Ten percent is 1,500, so 20 percent of 15,000 is 2 × 1,500 = 3,000. Bingo! This is the correct answer.

PERCENT WORD PROBLEMS DRILL

(Answers and explanations can be found in Part VIII.)

1. A one-year certificate of deposit pays 8% in interest. If an investor deposited $650 for one year, how much interest did the investor receive?

   (1) $50.75

   (2) $52.00

   (3) $53.00

   (4) $95.50

   (5) $520.00

2. Janice sells household products door to door. If she must pay her supplier 60% of the money that she takes in, how much would she keep for herself if she took in $1,200?

   (1) $720.00

   (2) $560.50

   (3) $480.00

   (4) $48.00

   (5) Not enough information is given.

3. A student furnishing his first apartment goes shopping and buys a bed for $120, a couch for $300, and a lamp for $70. If the sales tax is 7%, how much did the student pay in total for the furniture?

4. Carmen owns a computer store and had $9,000 in sales this May. The year before, she had $8,500 in sales in May. If Carmen had a profit of $5,400 this May, what percent of her sales were profits?

   (1)   30%

   (2)   60%

   (3)   65%

   (4)   80%

   (5)   95%

Ratios and Proportions

As we said earlier, a fraction can be expressed in many different forms. For example, $\frac{1}{2} = \frac{2}{4} = \frac{3}{6}$ ...etc. A ratio or proportion problem merely asks you to express a particular fraction in a slightly different form. Here's an example:

A map uses a scale in which 1 inch = 200 miles. If the distance between two cities measures 5 inches on the map, how many miles separate the two cities?

(1)   1,000

(2)   800

(3)   600

(4)   400

(5)   200

Here's How to Crack It

Let's talk about this problem in terms of inches per mile, which can be expressed as follows:

$$\frac{1 \text{ inch}}{200 \text{ miles}}$$

This is actually a kind of fraction, complete with a numerator and a denominator. And this fraction, like all fractions, can be expressed in an infinite number of different equivalent fractions. For example, it could equal a fraction with a numerator of 5:

$$\frac{1 \text{ inch}}{200 \text{ miles}} = \frac{5 \text{ inches}}{?}$$

We have just set up a proportion. One inch represents 200 miles, so five inches represents...we don't know yet. Instead of "?" let's put an x in its place, to represent the number we don't know yet. To find out how many miles are represented by five inches, we cross-multiply the denominator of the left-hand fraction with the numerator of the right, and then the denominator of the right-hand fraction with the numerator of the left:

$$\frac{1 \text{ inch}}{200 \text{ miles}} \times \frac{5 \text{ inches}}{x \text{ miles}} \qquad 1{,}000 = 1x$$

And $x = 1{,}000$ miles. To check this, you can stick this number into the proportion you just wrote:

$$\frac{1 \text{ inch}}{200 \text{ miles}} = \frac{5 \text{ inches}}{1{,}000 \text{ miles}}$$

Does $\dfrac{5}{1{,}000}$ reduce to $\dfrac{1}{200}$? You bet. The correct answer is choice (1).

———————◯———————

Let's do another:

———————◯———————

If Jane can finish her work assignment in half an hour, what part of it can she finish in 20 minutes?

(1) $\dfrac{1}{6}$

(2) $\dfrac{1}{4}$

(3) $\dfrac{1}{3}$

(4) $\dfrac{2}{3}$

(5) $\dfrac{3}{4}$

Here's How to Crack It

First of all, did you notice that this is the same type of problem we just did above? Jane can do one job in 30 minutes, so how much can she do in 20 minutes? To solve this, we must set up a proportion.

To make our job easier, we should use the same time measurement throughout the problem, so instead of talking about half an hour, let's permanently convert that to 30 minutes. Now, on to the proportion.

$$\frac{1 \text{ job}}{30 \text{ minutes}} = \frac{x \text{ (part of the job)}}{20 \text{ minutes}}$$

As we did before, let's cross-multiply.

$$\frac{1 \text{ job}}{30 \text{ minutes}} = \frac{x \text{ (part of the job)}}{20 \text{ minutes}} \qquad 30x = 20 \qquad x = \frac{20}{30} \text{ or } \frac{2}{3}$$

The correct answer is choice (4).

Could we have done some ballparking here? Of course! If the whole job takes 30 minutes, obviously 20 minutes is time to do more than half the job. Choices (1), (2), and (3) are all less than half and can be eliminated right away. In fact, you might even have noticed that 20 minutes out of 30 minutes was $\frac{2}{3}$ without even setting up the proportion. But it's always a good idea to do the work, just to make sure.

RATIOS AND PROPORTIONS DRILL
(Answers and explanations can be found in Part VIII.)

1. If a shrub 5 feet tall casts a 2-foot shadow, how tall is a tree standing next to the shrub that casts a 10-foot shadow at the same moment?

    (1)　50 feet

    (2)　25 feet

    (3)　20 feet

    (4)　10 feet

    (5)　　4 feet

2. Two songwriting collaborators decide that they will share profits in a song in a ratio of 3 parts for the lyric writer to 2 parts for the music writer. If the music writer gets $2,500, how much does the lyric writer receive?

    (1)　$2,500

    (2)　$3,750

    (3)　$7,500

    (4)　$10,000

    (5)　Not enough information is given.

3. A particular lawn requires 6 bags of fertilizer. A lawn next door requires 4 bags of fertilizer. How big is the lawn next door?

    (1)　20 square feet

    (2)　25 square feet

    (3)　37 square feet

    (4)　50 square feet

    (5)　Not enough information is given.

Putting It All Together

Now that you've seen the basics of arithmetic one topic at a time, we're going to give you a drill that mixes up all the different problems we've discussed so far. Often, the toughest part of the GED Math test is recognizing what kind of problem you are facing.

"Just Tell Me, Do I Have to Multiply or Divide?"

While there aren't that many math topics on the GED, it isn't always easy to recognize which kind of question you're dealing with right on cue. However, the process of spotting that *this* problem is a proportion problem while *that* one is a fraction problem is a key element to doing well on GED Math. It is almost as important as solving the problem itself. And unfortunately, while you're taking the test, there will be no one to give you a hint about what to do—so you're going to have to learn to let the problem itself give you the hint.

As we said at the beginning of this chapter, the last line of a question is usually the key to understanding the entire question. In addition, look for "signature" elements—if a problem contains fractions, it is almost certainly a fraction problem; if it contains percents, it is probably a percent problem.

"Standardized" Means Predictable

The nice thing about any standardized test is that each one is very similar to the one before. This means that after you have gone through this book, done our diagnostic tests, and perhaps a few of the official GED practice tests, you will have seen every type of problem and topic that they could possibly throw at you at least three or four times each. Each GED tests percents exactly the same way every time. Number line problems employ the same ideas year after year.

This means that it's important for you to remember the problems you've already done. Math questions that you do in this book should be added to a mental file. Then, when a problem just like one of them surfaces on the real GED, instead of staring at it perplexedly, you'll be saying, "Ah, what an interesting variation on that decimal problem I studied last week."

BASIC ARITHMETIC DRILL

(Answers and explanations can be found in Part VIII.)

1. Which of the following has the same value as $\frac{3}{5}$?

    (1) 3%

    (2) 6%

    (3) 0.6

    (4) $\frac{.9}{10}$

    (5) $\frac{5}{3}$

2. Ralph goes out to lunch and receives a bill for $23.00. What is the total amount he pays if he includes a 20% tip?

    (1) $4.60

    (2) $21.70

    (3) $25.30

    (4) $27.60

    (5) $43.00

3. If a boat takes 2 hours to travel 30 miles, how long will it take to travel 72 miles?

    (1) 1.7 hours

    (2) 4.0 hours

    (3) 4.8 hours

    (4) 6.0 hours

    (5) 7.2 hours

4. Susan did $\frac{1}{4}$ of her homework on Tuesday and $\frac{1}{5}$ of her homework on Wednesday. What fraction of her homework remains to be done?

    (1) $\frac{9}{20}$

    (2) $\frac{11}{20}$

    (3) $\frac{23}{40}$

    (4) $\frac{2}{3}$

    (5) $\frac{19}{20}$

5. In the figure above, point B represents the number 0. If the midpoint of segment AB is at point −2 on the number line and the midpoint of BC is at point 2 on the number line, then what is the length of AB?

6. The average price of a new home in an urban community is $80,675. What is that price to the nearest hundred?

   (1) $79,000
   (2) $80,600
   (3) $80,670
   (4) $80,700
   (5) $81,000

7. If $5R - 5S = 35$, then what is the value of $R - S$?

   (1) 3
   (2) 5
   (3) 6
   (4) 7
   (5) Not enough information is given.

8. $5(2 - 4 + 1) + \frac{2}{3}(7 - 1) = ?$

   (1) −5
   (2) −1
   (3) 0
   (4) 4
   (5) 5

9. If 30 people in a room of 70 people are smokers, approximately what percent of the people in the room are smokers?

   (1) 3%
   (2) 10%
   (3) 20%
   (4) 33%
   (5) 43%

10. A bankrupt company agrees to pay its creditors 80% of what they are actually owed. If the company pays $9,600, what did they originally owe?

    (1) $8,000
    (2) $9,500
    (3) $10,500
    (4) $11,000
    (5) $12,000

Chapter 24
Applied Arithmetic

In this chapter, we go over more arithmetic problems involving setup problems, averages, rate problems, charts and graphs, exponents, radicals, scientific notation, and probability.

Now we're going to show you some additional arithmetic concepts that build on the ideas you've already learned in the last chapter. As in that chapter, we'll introduce a concept first, then give you some GED-like examples followed by a short drill. At the end of the chapter, you'll find a big drill that mixes and matches all the different concepts. These are the subjects we'll cover:

- Setup problems
- Averages (mean and median)
- Rate problems
- Charts and graphs
- Exponents and square roots
- Scientific notation
- Probability

Setup Problems

Wouldn't it be interesting if a test question asked you to do the entire setup of a problem, but didn't want you to actually solve it? In fact, if you go on to college, you will find that this is often exactly what college math tests are like. College professors are much more interested in seeing *how you think* than how careful you are with your addition and subtraction.

Well, score one for the GED because each GED exam has six to eight problems that do *not* require you to identify the correct answer but instead ask you to identify the correct setup. Here's an example:

Jim started a business selling mattresses. He sold 12 standard mattresses and 7 deluxe mattresses last week. Which expression below represents how many dollars he took in last week if the standard mattress costs $100 and the deluxe costs $160?

(1)　12(100) + 7(100)

(2)　12(160) + 7(100)

(3)　12(100) + 7(160)

(4)　12(160) + 7(120)

(5)　19(100) + 7(100)

Here's How to Crack It

To find out the total price, we have to multiply the number of standard mattresses times the price of a standard mattress, and the number of deluxe mattresses times the price of a deluxe mattress. There were 12 standards at $100 each, so that's 12(100). There were seven deluxes at $160 each, so that's 7(160). Altogether that's 12(100) + 7(160). The correct answer is choice (3).

Take Your Time…

Try not to be in too much of a rush on setup problems. The answer choices are all close variations of one another, and it's easy to pick the wrong one if you're in a hurry. In addition, sometimes the GED test writers may not have written their equation in quite the same way that you did. For example, in this problem, you might have written *your* equation starting with the expensive mattresses— 7(160) + 12(100)— in which case, if you looked through the answer choices quickly, you might have thought *your* answer wasn't there. So be prepared to be flexible as you look at the answer choices on a setup problem. You may have to add the numbers in a different order or convert a fraction to a decimal.

…But Not Too Much Time

Some test takers actually *solve* setup problems; they find the correct answer (even though the problem does not require it) and then find the answer choice that adds up to the same number they calculated. We think this generally takes a little too much time. However, if there's one problem that you're really not sure of, you can check the equation you wrote by solving the problem and then making sure that the answer you chose agrees with the number you calculated.

Here's another setup problem, this time about percentages:

Mr. James goes into an investment with two partners. Together the three of them put a total of $30,000 into an investment that pays annual interest of 12%. At the end of the year, the three people share the interest evenly. How much did Mr. James receive in interest?

(1) $\dfrac{30,000 \times 12}{3}$

(2) $\dfrac{30,000 \times 0.12}{3}$

(3) $30,000 \times 12 \times 3$

(4) $\dfrac{30,000 \times 3}{12}$

(5) $\dfrac{30,000 \times 3}{0.12}$

Setup Quiz

Q: Which two setups below are identical?

(A) 40($1.25) + 25($0.90)

(B) 25($0.90) + 40($1.25)

(C) (40 + 25)($1.25 + $0.90)

Answer on page 442

Here's How to Crack It

Mr. James and his two partners share the interest evenly. If this were a normal problem, first we would find 12% of $30,000, and then we would figure out Mr. James's share. If you want to, you can do the problem this way—actually solve it and then figure out the numeric value of each of the answer choices, one by one, until you find the one that matches your solution. Unfortunately, as we said, this can take some time.

Rather than solving this problem, it may be better to set it up as if you were *going* to solve it using a traditional equation. When we first discussed percents in Chapter 23, we said that the word *of* always means *multiply*. If we want to find 12% of $30,000, we could write that in two ways:

$$\frac{12}{100} \times 30,000 \quad \text{or} \quad 0.12 \times 30,000$$

They both mean the same thing.

Whatever this number is—and remember, in this problem, we don't need to know what it is—it represents the entire amount of interest. The problem is asking for only James's share. Because all three investors share the interest evenly, we have to divide the entire amount by 3.

$$\frac{0.12 \times 30,000}{3}$$

The correct answer is choice (2).

SETUP DRILL
(Answers and explanations can be found in Part VIII.)

1. Sam works 8 hours per day, 6 days a week, delivering flowers. If he earns $5.50 per hour, how much does he make in 4 weeks?

    (1) $8 \times 6 \times 4 \times 5.50$
    (2) $8 \times 6 \times 5.50$
    (3) $(8 + 6)5.50 + 4(5.50)$
    (4) $[4(8) + 4(6)]\,5.50$
    (5) $5.50 \times 8 + 5.50 \times 4$

2. This year, the price of a particular model of car went up 4% from last year's price of $12,000. Which of the following represents the new price?

    (1) $0.04(\$12,000)$

    (2) $0.04(\$12,000) + 0.04$

    (3) $0.04(\$12,000) + \$12,000$

    (4) $\dfrac{\$12,000}{0.04} + \$12,000$

    (5) $0.96(\$12,000) + \$12,000$

3. Lola keeps the record of her store's petty cash fund. The fund began this month with a balance of $650. She paid out $430 and $22 for expenses and then added $250 from another account. Which of the following expressions represents the number of dollars left in the cash fund at the end of the month?

   (1)   250 + 650 + 430 + 22

   (2)   650 − 430 − 22 − 250

   (3)   650 + 430 + 22 − 250

   (4)   650 + 250 − 430 + 22

   (5)   650 − 430 − 22 + 250

Averages

"Mean" or "average" problems are very popular on the GED. In spite of its name, a mean problem is almost always pretty gentle and easy. To find the **mean** of several different numbers, first you add them up, and then you divide the sum of the numbers by the actual number of items that you added. For example, to find the average of 5, 10, and 15, you add

$$
\begin{array}{r}
5 \\
+10 \\
+15 \\
\hline
30
\end{array}
$$

and then, because there are three items being added, divide the sum of the numbers by three:

$$
3\overline{)30} = 10
$$

That's it. And in case you forget, the formula is always on the first page of the GED Math test. Let's try a couple of problems.

Missy played 4 Starmaster games at a video arcade. If her scores were 120, 125, 135, and 140, what was her mean (average) score?

(1)   120

(2)   128

(3)   130

(4)   135

(5)   140

Here's How to Crack It

As soon as you see the words *mean* and *average*, you know just what to do: Add the four numbers together, and divide by four.

$$
\begin{array}{r}
120 \\
125 \\
135 \\
+140 \\
\hline
520
\end{array}
\qquad
\begin{array}{r}
130 \\
4\overline{)520}
\end{array}
$$

The correct answer is choice (3).

Could we have ballparked here? Of course. The average of four numbers is going to be somewhere in the middle of the values of the four numbers. If you take an average of the numbers 140 plus three other smaller numbers, the answer must be less than 140. So eliminate choice (5). By the same token, if you take an average of the numbers 120 plus three other numbers that are larger than 120, the answer is going to be more than 120. So eliminate choice (1).

Give this one a try:

Jill shops once a week at a store. If the mean (average) amount that she spends per week is $27.20, how much did she spend in the past 8 weeks?

Here's How to Crack It

This problem is different from the first example in one important way: Instead of having to add up all the items to get the total amount and then divide the total to get our average, this time we already *have* the average. This time, what the problem is asking us for is the total amount.

Here's the way to find a mean average, written down in formula form:

$$\frac{\text{sum of all items}}{\text{number of items}} = \text{average}$$

Ballparking Averages
The average of a string of numbers has to be less than the biggest number and more than the smallest number.

Thus, there are three elements. But in every average problem, one of the elements is missing. In the first problem, we had the sum of all the items (520) and the number of items (4), which meant that the element that was missing was the average itself.

Let's put the information we have from the second problem into the same formula.

$$\frac{\text{sum of all items}}{8} = 27.20$$

This time, what's missing is the sum of all the items. How do we find it? By multiplying the number of elements (8) times the average (27.20). The correct answer is $217.60.

Now try this one:

A realtor hires a plumber to make x repairs. The plumber bills the realtor $1,450 in total. Which expression determines the average cost of each repair?

(1) $1{,}450x$

(2) $1{,}450 + x$

(3) $1{,}450 - x$

(4) $\dfrac{1{,}450}{x}$

(5) $\dfrac{x}{1{,}450}$

Here's How to Crack It

This problem is different from the first example in two ways. First, there is no actual number of repairs. Instead, that number is represented by a variable, x; second, in this problem we don't have to add up the individual elements (i.e., the cost of *each* of the individual repairs) because it has already been done for us.

In spite of these differences, this is still an average problem, and we can solve it using the same formula we used on the above.

$$\frac{\text{sum of all items}}{\text{number of items}} = \text{average}$$

Okay, let's start by adding the elements to get the sum of all the elements—oh, wait, the elements have *already* been added. The total cost of all the repairs is $1,450. All that's left to do is divide the total cost ($1,450) by the number of repair jobs—oh, wait, there is no precise number. Well, we do at least have a variable representing this number, so let's divide by the variable:

$$\frac{1,450}{x}$$

The correct answer is choice (4).

Median

The **median** of a bunch of numbers is the number right in the middle. For example, the median of 3, 16, and 17 would be 16. The median of 139, 234, 326, 327, and 328 would be 326.

The median is often not the same thing as the mean. Let's take the numbers 2, 3, and 10. The mean of these numbers is $\frac{2+3+10}{3}$, or 5, but the median is simply the middle number, or 3.

If you are asked to find the median of a set of numbers that is not in ascending order, first put the numbers in ascending order, and then take the middle number. For example, the median of 3, 7, and 6 would be 6.

What if there is no middle number? Take the following list of numbers:

$$4, 8, 10, 20$$

This time, two numbers are sharing the middle. In cases like this (where there are an even number of items), you take the mean of the two middle numbers. This time, the median is 9.

How do median problems look on the GED?

If there were 24 traffic summonses issued in September, 45 in October, and 39 in December, what was the median number of summonses issued over the three months?

(1)   36

(2)   39

(3)   45

(4)   47

(5)   108

Here's How to Crack It

First, put the numbers in ascending order: 24, 39, 45. Now, just take the middle number. The correct answer is choice (2).

MEAN AND MEDIAN DRILL
(Answers and explanations can be found in Part VIII.)

Do these problems on your own. Then, on another piece of paper, do them again using your calculator.

1.   A consumer group buys identical radios at 14 different stores. If the mean (average) price per radio is $23.40, how much did the consumer group spend for all the radios?

(1) $3,276.00

(2) $560.30

(3) $327.60

(4) $56.03

(5) $22.40

2. In a class of five students, what was the median score on a test if one student scored 86, two students scored 85, and two students scored 92?

    (1) 72

    (2) 84

    (3) 86

    (4) 88

    (5) 94

3. What is the average weekly business expense of a sewing supply shop during a three week period if $65.00, $73.23, and $35.77 were the weekly expense totals for the three weeks?

    (1) $56.43
    (2) $57.84
    (3) $58.00
    (4) $58.70
    (5) $60.24

Ice Cream Cones Sold at the Store "Cone Central" Over 5 Consecutive Days

Monday	Tuesday	Wednesday	Thursday	Friday
105	80	95	110	205

4. What is the mean (average) number of ice cream cones sold at the store "Cone Central" during the period shown in the graph above?

    (1) 95
    (2) 100
    (3) 114
    (4) 119
    (5) 123

Rate Problems

It's easy to spot rate problems: They're usually about cars, boats, or trains, often expressed in terms of miles per hour or kilometers per hour, and almost always use the word *travel*.

You may not think so, but you already know the formula to solve every rate problem. Don't believe us? Let's say you drive in a car for 2 hours at 50 miles per hour. How far have you traveled? That's right: 100 miles. Fifty miles per hour is the *rate* at which you traveled, 2 hours is the *time* it took you to travel, and 100 miles is the *distance* you traveled.

The formula looks like this:

$$\text{Rate} \times \text{Time} = \text{Distance}$$
$$50 \quad\quad 2 \quad\quad\quad 100$$

This formula can always be found on the first page of the GED Math test, but it is just as well to have it memorized—and besides, you already know it. Let's try two problems.

A train traveled at a speed of 120 kilometers per hour for $2\frac{1}{2}$ hours. How many kilometers did the train travel?

(1) 300

(2) 280

(3) 240

(4) 200

(5) 110

Here's How to Crack It

As soon as you see the words *train* and *travel,* you should immediately be writing down $R \times T = D$ on your scratch paper, even before you finish reading the problem. Now all you'll have to do is plug in the numbers they gave you:

$$R \times T = D$$

$$120 \times 2\frac{1}{2} = ?$$

Multiplying $120 \times 2\frac{1}{2}$, you get 300, which is answer choice (1).

Could we have ballparked this question? Sure. If the train is traveling at 120 kilometers per hour, then in one hour it must have traveled 120 kilometers. Choice (5) is less than 120, even though our train has been traveling for more than two hours. Eliminate choice (5). And by the same line of reasoning, because our train has been traveling for more than two hours, it must have traveled more than 240 kilometers. Eliminate choices (3) and (4) as well.

Here's another example:

Rate Problem Quiz

Q: How do you spot a
$R \times T = D$ problem?

Answer on page 452

Flying at 400 miles per hour, approximately how long will it take for a plane to travel between two cities that are 2,600 miles apart?

(1) between 3 and 4 hours

(2) between 4 and 5 hours

(3) between 5 and 6 hours

(4) between 6 and 7 hours

(5) between 7 and 8 hours

Here's How to Crack It

Again, after reading the first line, you should have been reaching for your scratch paper to write down $R \times T = D$. Let's plug in the numbers the problem gives us.

$$R \times T = D$$

$$400 \times \; ? \; = 2{,}600$$

Let's ballpark a little first, before we solve this. The answer choices give us some clues as to what this missing number T should be. Let's start with choice (3). If T were 5 hours, given that the rate is 400, what would the distance be? 5×400, or 2,000. We need a larger T if we want the distance to be 2,600. Let's try 6 hours: $6 \times 400 = 2{,}400$. Well, we're getting closer. How about 7 hours? $7 \times 400 = 2{,}800$. Now this is too big. The correct time must be between 6 and 7 hours.

How do you calculate this problem the traditional way? Solve for the missing T. If $R \times T = D$, then $T = \dfrac{D}{R} = \dfrac{2,600}{400} = 6.5$ hours. The correct answer is choice (4).

RATE PROBLEMS DRILL
(Answers and explanations can be found in Part VIII.)

1. If a man runs 12 miles in 3 hours, what is his rate in miles per hour?

2. A glacier is moving at a rate of 4 feet per year. At this rate, how long will it take the glacier to travel one mile?
    (1 mile = 5,280 feet)

    (1) 800 years

    (2) 920 years

    (3) 1,100 years

    (4) 1,320 years

    (5) 1,540 years

Rate Problem Quiz

A: It will be about trains, planes, or automobiles and/or be in terms of miles.

3. Marie drives from her home to the supermarket 10 miles away and then drives back home after shopping. If it takes her two hours for the entire trip, including one hour spent shopping in the supermarket, what was her average speed driving to and from the supermarket?

    (1)   10 mph
    (2)   15 mph
    (3)   20 mph
    (4)   25 mph
    (5)   30 mph

Charts and Graphs

Some test takers are scared by charts and graphs, but we hope our chapter on "Crazy Graphics" helped you to see that these are not really so intimidating after all. The two great things about the charts and graphs on the Math test are (1) they are roughly drawn to scale, so you can always ballpark, and (2) they cover exactly the same material we have already gone over in the last chapter and this one. Some charts and graphs will be about percents; others will be about rates; others may be about fractions. So it's not as if these are really separate categories of problems at all, and you will find that with a little practice, you should do very nicely. Look at the following problems:

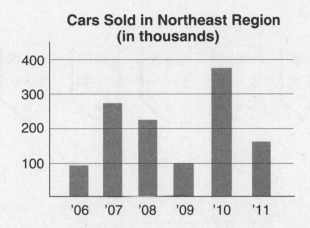

Cars Sold in Northeast Region (in thousands)

In the figure above, by approximately how much did sales of cars increase from 2009 to 2010?

(1)   20,000

(2)   100,000

(3)   200,000

(4)   260,000

(5)   350,000

Here's How to Crack It

As we said in our "Crazy Graphics" chapter, always take a moment to read the title of the graph and study the two variables. We are looking at the number of cars sold in a particular region, broken down *by year*. The number of cars is expressed *in thousands*.

In 2009, according to the graph, 100,000 cars were sold. In 2010, more than 300,000 were sold. How many more? It's difficult to say exactly because the scale on the left is marked only every 100,000 cars, but it looks to be about half the distance between the markings, or about 50,000 more. So the total 2010 figure is about 350,000. The question wants to know the increase from 2009 to 2010. How do we get that? We subtract. Roughly 350,000 minus 100,000 is roughly 250,000. Is this close to any of the answers? Yes. The correct answer is choice (4).

In effect, this was officially sanctioned ballparking. There was no way to get the precise answer mathematically. The GED test writers expected you to use your eyes and estimate in order to get the right answer.

Let's try another.

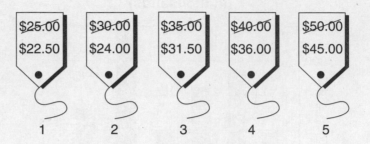

A man is searching through a bin of shirts that are on sale, some for 10% off and some for 20% off. Which sales tag above has been reduced by 20%?

(1)   1
(2)   2
(3)   3
(4)   4
(5)   5

Here's How to Crack It

In spite of the fact that there is a graphic that goes with it, this is just a percent problem. The question asks us to identify the tag that has been reduced by 20 percent. Let's begin with the first tag. It started at $25.00, and has been reduced to $22.50. Let's take away 20 percent from 25 and see if we get 22.50. If we do, it's the answer. If we don't, we can throw it back in the bin and try another. Twenty percent of $25.00 is $5.00, so the reduced price ought to be $20.00 if this were the correct answer. It isn't, so we can eliminate choice (1). Let's go to the next tag: It started at $30.00 and has been reduced to $24.00. What is 20 percent of 30? That's right: 6. If we take away the $6, we are left with $24.00. Bingo! The answer is choice (2).

CHARTS AND GRAPHS DRILL
(Answers and explanations can be found in Part VIII.)

Types of Telephones in Use

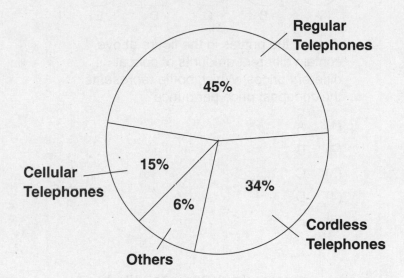

1. In the figure above, the number of regular telephones in use is how many times the number of cellular phones?

   (1)   2 times
   (2)   3 times
   (3)   4 times
   (4)   5 times
   (5)   Not enough information is given.

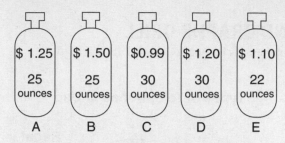

2. Each of the bottles in the figure above contain different amounts of cola at different prices. Which bottle represents the cheapest price per ounce?

(1) A
(2) B
(3) C
(4) D
(5) E

Average Stock Prices This Week

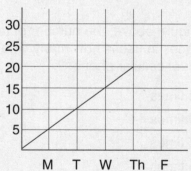

3. The price of a particular stock has been increasing at the same rate each day for the first four days of the week, as shown in the graph above. If the increase continues at its present rate, what should the price be on Friday?

(1) 15
(2) 20
(3) 25
(4) 30
(5) 35

Exponents

An exponent is shorthand for multiplication. The expression $4 \times 4 \times 4 \times 4 \times 4$ can also be written as 4^5. This is expressed as "4 to the fifth power." The large number (4) is called the **base**, and the little number (5) is called the **exponent**.

Although there aren't very many exponent questions on the GED, there are a few rules that you should remember.

Multiplying Numbers with the Same Base

When you multiply numbers that have the same base, you simply add the exponents.

$$6^2 \times 6^3 = 6^{(2+3)} = 6^5$$

Why is this true? Let's write this out in long form:

$$6^2 = 6 \times 6 \qquad 6^3 = 6 \times 6 \times 6$$

$$\text{so, } 6^2 \times 6^3 = 6 \times 6 \times 6 \times 6 \times 6 \text{ or } 6^5$$

Dividing Numbers with the Same Base

When you divide numbers that have the same base, you simply subtract the bottom exponent from the top exponent.

$$\frac{6^3}{6^2} = 6$$

Why is this true? Let's write it out in long form:

$$\frac{6^3}{6^2} = \frac{6 \times 6 \times 6}{6 \times 6}$$

The Zero Power

Anything to the zero power is 1.

$$4^0 = 1 \qquad x^0 = 1$$

The First Power

Anything to the first power equals that number.

$$4^1 = 4$$
$$-3^1 = -3$$

But Watch Out For…

There are several operations that seem like they ought to work with exponents but don't.

Does $x^2 + x^3 = x^5$? NO!!
Does $x^4 - x^2 = x^2$? NO!!!

Does $\dfrac{x^2 + y^3 + z^4}{x^2 + y^3} = z^4$? NO!!!!

In fact, none of these three expressions can be reduced.

You would expect that raising a number to a power would increase that number, and usually it does, but there are exceptions.

- If you raise a positive fraction of less than 1 to a power, the fraction gets smaller.

$$\left(\frac{1}{2}\right)^2 = \frac{1^2}{2^2} = \frac{1}{4}$$

- If you raise a negative number to an odd power, the number gets smaller.

$$(-3)^3 = (-3)(-3)(-3) = -27$$

(Remember -27 is smaller than -3.)

- If you raise a negative number to an even power, the number becomes positive.

$$(-3)^2 = (-3)(-3) = 9$$

Exponent problems on the GED tend to be pretty basic.

Exponent Facts

$5^0 = 1$

$5^1 = 5$

$5^2 = 25$

If $x^2 = 25$, then $x = 5$ or -5.

3^3 equals which of the following values?

(1) 9×9

(2) 3×3

(3) 3×9

(4) 9^2

(5) 1^{27}

Here's How to Crack It

The expression 3^3 equals 27. All we have to do is find the answer choice that also equals 27. You got it. The correct answer is choice (3).

Radicals

The **square root** of a positive number x is the number that, when squared, equals x.

For example:

- The square root of 16 equals 4 because $4 \times 4 = 16$.
- The square root of 9 equals 3 because $3 \times 3 = 9$.
- The square root of 4 equals 2 because $2 \times 2 = 4$.

The symbol for a positive square root is $\sqrt{}$, also called a radical.

$$\sqrt{16} = 4$$

$$\sqrt{9} = 3$$

Many numbers do not have an exact square root. For example, there is no exact $\sqrt{13}$. The best we can say about $\sqrt{13}$ is that it is *between* 3 and 4. Here's an example:

To find the square root of a number on your Casio FX-260, first enter the number, then press the "shift" key, and then press the "x^2" key.

The square root of 7 is between which of the following pairs of numbers?

(1)   2 and 3

(2)   3 and 4

(3)   4.5 and 5.5

(4)   6 and 8

(5)   9 and 10

Here's How to Crack It

There is no exact square root of 7, so let's see what numbers it is between that do have a square root. The expression $\sqrt{9}$ is the next biggest number that comes out evenly: $\sqrt{9} = 3$. The expression $\sqrt{4}$ is the next smallest number that comes out evenly: $\sqrt{4} = 2$. Thus, the square root of 7 is between 2 and 3. The correct answer is choice (1).

EXPONENTS AND SQUARE ROOTS DRILL

(Answers and explanations can be found in Part VIII.)

1.   Which of the following values is equal to 8?

(1) 2^3

(2) $(2 + 2)^2$

(3) $2^2 + 2$

(4) $1^2 + 6$

(5) $2^3 + 1^0$

2. $3^3 + 2^2 = ?$

3.   What is the value of $\sqrt{16} - \sqrt{4}$?

    (1)   12

    (2) $\sqrt{12}$

    (3)   4

    (4)   2

    (5)   1

Scientific Notation

Scientific notation combines your knowledge of decimals and your knowledge of exponents to allow you to express very large numbers without endless strings of zeros. Take the number 3,200,000,000. Numbers like this can be difficult to read and even more difficult to add or subtract. Here is the same number in scientific notation:

$$3.2 \times 10^9$$

How do we expand this out to its full size? Let's start with an easier example.

$$3.2 \times 10^2$$

All you have to do to simplify this expression is move the decimal point over to the right by the same number as the power of ten. In this case, two places.

$$3.2 \times 10^2 = 320$$
$$3.2 \times 10^3 = 3,200$$
$$3.2 \times 10^4 = 32,000$$

How do we contract a big number into scientific notation? Just perform the same process in reverse. Let's take 4,750,000. If we wanted to express this as 4.75 to the nth power of ten, what would the nth power be? On the large number, put your pencil point where you want the decimal to be (in this case, between the digit 4 and the digit 7), and now count how many places you have to move the pencil to the *right* to get to the end of the number. Did you move your pencil 6 places? You are now a certified scientific notationalist.

$$4,750,000 = 4.75 \times 10^6$$

Let's try a problem.

Which of the following expresses the number 5.6×10^4?

(1)   0.00056
(2)   5,600
(3)   56,000
(4)   560,000
(5)   564,000

Here's How to Crack It

On a piece of scratch paper, write down 5.6 with some space to the right of it. Now, take your pencil, and move the tip of the pencil over four times, like this:

5.6

Fill in the 0s. The correct answer is choice (3).

Probability Quiz

Q: If there is one probability question on your 56-question Math GED, what's the probability that the first question on the test will be a probability question?

Answer on page 464

Probability

If you flip a coin, what are the odds that it's going to come out tails? If you said anything but "$\frac{1}{2}$," "1 out of 2," or "fifty-fifty," then there's a poker game we'd like to invite you to next Thursday.

To figure out the probability that something is going to happen, you take the number of chances that the thing could happen and compare that to the *total* number of possible outcomes of *all* kinds. For example, let's take that coin we just mentioned. If you toss the coin once, how many chances are there on this *one* toss that it will be heads? One chance. And how many total possible outcomes are there? There are two possible outcomes—heads or tails. Therefore, you have a 1 out of 2, $\frac{1}{2}$, or fifty-fifty chance of seeing tails.

On the GED, probabilities are generally expressed as fractions. The number of possibilities that *one* thing could happen is the numerator. The number of *total* possibilities is the denominator. Let's try a problem.

---

9 workers decide to draw straws to see who will be the one to stay late and clean up. If there are 9 straws, 8 long and 1 short, what is the probability that Jim, who goes first, will draw the short straw?

(1) $\frac{1}{18}$

(2) $\frac{1}{9}$

(3) $\frac{1}{8}$

(4) $\frac{1}{2}$

(5) $\frac{8}{9}$

Here's How to Crack It

To solve any GED probability problem, you have to find the number of chances that a particular thing could happen (in this case, there is only one short straw, so Jim has only one chance of picking a short straw). This is your numerator. Then you have to find the total number of outcomes of *any* kind (in this case, the total number of straws is 9). This is your denominator. The correct answer to this question is choice (2).

Let's try another.

If a box of chocolates contains 3 caramels, 3 nut clusters, and 5 raspberry creams, which of the following fractions represents the chance of picking a caramel on the first try?

(1) $\dfrac{1}{11}$

(2) $\dfrac{1}{3}$

(3) $\dfrac{3}{11}$

(4) $\dfrac{5}{11}$

(5) $\dfrac{11}{3}$

Probability Quiz
A: 1 out of 56

Here's How to Crack It

As before, let's figure out the number of possible chances for you to pick a caramel. There are three caramels, so there are three possibilities for picking one. That becomes your numerator.

Now, we need the total number of possibilities of any kind. There are a total of 11 chocolates, so that becomes your denominator. The correct answer is $\dfrac{3}{11}$ or choice (3).

SCIENTIFIC NOTATION AND PROBABILITY DRILL

(Answers and explanations can be found on in Part VIII.)

1. Which of the following expresses the number 765,000 in scientific notation?

   (1) 7.65×10^4

   (2) 76.5×10^3

   (3) 7.65×10^5

   (4) 76.5×10^5

   (5) 0.765×10^3

2. Erica's closet has no light. If Erica has 4 dresses, 2 of which are blue, 1 of which is green, and 1 of which is red, what is the probability that she will pick a blue dress?

   (1) $\dfrac{1}{4}$

   (2) $\dfrac{1}{3}$

   (3) $\dfrac{2}{5}$

   (4) $\dfrac{1}{2}$

   (5) $\dfrac{4}{1}$

3. Which of the following is equivalent to $(3.4 \times 10^3) + (4.1 \times 10^4)$?

   (1) 75,000,000

   (2) 7,500,000

   (3) 4,440,000

   (4) 444,000

   (5) 44,400

Putting It All Together

Now that you've seen the basics of applied arithmetic one topic at a time, we're going to give you a drill that mixes up all the different applied arithmetic concepts we've discussed in this chapter. This drill will help to reveal whether you're having trouble recognizing individual types of problems, as we discussed in the last chapter. Some people are fine once they know that a question is about probabilities or percents, for example, but they have trouble spotting the key words that should tell them what type of problem they're dealing with. As you do this drill, make it a point to identify each question before you start calculating:

"This is an average question."
"That is a rate problem."
"This one is an exponent question."

APPLIED ARITHMETIC DRILL

(Answers and explanations can be found in Part VIII.)

1. Darryl puts $5,000 into an insured bank account that pays annual interest of 8%. How much interest will he earn in 2 years?

   (1) $2[0.08(5,000)]$

   (2) $\dfrac{0.08(5,000)}{2}$

   (3) $2[0.92(5,000)]$

   (4) $\dfrac{2(5,000)}{0.08}$

   (5) $2[1.08(5,000)]$

2. If Laverne walks steadily at a rate of 5 kilometers per hour, how long will it take her to walk 17.5 kilometers?

   (1) $1\dfrac{3}{4}$ hours

   (2) 2 hours

   (3) $3\dfrac{1}{2}$ hours

   (4) 52 hours

   (5) $87\dfrac{1}{2}$ hours

Computer Preferences

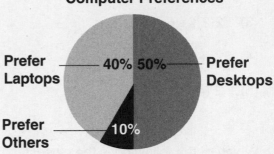

3. The figure above shows the results of a survey of a group of professionals who were asked what type of computer they preferred. What percentage of the group preferred to work on mainframe computers?

   (1) 10%

   (2) 15%

   (3) 25%

   (4) 45%

   (5) Not enough information is given.

4. Sara buys office supplies for her company. If she spent an average of $47.50 per month over the past four months, how much did she spend in total over the four months?

5. Which of the following is equal to 22?

   (1) 2^{11}

   (2) $2^{10} + 2$

   (3) $2(2^3) + 6$

   (4) $2^3 + 3^2$

   (5) $2^3(4)$

6. Which of the following is the closest approximation of $\sqrt{10}$?

   (1)   2

   (2)   3

   (3)   5

   (4)   10

   (5)   100

7. Michael calls a taxi to pick him up at his house. He knows that the taxi company has 1 limousine, 2 sedans, 3 vans, and 1 compact. What is the probability that he will ride in a sedan?

   (1) $\dfrac{1}{7}$

   (2) $\dfrac{2}{7}$

   (3) $\dfrac{5}{7}$

   (4) $\dfrac{6}{7}$

   (5) $\dfrac{7}{2}$

8. A set contains the following five numbers: 12, 4, 8, 16, 23. What is the median of the set?

9. Sheila works in a factory for $14.50 per hour for any hours up to 40. After 40 hours, she is paid at $19.00 an hour. If Sheila worked 43 hours last week, which expression below shows how much she earned?

   (1) $40(14.50) + 3(19.00)$

   (2) $43(19.00)$

   (3) $40(14.50) \times 3(19.00)$

   (4) $40(14.50) + 19.00$

   (5) $3(14.50) + 40(19.00)$

10. If one cell is 2.3×10^4 microns wide and another cell is 3.2×10^4 microns wide, then one cell is how much bigger than the other in microns?

   (1)   0.9

   (2)   19.0

   (3)   190.0

   (4) 9,000.0

   (5) 12,000.0

Chapter 25
Algebra

In this chapter, we introduce the basics of algebra—plus we'll show you powerful techniques that make certain types of difficult algebra questions really easy.

Algebra accounts for what is generally considered the toughest 20 to 30 percent of the GED Math test. Most people just don't like algebra, and they never did. Well, we have some good news for you.

You don't always need to use algebra to solve the algebra problems.

In just a few pages, we'll show you a great technique that will allow you to do some of the tougher algebra problems without writing equations. However, let's begin by going over the basics of the easy "solving for *x*"-type of GED problems.

If you've done the first two math chapters, then you've already been solving simple equations, also known as equalities. Every time you set up a proportion or an average formula, you were using algebra. Here is the most basic type of algebra equation:

If $2x - 14 = 10$, then $x = ?$

(1)   5

(2)   12

(3)   15

(4)   22

(5)   25

The GED test writers use some variation of this problem on practically every test. To find the answer to this question, we must "solve for *x*," which simply means getting *x* all alone on one side of the equation, and everything else on the other side. The *x* is already on the left-hand side of the equal sign in this equation, so let's try to move the *other* numbers on the left side over to the right side.

First, let's tackle the number 14 that is subtracted from $2x$. To make this *subtraction* of 14 disappear, we must *add* 14 to the left side. Of course, we want to avoid unbalancing the equation, so we must then add 14 to the *right* side of the equation as well.

$$
\begin{array}{r}
2x - 14 = 10 \\
+\ \ \ 14 \quad 14 \\
\hline
2x - 0\ = 24
\end{array}
$$

As long as you add or subtract your number to *both* sides of the equation, the equation actually stays the same. So now, the equation looks like this:

$$2x = 24$$

Now, let's tackle the number 2, which is being multiplied by *x*. To make this *multiplication* of 2 disappear, we must *divide* by 2 on the left side. Of course, we want to avoid unbalancing the equation, so we will also divide by 2 on the right side.

$$\frac{2x}{2} = \frac{24}{2}$$

As long as you multiply or divide your number on *both* sides of the equation, the equation stays proportionately the same. At this point, we can cancel the 2s on the left side and reduce the fraction on the right side as shown:

$$\frac{\cancel{2}x}{\cancel{2}} = \frac{\overset{12}{\cancel{24}}}{\cancel{2}} \quad \text{so} \quad x = 12$$

The correct answer to this question is choice (2).

Another kind of algebraic-equation question that comes up fairly often on the GED looks like this:

Solving for *x* Tip
Whatever you do to the left side of an equation, you have to do to the right side as well.

Given the formula $2a = 3b(c - 4)$, find *a* if $b = 5$ and $c = 6$.

(1)　　30

(2)　　23

(3)　　15

(4)　　　5

(5)　　−3

Here's How to Crack It

These problems give you an equation and values for two of the three variables. All you have to do is plug the values for the two variables you know into the equation and then solve for the third.

Start by writing the equation on your scratch paper, substituting 5 for *b* and 6 for *c*. It should look like this:

$$2a = (3 \times 5)(6 - 4)$$
$$2a = (15)(2)$$
$$2a = 30$$

If you were in a hurry, you might now pick answer choice (1), 30, but the problem asks for the value of *a*, not 2*a*. To solve for *a*, you must divide both sides by 2. The correct answer is 15, or choice (3).

SIMPLE EQUATION DRILL

(Answers and explanations can be found in Part VIII.)

1. If $2x - 5 = 11$, then $x =$

   (1) 10

   (2) 8

   (3) 6

   (4) 5

   (5) 2

2. What is the sum of $5x + 2y + x - 3y$?

   (1) $3x^2y^2$

   (2) $6x - y$

   (3) $6x + y$

   (4) $5x^2 - y^2$

   (5) $4x - y$

3. If $3x + 6 = 51$, then $x =$

4. Evaluate $3x^2 - 4y$, if $x = 2$ and $y = 3$.

   (1) 28

   (2) 11

   (3) 9

   (4) 0

   (5) −3

Inequalities

While an equality or an equation allows you to solve for x and get one answer, an inequality has a range of answers. For example, in the inequality $x > 5$, we know that x must be greater than 5, but there are an infinite amount of numbers that x could be. Thus, an inequality defines a range of values for the variable without giving you one specific value. Here are the symbols for inequalities:

> | > | greater than |
> | < | less than |
> | ≥ | greater than or equal to |
> | ≤ | less than or equal to |

An inequality is solved in exactly the same way as an equality. Let's use the same example we used at the beginning of the chapter, with one small change.

If $2x - 14 > 10$, then which of the following expressions gives all the possible values of x?

(1) $x > 5$

(2) $x > 12$

(3) $x < 15$

(4) $x < 22$

(5) $x = 25$

Here's How to Crack It

Pretend it's just a normal equality. This is what your work should look like:

$$2x - 14 > 10$$
$$+ \quad 14 \quad 14$$
$$\overline{2x - 0 \ > 24}$$

$$\frac{2x}{2} > \frac{24}{2}$$

So, the correct answer is choice (2), $x > 12$.

The only difference between an inequality and an equality is when you have to multiply or divide by a negative number.

If −3x + 6 < 18, then which of the following expressions gives all the possible values of x?

(1) $x < 2$

(2) $x < -4$

(3) $x > 2$

(4) $x > -4$

(5) $x = 4$

Here's How to Crack It

Until the very last step, this will be just like solving an equality. This is what the work should look like right up until that last step:

$$
\begin{array}{rcr}
-3x + 6 & < & 18 \\
-6 & & -6 \\
\hline
-3x & < & 12
\end{array}
$$

Now, comes the tricky part. When you multiply or divide an inequality by a negative number, the unequal sign flips over (that is, goes from > to <, or vice versa).

In this case, to get x alone on the left side of the equation, we're going to divide both sides by −3.

$$\frac{-3x}{-3} < \frac{12}{-3}$$

But the moment you divide by a negative number, the sign flips over.

$$x > -4$$

So, the correct answer to this question is choice (4).

Inequalities Tip
An inequality is just like an equality EXCEPT that when you multiply or divide by a negative number, the sign flips.

Take a look at a typical GED inequality below.

For which value of x below is the inequality $4x > 3$ true?

(1) -4

(2) -1

(3) 0

(4) $\dfrac{1}{2}$

(5) 1

Here's How to Crack It

We want to isolate x on one side of the equation, so let's get rid of the 4 by dividing both sides by 4.

$$\frac{4x}{4} > \frac{3}{4}$$

So $x > \dfrac{3}{4}$. When you look at the answer choices, your heart may sink because $\dfrac{3}{4}$ is not one of the options. However, let's read the question again. "For which value of x below is the inequality...true?" In other words, which of the answer choices is within the range of values expressed by the inequality $x > \dfrac{3}{4}$? Is -4 greater than $\dfrac{3}{4}$? No. Is 0 greater than $\dfrac{3}{4}$? No. Is 1 greater than $\dfrac{3}{4}$? Yes! The correct answer is choice (5).

INEQUALITIES DRILL

(Answers and explanations can be found in Part VIII.)

1. Freida is not allowed on the roller coaster because she is under the minimum age of 5. Which of the following inequalities expresses all the ages that *are* allowed on the roller coaster?

   (1) $x < 5$

   (2) $x > 5$

   (3) $x = 5$

   (4) $x \geq 5$

   (5) $x > -5$

2. If $5x + 3 < 28$, then which of the following expressions gives all the possible values of x?

   (1) $x < 5$

   (2) $x < -5$

   (3) $x > 0$

   (4) $x > 5$

   (5) $x = -5$

3. If m is the positive number 4, which of the following inequalities contains the number m?

   (1) $x < 3$

   (2) $x > 7$

   (3) $2x > 6$

   (4) $3x \leq -6$

   (5) $x < -4$

Backsolving

You've seen throughout this book that POE—Process of Elimination—can be a very important tool in answering difficult multiple-choice GED problems. **Backsolving** is the ultimate extension of POE. Let's look again at the very first example from this chapter.

If $2x - 14 = 10$, then $x = ?$

(1)   5

(2)   12

(3)   15

(4)   22

(5)   25

The traditional way to solve this problem is to use algebra to "solve for *x*." In fact, this problem is pretty easy, and you will probably want to do it the traditional way (which we just showed you above).

However, there is another way to do this problem, and we're going to show it to you because this same way can be used to solve many more difficult algebra problems that appear on the GED.

The Correct Answer Is Staring You in the Face

The problem asks for the value of *x* and then presents you with five possible answers. In other words, one of those five possibilities is the number you're looking for.

Well, since one of these five answers is correct, why not try plugging each of them back into the question until we find the one that works?

We'll start in the middle with choice (3). Let's suppose for a moment that 15 is the correct answer and plug it into the question.

$$2(15) - 14 = 10$$

Is this true? No! 30 – 14 = 16. We've just proven that answer choice (3) is wrong.

But We've Done Something Even Better Than That

Choice (3) is not just wrong—it's too big. Do we need to check choices (4), 22 or (5), 25, both of which are even bigger than (3)?

Just by trying out choice (3), we eliminated any answers that were bigger. On the GED, multiple-choice math answers are always listed in ascending or descending order. Therefore, every time you try substituting the middle answer choice (choice (3)) back into the problem, you will eliminate two other answers immediately. If the number you get is too big, you can get rid of any choices that are even bigger. If the number you get is too small, you can get rid of any choices that are even smaller.

The only two possibilities left are choices (1) and (2). Let's try (2).

$$2(12) - 14 = 10$$

Is This True?

When we substitute 12 into the equation, we get exactly the correct answer: $24 - 14 = 10$. Therefore, the answer to this problem is choice (2).

This technique is called **backsolving,** and while it is probably unnecessary on a simple equation such as this, it will save your life on tougher questions. The method is always exactly the same: Start with the middle number. Plug it into the equation in the problem. If it makes the equation work, then you're done; you have the right answer. If the number is too big, eliminate any choices that are bigger, and zero in on the two remaining choices. Try one of them. If it's still too big, then the answer must be the remaining choice. Pick it, and move on.

Let's try this technique on some more difficult problems.

———————————————○———————————————

There are 8 passengers on a small plane, who have paid a total of $900 for the flight. If an economy ticket costs $100 and a first-class ticket costs $200, how many first-class tickets were bought?

(1)   7

(2)   5

(3)   4

(4)   2

(5)   1

Here's How to Crack It

At first glance, this may not seem to resemble the equation problem we just finished. This is a word problem, for one thing, and there doesn't seem to be an equation in the problem at all.

In fact, the words of this problem actually contain an equation. The difficulty is that it's pretty tricky to translate these words into math. The correct equation that will solve this problem is

$$200x + [100(8 - x)] = 900$$

But if you don't think you could have come up with this, don't spend any time kicking the ground because you can solve this algebra problem *without* algebra.

Let's *backsolve*. One of those five answers must be correct, so let's try putting one of them into the problem and see what happens. Which choice do you want to start with? That's right: choice (3) because it's in the middle. If choice (3) is too big, we can eliminate the choices that are even bigger. If choice (3) is too small, we can eliminate the choices that are even smaller. If choice (3) is just right, then we can go on to the next problem because we'll be done.

Choice (3) says that four passengers flew first class. And because there were a total of eight passengers, that means that four passengers flew economy class.

$$4 \times \$200 = \$800$$

$$4 \times \$100 = \$400$$

If this is the correct answer, the total dollar amount should add up to the total given in the problem: $900. Does it? No, it's way too big. Which choices can we then eliminate? That's right: Cross off choices (1) and (2). The only remaining possibilities are choices (4) and (5). We'll try choice (4) next.

Choice (4) says that two passengers flew first class. And because there were a total of eight passengers, that means that six passengers flew economy class.

$$2 \times \$200 = \$400$$

$$6 \times \$100 = \$600$$

If this is the correct answer, the total dollar amount should add up to the total given in the problem: $900. Does it? No, but we're getting warmer; $1,000 is a lot closer to $900 than we were before.

We know the answer is *not* (1), (2), (3), or (4). Can you guess what the correct answer to this problem is?

Backsolving Quiz

Q: With which answer choice do you start when you backsolve?

Answer on page 481

Just to be sure, let's check choice (5). Choice (5) says that one passenger flew first class. And because there were a total of eight passengers, that means that seven passengers flew economy class.

$$1 \times \$200 = \$200$$

$$7 \times \$100 = \$700$$

Does this add up to $900? You bet. The correct answer to this tough algebra word problem is choice (5).

Can You Use This Technique on *Every* GED Problem?

No. Many problems on the GED cannot be backsolved because their answer choices contain variables or formulas or because the correct answer choice is the final result of a calculation rather than a missing ingredient in an equation. And, of course, it is impossible to work backward from the answer choices when there are no answer choices. Generally, each GED contains as many as three or four problems that can be backsolved. These are frequently considered some of the hardest problems on the test because they involve algebra. Of course, if you backsolve, these problems are actually kind of easy.

How Do You Spot a Backsolve Problem?

Problems that can be backsolved have several characteristics. First, they must be multiple choice; the answer choices are invariably made up of simple numbers (such as 16, 27, or 5) rather than formulas or variables. In addition, the last lines of the problems ask straightforward questions (such as "How many of the workers are women?" or "How many tickets were bought originally?").

Most important, the best way to spot a backsolve problem is to recognize that the only other way to solve that particular problem—the *traditional* way—would be to write an algebraic equation. If you need to write an algebraic equation, then you could backsolve instead.

Let's try another:

Forty-two people have signed up for the little league annual dinner. If there are twice as many children as adults signed up, how many children are signed up?

(1) 14

(2) 18

(3) 20

(4) 28

(5) 32

Here's How to Crack It

Is this a backsolving problem? It certainly has all the earmarks: It is a multiple-choice question, the last line asks a straightforward question, and the answers are simple numbers rather than variables or equations. Most important, the only other way to do this problem would be to write an algebraic equation. And by the way, if you came up with the equation ($x + 2x = 42$), you could *still* get the wrong answer because when you solve for x, you get 14 (which happens to be answer choice (1)). Unfortunately, the variable x in this equation represents the number of *parents*, not the number of children. In this problem, you could have written a perfectly good equation and still have gotten the problem wrong.

Let's try backsolving instead. The question asks how many children have signed up for the dinner. One of the answer choices has to be right. Why not start with choice (3), 20? The problem tells us that there are twice as many children as adults, so if there are 20 children, how many adults can there be? That's right: 10. If we add the number of children and the number of adults, we are supposed to get the same total number of people as there are in the problem (42 people). Do we? No, we only have 30. Choice (3) is not just the wrong answer—it is too small. So we can eliminate any choices that are smaller than (3), which means choices (1) and (2) bite the dust as well.

The answer is either (4) or (5). Let's try choice (4), 28. If there are 28 children and there are twice as many children as adults, that means that there are 14 adults. If we add 28 and 14, we are supposed to get 42. Do we? Yes! The correct answer to this difficult algebra question is choice (4).

Backsolving Quiz

A: The one in the middle. That way, if it isn't right, you can tell whether to go up or down.

BACKSOLVING DRILL

(Answers and explanations can be found in Part VIII.)

1. Two physical therapists have a total of 16 patients to see in one day. Marcie has to see 2 more patients than Lewis. How many patients will Marcie see?

    (1) 9

    (2) 7

    (3) 5

    (4) 3

    (5) 2

2. Which of the values of m below would make the inequality $3m < 12$ true?

    (1) 9

    (2) 7

    (3) 6

    (4) 4

    (5) 2

3. If there are 4 times as many women as men employed by the Ace Insurance Company, then how many of the 75 workers are women?

    (1) 80

    (2) 75

    (3) 60

    (4) 45

    (5) 15

4. If the tax on a $45.00 restaurant check is $4.05, what is the tax rate?

    (1) 8%

    (2) 9%

    (3) 10%

    (4) 11%

    (5) 12%

5. If $2x - 7 = 3$, then $x =$

    (1) 1

    (2) 2

    (3) 3

    (4) 4

    (5) 5

Translation

Math itself is a kind of language that can be translated into English. For example, when you see 3 + 4 = 7, you automatically translate the symbols on the page into English (three plus four equals seven). A small number of GED math problems will ask you to do the reverse: translate a word problem from English into algebra. These problems are easy to spot, for the answer choices always contain variables. Here's an example:

Marjorie makes an investment and doubles her money. If she ends up with $480, which equation below could be used to discover the amount of her original investment of x dollars?

(1) $\dfrac{x}{2} = 480$

(2) $x - 2 = 480$

(3) $x + 2 = 480$

(4) $2x = 480$

(5) $x = 480 + 2$

To translate a problem from English to math, you need to know what some English terms mean in math. Here are the terms that come up on the GED:

GED Term	What It Means	Example
of	multiply	"$\frac{1}{5}$ of the 30 women" (translated: $\frac{1}{5} \times 30$)
percent	over 100	"40 percent" (translated: $\frac{40}{100}$)
double	times 2	"is double the original amount, x" (translated: $2x$)
triple	times 3	"is triple the original amount, x" (translated: $3x$)
more than	add	"…three more than m" (translated: $m + 3$)
less than	subtract	"…three less than n" (translated: $n - 3$)
is, are	equals	"The number of boys is five more than the number of girls" (translated: $b = g + 5$)

The key to any translation problem is its variable. The variable (x, y, z, or whatever) is always defined for you by the GED test writers. For example, in the previous problem, the variable represents the original amount of money Marjorie had before the investment. In a translation problem, you have to figure out what to do to this variable to get the final outcome of the problem. Let's look at Marjorie's question again.

Marjorie makes an investment and doubles her money. If she ends up with $480, which equation below could be used to discover the amount of her original investment of x dollars?

(1) $\dfrac{x}{2} = 480$

(2) $x - 2 = 480$

(3) $x + 2 = 480$

(4) $2x = 480$

(5) $x = 480 + 2$

Math/English Dictionary
- "is" means "="
- "of" means "×"
- "more than" means "+"
- "less than" means "−"

Here's How to Crack It

The gist of the problem is this: Marjorie put her nest egg into an investment that doubled her money.

We need to express this in mathematical terms, and the key, as always, is the variable. In this case, the variable x represents the money Marjorie had *before* she invested. The $480 represents the money she had *after* she invested. Mathematically, what do we have to do to x in order to double it? That's right: $2x$. (If you aren't sure of this or any other translation we talk about in the next couple of problems, just look it up on the chart on the previous page.) And after it was doubled, how much money did she have? That's right: $480. The equation should read:

$$2x = 480$$

The correct answer is choice (4).

Let's try another one.

Sally is three years less than twice the age of her brother Hector. If h represents Hector's age, which expression shows Sally's age?

(1) $h - 3$

(2) $3h$

(3) $2h - 3$

(4) $3h - 2$

(5) $3 - h$

Here's How to Crack It

The variable h represents Hector's age. What can we do to h in order to get Sally's age? Let's translate. She is *three years less than* (which we know from the chart above means "$- 3$") *twice Hector's age* (which we know means "$2h$").

It may help to say these two phrases in reverse order. She is twice Hector's age, minus three years. The correct equation is:

$$2h - 3$$

The correct answer is choice (3).

TRANSLATION DRILL

(Answers and explanations can be found in Part VIII.)

1. Sandra weighs 5 pounds more than her younger brother John. If John's weight is represented by x, what is an expression for the *combined* weight of the two children?

    (1) $x + 5$

    (2) $2(x + 5)$

    (3) $2x + 5$

    (4) $2(x) + 2(5)$

    (5) $x - 5$

2. The number of rabbits at a zoo doubled in 2000 and rose to five times the original number by the end of 2001. If the original number of rabbits is represented by m, then how many rabbits did the zoo have by the end of 2001?

    (1) $2m$

    (2) $4m$

    (3) $5m$

    (4) $7m$

    (5) $10m$

3. Frank is two years more than three times the age of Sam. If x represents Sam's age, which expression shows Frank's age?

    (1) $x + 2$

    (2) $3x$

    (3) $2x - 3$

    (4) $3x + 2$

    (5) $3x - 2$

PUTTING IT ALL TOGETHER: ALGEBRA DRILL

Now that you've seen all the elements of algebra separately, we'd like you to try a drill in which they are all mixed together. This will give you practice in recognizing the different types of problems so that you can zero in on exactly which technique you need to solve them quickly. Pay particular attention to spotting backsolving questions, which our students find takes a bit of practice.

(Answers and explanations can be found in Part VIII.)

1. If $5x + 9 = 44$, then $x =$

   (1) 12

   (2) 10

   (3) 7

   (4) 6

   (5) 4

2. Laura has $4 more than three times the amount of money Steven has. If x represents the amount of money Steven has, which expression shows how much money Laura has?

   (1) $3x + 4$

   (2) $3x - 4$

   (3) $4x + 3$

   (4) $x + 4(3)$

   (5) $\dfrac{x + 4}{3}$

3. Evaluate $5x^2 - 4y$, if $x = 3$ and $y = 4$.

   (1) 29

   (2) 21

   (3) 11

   (4) 6

   (5) 2

4. The Oakdale Preschool accepts 4-year-olds and 5-year-olds and has a total of 63 students. If the school has 7 more 4-year-olds than 5-year-olds, then how many of the children are 4 years old?

   (1) 10

   (2) 14

   (3) 28

   (4) 35

   (5) 42

5. If $3m + 7 < 28$, then which of the following expressions gives all the possible values of m?

   (1) $m < 9$

   (2) $m < 7$

   (3) $m > -5$

   (4) $m > -7$

   (5) $m = -9$

6. What is the sum of $2(x + y) + 3x + 2y$?

   (1) $5x + 3y$

   (2) $6x + 3y$

   (3) $6x + 4y$

   (4) $12x + 12y$

   (5) $5x + 4y$

7. If $p = 4$, which of the following inequalities contains the number p?

    (1) $p < 4$

    (2) $p > 5$

    (3) $2p < 3$

    (4) $p = -4$

    (5) $p < 5$

8. If 36 of the 120 workers in a factory work overtime, what percentage of the workers work overtime?

    (1)   10%

    (2)   20%

    (3)   30%

    (4)   40%

    (5)   50%

9. This year, a furniture business's revenues are double last year's. Next year, the business's revenues should be triple last year's revenues. Which of the following expressions represents the projected revenues for <u>next</u> year, if last year's revenues were x dollars?

    (1) $x + 3$

    (2) $3x$

    (3) $4x$

    (4) $3x + 2$

    (5) $4x + 2$

10. Tony is 4 years older than Heather, and Heather is 5 years younger than Larry. If the sum of their ages is 69, how old is Tony?

    (1)   15

    (2)   18

    (3)   20

    (4)   24

    (5)   25

Chapter 26
Geometry

In this chapter, we'll cover all the geometry you need to know for the GED—including lines and angles, triangles, rectangles, circles, volume, and graphing.

The good news is that the geometry on the GED covers only a fraction of what is covered in high school. Even if you never took geometry, you can learn everything you need to get the GED geometry questions right just by reading this chapter and doing the exercises that follow.

Measuring Diagrams

One reason GED geometry isn't too tough is that the diagrams are always roughly drawn to scale. As we showed you in our introduction to the Math test, this means that anytime there's a diagram, you always have a wonderful, concrete way to ballpark the problem. As we cover each of the geometry topics in this chapter, we'll show you how to measure the different types of diagrams.

What If There Is No Diagram?

Geometry Diagrams
If there's a diagram, use your eyes to estimate what the answer ought to be.
If there's no diagram, draw one yourself.

If a geometry problem doesn't come with a diagram, then you should immediately draw your own. Believe us, it's a lot tougher to solve a geometric problem if you can't see it. Take a few seconds to sketch out the information provided for you in the question, and if possible, try to draw your figure to scale so you'll have some idea of which answer choices are out of the ballpark.

The Formula Page

Following the page of instructions on the GED Math test is a page consisting of all the mathematical formulas you may need during the test. Here you will find the area of a square, the circumference of a circle, and the volume of a cube.

A lot of test takers assume, therefore, that they don't have to know or understand the formulas before the test. This isn't true. You will be much more confident if you walk into the test room with most of these formulas already memorized and even more confident if you have practiced using the formulas on our two diagnostic tests and the drills in this chapter.

Everything You Need to Know About GED Geometry

Here are the topics that are tested on the GED:

- Lines and angles
- Triangles
- Rectangles and squares
- Circles
- Volume
- Setup geometry
- Graphing
- Slope and the distance formula

As in the previous chapters, we'll first cover a concept, then give you examples of how this concept is used on the GED, and then give you a short drill. At the end of the chapter, there will be a larger drill that covers all the geometry topics together.

Lines and Angles

Here is a line:

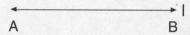

This particular line is labeled l, and like all lines, it extends forever to the left and to the right. A and B are points on the line, and the distance between them, AB, is called line segment AB.

How many degrees does a line contain? If the second hand on the face of a watch moves from 12 all the way around to 12 again, it has gone 360 degrees. A straight line drawn on the face of that watch from 12 straight down to six cuts the face of the watch in half: All straight lines create an angle of 180 degrees.

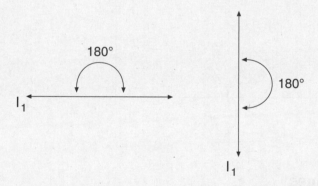

If that line is cut by another line, it divides that 180 degrees into two angles that together add up to 180 degrees.

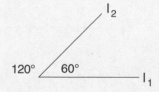

Perpendicular Lines

If the two lines cut across each other in such a way that they form two angles of 90 degrees each, then the two lines are called **perpendicular**. A 90-degree angle is also known as a **right angle**. On GED diagrams, this is sometimes indicated by a little box drawn into the corner of the angles.

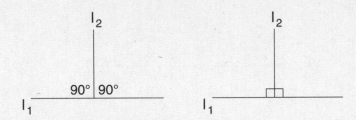

Using a Right Angle as a Measuring Tool

Whenever you see any angle on the GED, it helps to compare it in your mind to a 90-degree angle. Take angle A below. Is it bigger or smaller than the 90-degree angle? If it's bigger, then you can eliminate any answer choices that say that A is less than 90. If it is smaller, then you can eliminate any answer choices that say that A is more than 90. In this case, angle A is smaller than 90 degrees.

Parallel Lines

If two lines are drawn so that they could extend into infinity without ever meeting, these lines are considered **parallel**.

If these two parallel lines are cut by a third line, eight different angles are formed, or at least it looks that way.

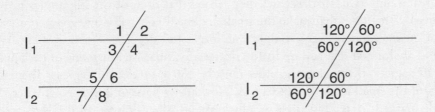

However, in reality, there are only two: a big angle and a little angle. This is because the third line that cuts across the two parallel lines intersects them both in exactly the same way. Look at the big angle 1 in the diagram above and notice that it is exactly the same size as angle 4, angle 5, and angle 8. Look at the small angle 2 in the diagram above and notice that it is exactly the same size as angle 3, angle 6, and angle 7.

In fact, a Princeton Review teacher named Fred came up with a theorem about all this. We call it Fred's theorem: "When two parallel lines are cut by a third line, then angles that *look* equal *are* equal." We're all very proud of Fred.

Let's see how Fred's theorem might apply on the GED.

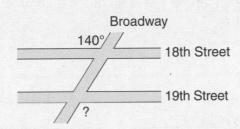

In the figure above, Broadway intersects the two parallel streets as shown. What is the angle of the intersection of Broadway and 19th street marked by the "?" sign?

(1)   140 degrees

(2)   120 degrees

(3)   90 degrees

(4)   40 degrees

(5)   20 degrees

Here's How to Crack It

As soon as you see the word *parallel* in the problem, you should immediately think of Fred's theorem. Even though it looks like there are eight different angles, there are really only two. In this case, they tell us that each of the big angles is 140 degrees. What does that make the small angles? If you said 40 degrees, you were right on the money. Every straight line forms 180 degrees. When it is cut, two angles are formed that add up to 180 degrees. Because we know one of the angles is 140 degrees, that means the other must be 180 − 140, or 40 degrees. Therefore each of the small angles is 40 degrees. Now all we have to decide is whether the angle marked "?" is a big angle or a little angle. What do you think? The correct answer to this question is choice (1), 140 degrees.

Could we have *ballparked* this question? Sure. Look at the angle marked "?" and compare this in your mind to a 90-degree angle. If you are having trouble picturing a 90-degree angle, just look at any corner of this page. The edges of this book form a 90-degree angle. Is the angle we're looking for smaller or larger than the 90-degree angle? Obviously, it's larger. This means we can get rid of choices (3), (4), and (5).

LINES AND ANGLES DRILL

(Answers and explanations can be found in Part VIII.)

Identify angle *x* in each of the diagrams below.

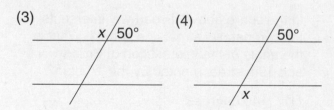

Triangles

A triangle is a geometric figure with three sides. The three angles inside a triangle always add up to 180 degrees, no matter how the triangle is drawn.

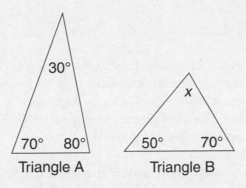

Triangle A   Triangle B

In triangle A, if you add up the three angles, you will notice that they add up to a total of 180 degrees. In triangle B, in order for the same thing to be true, how many degrees does angle x have to be? To find this out, add up the two other angles ($50 + 70 = 120$), and then subtract this from 180 ($180 - 120 = 60$).

Let's see how this would look on the GED.

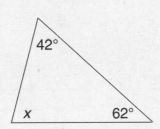

In the figure above, the triangle has three internal angles. One angle measures 42 degrees. Another angle measures 62 degrees. How many degrees does the third angle measure?

(1)   104 degrees

(2)   76 degrees

(3)   52 degrees

(4)   25 degrees

(5)   Not enough information is given.

Here's How to Crack It

The three interior angles of *every* triangle have a total of 180 degrees. If the GED test writers give you two out of the three angles, then you can find the third. Add up the two angles we know about (42 + 62 = 104). Now, just subtract the sum of the two angles from 180 (180 − 104 = 76). The correct answer to this question is answer choice (2).

Could we have *ballparked*? Of course. Look at the missing angle in the figure. Is it greater than or less than 90 degrees? Obviously it's a bit less, so we can eliminate choice (1). Now, compare it with the 62-degree angle directly across from it. Is it larger or smaller than 62 degrees? Come to think of it, it's still a little bit larger, isn't it. This lets us eliminate choices (3) and (4).

The GED test writers have certain favorite triangles that they use over and over again on the tests. These are the **isosceles** triangle and the **right** triangle.

The Isosceles Triangle

There are two important things to know about an isosceles triangle: First, it has two equal sides; second, the angles opposite those sides turn out to be equal as well.

 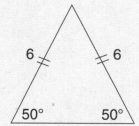

Generally, the GED test writers will tell you one of these two important things and then ask you to supply the other. Here's an example:

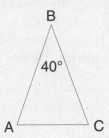

In the triangle above, if AB = BC, then what is the measure, in degrees, of angle A?

Here's How to Crack It

If side AB equals side BC, then the two angles opposite those sides (angles A and C) must be equal to each other as well. Although the problem doesn't mention it, this is in fact an isosceles triangle. First, let's find out the value of angle A plus angle C. The entire triangle has 180 degrees in it. If we subtract angle B (40 degrees) from the entire triangle, that leaves 140 degrees. Now, remember that angle A and angle C are equal to each other. How do we get the value of angle A alone? Divide by 2. The correct answer to this question is 70 degrees.

The Right Triangle

A right triangle contains one angle that equals 90 degrees.

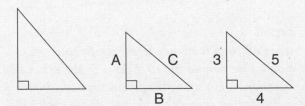

Pythagoras, a Greek mathematician, discovered that the sides of a right triangle are always in a particular proportion, which can be expressed by the formula $A^2 + B^2 = C^2$, in which A and B are the two shorter sides of the triangle, and C is the longer side opposite the 90-degree angle. This longer side is called the **hypotenuse**.

The most popular right triangle on the GED is the 3-4-5 right triangle, shown above. Let's see if Pythagoras knew what he was talking about, by trying out his theorem with the 3-4-5 triangle. According to the formula, $3^2 + 4^2$ should equal 5^2. Does it? Yes! 9 + 16 does equal 25. The Pythagorean formula is printed on the front page of the Math test along with all the other formulas, but you will probably never need to look at it if you remember the 3-4-5 triangle. The GED test writers rarely use any other right triangle. Here's a sample problem:

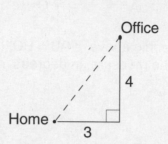

To get to her office, Susan must drive due east for 3 miles and then due north for 4 miles, as shown in the figure above. If she could drive directly from her home to her office, how many miles would that route be?

(1)   2 miles

(2)   3 miles

(3)   5 miles

(4)   6 miles

(5)   8 miles

Here's How to Crack It

The shortcut from her office to her home forms the hypotenuse of a right triangle, as the diagram shows. One side of the triangle is 3; the other side is 4. Do you need to plug these numbers into the Pythagorean theorem? Not if you memorized the 3-4-5 triangle. The correct answer to this question is choice (3).

The Perimeter of a Triangle

The perimeter is the distance around the outside edge of any two-dimensional object. The perimeter of a triangle is the sum of the lengths of the three sides. What was the perimeter of the triangle in that last problem? 3 + 4 + 5 = 12.

The Area of a Triangle

Like the other geometry formulas you'll need, the formula for the area of a triangle is printed on the first page of the Math test, but let's practice using it now. The formula for the area of a triangle is:

$$\frac{1}{2} \, (\text{base} \times \text{height})$$

where the base equals the length of the bottom side of the triangle, and the height equals the length of a perpendicular line from the base of the triangle to the triangle's highest point.

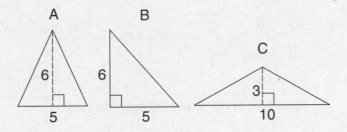

Triangle Quiz

Q: What's the area of a triangle with base 3 and height 6?

Answer on page 503

- In triangle A, the base equals 5, and the height equals 6, so the area is $\frac{1}{2}(5 \times 6)$, or 15.

- In triangle B, the base and height again equal 5 and 6, and the area of the triangle is again 15. However, note that because this is a right triangle, the height in this case is also the side of the triangle.

- In triangle C, the base equals 10, and the height equals 3, so the area is $\frac{1}{2}(10 \times 3)$, or 15.

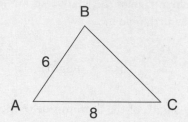

What is the area of the triangle above?

(1)   7

(2)   14

(3)   24

(4)   48

(5)   Not enough information is given.

Here's How to Crack It

To find the area of a triangle, you need the base and the height. In this triangle, we know the base (8) but not the height. The number 6 is simply the length of one of the other sides of this triangle and would have been the height only if this were a right triangle with angle A equal to 90 degrees. Therefore, the correct answer to this question is choice (5), Not enough information is given.

Similar Triangles

Two triangles are called similar if their angles have the same measurements and if their sides are in the same proportion. For example, the two triangles below are similar.

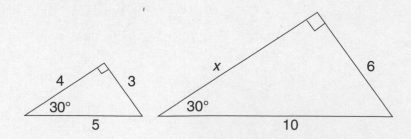

Because the sides of the two triangles are in the same proportion, you can find the missing side, *x*, of a similar triangle by setting up a proportion:

$$\frac{4}{5} = \frac{x}{10}$$

small triangle   big triangle

So, *x* = 8.

Here's how this might look on the GED.

Triangle Quiz

A: $\frac{1}{2}(3 \times 6) = 9$

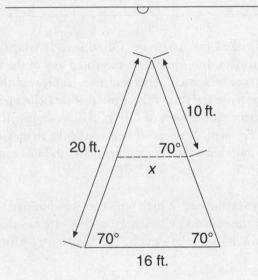

The diagram above shows the plans for a triangular billboard. If it is found that the billboard is too big and must be cut along the dotted line, as shown, what will be the length of the new base of the triangle?

(1)   2

(2)   3

(3)   8

(4)   9

(5)   16

Here's How to Crack It

If you look at the larger triangle and then at the smaller triangle, you may notice that all of the angles of the smaller triangle are the same as those of the bigger triangle. Why? Well, they *share* the top angle, and the diagram tells us that the lower angle on the right of the smaller triangle is the same as the lower angle on the right corner of the larger triangle. This means that the lower left angles must be the same as well.

These two triangles are therefore similar, which means that their sides will always be in proportion. So let's set up a proportion equation:

$$\frac{20 \text{ ft.}}{16 \text{ ft.}} = \frac{10 \text{ ft.}}{x \text{ ft.}} \quad \text{so } x = 8$$

The correct answer to this question is choice (3).

───────────○───────────

Could we have ballparked this question? Of course. If you didn't notice that these were similar triangles, you could have measured any of the lengths from the diagram with your piece of scratch paper and then compared that length to the dotted line. Why don't you try this: Take a piece of scratch paper, and line it up against the line segment that is marked "10 ft." Use your pencil to mark off the length of the "10 ft." segment. Now, use this as your ruler to measure the length of the dotted line. Is it more than 10? No, it's less than 10. How much less than 10? Not too much.

Now, look at the answer choices. Which ones can we eliminate? Choices (1), (2), and (5) are all out of the ballpark. Choices (3) and (4) are too close to call. If you aren't sure how to solve it, just take a guess. You have a fifty-fifty chance of being right.

TRIANGLES DRILL

(Answers and explanations can be found in Part VIII.)

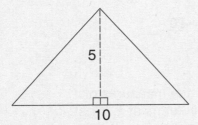

1. Michael is constructing a triangular garden as shown above. If the base of the garden is 10 feet long and the perpendicular distance from the base to the endpoint of the garden is 5 feet, then what is the area of the garden?

   (1)   50

   (2)   25

   (3)   15

   (4)   10

   (5)   Not enough information is given.

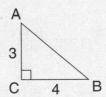

2. The distance from point A to point B is how much longer than the distance from point A to point C?

3. If a triangle has interior angles of 27 degrees and 53 degrees, then what is the measurement, in degrees, of the third angle?

   (1)   24

   (2)   50

   (3)   100

   (4)   110

   (5)   190

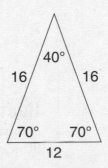

4. Frank is making a photocopy of a triangular-shaped design, as shown above. He plans to use the photocopier's "shrink" function to reduce the size of the figure so that its base will measure exactly 6 inches across. What will be the measurement of each of the other two sides?

   (1)   20

   (2)   18

   (3)   14

   (4)   10

   (5)   8

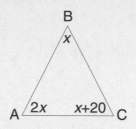

5. In triangle ABC above, the measures of the angles are shown in terms of x. What is the measure, in degrees, of angle A?

(1) 45 degrees

(2) 52 degrees

(3) 63 degrees

(4) 80 degrees

(5) 87 degrees

Rectangles and Squares

A rectangle is a four-sided object whose four interior angles are each equal to 90 degrees.

Square Rectangle Quiz

Q: Is a rectangle always a square, or is a square always a rectangle?

Answer on page 508

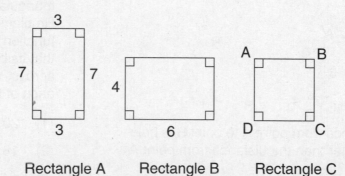

Rectangle A   Rectangle B   Rectangle C

The area of a rectangle is found by multiplying its length times its width. This formula is printed on the first page of the GED Math test. The area of rectangle A is 7×3, or 21. The area of rectangle B is 4×6, or 24.

The lengths of the opposite sides of a rectangle are always equal to each other. For example, in rectangle C, side AB is equal to side DC, and side AD is equal to side BC. To find the perimeter of a rectangle, you simply add the four sides together. The perimeter of rectangle A is 20. The perimeter of rectangle B is also 20.

A square is a rectangle whose four sides all happen to equal one another. The area of a square can still be found by multiplying length times width, but because the length and width in a square are the *same*, you can also say that the area of a square equals side².

RECTANGLES AND SQUARES DRILL

(Answers can be found in Part VIII.)

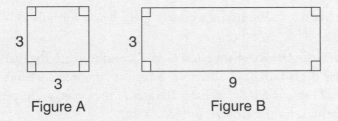

Figure A   Figure B

Answer the following questions based on the two figures above.

1. Identify figure A.

2. Identify figure B.

3. What is the area of figure A?

4. What is the perimeter of figure B?

5. How many figure As would fit inside figure B?

Circles

The distance from the center of a circle to any point on the circle is called the **radius.** The distance from one side of a circle through the center of the circle to the other side is called the **diameter.** The diameter of a circle is always equal to twice the radius. In the circle below, the radius is equal to 3, so the diameter is 2×3, or 6.

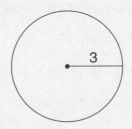

The **circumference** of a circle is the distance all the way around the outside edge of the circle. In other words, circumference is the name for a circle's perimeter. The formula for the circumference of a circle is πd, where d is the diameter of the circle, and π is a number with the approximate value of 3.14, sometimes also approximately expressed as $\frac{22}{7}$. A long time ago, mathematicians discovered that this number, when multiplied by the diameter, gave the value for a circle's circumference. The circumference formula and the value for π are printed on the first page of the Math test. The area of a circle is given by the formula πr^2.

What is the circumference of the circle on the previous page? The diameter of this circle is twice the radius, or 6. Therefore, using the circumference formula, the circumference of this circle is 6π. What is the area of the circle on the previous page? Using the formula for the area, we get $\pi 3^2$, or 9π.

Square Rectangle Quiz

A: A square is always a rectangle. But a rectangle doesn't have to be a square.

CIRCLES DRILL
(Answers can be found in Part VIII.)

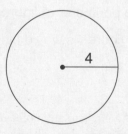

Using the figure above, answer the following questions.

1. What is the radius of this circle?

2. What is the diameter?

3. What is the circumference of this circle?

4. What is the area of this circle?

Volume

While area is always a two-dimensional measurement of flat objects on a page, volume is a three-dimensional measurement. Imagine a square metal lunch box. The volume of the box would represent how much space there is inside.

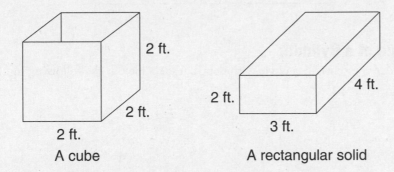

A cube   A rectangular solid

For four-sided solid objects, it is always easy to find the volume.

The formula for the volume of a cube is very simple. If you remember, the area of a square is side^2. The volume of a cube is side^3. For the cube shown above, the volume would be 2^3, or 8 cubic feet.

The formula for the volume of a rectangular solid is also simple. It is length × width × depth. For the rectangular solid shown above, the volume would be $2 × 3 × 4$, or 24 cubic feet.

Here's how this might look on the GED:

If Judy wants to fill a rectangular pool with water, approximately how many cubic feet of water will she need if the pool's dimensions are 10 feet wide by 12 feet long by 5 feet deep?

(1) 1,200

(2)   600

(3)   300

(4)   150

(5)   27

Here's How to Crack It

The key words in this problem are *volume* and *rectangular*. As soon as you see these words, you should know just what to do. The volume of a rectangular solid is length × width × depth. In this case, that means 12 × 10 × 5 = 600. The correct answer is choice (2).

Volume of a Cylinder

A cylinder is essentially a circle with depth. Take a look at the following figure:

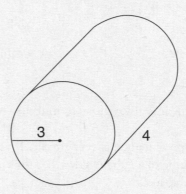

To find the volume of any cylinder, you must multiply the area of the circle at one end of the cylinder by its height. The formula for the area of a circle is πr^2. So the volume of a cylinder is $\pi r^2 h$. Thus, the volume of the cylinder in the figure above is $\pi 3^2(4)$, or 36π.

VOLUME DRILL

(Answers and explanations can be found in Part VIII.)

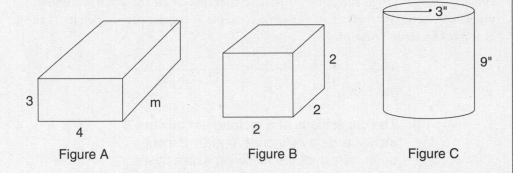

Figure A

Figure B

Figure C

Answer questions 1 through 3 based on the three figures above.

1. If the volume of figure A is 60 cubic feet, then what is the length of segment m?

2. Figure B is a tank in the shape of a cube. If this tank is to be filled halfway to capacity, how many cubic units will be in the tank?

3. The cylindrical box in figure C is 9 inches tall. If the radius of the cylinder is 3 inches, what is the maximum volume that can fit in the box?

4. Chen plans to wallpaper a rectangular room with the dimensions 10 feet by 12 feet by 9 feet high. If there are no windows, and only one door measuring 2 feet by 7 feet, and she does not wallpaper the ceiling or floor, approximately how much will it cost to wallpaper the room?

   (1) $382
   (2) $395
   (3) $400
   (4) $412
   (5) Not enough information is given.

Setup Geometry

A few GED problems will ask you to set up a geometry problem but then not solve it. Just like the setup problems we saw in the "Applied Arithmetic" chapter—which tested the same arithmetic concepts as all the other arithmetic problems—setup geometry tests the same concepts as regular geometry. Here's an example of a setup problem:

The dimensions of a rectangular box are 3 inches wide by 4 inches long by 2 inches deep. Which of the following expressions represents the volume (in cubic inches) of the box?

(1) 3(2)(4)

(2) 3 + 2 + 4

(3) 3(2) + 4

(4) 3(2)(4)(2)

(5) 3(4) + 2

Here's How to Crack It

Essentially, this is almost exactly the same problem you just saw before. The key words again are *volume* and *rectangular*. The only real difference is that this time the question does not ask you to find the volume, but to set up the work involved in finding the volume.

As we said in the "Applied Arithmetic" chapter, take your time with these problems. It's easy to pick an answer choice that is almost (but not quite) right. We need to multiply length times width times depth. In this problem, that means $4 \times 3 \times 2$. The correct answer is choice (1).

Graphing

Graphing is a way of representing a point in two dimensions on what is known as a Cartesian grid or coordinate plane. This may sound intimidating, but it's actually pretty simple. Here's a Cartesian grid:

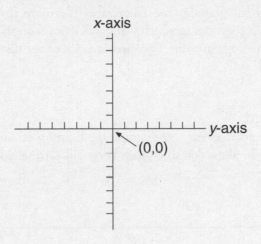

Graphing is a way of assigning points to this grid. Every point has two numbers assigned to it: an *x*-coordinate and a *y*-coordinate. Let's take the point A (3,1). The first number is considered the *x*-coordinate. The second number is the *y*-coordinate. To plot this point on the graph, we start at (0,0) and count over three to the right on the *x*-axis, and then count up one place. To find point B (5,4), we count over five places to the right on the *x*-axis and then up four places.

Try plotting these two points on the graph above. Then, check your work by looking at the graph below.

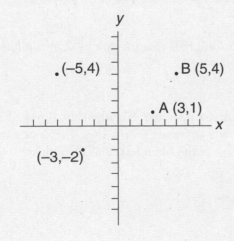

GED Pop Quiz

Q: Which GED graduate
played an aeronautics
instructor who taught
Tom Cruise all kinds of
complicated math in
Top Gun?

Answer on page 516

If the first number in an (*x,y*) point (in other words, the *x*-coordinate) is negative, then to graph this point, you count to the *left* along the *x*-axis. If the second number in an (*x,y*) point (in other words, the *y*-coordinate) is negative, then you count downward. Look at the graph above and see how points (−5,4) and (−3,−2) were plotted.

GED questions about graphing are fairly rare. There are three types of GED graphing questions: questions in which you graph a point on the coordinate plane, questions about the slope of a line, and questions about the distance between two points.

Graph the Point

The GED test writers may ask you to graph the location of an (*x,y*) point on the coordinate plane. To allow you to do this, they will provide you with a grid that looks like this:

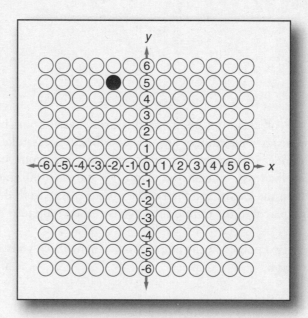

On the grid above, you will note that the point (−2,5) is plotted.

Slope

The slope of a line tells you how sharply a line is inclining. To find the slope, you need to know two points anywhere on the line. The slope formula (which always appears on the first page of the Math test) looks like this:

$$\textbf{Slope} = \frac{\text{change in } y}{\text{change in } x}$$

For example, to find the slope of a line that went through points (5,6) and (3,2), all you have to do is subtract one *y*-coordinate from the other (the result of this subtraction becomes your numerator—also sometimes known as the "rise") and subtract one *x*-coordinate from the other (the result of this subtraction becomes your denominator—also known as the "run"):

$$\frac{6-2}{5-3} = \frac{4}{2} = 2$$

Distance

To find the distance between two points on a Cartesian grid, there is a long formula that we think is *one* equation you shouldn't bother to memorize. It's too complicated, it comes up too rarely on the test, and besides, it's printed at the beginning of the test.

Just for practice, here it is:

$$\text{Distance between two points} = \sqrt{\left(x_2 - x_1\right)^2 + \left(y_2 - y_1\right)^2}$$

where (x_1, y_1) and (x_2, y_2) are two points in a plane.

Let's find the distance between points (1,2) and (5,6). What we have to do is carefully plug these numbers into that long equation. Here's what it should look like:

$$= \sqrt{\left(5-1\right)^2 + \left(6-2\right)^2}$$
$$= \sqrt{4^2 + 4^2}$$
$$= \sqrt{32}$$

You can see why this doesn't come up often.

When You're Given a Graph

Most of the graphing problems on the GED concerning slope or distance will actually give you a graph to look at. This can be very helpful in ballparking your answers. Take a look at the following question:

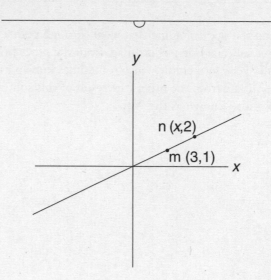

In the graph shown above, what is the

x-coordinate of point n if the slope of the

line mn is $\frac{1}{3}$?

(1)   9

(2)   6

(3)   3

(4)   2

(5)   −1

Here's How to Crack It

First, let's get an idea of which answer choices are out of the ballpark. We are looking for the *x*-coordinate of point n. Well, before we start using complicated formulas, let's do a little measuring. The *x*-coordinate for point m is 3. This means that the horizontal distance from 0 to m is 3. Mark off this distance on your scratch paper. Now, try measuring the horizontal distance between 0 and point n. Did you get about 6? That's what we got. Because these figures are drawn only roughly to scale, we can't guarantee that the answer is going to be exactly 6, but it ought to be close to 6 anyway. So which answer choices can we get rid of? Choices (1), (3), (4), and (5) are all out of the ballpark. The only possible answer this time is choice (2).

If you needed to get this one the traditional way, you would have to use the slope formula backward.

$$\text{Slope} = \frac{\text{change in } y}{\text{change in } x} \qquad \frac{1}{3} = \frac{2-1}{x-3}$$

The correct answer is choice (2).

GRAPHING DRILL
(Answers and explanations can be found in Part VIII.)

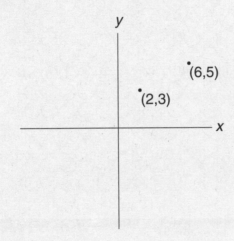

1. A line passes through the points (6,5) and (2,3). What is the slope of this line?

    (1) $-\dfrac{1}{5}$

    (2) 0

    (3) $\dfrac{1}{4}$

    (4) $\dfrac{1}{2}$

    (5) 3

2. What is the distance between points (5,0) and (12,0) on the coordinate plane?

    (1) 12

    (2)   9

    (3)   7

    (4)   4

    (5) Not enough information is given.

3. On the grid below, plot the following points: Point A (–3,–4), Point B (2,3), and Point C (3, 5).

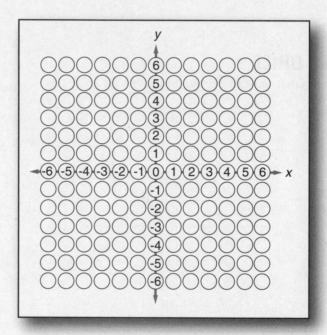

Putting It All Together

Now that you've seen the basics of geometry one topic at a time, we're going to give you a drill that mixes up all the different geometric concepts we've discussed in this chapter. This drill will help show you whether you're having trouble *recognizing* individual types of problems, as we've discussed in all the previous chapters. As you do this drill, make it a point to identify each question before you start calculating:

> *"This one is a triangle question."*
>
> *"That is a setup volume problem."*
>
> *"This one is a graphing question."*

Examine every diagram to see if you can eliminate any answers that are out of the ballpark. Remember, if two answers are close together, you can't rely on the diagram to tell you which is exactly right. The figures are only drawn *roughly* to scale.

If there is no diagram provided, try to make your own. By taking something conceptual and making it concrete, you may be able to ballpark your *own* diagram.

GEOMETRY DRILL

(Answers and explanations can be found in Part VIII.)

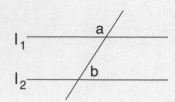

1. In the diagram above, if the sum of angle a plus angle b is equal to 180 degrees, then what is the relationship between the two straight lines l_1 and l_2?

    (1) The lines are perpendicular.

    (2) The lines are isosceles.

    (3) The lines are segments.

    (4) The lines are parallel.

    (5) Not enough information is given.

2. The radius of a circular traffic island is 7 feet. What is the approximate area of the traffic island? (Use $\pi = \frac{22}{7}$.)

    (1) 1,078

    (2) 154

    (3) 148

    (4) 21

    (5) 15

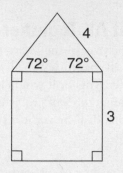

3. The figure above shows a square attached to a triangle. If the triangle is isosceles, what is the perimeter of the <u>entire</u> figure?

    (1) 7

    (2) 12

    (3) 17

    (4) 34

    (5) 40

4. A three-sided figure has sides in a ratio of 1 : 1 : 2. What type of figure is this?

    (1) an equilateral triangle

    (2) a square

    (3) an isosceles triangle

    (4) a rectangle

    (5) Not enough information is given.

5. If a cube has a volume of 27, which of the following is the length of one side of the cube?

    (1) 3

    (2) 9

    (3) 81

    (4) 144

    (5) 729

6. An isosceles triangle has one internal angle of 45 degrees. What is the sum of the other two interior angles?

   (1) 180 degrees

   (2) 135 degrees

   (3) 90 degrees

   (4) 45 degrees

   (5) 15 degrees

7. A rectangular flower garden has an area of 168 square feet. If the width of the garden is 12 feet, then what is the length of the garden?

   (1) 30

   (2) 23

   (3) 20

   (4) 15

   (5) 14

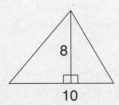

8. The triangle above has a base of 10 and a height of 8. Which of the following expressions gives the area of the triangle?

   (1) $\frac{1}{2}(10)(8)$

   (2) $2(10 + 8)$

   (3) $10 + 8$

   (4) $\frac{1}{2}(10 + 8)$

   (5) $\frac{1}{2}(10 - 8)$

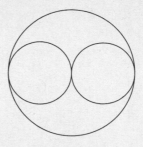

9. Two circles with identical radii are inscribed inside a third circle, as shown above. If the diameter of the large circle is 20, what is the radius of one of the small circles?

   (1) 50

   (2) 40

   (3) 20

   (4) 10

   (5) 5

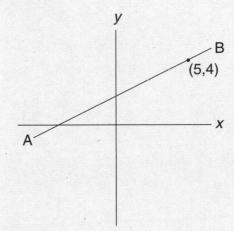

10. Point (5,4) is on line AB as shown. Which of the following represents the slope of line AB?

   (1) $\frac{4}{5}$

   (2) $\frac{5}{4}$

   (3) $\frac{4 - 5}{5 - 4}$

   (4) $\frac{4 - 5}{5}$

   (5) Not enough information is given.

Part VII Summary

○ The GED Math test concentrates on only a few areas of math:
  • Number Operations   20–30%
  • Measurement/Geometry   20–30%
  • Data Analysis/Statistics   20–30%
  • Algebra/Functions   20–30%

○ And even these topics are not covered inclusively.

○ There are 50 questions on the Math test, to be done in 90 minutes. About half the questions will be in Part One, in which calculators are permitted. The other half will be in Part Two, in which calculators are not permitted.

○ Eighty percent of the problems will be multiple choice. In these problems, a version of POE called ballparking enables you to eliminate answer choices on the Math test that are out of the ballpark.

○ Even if you know how to do the problem, ballparking is useful as a reality check.

○ Ballparking is even more useful if you don't know how to do the problem—as a guessing strategy.

○ Look out for partial answers—answers that are on the way to the correct answer but stop too soon.

○ Look out for red herrings—pieces of information in the problem that aren't necessary for its solution.

○ Do each section of the Math test in two passes:
  • The first pass for the problems you know immediately how to do;
  • The second pass for the problems you aren't sure of.

○ Because you can't write in your test booklet, you'll have to get comfortable with using scratch paper. Practice using scratch paper on our diagnostic tests. Put the paper right underneath the problems, and label each problem on your scratch paper so you can find your work again if you come back to it on the second pass.

o   Numbers to the left of zero on the number line are negative. Numbers to the right of zero on the number line are positive. Zero is neither positive nor negative.

o   When multiplying positive and negative numbers,
    •   positive × positive = positive
    •   positive × negative = negative
    •   negative × negative = positive

o   When doing several operations, use PEMDAS to decide which operation to perform first.

o   A fraction is a $\frac{\text{part}}{\text{whole}}$. To compare fractions, use the Bowtie as outlined in Chapter 23.

o   You must know how to add, subtract, multiply, and divide fractions.

o   Always reduce fractions (when you can) before doing a complicated operation. This will reduce your chances of making a careless error.

o   A decimal is just another way of expressing a fraction.

o   A percentage is just a fraction whose denominator is always 100. You should memorize the percentage shortcuts we outline in Chapter 23.

o   In the six to eight setup problems on the GED, you don't have to find the answer—just the equation that will get the answer.

o   An average (or arithmetic mean) is the sum of all items, divided by the number of items. The median is the middle number of a group of numbers.

o   Any problem about trains, planes, or automobiles can be solved by the equation rate × time = distance.

o   An exponent is a shorter way of expressing the result of multiplying a number several times by itself.

o   When you multiply numbers with the same base, you simply add the exponents. When you divide numbers with the same base, you simply subtract the exponents.

- The square root of a positive number x is the number that, when squared equals x. The square root of $9 = \sqrt{9} = 3$.

- To find the probability that something is going to happen, you take the number of chances that the thing could happen and compare that to the total number of possible outcomes. Probabilities are usually expressed as fractions in which the number of chances that the thing could happen is the numerator and the total number of possible outcomes is the denominator.

- Many algebra problems can be solved by back-solving—working backward from the answer choices to see which one solves the problem.

- Some problems can be "translated" from English to math:
  - *is* means =
  - *of* means ×
  - *more than* means +
  - *less than* means −

- A line contains 180 degrees. A circle contains 360 degrees.

- Triangles contain 180 degrees. A right triangle contains one 90-degree angle. An isosceles triangle has two equal sides, and two equal angles. An equilateral triangle contains three equal sides with three angles of 60 degrees each.

- The area of a triangle is $\dfrac{\text{base} \times \text{height}}{2}$.

- The circumference of a circle is $2\pi r$. The area of a circle is πr^2.

- The volume of a rectangular solid is length × width × depth.

- To graph an x,y-coordinate on a coordinate plane, count over to the right (for positive) or left (for negative) to plot the x-coordinate, then up (for positive) or down (for negative) to plot the y-coordinate.

Part VIII
Answer Key to Drills

Language Arts, Writing

Sentence Fragment Drill (Pages 91–92)

1. **2** The second sentence does not contain an independent clause. The only answers that fix this problem are choices (2) and (5), which combine the two sentences into one. Which conjunction is correct? We need *while*.

2. **5** This sentence is composed of two dependent clauses. The correct answer choice will turn one of the dependent clauses into an independent clause. Choice (5) does this by creating a real verb.

3. **3** "Angry, too" is a sentence fragment. Who is angry? That's right, the bride and groom. Why not put this adjective next to the other adjective that describes them: frustrated. Now, how do we connect these two adjectives? If they are describing similar states, we need the word *and*.

4. **5** Again, there is no independent clause in this sentence as it stands. Only one of the answer choices gives the sentence an independent clause, in this case by giving the second clause a true verb.

5. **1** This sentence is fine as written.

Comma Splice and Run-On Drill (Page 96)

1. **2** This sentence is a run-on. The best way to fix it is to split it up into two separate sentences. Only choice (2) breaks up the sentence.

2. **2** As written, this is also a run-on, but because there is a clear relationship between the two clauses, it makes sense to combine them using a word that illustrates their relationship (the second clause explains the first). The word *because* illustrates this relationship.

3. **4** This one is tough because you might think that the sentence is listing three things a home should have. However, the meaning of the sentence makes it clear that there should in fact be two sentences. "Fire extinguishers and escape ladders…" are not part of the original thought and belong in the second sentence.

Coordinating Conjunction Drill (Pages 97–98)

1. **but**   The second sentence expresses a contrasting idea.

2. **and**   The second sentence adds information.

3. **so**   The second sentence gives the result of the first one.

4. **or**   These sentences present a choice.

5. **for**   The second sentence provides a reason for the first one.

6. **nor can she scuba dive.**   Neither sentence presents an acceptable choice.

Subordinating Conjunction Drill (Pages 100–101)

1. **Before** Use *before* to indicate the time sequence of the two events.

2. **After** Use *after* to indicate the time sequence of the two events.

3. **When, If, or Whenever** Another time sequence question. You can use any of these three words.

4. **If** Use *if* to show that the first clause is a condition.

5. **Although, Though, or Even though** These clauses express contrast, so use one of these words.

6. **Because or Since** These clauses describe a cause and an effect, so use one of these two words.

Improper Coordination Drill (Pages 104–105)

1. **4** These two sentences could stand alone, but the question asks you to combine them. As we know, the best way to do this is with a conjunction. In this case, the second sentence is in contrast to the first, requiring a word like *although*.

2. **1** If you missed this, try switching the clauses around: "Some networks believe that they will be able to recapture their lost viewers, unless it is too soon to say for certain." Does that sound right? No. This sentence uses the wrong conjunction. *Although* best expresses the contrast between the two clauses.

3. **2** Choice (5) creates a sentence fragment. Choices (1) and (3) change the meaning of the sentence. Choice (4) would make the sentence much too complicated. The *although* in the new sentence replaces the *but* in the old sentence; therefore, almost nothing else has to change.

Parallel Construction and Misplaced Modifier Drill (Page 111)

1. **3** As soon as we see a list of three things, we should think parallel construction. Are all three items on the list set up the same way? No. The first two begin "getting…" and "saving…," but the third begins "to decide…"

2. **5** This sentence begins with a modifying phrase, "after picking the time and the place," so the word that follows the comma should be the noun that is being described by the modifying phrase. Who is doing the picking? That's right: "most people." So the answer is either choice (4) or (5). Which is correct? If you aren't sure, just guess. Do you forget doing something, or do you forget to do something?

Sentence Structure Drill (Pages 112–114)

1. **3** Because there are two sentences, first check to make sure that both contain independent clauses. Do they? The first one doesn't; it's a sentence fragment. To fix the problem, we need to combine the two sentences. Neither choice (1) nor (2) do this. Because both clauses aren't independent, we don't need a conjunction to join them together. This gets rid of choices (4) and (5).

2. 4   This sentence contains a list of things, so right off the bat we should be thinking parallel construction. The first two items on the list are nouns, but the third is a kind of verb. The easiest way to fix this is just to remove the verb.

3. 1   Is the subordinating conjunction *when* the correct way to start this sentence? No, *if* is better.

4. 2   This is a run-on. As usual, you should begin by checking to see if there is more than one independent clause in the sentence. Two independent clauses can sometimes be joined with a conjunction, but the only two choices that try this [choices (4) and (5)] use contrast words that don't relate the two clauses correctly. Often the best way to separate two independent clauses is to break the sentence in two. There is only one answer choice that does this.

5. 5   Choices (1) and (2) change the meaning of the sentence. The remaining choices are all exactly the same, except that they each use a different coordinating conjunction. Which is best? This time, we need a contrast word.

6. 4   This sentence begins with a modifying phrase, so we should check to see if the noun that follows the comma is what is being described by the modifying phrase. Do you think that "scholars" were enormously popular at the time, or was it the plays? Choices (1), (2), and (3) are misplaced modifiers. To decide between choices (4) and (5), look for the differences between them. The only difference is the tense of the verb at the end. Should it be present tense? No.

7. 4   As always, check to see if there is an independent clause. Is there? No. This is a sentence fragment. To make the second clause independent, we must change *being* to the real verb *is*.

8. 1   "After examining Marlowe's writing" is a modifying phrase. The word that follows the comma must be the noun that the modifying phrase is describing. Who did the examining? That's right: the important scholar. If you picked choice (4), you got the grammar right, but we wouldn't know who "she" was.

9. 5   Check to see if there is an independent clause. In fact, there are two, joined by a coordinating conjunction. We could break this up into two sentences, but if you look at the answer choices, you will see that that doesn't seem to be an option. Look through the other choices to see if anything else strikes you. Nope. This one is correct as written.

10. 2   This sentence also has two independent clauses, but this time they are not joined by a coordinating conjunction. Only is just an adjective. This is a run-on sentence. None of the answer choices breaks the sentence in two, so we should look for an answer choice with a coordinating conjunction. Only choices (2) and (3) provide that. Given the meaning of the sentence, we want the contrast word *but*.

Subject-Verb Agreement Drill (Page 122)

1. 2   The subject of this sentence is collector. "Of gourmet recipes" just modifies collector. The verb we need is the singular *does*.

2. 1   Two subjects joined by an *or* take the singular verb *is*.

3. 3   What does the clause "that have been passed down from generation to generation" describe? That's right: *recipe*. However, *recipe* is singular, so we need the singular verb *has*.

Pronoun Drill (Pages 128–129)

1. **3** To what is the pronoun *them* referring? It could refer only to the singular "the salary." Therefore, we need the singular pronoun *it*.

2. **3** By itself, this sentence is fine—but in the middle of a paragraph that is using the general pronoun *you*, it is very confusing to suddenly shift to *we*.

3. **4** *Them* is a plural pronoun. What noun in this sentence could it refer to? You're right: There aren't any plural nouns in the entire sentence. Get rid of choices (1) and (2). Whose poverty won't your friend kid you about? Your poverty.

Tense Drill (Page 133)

1. **4** Because the answer choices all give you variations on the tense of a verb, you can be pretty sure this is a tense question. We want the verb tense to stay consistent with the sentence. Do you see any other verbs in the sentence? Sure: "We have one of…" Because this is in the present tense, we should put *paid* into the present tense as well.

2. **4** The first sentence was in the present tense. The first half of the second sentence is also in the present tense. Does it make sense to say that nobody liked to pay taxes? No, we need the present form of that verb as well.

3. **5** Is the verb consistent with the first two sentences? Yes. Take a second to check the other answer choices to see if anything else catches your eye. No. There is no correction necessary.

Usage Drill (Pages 134–136)

1. **3** This is a subject-verb question. The subject of the sentence is *people*. The verb must be the singular *wonder*.

2. **2** Looking at the answer choices, it is clear that this is a tense question. Do we need the past tense, as it is used in the original sentence? Look at the sentences that surround it. Sentences 1 and 2 both use the present tense. There's no good reason to switch tenses here, so the correct verb would be *believe*.

3. **2** *Crime and violence* is a compound subject with *and* in between. Therefore, we need the plural verb *are*.

4. **4** Check each of the answer choices for something that may be wrong. Is it crystal clear what the pronoun *they* is referring to? Not really. It could refer to tourists, cities, or movie stars. Choice (4) makes it clear that it is the sightings that don't happen often.

5. **5** None of the first four choices is relevant. In this sentence, you can't use *you* instead of *one*—it wouldn't make sense. *No one* is singular, so we need the singular verb *says*. *Live* is ungrammatical. And there is no need to change the tense of the sentence because the other sentences in this passage are also in the present. This sentence is fine just the way it is.

6. **4** This sentence has a compound verb. You *can see* live plays and *ate* late at night. The first verb is in the present tense, and the second is in the past. One of the verbs has to change, and fortunately, only the second one is underlined. First, eliminate any choices in the past tense. That gets rid of choices (1), (2), and (3). Choice (5) does not agree with the subject in number, so the answer is choice (4).

7. **1** In this pronoun question, the sentence suddenly shifts from the *you* pronoun used throughout the rest of the passage to the *one* pronoun instead. Just change it back.

8. **5** The sentence begins in the present tense but then switches for no good reason to the past. Choice (5) changes *arrived* to *arrive*.

9. **3** If you look at the answer choices, you will notice that we are given a choice of *are* or *is*. Clearly, this is a subject-verb agreement question. What is the subject of the sentence? The taxi. (The phrase "like the old horse-drawn carriage of the past" is modifying *taxi*.) Thus, we need the singular verb *is*. This leaves us with only two possibilities: choices (3) or (5). Choice (5) creates another agreement problem because "the taxi" is only one "way" to get around. The correct answer is choice (3).

10. **4** "That travels underground" is referring to the plural *subways*. Does the singular verb *travels* agree with the plural *subways*? No. We need the verb *travel*.

Punctuation Drill (Page 143)

1. **2** There are two clauses in this sentence, and these two clauses must be separated by a comma. If you didn't notice that as you were reading the sentence, two of the choices contained commas inserted in different places. This may be a clue. Where does one clause end and the other begin? The correct answer is choice (2).

2. **3** This sentence includes a list of several things. There must be a comma between each item on the list. The only one that is missing is the one between *rope* and *food*.

3. **5** Sentence 3 begins with the introductory phrase "For many days." There should be a comma between the phrase and the main clause. The only choice that provides this is choice (5).

4. **1** The phrase "that is" represents a parenthetical thought, which again requires commas on each side of it. The correct answer is choice (1).

Capitalization Drill (Page 147)

1. **3** The only time you have to check capitalization is when this option is included among the answer choices. In this case, there are two possibilities to check: *friday* and *weekend*. One of the rules we just went over in this chapter is that days of the week are always capitalized. Therefore, we need to capitalize *Friday*.

2. **5** The two possible capitalization problems in the answer choices are *presidents* and *congressmen*. Does it make sense to capitalize one of these nouns but not the other? No, which means we can eliminate choices (1) and (3). As you know from reading the rules in this chapter, it is not necessary to capitalize these titles unless they are referring to a particular congressman or president.

3. **1** Real GED questions will never have as many capitalization options in the answer choices as this question does. Let's check them out. Choice (1) refers to the season *fall*. Should this be capitalized? Actually, no. Seasons are never capitalized. This is our answer; there is no need to go through the other choices.

4. **4** There is only one capitalization possibility to check: Is *Birthday* correct? Well, no. Words like *birthday* and *anniversary* are never capitalized. By the way, if you weren't sure whether to capitalize *congressmen* in sentence 2, sentence 4 would have helped you to realize that it wasn't necessary.

Spelling Drill (Page 152)

1. **3** The answer choices contain a potential soundalike to check out. Do we need *there* or *their*? In this case, *their* is correct because the sentence is describing the benefits belonging to the small companies.

2. **1** If *your* is used as an adjective to describe thinking, then *your* would be correct. However, if this is supposed to be a contraction of *you are*, then we need *you're* instead. This is a contraction.

3. **1** *Lets* is supposed to be a contraction of *let us*. The proper way to express this is *Let's*. We would have had to capitalize *frank* only if it were the name of a person. In this case, *frank* is an adjective meaning *honest*.

Mechanics Drill (Pages 153–155)

1. **3** From the answer choices, you can see that this question hinges on knowing the difference between *accept* and *except*. If you know the correct spelling, you are down to choices (3) and (4). Which is right? If we have the plural *dentists'*, we need *offices*. This was a pretty hard question.

2. **2** Did you notice the list of three things? We need a comma between each item.

3. **3** The answer choices show us that we need to decide between *It's* and *Its*. In this case, the sentence is really trying to say, "It is always difficult…" Thus, we need the contraction of *it is*: *It's*.

4. **5** We need the comma after the introductory phrase *For example*. *Thanksgiving* must be capitalized. It is the correct pronoun in this case. *To get* is the correct idiom to use after *took*. Thus, no correction is necessary.

5. **2** There are two clauses in this sentence, and they must be separated by a comma.

6. **4** *Serial* is a soundalike of *cereal*. Everything else is correct.

7. **3** Again, there are two clauses in this sentence, and they need to be separated by a comma.

8. **5** The season *spring* does not need to be capitalized.

9. **1** This sentence is fine the way it is. *Finally* is an introductory phrase and, as such, needs a comma to separate it from the rest of the sentence.

10. **3** Looking at the answer choices, you might have noticed that there are three different variations on *Everyone's*. Which is correct? In this case, *Everyone's* is a singular possessive adjective requiring the apostrophe. The other variation in the answer choices is the choice of the present or past form of the verb *has*. Because the rest of the sentence is in the past, we need the past tense for this verb as well.

Sentence Drill (Page 157)

1. **2** Each of the sentences in this paragraph is about the advantages of paperback books, but none of the sentences states that theme as a topic sentence. We are looking for an answer choice that summarizes the sentences in the paragraph. Choice (2) is a great topic sentence: It summarizes the other sentences and states the theme of the paragraph.

2. 1   The first paragraph is about the advantages of paperbacks. Before you even read the answer choices, think for a moment about what the next paragraph might be about. While second paragraphs can go off on a tangent, they should be related to the topic of the first paragraph. Choice (1) clarifies the paragraph and helps orient the reader.

Organizing Paragraphs Drill (Page 160)

3. (C), (B), (A)   Paragraph C indicates what the passage is about, so it goes first. You can use organization and contrast words to figure out the order of the other two paragraphs. For example, paragraph B refers to "the first step," while paragraph A refers to "the next step." This shows that B should go before A. You might have also noticed that paragraph B begins with a contrast word: *However.* This helps to show that B should follow C; the author says one thing in paragraph C, and then contradicts it in paragraph B.

Organization Letter Drill (Pages 161–162)

4. 1   This passage consists of a letter from a job seeker to a boss. But without a paragraph telling the reader what the letter is about, this would be a pretty confusing letter. Choice (1) clarifies the letter and helps orient the reader.

5. 3   This paragraph describes the author's abilities, but it is missing a topic sentence. Choice (3) is the best answer.

6. 1   The topic sentence of paragraph A is the first sentence, as usual. But the second sentence comes out of left field. If you look forward to the third sentence, it seems to continue on with the same logic as the first. Clearly, we should bump the second sentence back to the end of the paragraph.

Language Arts, Essay

Specifics Drill (Page 184)

1. You might have given examples of places where there have been famines in the past. You could also have used a stronger and more descriptive word than *bad*, such as *unacceptable, horrifying,* or *abhorrent.*

    The starvation we have seen in Somalia and Ethiopia is totally unacceptable in these modern times.

2. What do they do *instead* of reading?

    Nobody reads anymore—if people aren't playing video games, they're watching television.

3. *What* do they waste their money on?

    Hollywood producers pay millions of dollars to screenwriters who can't write, actors who can't act, and directors who can't direct. Is it any wonder they then complain about their losses?

4. *Who* should be fired?

    One way to cut government spending is to fire people who are incompetent.

5. *Why* don't they have any fun?

    Older people often don't go out to do fun things because they're afraid of falling down.

6. *How* do nurses help people?

   Every day, nurses save lives by monitoring patients, asking intelligent questions, and sometimes even administering CPR.

Contrast Drill (Page 187)

1. Although some great movies were expensive to make, I believe great movies could be made more cheaply.

2. While many types of government spending, such as Social Security and Medicare, are essential, some government spending is wasteful.

3. Although consulting a lawyer is always an expensive undertaking, lawyers can sometimes save you money.

4. While most scientists downplay the possibility that we will ever see "men from Mars," some people believe that there is alien life on other planets.

Structure Drill (Page 191)

1. You might begin the second sentence with *for example* or *for one thing*.

2. You could combine the two sentences with the word *because* or begin the second sentence with the word *clearly*.

3. Begin the second sentence with *for one thing*. Begin the third sentence with *for another thing*.

4. You might begin the second sentence with the words *for example* and the third sentence with the words *in fact* or *as a matter of fact*.

5. There are many ways to rewrite this. Here are a few examples:

   Doctors help humankind a lot. They heal the sick, and in addition, they sometimes discover cures for diseases.

   Doctors help humankind in two ways. First, they heal the sick, and second, they sometimes discover cures for diseases.

   Doctors help humankind a lot. They not only heal the sick, but also sometimes discover cures for diseases.

Varying Sentence Length Drill (Page 192)

1. My friends think becoming a police officer is a waste of time, but I think it is one of the most valuable things a person could do.

2. The police save lives, stop crime, and arrest criminals. They also interact with the community.

3. Young kids sometimes have bad attitudes because they don't have very stable home lives.

4. A police officer can show these kids that it is possible to grow up to be somebody and make a difference. In addition, a police officer can make sure they don't get bullied by other kids.

Editing Drill (Page 196)

Although
~~Altho~~ there are many professions that are
beneficial to humankind, I think the profession that
is the most beneficial of all is ~~to be~~ a politician.
That of

The world today is in the midst of making very
important changes. In ~~r~~ussia, the ~~r~~ussian people
R   R
must decide~~s~~ what kind of government they will
live under. In the United States, we must curb the
deficit and decide how to fund a health care
system for everyone. And all countries must
decide how to tackle the es~~s~~ential problems of
S
polu~~t~~ion and conservation.
^

Who will have the most say in each of these
important changes? I think it will be the politicians.
In Russia, it will be up to the men and women in
politics ~~transforming~~ the country into a democratic,
to transform
free-market economy, where everyone has
enough to eat and the chance to become whoever
he or she wants to be, without fear of being arrested or
imprisoned for political views. In the United
States, it will be our ~~C~~ongressmen and ~~S~~enators
c   s
who ~~has~~ the power to bring spending under control
have
and find a way to have affordable health care.
And it will be up to the politicians of the world to
come to terms with the threats to the ozone layer,
the forests, and the endangered species.

Social Studies

Facts, Conclusions, Opinions, and Inferences Drill (Page 228)

1. Inference—This statement goes subtly further than the passage itself by getting into the specifics of "each legislative session."

2. Conclusion—This is a restatement of the conclusion of the passage, found in its first sentence.

3. Fact—This is directly stated in the passage.

4. Opinion—This is an *interpretation* of the facts in the passage by the Council on Legislative Reform.

5. Fact—This is directly stated in the passage.

Political Systems Drill (Pages 232–233)

1. **1** Because the members of the glee club are voting, this must be some kind of democracy. Are they voting directly, or are they voting for representatives who will make decisions for them? This is a direct democracy.

2. **3** Because a small group of people is controlling the country, this must be an oligarchy.

3. **5** You might have been fooled by the "elected" president—but this president has seized power for the rest of his life. This is no longer a democracy. It is a dictatorship.

4. **2** The word *elections* means some kind of democracy. Which kind? That's right: They are electing representatives, so this is a representative democracy.

U.S. Government Drill (Page 236)

1. **1** Choice (1) is an accurate restatement of the information in the passage.

2. **2** We must focus on the facts as presented to us. The passage gives no information on the popularity of the secretary of war or the later actions of the vice president or the chief justice. All we know from the question is that Andrew Johnson was acquitted by one vote. All we know from the passage is that a conviction requires the vote of two-thirds of the Congress. The correct answer is choice (2).

U.S. Documents Drill (Page 239–240)

1. **1** According to the information, the 18th Amendment was repealed by the 21st Amendment.

2. **2** When women were given the right to vote in the 19th Amendment, it increased the number of voters in the nation.

3. **4** According to the information, Franklin D. Roosevelt was the only president among the five choices who served for more than two terms.

Economics Drill (Page 243)

1. **2** The key word in the passage is *free*. Any answer choice that suggests having to pay for basic services can be thrown out. Thus, choices (3) and (5) must be wrong. As defined in the passage, socialism also provides a state-run transportation system. This rules out choice (4). We are down to choices (1) and (2). Getting rich is clearly not the purpose of socialism, so the best answer is choice (2).

2. **3** Choices (1) and (2) both seem to be describing countries based entirely on central planning, with no element of capitalism. Choice (4) seems to be describing a country based entirely on capitalism, with no elements of socialism. The country in choice (5) also seems to have no elements of socialism. The best answer is choice (3): This country's philosophy embraces elements of both.

3. **5** For this question, we are interested only in the northeastern region, represented by the figure on the left. Just subtract the '09 figure from the '10 figure.

4. **1** This is a tough evaluation problem that requires you to make generalizations about the economy based on unemployment figures. If a country's unemployment figures are up, we can make a general assumption that the country's economy is not healthy. Of course, from this chart, we have no idea about the economies of other nations.

Supply and Demand Drill (Page 246–247)

1. **1** If supply falls, then demand cannot be satisfied, and prices rise. Choice (1) is the only one that discusses a rise in price. Choice (4) goes a little too far. While it is possible that a large increase in the cost of oil (and therefore gasoline) would cause fewer cars to be produced, it isn't likely that production of cars would halt completely.

2. **5** If the old computer becomes obsolete, its value will fall.

3. **3** Only choice (3) would increase the earnings of the rich, presumably leading to increased jobs for the poor.

Markets Drill (Page 249–250)

1. **5** In this analysis question, you must read the graph to see how the proposed law would affect the U.S. balance of payments deficit with country X. Under the proposed law, the deficit would be lower than under current law.

2. **4** If businessmen wish to lower the balance of payments deficit, this chart seems to show that the new law is a good thing. Therefore, the answer to this application question is choice (4).

Map and Globe Drill (Pages 256–258)

1. **2** Farming would be pretty hard in the mountains or the desert. However, farming is generally good near a river. The river is in the southeast region.

2. **5** Ten miles is not far enough to change the weather patterns very much.

3. **4** Latitude means the horizontal lines. Longitude means the vertical lines.

4. 1   The North Pole is at the top of the globe. Zero degrees latitude is at the equator.

5. 3   The only city on this map to the northwest of Philadelphia is Rochester.

Immigration Drill (Page 259)

1. 1   According to the passage, the Asian immigrants came to work on the railroads. The best answer is choice (1).

2. 3   Choice (1) can be eliminated because the passage tells us the railroad was built largely by noncitizens. Choices (2) and (5) are vague. Choice (4) is wrong because obviously there was some way to reach California, since the Asians arrived there.

Civil Rights Drill (Page 262)

1. 3   This is a direct restatement of information from the passage.

2. 2   These antidiscrimination regulations *may* have had support from church groups or others, but if we have to choose who *most likely* gave support, it has to be civil rights groups.

Conservation and the Environment Drill (Page 265)

1. 4   Go through each of the answer choices, checking it against the information supplied in the passage. Choice (1) is wrong because there are more endangered species than threatened species. Choice (2) is wrong because not all endangered species are being aided. We don't know if choice (3) or choice (5) is correct. We simply have no information about either.

2. 2   Simply subtract the six (that were listed twice) from the 130 threatened species.

Education Drill (Page 267)

1. 1   Educators assume that the fewer students per teacher, the better the education the students receive. Of the five states listed, Vermont has the lowest pupil-per-teacher ratio.

2. 5   Of the five listed, the state that spends the smallest amount of money per student is Utah.

3. 1   Vermont leads in both categories: It spends the most amount of money and has the smallest pupil-per-teacher ratio.

History Drill (Page 272–273)

1. 3   Only one of these five historic acts had relevance to someone who escaped from slavery in 1860: the Dred Scott decision.

2. 2   The first of these acts to essentially overturn the Missouri Compromise was the Kansas-Nebraska Act, which allowed new western states to decide the issue of slavery for themselves.

3. 4 The Homestead Act gave settlers land to farm. Without this, many would not have been able to go west.

4. 5 The Emancipation Proclamation made all slavery illegal, thus effectively nullifying both the Kansas-Nebraska Act and the Dred Scott decision.

Practical Document Drill (Page 274–275)

1. 1 The title of this form is "Lakeville Municipal Employment Application." In other words, it is a job application.

2. 4 The form asks about the applicant's last employer and position, so clearly previous experience will be a factor in deciding whether to hire the applicant; the form also asks about the applicant's education, and previous salary; there is also a place to supply the name and telephone of a personal reference, so it seems likely the person doing the hiring will be calling that person to see what the applicant is like. The only answer choice NOT mentioned in the form is the age of the applicant (and by the way—by law, no United States employer is allowed to ask the age, race, or religion of a prospective employee).

Science

Scientific Method Drill (Page 293)

1. 5 If the bird was found in the lava from the Pompeii eruption, it is a pretty safe bet that the bird came from that period. How else would it end up preserved in that rock? This was an evaluation question.

2. 3 To see if this bird is from a particular species, scientists would need to compare the bird's remains to the remains of other members of the species. Because the species is now extinct, it will be impossible to compare the remains to *living* members of the species. This was also an evaluation question.

Cells Drill (Pages 296–297)

1. 4 As long as the cell is glowing, it is still alive. It is possible that a higher dosage would kill the cell, but it is more likely that this particular strain of tuberculosis is resistant to that drug. This was an analysis question.

2. 1 For this analysis question, it helps to realize that if the tests take a long time, the patient will not be able to begin effective treatment.

3. 2 According to the passage, the new technique has only recently been discovered, so choices (1) and (3) can be eliminated. Choice (4) gets the passage backward. This procedure is faster than conventional tests. Choice (5) is not mentioned at all in the passage.

Plants Drill (Pages 302–303)

1. 3 The more rings, the older the tree is. Larger rings merely signify that the tree grew more during those years.

2. 3 The largest ring is the one marked C.

Natural Selection Drill (Pages 305–306)

1. 1   The best way to do this question is to eliminate the incorrect answer choices. Choice (2) is wrong because we know dinosaurs did not just go into hibernation—they died. Choice (3) is wrong because we know that plants depend on sunlight for their energy. Choice (4) is wrong because life forms cannot exist without food. Choice (5) is not a scientifically proven fact.

2. 2   If a dinosaur were to survive the ice age caused by the obscuring of the sun, it would have needed to be able to withstand cold temperatures. There was no plant life to eat and no sun to cause burning (under this hypothesis).

3. 2   A small-scale example of this hypothesis is choice (2), in which a volcanic eruption partially blocks the sun, causing a small variation in temperature. Choices (1) and (3) involve no climatic changes. Neither choices (4) nor (5) are caused by an outside event.

Food Chain Drill (Page 309)

1. 3   If you examine the chart, you will see that the only sea creature in this food web that is eaten by *both* land and sea creatures is the salmon.

2. 5   Algae are the most important part of this food web because, without them, none of the others would exist. Salmon, for example, would not be able to eat minnows because the minnows would have starved without the algae.

3. 4   Sharks and barracudas are the only fish in this web that have arrows going in both directions. You may not have been sure exactly what the arrows meant, but this was the best guess.

Fossils Drill (Page 311)

1. 5   Newer rock layers are generally laid on top of older layers. Unless there has been some sort of geological disturbance, layer E is going to be older than layer D.

2. 1   At different times, the ocean has covered different parts of the earth. For example, some scientists believe that the Sahara desert was underwater at one time. If rock layer B contains sea fossils, then at that time, this location was near or underwater. However, this doesn't mean that this location was always underwater or that no land fossils will be found. We can eliminate choice (5) because there were long periods of Earth's history when humans did not exist.

The Changing Earth Drill (Pages 317–318)

1. 2   Choices (1) and (4) infer too much. How can we know whether these are the only places where earthquakes occur or whether there will be fewer quakes in the future? Choices (3) and (5) are not true if you examine the chart.

2. 1   Earthquakes are caused by friction between two tectonic plates. Thus, if the friction were to stop, there should be no more earthquakes at that spot. Choices (2) and (5) would both result in enormous friction, thus causing more earthquakes. Choices (3) and (4) are irrelevant to this question.

3. 3   When molten lava explodes from the earth, it is called a volcanic eruption.

Glaciers, Erosion, and the Ice Ages Drill (Page 320)

1. **1** Glaciers are composed of frozen water. They begin melting when the temperature goes above freezing. Choices (2) and (3) are both completely opposite to the truth: These days, glaciers are found only at the two poles, not at the equator, and when glaciers melt, the level of water in the ocean goes up, not down. If glaciers are affected by the moon's gravitational pull, it didn't say so in the passage, so we can eliminate choice (4). The movement of glaciers is slow but constant—they move all the time, thus eliminating choice (5).

2. **5** Snow itself is formed only from freshwater.

Oceans, Tides, and the Moon Drill (Page 322)

1. **4** The next high tide will be $12\frac{1}{2}$ hours after 4:00 A.M.—about 4:30 P.M.

2. **3** If the moon's gravitational force causes ocean tides, then if the force becomes weaker, the tidal action would become less pronounced. Choice (1) is too extreme. Choice (2) gets it backward. Choice (4) has nothing to do with a weaker gravitational force. In choice (5), it is possible that crops and livestock would be affected, but choice (3) is the most likely answer.

The Solar System Drill (Page 326)

1. **5** Of the planets listed in the answer choices, Jupiter is the farthest away from the sun and, therefore, has the lowest surface temperature (although Venus has a higher surface temperature than has Mercury).

2. **1** If all the planets orbited the sun at the same speed, then the closest planet to the sun would take the least amount of time to travel one entire revolution around the sun. In reality, of course, the planets all travel at different speeds.

Solids, Liquids, and Gases Drill (Page 329)

1. **2** Gases can expand or contract under pressure. Heat causes gases to expand, while cooling causes gases to contract.

2. **1** Choice (1) is just a fancier way of stating what was said in the question itself.

3. **5** It can be inferred from the question that base compounds would register above a 7 (7 is considered neutral). The only answer above 7 is choice (5).

Physical Laws Drill (Page 331)

1. **4** This is a difficult question because several choices seem possible. First, let's eliminate the impossible: Choices (3) and (5) concern other fields entirely. Choices (1) and (2) are not right: Weight and mass are not really what we're looking for. The best answer to this evaluation question is choice (4), inertia.

2. **1** Because the man did not actually move the rock, according to the definition of work offered in the question, the man actually did no work, even if he is completely exhausted from the effort.

Language Arts, Reading

Fiction Drill (Pages 350–351)

1. **2** The passage tells us that Smiley recognizes the photograph of Elizabeth because he has seen a lot of other photographs of her lately. This implies he has never met her. You might not have made that inference, but if you look at the other answer choices, they can all be eliminated anyway. Choice (3) isn't true because she has not yet been hired by the company. Choice (4) is incorrect because the people Smiley is interviewing *are* her parents, and it is pretty clear they are not his friends. Choice (5) is almost certainly wrong because Smiley does not in any way show us any emotion toward Elizabeth at all. Choice (1) is harder to eliminate, but again, he shows no emotion toward Elizabeth.

2. **1** Mr. Pelling is certainly expressing a negative reaction to the name of Smiley's supposed company. Which answer choice reflects dislike? Only choice (1) or (4). Is it the card he dislikes, or does he disbelieve that the company actually exists? In fact, the answer is choice (1).

3. **4** The description shows a man who lives almost completely in one room alone. This does not sound like a description of intelligence, strength, humor, or an indication of his profession.

Drama Drill (Pages 357–358)

1. **4** The birthday present is for Big Daddy.

2. **1** Margaret says that she didn't have much growing up—that's why she says she's surprised to see the cashmere robe.

3. **2** Mae knows that Margaret bought the robe herself, so she is laughing at Margaret's attempts to make it seem as if Brick bought the present.

4. **3** In the passage, Big Daddy intimidates everyone in his immediate family and then intimidates the Reverend Tooker as well. Clearly, he is used to getting what he wants.

5. **4** Mae seems to be trying to make both Margaret and her husband Brick look bad in front of Big Daddy. Margaret responds by trying to make fun of Mae. There certainly seems to be a rivalry in progress, although we don't know yet exactly why.

Nonfiction Drill (Pages 367–368)

1. **3** Reading just a little further in the first paragraph, it becomes clear that the author thinks one of death's stings these days is the bill relatives have to pay for the funeral. While you could make an argument for both choices (1) and (2), choice (3) is the best answer.

2. **1** This question is a bit difficult because the author does not spell out her meaning here, but the entire passage is about the funeral industry, so it is a logical inference that the dismal Traders are, in fact, undertakers.

3. 3　It is in the fourth and fifth paragraphs that the author talks about new funeral products. In those paragraphs, she says that the funeral industry uses the vocabulary of "Madison Avenue"—a common reference to the advertising industry. She also quotes the industry's jargon to describe its products, and the jargon sounds just like advertising copy.

4. 2　The author is certainly making fun of the funeral industry, mocking its language and its practices. Her tone is not nostalgic, happy, indifferent, or lyrical. It is ironic.

5. 5　After reading the passage, it is clear that the author detests expensive, overblown funerals. The best answer is choice (5).

Poetry Drill (Pages 372–373)

1. 4　Having taken one path, the poet is implying that he will always wonder what lay down the other path and what would have happened if he had taken that path instead.

2. 3　The poetic words "Because it was grassy and wanted wear" are a little tough to understand, but the title of the poem provides a clue: "The Road Not Taken." He took the path where fresh grass was growing and the ground was not worn, suggesting that few had walked on it.

3. 3　The poet says that someday he will "be telling this with a sigh, somewhere ages and ages hence…." This implies that he is not an old man. However, the language and surety of the poet's voice show that he cannot be a very young person either. The best answer is that he is a middle-aged man.

4. 4　The poet does not say that one was necessarily better than the other, so we can eliminate choices (1) and (3). Surely it would not have been exactly the same, so we can eliminate choice (2). The poem implies that the other path would not have been more unusual. After all, he chose the path less traveled in the first place. The correct answer is choice (4).

Math

Number Line Drill (Page 396)

1. 1　　　Just use the values you were given to find the value of point A. The answer is −4.

2. 4　　　Estimate. Roughly where will the midpoint fall? That's right: between 3 and 4.

3. 3　　　As in the last question, estimate. Point E will be between points 0 and 1.

Rounding Off Drill (Page 399)

1. 3,000　　3,400 is less than 3,500.

2. 3.5　　3.46 is greater than 3.45.

3. **600**   565 is greater than 550.

4. **$433**   432.70 is greater than 432.50.

5. **4.80**   This number already has a zero in the hundredths place.

Adding, Subtracting, Multiplying, and Dividing Positive and Negative Numbers Drill (Page 401)

1. **2**   Adding a negative is like subtracting.

2. **–11**

3. **18**

4. **–12**   Multiplying a negative by a positive always yields a negative.

5. **1**

6. **5**

7. **10**   Multiplying a negative times a negative always yields a positive.

8. **3**   Dividing a negative by a negative always yields a positive.

9. **–4**   Dividing a positive by a negative or a negative by a positive always yields a negative.

10. **–4**

Order of Operations and Associative and Distributive Properties Drill (Page 405)
Use **PEMDAS** for these.

1. **–3**

2. **42**

3. **–12**

4. **–64**

5. **3**

Reducing Fractions Drill (Page 407)

1. $\dfrac{2}{3}$ Divide top and bottom by 2.

2. $\dfrac{3}{4}$ Divide top and bottom by 3.

3. $\dfrac{1}{2}$ Divide top and bottom by 10. Or start with 2 or 5 and then reduce again.

4. $\dfrac{5}{4}$ Divide top and bottom by 2.

5.   Can't be reduced. If you said $\dfrac{2}{3}$, you found the square root of top and bottom by mistake.

Adding and Subtracting Fractions Drill (Page 411)

1. $\dfrac{4}{5}$ Use the Bowtie method.

2. $\dfrac{48}{35}$ 35 is the common denominator.

3. $\dfrac{4}{9}$ 9 is the common denominator.

4. $\dfrac{5}{9}$ If you use the Bowtie for the first two numbers, you will already have the same denominator as in the third number.

5. 0 $\dfrac{1}{3}$ is the same as $\dfrac{5}{15}$.

Multiplying, Dividing, and Converting Fractions Drill (Page 413)

1. $\dfrac{3}{5}$ First cancel the 4s on top and bottom.

2. 3   Invert and multiply. But before you multiply, cancel the 10s, and divide top and bottom by 3.

3. $\dfrac{10}{54}$ or $\dfrac{5}{27}$ Invert and multiply, but before you multiply, divide top and bottom by 2.

4. $\dfrac{2}{5}$ Cancel the 3s and the 4s, and you won't have to multiply at all!

5. $\dfrac{1}{2}$ First, convert $1\dfrac{1}{3}$ to an improper fraction: $\dfrac{4}{3}$. Then cancel the 3s.

Fraction Word Problem Drill (Page 417–418)

1. **3**   Half of the 80 people tested originally had Lyme disease—that's 40 people. Of the other 40 people, one quarter later developed Lyme disease. One quarter of 40 is 10. So a total of 50 got Lyme disease out of 80 people. $\frac{50}{80} = \frac{5}{8}$.

2. **5**   One tenth of 100 is 10, so in August they baked 110 pies. In September they increased production by another tenth. One tenth of 110 is 11. So in September, they baked 110 + 11 pies, or 121.

3. **2**   To work with these fractions, you need to find a common denominator: $\frac{1}{3} = \frac{5}{15}$. $\frac{2}{5} = \frac{6}{15}$. So if $\frac{5}{15}$ go by public transportation, and $\frac{6}{15}$ go by car, that adds up to $\frac{11}{15}$ —which means that $\frac{4}{15}$ walk to work.

Decimals Drill (Page 421)

1. **7.06**

2. **4.36**

3. **8.194**   Forget the decimals and just multiply. Then add up the numbers to the right of the decimals in the original numbers. That is how many places to move the decimal to the left in your new number.

4. **3,200**   Set this up like a normal division problem. Then move the decimal place of the divisor as many times as it takes to turn the divisor into an integer. Now move the decimal in the dividend the same number of places, and divide as usual.

5. **40**   Use the same methods you used in Question 4.

Percentages Drill (Page 425)

1. **8**   Move the decimal over one place to the left.

2. **6**   Move the decimal over one place to the left, and then multiply by 2.

3. **280**   Move the decimal over one place to the left, and then multiply by 4.

4. **0.7**   Move the decimal over two places to the left.

5. **12**   Move the decimal over two places to the left, and then multiply by 6.

6. **100 + 15 = 115**

7. **20 + 10 = 30**

8. $18 + 3 = 21$

9. 20

10. $\frac{1}{4}$ of 80 = 20

Percent Word Problems Drill (Page 429)

1. **2**   6.5 times 8 = 52. By ballparking, you could have eliminated choice (5).

2. **3**   Think about what's left over: 40 percent of 1,200. Choice (1) was 60 percent of 1,200, which was a partial answer.

3. **524.3** $490 plus 7 percent of $490, or $34.30, for a total of **$524.30.** However, make sure you enter it in the grid as 524.3 because there are only five spaces allotted for answers.

4. **2**   The $8,500 for the year before is a red herring: It doesn't have anything to do with this problem. The best way to do this problem is by working backward. Let's start with choice (2). What is 60 percent of $9,000? If you got $5,400, you are absolutely correct. You are also done. The answer to this problem is choice (2).

Ratios and Proportions Drill (Page 433)

1. **2** $\frac{5}{2} = \frac{x}{10}$

2. **2** $\frac{3}{2} = \frac{x}{2,500}$

3. **5**   Not enough information is given. We have no method of comparison.

Basic Arithmetic Drill (Pages 435–436)

1. **3**   Just divide 5 into 3, or think "one-fifth = 0.2, so three-fifths = 0.6."

2. **4**   Just move the decimal one place, multiply by 2, and add that to $23.00.

3. **3** $\frac{2}{30} = \frac{x}{72}$. Ballparking will get rid of choices (1) and (2).

4. **2**   Add $\frac{1}{4}$ and $\frac{1}{5}$, but look out for choice (1): It is a partial answer. We want what is left over.

5. **4**   If the midpoint of AB is –2, then point A is located at –4. Similarly, point C is located at 4. The length of AB is 4.

6. **4**   To the nearest hundred, $75 rounds up to the next hundred.

7. **4**   Divide both sides of the equation by 5. You should get $R - S = 7$.

8. **2** Use PEMDAS, and be careful. The answer is –1.

9. **5** $\dfrac{30}{70} = \dfrac{3}{7} = \dfrac{x}{100}$, which you can round up to 43 percent. Ballparking shows it will be just under 50 percent.

10. **5** We can eliminate choices (1) and (2) because they are less than the amount paid. This is a good problem to do backward. Let's start with choice (4), $11,000. What is 80 percent of $11,000? $8,800, which is too small. Let's try choice (5), which is the only number that is bigger. What is 80 percent of $12,000? You guessed it: $9,600.

Setup Drill (Pages 441–442)

1. **1** 8 times 6 times 4 times $5.50.

2. **3** The new cost is the old cost ($12,000) plus 0.04 times the old cost.

3. **5** 650 – 430 – 22 + 250

Mean and Median Drill (Pages 447–448)

1. **3** An average is always equal to the sum of all the elements divided by the number of elements. So $23.40 = $\dfrac{x}{14}$. x = $23.40 times 14, or $327.60.

2. **3** The median is the middle number. Choice (4) is actually the mean, and choice (5) is out of the ballpark.

3. **3** All the choices are too close to ballpark. Just add and divide by 3.

4. **4** Add up the total number of cones and divide by the number of days: 595 divided by 5 = 119.

Rate Problems Drill (Page 451–452)

1. **4** If you set this up in the $R \times T = D$ format, it looks like this: ? × 3 = 12. The correct answer is 4 mph.

2. **4** Just divide 5,280 by 4.

3. **3** She drives 20 miles. If we deduct the hour she spent shopping, she drove the 20 miles in one hour.

Charts and Graphs Drill (Page 455–456)

1. **2** Let's say there were 100 telephones in all. If 45 of them were regular, then that number (45) is how many times greater than the number of cellular phones (15)? The answer is 3 times greater.

2. 3   To ballpark this problem, first compare bottles A and B (which have the same number of ounces), and bottles C and D (which also contain the same number of ounces). Bottle A is cheaper than B, and bottle C is cheaper than D, so we can eliminate choices (2) and (4). To find the exact price per ounce of each bottle, divide the price by the number of ounces. Bottle A costs 5 cents per ounce. Bottle C costs 3.3 cents per ounce. Bottle E costs 5 cents per ounce. The answer is bottle C.

3. 3   Just ballpark, based on the chart.

Exponents and Square Roots Drill (Pages 460–461)

1. 1   Just try out the answer choices until you find the one that equals 8.

2. 31   27 + 4 = 31

3. 4   4 − 2 = 2

Scientific Notation and Probability Drill (Page 465)

1. 3   It's probably easiest to expand each of the answer choices until you find the one that works.

2. 4   Two out of four, or $\frac{1}{2}$.

3. 5   3,400 + 41,000 = 44,400

Applied Arithmetic Drill (Pages 467–468)

1. 1   In this setup problem, we need to multiply 0.08 times $5,000 twice.

2. 3   If we set this up in the rate times time format, we have 5 × ? = 17.5. The correct answer is $3\frac{1}{2}$ hours. You could have eliminated choices (4) and (5) by ballparking.

3. 5   There is not enough information given to answer this chart problem.

4. 190 $47.50 times 4 gives us the answer to this average problem: $190.

5. 3   Don't bother multiplying further than you have to—it's clear choice (1) is way too big, for example. The correct answer to this exponent problem is choice (3).

6. 2   The square root of 9 is 3. This is the closest the answer choices come to the square root of 10.

7. 2   There are a total of 7 possible cars. There are 2 sedans. The odds on this probablility problem are 2 out of 7.

8. 12   Rearrange the numbers in ascending order. The middle number is 12.

9. **1**   To answer this setup problem, just convert the words into math. She works 40 hours at $14.50 and 3 hours at $19.00. The correct answer is choice (1). Choice (3) is wrong because we are supposed to add the two numbers, not multiply.

10. **4**   Expand out the scientific notation: 23,000 microns versus 32,000 microns. The difference is 9,000 microns.

Simple Equation Drill (Page 472)

1. **2**   Add 5 to both sides of the equation, and then divide both sides by 2.

2. **2**   First, combine all the x's, and then combine all the y's.

3. **15**   Subtract 6 from both sides of the equation, and then divide both sides by 3.

4. **4**   Just plug in 2 for x and 3 for y.

Inequalities Drill (Page 476)

1. **4**   If the minimum age is five, then anyone five or older can ride the roller coaster.

2. **1**   Just solve as if this were an equality.

3. **3**   Try out each of the answer choices until you find an equation that includes 4.

Backsolving Drill (Page 482)

1. **1**   First, let's ballpark. If Marcie sees more patients, then she must see more than half of them. The answer must be more than 8, which eliminates every answer choice but choice (1). If you didn't notice that, how could you have solved the problem? By backsolving. Let's try choice (3) and say that Marcie saw 5 patients. If Marcie saw 2 more than Lewis, then Lewis saw 3 patients. When you add together Marcie and Lewis's patients, you are supposed to have 16. Could this be the right answer? No way. We need a bigger number. Let's try answer choice (2). If Marcie had 7 patients, Lewis has 5, and this is still too small. The correct answer must be choice (1).

2. **5**   This is another good backsolve. Just try putting the values in the answer choices into the equation until you find one that works.

3. **3**   Ballparking gets rid of choice (1) because there can't be more women than there are total workers. Ballparking also gets rid of choice (2) because the problem says there are some men workers as well. If you solve this algebraically, watch out for choice (5), which turns out to be the number of men. However, a good way to avoid any chance of making a mistake is not to use algebra—try backsolving instead. As always, start with choice (3). If there are 60 women and 4 times as many women as men, then the number of men is $\frac{1}{4}$ of 60 or 15. If 60 + 15 = 75, then this is the answer. And it is.

4. 2   Again, it is much easier to backsolve. Start with choice (3), 10%. Ten percent of $45.00 is $4.50. This is too much, so go down one and find 9 percent of $45.00. This is the correct answer.

5. 5   You could use algebra, but backsolving is just as easy. Start with choice (3), and see if it makes the equation work. No, we need a bigger number. Choice (4) doesn't work either, so the answer must be choice (5).

Translation Drill (Page 487)

1. 3   Choice (1) is just Sandra's weight alone. The combined weight of both of them is choice (3).

2. 3   The 2000 figure is just a red herring. It doesn't matter that the number of rabbits doubled in 2000 because by 2001 (the year we are interested in), the population is up five times.

3. 4   Choice (1) doesn't multiply Sam's age by 3. Choice (2) doesn't add 2 years. Choices (3) and (5) subtract years.

Putting It All Together: Algebra Drill (Pages 488–489)

1. 3   Use algebra or backsolve.

2. 1   Use translation: $3x + 4$.

3. 1   Just plug in 3 for x and 4 for y.

4. 4   This is a good backsolving problem. If you start with choice (3), you'll see it's too small, so go up to the next biggest answer and try that.

5. 2   Treat this just like an equality: Solve for m.

6. 5   Just add up the total number of x's and y's.

7. 5   Plug 4 into each of the answer choices until you find the one that is true.

8. 3   You can ballpark this: 30 workers would be one-quarter, or 25 percent. 36 workers would be slightly more. Or work backward: What is 10 percent of the 120 workers? That's right: 12. Twenty percent? 24. Thirty percent? 36. Bingo!

9. 2   The first sentence of this problem is a red herring. In this problem, it doesn't matter what happened this year. The problem is asking about next year in terms of last year. Next year is supposed to be triple last year's revenues, or $3x$.

10. 4   This is a great backsolving problem. Start with choice (3). You'll notice that you need a larger number. Choice (4) is correct.

Lines and Angles Drill (Page 496)

1. **40 degrees** $180 - 140 = 40$

2. **90 degrees** $180 - 90 = 90$

3. **130 degrees** $180 - 50 = 130$

4. **130 degrees** You can use Fred's theorem, provided the lines are parallel.

Triangles Drill (Page 505–506)

1. **2** Area is base times height divided by two. If you picked choice (1), you forgot to divide by two.

2. **2** This is a 3-4-5 triangle. The answer is $5 - 3 = 2$.

3. **3** $180 - (27 + 53) = 100$.

4. **5** First, let's ballpark. We are going to "reduce" the entire triangle. This means the measurement of each of the other two sides must be less than 16, which eliminates choices (1) and (2). Now, if you are reducing the entire triangle by $\frac{1}{2}$, then the two sides in question will each have a length of 8.

5. **4** Adding up the three sides of the triangle, we get $4x + 20 = 180$. Solving for x, we get 40 degrees—but the question is asking for angle A, which is $2x$ or 80 degrees.

Rectangles and Squares Drill (Page 507)

1. **square** All sides are the same length.

2. **rectangle** The sides are different lengths.

3. **9** Multiply length by width: $3 \times 3 = 9$

4. **24** Add the four sides together: $3 + 3 + 9 + 9 = 24$. (The area of figure B would be 27.)

5. **3** Divide the area of the rectangle by the area of the square: $27 \div 9 = 3$.

Circles Drill (Page 508)

1. **4**

2. **8** Multiply the radius by 2: $4 \times 2 = 8$.

3. **8π** The diameter is 8, so multiply thay by π to get the circumference.

4. **16π** Use the formula for area: $\pi 4^2 = 16\pi$.

Volume Drill (Page 511)

1. 5 $3 \times 4 \times\, ? = 60$

2. 4   The entire volume of the cube equals 8.

3. 81π The area of the circle is 9π. $9\pi \times 9 = 81\pi$.

4. 5   Because we don't know how much the wallpaper costs, there is not enough information given for us to answer the question.

Graphing Drill (Pages 517–518)

1. 4   To find the slope, take the difference in y-values, and put that over the difference in x-values. In this case, that is $\dfrac{2}{4}$ or $\dfrac{1}{2}$.

2. 3   Did you need the distance formula this time? No way! The y-values were the same for both numbers. All we had to do was subtract 5 from 12. If you didn't notice this, you could have sketched it out. Seeing what the problem really looks like almost always makes it easier to solve.

3.   To graph point A, count 3 left and 4 down. To graph point B, go right 2 and up 3. For point C, count 3 right and 5 up.

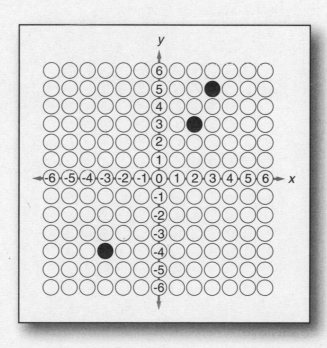

Geometry Drill (Pages 520–521)

1. **4** The lines are parallel.

2. **2** The area is $7^2 \times \dfrac{22}{7}$, or 154.

3. **3** Each side of the square has the same length, 3. The two sides of an isosceles triangle that are opposite equal angles also have the same length, 4. The correct answer is 17.

4. **3** Any three-sided figure is a triangle. If two of the sides have the same length, as the ratio tells us, then it is an isosceles triangle.

5. **1** You could backsolve this. The volume of a cube is side^3. Try cubing each answer choice until you find one that gives you the value 27. Obviously, you won't have to go too far to realize you are going to need a pretty small number.

6. **2** The sum of all three angles must equal 180, so subtract 45 from 180.

7. **5** Divide 168 by 12. The correct answer is 14.

8. **1** Area of a triangle equals base times height divided by 2.

9. **5** The diameter of the large circle equals the sum of the diameters of the two small circles, so each small circle has a diameter of 10 and a radius of 5.

10. **5** You need *two* points on a line to find its slope.

Part IX
The Princeton Review GED Practice Tests and Explanations

Chapter 27
Practice Test 1

LANGUAGE ARTS, WRITING PART I

Tests of General Educational Development

Directions

The Language Arts, Writing Test is intended to measure your ability to use clear and effective English. It is a test of English as it should be written, not as it might be spoken. This test includes both multiple-choice questions and an essay. These directions apply only to the multiple-choice section; a separate set of directions is given for the essay.

The multiple-choice section consists of paragraphs with numbered sentences. Some of the sentences contain errors in sentence structure, usage, or mechanics (spelling, punctuation, and capitalization). After reading the numbered sentences, answer the multiple-choice questions that follow. Some questions refer to sentences that are correct as written. The best answer for these questions is the one that leaves the sentence as originally written. The best answer for some questions is the one that produces a sentence that is consistent with the verb tense and point of view used throughout the text.

You should spend no more than 40 minutes on the multiple-choice questions and 45 minutes on your essay. Work carefully, but do not spend too much time on any one question. You may begin working on the essay part of this test as soon as you complete the multiple-choice section.

Do not mark in this test booklet. Record your answers on the separate answer sheet provided. Be sure that all requested information is properly recorded on the answer sheet.

To record your answers, mark one numbered space on the answer sheet beside the number that corresponds to the question in the test booklet.

FOR EXAMPLE:

Sentence 1: **We were honored to meet governor Phillips.**

Which correction should be made to sentence 1?

(1) insert a comma after <u>honored</u>
(2) change <u>honored</u> to <u>honer</u>
(3) change <u>governor</u> to <u>Governor</u>
(4) change <u>were</u> to <u>was</u>
(5) no correction is necessary

In this example, the word *governor* should be capitalized; therefore, answer space (3) would be marked on the answer sheet.

Do not rest the point of your pencil on the answer sheet while you are considering your answer. Make no stray or unnecessary marks. If you change an answer, erase your first mark completely. Mark only <u>one</u> answer space for each question; multiple answers will be scored as incorrect. Do not fold or crease your answer sheet. All test materials must be returned to the test administrator.

Writing, Part I

<u>Directions</u>: Choose the <u>one best answer</u> to each question.

<u>Questions 1 through 8</u> refer to the following consumer awareness letter.

Consumer Environmental Awareness Society
Box 22
Washington, D.C.

Dear Concerned Citizen,

(A)

(1) Because of changes in the attitudes of their customers, Companies are making new efforts to compromise between convenience and concern for the environment. (2) However, you still need to be concerned about the consequences of using certain products. (3) When a label claims that a product is environmentally safe. (4) But how can you be sure this is true?

(B)

(5) Read the content label of any product before you make your purchase. (6) Then, read the newspaper and other periodicals to familiarize oneself with the current research and with the properties of various chemicals. (7) Staying informed, getting involved in community programs, and remembering to recycle are simple ways to help the environment now and preserve them for future generations. (8) There are people who believe that mistreatment of the environment will not affect them directly they are sadly mistaken.

(C)

(9) Deciding that the environment is important is the first step. (10) Start with one simple activity, such as installing water-conserving faucets. (11) Awareness respect, and care for the environment can be contagious. (12) You will probably start to notice others around you following your good example.

---

1. Sentence 1: **Because of changes in the attitudes of their customers, Companies are making new efforts to compromise between convenience and concern for the environment.**

   Which correction should be made to sentence 1?

   (1) replace <u>Because of</u> with <u>Due to the fact that</u>
   (2) remove the comma after <u>customers</u>
   (3) change <u>Companies</u> to <u>companies</u>
   (4) insert a comma after <u>convenience</u>
   (5) no correction is necessary

2. Sentences 3 and 4: **When a label claims that a product is environmentally <u>safe. But how</u> can you be sure this is true?**

   Which of the following is the best way to write the underlined portion of these sentences? If you think that the original is the best way, choose option (1).

   (1) safe. But how
   (2) safe, and how
   (3) safe, how
   (4) safe, how it
   (5) safe, or how

GO ON TO THE NEXT PAGE

3.   Sentence 5: **Read the content label of any product before you make your purchase.**

If you rewrote sentence 5 beginning with

Make sure that

the next words should be

(1)   you had already read
(2)   you read
(3)   you did read
(4)   you are reading
(5)   you will read

4.   Sentence 6: **Then, read the newspaper and other periodicals to familiarize oneself with the current research and with the properties of various chemicals.**

Which correction should be made to sentence 6?

(1)   remove the comma after Then
(2)   change periodicals to periodical
(3)   replace oneself with yourself
(4)   change properties to property
(5)   no correction is necessary

5.   Sentence 7: **Staying informed, getting involved in community programs, and remembering to recycle are simple ways to help the environment now and preserve them for future generations.**

Which correction should be made to sentence 7?

(1)   change staying to to stay
(2)   insert a comma after recycle
(3)   change ways to a way
(4)   change help to helping
(5)   replace them with it

6.   Sentence 8: **There are people who believe that mistreatment of the environment will not affect them directly they are sadly mistaken.**

Which of the following is the best way to write the underlined portion of this sentence? If you think the original is the best way, choose option (1).

(1)   directly they
(2)   directly. They
(3)   directly, or they
(4)   directly and they
(5)   directly; still, they

7.   Sentences 9 and 10: **Deciding that the environment is important is the first step. Start with one simple activity, such as installing water-conserving faucets.**

The most effective combination of sentences 9 and 10 would include which of the following groups of words?

(1)   step; but start
(2)   step; then start
(3)   step; simple activities
(4)   step; water conservation
(5)   step; such as

8.   Sentence 11: **Awareness respect, and care for the environment can be contagious.**

Which correction should be made to sentence 11?

(1)   insert a comma after Awareness
(2)   replace respect with suspect
(3)   insert a comma after care
(4)   replace for with of
(5)   change contagious to contagiousness

GO ON TO THE NEXT PAGE

Writing, Part I

Questions 9 through 13 refer to the following paragraphs.

(A)

(1) Learning to use a computer can frequently be a test of your patience and persistence. (2) What do you do, for example, when you think you have followed the instructions to the letter? (3) And the predicted result does not occur? (4) It is equally frustrating when you make a simple mistake and undo hours of work. (5) You think learning to use a computer is difficult, imagine what it would be like to do everything by hand or typewriter. (6) As a matter of fact, the computer has allowed for miraculous advances in information management. (7) When it was finally developed, it is the result of countless hours of creative thinking and research.

(B)

(8) The first personal computers were introduced to the consumer market in the early seventies. (9) Companies back then agree to take the financial risk because they believed in the future of this machine that would change the face of communication and industry. (10) In just five short years, computer sales increased dramatically, making them one of the fastest growing industries in the last decade. (11) The result of this innovation is that tasks that took offices months to complete, can now be achieved in a matter of days. (12) Efficiency, in a word, is the main result. (13) Nowadays, a computer is no longer a luxury or a novelty, but rather a necessity for keeping up in the worlds of business, education, and communication.

9. Sentences 2 and 3: **What do you do, for example, when you think you have followed the instructions to the <u>letter? And</u> the predicted result does not occur?**

   Which of the following is the best way to write the underlined portion of these sentences? If you think the original is the best way, choose option (1).

   (1) letter? And
   (2) letter, or
   (3) letter and
   (4) letter; and
   (5) letter and what

10. Sentence 4: **It is equally frustrating when you make a simple mistake and undo hours of work.**

    If you rewrote sentence 4 beginning with

    <u>Nor is it</u>

    the next words should be

    (1) just as frustrated
    (2) frustrated any less
    (3) any less frustrating
    (4) completely frustrating
    (5) after which, more frustrating

GO ON TO THE NEXT PAGE

Writing, Part I

11. Sentence 5: **You think learning to use a computer is difficult, imagine what it would be like to do everything by hand or typewriter.**

    Which of the following is the best way to write the underlined portion of this sentence? If you think the original is the best way, choose option (1).

    (1) You think learning to use a computer is difficult, imagine
    (2) You think learning to use a computer is difficult, imagining about
    (3) Learning to use a computer is hard, you think, then imagine
    (4) If you think learning to use a computer is difficult, imagine
    (5) Why you think learning to use a computer is difficult, imagine

12. Sentence 7: **When it was finally developed, it is the result of countless hours of creative thinking and research.**

    Which correction should be made to sentence 7?

    (1) change <u>finally</u> to <u>final</u>
    (2) remove the comma after <u>developed</u>
    (3) change <u>is</u> to <u>was</u>
    (4) change <u>thinking</u> to <u>thinkers</u>
    (5) change <u>research</u> to <u>researched</u>

13. Sentence 9: **Companies back then <u>agree</u> to take the financial risk because they believed in the future of this machine that would change the face of communication and industry.**

    Which of the following is the best way to write the underlined portion of this sentence? If you think the original is the best way, choose option (1).

    (1) agree
    (2) is agreeing
    (3) agreeing
    (4) agreed
    (5) was agree

GO ON TO THE NEXT PAGE

Writing, Part I

Questions 14 through 20 refer to the following fund-raising letter.

Miguel Alvarez
22 Sunset Drive
Miami, Florida

Dear Mr. Alvarez,

(A)

(1) The Late President John F. Kennedy said in his inaugural address of 1961, "Ask not what your country can do for you, but what you can do for your country." (2) This call for service to the country has been repeated in the political speeches of recent years. (3) Lets clarify, however, exactly what sort of "service" these politicians are calling for. (4) They are not asking for service of the military sort, but rather asking just how far you are willing to go to help your neighbor.

(B)

(5) The concept of helping one's neighbor was certainly not invented by Kennedy. (6) Nor has it been settled since his death; it was hotly debated to this very day. (7) The biblical patriarchs, Greek philosophers, and contemporary lawyers have all puzzled over this ethical issue. (8) On the one hand, most people believe that good deeds will be rewarded. (9) On the other hand, everyone can think of examples of "good guys" who get hurt while "bad guys" go unpunished. (10) Fortunately, despite such disturbing exceptions to the golden rule, most people still try to help their neighbors, if the sacrifice is not too great.

(C)

We hope you will contribute to our neighborhood hurricane relief fund again this year.

Yours truly,

Otis Pindar
Committee Chair

GO ON TO THE NEXT PAGE

Writing, Part I

14. Sentence 1: **The Late President John F. Kennedy said in his inaugural address of 1961, "Ask not what your country can do for you, but what you can do for your country."**

    Which correction should be made to sentence 1?

    (1) change <u>Late</u> to <u>late</u>
    (2) change <u>President</u> to <u>president</u>
    (3) change <u>said</u> to <u>says</u>
    (4) change <u>address</u> to <u>addresses</u>
    (5) remove the comma after <u>1961</u>

15. Sentence 3: **Lets clarify, however, exactly what sort of "service" these politicians are calling for.**

    Which correction should be made to sentence 3?

    (1) change <u>Lets</u> to <u>Let's</u>
    (2) remove the comma after <u>however</u>
    (3) insert a comma after <u>"service"</u>
    (4) change <u>are calling</u> to <u>had called</u>
    (5) no correction is necessary

16. Sentence 4: **They are not asking for service of the military sort, but rather asking just how far you are willing to go to help your neighbor.**

    If you rewrote sentence 4 beginning with

    <u>Rather than asking for service of the military sort,</u>

    the next words should be

    (1) are you willing
    (2) what had been being asked
    (3) but these politicians
    (4) these politicians are asking
    (5) what was being asked

17. Sentence 6: **Nor has it been settled since his death; <u>it was hotly debated</u> to this very day.**

    Which of the following is the best way to write the underlined portion of this sentence? If you think the original is the best way, choose option (1).

    (1) it was hotly debated
    (2) hotly it was debated
    (3) it is hotly debated
    (4) it was hotly debated over
    (5) it will debate hotly

18. Sentence 7: **The biblical patriarchs, Greek philosophers, and contemporary lawyers have all puzzled over this ethical issue.**

    If you rewrote sentence 7 beginning with

    <u>This ethical issue</u>

    the next words should be

    (1) has been puzzled over
    (2) were being puzzled
    (3) with the biblical
    (4) having been puzzled over
    (5) has, by the biblical

GO ON TO THE NEXT PAGE

19. Sentence 9: **On the other hand, everyone can think of examples of "good guys" who get hurt while "bad guys" <u>go unpunished</u>.**

   Which of the following is the best way to write the underlined portion of this sentence? If you think the original is the best way, choose option (1).

   (1) go unpunished
   (2) goes unpunished
   (3) went unpunished
   (4) are going unpunished
   (5) go being unpunished

20. Sentence 10: **Fortunately, despite such disturbing exceptions to the golden rule, most people still try to help their neighbors, if the sacrifice is not too great.**

   Which correction should be made to sentence 10?

   (1) change <u>try</u> to <u>tries</u>
   (2) change <u>help</u> to <u>helping</u>
   (3) replace <u>if</u> with <u>whether</u>
   (4) change <u>sacrifice</u> to <u>sacrifices</u>
   (5) no correction is necessary

GO ON TO THE NEXT PAGE

Writing, Part I

<u>Questions 21 through 25</u> refer to the following paragraphs.

(A)

(1) A maxim we all know states that, "The more things change, the more they stay the same." (2) Most of us, see this principle in action every day. (3) One way to illustrate this point is to examine one of life's seemingly mundane issues—transportation. (4) Transportation is an area that has seen enormous changes over the last hundred years. (5) Even 50 years ago, possession of an automobile was far less common than it is today. (6) The proliferation of the automobile and the new accessibility of once distant cities has had widespread effects.

(B)

(7) However, although we travel around our own country, we remain closed off to much of the world that surrounds you. (8) Airline travel remains very expensive, and people do not fly as much as the airlines want them to.

(C)

(9) In short, the average American does not reach Europe, much less the mountains of Africa.

(D)

(10) Compared to Americans of the last century, we have indeed achieved a great deal, but our progress is more in theory than in practice.

(E)

(11) We must always remember that real progress is extremely rare.

21. Sentence 2: **Most of us, see this principle in action every day.**

    Which correction should be made to sentence 2?

    (1) remove comma after <u>us</u>
    (2) replace <u>us</u> with <u>you</u>
    (3) change <u>see</u> to <u>saw</u>
    (4) replace <u>principle</u> with <u>principal</u>
    (5) no correction is necessary

22. Sentence 4: **Transportation is an area that has seen enormous changes over the last hundred years.**

    Which correction should be made to sentence 4?

    (1) replace <u>is</u> with <u>has</u>
    (2) insert a comma after <u>area</u>
    (3) change <u>hundred</u> to <u>hundreds of</u>
    (4) change <u>changes</u> to <u>changing</u>
    (5) no correction is necessary

GO ON TO THE NEXT PAGE

23. Sentence 6: **The proliferation of the automobile and the new accessibility of once distant cities <u>has had</u> widespread effects.**

    Which of the following is the best way to write the underlined portion of this sentence? If you think the original is the best way, choose option (1).

    (1)   has had
    (2)   will have
    (3)   have had
    (4)   had had
    (5)   will have had

24. Sentence 7: **However, although we travel around our own country, we remain closed off to much of the world that surrounds you.**

    Which correction should be made to sentence 7?

    (1)   replace <u>although</u> with <u>notwithstanding</u>
    (2)   remove the comma after <u>country</u>
    (3)   change <u>remain</u> to <u>remains</u>
    (4)   insert a comma after <u>off</u>
    (5)   replace <u>you</u> with <u>us</u>

25. Sentence 9: **In short, the average American does not reach Europe, much less the mountains of Africa.**

    If you rewrote sentence 9 beginning with

    <u>The average American,</u>

    the next words should be

    (1)   in short, does not reach
    (2)   in short will not reach
    (3)   in short, reaching
    (4)   the mountains will not reach
    (5)   in short, reaches not

GO ON TO THE NEXT PAGE

Writing, Part I

Questions 26 and 27 refer to the following business memo.

Minutes of Coordinating Committee 3/15/01

(A)

(1) The first order of business was the reading of the minutes of the previous meeting. (2) The committee then voted to move on to new business.

(B)

(3) The committee agreed at that time to table discussion of the office renovations in order to move on to the more vital topic of sagging sales. (4) The first item of new business was the topic of upcoming office renovations. (5) There was heated discussion as to the expense of some items of the planned renovation, including the new computers for the secretarial staff, but no consensus was reached.

(C)

(6) The sales figures for February were 24 percent below last year's levels.

26. Which of the revisions below would most improve the organization of paragraph B?

    (1) move sentence 3 so it comes after sentence 4
    (2) move sentence 3 so it comes after sentence 5
    (3) move sentence 5 to the beginning of paragraph B
    (4) end paragraph B with a new sentence beginning, "Secretaries don't deserve new computers anyway…"
    (5) begin paragraph B with a new sentence beginning, "No one really felt coming to this meeting…"

27. Which of the following sentences would most likely follow sentence 6?

    (1) The secretarial computer purchase is expected to cost $3,700.
    (2) Plans for the office renovations have taken longer than expected.
    (3) The minutes from last week's meeting were not accepted by the committee.
    (4) In an effort to boost sales, it was resolved to spend more money on advertising in the next two months.
    (5) The committee moved on to discuss several items of old business.

GO ON TO THE NEXT PAGE

LANGUAGE ARTS, WRITING PART II

Tests of General Educational Development

Essay Directions and Topic

This part of the Language Arts, Writing Test is intended to determine how well you write. You are asked to write an essay that explains something or presents an opinion on an issue. In preparing your essay, you should take the following steps:

1. Read the directions and the essay topic given below carefully.

2. Plan your essay thoughtfully before you write, using personal experience, observation, and knowledge.

3. Use scratch paper to make any notes.

4. Write your essay on the lined pages of the separate answer sheet.

5. Review what you have written and make any changes that will improve your essay.

6. Check your paragraphs, sentence structure, spelling, punctuation, capitalization, and usage, and make any necessary corrections.

Be sure you write the <u>letter</u> of the essay topic (given below) on your answer sheet. Write the letter in the box at the upper right-hand corner of the page where you write your essay.

You will have 45 minutes to write on the topic below. Write legibly and use a ballpoint pen so that the evaluators will be able to read your writing.

Write your essay on the lined pages of the separate answer sheet. The notes you make on scratch paper will not be scored.

Your essay will be scored by at least two trained evaluators who will judge it according to its <u>overall effectiveness</u>. They will judge how clearly you make the main point of your composition, how thoroughly you support your ideas, and how clearly and correctly you write throughout the essay.

TOPIC E

These days it seems that everything about us is being monitored, from our credit histories to our shopping preferences. The information age is quickly destroying our right to privacy.

Do you agree or disagree with this statement? Write an essay of about 250 words presenting your view and supporting it with specific examples from your own experience or your observations of others.

END OF TEST

SOCIAL STUDIES

Tests of General Educational Development

Directions

The Social Studies Test consists of multiple-choice questions intended to measure general social studies concepts. The questions are based on short readings that often include a map, graph, chart, cartoon, or figure. Study the information given and then answer the question(s) following it. Refer to the information as often as necessary in answering the questions.

You should spend no more than 45 minutes answering the questions in this booklet. Work carefully, but do not spend too much time on any one question. Be sure you answer every question. You will not be penalized for incorrect answers.

Do not mark in this test booklet. Record your answers to the questions on the separate answer sheet provided. Be sure all requested information is properly recorded on the answer sheet.

To record your answers, mark the numbered space on the answer sheet beside the number that corresponds to the question in the test booklet.

FOR EXAMPLE:

Early colonists of North America looked for settlement sites with adequate water supplies and access by ship. For this reason, many early towns were built near

(1) mountains
(2) prairies
(3) rivers
(4) glaciers
(5) plateaus

The correct answer is "rivers"; therefore, answer space (3) would be marked on the answer sheet.

Do not rest the point of your pencil on the answer sheet while you are considering your answer. Make no stray or unnecessary marks. If you change an answer, erase your first mark completely. Mark only <u>one</u> answer space for each question; multiple answers will be scored as incorrect. Do not fold or crease your answer sheet. Return all test materials to the test administrator.

Social Studies

Directions: Choose the <u>one best answer</u> to each question.

Questions 1 through 5 are based on the following information.

   The Department of Labor operates under the mandate that the most important capital is human capital. Particular attention is paid to the future workforce of America—the children. To this end, legislation was enacted to safeguard youngsters' opportunities to receive schooling without the burden of a full-time or health-threatening occupation. The Fair Labor Standards Act (FLSA) has provisions designed to protect children. Employment for minors now must conform to the following restrictions, which apply to all labor except farm labor. First, 16- or 17-year-olds may legally obtain employment as long as the job is not determined to be dangerous or ruinous to their health or well-being. Second, 14- or 15-year-olds may also work during specific hours at certain jobs as long as their employment does not negatively affect their health, schooling, or well-being. Employment of children under 14 years of age is usually prohibited. The Department of Labor has already classified 17 nonagricultural occupations as being unsuitable for minors.

1. According to the regulations described, all of the following could legally be used to deny a minor employment EXCEPT

 (1) age
 (2) gender
 (3) hazard level
 (4) type of job
 (5) working hours

2. Which of the following beliefs is the basis for the regulations?

 (1) Minors should judge the appropriateness of their own employment.
 (2) Employment of minors must be controlled to protect them from harm.
 (3) Minors should not be employed under any circumstances.
 (4) School children should focus on their studies and not be burdened with jobs.
 (5) Minors can work as hard as adults with no ill effects.

3. It can be inferred that support for the passage of the FLSA most likely came from

 (1) factory owners
 (2) child protection agencies
 (3) workers' unions
 (4) small companies
 (5) agricultural workers

GO ON TO THE NEXT PAGE

Social Studies

4. Which of the following statements is the most likely reason why there was a need for regulating child labor?

    (1) In the past, children suffered because of long working hours and dangerous conditions.
    (2) Children do not make up a responsible workforce.
    (3) Children were taking jobs away from adults.
    (4) Minors are a good source of labor.
    (5) Employers usually treat their young employees justly.

5. Which of the following is an opinion with which the Department of Labor would most likely disagree?

    (1) Children should be protected from hazardous work conditions.
    (2) Children should not be permitted to work in any capacity.
    (3) Seventeen nonagricultural occupations have already been ruled unsuitable for minors.
    (4) The Fair Labor Standards Act protects children.
    (5) The Department of Labor protects the American labor force.

Question 6 refers to the following graph.

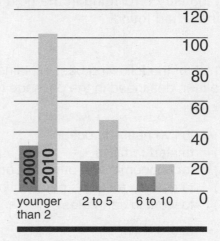

Off to the Doctor
We Go

(Annual visits rated per 100 children for visits with a principal diagnosis of middle-ear infection by age, 2000 and 2010)

6. According to the graph, which of the following children would least likely have been treated for an ear infection?

    (1) an eight-year-old in 2000
    (2) a four-year-old in 2010
    (3) a one-year-old in 2000
    (4) a three-year-old in 2000
    (5) a nine-year-old in 2010

GO ON TO THE NEXT PAGE

Social Studies

Questions 7 and 8 are based on the following information.

Most of them were disappointed in their search for gold. Many of those who failed as prospectors settled in towns such as San Francisco and Monterey. There they found jobs working for the canneries that sprang up as a result of the booming fishing industry or digging in the gold mines that others had found.

7. Which of the following best explains why the men described in the passage traveled west?

    (1)   to live near the ocean
    (2)   to start families
    (3)   for economic and other opportunities
    (4)   to escape religious persecution
    (5)   to work in canneries

8. According to the information, which of the following is a conclusion that best explains why many of those who headed west settled in coastal towns?

    (1)   They were able to find jobs there.
    (2)   There was no available land.
    (3)   Monterey rivers were rich in gold.
    (4)   The mountains were not open to settlement.
    (5)   The train stations were on the coast.

Questions 9 and 10 refer to the following speakers.

SPEAKER I: Morality is a function of the rules that regulate the competition for scarce resources.

SPEAKER II: The best way to understand the morality of a given people is to examine their past achievements.

SPEAKER III: The environment in which individuals live dictates their moral codes; the people of a mountainous region will have a different concept of morality than people who live by the ocean.

SPEAKER IV: The roots of morality lie within the mind of the individual and stem from that individual's formative experiences.

SPEAKER V: Morality is best observed in the interactions between the members of a particular culture as well as in interactions among different cultures.

9. It can be inferred from the passage above that Speaker II's profession is most likely to be

    (1)   an economist
    (2)   a geographer
    (3)   a historian
    (4)   a political scientist
    (5)   a sociologist

10. Which of the speakers is most likely to be a psychologist?

    (1)   I
    (2)   II
    (3)   III
    (4)   IV
    (5)   V

GO ON TO THE NEXT PAGE

Social Studies

Question 11 is based on the following graph.

How Children Are Being Educated

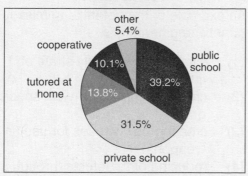

11. Which statement is supported by information in the graph?

    (1) Private schools provide a better education.
    (2) Children prefer the educational arrangements their parents have made for them.
    (3) Tutoring at home is the most popular method of educating children.
    (4) Most children attend either public or private schools.
    (5) About one-third of all children are in cooperative forms of education.

Questions 12 and 13 refer to the following information.

Economic systems can be classified according to the degree of government intervention and the type of control that the government exerts.

A command economy is one in which the government takes a very active role. If the government chooses to use its control of the economy to redistribute all of the money equally among all of the members of society, this is a command socialist system. If the government controls the economy but allows the money to be unevenly distributed, this is known as a command capitalistic system.

An economy in which the government takes no active role is known as a pure market economy. The only things that control the distribution of money in a pure market economy are market forces that no one person or organization can control.

12. It can be inferred from the passage that which of the following would not be found in a pure market economy?

    (1) monopolies
    (2) small businesses
    (3) unemployed workers
    (4) taxes and welfare
    (5) stocks and bonds

13. Of the following groups, which would probably benefit the least from a transition from a market economy to a socialist economy?

    (1) government employees
    (2) the unemployed
    (3) the elderly
    (4) small shop owners with small profits
    (5) highly skilled labor

GO ON TO THE NEXT PAGE

Question 14 refers to the following photo.

Source: Shutterstock

14. While today's car owners sometimes have to deal with gas shortages, car owners in the early 20th century had to cope with a number of quite different kinds of shortages.

Which of the following would have been the biggest concern for the people shown in the photo above?

(1) a shortage of paved roads, which frequently led to getting stuck in the mud

(2) a lack of unleaded gas, which resulted in pollution

(3) a lack of seatbelts and other safety features

(4) a shortage of lightweight building materials, which led to much heavier cars than we have today

(5) a chronic scarcity of gas stations

15. International efforts are being made to safeguard against the misuse of advances in genetic engineering.

An example of the potential to misuse genetic engineering is

(1) eliminating a deadly strain of influenza

(2) creating a new high-yield species of grain

(3) creating new viruses for use as weapons

(4) reducing birth defects through genetic screening

(5) improving the shelf life and durability of certain vegetables

GO ON TO THE NEXT PAGE

16. "Ulysses S. Grant concluded by 1863 that the very nature of a war to preserve the Union states would have the effect of changing those states and thus altering the Union."

Which of the following historical developments best supports Grant's conclusion?

(1) Grant had predicted a Northern triumph.
(2) The population of Missouri has since shifted from a more rural-oriented culture to a more urban-oriented culture.
(3) In 1917, the United States entered the First World War.
(4) Women received the right to vote in 1919.
(5) The emancipation of the slaves affected the society of the entire nation.

17. The 24th Amendment states that "Non-payment of taxes cannot be used as a reason for denying to any citizen the right to vote for president, vice president, or a member of Congress." This amendment to the U.S. Constitution upholds which of the following common law principles?

(1) No taxation without representation.
(2) All citizens have the right to bear arms.
(3) A person is innocent until proven guilty.
(4) One person, one vote.
(5) Possession is nine points of the law.

GO ON TO THE NEXT PAGE

Question 18 refers to the following graph.

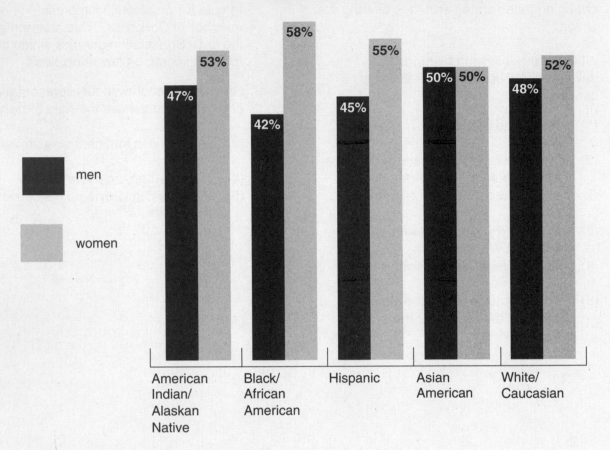

Profile of SAT Takers by Ethnic Group

men

women

| American Indian/ Alaskan Native | Black/ African American | Hispanic | Asian American | White/ Caucasian |

47% · 53% · 42% · 58% · 45% · 55% · 50% · 50% · 48% · 52%

18. Which statement is clearly supported by evidence in the graph?

    (1) American women perform better on the SAT than American men do.

    (2) There has been a decline in the number of Asian American men taking the SAT.

    (3) SAT scores are good indicators of performance in college.

    (4) The number of women in general taking the SAT has increased.

    (5) More women than men take the SAT.

GO ON TO THE NEXT PAGE

Social Studies

19. A plutocracy may be defined by the political principle of rule by the wealthy, that is, those who have accumulated wealth either through inherited property or financial success.

According to this statement, which of the following is <u>inconsistent</u> with a plutocratic form of government?

(1) Citizens must abide by the decision of the select group in power.
(2) Monetary interests are valued above human interests.
(3) Leaders are determined by popular vote.
(4) A farmer is excluded from holding office.
(5) Economic shifts result in a change in political leaders.

Question 20 refers to the following quotation.

"The [oil monopoly] molds public opinion in a manner creating a complete misunderstanding of the petroleum situation and influences the judgment and acts of unknowing and unwise public officials to a point where they fall to these interests of monopoly as against the welfare of the people whom they are supposed to serve."

—Andrew Mellon

20. Which of the following is an opinion most likely held by the speaker above?

(1) Those who profit from monopolies should not try to serve the public by running for office.
(2) Monopolies should never be allowed to exist.
(3) The interests of the people are secondary to those of public officials.
(4) All should profit from the rewards gained by a monopoly.
(5) Public officials should value the interests of the people they serve over the interests of any one business.

Question 21 refers to the following paragraph.

The U.S. government is structured with separate powers at the state and federal levels. Some political scientists have referred to this organization as a "wagon wheel," with the hub, or center, representing the federal government and the spokes representing the various state governments. This means that each state is separate, but the federal government maintains some level of centralized power.

21. Which of the following best illustrates how the "wagon wheel" analogy applies to the U.S. system of government?

(1) A wagon wheel is one of four wheels needed to stabilize a wagon.
(2) The hub of a wagon wheel holds in place the spokes, which strengthen the structure of the wheel.
(3) A wagon wheel's hub and spokes are made of different materials.
(4) A wagon wheel is created in several pieces and then assembled.
(5) A wagon wheel works best on smooth surfaces.

GO ON TO THE NEXT PAGE

Social Studies

Questions 22 through 24 relate to the following map.

Non-English-Speaking Children*

*Children aged 5 to 17 who speak a foreign language at home and
who don't speak English well or who don't speak it at all.

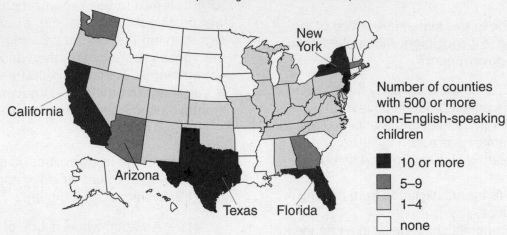

Number of counties
with 500 or more
non-English-speaking
children

■ 10 or more
▨ 5–9
▦ 1–4
□ none

22. Which of the following best explains the distribution of non-English-speaking children shown on the map?

   (1)   Income taxes are lower on the coasts than in the middle of the country.
   (2)   Fewer children are born in states with cold climates.
   (3)   There are fewer English courses offered in the northern part of the United States.
   (4)   Recent immigrants to the United States have tended to settle in border and coastal states.
   (5)   Federal funding for public schools has decreased.

23. Which factor would have the least effect upon the distribution of non-English-speaking children in the United States?

   (1)   migration patterns
   (2)   climate
   (3)   E.S.L. programs
   (4)   immigration laws
   (5)   social services

24. Which generalization is supported by the evidence in the map?

   (1)   Non-English-speaking children are distributed evenly across the United States.
   (2)   There are more non-English-speaking children in Arizona than in California.
   (3)   In Texas and California, more children are unable to speak English than are able to speak English.
   (4)   The East Coast and the West Coast of the United States are home to the same number of non-English-speaking children.
   (5)   There are fewer non-English-speaking children in the northern middle portion of the United States than in other parts of the country.

GO ON TO THE NEXT PAGE

Social Studies

Questions 25 through 27 refer to the following paragraph.

The Constitution, the laws made in accordance with that Constitution, and any treaties that the United States has signed constitute the supreme law of the land, to which the judges in any state must adhere. Any state laws incompatible with this supreme law of the land are unconstitutional, and therefore null and void.

25. Which of the following is an example of the concept of supreme law?

(1) The president of the United States makes political appointments to the Supreme Court.

(2) The freedoms outlined in the Bill of Rights can't be denied by the government.

(3) The House of Representatives contains two representatives from each state.

(4) The president is elected to four-year terms.

(5) The Court of Appeals can overturn previous court decisions.

26. Which of the following is an example of a state law that would be incompatible with the Constitution?

(1) a law that prohibits protests by a steelworkers' union

(2) a law that lowers the speed limit on a highway to 50 miles per hour

(3) a law that limits state senators to two six-year terms each

(4) legislation that requires reductions in emissions from factories

(5) a law that reserves a certain area of a town for residences

27. Which of the following is an example of a law compatible with the Constitution?

(1) legislation that prohibits the practice of certain religions

(2) a law that protects the rights of convicted criminals

(3) a law that suspends the right to trial by jury

(4) a law that prevents non-English-speakers from voting

(5) a law that allows the president to ignore congressional and Supreme Court decisions

<u>Questions 28 and 29</u> are based on the following paragraphs.

According to several prominent professors of economics, it is impossible to be completely accurate when predicting the long-term performance of any given stock. The professors' arguments are that the various political, social, and economic pressures that affect the success of any company are constantly changing and that their combined effects are extremely unpredictable.

This would explain why an amateur investor can very often do as well as a professional stock trader in long-term investments. The professors likened predicting stock performance to predicting weather patterns. Weather predictions are usually accurate up to a few days into the future, but the farther ahead the prediction, the greater the likelihood that unforeseen events render the prediction inaccurate. The same may be true of long-term stock predictions.

28. After analyzing the success of long-term stock predictions, some business professors reported that

  (1) professional predictions of stock performance are usually accurate
  (2) stocks that are currently performing well will continue to do so
  (3) amateur stock investors do very poorly in long-term investments
  (4) even careful analysis of current stock performance is no guarantee of accurate long-term predictions
  (5) there is no relationship between long-term and short-term performance

29. If it is true that a company's performance is affected by many factors, one can conclude that

  (1) two companies producing the same goods will perform equally well
  (2) a company's success is dependent on amateur investors
  (3) it is possible to lose money by investing in a company that has been very successful
  (4) an amateur stock investor will automatically make more money than a professional
  (5) more information will allow professional investors to make accurate predictions

GO ON TO THE NEXT PAGE

Social Studies

Questions 30 refers to the photo below.

Source: Photofest Archives

30. The golden age of transatlantic passenger ships was quickly coming to an end in this photo taken of six ocean liners at dock in New York City circa 1953. Which of the following events was probably the most important reason for the end of the era of crossing the Atlantic by ship?

    (1)   A series of highly publicized liner accidents made the public too nervous to take ships.

    (2)   A major war made overseas travel impossible.

    (3)   The advent of passenger airlines cut down the time it took to get to Europe, leaving ships outmoded.

    (4)   The cost of travel by boat became prohibitively expensive.

    (5)   It became unfashionable to travel by boat.

GO ON TO THE NEXT PAGE

Social Studies

Question 31 refers to the following cartoon.

A MAN KNOWS A MAN

"Give me your hand, Comrade! We have each lost a Leg for the good cause; but, thank God, we never lost Heart."

31. This cartoon from the Civil War era depicts two veterans of the Civil War (which was fought over the emancipation of African American slaves) greeting each other. What did the cartoonist mean to imply by the caption?

    (1) These two men were equals in each other's eyes.
    (2) These two soldiers who had lost their legs were not to be pitied because they were still men.
    (3) These soldiers had previously met.
    (4) Although they may have met before, these veterans had nothing in common.
    (5) The two men were shaking hands to be polite.

32. Before the Industrial Revolution, many families produced their own goods, such as soap and cloth. However, after the Industrial Revolution, families were more likely to buy these goods than produce them at home.

    Of the following statements, which best explains the change in consumption patterns?

    (1) Mass-produced goods tend to be more durable because greater craftsmanship and care go into their production.
    (2) No one wanted to make something that could be bought at a store.
    (3) The production of consumer goods at home can be dangerous.
    (4) After the Industrial Revolution, many families had less time at home and more money to spend.
    (5) Factory goods are better because there are certain quality controls that protect the consumer.

SCIENCE

Tests of General Educational Development

Directions

The Science Test consists of multiple-choice questions intended to measure general concepts in science. The questions are based on short readings that often include a graph, chart, or figure. Study the information given and then answer the question(s) following it. Refer to the information as often as necessary in answering the questions.

You should spend no more than 53 minutes answering the questions in this booklet. Work carefully, but do not spend too much time on any one question. Be sure you answer every question. You will not be penalized for incorrect answers.

Do not mark in this test booklet. Record your answers to the questions on the separate sheet provided. Be sure all requested information is properly recorded on the answer sheet.

To record your answers, mark the numbered space on the answer sheet beside the number that corresponds to the question in the test booklet.

FOR EXAMPLE:

Which of the following is the smallest unit in a living thing?

(1) tissue
(2) organ
(3) cell
(4) muscle
(5) capillary

The correct answer is "cell"; therefore, answer space (3) would be marked on the answer sheet.

Do not rest the point of your pencil on the answer sheet while you are considering your answer. Make no stray or unnecessary marks. If you change an answer, erase your first mark completely. Mark only <u>one</u> answer space for each question; multiple answers will be scored as incorrect. Do not fold or crease your answer sheet. Return all test materials to the test administrator.

Science

Directions: Choose the one best answer to each question.

Questions 1 through 4 refer to the following information.

All matter is made up of atoms. Atoms are made up of three different kinds of particles called (1) protons, (2) electrons, and (3) neutrons. Protons have a positive electrical charge. Electrons have a negative charge. Neutrons have no charge at all. Atoms of the 92 natural elements have from 1 to 92 protons. The number of electrons in each atom is the same as the number of protons, but the number of neutrons (which have approximately the same mass as a proton but no electric charge) can vary. The only difference between elements is the number and combination of protons, neutrons, and electrons. Overall, each atom is neutral, with offsetting positive and negative charges.

Most atoms have an equal number of protons and neutrons, but some atoms can have varying numbers of neutrons. An atom with a different number of neutrons than protons is called an isotope.

1. Which of the following is true about a neutron?

    (1)   It is larger than an atom.
    (2)   It has a positive charge.
    (3)   It has roughly the same mass as a proton.
    (4)   It is the same as an isotope.
    (5)   It has a negative charge.

2. If hydrogen has one proton, then how many electrons does it have?

    (1)   1
    (2)   2
    (3)   3
    (4)   4
    (5)   5

3. Which of the following partial atomic make-ups is not that of an isotope?

    (1)   2 neutrons, 1 proton
    (2)   3 protons, 4 neutrons
    (3)   3 protons, 3 neutrons
    (4)   2 protons, 3 neutrons
    (5)   5 protons, 10 neutrons

4. In order for a helium atom, which has two positively charged protons, two neutrons, and two electrons, to become an isotope, it would need which of the following?

    A.   an extra proton
    B.   an extra electron
    C.   an extra neutron

    (1)   A only
    (2)   B only
    (3)   C only
    (4)   A and C only
    (5)   B and C only

5. Unlike most liquids, water expands when it freezes and becomes less dense as a result. This is the reason ice cubes will float in a glass of water.

    Which of the following phenomena would best be explained by the information above?

    (1)   Liquid mercury does not expand when it is frozen.
    (2)   Frozen or liquid, water has the same mass.
    (3)   When glass is heated, it gets softer but does not melt.
    (4)   Icebergs do not sink in the ocean.
    (5)   Water, left standing, will eventually evaporate.

GO ON TO THE NEXT PAGE

Science

Questions 6 through 8 refer to the following information.

One way to measure sound is by its frequency, which is the number of complete cycles of a sound wave within one second (see graph). One cycle per second is called 1 hertz. Human ears can detect sounds from about 20 hertz (the lowest sound) to 20,000 hertz (the highest sound). Below 20 hertz, humans feel only the vibration of the sound. Above 20,000 hertz, they can't hear the sound at all. All sound travels at the same speed, regardless of frequency.

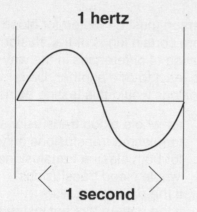

1 hertz

1 second

6. If a bat can hear sounds that humans cannot detect at all without special equipment, then these sounds are likely to be within which of the following frequency ranges?

    (1)   1–20 hertz
    (2)   20–10,000 hertz
    (3)   10,000–15,000 hertz
    (4)   15,000–20,000 hertz
    (5)   20,000–50,000 hertz

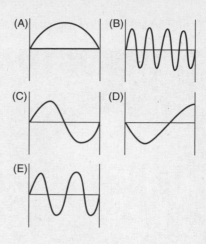

7. Which of the graphs above represents the greatest frequency?

    (1)   A
    (2)   B
    (3)   C
    (4)   D
    (5)   E

8. If you were going to buy a pair of speakers for your stereo system, which of the following sets of speaker specifications would offer the most complete reproduction of sound audible to humans?

    (1)   20–10,000 hertz
    (2)   1–15,000 hertz
    (3)   10,000–20,000 hertz
    (4)   20–20,000 hertz
    (5)   20,000–30,000 hertz

GO ON TO THE NEXT PAGE

Question 9 refers to the following photo and chart.

Source: Shutterstock

Average Temperature of Various Large Bodies of Water

Atlantic Ocean	46 degrees Fahrenheit
Arctic Ocean	36 degrees Fahrenheit
Baltic Sea	45 degrees Fahrenheit
Great Lakes of North America	44 degrees Fahrenheit
Gulf of Mexico	60 degrees Fahrenheit

9. Hurricanes, like the one pictured above, gather strength as they pass over warm water. Using the chart above, over which of the following bodies of water would a hurricane gather the most strength?

    (1)   the Baltic Sea
    (2)   the Atlantic Ocean
    (3)   the Great Lakes of North America
    (4)   the Arctic Ocean
    (5)   the Gulf of Mexico

10. Blood is made up of two main elements: (1) plasma, which is largely water and proteins, and (2) the solid components of blood— red blood cells, white cells, and platelets (important for forming blood clots).

     If a patient has lost a lot of blood, the patient will probably need a transfusion of "whole blood," which includes red blood cells and plasma. However, sometimes the patient only needs an increase in the *volume* of liquid in the bloodstream, in which case plasma alone can be substituted.

     A person must be tested for blood type before certain kinds of transfusions because of differences in the way red blood cells react to one another. Under what conditions would this testing be necessary?

     (1)   for whole blood transfusions only
     (2)   for plasma transfusions only
     (3)   for both plasma transfusions and whole blood transfusions
     (4)   if the patient requests it
     (5)   if the patient has not lost any blood

GO ON TO THE NEXT PAGE

Science

Questions 11 through 15 are based on the following information.

Coal is formed from the material of plants and other organisms that lived on land and whose remains were covered by mud, which later became rock. Coal is classified by carbon content.

Types of Coal

Peat	=	The remains of plants and organisms that, because they were covered in bogs, were prevented by a lack of oxygen from completely decaying. Still a porous, soft brown mass, peat has a carbon content of 52%–60%.
Lignite	=	In time, peat turns into lignite, a soft coal-like substance that is 60%–65% carbon.
Subbituminous coal	=	With more time, heat, and pressure, lignite changes into subbituminous coal, which is about 65%–75% carbon.
Bituminous coal	=	After even more heat and pressure, subbituminous coal turns into bituminous coal with a carbon level of 75%–85%.
Anthracite	=	This is bituminous coal subjected to another million years of heat and pressure. Anthracite has a carbon level of 85%–95% and will burn only at extremely high temperatures.

11. If a piece of coal is analyzed for its carbon content and discovered to be 63% carbon, what type of coal is it?

    (1) peat
    (2) lignite
    (3) subbituminous
    (4) bituminous
    (5) anthracite

12. Steel is made in a process in which iron is combined with carbon at an extremely high temperature. Which of the following types of coal might be most useful in this process?

    (1) peat
    (2) lignite
    (3) subbituminous
    (4) bituminous
    (5) anthracite

13. Which of the following classifications is most probably a state in which the other four classifications at one time previously existed?

    (1) peat
    (2) lignite
    (3) subbituminous
    (4) bituminous
    (5) anthracite

14. Which of the types of coal classified above is most likely found closest to the surface?

    (1) peat
    (2) lignite
    (3) subbituminous
    (4) bituminous
    (5) anthracite

15. Which of the types of coal described above has the most carbon?

    (1) peat
    (2) lignite
    (3) subbituminous
    (4) bituminous
    (5) anthracite

GO ON TO THE NEXT PAGE

Questions 16 and 17 are based on the following information.

Most seeds will germinate when they have moisture, oxygen, and the right temperature, but different seeds need differing proportions of each of these ingredients. Most seeds require a temperature of between 15 degrees and 27 degrees centigrade to germinate, although some seeds, such as the maple, can germinate in far colder climates, and some other seeds, such as corn, require warmer temperatures. Before germination, seeds must absorb water, but too much absorption of water will encourage the growth of fungus, which can halt the germination process.

16. Which of the following environments would best be suited for the germination of a corn seed?

    (1) a moist, sealed container at 26 degrees centigrade
    (2) an arid desert plain
    (3) a moist, plowed field at 30 degrees centigrade
    (4) a test tube filled with water
    (5) an environment suitable for a maple seed

17. Based on the information above, which of the following is most likely true?

    (1) Maple seeds can germinate in any temperature.
    (2) Corn is difficult to grow.
    (3) Oxygen is not necessary for germination.
    (4) Water, in limited amounts, is vital to the germination process.
    (5) Germs are needed for germination.

18. During periods of intense activity, the cells of the body need more oxygen than the body is supplying, a situation known as oxygen debt. During these periods, the body's cells briefly switch to "anaerobic respiration," which produces lactic acid. The buildup of lactic acid in the tissues signals the brain to increase the breathing and heart rate, thus supplying the body with more oxygen.

    After which of the following activities would lactic acid most likely be found in the body?

    (1) walking to work
    (2) playing an intense game of chess
    (3) taking an aerobics class
    (4) eating breakfast
    (5) watching a scary movie

19. During periods that are unfavorable for growth, some plants become dormant. During this period, woody plants are protected by their bark. Perennial plants die above the ground, but their roots remain alive. Annual plants die, but their seeds will survive to continue the life of the species.

    Which of the following would most likely be a time of the year during which plants might lie dormant?

    (1) summer
    (2) summer and fall
    (3) winter
    (4) spring
    (5) spring and summer

GO ON TO THE NEXT PAGE

Science

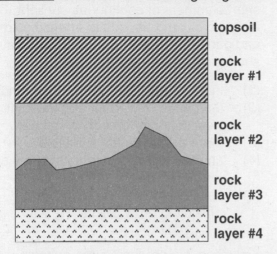

Food Chain

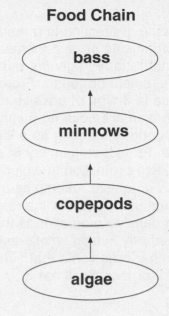

20. The diagram above shows various layers of rock that have been deposited over time. Which of the following is most likely the correct sequence of the ages of the rock layers, arranged from oldest to newest?

    (1)   2, 1, 3, 4
    (2)   4, 3, 2, 1
    (3)   1, 2, 3, 4
    (4)   3, 1, 2, 4
    (5)   4, 3, 1, 2

22. Which of the following conclusions is most likely to be true regarding the food chain above?

    (1)   Bass are the only fish that eat minnows.
    (2)   Algae eat even smaller animals.
    (3)   Minnows are bigger than bass.
    (4)   Copepods are smaller than minnows.
    (5)   Bass could simply eliminate the middlemen by eating algae.

21. Auxins are natural plant hormones that regulate growth in plants. Scientists have developed a new type of synthetic auxin that prevents the growth of weeds while encouraging grass. This synthetic auxin could possibly be used in place of

    (1)   synthetic grass
    (2)   plant-killing pesticides
    (3)   weeds
    (4)   hybrid seeds
    (5)   water

GO ON TO THE NEXT PAGE

Science

Questions 23 and 24 refer to the following passage.

Passive protection is a method by which organisms protect themselves from predators, not by fighting, but by their appearance, smell, or sound. Protective resemblance is a type of passive protection in which an animal's coloring mimics the natural environment, acting as a kind of camouflage. Protective mimicry is another type of passive protection in which a defenseless organism resembles a more powerful organism. Another interesting example of passive protection is the Monarch butterfly, which smells and tastes so bad to other organisms that virtually no other animal or insect will eat it.

23. Which of the following is an example of passive protection?

    (1) A bird builds a nest high above the ground, out of reach of many animals.
    (2) A beaver builds a home that is accessible only from underwater.
    (3) A tropical fish has colorings that resemble the coral reef that it inhabits.
    (4) A stingray has a sharp barb it uses to defend itself against aggressors.
    (5) A shark has sensors that can detect blood in the water as much as a mile away.

24. Which of the following is an example of protective mimicry?

    (1) A hunter imitates the sounds of a duck to lure ducks within range.
    (2) A certain type of fly without any real protective features resembles a stinging insect.
    (3) A tiger's stripes blend with the grasses and shadows rendering it almost invisible from a distance.
    (4) An elephant has long tusks to defend its territory.
    (5) A moray eel lives in a tunnel into which it can retreat if attacked.

25. In the tundra region of Siberia, there are short summers of continuous sunlight, followed by long periods of intense cold and dark. Plants in this environment have a short growing season because

    (1) there is very little water in the tundra
    (2) the period of warmth and sunlight necessary for growth is so brief
    (3) there are no seeds available
    (4) animals will eat the plants if they are visible above the ground
    (5) pollution in Siberia has made it difficult to grow plants

26. Estivation is a process some animals undergo during hot weather, in which they lie dormant with their respiration, heartbeat, and metabolic rates all reduced. Which of the following might be an example of estivation?

    (1) A particular type of frog lies motionless and apparently asleep in the cool mud at the bottom of a pond during the hot months of summer.
    (2) A leaf turns brown and then falls off its branch in the fall.
    (3) A pool of water slowly evaporates during a drought.
    (4) A bear goes into a cave and hibernates during the winter.
    (5) A squirrel spends the summer and fall busily gathering nuts for the winter.

GO ON TO THE NEXT PAGE

27. Crop rotation is a process in which various crops are planted on the same land in alternating years to prevent the depletion of organic material in the soil. For example, a farmer might plant corn one year, then wheat or oats the following year, and then a legume such as clover the year after that.

Because grass and clover are not valuable crops, which of the following would best explain why a farmer would plant them?

(1) Grass and clover deplete the soil so rapidly that they can be planted only once every three years.
(2) Corn and wheat seeds are too expensive to plant every year.
(3) Wheat causes less depletion than corn does.
(4) Corn causes less depletion than oats do.
(5) Grass and clover add valuable nitrates back into the soil.

28. Coniferous forests grow in colder climates and show little change in their appearance throughout the year. Rain forests, which tend to grow in tropical climates, get lots of rain and tend to grow year-round. Deciduous forests grow in temperate regions, undergoing seasonal change each year.

In which type of forest would you expect to see the leaves turn brown and fall off during the fall?

A. coniferous forests
B. rain forests
C. deciduous forests

(1) A only
(2) B only
(3) C only
(4) A and B only
(5) B and C only

GO ON TO THE NEXT PAGE

Science

Question 29 refers to the following chart.

Projected AIDS Deaths 2011–2020

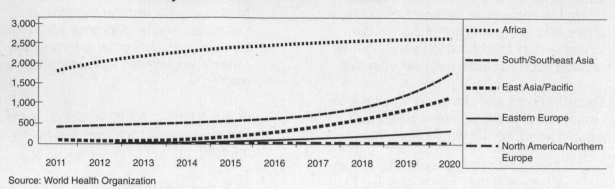

Source: World Health Organization

29. According to the chart above, which region will have the largest projected number of AIDS deaths in the year 2020?

   (1) South/Southeast Asia
   (2) Africa
   (3) Eastern Europe
   (4) East Asia/Pacific
   (5) North America/Northern Europe

GO ON TO THE NEXT PAGE

Science

30. The following definition is given for irrigation:

    To water soil by artificial methods.

    The definition above would most likely appear in which of the following sources?

    (1) a physics book
    (2) an organic chemistry book
    (3) a pamphlet on biology
    (4) an agricultural science book
    (5) an article on astronomy

31. An experiment was undertaken by a scientist to see if men will go bald if exposed to a particular chemical compound. A group of 1,000 adult men were given this compound over 40 years, and it was found that a high percentage of the men did indeed go bald. From this, the scientist concluded that the compound causes baldness in men.

    Which of the following is the main flaw of this study?

    (1) Scientists should experiment only on laboratory animals.
    (2) The number of subjects in the study was too small to be able to make any general conclusions.
    (3) The time period of the study was too short.
    (4) The scientist did not compare his subjects to a control group of subjects who did *not* receive the compound.
    (5) The scientist did not include women in his experiment.

32. Exposure to air causes the breakdown of organic matter. If a dinosaur from the early Mesozoic period is found perfectly preserved in a glacier, which of the following conclusions is most likely?

    (1) The body of the dinosaur was protected from the air by ice.
    (2) In the Mesozoic period, organic matter behaved differently than it does today.
    (3) The dinosaur died of drowning.
    (4) If the dinosaur had been preserved by mud, it would not have been perfectly preserved.
    (5) There was no air during the Mesozoic period.

33. In a certain species of bird, it is the male of the species who has the more brightly colored plumage, which he uses to attract the female of the species. A scientist wishing to observe the egg-laying process of a bird from this species should

    (1) look for a bird from this species with brightly colored plumage
    (2) observe other species of birds with the same coloring
    (3) look for a bird from this species with less brightly colored plumage
    (4) capture a male of the species
    (5) ask other scientists for help

LANGUAGE ARTS, READING

Tests of General Educational Development

Directions

The Language Arts, Reading Test consists of excerpts from classical and popular literature, business documents, and articles about literature or the arts. Each excerpt is followed by multiple-choice questions about the reading material.

Read each excerpt first and then answer the questions following it. Refer back to the reading material as often as necessary in answering the questions.

Each excerpt is preceded by a "purpose question." The purpose question gives a reason for reading the material. Use these purpose questions to help focus your reading. You are not required to answer these purpose questions. They are given only to help you concentrate on the ideas presented in the reading material.

You should spend no more than 35 minutes answering the questions in this booklet. Work carefully, but do not spend too much time on any one question. Be sure you answer every question. You will not be penalized for incorrect answers.

Do not mark in this test booklet. Record your answers on the separate answer sheet provided. Be sure that all requested information is properly recorded on the answer sheet. To record your answers, mark the numbered space on the answer sheet beside the number that corresponds to the question in the test booklet.

FOR EXAMPLE:

It was Susan's dream machine. The metallic blue paint gleamed, and the sporty wheels were highly polished. Under the hood, the engine was no less carefully cleaned. Inside, flashy lights illuminated the instruments on the dashboard, and the seats were covered by rich leather upholstery.

The subject ("It") of this excerpt is most likely

  (1) an airplane
  (2) a stereo system
  (3) an automobile
  (4) a boat
  (5) a motorcycle

The correct answer is "an automobile"; therefore, answer space (3) would be marked on the answer sheet.

Do not rest the point of your pencil on the answer sheet while you are considering your answer. Make no stray or unnecessary marks. If you change an answer, erase your first mark completely. Mark only <u>one</u> answer space for each question; multiple answers will be scored as incorrect. Do not fold or crease your answer sheet. Return all test materials to the test administrator.

Reading

Questions 1 through 5 refer to the following excerpt from a play.

WHAT ARE THE CIRCUMSTANCES OF THIS FAMILY?

MARION: [Rattling with the pots, the nervous vein flames in her neck.] The foulness of this place.

(5) **DANGERFIELD:** Take it easy, Ma. It's just adjustment. Got to get used to it here.

MARION: Children running barefoot in the streets in the middle of winter.

DANGERFIELD: Untruths. Lies.

(10) **MARION:** You weren't like this before we came to Ireland. This vulgar filthy country.

DANGERFIELD: Easy now.

(15) **MARION:** I know now why they're only fit to be servants.

DANGERFIELD: Oh, bitterness.

MARION: You know it's all true. O'Keefe's been here. I can still smell him. America doesn't seem to (20) help them. He's not even fit to be a servant.

DANGERFIELD: I think Kenneth's a gentleman in every respect.

(25) **MARION:** He has the revolting lechery of an Irish peasant. And he tries to give the impression of good breeding. Watch him eating. It's infuriating. Grabs everything. That first time we had him to dinner he (30) just came in as if we were servants and proceeded to eat even before I had time to sit down. And pulling hunks out of the bread. How can you be blind to these things?

(35) **DANGERFIELD:** [To telescope] Testing my sight.

MARION: That damn stupid thing.

DANGERFIELD: How dare you. How would you like it if I missed a comet?

(40) **MARION:** We've only got thirty shillings left.

DANGERFIELD: Interesting foreign body here.

MARION: Did you hear me, we've got (45) thirty shillings left.

DANGERFIELD: I heard you. Our good accents and manners will see us right. Didn't you know, Marion, they can't put Protestants in jail?

(50) **MARION:** And to have my child raised among a lot of savage Irish and be branded with a brogue for the rest of her life.

DANGERFIELD: Marion, do you ever (55) think of death?

MARION: No.

DANGERFIELD: Marion, do you ever think you're going to die?

MARION: Would you mind stopping (60) that sort of talk. You're in that nasty mood.

DANGERFIELD: Not at all.

J. P. Donleavy, THE GINGER MAN, 1972. (Abridged)

GO ON TO THE NEXT PAGE

Reading

Directions: Choose the <u>one best answer</u> to each question.

1. The playwright has Dangerfield pick up the telescope (line 35) to show

    (1) his innate curiosity
    (2) his desire to be an astronomer
    (3) his concern about his eyesight
    (4) his love of ocular instruments
    (5) his uneasiness with his current situation

2. From this passage, it is clear that Marion is

    (1) bored of her relationship with Dangerfield
    (2) sensitive to negative stereotyping
    (3) glad her child is learning a new accent
    (4) concerned about her financial situation
    (5) happy to be in Ireland

3. "Our good accents and manners will see us right" (lines 46–48). Dangerfield says this

    (1) to attempt to make light of their current predicament
    (2) to show Marion they can make money by teaching at a finishing school
    (3) to compliment himself and Marion on resisting talking with a brogue
    (4) to hear himself speak impeccable English
    (5) to point out that good eyesight and manners are not incompatible

4. It is clear from the passage that Marion

    (1) loves Irish food but dislikes the cold weather
    (2) likes Ireland except for the peasants
    (3) contemplates death often
    (4) is concerned about her child's exposure to Irish children
    (5) is angry that she bought Dangerfield the telescope

5. It can be inferred from the excerpt that Marion and Dangerfield came to Ireland

    (1) so Dangerfield could use his telescope
    (2) because Marion loves Ireland
    (3) under stressful circumstances
    (4) for their daughter's health
    (5) because they had started a business with O'Keefe

GO ON TO THE NEXT PAGE

Reading

Questions 6 through 10 refer to the following poem.

WHAT MAKES THIS BOY FEEL BETTER?

First Song

Then it was dusk in Illinois, the small boy
After an afternoon of carting dung
Hung on the rail fence, a sapped thing
Weary to crying. Dark was growing tall
(5)   And he began to hear the pond frogs all
Calling on his ear with what seemed their joy.

Soon their sound was pleasant for a boy
Listening in the smoky dusk and the nightfall
Of Illinois, and from the fields two small
(10)   Boys came bearing cornstalk violins
And they rubbed the cornstalk bows with resins
And the three sat there scraping of their joy.

It was now fine music the frogs and the boys
Did in the towering Illinois twilight make
(15)   And into dark in spite of a shoulder's ache
A boy's hunched body loved out of a stalk
The first song of his happiness, and the song woke
His heart to the darkness and into the sadness of joy.

Galway Kinnell, "First Song," from WHEN ONE HAS LIVED A LONG TIME ALONE, 1990

6.   It is clear from the poem that the boy lives in

   (1)   a bustling city
   (2)   a strange land
   (3)   a rural area in the Midwest
   (4)   a wildlife preservation
   (5)   a concert town

7.   The boy is unhappy at the beginning of the poem because

   (1)   his neighbors refuse to play with him
   (2)   he has been bitten by a bug
   (3)   he is exhausted because of much hard work
   (4)   the sounds of the frogs are unpleasant to him
   (5)   he is afraid of the dark

GO ON TO THE NEXT PAGE

8. The time of day described in the second stanza (lines 7–12) is

    (1) early morning
    (2) late afternoon
    (3) just before midnight
    (4) midday
    (5) evening

9. What is meant by "cornstalk violins" (line 10)?

    (1) a special type of violin used for purposes of nature
    (2) an imported violin
    (3) a type of cornstalk
    (4) a homemade violin
    (5) a dish made with corn

10. Which of the following comes closest to the meaning of the last three lines?

    (1) The boy is happy with the musical talents he discovered he had.
    (2) The musical sound of the night brings happiness to the boy.
    (3) The boy is afraid of being alone in the dark.
    (4) It is sad that the boys have no real instruments.
    (5) Twilight is too late for young boys to be outside.

GO ON TO THE NEXT PAGE

Questions 11 through 16 refer to the following excerpt.

HOW DOES THIS WRITER FEEL ABOUT HER NEIGHBORHOOD?

In that place where they tore the nightshade and blackberry patches from their roots to make room for the Medallion City Golf Course, there was once a
(5) neighborhood. It stood in the hills above the valley town of Medallion and spread all the way back to the river. It is called the suburbs now, but when black people lived there, it was called the Bottom. One road,
(10) shaded by beeches, oaks, maples, and chestnuts, connected it to the valley. The beeches are gone now, and so are the pear trees where children sat and yelled down through the blossoms to passersby.
(15) Generous funds have been allotted to level the stripped and faded buildings that clutter the road from Medallion up to the golf course. They are going to raze the Time and a Half Pool Hall, where feet in
(20) long tan shoes once pointed down from chair rungs. A steel ball will knock to dust Irene's Palace of Cosmetology, where women used to lean their heads back on sink trays and doze while Irene lathered
(25) Nu Nile into their hair. Men in khaki work clothes will pry loose the slats of Reba's Grill, where the owner cooked in her hat because she couldn't remember the ingredients without it.

(30) There will be nothing left of the Bottom (the footbridge that crossed the river is already gone), but perhaps it is just as well, since it wasn't a town anyway: just a neighborhood where on quiet days
(35) people in valley houses could hear singing sometimes, banjos sometimes, and, if a valley man happened to have business up in those hills—collecting rent or insurance payments—he might see a dark woman
(40) in a flowered dress doing a bit of a cakewalk, a bit of black bottom, a bit of "messing around" to the lively notes of a mouth organ. Her bare feet would raise the saffron dust that floated down on the
(45) coveralls and bunion-split shoes of the man breathing music in and out of his harmonica. The black people watching her would laugh and rub their knees, and it would be easy for the valley man to hear
(50) the laughter and not notice the adult pain that rested somewhere under the eyelids, somewhere under their head rags and soft felt hats, somewhere in the palm of the hand, somewhere behind the frayed
(55) lapels, somewhere in the sinew's curve. He'd have to stand in the back of Greater Saint Matthew's and let the tenor's voice dress him in silk, or touch the hands of the spoon carvers (who had not worked
(60) in eight years) and let the fingers that danced on wood kiss his skin. Otherwise the pain would escape him even though the laughter was part of the pain.

Toni Morrison, SULA, 1974.

GO ON TO THE NEXT PAGE

11. Which of the following best expresses the narrator's feeling about the changes in the neighborhood?

    (1) relief at the change of hands
    (2) inspiration because of its improvement
    (3) nervousness about the reconstruction
    (4) sadness about what she perceives as its loss of character
    (5) anger over the inhabitants who chose to remain

12. The area formerly known as the Bottom

    (1) is so named because of trees that overhang the area and block out the sun
    (2) is a multiracial community
    (3) once had a church
    (4) is being torn down to make room for a new suburb
    (5) was flooded by the river and thus people moved away

13. The narrator mentions the Time and a Half Pool Hall and Irene's Palace of Cosmetology (lines 19 and 22) in order to

    (1) show examples of successful businesses owned by the townspeople
    (2) illustrate the richness of the old neighborhood
    (3) illustrate what she perceives as the improvement that the town will undergo
    (4) avoid talking about painful experiences
    (5) contrast the art of pool with that of golf

14. The narrator's general attitude toward the Bottom is

    (1) belittlement
    (2) amusement
    (3) nostalgia
    (4) anxiety
    (5) confusion

15. The narrator believes the valley man would "not notice the adult pain that rested somewhere under the eyelids" (lines 50–51) because

    (1) he is overjoyed by the laughter
    (2) he is preoccupied with the new golf course
    (3) he is visually impaired
    (4) he is on his way to a town meeting
    (5) he doesn't understand the complex emotions of the townspeople

16. In the last nine lines of the passage, the valley man's experience could best be described as

    (1) a spiritual connection to God
    (2) a new empathy with the black townspeople
    (3) a daydream where he envisions himself clad in silk
    (4) being uplifted through the joy of song
    (5) exploring the economic policy

GO ON TO THE NEXT PAGE

Reading

Questions 17 through 20 refer to the following excerpt.

WHAT DOES THE REVIEWER THINK ABOUT THIS FILM?

Like it or not, the Star Wars series by director George Lucas has become a distinct part of American culture. Its many additions to our vocabulary ("Feel the
(5) force, Luke") and even to our visual frame of reference have made the series iconic. That is perhaps why there was such a hue and cry when, after a hiatus of nearly 20 years, Lucas released the first of three new
(10) Star Wars films, *The Phantom Menace*. An entire nation seemed outraged by Lucas's attempts to tamper with his own formula— even as we lined up to see it. How dare he get so ponderous? Where were the iconic
(15) images we had come to expect? Where was the sense of fun and gee-whiz effects we loved so much in the early films?

Now, with the release of *Episode II: Attack of the Clones*, Lucas seems to have
(20) found his visual footing again, although many will debate whether he has regained his sense of fun. The visual images are simply stunning. We are transported to a beautiful and stark planet of rain, then
(25) thrown into a vast coliseum in which the heroes battle strange alien beasts, then conducted into a towering and awe- inspiring Senate chamber. Each of these images is so rich and full of nuance, that—
(30) at least on a visual level—the film works as a kind of tapestry that can be viewed again and again.

Unfortunately, only die-hard fans will want to listen to the dialogue more than
(35) once. There is little life in the words the characters utter, and this is not just due to the strangely stiff and formal performances by actors who have been great in other roles. Natalie Portman, usually so full of
(40) verve, and even the great Liam Neeson, recite their lines in a curious monotone. But, ultimately, it is the lines themselves that seem wooden.

In the end, *Attack of the Clones*
(45) feels a bit cloned itself—a pastiche of the series' early plot points minus the brio that made it all seem so fun in the first place.

17. When the reviewer writes, "even as we lined up to see it" (line 13), she is implying that

    (1) the movie did poorly at the box office
    (2) the audience felt outraged about long lines
    (3) the public still wanted to see the movie even with its flaws
    (4) the movie was not being shown in enough theaters
    (5) viewers formed picket lines to protest the movie

18. According to this reviewer, who would be most likely to enjoy this movie?

    (1) moviegoers who like historical dramas
    (2) moviegoers who like comedies
    (3) fans of Natalie Portman and Liam Neeson
    (4) avid fans of the previous Star Wars movies
    (5) people who like well-written dialogue

GO ON TO THE NEXT PAGE

19. The film *The Phantom Menace* is known, according to the reviewer, for its

    (1) gee-whiz effects
    (2) differences from previous Star Wars movies
    (3) sense of fun and brio
    (4) iconic images
    (5) many additions to the American vocabulary

20. Which of the following statements best explains the reviewer's comparison of *Attack of the Clones* to a tapestry (line 31)?

    (1) The set design included many wall tapestries and hangings in its indoor scenes.
    (2) The film is so visually rich that the reviewer notices new details on each viewing.
    (3) The muted colors used by the cinematographer were chosen to make the film look like a tapestry.
    (4) The film is a combination of many different plot devices of the earlier movies.
    (5) Like a tapestry, the film was complicated to make and required many months of work.

GO ON TO THE NEXT PAGE

Reading

Questions 21 and 22 refer to the following excerpt from a company handbook for new employees.

WHAT DOES THIS COMPANY WISH TO ENCOURAGE?

New Employees of Maxtext, Inc. are strongly urged to consider making regular contributions to the Maxtext, Inc. 401(k) deferred compensation retirement plan as
(5) soon as they become eligible. Note that eligibility does not begin with the first day of employment. Employees of Maxtext become "vested," meaning that they are eligible to participate in the 401(k) plan,
(10) after a six-month probationary period.

A 401(k) retirement plan is a voluntary system by which you can defer some portion of your weekly salaries toward retirement. This money is then invested for
(15) you in your choice of a number of different tax-deferred investment vehicles, including mutual funds, bond funds, or money market funds.

The Maxtext company is so
(20) committed to the concept of regular contributions to 401(k) funds that it will match any contribution you make up to 7% of your yearly salary, effectively doubling each dollar you save.

(25) If you leave the company before retirement, you will have the option to "roll over" your 401(k) funds into your new employer's 401(k) plan, without loss of tax-deferred status. Similarly, you can elect to
(30) roll over any 401(k) funds that you have already contributed at another company into the Maxtext company plan as soon as you become vested.

21. Which of the following reasons would most likely prevent a new employee from participating in this company's 401(k) plan?

(1) not earning enough money to qualify for the plan
(2) choosing bond funds as opposed to mutual funds
(3) choosing mutual funds as opposed to money market funds
(4) leaving the company before becoming "vested"
(5) not having tax-deferred status

22. Which of the following inferences about the company's attitude toward employee 401(k) contributions is supported by the excerpt?

(1) The company is indifferent to the retirement savings habits of its employees.
(2) Retirement savings by employees are actively discouraged by the company.
(3) The company strongly encourages retirement savings by its employees.
(4) The company would prefer employees to invest in mutual funds as opposed to money market funds.
(5) The company has plans to raise the matching-funds percentile to 8% from 7%.

END OF TEST

MATHEMATICS

Tests of General Educational Development

Directions

The Mathematics Test consists of questions intended to measure general mathematics skills and problem-solving ability. The questions are based on short readings that often include a graph, chart, or figure.

You should spend no more than 45 minutes answering the questions in this booklet. Work carefully, but do not spend too much time on any one question. Be sure you answer every question. You will not be penalized for incorrect answers.

Formulas you may need are given on page 608. Only some of the questions will require you to use a formula. Not all the formulas given will be needed.

Some questions contain more information than you will need to solve the problem. Other questions do not give enough information to solve the problem. If the question does not give enough information to solve the problem, the correct answer choice is "Not enough information is given."

The use of calculators is allowed only in Part One.

Do not mark in this test booklet. The test administrator will give you blank paper for your calculations. Record your answers on the separate answer sheet provided. Be sure all requested information is properly recorded on the answer sheet.

To record your answers, mark the numbered space on the answer sheet beside the number that corresponds to the question in the test booklet.

FOR EXAMPLE:

If a grocery bill totaling $15.75 is paid with a $20.00 bill, how much change should be returned?

- (1) $5.25
- (2) $4.75
- (3) $4.25
- (4) $3.75
- (5) $3.25

The correct answer is $4.25; therefore, answer space (3) would be marked on the answer sheet.

Do not rest the point of your pencil on the answer sheet while you are considering your answer. Make no stray or unnecessary marks. If you change an answer, erase your first mark completely. Mark only <u>one</u> answer space for each question; multiple answers will be scored as incorrect. Do not fold or crease your answer sheet. Return all test materials to the test administrator.

FORMULAS

AREA (A) of a:

square	$A = s^2$; where s = side
rectangle	$A = lw$; where l = length, w = width
parallelogram	$A = bh$; where b = base, h = height
trapezoid	$A = \frac{1}{2}(b_1 + b_2)h$; where b = base, h = height
triangle	$A = \frac{1}{2}bh$; where b = base, h = height
circle	$A = \pi r^2$; where π = 3.14, r = radius

PERIMETER (P) of a:

square	$P = 4s$; where s = side
rectangle	$P = 2l + 2w$; where l = length, w = width
triangle	$P = a + b + c$; where a, b, and c are the sides

CIRCUMFERENCE (C) of a circle $C = \pi d$; where π = 3.14, d = diameter

VOLUME (V) of a:

cube	$V = s^3$; where s = side
rectangular container	$V = lwh$; where l = length, w = width, h = height
square pyramid	$V = \frac{1}{3}(\text{base edge})^2 h$
cone	$V = \frac{1}{3}\pi r^2 h$
cylinder	$V = \pi r^2 h$; where π = 3.14, r = radius, h = height

PYTHAGOREAN RELATIONSHIP $c^2 = a^2 + b^2$; where c = hypotenuse, a and b are legs of a right triangle

DISTANCE (d) BETWEEN TWO POINTS ON A PLANE $d = \sqrt{\left(x_2 - x_1\right)^2 + \left(y_2 - y_1\right)^2}$; where (x_1, y_1) and (x_2, y_2) are two points in a plane

SLOPE OF A LINE (m) $m = \dfrac{y_2 - y_1}{x_2 - x_1}$; where (x_1, y_1) and (x_2, y_2) are two points in a plane

MEAN $mean = \dfrac{x_1 + x_2 + ... x_n}{n}$; where the x's = the values for which a mean is desired, and n = number of values in the series

MEDIAN $median$ = the point in an <u>ordered</u> set of numbers at which half of the numbers are above and half of the numbers are below this value

SIMPLE INTEREST (i) $i = prt$; where p = principal, r = rate, t = time

DISTANCE (d) as function of rate and time $d = rt$; where r = rate, t = time

TOTAL COST (c) $c = nr$; where n = number of units, r = cost per unit

Mathematics, Part I

Part One—Use of calculator permitted

<u>Directions</u>: Choose the <u>one best answer</u> to each question.

1. To fill up 4 CDs with recorded music, when each CD contains $2\frac{3}{4}$ hours of recording time, how many hours of music are needed?

   (1) $8\frac{1}{4}$

   (2) $8\frac{3}{4}$

   (3) 9

   (4) $10\frac{1}{4}$

   (5) 11

<u>Questions 2 and 3</u> are based on the following information.

A group of 8 students spends a weekend going door-to-door raising money for charity. The students who work on Saturday visit 25 houses each. Those who work on Sunday visit 30 houses each.

2. If the students are to reach their goal of $1,700.00, what is the minimum average amount each student must raise?

   (1) $209.50

   (2) $211.50

   (3) $212.00

   (4) $212.50

   (5) $220.00

3. What is the total number of houses visited by the students?

   (1) 130

   (2) 150

   (3) 200

   (4) 240

   (5) Not enough information is given.

4. Traveling at a speed of 35 miles per hour, approximately how long will it take Terence to drive 180 miles?

   (1) 1 to 2 hours

   (2) 2 to 3 hours

   (3) 3 to 4 hours

   (4) 4 to 5 hours

   (5) 5 to 6 hours

5. Vanessa goes on 4 nature hikes with her youth group. The first takes 5 hours, the second takes 2 hours, the third takes 6 hours, and the fourth takes 3 hours. If the group walks at 4.2 miles per hour, which of the following expressions represents the <u>total distance</u> Vanessa walks?

   (1) $5 + 2 + 6 + 3$

   (2) $16(4.2)$

   (3) $4.2 + 8$

   (4) $4.2 + 16$

   (5) $8(4.2)$

GO ON TO THE NEXT PAGE

Question 6 is based on the following graph.

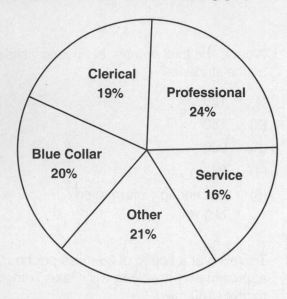

6. The figure above shows the worker distribution in a given country. According to the figure, what percent of the workers work neither in clerical nor in professional occupations?

(1)   3%

(2)   19%

(3)   43%

(4)   57%

(5)   116%

7. If a large can of soup costs $3.00 and a small can costs $1.20, how many ounces of soup does the larger can contain?

(1)   8

(2)   12

(3)   15

(4)   30

(5)   Not enough information is given.

8. The average temperature, in degrees Fahrenheit, in the month of July in Clark City is 4 times the average temperature in the month of February. If the average temperature in July was 82 degrees, which of the following equations could be used to determine the average temperature in February (t)?

(1) $t - 4 = 82$

(2) $t + 4 = 82$

(3) $4t = 82$

(4) $\dfrac{t}{4} = 82$

(5) $4(t + 4) = 82$

9. If 20% of a shipment of 50,000 tomatoes is crushed during transport, how many tomatoes will <u>still be intact</u>?

GO ON TO THE NEXT PAGE

Mathematics, Part I

10. The square root of 14 is between which of the following?

    (1) 1.4 and 1.5

    (2) 2 and 3

    (3) 3 and 4

    (4) 4 and 5

    (5) 13 and 15

11. Miriam and Betty buy a total of 42 stamps. Miriam bought 6 more stamps than Betty did. How many stamps did Miriam buy?

    (1) 18

    (2) 24

    (3) 30

    (4) 36

    (5) 48

Question 12 refers to the following number line.

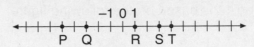

12. Which letter on the number line above represents 4?

    (1) P

    (2) Q

    (3) R

    (4) S

    (5) T

13. Since its formation 10,000 years ago, Niagara Falls has eroded upstream for a distance of 10 miles. If Niagara Falls is expected to disappear entirely after another 22,000 years, how many total miles will have eroded when it disappears?

    (1) 10

    (2) 22

    (3) 28

    (4) 32

    (5) 50

GO ON TO THE NEXT PAGE

Mathematics, Part II

Question 14 is based on the following figure.

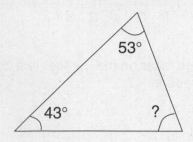

14. One of the three internal angles of the triangle above measures 53°. Another measures 43°. What is the degree measure of the third interior angle of the triangle?

    (1)   22°

    (2)   38°

    (3)   84°

    (4)   244°

    (5)   Not enough information is given.

15. A science class is comparing the relative strength of two telescopes. Model X magnifies up to 3×10^3 times, and the Y model magnifies up to 6×10^2 times. Which of the following statements is correct?

    (1)   The X model is 5 times stronger than the Y model.

    (2)   The Y model is 5 times stronger than the X model.

    (3)   The X model is 1.3 times stronger than the Y model.

    (4)   The Y model is 1.3 times stronger than the X model.

    (5)   The X model is 18 times stronger than the Y model.

16. If Mark can mow $\frac{2}{3}$ of a lawn in 1 hour, how many hours does it take him to mow the entire lawn?

    (1) $\frac{2}{3}$

    (2) $1\frac{1}{3}$

    (3) $1\frac{1}{2}$

    (4)   2

    (5)   3

GO ON TO THE NEXT PAGE

Mathematics, Part II

Question 17 refers to the diagram below.

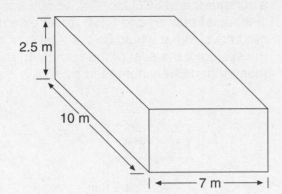

2.5 m

10 m

|← 7 m →|

19. A furniture company charges 5% of the price of any item for delivery. What is the charge for delivering a sofa priced at $850, a dining room set priced at $1,155, and a chair priced at $355?

(1) $11.80

(2) $42.60

(3) $68.50

(4) $118.00

(5) $2,360.00

17. The dimensions of a rectangular sandbox are shown in the diagram above. Which one of the following expressions represents the volume of sand (in cubic meters) it will hold when completely filled?

(1)   7(10)(2.5)

(2)   7(10 + 2.5)

(3)   10(7 + 2.5)

(4)   2(7) + 2(10)

(5)   2(7) + 2(10) + 2(2.5)

18. Evaluate $3x^2 - 2a$, if $x = 3$ and $a = 4$.

GO ON TO THE NEXT PAGE

Mathematics, Part II

Question 20 is based on the following figure.

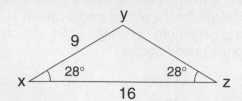

20. If triangle xyz above is an isosceles triangle, what is the perimeter (in meters) of the triangle?

21. Mrs. Carter decides to buy a computer system for her son. She spends $1,500 for a computer and LCD monitor, $650 for a color laser printer, and $250 for an external hard drive. What would be the total cost of the system if the cost of the computer and monitor had been increased by 10%?

22. Universal Products has 78 employees. If twice as many women work for Universal as men, how many women work for Universal?

   (1) 52

   (2) 42

   (3) 26

   (4) 16

   (5) Not enough information is given.

GO ON TO THE NEXT PAGE

Mathematics, Part II

Question 23 is based on the following drawing.

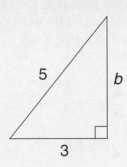

23. According to the Pythagorean theorem, which of the expressions below is true for the triangle shown?

(1) $5^2 + b^2 = 3^2$

(2) $3^2 - 5^2 = b^2$

(3) $3^2 + 5^2 = b^2$

(4) $3^2 - b^2 = 5^2$

(5) $3^2 + b^2 = 5^2$

24. The bird-watching society is monitoring bird migration. On a certain day, 100 birds fly by the watch station, 65 of which are geese and 35 of which are ducks. Which of the following expressions represents the correct way to calculate the <u>probability</u> of a passing bird being a duck?

(1) $\dfrac{35}{65}$

(2) $\dfrac{35}{100}$

(3) $\dfrac{65}{100}$

(4) $\dfrac{(65 - 35)}{100}$

(5) $\dfrac{(35 + 65)}{100}$

25. What is the sum of $2a + 2b + a + b$?

(1) $2a + 3b$

(2) $3a + 3b$

(3) $a^2 + b^4$

(4) $a^3 + b^4$

(5) ab

26. Three members of a swim team weigh 135, 135, and 150 pounds. What is their mean (average) weight?

GO ON TO THE NEXT PAGE

Question 27 is based on the following graph.

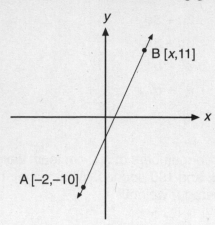

27. A line is drawn on a graph using points A and B as shown. What is the x-coordinate of point B if the slope of the line is 3?

(1) −2

(2) $2\frac{3}{4}$

(3) 3

(4) 5

(5) 9

28. Working for 4 hours a day, a typist earns $65.40 a day after taxes. At the same rate of pay, what would he earn per day if he worked for 7 hours a day? (Let N represent after-tax earnings.)

(1) $N = \frac{4}{7}(65.40)$

(2) $N = \frac{7}{4}(65.40)$

(3) $N = 4(65.40)$

(4) $N = 7(65.40)$

(5) Not enough information is given.

END OF EXAMINATION

NO TEST MATERIAL ON THIS PAGE

Answer Key for Practice Test 1

Writing Part 1 Answer Key		Social Studies Answer Key		Science Answer Key		Reading Answer Key		Math Answer Key	
1.	3	1.	2	1.	3	1.	5	Part One	
2.	3	2.	2	2.	1	2.	4	1.	5
3.	2	3.	2	3.	3	3.	1	2.	4
4.	3	4.	1	4.	3	4.	4	3.	5
5.	5	5.	2	5.	4	5.	3	4.	5
6.	2	6.	1	6.	5	6.	3	5.	2
7.	2	7.	3	7.	2	7.	3	6.	4
8.	1	8.	1	8.	4	8.	5	7.	5
9.	3	9.	3	9.	5	9.	4	8.	3
10.	3	10.	4	10.	1	10.	2	9.	40,000
11.	4	11.	4	11.	2	11.	4	10.	3
12.	3	12.	4	12.	5	12.	4	11.	2
13.	4	13.	5	13.	1	13.	2	12.	5
14.	1	14.	5	14.	1	14.	3	13.	4
15.	1	15.	3	15.	5	15.	5		
16.	4	16.	5	16.	4	16.	2	Part Two	
17.	3	17.	4	17.	4	17.	3	14.	3
18.	1	18.	5	18.	3	18.	4	15.	1
19.	1	19.	3	19.	3	19.	2	16.	3
20.	5	20.	5	20.	2	20.	2	17.	1
21.	1	21.	2	21.	2	21.	4	18.	19
22.	5	22.	4	22.	4	22.	3	19.	4
23.	3	23.	2	23.	3			20.	34
24.	5	24.	5	24.	2			21.	2,550
25.	1	25.	2	25.	2			22.	1
26.	2	26.	1	26.	1			23.	5
27.	4	27.	2	27.	5			24.	2
		28.	4	28.	3			25.	2
		29.	3	29.	2			26.	140
		30.	3	30.	4			27.	4
		31.	1	31.	4			28.	2
		32.	4	32.	1				
				33.	3				

Chapter 28
Practice Test 1:
Answers and
Explanations

Writing—Part I Explanations

1. **3** The word "Companies" does not refer to specific companies, so it should be lowercase. "Because of" and "Due to the fact that" (1) serve the same function in the sentence and are both correct. The comma after "customers" is necessary because it joins the dependent clause beginning with a subordinating conjunction with the independent clause, which eliminates (2). No comma is needed after "convenience," because "convenience and concern" are only two items; commas are necessary only in a list of three or more items.

2. **3** This sentence fragment can be fixed by changing the period to a comma and eliminating "But." To use a coordinating conjunction such as "but," the first clause must be independent and stand alone as a complete thought. Using other coordinating conjunctions, as in (2) and (5), does not fix the fragment problem. Choice (4) adds an unnecessary "it" and also does not correct the fragment.

3. **2** This question tests tense. Because the passage is written in the present tense, look for an answer in the present tense. Remember, the GED tests the present and past tense only, so the present progressive (4) will not be the correct choice. The simple present tense (2) is the way to go.

4. **3** This question tries to confuse you with pronouns, so use the rest of the passage to guide you. The passage talks to "you" and asks you to "read the newspaper" in order to "familiarize" yourself with the research. "Oneself" does not make sense in this context because the passage specifically references "you" at all other times.

5. **5** Examine pronoun references. What does "them" reference? What is being preserved? The answer is "the environment," a singular noun. Because "the environment" is singular, it must be replaced with the pronoun "it" rather than "them." Choosing (1) removes the parallelism from the sentence. There are three "ways" mentioned, so you would not refer to only one way (3). There is no reason to use a comma after "recycle" (2) or to conjugate "help" differently (4).

6. **2** To fix this sentence structure error, divide the sentence into its two independent clauses with periods. Choices (3) and (4) insert coordinating conjunctions that do not fit with the sentence's meaning. The addition of "still" in (5) also does not fit with the sentence's meaning.

7. **2** A semicolon followed by the time word "then" is the best way to combine these two independent clauses. "But" (1) suggests incorrectly that the sentence is changing direction. Choices (3), (4), and (5) do not include a verb, so the second clause would not be independent and could not be divided from the first by a semicolon.

8. **1** Commas are necessary between lists of three or more items for clarity. There is no need for a comma after the list, so you can eliminate (3). The vocabulary used in the sentence is correct, so (2) and (5) are not correct. "Care for" is the correct idiomatic expression, not "care of," so cross off (4).

9. **3** Because the two sentences follow the same train of thought, it makes sense to connect them with the coordinating conjunction "and." This eliminates (2) and (5). The word "and" should not begin a sentence or an independent clause, so (1) and (4) are not correct.

10. **3** The word "nor" turns the sentence into a negative. How can you keep the sentence's meaning the same while using negative words? "It is frustrating when you make a simple mistake" becomes "Nor is it any less frustrating when you make a simple mistake." Both mean that it is frustrating to make a simple mistake.

11. **4** The best way to fix this comma splice error is by adding the subordinating conjunction "if" to the beginning of the sentence. The first clause becomes the dependent one and the second clause becomes the independent one. Together, linked with "if," they become a complete sentence.

12. **3** To correct this tense error, study the rest of the text first. In what tense is the passage written? It's written in the past tense, so you need to change "is" to "was." Because none of the other answer choices are in the past tense, this answer must be the correct choice.

13. **4** This sentence tests tense error and has a clue to the answer in the sentence: The words "back then" indicate, along with the rest of the text, that the verb "agree" should be in the past tense. "Was agree" may seem like it is in the past tense because of "was," but the conjugation is wrong.

14. **1** Because "late" is not part of the title of President Kennedy or the first word of the sentence, it should not be capitalized. "President" is part of the title, so it must be capitalized. Since the president's words are in the past, the verb "said" should remain in the past tense. The word "inaugural" refers to a single "address," so the word should remain singular. The comma is necessary because it is introducing a quotation.

15. **1** "Lets" is supposed to be the contraction "Let's," short for "Let us." "However" should be fenced in by commas. Do not break up a phrase with a comma. There is no need to change the tense.

16. **4** The sentence begins with a modifying phrase, so it must be followed immediately by the subject the phrase is describing. Only (4) begins with "these politicians," those who are asking for something other than military service. None of the other choices begins with the noun that defines the modifying phrase.

17. **3** This question tests tense. Start by determining which tense is used in the surrounding sentence. The words "has" and "to this very day" reveal that the sentence is in present tense. Choices (1), (2), and (4) are all in the past tense. Choice (5) is in the future tense. Therefore, (3), the only one in the present tense, is the correct answer.

18. **1** The groups puzzling over the ethical issue include both those of the past and the "contemporary lawyers" of the modern day. Therefore, the verb tense must reflect the continuation over time. The verb must also be singular because "issue" is singular. Choice (2) is plural. Choice (3) does not have a verb. Choice (4) turns the sentence into a fragment with only a dependent clause. Choice (5) splits the verb "to have puzzled" with the subject of the sentence.

19. **1** The verbs in the answer choices vary by tense and by number. "Bad guys" is plural, so you'll need a plural verb. The verb "get" in the first part of the sentence is in the present tense, so you'll need a verb in the present. These requirements eliminate (2) and (3). Choices (4) and (5) are not parallel in construction with the first part of the sentence.

20. **5** This sentence is correct as written. Because "people" is plural, "try" is correctly plural, (1). "To help" follows a conjugated verb, so it should remain in the infinitive (2). "If" is a better word choice than "whether" (3). The verb "is" is singular, so the word "sacrifice" should remain singular (4).

21. **1** "Most of us" is the subject of the sentence and should not be divided from the verb by a comma. The essay uses "us" and "we" throughout the piece, so it should not be changed to "you" in one instance (2). These paragraphs are written in the present tense, so "see" should remain in the present tense (3). "Principle" is used correctly here as a rule or a generalization; "principal" refers to a person who leads (4).

22. 5   This sentence is correct. The sentence describes the state of being of transportation, not what it owns. Therefore, "is" is the correct verb, choice (1). If the reader could understand what "area" means if the rest of the sentence is removed, then a comma would be necessary. However, "area" needs more description to be distinguished from other areas. As a vital part of the sentence, it should not be set off by a comma (2). The sentence refers only to a single set of a hundred years, not several hundred years (3). "Changing" would work in this sentence only if you insert "an" before "enormous" (4).

23. 3   This question asks you to study the tense and number of the verb "to have." The essay is in the present tense, so this verb should also be in the present tense. This eliminates (2) and (5), in the future tense, and (4), in the past tense. Because there are two nouns in the subject, "proliferation" and "accessibility," the verb should be plural. Choice (1) is singular.

24. 5   The entire passage is written using "we" and "us," including the given sentence. "You" changes the point of view. None of the other choices make the sentence grammatically incorrect.

25. 1   Choices (2) and (4) are in the future tense. However, the phrase "in short" summarizes the text, which is all in the present tense. Choice (3) turns the sentence into a fragment. Choice (5) uses sentence structure that simply isn't used anymore.

26. 2   First, figure out the logical order the thoughts of the sentences should follow. The topic of new business should be first. The contents of the discussion should be next. And the conclusion of the conversation should be last. (2) best follows this logic. Choices (1) and (3) keep the paragraph confusing. Choices (4) and (5) are extreme statements that are unlikely to appear in a business memo.

27. 4   Because the sixth sentence explains a problem, the answer choice offering a possible solution should follow it. Only (4) addresses the issue of poor sales figures with a suggestion to spend more money on advertising.

Writing—Part II Test Explanations
ESSAY SCORE: 4

The issue of privacy in the marketplace is controversial. On one hand, as consumers, we benefit when companies market to our purchasing habits. On the other hand, it is dangerous to allow the wrong companies to have access to our financial information. However, in the final analysis, I believe that companies should be allowed to find and to market to their willing audiences but with enough precautions to protect their customers from fraud.

Companies should be permitted to share information about their markets with their customers. If someone invents something I would love, I want someone to find me and tell me about it so that I have the option to buy it. For example, I receive many catalogues in the mail relating to hunting, fishing, and camping. These are my interests and I am eager to read about the latest fishing lure. Companies that do not interest me do not want to waste money trying to sell to someone who will never buy. I would rather they have my information so as not to use it rather than simply mailing to everyone in the phone book.

However, some companies are too eager to sell their wares and hurt their customers. For example, there are television commercials that advertise albums filled with musical hits. After purchasing one album, those who do not understand the small print discover that they have joined a music club and that their credit cards get charged automatically for each new album.

In conclusion, I believe that companies should market to their audiences, but only if their audiences wish to participate. It should be easier than it is to remove oneself from mailing lists and music clubs. Companies must respect the wishes of their customers so that they do not develop a bad reputation and lose business anyway.

Reasons the author received a score of 4:

- o The essay is well organized.
  - The introduction clearly explains what aspects of privacy the essay will explore.
  - The body paragraphs flow naturally and with transitions from the introduction.
  - The conclusion summarizes the author's viewpoint clearly and emphatically.
- o The essay is well supported.
  - The examples given are realistic and accessible to any reader.
  - The examples are detailed and thorough.
  - The examples connect clearly to the main idea.
- o The essay demonstrates a strong grasp of grammar, spelling, and punctuation.
  - The author varies sentence structure and length.
  - The essay uses complex vocabulary correctly.

ESSAY SCORE: 2

I agree. We shouldn't have our lives watched by everyone else. Who want money from us. I try to tear up my credit cards but they always send me new ones and you just can't break the cycel.

Credit card companies are known for selling your information about what I purchase from where to other companies who might be interested in you. So the credit card people make money from charging you intrest and from selling your personel info. Not fair. Also, the govt doesn't help the information. I saw a show on tv where this guy borrowed a book from the library and the government tracked him because it was a book about built bombs. I saw another show where some guy hacked into the governments computers so its not a safe place to store library book tracking info or social security numbers or anything else.

Personnel information should personal. Or new information should be invented that no one knows so you can keep at least something secret anymore.

Reasons the author received a score of 2:

- o The essay is poorly organized.
  - The body paragraph should be separated by ideas.
  - The essay needs better transitions between ideas and sentences.
  - The piece needs a solid introduction and conclusion.
- o The essay is poorly supported.
  - The ideas should be clearly described in the introduction.
  - Opinions should be supported by factual examples or occurrences.
  - The examples used should convince any reader that they are plausible.
  - The suspicious tone is not justified by the examples.
- o The essay has numerous grammar, spelling, and punctuation errors.
  - There are many run-on sentences.
  - There are many sentence fragments.
  - There is no use of unique or complex vocabulary.
  - The point of view frequently changes.
- o The essay is noticeably shorter than 250 words.

Social Studies Test Explanations

1. **2** This EXCEPT question is asking you to decide which answer choice can NOT be used to deny a child employment. Each of the choices is mentioned in the passage as a possible reason to keep children from working—except for one: (2) gender. Age is mentioned in the second half of the passage as a restrictor to employment, so eliminate (1). As for (3), the actual phrase "hazard levels" is not in the passage, but the third sentence from the end says, "as long as the job is not determined to be dangerous or ruinous to their health or well-being," which basically means the same thing. This sentence also rules out (4). In the second-to-last sentence, the passage discusses working hours, which rules out (5). Only gender is NOT discussed as a reason to deny a child employment.

2. **2** Choice (1) says that it should be up to kids to decide when and if they want to take a job—but the passage says this is decided by the Department of Labor, so you can eliminate this one. Choice (3) says kids can't work under any circumstances, which directly contradicts the entire passage, so you can eliminate this one, too. Choice (4) is saying the same thing as (3) using different words. Choice (5) may be true, but it wasn't stated in the passage. The correct answer, which sums up the reason for the need for regulations, is (2).

3. **2** Who would be likely to support regulations to protect children? Factory owners *may* be kind-hearted, but then again, there have been a lot of factory owners who have exploited child labor—so eliminate (1). Child protection agencies would seem very likely to protect children; let's hold onto (2) while we look at the other choices. Worker's unions might well also support regulations to protect children, so let's hold on to (3) as well. Small companies and agricultural workers *might* be kind-hearted too, but we don't know that they will be, so eliminate (4) and (5). We have two choices left: (2) and (3). Which is better? The correct answer is (2).

4. **1** Why do we need to protect children in the workplace? Let's eliminate the craziest answers first: Do we need to protect kids because they were taking jobs away from adults (3)? That's not a reason to protect kids. Do we need to protect kids because they are a good source of labor (4)? No way. Do we need to protect kids because employers are taking good care of them (5)? That doesn't make sense. We have two choices left: Choice (1) says we need to protect kids because they have been exploited in the past. That seems pretty good. Choice (2) says we should protect kids because they aren't responsible, implying that they don't do good work. The best answer is (1).

5. **2** The most important word in this question is the last word: *disagree*. We are looking for a statement that the Department of Labor will disagree with. Will the Department of Labor disagree that kids should be protected from hazards, as in (1)? No way! Would they disagree that kids should not be permitted to work in *any* capacity (2)? Way! The passage outlines how the Department of Labor *does* let kids work. This is the correct answer. What about the other choices? The passage tells us in the last sentence that the Department of Labor has already classified 17 nonagricultural occupations unsuitable for minors—so why would they disagree with that? Eliminate (3). The passage tells us in the third sentence that the Fair Labor Standards Act protects children—and we know the Department of Labor is in favor of protecting children—so eliminate (4). For the same reason, we have to eliminate (5).

6. **1** The chart shows the number of visits to the doctor for an ear infection for various age groups of children in two different years, 1990 and 2005. You'll notice that apparently more kids were diagnosed with ear infections in 2005 than were in 1990—but that's not what the question is about. The question asks you to identify the type of child *least* likely to have been treated for an ear infection. What you want to find is the smallest bar on the chart. Do you see it? That's right, it belongs to the group of 6 to 10 year olds from 1990. Now, look at the answer choices: Which choice is part of that group? The correct answer is (1).

7. **3** The passage says the young men went west in search of opportunities like finding gold and striking it rich. Which of the answer choices says that? The correct answer is (3). Choices (1), (2), and (4) didn't appear in the passage itself—and while these all *might* have been reasons for someone to head west, the correct answer to a GED Reading passage is almost always going to come from within the passage. Choice (5) was in the passage—but earlier in the second paragraph, it explained that people got jobs in the cannery only when their quest to get rich by discovering gold had not worked out.

8. **1** The only reference to towns in the passage comes in the second paragraph, and it refers to San Francisco and Monterey. The next sentence reads, "There they found jobs…" So why did people settle in those towns? The correct answer is choice (1). You might have been tempted by choice (3) because it referred to Monterey and the gold to be found there—but by the time they got to these towns, the passage says the settlers had given up on being prospectors and just needed jobs. Choices (2), (4), and (5) contain information not found in the passage itself.

9. **3** It's easy to get confused in these classification passages because there are so many terms. Don't get too stuck on reading—just try to get to the questions as fast as you can. Why memorize the five different kinds of speakers when there are only two questions? For the first question, we have to deal with only one of the speakers, Speaker II. He or she is saying that the way to understand a people's morality is to examine *past* achievements. Let's look at the answer choices. Which of these individuals studies the past? All of them *might*, but one in particular is defined by the past: The correct answer is (3), a historian.

10. **4** Now we are looking for a statement that is likely to have been made by a psychologist, a professional who deals with the mind. As you read the statements, remember to skip Speaker II—you already know she's a historian. Speaker I is talking about scarce resources; seems more like an economist than a psychologist. Speaker III is talking about the impact of the physical world around a people; sounds more like a geographer. Speaker IV is talking about what lies within the mind of an individual: Bingo! That's our answer. To make sure, take a look at (5), which deals with different cultures; seems more like a sociologist than a psychologist. The correct answer is (4).

11. **4** Before you turn to the question, make sure you understand the pie chart. The title says it is about how children are being educated. It says that 39.2 percent are being educated in public school, 31.5 percent are being educated in private school, and the rest of the children are being educated in other ways. Which statement is supported by the information in the pie chart? Choices (1) and (2) imply value judgments that are not supported by the chart. Who knows which is better, or which ones the children prefer? Choice (3) contradicts what we can see from the chart. If tutoring at home were the most popular method, it would have the largest percentage of kids doing it. Choice (5) also contradicts the information in the chart. A third converted to a percentage is about 33 percent—but on the chart we can see cooperative education makes up only 10.1 percent. The correct answer is (4).

12. **4** This was a tough question, because it asked you to do some analysis. A pure market economy, according to the passage, is one in which the forces of the market control what happens; in other words, there is no government control whatsoever. So which of the answer choices would NOT be found in a pure market economy? Monopolies could occur in a pure market economy because there would be no government rules to prevent them. Small businesses would probably flourish—at least until monopolies put them out of business. There would certainly be unemployment because the markets would hire people only when they needed them. And presumably, stocks and bonds (which provide capital for new businesses) would be found in large numbers. The only things you would NOT find in a pure market economy, as unlikely as it seems, would be taxes and welfare (both of which are controlled by the government). The answer to this difficult question is (4).

13. 5   The passage says that in a socialist economy, all the money is distributed equally among the members of a society. So which of the groups in the answer choices would benefit the *least* from the switch to a socialist economy? Choices (2), (3), and (4) would all benefit quite a bit, because these are relatively poor people who would get a bigger slice of the pie than they have now. Eliminate (2), (3), and (4). Between the two choices we have left, who benefits the *least*? The correct answer is (5), highly skilled labor, because presumably they were being well paid for their unique skills, and would lose money in the redistribution of wealth. Government employees in socialist systems usually tend to gain power because they get to decide who receives the wealth.

14. 5   As you study the photograph, you will probably notice two things: (A) the car in the photo is quite old, and (B) it isn't working. The people in this old photograph are pushing the car instead of riding in it. The question itself says that while today we sometimes face a shortage of gas, the people back then had to deal with another kind of shortage. What was it? If the answer were (1), the photo would probably show the car stuck in the mud, but it doesn't. Does it seem as if the people in that photo are concerned about pollution? We didn't think so. Are they concerned about seatbelts? Not when most of them are pushing the car. Are they concerned about heavy cars? Now, we're getting warmer. If you were pushing a car, you would probably want it to be as light as possible. But let's read the last answer choice before we pick: Could the people in the photo be concerned with a shortage of gas stations? Aha! This answer gets to the heart of *why* they are pushing the car in the first place: It is out of gas. The correct answer to this question is (5).

15. 3   At first glance, you might think this question requires an advanced understanding of genetic engineering. However, once you look at the answer choices, you will see that most of them can be ruled out immediately. The question asks for an example of the *misuse* of genetic engineering. This means you are looking for an example of something bad. Choices (1), (2), (4), and (5) all involve something that could really only be called good: eliminating a strain of influenza, creating a new type of grain, reducing birth defects, improving vegetables. None of these can be an example of misuse. The best answer is (3), which discusses using a new virus as a weapon.

16. 5   In the passage, Grant says the Civil War would change the nation as a whole. Which historical development best supports that? The triumph by one side in a civil war isn't an example of how the country was changed by the war. Eliminate (1). The shift of population in Missouri may somehow be related to the war, but it's difficult to see exactly how. Eliminate (2). The entry of the United States into World War I does not seem to be directly related to the Civil War either. Eliminate (3). Women's winning the right to vote also doesn't seem like a direct result of the Civil War. Eliminate (4). The correct answer is (5). The Civil War was waged to free the African American slaves—which profoundly changed the entire nation.

17. 4   You may have been tempted to pick (1) because it concerned taxation, but the principle of "taxation without representation" means that a government doesn't have the right to tax its citizens unless those citizens have the right to elect the government and thus have a say in how much they will be taxed. This was one of the principles that drove the 13 colonies to declare independence from England in 1776. Choices (2), (3), and (5) have nothing to do with the 24th Amendment as outlined in the question. Only (4) does: just because a person doesn't pay his taxes does not mean his right to vote can be taken away.

18. 5   Read the graph carefully before looking at the questions. We see bars representing men and women who take the SAT, broken down by ethnic group. From this graph, we can see that in all but one group, more women than men take the SAT. The one group where this does not appear to be true is that of Asian Americans. Looking at the answers, (1) and (3) make value judgments not supported by the graph. We are not given any information on how men and women perform on the test, nor how well the test measures performance in college—just the fact that they took it. So we can eliminate both (1) and (3). Choices (2) and (4) make statements of fact not supported by the graph. We have no idea of whether numbers are declining or increasing from year to year. This graph is of a single snapshot in time. The correct answer is (5): According to the chart, clearly more women than men take the SAT.

19. **3** The question is basically asking, "Which of the following is NOT an example of a plutocratic government?" The best answer is (3), in which the leaders are elected by popular vote. In a plutocracy, the leaders are chosen because they are the wealthiest citizens. This means that there is no vote. All the other choices reflect situations that could occur in a plutocracy.

20. **5** You don't have to know anything about Andrew Mellon to realize that, in this statement at least, he is on the side of the people. He writes that "unwise" public officials "fall to these interests of monopoly as against the welfare of the people of whom they are supposed to serve." So we are looking for an answer choice that is sympathetic to the people and critical of officials who lose sight of the people's welfare. Choice (1) seems possible at first, but goes too far: Mellon doesn't suggest that public officials who profit from a monopoly shouldn't run for office. Choice (2) also goes too far. Mellon doesn't say monopolies should never exist. Choice (4) again goes too far, because Mellon never says the profits of monopolies should be shared by all. Choice (3) is wrong because it sides with the public officials over the interests of the people. This leaves us with Choice (5), which is a simple restatement of what Mellon says in the passage.

21. **2** The passage compares the relationship between the federal and state governments to, respectively, the hub and spokes of a wagon wheel. This is called an analogy (which means a comparison between two things to help you understand one of them better). You have to find an answer choice that illustrates the analogy. Choice (1) is no good because, in the analogy, the entire government is represented by one wheel. What purpose would three other wheels serve? This might have been a good analogy if we were talking about four separate countries, each with its own wagon wheel helping to support the world-wagon—but that's a different analogy. Choice (2) basically restates the analogy—and is the correct answer. Choices (3), (4), and (5) all extend the analogy in some meaningless way.

22. **4** The map of the United States shows which areas have a high number of non-English-speaking children. You'll notice that the highest concentrations tend to be on the outside edges of the country, not the interior. Question 22 asks you to pick the best geographic explanation for the areas that have the highest numbers of non-English-speaking children. Choice (2) is irrelevant because we aren't concerned with the total number of children in the country—only the children who can't speak English. Choice (3) is irrelevant because, according to the map, some of the heaviest areas of non-English-speaking kids are in the north, such as New York and Washington. Choice (5) is wrong because a decrease in federal funding would presumably affect *all* states, not just the ones that now appear to have a high number of non-English-speaking kids. Choice (1) seems possible at first, because lower income taxes might attract new immigrants, but then again, wouldn't they attract just about everyone? Let's hold onto this as we look at (4): If recent immigrants settled in border and coastal states, wouldn't that be a pretty logical explanation for why these areas contain the most non-English-speaking kids? Choice (4) is a much better answer than (1).

23. **2** All of the answer choices would have an effect on the distribution of these kids EXCEPT (2), climate. In general, new immigrants would seem to make decisions based more on the availability of ESL programs, immigration laws, social services, and even migration patterns (where immigrants have gone before) than on climate. One of the states with the largest number of non-English speakers (according to the chart) is New York (which has a colder climate) while others include California and Florida, with warmer climates.

24. **5** To answer this question, you have to consider each answer choice in turn. Are non-English-speaking children evenly distributed across the entire country? The map says no. Eliminate (1). Are there more of these kids in Arizona than in California? No, according to the map, California has the highest level of counties with at least 500 non-English-speaking kids. Arizona has between five and nine counties with 500 or more non-English-speaking children, but not as many as California, so we can eliminate (2). And while Texas and California *do* have the highest levels of kids who don't speak English, could that really mean that they have more kids who can't speak English than kids who *can*? The map does not show information that compares these two groups of children, so eliminate (3). Choice (4) is basically irrelevant to the question, so eliminate this one too. The correct answer is (5) because it best reflects what the map tells us: In the middle states in the north of the United States there are fewer non-English-speaking children.

25. 2   The passage tells us that the Constitution and other laws "made in accordance" with the Constitution can't be set aside by judges or any other laws. So, which is an example of this? The correct answer is (2), which says that the Bill of Rights (the first ten amendments of the Constitution) can't be denied by any arm of the government. Choices (1), (3), and (4) are all irrelevant to this concept. Choice (5) says that the Court of Appeals can overturn previous court decisions, but this is true only of decisions made by lower courts. Appeals courts can't overturn "the supreme law of the land," as the passage calls it.

26. 1   Lowering the speed limit, limiting senators to two terms, reducing pollution, or creating town zoning—none of these deprives people of their constitutional rights. However, prohibiting protests by a union takes away a fundamental right guaranteed by the Constitution: the right to free speech. Thus, the correct answer is (1).

27. 2   Freedom of religion is a fundamental right guaranteed by the Constitution—so we can eliminate (1). A right to a trial by jury is also guaranteed by the Constitution—so we can eliminate (3). The right to vote is also guaranteed to citizens by the Constitution—so we can probably eliminate (4), because even if they don't speak English, people can be citizens. The president is not allowed to simply ignore Supreme Court decisions or Congressional decisions, so we can also eliminate (5). The correct answer is (2).

28. 4   The passage states that the economics professors say there are too many factors to be able to make long-term stock-market predictions. Choice (4) accurately restates that idea. Choices (1), (2), and (3) all make statements that contradict the passage. Choice (5) may have been tempting, but it went too far: The economists did not say there was *no* relation between long- and short-term predictions. They simply said long-term predictions become less accurate over time, much as weather forecasts do.

29. 3   Because so many different factors can affect stock prices, there can be no guarantee that two companies producing the same goods will do equally well—so we can eliminate (1). While amateur investors are mentioned in the passage, their effect is not the most important factor on a stock's success—so eliminate (2). The passage says that amateurs may do as well as a professional stock trader, but it does not say they will do better—so we can eliminate (4). Choice (5) is tempting, because more information is likely to help investors to make *better* predictions, but the passage does not imply that more information will help investor to make completely accurate predictions—so eliminate (5). The correct answer must be (3), because past success does not ensure future performance—a concept always mentioned in stock prospectuses, but often forgotten in practice.

30. 3   What caused the end of the era of transatlantic ship-crossings? Do you think it was a series of accidents, a major war that disrupted routes, the cost of travel by boat, or the fact that sea travel fell out of fashion? Nope, it was something much more basic—the airplane. The correct answer is (3).

31. 1   In this cartoon, the two Civil War veterans, one African American, one white—each missing a leg—are shaking hands. Always read the caption carefully in a cartoon or photograph. The two soldiers are calling each other comrade and saying they each lost a leg for a good cause. The best answer is (1), which reflects what the Civil War was fought over: the right of all men to be free and equal to each other. Choices (3), (4), and (5) all suggest information that is impossible to know about these two individuals, while not reflecting the point of the cartoon. Choice (2), while true, again did not reflect the larger point behind the conflict.

32. 4   The Industrial Revolution changed fundamental patterns of life. Instead of each family producing many of its own primary supplies, people began to work in factories that provided them with a wage, which they used to buy manufactured versions of what they used to make themselves. Choice (4) best explained this new fundamental change. Choices (1), (2), (3), and (5) may or may not be true, but didn't explain why people changed their fundamental way of life.

Science Test Explanations

1. **3** The answer to this question can be found inside the parentheses in the middle of the passage: "...the number of neutrons (which have approximately the same mass as a proton but no electric charge) can vary." Choice (1) is wrong because a neutron and a proton each have about the same mass, and they both are a part of an atom, so an atom is larger than a neutron. Choices (2) and (5) are wrong because neutrons (as their name implies) have no charge, positive or negative. Choice (4) is wrong because an isotope is a kind of atom composed of neutrons, protons, and electrons.

2. **1** The passage tells us that an atom has the same number of electrons as protons.

3. **3** An isotope, as the last line in the passage tells us, has a different number of neutrons and protons. Each of the answer choices here is an isotope except for choice (3), which has the same number of protons as neutrons.

4. **3** An isotope must have a different number of neutrons and protons. You may have been tempted to think that adding an extra proton would create an isotope—but remember, the passage told us that in every atom, the number of protons and electrons must be the same. So you can't add just a proton. Eliminate (1). Adding an electron wouldn't cause the protons and neutrons to have different numbers, so eliminate (2). In choice (3), adding an extra neutron would create an isotope. For this reason, we must eliminate (4) because it says "A and B only," even though adding a proton and an electron would accomplish the task. Adding all three particles would not create an isotope, so eliminate (5). The only way to create an isotope in the answer choices in this case is to add an extra neutron. The correct answer is choice (3).

5. **4** Choices (1) and (3) are not actually related to the information given, so we can eliminate them both. Choices (2) and (5) are at least about water but have little to do with the information given, either. Choice (4) represents a phenomenon that is directly explained by the information: Icebergs don't sink in the ocean for the same reason ice cubes float in a glass of water; when frozen, water expands and becomes less dense.

6. **5** If humans can't detect the sound at all, then it must be above 20,000 hertz (above which, the paragraph tells us, humans can't hear at all). Below 20 hertz, we've been told, humans can't *hear* the sound but they can *feel* it. The only answer choice that is above 20,000 hertz is choice (5).

7. **2** Frequency is measured, according to the paragraph, by the number of cycles of a sound wave within one second. Therefore, the correct answer will be the choice with the largest number of cycles in the same period of time, or (2).

8. **4** The best speakers would be the ones that reproduce every sound a human can hear—which, we are told in the paragraph, means everything between 20 hertz and 20,000 hertz. The best answer is (4).

9. **5** If hurricanes gather strength over warm water, then we need to pick the warmest body of water from among the choices. Based on the chart, which body of water is the warmest? The correct answer is (5).

10. **1** According to the passage, tests for blood type are necessary because of the way red blood cells interact with each other. Therefore, testing for blood type is necessary only when there is going to be an exchange of red blood cells. In practice, this means you need the blood test for whole blood transfusions only. Plasma transfusions do not pass on red blood cells. This rules out (2) and (3). Choices (4) and (5) don't seem to be based on the passage at all. The correct answer is (1).

11. **2** Based on the chart, a carbon level of 63 percent means the coal is classified as (2), lignite.

12. 5   The answer to this tough question might not be immediately obvious. However, if steel is formed when iron combines with carbon at a very high temperature, then it would be helpful if the coal that provides the carbon didn't just burn up right away and if it had a high carbon content. Therefore, the best type of coal to use would be anthracite, which has the highest carbon content and burns only at very high temperatures. The best answer is (5).

13. 1   As you read the classifications, you may notice that each new type of coal is basically the previous type of coal, only with more heat, pressure, and time. For example, lignite is just peat that has been subjected to more heat, pressure, and time. So, which of the types of coal was at some time in the past *all* the other types of coal? If you said (1), peat, then you are doing just fine.

14. 1   Peat gradually changes into lignite and then into subbituminous coal and then into anthracite with the addition of heat and pressure. Heat and pressure basically come from the coal being farther and farther underground. So, which type of coal would most likely be near the surface? The correct answer is (1), peat.

15. 5   After all the other questions, this one should be a piece of cake. From the chart, the coal with the highest level of carbon is (5), anthracite.

16. 3   From the passage, we know that seeds need moisture, oxygen, and the right temperature, somewhere between 15 and 27 degrees centigrade. However, the passage tells us that corn seeds require an even higher temperature. Therefore, the correct answer will have a temperature greater than 27 degrees centigrade, with adequate moisture and oxygen. Choice (1) has not only a temperature that is too low, but a sealed container, so there might not be enough oxygen. Choice (2) is in an arid desert. The word "arid" means "without moisture," a climate which would make it very hard to germinate a seed. The passage says you need a certain amount of water, but (4), a test tube full of water, is clearly too much. And the passage says that an environment suitable for a maple seed is actually colder than most seeds can handle, let alone a corn seed which needs more heat than most, so we can eliminate (5). The correct answer is (3).

17. 4   We know that maple seeds can germinate in colder than usual temperatures, but does that mean they can germinate in *any* temperature? Not likely, so we can eliminate (1). Corn may need a higher temperature than average, but it can't be *too* hard to grow, or it wouldn't be one of the most-grown grains in the world, so we can eliminate (2). The passage specifically says oxygen is necessary for germination, so we can eliminate (3). And the passage does not mention the role of germs in germination, so we can most likely eliminate (5). The correct answer is (4), which is stated in the passage itself.

18. 3   Lactic acid is produced during periods of "intense activity," according to the passage. Which of the answer choices describes a period of intense activity? The best answer is (3), taking an aerobics class.

19. 3   When do plants lie dormant? You guessed it: in the winter. The correct answer is (3).

20. 2   If you picked (3), you simply reversed the sequence. For the most part (unless there has been volcanic activity) the earliest rock layers are found deepest in the ground. Thus, if we arrange these rock layers from oldest to newest, the answer would be 4, 3, 2, 1, or choice (2).

21. **2** If auxin prevents weeds, while encouraging grass, what could auxin replace? The correct answer is (2), pesticides—the chemicals that kill harmful insects or weeds. Auxin would not take the place of grass or weeds, because it is simply a chemical. And certainly it could not take the place of seeds (which are the mechanism that allows many plants to grow) or water (without which there could not be any life as we know it).

22. **4** This food chain begins with microscopic algae and moves up to bigger and bigger sea creatures, ending with the bass. Which of the answer choices seems most likely to be true? It seems very unlikely that only bass eat minnows, so we can eliminate (1). Do algae eat even smaller animals? Based on this food chain, that does not seem to be true (in fact, algae mostly get their energy from the sun), so we can eliminate (2). Minnows are much smaller than bass, so we can eliminate (3). Based on the food chain we are looking at, bass need to eat minnows—they could probably not survive on algae. The best answer, given that food chains usually go from the smallest organism in the chain to the largest, is (4). You may have had no idea what copepods are, but you still had a pretty good shot of getting the correct answer.

23. **3** Having read the passage about passive protection, you should read through each of the answer choices to see if it is an example of passive protection. Choices (1) and (2) do not involve camouflage, mimicry, or bad taste. They are about avoiding other animals completely, which is not described as part of passive protection. (4) details an active defense that involves killing another creature. (5) is not about protection but about a predator's hunting mechanism. The correct answer is (3), which involves the camouflaging of a tropical fish.

24. **2** Protective mimicry, according to the passage, is when a defenseless organism resembles a fiercer organism and so gets left alone by other creatures. Only (2) is a true example of protective mimicry. If you picked (1), you were thinking of another kind of mimicry, when a hunter imitates the sound of the animal he is trying to kill to get it to come near enough to shoot. If you picked (3), you were probably thinking of "protective resemblance" which was also mentioned in the passage.

25. **2** The passage says that the "short summers" are followed by intense cold and dark. So, why do plants in the tundra have a short growing season? The correct answer simply rephrases the passage: because the period of warmth and sunlight necessary for growth is so brief. This is answer (2). Many of the other answer choices bring up valid worries about growing plants in the tundra, but none of them is mentioned in the passage.

26. **1** Estivation is defined in the passage as a process in which animals lie dormant (i.e., asleep) during the hot summer months. Which of the answer choices gives the best example of estivation? We can eliminate choices (2) and (3) because neither concerns an animal. Choice (4) is tempting because hibernation seems a lot like estivation, but there is one big difference: The passage says estivation only occurs during the hot summer months. Choice (5) is wrong because the squirrel is not lying dormant; to the contrary, it is scurrying around finding nuts. The best answer is choice (1).

27. **5** Why would a farmer plant a crop that can't be sold? He would have to have a good reason. Which of the answer choices provides a good reason? Choice (1) doesn't make any sense, because there would be no reason for a farmer to plant grass and clover in the first place. Choice (2) doesn't make sense either, because the farmer won't make *any* money from planting grass or clover. Choices (3) and (4) take us outside the scope of the question by bringing up relative degrees of depletion by the cash crops corn, wheat, and oats, but not explaining why clover or grass would be planted. The correct answer is (5), which finally gives us a good reason for planting this non-cash crop: because it puts valuable nutrients back into the soil so that the farmer can start planting corn and wheat again next year.

28. 3   Only deciduous forests have seasons in which the leaves turn brown and fall off the trees. If you didn't know this, you could still get it from the passage: Rain forests (it says) grow all year long, so the leaves never turn brown and fall off. Coniferous trees "show little change in their appearance throughout the year." The correct answer is (3).

29. 2   First, read the graph: It projects deaths from AIDS in five different regions over time. Which region will have the most deaths in 2010? To find out, just look for the line that rises the highest on the graph. The correct answer is (2), Africa.

30. 4   Where would this definition appear? If you aren't sure, try crossing off answers you *know* must be wrong. For example, would the definition of the word irrigation really appear in an article on astronomy? Cross off (5). Has irrigation got anything to do with biology? Not really, so cross off (3). Come to think of it, does irrigation have anything to do with physics or chemistry? Nope, so cross off (1) and (2). The correct answer is (4). Agricultural science is the science of farming.

31. 4   The scientist believed that the cause of the men's baldness was the chemical he gave them. However, the question in any causal type of reasoning is whether there might have been an *alternate* cause—for example, maybe the men were going to go bald as they got older anyway. To make sure there isn't some alternate cause, as you read in Chapter 17, in any scientific experiment there is supposed to be a control group of subjects who *don't* get exposed to whatever is being tested. The correct answer to this question is (4). You could argue that scientists should never experiment on people (although we wouldn't ever know if studies were never run on people), or that the number of subjects was too small (although 1,000 subjects is a pretty big sample), or that 40 years is too short a time (although 40 years is a pretty long time to run an experiment), or that the study should have included women. But the *main* flaw was the lack of a control group.

32. 1   Exposure to the air starts breaking down tissue, so if the dinosaur is perfectly preserved, somehow it was kept away from air. How could that happen? The correct answer is (1): The ice kept the air away from the dinosaur. Choices (2) and (5) ask us to believe that, in the Mesozoic period, fundamental principles of life did not hold true. Eliminate (2) and (5). Choice (3) is irrelevant. Choice (4) doesn't really make sense because the mud would have done the same job as the ice in the glacier.

33. 3   Laying eggs is the job of the female bird—so if we are looking for the female of this species, we should be looking for a bird that is *less* brightly colored, according to the passage—which is (3). Choices (1) and (4) would result in finding out a lot about the *male* of the species rather than the female. Choices (2) and (5) seem a bit irrelevant.

Reading Test Explanations

1. 5   This is an analysis question. First, look at the relationship between Marion and Dangerfield. Clearly, they feel very differently about their situation. Although Dangerfield may be curious , he may want to be an astronomer, and he may love ocular instruments, there is little evidence to support choices (1), (2), and (4). It is unlikely that Dangerfield is "concerned about his eyesight," which eliminates (3). When he says he is "testing my sight," he is most likely referring to the part of the telescope called a sight.

2. 4   In this comprehension question, you must first understand how upset Marion is at her situation. Then look at the answer choices and eliminate the ones that do not fit. She is not bored, glad about her child's accent, or happy in Ireland. Although she is "sensitive to negative stereotyping", she spends more time complaining and worrying about her finances.

3. **1**   Dangerfield is clearly tired of listening to Marion's complaints. This quotation is an attempt to cheer her up. There is no mention of finishing school, which eliminates (2). Dangerfield never suggests that he is pleased not to speak with an accent, as in (3) and (4). "Good eyesight," choice (5), is not the same as "good accents" in the quotation.

4. **4**   This question asks you to evaluate Marion's perspective in the excerpt. Use the Process of Elimination for a quick answer. The passage does not mention Marion's love of either Irish food or Ireland itself, choices (1) and (2). Dangerfield asks her twice about death and she dismisses him, so she does not reveal whether she thinks about death (3). She calls the telescope a "damn stupid thing," but there is no statement in the passage that she purchased it for him. Choice (4) is correct because Marion specifically mentions her daughter growing up with the Irish.

5. **3**   It is unclear from the passage why they came to Ireland; however, we do know that it was for a negative reason. Although any of the choices may be revealed to be true later in the play, we cannot know from the given passage.

6. **3**   This comprehension question is best answered using Process of Elimination. Choices (1) and (5) are easiest to dismiss as there is no support for either in the poem. Although the place may be a "strange land" to the reader, it is not unusual for the boy, as in choice (2). The boy may be on a wildlife preservation, but such a place probably would not involve him "carting dung" or fields of corn, choice (4). The wording of the poem does not specifically mention or describe a preservation. Choice (3) is the best option because the area is certainly rural in its descriptions of corn, frogs, and fields, and the area is in the Midwest, specifically Illinois.

7. **3**   To solve this synthesis question, look for clues in the first stanza. The boy has been carting dung all afternoon. He is "a sapped thing / Weary to crying." We can infer that he is unhappy because he is tired from working so hard.

8. **5**   This comprehension question asks you to look for clues in the second stanza about time. Line 8 talks of "smoky dusk" and "nightfall." Night has just begun, so the correct answer is "evening."

9. **4**   Use Process of Elimination to help you solve this one. There is no evidence in line 10 that "cornstalk violins" are "an imported violin", "a type of cornstalk", or "a dish made with corn," eliminating choices (2), (3), and (5). Choice (4) is the best answer because the boys made their own music out of the cornstalks.

10. **2**   This is a synthesis question. There is no outside commentary on the boys' situation, so cross off (4) and (5). There is no evidence that the boy was afraid of the dark, so cross off (3). Choice (2) is closest to the meaning of the last three lines, which speak of the boy's happiness with the night's music.

11. **4**   To answer this evaluation question, use Process of Elimination. The narrator is not pleased with the changes, so you can eliminate (1) and (2). Choice (5) is incorrect because she is not angry with those who remain. Ultimately, she is more saddened than nervous about the changes, so (4) is the best answer.

12. **4**   The passage mentions several times that the neighborhood called the Bottom was torn down in lines 1–5, 8–10, and 16–34. We can eliminate choices (1), (2), and (5), because we do not know the reason for its name, if it is multiracial, or if it is flooded. The church Greater Saint Matthew's is mentioned, but not in the past tense. Because it still has its church, cross off (3).

13. **2**   This analysis question asks you to examine the purpose for the author's specificity. By sharing the detailed names of familiar places, the narrator reveals her appreciation for the delightful places that compose the Bottom.

14. **3**   Use Process of Elimination to answer this synthesis question. We can eliminate (1), (4), and (5) because the narrator does not belittle her subject, is not anxious about the place, and does not experience confusion about the Bottom. Although parts of the Bottom may amuse the narrator, his or her central attitude is one of nostalgia, so we can eliminate (2).

15. **5** The last sentence of the passage helps to clarify the answer to this question: "Otherwise the pain would escape him even though the laughter was part of the pain." The townspeople have very complex emotions and most people, including the hypothetical valley man, would not bother to look deeply into the experiences of the townspeople to discover the complexity.

16. **2** The last nine lines show how the valley man would have to involve himself with the locals' intimate daily lives to appreciate their lives fully. This section does not mention a connection to God or economic policy, so we can eliminate (1) and (5). Although he experiences beautiful voices in song, choice (2) is a fuller explanation of the man's visit.

17. **3** This yin/yang sentence contrasts the outrage of the nation with the long lines to see the film. This line does not suggest that the movie did poorly, that the public had an opinion about the lines, that the movie was not in enough theaters, or that there were picket lines.

18. **4** To answer this synthesis question, use Process of Elimination. These movies are not historical but futuristic, which eliminates (1). These movies are not comedies, so get rid of (2). They do not lavish the audience with the talents of Portman and Neeson, so cross out (3). Finally, the author spends the entire third paragraph on the poorly written dialogue, which eliminates (5).

19. **2** Reread the first paragraph to answer this question. The author discusses how different, in a bad way, *The Phantom Menace* is from the previous three movies. It doesn't have the same effects, sense of fun, iconic images, and memorable vocabulary.

20. **2** To best answer this question, it helps to know what a tapestry is. A tapestry is a heavy fabric woven with elaborately detailed designs or scenes. When the reviewer compares the movie to a tapestry, she focuses on its visual richness. When the reviewer says that the movie works "as a kind of tapestry," it's clear that she is comparing the two, not commenting on the tapestries in the movie, so eliminate (1). Tapestries are not known for muted colors, and muted colors are rarely described as "rich," so cross out (3). A tapestry is not a combination of plot devices, so get rid of (4). Although this statement is likely true, the paragraph in which the author compares the movie to a tapestry focuses on the visual impact, not on the creation time, which eliminates (5).

21. **4** Because employees have to wait six months before participating in the 401(k), leaving before the six-month mark is the best reason for not joining. The text does not mention a salary requirement, fund choice, or the employee's tax-deferred status in this context.

22. **3** The company clearly encourages the plan in the excerpt. The third paragraph describes the company's level of commitment to the program in detail. The easiest way to answer this synthesis question is to cross out the answers that are obviously wrong. From the third paragraph, we know that the company is not indifferent or discouraging, so eliminate (1) and (2). We also know that the company offers the employees a variety of investment choices without stating a preference, so get rid of (4). The excerpt does not mention raising the matching-funds percentile at all, which eliminates (5).

Math Test Explanations

1. **5**   To find out how many total hours of music there are, multiply 4 by the number of hours each cassette can hold. However, first you have to convert $2\frac{3}{4}$. You can convert it to a fraction $\frac{11}{4}$ or a decimal (2.75), and then use your calculator to find the answer, 11. If you converted to a fraction, you might have noticed that you could do some easy canceling that might have saved you some time: $4 \times \frac{11}{4} = 11$ (canceling the 4s would have saved you doing any multiplication at all).

2. **4**   There are 8 students, so to find out the minimum average each must raise, you have to divide their goal amount ($1,700) by the number of students. Use your calculator—but be careful. The answer is $212.50.

3. **5**   Some of the students go to 25 houses, some go to 30 houses, but there is not enough information given to figure out how many students go to each. The correct answer is choice (5). Note that if you tried multiplying 30 times 8, you got answer choice (4), and if you tried multiplying 25 times 8, you got answer choice (3). The test writers included these partial answers as choices to see if you really understood the problem.

4. **5**   Whenever you see a problem with planes, trains, or automobiles, you know the formula is $R \times T = D$. 35 miles per hour is the rate, and the distance is 180 miles. How long will it take? Just divide 180 by 35. Your answer is a little more than 5 hours. Which answer choice is a little more than 5? The answer is choice (5).

5. **2**   In this setup problem, all you have to do is set up the equation—you don't have to figure out the exact answer. Once again, the formula you need is $R \times T = D$. The youth group's rate is 4.2, and their time is the total number of hours they walked, 16. The correct answer is choice (2).

6. **4**   To find out the percentage who are NOT clerical or professional, first find out who ARE clerical and professional: 24% + 19% = 43%. If you were in a hurry, you might pick choice (3), the partial answer—but you aren't done yet. Now, to find out who are NOT clerical and professional, subtract 43 percent from the whole (100 percent). The correct answer is 57 percent, choice (4).

7. **5**   There is simply no way to get an answer to this question from the information given.

8. **3**   This setup problem asks you to write an equation. They tell you that the summer temperature is 4 times the winter temperature. You could translate this word-for-word: The summer temperature (82) is (=) 4 times ($\times$) the winter temperature (t, the thing you don't know). The correct equation is $82 = 4t$, choice (3). If you didn't translate, you might also have written the equation as $\frac{82}{4} = t$, but that form of the equation wasn't one of the answer choices.

9. **40,000**

   If 20 percent of a shipment is crushed, then 80 percent is still intact. All you have to do is find 80 percent of 50,000. On your calculator, simply key in

   $0.80 \times 50,000 =$

   and you will have your answer, which is 40,000.

10. **3**   The $\sqrt{14}$ is a complicated number; is there a number close by that is less complicated? Sure, $\sqrt{16}$ is easy: It's 4. So the square root of 14 will be a bit less than 4. The correct answer is between 3 and 4, choice (3).

11. **2**   The test writers want you to use algebra to solve this problem, but there is a much easier way: backsolve. One of these answer choices has to be right. Let's try the middle one: Let's say Miriam bought 30 stamps. The problem tells us that Miriam bought 6 more than Betty, which means Betty must have bought 30 – 6, or 24. Together, 30 + 24 *should* add up to 42. Do they? Nope, it's too much. So the correct answer has to be smaller. Let's try choice (2): If Miriam bought 24 stamps, that means Betty bought 18. Together, does 24 + 18 add up to 42? It does, which means the answer is choice (2).

12. **5**   On the number line, zero is the point just to the left of R. Now, just count over to the right until you get to 4. The correct answer is choice (5).

13. **4**   One way to think of this problem is as a proportion. If the falls eroded 10 miles in 10,000 years, how many miles will have eroded in 32,000 years? The proportion would look like this:

$$\frac{10}{10,000} = \frac{x}{32,000}$$

If you're wondering why we've written 32,000 instead of 22,000, it's because the question asks how many total miles will have eroded when the falls disappear. The total time it will take to disappear is 10,000 (the amount of time that has gone by so far) + 22,000 (the amount of time from now until it totally disappears). Solving for x, we get 32 miles, choice (4). If you thought the total number of years was 22,000, choice (2) was there waiting for you—and you would have gotten the problem wrong.

14. **3**   The total number of degrees in a triangle is 180. So to figure out the third angle here, simply add up the two you know and subtract from 180. The correct answer is choice (3). By the way, if you didn't remember that, please *do* remember that the drawings on the GED are to scale unless they say they aren't. Just eyeballing that mystery angle, what would you say it was? Greater than 90 degrees? Of course not, so you can eliminate choice (4). Greater than 43 degrees—the angle on the left? Definitely. So we can eliminate choices (2) and (1).

15. **1**   Before we can compare the two telescopes, we have to do the multiplication. Model X is 3×10^3, or 3,000 and Model Y is 6×10^2, or 600. Before we do any math, which telescope is stronger? That's right, the X telescope—which means we can eliminate choices (2) and (4) right off the bat, because both choices say the Y telescope is stronger. Now, we can either write an equation or do a combination of translation and backsolving. Let's try translating and backsolving. We'll start with choice (3), which says the X model (3,000) is (=) 1.3 times (×) 600. Is that true? Does 3,000 = 1.3 × 600? Nope. The X model is bigger, so let's try choice (1), which says the X model (3,000) is (=) 5 times (×) 600. Is that true? Does 3,000 = 5 × 600? Well, as a matter of fact, it does. The correct answer is choice (1).

16. **3**   Before we do any math, let's just think about this for a minute. If Mark can do $\frac{2}{3}$ of a lawn in 1 hour, it will take him only a little bit more time to finish the entire lawn, certainly less than 2 hours. Which answer choices can we eliminate? Clearly, we can get rid of choices (4) and (5) because the entire lawn will take less than 2 hours to finish. We can also get rid of choice (1) because it has to take longer than $\frac{2}{3}$ of an hour. Even if you didn't know how to do this problem, you are already down to a 50–50 guess, which is not bad. Now, let's do the math! As you may remember from our section on proportions in Chapter 23, it helps to convert everything to the same unit of measurement, so let's think of the whole problem in minutes. Here's the equation:

$$\frac{1 \, \text{job}}{x \, \text{minutes}} = \frac{\frac{2}{3}}{60 \, \text{minutes}}$$

If you cross-multiply, you end up with $x = 90$ minutes, which converts to $1\frac{1}{2}$ hours, choice (3).

17. **1** The formula for the volume of a rectangle is on the first page of each GED Math test—so you don't have to worry about forgetting it. Volume equals length × width × height. In this setup problem that's all you needed. The correct answer is choice (1).

18. **19** For this grid-in problem, simply plug in 3 for x and 4 for a, and do the math. The correct answer is 19.

19. **4** Before you find the 5 percent delivery price, you must add up all the items to get the total. $850 + $1,155 + $355 = $2,360, which is answer choice (5)—but NOT the correct answer. It is a partial answer to trick anyone who was in too much of a hurry. To get the answer to the actual problem, we need to find 5 percent of $2,360. Remember the shortcut we taught you? To find 10 percent of $2,360, just take away one decimal place: $236. Five percent is *half* of that, or $118. The correct answer is choice (4).

20. **34** An isosceles triangle has two identical angles and two identical sides opposite those angles. In this case, the missing side is 9 meters. The perimeter of the entire triangle is 9 + 9 + 16, or 34.

21. **2,550**

   The trickiest part of this problem is reading it. We want to figure out the total cost of the computer system, so we add up the cost of all the components: $1,500 for the computer and LCD monitor + $650 for the laser printer + $250 for a hard drive—but we aren't done yet. The test writers want to know how much it would have been if the cost of the computer and monitor had gone up 10 percent. So we also have to figure out 10 percent of $1,500 (take away one decimal place to get $150) and add that to the total. The correct answer is $2,550.

22. **1** This is a hard algebra problem but an easy backsolving problem. Always start with the middle answer choice, choice (3). Let's say there are 26 women at Universal. If there were twice as many women as men, that means there would be 13 men. Altogether, there are *supposed* to be 78 employees, but our numbers add up to only 39. Could choice (3) be the right answer? Nope, too small. We need a bigger number. Let's move up to choice (2) and say there are 42 women, which means there would be 21 men. We're supposed to get 78 employees but 42 + 21 equals only 53 employees. Still too small. That must mean the correct answer is choice (1), but let's just check: Let's say there are 52 women at Universal, which means there would be 26 men. Altogether, that's supposed to add up to 78 people—and this time it *does*. The correct answer is choice (1).

23. **5** The Pythagorean theorem can be found on the first page of every GED Math test booklet, so don't worry about forgetting it. The theorem states that in a right triangle, $a^2 + b^2 = c^2$, where c is the hypotenuse (the long side) of the triangle (the one opposite the 90-degree angle). Plugging in the numbers from the triangle into the formula, the correct answer is choice (5).

24. **2** The probability of something happening can be found by putting the number of outcomes you are looking for over the total number of possible outcomes. The number of ducks that flew overhead was 35, and the total number of birds that flew by was 100. Thus, the probability was $\frac{35}{100}$, choice (2).

25. **2** Simply add like terms together: $2a + a = 3a$. $2b + b = 3b$. The correct answer is choice (2).

26. **140**

   To find an average add up everything and divide by the number of things: 135 + 135 + 150 = 420. To find the average, divide 420 by 3. The correct answer is 140.

27. **4** The equation for slope can be found on the first page of every GED Math test booklet, so remember to look for it if you don't remember it. Slope = $\dfrac{\textit{the change in } y-\textit{values}}{\textit{the change in } x-\textit{values}}$. Let's plug in what we know: $3 = \dfrac{11-(-10)}{x-(-2)}$ or $3 = \dfrac{21}{x+2}$. So x must equal 5, or choice (4).

28. **2** The answer choices should clue you in that this is a setup problem: There is no need to do any actual math. To find out how much the typist is earning per hour, divide $65.40 (his daily pay) by 4 (the number of hours he is currently working). This is the typist's hourly rate. Now, multiply that by 7 hours to find out what he would be paid if he worked 7 hours a day: $7 \times \dfrac{\$65.40}{4}$. The correct answer is choice (2).

Chapter 29
Practice Test 2

LANGUAGE ARTS, WRITING PART I

Tests of General Educational Development

Directions

The Language Arts, Writing Test is intended to measure your ability to use clear and effective English. It is a test of English as it should be written, not as it might be spoken. This test includes both multiple-choice questions and an essay. These directions apply only to the multiple-choice section; a separate set of directions is given for the essay.

The multiple-choice section consists of paragraphs with numbered sentences. Some of the sentences contain errors in sentence structure, usage, or mechanics (spelling, punctuation, and capitalization). After reading the numbered sentences, answer the multiple-choice questions that follow. Some questions refer to sentences that are correct as written. The best answer for these questions is the one that leaves the sentence as originally written. The best answer for some questions is the one that produces a sentence that is consistent with the verb tense and point of view used throughout the test.

You should spend no more than 40 minutes on the multiple-choice questions and 45 minutes on your essay. Work carefully, but do not spend too much time on any one question. You may begin working on the essay part of this test as soon as you complete the multiple-choice section.

Do not mark in this test booklet. Record your answers on the separate answer sheet provided. Be sure that all requested information is properly recorded on the answer sheet.

To record your answers, mark one numbered space on the answer sheet beside the number that corresponds to the question in the test booklet.

FOR EXAMPLE:

Sentence 1: **We were honored to meet governor Phillips.**

Which correction should be made to sentence 1?

(1) insert a comma after <u>honored</u>
(2) change the spelling of <u>honored</u> to <u>honered</u>
(3) change <u>governor</u> to <u>Governor</u>
(4) change <u>were</u> to <u>was</u>
(5) no correction is necessary

In this example, the word *governor* should be capitalized; therefore, answer space (3) would be marked on the answer sheet.

Do not rest the point of your pencil on the answer sheet while you are considering your answer. Make no stray or unnecessary marks. If you change an answer, erase your first mark completely. Mark only <u>one</u> answer space for each question; multiple answers will be scored as incorrect. Do not fold or crease your answer sheet. All test materials must be returned to the test administrator.

Writing, Part I

Directions: Choose the <u>one best answer</u> to each question.

<u>Questions 1 through 5</u> refer to the following handout for new pet owners.

From the Pets for Life Society: Helpful Hints for the New Dog Owner

(A)

(1) Adopting a dog usually means making some changes in your lifestyle. (2) Just walking a dog, for example, taking a lot of your time. (3) However, after the initial adjustments are made, the time required to care for a dog doesn't have to amount to much.

(B)

(4) The first thing to do when bringing a new puppy into the home is simple: Make the pet feel welcome. (5) In contrast to earlier beliefs, animal psychologists now agreeing that the first two weeks of contact between dog and owner are crucial. (6) They quickly learn to recognize their owner with their most keen sense—their sense of smell. (7) Studies also show that puppies like to sleep with objects that smell familiar they suggest putting an old shirt in the puppy's bed.

(C)

(8) As they get older, puppies need chew toys because, like humans, they will lose their baby teeth. (9) A rawhide bone or even an old shoe will be sufficient. (10) Your puppy will play with these toys incessantly. (11) Be sure that these toys are available; if they aren't, your puppy may chew up things you'd rather have intact.

(D)

(12) Of course, growing dogs have many needs that must be met to ensure their health and happiness. (13) Frequent walks and good nutrition and a yearly visit to the veterinarian will help keep your puppy in glowing health. (14) On the other hand, the happiness of your dog is dependent not upon what type of food he or she eats, but upon plenty of attention and affection from you.

GO ON TO THE NEXT PAGE

Writing, Part I

1. Sentence 2: **Just walking a dog, for example, taking a lot of your time.**

   Which correction should be made to sentence 2?

   (1) remove the comma after <u>dog</u>
   (2) change <u>taking</u> to <u>can take</u>
   (3) change <u>a lot</u> to <u>lots</u>
   (4) replace <u>your</u> with <u>you're</u>
   (5) no correction is necessary

2. Sentence 5: **In contrast to earlier beliefs, animal psychologists now agreeing that the first two weeks of contact between dog and owner are crucial.**

   Which correction should be made to sentence 5?

   (1) change <u>contrast</u> to <u>contrasting</u>
   (2) remove the comma after <u>beliefs</u>
   (3) change <u>agreeing</u> to <u>agree</u>
   (4) insert a comma after <u>dog</u>
   (5) no correction is necessary

3. Sentence 7: **Studies also show that puppies like to sleep with objects that smell <u>familiar they suggest</u> putting an old shirt in the puppy's bed.**

   Which of the following is the best way to write the underlined portion of the sentence? If you think the original is the best way, choose option (1).

   (1) familiar they suggest
   (2) familiar they are suggesting
   (3) familiar, they had suggested
   (4) familiar. They suggest
   (5) familiarized they suggest

4. Sentence 8: **As they get older, puppies need chew toys because, like humans, they will lose their baby teeth.**

   If you rewrote sentence 8 beginning with

   <u>Because, like humans, they will lose their baby teeth,</u>

   the next words should be

   (1) make puppies chew
   (2) as they are chewing
   (3) puppies need
   (4) older than puppies
   (5) chewing on toys

5. Sentence 13: **<u>Frequent walks and good nutrition and a yearly</u> visit to the veterinarian will help keep your puppy in glowing health.**

   Which of the following is the best way to write the underlined portion of the sentence? If you think the original is the best way, choose option (1).

   (1) Frequent walks and good nutrition and a yearly
   (2) Frequent walks and good nutrition, and a yearly
   (3) Frequent walks good nutrition, and a yearly
   (4) Frequent walks good nutrition and a yearly
   (5) Frequent walks, good nutrition, and a yearly

GO ON TO THE NEXT PAGE

Writing, Part I

Questions 6 through 11 refer to the following paragraphs.

(A)

(1) All the babies I have ever met appear to possess one of four personality types. (2) The first type are the colicky, or angry, babies, who are furious regardless of weather they have been fed or are comfortable. (3) These babies are marathon criers and manage not to exhaust them with incessant screaming. (4) They go about their shrieking tirelessly and ignored the pleas of their parents.

(B)

(5) The second personality type exhibited by babies is the happy baby. (6) In contrast to colicky babies, happy babies encountering the world with glee and rarely express displeasure. (7) The parents of such a baby are likely to consider themselves fortunate, because this type of child is so charming and pleasant to be around.

(C)

(8) The third and probably the easiest to care for of the baby types is the "sleeper." (9) Visitors to houses of sleepers seldom notice that there is a baby in the house at all. (10) Such babies spend the majority of the day in their cribs, oblivious to the world around them. (11) Parents of these babies are pleased with the peace and quiet, but sometimes wish for more opportunities to interact with their child.

(D)

(12) Last, there is of course the "properly adjusted" baby, who indulges in fairly equal amounts of crying, smiling, and sleeping.

6. Sentence 2: **The first type are the colicky, or angry, babies, who are furious regardless of weather they have been fed or are comfortable.**

   Which correction should be made to sentence 2?

   (1) change <u>are</u> to <u>can be</u>
   (2) change <u>are</u> to <u>were</u>
   (3) change <u>regardless</u> to <u>regarding</u>
   (4) replace <u>weather</u> with <u>whether</u>
   (5) insert a comma after <u>fed</u>

7. Sentence 3: **These babies are marathon criers and manage not to exhaust <u>them</u> with incessant screaming.**

   Which of the following is the best way to write the underlined portion of the sentence? If you think the original is the best way, choose option (1).

   (1) them
   (2) these
   (3) themselves
   (4) these babies
   (5) their crying

GO ON TO THE NEXT PAGE

Writing, Part I

8. Sentence 4: **They go about their shrieking tirelessly and ignored the pleas of their parents.**

    Which correction should be made to sentence 4?

    (1) change <u>ignored</u> to <u>ignore</u>
    (2) replace <u>pleas</u> with <u>pleases</u>
    (3) replace <u>pleas</u> with <u>please</u>
    (4) replace <u>their</u> with <u>there</u>
    (5) change <u>parents</u> to <u>parent's</u>

9. Sentence 6: **In contrast to colicky babies, happy babies <u>encountering the world</u> with glee and rarely express displeasure.**

    Which of the following is the best way to write the underlined portion of the sentence? If you think the original is the best way, choose option (1).

    (1) encountering the world
    (2) encounters the world
    (3) encountering worlds
    (4) encounter the world
    (5) encounters worlds

10. Sentence 8: **The third and probably the easiest to care for of the baby types is the "sleeper."**

    Which correction should be made to sentence 8?

    (1) insert a comma after <u>for</u>
    (2) change <u>baby</u> to <u>babies</u>
    (3) change <u>is</u> to <u>were</u>
    (4) change <u>is</u> to <u>are</u>
    (5) no correction is necessary

11. Sentence 9: **Visitors to houses of sleepers seldom notice that there is a baby in the house at all.**

    Which correction should be made to sentence 9?

    (1) change <u>houses</u> to <u>houses'</u>
    (2) insert a comma after <u>sleepers</u>
    (3) change <u>notice</u> to <u>notices</u>
    (4) replace <u>there</u> with <u>their</u>
    (5) no correction is necessary

GO ON TO THE NEXT PAGE

Writing, Part I

Questions 12 through 18 refer to the following paragraphs.

(A)

(1) Have you ever labored over writing a composition and asked yourself why it is that writing is so hard, when speaking is so easy? (2) Strangely enough, however, achieving fluency in writing starts with the ability to speak and listen careful.

(B)

(3) The most recent innovative techniques taught by instructors of composition focuses on stripping the writer of embellishment, or flowery language. (4) The overall goal to consider when writing any piece of work, be it poetry, prose, or technical writing, is that the work should convey an idea with clarity. (5) Contrary to the beliefs of some young writers, the most effective writing is simple and concise, just like good speech.

(C)

(6) Mark Twain took the idea of merging speech with writing to an extreme. (7) Twain used dialect to express not only the thoughts and ideas of his characters, but also to reveal class distinctions and other social realities of his day. (8) There are, of course, writers such as James Joyce who are admired while their rich, complicated language. (9) The writing of Joyce is so complex that often an accompanying explanation is needed to even begin to penetrate the intent of the words on the page.

(D)

(10) One major difference between Joyce's work and that of Twain lies in the difference in their subject matters. (11) While Twain's simple language conveys the complexities of his "simple" society Joyce's complex language exposes the complexities of simple human passions.

12. Sentence 2: **Strangely enough, however, achieving fluency in writing starts with the ability to speak and listen careful.**

    Which correction should be made to sentence 2?

    (1) change <u>strangely</u> to <u>strange</u>
    (2) replace <u>in</u> with <u>with</u>
    (3) change <u>starts</u> to <u>has started</u>
    (4) change <u>careful</u> to <u>carefully</u>
    (5) no correction is necessary

13. Sentence 3: **The most recent innovative techniques taught by instructors of composition focuses on stripping the writer of embellishment, or flowery language.**

    Which correction should be made to sentence 3?

    (1) insert a comma after <u>most</u>
    (2) replace <u>taught</u> with <u>taut</u>
    (3) change <u>focuses</u> to <u>focus</u>
    (4) replace <u>on</u> with <u>in</u>
    (5) insert a comma after <u>writer</u>

GO ON TO THE NEXT PAGE

Writing, Part I

14. Sentence 4: **The overall goal to consider when writing any piece of work, be it poetry, prose, or technical writing, is that the work should convey an idea with clarity.**

If you rewrote sentence 4 beginning with

The overall goal of any kind of writing should be

the next words should be

(1) to convey an idea with clarity
(2) should be considering when writing
(3) because of the clarity of ideas
(4) because considering an idea
(5) writing any piece of work

15. Sentence 5: **Contrary to the beliefs of some young writers, the most effective writing is simple and concise, just like good speech.**

Which correction should be made to sentence 5?

(1) remove the comma after <u>writers</u>
(2) replace <u>some</u> with <u>one</u>
(3) change <u>is</u> to <u>was</u>
(4) insert a comma after <u>simple</u>
(5) no correction is necessary

16. Sentence 7: **Twain used dialect <u>to express</u> not only the thoughts and ideas of his characters, but also to reveal class distinctions and other social realities of his day.**

Which of the following is the best way to rewrite the underlined portion of the sentence? If you think the original is the best way, choose option (1).

(1) to express
(2) expressing
(3) has expressed
(4) to be expressing
(5) was expressing

17. Sentence 8: **There are, of course, writers such as James Joyce who are admired while their rich, complicated language.**

Which correction should be made to sentence 8?

(1) change <u>writers</u> to <u>writer</u>
(2) insert a comma after <u>admired</u>
(3) replace <u>while</u> with <u>for</u>
(4) insert a comma after <u>complicated</u>
(5) change <u>admired</u> to <u>admire</u>

18. Sentence 11: **While Twain's simple language conveys the complexities <u>of his "simple" society</u> Joyce's complex language exposes the complexities of simple human passions.**

Which of the following is the best way to write the underlined portion of the sentence? If you think the original is the best way, choose option (1).

(1) of his "simple" society
(2) of his "simple" society,
(3) of their "simple" society
(4) society was "simple,"
(5) around "simple" societies

GO ON TO THE NEXT PAGE

Writing, Part I

Questions 19 through 26 refer to the following paragraphs.

(A)

(1) A revolution taking place in the world of music. (2) In the past, music was a source of pleasure and played a vital role in the community. (3) However, until this century, most individuals had little control over when they got to hear music, or what music they heard. (4) Music was available only to those who had the money to pay musicians to play for them.

(B)

(5) The introduction of the phonograph changed all that. (6) The invention of the sound recording made music available to anyone at any time, for a much lower price than hiring an orchestra. (7) Furthermore, the range of available types of music was greatly expanded.

(C)

(8) Since the phonograph, recorded music has gone through many forms, each with advantages and disadvantages. (9) When the electric record player was introduced, for example, people complained that they didn't want to loose the pleasure of turning the crank on their phonograph. (10) The next advance in home listening was the invention of the compact-disc player, which offered listeners improvements in quality efficiency, and durability. (11) The listener was spared the tedious fast-forwarding and rewinding that accompanied audio cassette use because of the advanced technology of the CD.

(D)

(12) Innovations in music technology proceed today; the invention of MP3 players indicates that the members of the music industry continues to work toward greater convenience and portability. (13) Today, a music lover can listen to music whenever they want. (14) But if they only listen to polka, mostly, then many people may find them odd.

19. Sentence 1: **A revolution taking place in the world of music.**

    Which correction should be made to sentence 1?

    (1) replace <u>taking place</u> with <u>shall take place</u>
    (2) replace <u>taking place</u> with <u>is taking place</u>
    (3) insert a comma after <u>revolution</u>
    (4) insert a comma after <u>world</u>
    (5) replace <u>of</u> with <u>for</u>

20. Sentence 2: **In the past, music was a source of pleasure and played a vital role in the community.**

    Which correction should be made to sentence 2?

    (1) change <u>past</u> to <u>Past</u>
    (2) remove the comma after <u>past</u>
    (3) change <u>was</u> to <u>were</u>
    (4) change <u>played</u> to <u>plays</u>
    (5) no correction is necessary

GO ON TO THE NEXT PAGE

21. Sentence 3: <u>However, until</u> this century, most individuals had little control over when they got to hear music, or what music they heard.

    Which of the following is the best way to write the underlined portion of the sentence? If you think the original is the best way, choose option (1).

    (1) However, until
    (2) However, after
    (3) If, since
    (4) If since
    (5) Indeed, since

22. Sentences 6 and 7: **The invention of the sound recording made music available to anyone at any time, for a much lower price than hiring an orchestra. Furthermore, the range of available types of music was greatly expanded.**

    The most effective combination of sentences 6 and 7 would include which of the following groups of words?

    (1) orchestra, and expanded the range
    (2) made music more expanded
    (3) an orchestra and the range
    (4) at any time more available
    (5) the range made expanses

23. Sentence 9: **When the electric record player was introduced, for example, people complained that they didn't want to loose the pleasure of turning the crank on their phonograph.**

    Which correction should be made to sentence 9?

    (1) remove the comma after <u>introduced</u>
    (2) replace <u>loose</u> with <u>lose</u>
    (3) insert a comma after <u>pleasure</u>
    (4) change <u>of turning</u> to <u>to turn</u>
    (5) no correction is necessary

24. Sentence 10: **The next advance in home listening was the invention of the compact-disc player, which offered listeners improvements in quality efficiency, and durability.**

    Which correction should be made to sentence 10?

    (1) insert a comma after <u>was</u>
    (2) change <u>was</u> to <u>were</u>
    (3) remove the comma after <u>player</u>
    (4) insert a comma after <u>quality</u>
    (5) replace <u>and</u> with <u>or</u>

25. Sentence 11: **The listener was spared the tedlous fast-forwarding and rewinding that accompanied audio cassette use because of the advanced technology of the CD.**

    If you rewrote this sentence beginning with

    <u>Due to the advanced technology of the CD,</u>

    the next words should be

    (1) that are spared
    (2) forwarding and rewinding
    (3) the CD accompanies
    (4) cassette listeners
    (5) the listener

26. Sentence 12: **Innovations in music technology proceed today; the invention of MP3 players indicates that the members of the music industry continues to work toward greater convenience and portability.**

    Which correction should be made to sentence 12?

    (1) change <u>proceed</u> to <u>proceeds</u>
    (2) remove the semicolon after <u>today</u>
    (3) change <u>invention</u> to <u>Invention</u>
    (4) change <u>continues</u> to <u>continue</u>
    (5) change <u>work</u> to <u>works</u>

GO ON TO THE NEXT PAGE

Writing, Part I

Questions 27 and 28 refer to the following business letter.

January 7, 2011

Personnel Director
AVI Products
344 Kennedy Drive
Detroit, MI 48201

Dear Sir or Madam:

(A)

(1) I am writing to apply for the position of Product Manager that was advertised in *The Detroit News* this past Sunday.

(B)

(2) AVI Products has long been my idea of a dream company. (3) Your diverse line of products has done extremely well in the marketplace, and my friends who work for you speak very highly of the level of professionalism and high morale at your offices.

(C)

(4) My hobbies include surfing and calligraphy. (5) I am currently studying at night for an engineering degree. (6) I have two years of college under my belt, and I passed my GED three years ago.

(D)

(7) I have three years of experience as a product manager. (8) I am currently managing the "Biz Kidz" winter line of accessories at RVS, a medium-sized firm here in Detroit. (9) Before that, I worked as a junior product manager at Kendall Industries for four years.

(E)

(10) Please take a look at my resume. My references (including several executives from your own company) are standing by for a call. (11) You can reach me at (275) 555-2323.

Sincerely,

James Butler

GO ON TO THE NEXT PAGE

27. Which of the following revisions would most improve this letter?

    (1) move paragraph B to the beginning of the letter

    (2) move paragraph A to the end of the letter

    (3) place paragraph C before paragraph B

    (4) place paragraph D before paragraph C

    (5) remove paragraph D from the letter entirely

28. Which of the revisions below would most improve the organization of paragraph C?

    (1) move sentence 4 to the end of the paragraph

    (2) move sentence 6 before sentence 5

    (3) begin paragraph C with a new sentence beginning, "I am a mellow kind of guy..."

    (4) begin paragraph C with the new sentence, "Education has never been very important to me"

    (5) move sentence 10 to the beginning of paragraph C

GO ON TO THE NEXT PAGE

LANGUAGE ARTS, WRITING PART II

Tests of General Educational Development

Essay Directions and Topic

This part of the Language Arts, Writing Test is intended to determine how well you write. You are asked to write an essay that explains something or presents an opinion on an issue. In preparing your essay, you should take the following steps:

1. Read the directions and the essay topic given below carefully.

2. Plan your essay thoughtfully before you write, using personal experience, observations, and knowledge.

3. Use scratch paper to make any notes.

4. Write your essay on the lined pages of the separate answer sheet.

5. Review what you have written and make any changes that will improve your essay.

6. Check your paragraphs, sentence structure, spelling, punctuation, capitalization, and usage, and make any necessary corrections.

Be sure you write the <u>letter</u> of the essay topic (given below) on your answer sheet. Write the letter in the box at the upper right-hand corner of the page where you write your essay.

You will have 45 minutes to write on the topic below. Write legibly and use a ballpoint pen so that the evaluators will be able to read your writing.

Write your essay on the lined pages of the separate answer sheet. The notes you make on scratch paper will not be scored.

Your essay will be scored by at least two trained evaluators who will judge it according to its <u>overall effectiveness</u>. They will judge how clearly you make the main point of your composition, how thoroughly you support your ideas, and how clearly and correctly you write throughout the essay.

TOPIC F

"The best way to better humanity is to better yourself."

Do you agree or disagree with this statement? Write an essay of about 250 words presenting your view and supporting it with specific examples from your own experience or your observations of others.

END OF TEST

SOCIAL STUDIES

Tests of General Educational Development

Directions

The Social Studies Test consists of multiple-choice questions intended to measure general social studies concepts. The questions are based on short readings that often include a map, graph, chart, cartoon, or figure. Study the information given and then answer the question(s) following it. Refer to the information as often as necessary in answering the questions.

You should spend no more than 45 minutes answering the questions in this booklet. Work carefully, but do not spend too much time on any one question. Be sure you answer every question. You will not be penalized for incorrect answers.

Do not mark in this test booklet. Record your answers to the questions on the separate answer sheet provided. Be sure all requested information is properly recorded on the answer sheet.

To record your answers, mark the numbered space on the answer sheet beside the number that corresponds to the question in the test booklet.

FOR EXAMPLE:

Early colonists of North America looked for settlement sites with adequate water supplies and access by ship. For this reason, many early towns were built near

- (1) mountains
- (2) prairies
- (3) rivers
- (4) glaciers
- (5) plateaus

The correct answer is "rivers"; therefore, answer space (3) would be marked on the answer sheet.

Do not rest the point of your pencil on the answer sheet while you are considering your answer. Make no stray or unnecessary marks. If you change an answer, erase your first mark completely. Mark only <u>one</u> answer space for each question; multiple answers will be scored as incorrect. Do not fold or crease your answer sheet. Return all test materials to the test administrator.

Social Studies

Directions: Choose the one best answer to each question.

Questions 1 and 2 refer to the following interpretation of the U.S. Constitution.

The first ten amendments to the U.S. Constitution are called the Bill of Rights. They were originally added to grant both individual citizens and states certain rights that could not be violated by the federal government. The 14th Amendment, which was adopted in 1868 as part of the settlement of the Civil War, widened the applications of the Bill of Rights. One sentence of this amendment states: "No state shall make or enforce any law which shall abridge the privileges or immunities of citizens of the United States; nor shall any state deprive any person of life, liberty or property, without due process of law, nor deny to any person...equal protection under the law."

This amendment has since been interpreted as protecting the individual citizen's rights from encroachment by the states.

1. Which of the following descriptions of the authors of the amendments to the Constitution is supported by the passage?

   (1) They were legal scholars.
   (2) They believed that the government and the church should be united.
   (3) They believed that the best type of government would have ultimate authority.
   (4) They were wary of giving the government too much power over individual rights.
   (5) They believed that the federal government should control state governments.

2. All of the following actions by a particular state would violate the 14th Amendment EXCEPT

   (1) a zoning law prohibiting naturalized citizens from operating ethnic restaurants
   (2) legislation requiring citizens to pay taxes regardless of their beliefs
   (3) a bill requiring children of citizens of a particular ethnic origin to attend separate public schools
   (4) sentencing a person accused of murder without a trial
   (5) government takeover of a newspaper that expresses controversial views

GO ON TO THE NEXT PAGE

Social Studies

Question 3 refers to the following statement about Amelia Earhart.

When Amelia Earhart made her first successful trip across the Atlantic with her colleague, Captain Manning, she was greeted on arrival by the mayor of Southampton in England. Despite most of the favorable reactions of the press to her accomplishment, one of the London papers stated that she was "a pleasant young woman who should be capable of spending her time to better advantage in domestic pursuits." Many members of the American press characterized her as a "foolhardy girl" and as a publicity seeker. Perhaps as a result, Earhart resolved to tackle her next mission alone.

3. In the author's opinion, what factor contributed to Amelia Earhart's decision to fly alone?

   (1) the belief that women are generally superior
   (2) a love of her country
   (3) the public's ignorance of aviation
   (4) the patriotism of the British
   (5) a lack of respect by some members of the press for women's abilities

Question 4 refers to the advertisement below.

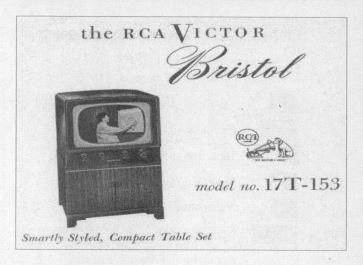

Advertisement for a black and white RCA television, ca. 1954
Source: Photofest Archives

4. In the 1954 advertisement for a television above, all of the following might have been part of the accompanying advertising copy EXCEPT

   (1) enhanced reception capabilities
   (2) modern styling
   (3) bright color picture
   (4) ability to block interference from other channels
   (5) durable, dependable performance

GO ON TO THE NEXT PAGE

Social Studies

Question 5 refers to the following chart.

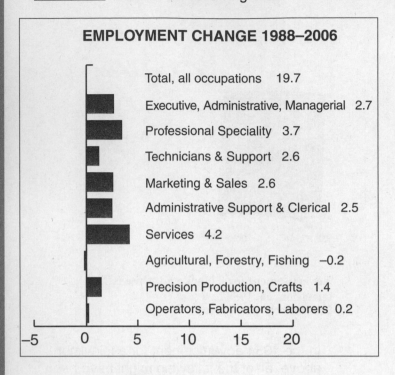

EMPLOYMENT CHANGE 1988–2006

Total, all occupations   19.7

Executive, Administrative, Managerial   2.7

Professional Speciality   3.7

Technicians & Support   2.6

Marketing & Sales   2.6

Administrative Support & Clerical   2.5

Services   4.2

Agricultural, Forestry, Fishing   –0.2

Precision Production, Crafts   1.4

Operators, Fabricators, Laborers   0.2

5. The information in the chart supports the conclusion that from 1988 to 2006 there has been

   (1) an increase in agricultural jobs
   (2) more growth in administrative support jobs than in any other occupation
   (3) more growth in administrative support jobs than in services and technicians and support jobs combined
   (4) less growth in precision production than in professional specialties
   (5) more growth in marketing and sales jobs than in executive, administration, and managerial jobs

6. The highest literacy rates are found in industrialized nations.

   Based on the above statement, which of the following is the best conclusion?

   (1) Industrialization discourages people from reading.
   (2) The economic and educational well-being of a nation are related.
   (3) Agrarian societies do not provide schooling.
   (4) People in industrialized nations have more money for books.
   (5) Economic developments have no effect on the educational well-being of a society.

7. While Jimmy Carter was president, White House domestic policy seemed powerless to control one of the worst periods of inflation in U.S. history. This shows that Jimmy Carter was a bad president.

   Which of the following statements is a possible criticism of the passage's conclusion about Carter?

   (1) A certain level of inflation is good for the economy.
   (2) Ronald Reagan defeated Carter in a landslide victory in 1980.
   (3) President Carter was much more popular than his predecessor, Gerald Ford, who was a mediocre president.
   (4) Carter's foreign policy accomplishments are ignored. His successful peace negotiations in the Middle East were of historic importance.
   (5) President Carter was also considered by some to be weak on foreign policy.

GO ON TO THE NEXT PAGE

Social Studies

Questions 8 and 9 refer to the following graph.

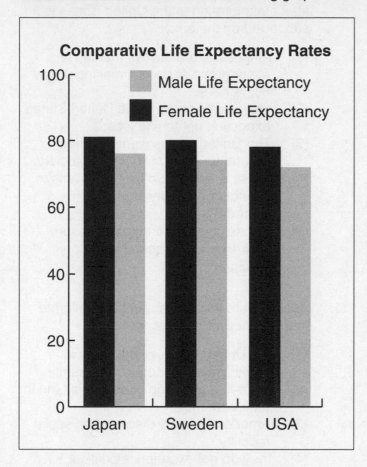

Comparative Life Expectancy Rates

Legend:
- Male Life Expectancy
- Female Life Expectancy

8. According to the above graph, a member of which of the following groups is likely to have the shortest life span?

    (1) Japanese women
    (2) Swedish women
    (3) American men
    (4) Japanese men
    (5) American women

9. Which statement is the most likely explanation for the differences in life expectancy shown in the graph?

    (1) Asian men tend to work more hours per week than do men from other countries.
    (2) Life expectancy is higher in North American countries.
    (3) Japan provides free or low-cost health care for all Japanese citizens.
    (4) There are fewer natural disasters in Japan than there are in other parts of the world.
    (5) Birth rates have been increasing in the United States and Sweden.

GO ON TO THE NEXT PAGE

Social Studies

Questions 10 through 12 refer to the following interpretation of the role of immigrants in American society.

The society of the United States, perhaps more than that of any other country, is a "melting pot" society. America is a nation of immigrants and is reputed to be a haven for the oppressed and a land of equal opportunity for all. Symbols such as the Statue of Liberty and rags-to-riches success literature reinforce this reputation. Immigrants to the United States come in search of new opportunities, increased social mobility, and an environment free from political unrest and oppression.

On the other hand, America is not free from bigotry. In the past, each new immigrant group has been greeted with prejudice and discrimination by the groups that settled before them.

There have been many steps taken in recent history to make American society as free and equal as our founders had intended. There has been much legislation passed over the last three decades to help to ensure the equal treatment of all individuals and groups. With this legislation and improved public awareness, perhaps American society can live up to its "melting pot" image.

10. Which of the following observations about immigration to the United States is supported by the article?

   (1) Americans are always friendly to every group of people making a new home here.
   (2) Immigrants come to the United States expecting not to find jobs.
   (3) The United States wants to shed its reputation as a "melting pot" society.
   (4) There is no reason for immigrants to expect opportunity in the United States.
   (5) Efforts have been made to ensure that America is receptive to immigrants.

11. According to the article, people immigrate to the United States because

   (1) the United States offers political stability and economic opportunity
   (2) there is a shortage of available land in their countries
   (3) American society discourages social mobility
   (4) they do not experience political unrest and oppression in their home countries
   (5) they are guaranteed employment

12. Which of the following statements is NOT directly supported by the article?

   (1) Bigotry can still be found in America.
   (2) There are steps being taken to decrease the amount of bigotry in the United States.
   (3) People have immigrated to the United States because they were unhappy with life in other countries.
   (4) People have immigrated to the United States because of the possibility of new opportunities and social mobility.
   (5) Immigrants make more money after coming to America.

GO ON TO THE NEXT PAGE

Social Studies

Question 13 refers to the following photo.

13. This 1852 advertisement expresses opposition to "foreign pauper labor" and "foreigners holding office." With which of the following policies would the writer of this advertisement be likely to disagree?

(1) a trade embargo to keep cheap foreign goods out of the United States
(2) a new law that prevents immigration unless the immigrant is rich
(3) a voter registration drive that targets only American-born persons
(4) a constitutional amendment giving new immigrants voting rights
(5) a quota that limits entry into the United States by foreigners

14. A strict free-market economy allows business to control and regulate its affairs without interference from the government.

According to this definition, which of the following would most likely be found in a country with a strict free-market economy?

(1) emissions standards for automobiles
(2) a national health-care system
(3) deposits on bottles to promote recycling
(4) antitrust laws
(5) prices based solely on supply and demand

GO ON TO THE NEXT PAGE

15. Government antitrust action is designed to prevent large corporations from creating monopolies. Which of the following is an example of an antitrust action?

    (1) forcing a large corporation to merge with another large corporation to prevent both from going bankrupt
    (2) forcing a large corporation to break up into several smaller autonomous companies
    (3) granting a large corporation tax credits and loan guarantees to help the corporation through a tough time
    (4) exempting a corporation from pollution controls
    (5) taxing a corporation on its overseas profits

Question 16 refers to the following graph.

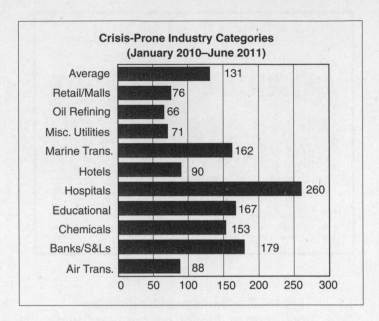

Crisis-Prone Industry Categories
(January 2010–June 2011)

Category	Value
Average	131
Retail/Malls	76
Oil Refining	66
Misc. Utilities	71
Marine Trans.	162
Hotels	90
Hospitals	260
Educational	167
Chemicals	153
Banks/S&Ls	179
Air Trans.	88

16. According to the graph, which of the following types of industries was least likely to experience a crisis?

    (1) education
    (2) chemical
    (3) banking
    (4) hotel
    (5) oil refining

GO ON TO THE NEXT PAGE

Social Studies

Questions 17 through 19 refer to the following points of view about education.

Speaker A: "Our school system cannot be rescued without funding from the federal government. The federal government spends enough on defense, but it focuses too little on important domestic issues."

Speaker B: "The public schools in the United States are doomed. There are just too many issues involved! I am going to send my children to private school."

Speaker C: "We need to make better use of the money we already have. We can invest more federal funds in education, but we need to examine how that money is actually spent. So much of the spending is wasteful."

Speaker D: "Our schools depend on us. We cannot abandon them by sending our kids to private schools. That response is the cause of the poor state of public schools today."

Speaker E: "We need to bring back many of those parents who send their kids to private schools. We can do this by encouraging community involvement—by asking for parental input and help with teacher recruiting."

17. Which speaker would most likely go to a local community meeting and support an audit of local education spending?

   (1)   Speaker A
   (2)   Speaker B
   (3)   Speaker C
   (4)   Speaker D
   (5)   Speaker E

18. Speaker B's point of view is different from the other speakers' arguments in that Speaker B

   (1)   opposes federal aid of any kind, but the others discuss the amount of aid needed
   (2)   thinks that community action is irrelevant, but the others argue that community involvement is necessary for the improvement of schools
   (3)   believes that public school is important for the nation's well-being and must be saved, but the others believe that efforts at saving it are in vain
   (4)   favors giving up on public schools, while the others want to act to save public schools, although suggesting different methods
   (5)   suggests that public schools should not be replaced by alternate methods of schooling, while the others believe that efforts should be made to develop alternatives

19. What is the main issue that divides Speakers A and C?

   (1)   how federal aid is actually spent
   (2)   the amount of state funding
   (3)   the role of the community in taxation
   (4)   the issue of religious schooling
   (5)   the distribution of state funds earmarked for welfare programs

GO ON TO THE NEXT PAGE

Social Studies

20. With improvements in technology, production becomes more efficient, increasing the output per worker of a given industry. Product quality rises, profits and wages increase, and the economy improves overall. In short, both workers and employers benefit.

Which of the following opinions contradicts the above conclusion about improvements in technology?

(1) New technology will cause companies to decrease the size of their workforce in order to cut costs.

(2) Product quality increases consumer satisfaction, which leads to greater company profits.

(3) When businesses succeed, more money is reinvested into the economy.

(4) Efficiency is a key factor in ensuring a business's success.

(5) Increasing the output per worker is possible without creating hazardous work conditions.

21. Which of the following statements about World War II would be the most difficult to prove?

(1) There were more civilian casualties in this war than in any other war.

(2) It is the only war in which nuclear weapons have been deployed.

(3) The war weakened communism in Russia and China.

(4) The war resulted in sweeping changes in territorial possession.

(5) More buildings were destroyed in this war than in any other.

GO ON TO THE NEXT PAGE

Social Studies

Questions 22 through 24 refer to the following explanations about the beliefs of different religions.

Different religions have different beliefs about what occurs to a believer after death. These beliefs profoundly affect not only how people view death, but how they try to live their lives.

According to Judeo-Christian faiths, the quality of one's behavior in life determines what happens after death. Kindness, honesty, and a sense of responsibility for one's fellow man are all extolled as important virtues. A virtuous life is rewarded with entrance into heaven. Lives led without virtue are punished; a person might be sent to await final judgment, banished to hell, or in some cases, forgiven, if repentance is genuine.

Buddhists and Hindus, like Jews and Christians, believe that conduct in life determines the quality of what comes afterward. These Eastern religions, however, teach that the soul is reincarnated through various levels of existence until an elevated state is attained. These levels represent different species, castes, or even the amount of good or bad fortune one experiences in day-to-day existence. A virtuous life is rewarded by an elevation to the next level of existence, and those who have been less than virtuous will live their next life on a lower level. For these religions, the effect of one's conduct is cumulative.

22. Which of the following is supported by Judeo-Christian values?

    (1)   a belief in reincarnation
    (2)   commitment to help those in need
    (3)   disapproval of other religions
    (4)   an understanding of the value of hard work
    (5)   a commitment to democracy

23. According to the passage, one of the similarities shared by Judeo-Christian faiths and Buddhist and Hindu faiths is a belief

    (1)   that what occurs after death is determined, in part, by one's conduct during life
    (2)   in the reincarnation of the spirit, which moves through different levels until an elevated state is attained
    (3)   in an afterlife in which people are sent to heaven if they have performed virtuous actions during life
    (4)   that the effect of your actions during life is cumulative
    (5)   that almost anything can be forgiven, so long as repentance is genuine

24. Which conclusion about the religions discussed is supported by the information presented?

    (1)   Beliefs about life after death can affect the conduct of those who hold them.
    (2)   Different religious beliefs make cohabitation impossible.
    (3)   All religions share the same fundamental beliefs.
    (4)   All the religions described in the article share a common belief in the concept of heaven.
    (5)   Most people do not consider religion when making decisions in life.

GO ON TO THE NEXT PAGE

Social Studies

Question 25 refers to the following passage.

Interpreting the U.S. Constitution is so complex a task that it has become its own legal specialty, constitutional law. One example of the complexity of the Constitution is an interpretation of the 13th Amendment, which states that there shall be no "involuntary servitude" except as a punishment for a crime. Due to this interpretation, Congress was reluctant for a long time to pass any draft resolutions in times of peace. Finally, in 1940, only one year before our entrance into World War II, Congress approved the first peacetime draft in our history.

25. What conclusion is supported by this statement about the interpretation of the Constitution?

   (1) A document that needs amendments is not a reliable guide for government policy.
   (2) A document that can be reinterpreted is not an adequate method for resolving legal questions.
   (3) A text that causes controversy does more harm than good.
   (4) Interpretations of the Constitution can change, which in turn affect decisions made by lawmakers.
   (5) If a democracy is committed to the rights of its people, the Constitution cannot reflect this goal.

Question 26 refers to the following graph.

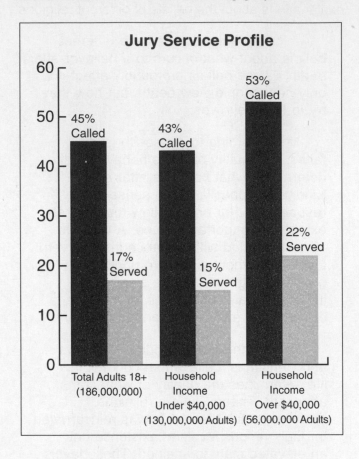

Jury Service Profile

26. Which of the following statements is supported by the survey on jury service represented in the table?

   (1) People with incomes under $40,000 are twice as likely to be called as are those with higher incomes.
   (2) A greater percentage of adults from households with incomes of more than $40,000 have served on juries than have those from households with lower incomes.
   (3) People with lower incomes are more likely to want to serve on juries.
   (4) Most jurors have incomes between $30,000 and $35,000.
   (5) No one in the survey had actively attempted to avoid jury service.

GO ON TO THE NEXT PAGE

Social Studies

Questions 27 through 30 refer to the following information about energy production.

Three of the most common sources of energy are fossil fuels, nuclear power, and hydroelectric power. Each of these three methods of energy production has its advantages and disadvantages.

Fossil fuels are the most widely used energy source in the United States. The burning of oil and coal derivatives releases energy that is used to boil water. The released steam turns turbines and produces energy. Today, fossil fuels are relatively abundant, which makes this form of energy production inexpensive. However, one of the problems with fossil fuels is that burning oil and coal derivatives releases chemicals that are harmful to the environment.

Nuclear power harnesses the energy contained in atoms. The energy released is used to convert water to steam, which in turn drives turbines. This form of energy production has proven to be even less expensive than fossil fuels, but there is no foolproof method for storing all of the dangerous by-products from nuclear power plants.

Hydroelectric power is produced by using the force of a river to turn turbines. This is the cleanest of the three methods of energy production, but not all communities have access to rivers, and rivers with hydroelectric plants are much more vulnerable to the effects of erosion.

27. Which of the following would most likely result in an increase in the use of nuclear power?

   (1) the invention of a safe radioactive-waste disposal method
   (2) the discovery of a cleaner method of burning coal
   (3) a decrease in taxes on fossil fuels
   (4) increased oil exploration in Alaska
   (5) the institution of erosion-control regulations for hydroelectric plants

28. What do all three forms of energy production have in common?

   (1) waste
   (2) smoke
   (3) smog
   (4) erosion
   (5) turbines

29. Which of the following communities would most likely use hydroelectric power?

   (1) a desert community with little or no fossil fuel resources
   (2) a town adjacent to a large river
   (3) a community with large oil reserves
   (4) a community in coal-rich West Virginia
   (5) a community with elevated oil prices

30. Which of the following inventions did the most to popularize the use of fossil fuel?

   (1) Thomas Edison's phonograph
   (2) Robert Fulton's steam engine
   (3) Alexander Graham Bell's telephone
   (4) Johannes Gutenberg's printing press
   (5) Samuel Clegg's gas meter

GO ON TO THE NEXT PAGE

Social Studies

Question 31 refers to the following excerpt from U.S. history.

Development in California during the gold rush of 1849 was characterized by exploitation of the wilderness for economic gains. Entire forests were razed for lumber, and beautiful valleys were dammed up and lost forever to provide water pressure for strip mining. Such atrocities continued unhindered until one man stepped forward to argue on the behalf of the wilderness. John Muir almost single-handedly convinced President Roosevelt to create one of the nation's first national parks in Yosemite Valley, thereby protecting that portion of land from the dangers of development.

31. Which of the following might describe John Muir's opinions regarding the California wilderness?

   (1) Economic interests should outweigh sentimental interests.
   (2) It is acceptable to destroy natural beauty in some cases.
   (3) Things that humans value should be used for human benefit.
   (4) Some things have value that cannot be measured in monetary terms.
   (5) The government should not pass legislation about the wilderness.

Question 32 refers to the following globe.

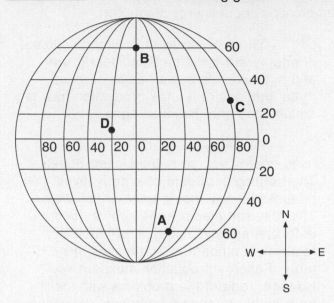

32. Which of the following lists the points on the globe from west to east?

   (1) D, A, C, B
   (2) C, B, D, A
   (3) A, C, B, D
   (4) D, B, A, C
   (5) D, A, B, C

END OF TEST

SCIENCE

Tests of General Educational Development

Directions

The Science Test consists of multiple-choice questions intended to measure general concepts in science. The questions are based on short readings that often include a graph, chart, or figure. Study the information given, and then answer the question(s) following it. Refer to the information as often as necessary in answering the questions.

You should spend no more than 53 minutes answering the questions in this booklet. Work carefully, but do not spend too much time on any one question. Be sure that you answer every question. You will not be penalized for incorrect answers.

Do not mark in this test booklet. Record your answers to the questions on the separate sheet provided. Be sure all requested information is properly recorded on the answer sheet.

To record your answers, mark the numbered space on the answer sheet beside the number that corresponds to the question in the test booklet.

FOR EXAMPLE:

Which of the following is the smallest unit in a living thing?

(1) tissue
(2) organ
(3) cell
(4) muscle
(5) capillary

The correct answer is "cell"; therefore, answer space (3) would be marked on the answer sheet.

Do not rest the point of your pencil on the answer sheet while you are considering your answer. Make no stray or unnecessary marks. If you change an answer, erase your first mark completely. Mark only <u>one</u> answer space for each question; multiple answers will be scored as incorrect. Do not fold or crease your answer sheet. Return all test materials to the test administrator.

Science

Directions: Choose the <u>one best answer</u> to each question.

Questions 1 and 2 refer to the following graph.

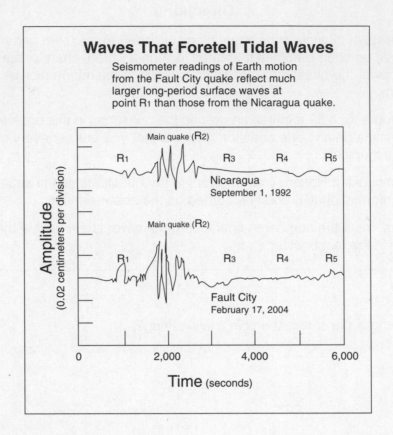

Waves That Foretell Tidal Waves

Seismometer readings of Earth motion from the Fault City quake reflect much larger long-period surface waves at point R1 than those from the Nicaragua quake.

1. According to the graph above, which of the following statements is true?

   (1) The Nicaragua main quake had a larger amplitude than the Fault City quake.
   (2) There were no surface waves recorded in either location before the main quake struck.
   (3) The Fault City main quake had a larger amplitude than the Nicaragua quake.
   (4) A seismometer was used to measure the Nicaragua quake but not the Fault City quake.
   (5) The long-period surface waves at point R1 were larger during the Nicaragua quake.

2. In order to foretell an earthquake, which of the following points on the graph would be of the most importance?

   (1) R_1
   (2) R_2
   (3) R_3
   (4) R_4
   (5) R_5

GO ON TO THE NEXT PAGE

Science

Questions 3 and 4 refer to the following diagrams.

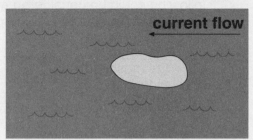

Judd Island in the Blue River in 1975

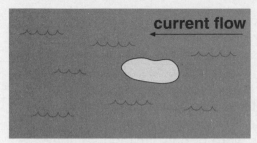

Judd Island in the Blue River in 2010

3. The diagram above shows an island located in the middle of the Blue River in 1975 and in 2010.

    What best accounts for the diminished size of the island in 2010?

    (1) water level in the river has fallen since 1975
    (2) tidal movements
    (3) continental drift
    (4) erosion action by the river
    (5) glacial activity

4. If a dam were constructed downstream from Judd Island, what effect might it have on the island?

    (1) The island could appear smaller as the water level of the river backed up behind the dam.
    (2) The island could become larger because there would be less erosion of its banks.
    (3) The island would stay the same size because the effect of dams on rivers is always very slight.
    (4) The island would attract more endangered species of birds because these birds are attracted to construction activity.
    (5) The island could become a source of solar power.

GO ON TO THE NEXT PAGE

Science

Questions 5 through 7 refer to the following article.

For years, scientists have debated whether the archaeopteryx, a creature that lived 150 million years ago, was an early species of bird or a dinosaur. Paleontologists argue that the archaeopteryx was a dinosaur that spent most of its time on the ground. Its feathers and wings were of only limited use, they say, and could not sustain flight.

Ornithologists, on the other hand, believe that the archaeopteryx was first and foremost a bird. As evidence, they point to fossil remains of the creature that show its claws were curved so that it could perch on tree limbs. Curved claws would have prevented the animal from walking or running quickly on the ground.

5. According to paleontologists, the archaeopteryx was incapable of

(1) perching
(2) running
(3) walking
(4) flying
(5) swimming

6. According to ornithologists, which of the following could be considered a modern-day descendant of the archaeopteryx?

(1) the lizard
(2) the mosquito
(3) the turtle
(4) the alligator
(5) the parrot

7. Scientists' theories about the archaeopteryx are based on

(1) studies of the creature in its native habitat
(2) examinations of fossilized remains
(3) laboratory experiments on a young archaeopteryx raised in captivity
(4) studies of the modern descendants of the archaeopteryx
(5) old written records

GO ON TO THE NEXT PAGE

Science

Questions 8 through 10 are based on the following information.

Matter can be classified according to the three states in which it can exist.

(1) Solids—have both shape and volume. Their molecules are held together tightly. A solid is elastic, and after it is struck, will slowly regain its former shape, unless the force was too great.

(2) Liquids—have volume but no shape. Their molecules are held together less tightly so that a liquid will flow into a container.

(3) Gases—have neither a set volume nor a shape. Their molecules are free to move about, and a gas will fill any container that encloses it.

Each of the following items describes a state of matter that refers to one of the three categories defined above. For each item, choose the one category that best describes the relationship. Each of the three categories above may be used more than once in the following set of items.

8. When matter X is placed inside a container and is subjected to double its normal pressure, its volume is halved. Matter X is most likely

    A. a solid
    B. a liquid
    C. a gas

    (1) A only
    (2) B only
    (3) C only
    (4) A and B only
    (5) A, B, and C

9. Below 32 degrees Fahrenheit (F), H_2O exists in one kind of state. From 32 degrees F to 212 degrees F, it changes into another state. Above 212 degrees F, it changes again into a third state. Which of the following lists the correct order for the different states of H_2O as it is subjected to increasing heat?

    (1) liquid, gas, solid
    (2) gas, liquid, solid
    (3) solid, liquid, gas
    (4) solid, gas, liquid
    (5) liquid, solid, gas

10. If element Y is struck while being observed under a microscope, it can be seen to compress but then spring back to resume its former shape.

     The state of the matter being described is best classified as

     A. a solid
     B. a liquid
     C. a gas

     (1) A only
     (2) B only
     (3) C only
     (4) A and B only
     (5) A, B, and C

GO ON TO THE NEXT PAGE

Science

Questions 11 through 13 refer to the following article.

A family lives in a house across the valley from a church. They notice an interesting phenomenon. During the summer months, they can hear the church bell when it is rung on Sundays. However, during the winter months, they cannot hear the church bell on Sundays.

The following comments were made in the order they appear below by various members of the family.

A. "I guess they don't ring the church bell in the winter."

B. "No, they just don't ring it as loud."

C. "Let's call our friend Sam who lives near the church."

D. "Maybe we don't hear as well during the winter."

E. "Maybe sound carries better during the summer."

11. Which of the other comments would most help to decide whether comment A is a correct conclusion?

   (1)   B and D
   (2)   B alone
   (3)   C alone
   (4)   D and E
   (5)   E alone

12. If the church bell was, in fact, rung during the winter, which of the comments is a possible explanation of why the family did not hear it?

   (1)   A only
   (2)   B only
   (3)   B and C only
   (4)   C, D, and E only
   (5)   B, D, and E only

13. Which of the comments is not an example of a hypothesis to explain why the family does not hear the bells in the winter?

   (1)   A
   (2)   B
   (3)   C
   (4)   D
   (5)   E

Question 14 refers to the following photo.

Source: Shutterstock

14. When lightning occurs, as in the photo above, the thunder that accompanies it often seems to come several seconds later. Which of the following best explains the delay?

   (1)   Sound travels faster than light.
   (2)   It takes a few seconds for the air around the lightning to begin vibrating.
   (3)   Thunder is not related to lightning.
   (4)   Light travels faster than sound.
   (5)   Thunder causes lightning.

GO ON TO THE NEXT PAGE

Science

15. During periods of full moon, tides are 6 to 8 inches higher along a particular stretch of coastline. If a hurricane were to hit this part of the coastline, when would the most severe flooding be likely to occur?

    (1) at high tide, during a full moon
    (2) at low tide, during a new moon
    (3) at high tide, when the moon is half full
    (4) at low tide, when the moon is half full
    (5) at low tide, during a full moon

16. The Cereus flower is unusual in that it blooms only at night. Which of the following best accounts for the behavior of this flower?

    (1) The Cereus can be pollinated only by a particular night-flying moth.
    (2) Like all plants, the Cereus produces chlorophyll using energy from the sun.
    (3) The Cereus, like most other flowers, has both pistils and stamens.
    (4) The Cereus grows only in sandy soil.
    (5) The Cereus resembles the common daisy in its root structure.

17. Some objects in space have circular orbits while others have elliptical orbits that resemble an oval. In our solar system, Pluto is usually farther from the Sun than Neptune, but not always. Pluto's orbit sometimes takes it about 2.7 billion miles away from the Sun. Neptune, at its unchanging orbit of 2.8 billion miles, sometimes becomes the most distant object from the Sun.

    Which of the following would explain the facts presented above?

    (1) Both objects are farther away from the Sun than Earth is.
    (2) Pluto's orbit is circular while Neptune's is elliptical.
    (3) Neptune has more moons than Pluto has.
    (4) Neptune is traveling at a faster speed than Pluto is.
    (5) Neptune's orbit is circular while Pluto's is elliptical.

18. Which of the following accounts for the fact that although the planet Jupiter is 11 times the size of Earth, a day on Jupiter lasts only 10 Earth-hours, compared to the 24-hour day we have on Earth?

    (1) Jupiter has 17 moons.
    (2) Jupiter spins more rapidly on its axis, completing a day faster than Earth does.
    (3) The distance between Earth and Jupiter changes throughout the year.
    (4) Jupiter is farther away from the Sun than Earth is.
    (5) The body of Jupiter is composed of a gaseous matter.

GO ON TO THE NEXT PAGE

Science

Questions 19 and 20 refer to the following chart.

Dairy Products	Measure	Calories	Proteins (in grams)	Fat (in grams)
cheese (cream)	1 ounce	100	2	10
cheese (cheddar)	1 ounce	115	7	8
cream (sour)	1 tbsp.	25	0	3
milk (whole)	1 cup	150	8	8

19. According to the chart above, which of the following statements is true?

    A.   Cheddar cheese has the same amount of fat per ounce as whole milk.

    B.   A cup of sour cream would have more protein than a tablespoon of sour cream.

    C.   A cup of whole milk contains the same amount of protein as fat.

    (1)   A only
    (2)   B only
    (3)   C only
    (4)   A and B only
    (5)   A, B, and C

20. If 1 cup equals 8 ounces, which of the following would supply the greatest amount of calories?

    (1)   1 cup of whole milk
    (2)   1 cup of cheddar cheese
    (3)   1 ounce of cream cheese
    (4)   1 tablespoon of sour cream
    (5)   1 ounce of cream cheese plus 1 ounce of cheddar

21. If a rock layer A contains fossils and another rock layer B, located above rock layer A, also contains fossils, which of the following conclusions is most likely?

    (1)   Both layers are composed of shale.
    (2)   The fossils found in the two layers come from the 1900s or later.
    (3)   The fossils found in rock layer A are likely to be older than the fossils in rock layer B.
    (4)   The rock in layer A is heavier than the rock in layer B.
    (5)   At one time, layer A was located above layer B.

GO ON TO THE NEXT PAGE

Science

Questions 22 through 24 refer to the following chart.

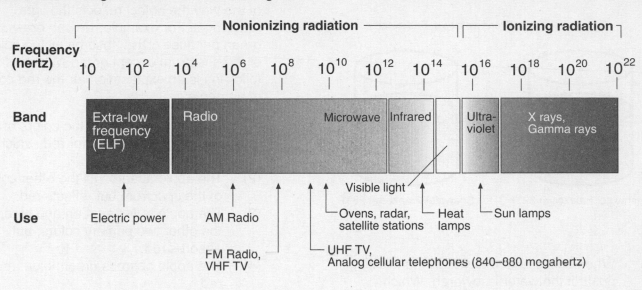

22. According to the chart above, visible light appears between which levels of frequency?

    (1) 10^2 and 10^3
    (2) 10^3 and 10^4
    (3) 10^8 and 10^{10}
    (4) 10^{14} and 10^{16}
    (5) 10^{18} and 10^{20}

23. The waves used in or produced by AM radios, microwave ovens, and cellular phones all fit into which of the following categories?

    (1) infrared light
    (2) microwaves
    (3) extra-low frequency
    (4) ionizing radiation
    (5) nonionizing radiation

24. Certain bees can see only waves that are both invisible to the human eye and have a slightly higher frequency than the visible light spectrum. Which of the following is most likely to be visible to bees?

    (1) infrared light
    (2) microwaves
    (3) radio waves
    (4) extra-low frequency waves
    (5) ultraviolet light

GO ON TO THE NEXT PAGE

Science

Question 25 refers to the following image.

Freezing Point of Freshwater vs. Saltwater

Freshwater Freezes at 32° F   Seawater Freezes at 28° F

25. When salt is added to water, the freezing point of the water is lowered. Which of the following is an example of this phenomenon?

   (1) A freshwater lake often freezes in winter, while the ocean almost never does.
   (2) Spreading salt on rainy roads causes water to freeze into ice.
   (3) Adding salt to boiling water temporarily slows the boiling process.
   (4) When a thread is suspended in a salt solution, salt crystals will form on the thread.
   (5) The Dead Sea is saltier than any other large body of water because it evaporates faster than other bodies of water do.

26. We perceive color in an object because of the way the object reflects the light reaching it. For example, we see grass as green because grass absorbs all the colors of the spectrum except green. Which of the following is an explanation for the red color of an apple?

   (1) The apple reflects all the colors of the spectrum except for red, which is absorbed.
   (2) The apple absorbs all the other colors of the spectrum but reflects red.
   (3) The apple reflects green and blue, the other two primary colors, but absorbs red.
   (4) The apple absorbs green, blue, and red.
   (5) The apple reflects green, blue, and red.

GO ON TO THE NEXT PAGE

Science

Questions 27 through 31 refer to the following information.

Viruses may be able to evolve in much the same way that other living species do, according to an American scientist. That may be why certain diseases have become resistant to drugs. When confronted with a single drug, a virus can mutate slightly and continue to be a threat to humans.

Yung-Kang Chow of Boston, Massachusetts, is attempting to force a virus deadly to humans to mutate into a harmless form of itself by barraging it with three different drugs at the same time. The theory is that the virus will be forced to evolve so far from its former self that it will turn into a benign form. In test-tube results, the experiment has been a complete success.

The questions that follow consist of statements about the above study. Classify each of the statements into one of the categories defined below. More than one statement may have the same classification.

(1) the problem = the major topic being studied

(2) a method = an operation or approach used to study the problem

(3) a finding = a proven outcome obtained as part of the study

(4) an assumption = an idea or theory that supports the finding but is not yet proven

(5) irrelevant information = information that has no bearing on this problem

27. Three different drugs were used at the same time in the experiment.

   (1) the problem
   (2) a method
   (3) a finding
   (4) an assumption
   (5) irrelevant information

28. Other living species have evolved over many thousands of years.

   (1) the problem
   (2) a method
   (3) a finding
   (4) an assumption
   (5) irrelevant information

29. The virus, when exposed to three drugs at once, demonstrated greatly reduced ability to harm human beings.

   (1) the problem
   (2) a method
   (3) a finding
   (4) an assumption
   (5) irrelevant information

30. Viruses evolve much the same way that other organisms evolve.

   (1) the problem
   (2) a method
   (3) a finding
   (4) an assumption
   (5) irrelevant information

31. In test tubes, the subject virus mutated in response to the three drugs.

   (1) the problem
   (2) a method
   (3) a finding
   (4) an assumption
   (5) irrelevant information

GO ON TO THE NEXT PAGE

Science

32. Coral is formed from the calcified skeletons of small creatures called polyps. Only the outer layer of a coral reef is actually alive. Which of the following would <u>not</u> represent a dangerous threat to the continued growth of a coral reef?

    (1) The force of a hurricane rips off the fragile outer layer of the reef.
    (2) Global warming raises the temperature to a level at which polyps cannot survive.
    (3) Pollution causes the poisoning of the polyps.
    (4) A burrowing undersea animal bores tunnels through the calcified portion of the reef.
    (5) A drop in sea level causes the live portion of the coral reef to be exposed to the air.

<u>Question 33</u> refers to the following image.

One Liter of Water

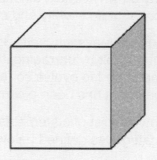 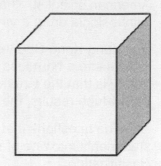

Unfrozen: 1 cubic liter   Frozen: 1.1 cubic liters

The two figures may look the same, but the cube on the left is a little smaller than the image on the right. The image on the right was created by copying the cube on the left, and stretching it vertically a tiny bit (because ice expands upwards when water is frozen in a container).

33. When water freezes, it expands in volume but not in mass. If a block of ice with a volume of 9 cubic centimeters were melted, the volume of the water would most probably

    (1) remain unchanged
    (2) be slightly smaller
    (3) expand slightly
    (4) change less than its mass
    (5) double

END OF TEST

LANGUAGE ARTS, READING

Tests of General Educational Development

Directions

The Language Arts, Reading Test consists of excerpts from classical and popular literature, business documents, and articles about literature or the arts. Each excerpt is followed by multiple-choice questions about the reading material.

Read each excerpt first and then answer the questions following it. Refer back to the reading material as often as necessary in answering the questions.

Each excerpt is preceded by a "purpose question." The purpose question gives a reason for reading the material. Use these purpose questions to help focus your reading. You are not required to answer these purpose questions. They are given only to help you concentrate on the ideas presented in the reading material.

You should spend no more than 35 minutes answering the questions in this booklet. Work carefully, but do not spend too much time on any one question. Be sure you answer every question. You will not be penalized for incorrect answers.

Do not mark in this test booklet. Record your answers on the separate answer sheet provided. Be sure that all requested information is properly recorded on the answer sheet. To record your answers, mark the numbered spaceon the answer sheet beside the number that corresponds to the question in the test booklet.

FOR EXAMPLE:

It was Susan's dream machine. The metallic blue paint gleamed, and the sporty wheels were highly polished. Under the hood, the engine was no less carefully cleaned. Inside, flashy lights illuminated the instruments on the dashboard, and the seats were covered by rich leather upholstery.

The subject ("It") of this excerpt is most likely

- (1)   an airplane
- (2)   a stereo system
- (3)   an automobile
- (4)   a boat
- (5)   a motorcycle

The correct answer is "an automobile"; therefore, answer space (3) would be marked on the answer sheet.

Do not rest the point of your pencil on the answer sheet while you are considering your answer. Make no stray or unnecessary marks. If you change an answer, erase your first mark completely. Mark only <u>one</u> answer space for each question; multiple answers will be scored as incorrect. Do not fold or crease your answer sheet. Return all test materials to the test administrator.

Reading

Directions: Choose the <u>one best answer</u> to each question.

Questions 1 through 7 refer to the following excerpt from a play.

WHAT WILL MRS. MORTAR DO?

Mrs. Mortar: I told you at the beginning you shouldn't have bought a place like this. Burying yourself on a farm! You'll regret it.

(5) **Martha:** We like it here. Aunt Lily, you've talked about London for a long time. Would you like to go over?

Mrs. Mortar: It's been twenty years, and I shall never live to see it again.

(10) **Martha:** Well, you can go any time you like. We can spare the money now, and it will do you a lot of good. You pick out the boat you want, and I'll get the passage. [Rapidly,
(15) anxious to end the whole thing] Now that's all fixed. You'll have a grand time seeing all your old friends, and if you live sensibly I ought to be able to let you have
(20) enough to get along on. [She begins to gather books, notebooks, and pencils.]

Mrs. Mortar: [slowly] So you want me to leave?

(25) **Martha:** That's not the way to put it. You've wanted to go ever since I can remember.

Mrs. Mortar: You're trying to get rid of me.

(30) **Martha:** That's it. We don't want you around when we dig up the buried treasure.

Mrs. Mortar: So? You're turning me out? At my age! Nice grateful girl you are.

(35) **Martha:** Oh, my God, how can anybody deal with you? You're going where you want to go, and we'll be better off alone. That suits everybody. You complain about Karen, and now you
(40) have what you want, and you're still looking for something to complain about.

Mrs. Mortar: [with dignity] Please do not raise your voice.

(45) **Martha:** You ought to be glad I don't do worse.

Mrs. Mortar: I absolutely refuse to be shipped off three thousand miles away. I'm not going to England. I shall go
(50) back to the stage. I'll write my agents tomorrow, and as soon as they have something good for me—

Martha: The truth is I'd like you to leave soon. The three of us can't live
(55) together, and it doesn't make any difference whose fault it is.

Mrs. Mortar: You wish me to go tonight?

Martha: Don't act, Aunt Lily. Go as soon as you've found a place you like. I'll
(60) put the money in the bank for you tomorrow.

Mrs. Mortar: You think I'd take your money? I'd rather scrub floors first.

Martha: I imagine you'll change your
(65) mind.

Lillian Hellman, THE CHILDREN'S HOUR, from SIX PLAYS, 1979.

GO ON TO THE NEXT PAGE

Reading

1. According to this excerpt, the problem between Martha and Mrs. Mortar is probably

   (1) money
   (2) jealousy
   (3) incompatibility
   (4) loneliness
   (5) disagreement about where to live

2. Mrs. Mortar can best be described as

   (1) supportive
   (2) easygoing
   (3) thoughtful
   (4) demanding
   (5) indifferent

3. Why does the author have Martha begin to "gather books, notebooks, and pencils" in lines 20–22?

   (1) as an example of Martha's hardworking nature
   (2) as a way to indicate that Martha is a neat person
   (3) to suggest that Martha wants to write something down
   (4) to make Martha appear selfish
   (5) to show that the conversation has made Martha uncomfortable

4. What does Martha suggest that Mrs. Mortar do?

   (1) become an actress
   (2) move back to London
   (3) go live with Karen
   (4) do more work on the farm
   (5) change bedrooms

5. Why does Martha mention "buried treasure" in lines 30–32?

   (1) She has hidden some of Mrs. Mortar's belongings.
   (2) She thinks she knows where Mrs. Mortar left her glasses.
   (3) She wants to keep the family inheritance for herself and Karen.
   (4) She is making light of Mrs. Mortar's accusation.
   (5) She is implying that Mrs. Mortar is greedy.

6. Why does the author have Martha tell Mrs. Mortar not to "act" in line 58?

   (1) to show Martha's impatience with Mrs. Mortar
   (2) because Mrs. Mortar is not a good actress
   (3) to remind the audience that Mrs. Mortar is leaving
   (4) as a way to make Martha appear jealous
   (5) to make the audience feel sorry for Mrs. Mortar

7. Why does Mrs. Mortar refuse Martha's money?

   (1) She has plenty of money already.
   (2) She knows that the money is stolen.
   (3) She wants more money than Martha offered.
   (4) She is too proud to accept it.
   (5) She does not have a bank account.

GO ON TO THE NEXT PAGE

Reading

Questions 8 through 12 refer to the following excerpt.

WHAT DOES SHE FIND IN THE GARDEN?

When grandmother was ready to go, I said I would like to stay up there in the garden awhile.

She peered down at me from (5) under her sunbonnet. "Aren't you afraid of snakes?"

"A little," I admitted, "but I'd like to stay, anyhow."

"Well, if you see one, don't have (10) anything to do with him. The big yellow and brown ones won't hurt you; they're bull snakes and help to keep the gophers down. Don't be scared if you see anything look out of that hole in the bank over there. That's (15) a badger hole. He's about as big as a bog 'possum, and his face is striped, black and white. He takes a chicken once in a while, but I never let the men harm him. In a new country a body feels friendly to the animals. (20) I like to have him come out and watch me when I'm at work."

Grandmother swung the bag of potatoes over her shoulder and went down the path, leaning forward a little. The road (25) followed the windings of the draw; when she came to the first bend, she waved at me and disappeared. I was left alone with this new feeling of lightness and content.

I sat down in the middle of the (30) garden, where snakes could scarcely approach unseen, and leaned my back against a warm yellow pumpkin. There were some ground-cherry bushes growing along the furrows, full of fruit. I turned back the (35) papery triangular sheaths that protected the berries and ate a few. All about me giant grasshoppers, twice as big as any I had ever seen, were doing acrobatic feats among the dried vines. The gophers

(40) scurried up and down the ploughed ground. There in the sheltered draw-bottom the wind did not blow very hard, but I could hear it singing its humming tune up on the level, and I could see the tall grasses (45) wave. The earth was warm under me, and warm as I crumbled it through my fingers. Queer little red bugs came out and moved in small squadrons around me. Their backs were polished vermilion, with black spots. I (50) kept as still as I could. Nothing happened. I did not expect anything to happen. I was something that lay under the sun and felt it, like the pumpkins, and I did not want to be anything more. I was entirely happy. (55) Perhaps we feel like that when we die and become a part of something entire, whether it is sun and air, or goodness and knowledge. At any rate, that is happiness; to be dissolved into something complete (60) and great. When it comes to one, it comes as naturally as sleep.

Willa Cather, MY ÁNTONIA, 1918.

GO ON TO THE NEXT PAGE

8. Why does the grandmother not want the badger to be harmed?

    (1) The badger kills the snakes.
    (2) The badger is in danger of becoming extinct.
    (3) She uses holes that the badger digs to plant vegetables.
    (4) She believes that the badger brings her good luck.
    (5) She enjoys his company.

9. The girl stays in the garden because she

    (1) likes snakes
    (2) is afraid of her grandmother
    (3) enjoys being outdoors
    (4) wants to feed the chickens
    (5) doesn't want to do chores

10. After her grandmother is gone, the girl feels

    (1) afraid
    (2) delighted
    (3) worried
    (4) hungry
    (5) sleepy

11. Why does the narrator mention grasshoppers, gophers, and tall grasses (lines 36–45)?

    (1) to foreshadow a natural disaster
    (2) to demonstrate her knowledge of wildlife
    (3) to contrast the scenery with that of urban settings
    (4) to emphasize the lushness of the garden
    (5) to illustrate the girl's fear of animals

12. With which of the following statements would the narrator most likely agree?

    (1) Growing vegetables is just like sleeping; they both require next to no effort.
    (2) Dangers are present even in a beautiful garden.
    (3) We should pay more attention to our worries.
    (4) Forgetting one's self can bring happiness.
    (5) Happiness can sometimes make one sleepy.

GO ON TO THE NEXT PAGE

Reading

Questions 13 through 18 refer to the following review.

WHAT IS SPECIAL ABOUT THIS MOVIE?

Sometimes life can throw you a curve ball. For Charlie Babbitt, it's being reunited with his brother Raymond. Their relationship is the heart of the classic 1980s
(5) film, *Rain Man.*

Charlie Babbitt (Tom Cruise) is a self-centered, greedy man embittered by a self-imposed exile from his father. After being virtually disinherited in his estranged
(10) parent's will, he is reintroduced to his brother Raymond (Dustin Hoffman). The older brother is the recipient of their father's three million dollar trust fund.

To complicate things further,
(15) Raymond is an autistic savant. Autism, a disorder believed to be neurologically based, limits normal intellectual development. An autistic savant, such as Raymond, displays genius capacity in a
(20) limited area of mental ability. The disorder is extremely rare. An astounding affinity for memorizing and calculating numbers is Raymond's unique talent.

But Raymond has no conception
(25) of money. By nature, he is selfless, unassuming and kind. Having been institutionalized all his life, Raymond cannot survive without constant, protective supervision, which is very wearing on
(30) Charlie. When Charlie spirits him away, the two brothers begin a weeklong cross-country odyssey that will change their lives.

The bond that develops between the brothers is not unpredictable. But the
(35) subtle nuances and small dramas that build up throughout the film culminate in a picture of quiet depth and beauty. One major production piece that links the brothers is the car in which they journey. It is their
(40) father's treasured 1949 Buick Roadmaster convertible.

Dustin Hoffman turned in a remarkable, Oscar-caliber performance. Hoffman takes an illness that mystifies
(45) doctors and brings it to life on the screen, without the pity that usually stunts such characterizations. Reportedly, he spent 13 months researching for his role. (The film itself boasts no less than six consultants
(50) on autistic behavior.) Hoffman's efforts included interviewing autism experts, spending time with autistic people, studying documentaries and reading books on the disorder. Obviously, it was time well spent.
(55) Hoffman is nothing short of brilliant.

Tom Cruise is equal to the task of taking an utterly despicable character and turning him around. It would turn out to be his most mature and comprehensible
(60) role for years to come. His performance is flawless.

Barry Levinson was the fourth director to tackle *Rain Man.* He delivered an exceptionally well-executed production
(65) from a screenplay by Ronald Bass and Barry Morrow. The dialogue is superb. The acting is exceptional. Australian-born cinematographer John Seale's remarkable photography adds luster to the picture's
(70) overall excellence.

Rain Man is a timeless masterpiece.

C. M. Fiorillo, "Rain Man," from FILMS IN REVIEW.

GO ON TO THE NEXT PAGE

13. From the excerpt, it is clear that

   (1) the movie is a documentary
   (2) the reviewer enjoyed the movie
   (3) the movie took 13 months to make
   (4) the movie will win an Academy Award
   (5) many people suffer from autism

14. According to the review, what qualities do the two stars of the movie seem to have in common?

   (1) mastery of many dialects
   (2) inadequate training in acting
   (3) a tendency to exaggerate
   (4) talent and attention to detail
   (5) a lack of understanding of human frailty

15. The function of Raymond's illness in the film is to

   (1) make the audience feel sorry for him
   (2) help Charlie discover something about himself
   (3) turn a comic movie into a tragic one
   (4) make him very good with money
   (5) illustrate his skill with numbers

16. One reason Hoffman's portrayal of Raymond is so convincing is that he

   (1) doesn't have very many lines
   (2) is a psychologist as well as an actor
   (3) asks too many questions
   (4) spent time with autistic people
   (5) is autistic himself

17. The reviewer describes the bond between Charlie and Raymond as "not unpredictable" (line 34) because

   (1) he had seen the movie before
   (2) the brothers were very close
   (3) most movies have happy endings
   (4) the audience naturally anticipates it
   (5) the brothers frequently fight

18. Which of the following is a source of tension in the film?

   (1) the expense of Raymond's doctors
   (2) the father's Buick
   (3) Raymond's dependence on Charlie
   (4) Charlie's ability to memorize
   (5) Raymond's inability to speak

GO ON TO THE NEXT PAGE

Reading

Questions 19 and 20 refer to the following poem.

HOW DOES THIS WOMAN FEEL ABOUT RECEIVING FLOWERS?

One Perfect Rose

A single flow'r he sent me, since we met.
All tenderly his messenger he chose;
Deep-hearted, pure, with scented dew still wet—
One perfect rose.

(5) I knew the language of the floweret;
"My fragile leaves," it said, "his heart enclose."
Love long has taken for his amulet
One perfect rose.

Why is it no one ever sent me yet
(10) One perfect limousine, do you suppose?
Ah no, it's always just my luck to get
One perfect rose.

Dorothy Parker, "One Perfect Rose," from COLLECTED POETRY, 1926.

19. Who or what is the messenger sent by the lover to the speaker?

    (1) the florist
    (2) the lover's best friend
    (3) a hired messenger
    (4) a friend of the speaker
    (5) a rose

20. Which of the following words best describes the overall mood of the speaker?

    (1) embarrassed
    (2) sarcastic
    (3) romantic
    (4) angry
    (5) sad

GO ON TO THE NEXT PAGE

Reading

Questions 21 and 22 refer to the following excerpt from an offering for an extended warranty plan.

WHAT DO THESE WARRANTIES COVER?

Is your home adequately protected? Homeowner's insurance is an important part of any homeowner's peace of mind, but we have found that homeowners want
(5) the additional security that comes with extended warranties on their appliances and home systems. The Triple A Extended Warranty Company offers three basic plans to give you the home coverage you need.

(10) Plan #1 provides coverage for a 12-month period during which we will repair or replace the mechanical systems and appliances of your home, including (and limited only to) the plumbing system,
(15) electrical system, refrigerator, oven, stove, and dishwasher, when they break down from normal wear.

Plan #2 offers all the coverage of plan #1, plus coverage for the washer/
(20) dryer, air conditioner, trash compactor, and roof system, when they break down from normal wear.

Plan #3 offers all the coverage of plan #2, plus coverage for the garbage
(25) disposal, well, and septic tank, when they break down from normal wear.

It doesn't matter how old your appliances or systems are. It doesn't matter what condition they are in. We will
(30) repair or replace your covered systems and appliances PROVIDED that you can produce bills of sale for each item; that the covered items have not been damaged by fire, flood, act of war, act of nature,
(35) vandalism, negligence, or improper use; and that the covered items are not already covered by an existing warranty by the manufacturer, once the cost of repair or replacement meets a $1,000 deductible.

21. Which of the following would NOT be eligible for repair or replacement under the terms of plan #2 above?

   (1)   an oven whose pilot light mechanism broke down from use
   (2)   a refrigerator destroyed by hurricane damage
   (3)   an air conditioner whose compressor gave out
   (4)   a roof worn down by wind and rain
   (5)   a rusted bathroom pipe

22. It can be inferred from this excerpt that the company would NOT replace or repair an item

   (1)   still covered by its original manufacturer's warranty
   (2)   that cost more than $1,000 in price
   (3)   more than ten years old
   (4)   less than five years old
   (5)   damaged by normal wear and tear

END OF TEST

MATHEMATICS

Tests of General Educational Development

Directions

The Mathematics Test consists of questions intended to measure general mathematics skills and problem-solving ability. The questions are based on short readings that often include a graph, chart, or figure.

You should spend no more than 45 minutes answering the questions in this booklet. Work carefully, but do not spend too much time on any one question. Be sure you answer every question. You will not be penalized for incorrect answers.

Formulas you may need are given on page 691. Only some of the questions will require you to use a formula. Not all the formulas given will be needed.

Some questions contain more information than you will need to solve the problem. Other questions do not give enough information to solve the problem. If the question does not give enough information to solve the problem, the correct answer choice is "Not enough information is given."

The use of calculators is allowed only in Part One.

Do not mark in this test booklet. The test administrator will give you blank paper for your calculations. Record your answers on the separate answer sheet provided. Be sure all requested information is properly recorded on the answer sheet.

To record your answers, mark the numbered space on the answer sheet beside the number that corresponds to the question in the test booklet.

FOR EXAMPLE:

If a grocery bill totaling $15.75 is paid with a $20.00 bill, how much change should be returned?

(1) $5.25
(2) $4.75
(3) $4.25
(4) $3.75
(5) $3.25

The correct answer is $4.25; therefore, answer space (3) would be marked on the answer sheet.

Do not rest the point of your pencil on the answer sheet while you are considering your answer. Make no stray or unnecessary marks. If you change an answer, erase your first mark completely. Mark only <u>one</u> answer space for each question; multiple answers will be scored as incorrect. Do not fold or crease your answer sheet. Return all test materials to the test administrator.

FORMULAS

AREA (A) of a:

square	$A = s^2$; where s = side
rectangle	$A = lw$; where l = length, w = width
parallelogram	$A = bh$; where b = base, h = height
trapezoid	$A = \frac{1}{2}(b_1 + b_2)h$; where b=base, h=height
triangle	$A = \frac{1}{2}bh$; where b = base, h = height
circle	$A = \pi r^2$; where π = 3.14, r = radius

PERIMETER (P) of a:

square	$P = 4s$; where s = side
rectangle	$P = 2l + 2w$; where l = length, w = width
triangle	$P = a + b + c$; where a, b, and c are the sides
CIRCUMFERENCE (C) of a circle	$C = \pi d$; where π = 3.14, d = diameter

VOLUME (V) of a:

cube	$V = s^3$; where s = side
rectangular container	$V = lwh$; where l = length, w = width, h = height
square pyramid	$V = \frac{1}{3}(\text{base edge})^2 h$
cone	$V = \frac{1}{3}\pi r^2 h$
cylinder	$V = \pi r^2 h$; where π = 3.14, r = radius, h = height

PYTHAGOREAN RELATIONSHIP	$c^2 = a^2 + b^2$; where c = hypotenuse, a and b are legs of a right triangle
DISTANCE (d) BETWEEN TWO POINTS IN A PLAN	$d = \sqrt{(x_2 - x_1)^2 + (y_2 - y_1)^2}$; where (x_1, y_1) and (x_2, y_2) are two points in a plane
SLOPE OF A LINE (m)	$m = \frac{y_2 - y_1}{x_2 - x_1}$; where (x_1, y_1) and (x_2, y_2) are two points in a plane
MEAN	mean $= \frac{x_1 + x_2 + ...x_n}{n}$; where the xs are the values for which a mean is desired, and n = number of values in the series
MEDIAN	median = the point in an <u>ordered</u> set of numbers at which half of the numbers are above and half of the numbers are below this value
SIMPLE INTEREST (i)	$i = prt$; where p = principal, r = rate, t = time
DISTANCE (d) as function of rate and time	$d = rt$; where r = rate, t = time
TOTAL COST (c)	$c = nr$; where n = number of units, r = cost per unit

Mathematics, Part I

Directions: Choose the <u>one best answer</u> to each question.

<u>Question 1</u> refers to the following graph.

Movie Survey, by %

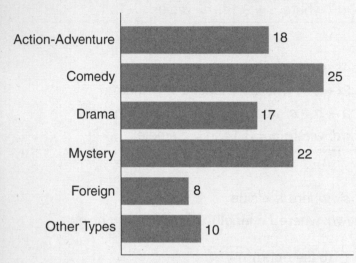

1. The graph above shows the results of a survey that asked 100 moviegoers to name their favorite type of movie. What percent of moviegoers said they preferred mysteries?

    (1)   20

    (2)   22

    (3)   36

    (4)   55

    (5)   78

2. Tickets for a train trip sell for the following prices:

    First-class tickets $6.00
    Second-class tickets $3.50

    Which of the following expressions represents the cost for a group of 110 first-class and 172 second-class tickets?

    (1)   110(6.00) + 172(3.50)

    (2)   (110 + 172)9.50

    (3)   110(3.50) + 172(6.00)

    (4)   110 + 172

    (5)   6.00 + 9.50

3. If $4x + 3 = 19$, then $x =$

4. A surveyor buys the same pair of sneakers at 45 different shoe stores across the country. If the mean (average) price for the pair of sneakers is $37.20, how much does the surveyor spend in total on sneakers?

    (1) $1,674.00

    (2) $77.80

    (3) $67.40

    (4) $37.78

    (5) $0.83

GO ON TO THE NEXT PAGE

Mathematics, Part I

Question 5 refers to the following diagram.

7 miles	8 miles	2 miles	6 miles	12 miles

A   B   C   D   E   F

5. The towns in Maple County are located along a 35-mile section of an interstate at the points A, B, C, D, E, and F as shown in the diagram above. The Maple County Post Office is located midway between points A and E. The location of the post office is between which of the following two points?

   (1)   E and F

   (2)   D and E

   (3)   C and D

   (4)   B and C

   (5)   A and B

Questions 6 and 7 refer to the following information.

A sailboat travels to its destination at a constant speed. For example, after one hour had elapsed, the sailboat had traveled 14 miles.

6. How far would you expect the sailboat to have traveled at a point 2 hours into the trip?

   (1)   18

   (2)   20

   (3)   24

   (4)   28

   (5)   Not enough information is given.

7. The trip was 50 miles long. If the sailboat maintained a constant speed throughout the trip, approximately how long did it take the sailboat to complete the trip?

   (1)   2 hours

   (2)   2.3 hours

   (3)   3.5 hours

   (4)   7 hours

   (5)   Not enough information is given.

8. A newspaper delivery van starts the day carrying 962 pounds of newspapers. It drops off 345 pounds and 218 pounds at its first two stops. It also picks up 1,048 pounds of old newspapers to drop off at the recycling center. The number of pounds of newspaper now in the van is equal to which of the following expressions?

   (1)   1,048 − 345 − 218 − 962

   (2)   962 − 345 − 218 − 1,048

   (3)   1,048 + 962 + 345 + 218

   (4)   962 + 345 + 218 − 1,048

   (5)   962 − 345 − 218 + 1,048

9. What is the price of an $85,720 house, rounded to the nearest thousand?

GO ON TO THE NEXT PAGE

Mathematics, Part I

10. Mary is dividing up a $36.00 bill for dinner at a restaurant. If she wants to divide the bill so that she and each of her friends pay an equal amount, which expression represents the amount in dollars that each person must pay?

(1) $\dfrac{36.00}{7}$

(2) $\dfrac{36.00}{6}$

(3) $\dfrac{36.00}{4}$

(4) $\dfrac{36.00}{3}$

(5) Not enough information is given.

11. The coordinates of point A are (–5,1). What is the location of point A? Mark your answer on the coordinate plane grid.

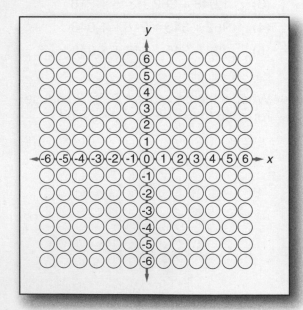

Questions 12 through 14 refer to the following label and information.

Stain Guard Stain Repellents	
Repellent X	1.44%
Repellent Y	0.06%
Fillers	98.50%
Total	100.00%

A textiles manufacturer uses the stain guard described above to protect a fabric. One $3\frac{1}{2}$ pound (1.59 kilogram) bag sells for $8.00 and treats 90 square yards (75 square meters).

12. The two stain repellents make up what percentage of the stain guard?

(1) 0.06%

(2) 0.325%

(3) 1.44%

(4) 1.50%

(5) 10.50%

13. If the sales tax on the $8.00 bag of stain guard is $0.64, what is the sales tax rate?

(1) 5%

(2) 6%

(3) 7%

(4) 8%

(5) 9%

14. A bolt of cloth that contains 600 square meters requires 8 bags of stain guard. In kilograms, what is the weight of 8 bags of stain guard?

(1) 2.38 kilograms

(2) 12.72 kilograms

(3) 28.00 kilograms

(4) 75.00 kilograms

(5) 80.00 kilograms

GO ON TO THE NEXT PAGE

Mathematics, Part II

Part Two—Use of calculators prohibited

15. Karen puts 60% of her paycheck into her savings account. If Karen put $120 into her savings account, what was the amount of her entire paycheck?

16. Gary lent his brother $1,000 and charged him 3.5% interest per year. Which of the following shows the total dollar amount of interest Gary will receive from his brother?

   (1) 1,000 × 0.035
   (2) 1,000 × 2.5
   (3) 1,000 × 35
   (4) 3,500
   (5) Not enough information is given.

17. A rainfall doubled the original amount of water in a reservoir in 1 day and quadrupled the original amount in 5 days. Which of the following expressions represents the approximate amount of water in the reservoir after the 5 days of rain, if there were x gallons of water in the reservoir before the rainfall?

   (1) x
   (2) $x + 4$
   (3) $x + 6$
   (4) $4x$
   (5) $5x$

18. A wheel rotates at a constant rate of 2,400 revolutions per hour. Which of the following expressions would represent the number of revolutions the wheel would make in one minute?

   (1) $\dfrac{2,400}{60}$
   (2) 2,400 − 60
   (3) 2,400 + 60
   (4) 2,400 × 60
   (5) $\dfrac{2,400}{30}$

GO ON TO THE NEXT PAGE

Mathematics, Part II

Question 19 refers to the following diagram.

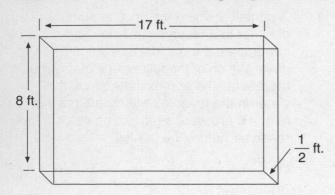

Question 20 refers to the following diagram.

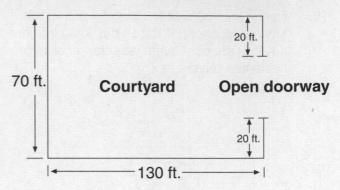

19. Marcia builds an 8-foot-by-17-foot wading pool that is $\frac{1}{2}$ foot deep, as shown in the diagram above. Approximately how many cubic feet of water will the pool contain if it is filled completely?

  (1) $2\frac{1}{2}$

  (2)   12

  (3)   25

  (4)   68

  (5)   544

20. A painter has been hired to repaint the trim around the base of the courtyard wall. Which of the following expressions represents the number of feet of trim the painter must paint?

  (1)   2(130) + 40

  (2)   2(130) + 70 + 40

  (3)   2(130) + 70

  (4)   2(130 + 70 + 40)

  (5)   2(130 + 70)

Question 21 refers to the following jars.

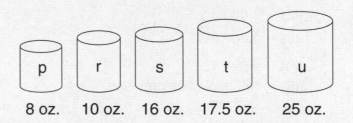

8 oz.   10 oz.   16 oz.   17.5 oz.   25 oz.

21. A factory is going to increase the volume of certain jars by 25%. Which of the jars above will have a new volume of 20 ounces?

  (1)   p

  (2)   r

  (3)   s

  (4)   t

  (5)   u

GO ON TO THE NEXT PAGE

Mathematics, Part II

22. Mark has 8 nickels, 12 dimes, and 20 pennies in a jar. If Mark removes one coin from the jar without looking, what is the probability that the coin will be a penny?

23. Which of the following is equal to 18?

    (1) (1 + 0)2

    (2) 32 + 62

    (3) (3 + 6)2

    (4) 36

    (5) 32(2)

24. Two of the interior angles of a triangle have measures of 34° and 55°. Which of the expressions below can be used to find the measure of the third interior angle?

    (1) 360 − (34 + 55)

    (2) 180 − (34 + 55)

    (3) 34 + 55 + 180

    (4) 34 + 55 − 180

    (5) 180 − (34 − 55)

Question 25 refers to the following diagram.

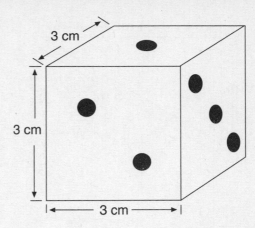

25. The cube-shaped die shown in the diagram above has 3-centimeter edges. In cubic centimeters, what is the volume of the die?

    (1) 3

    (2) 6

    (3) 9

    (4) 27

    (5) 54

GO ON TO THE NEXT PAGE

Mathematics, Part II

Question 26 refers to the following diagram.

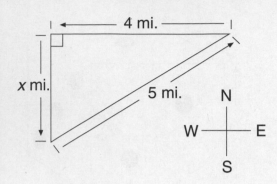

Question 27 refers to the following diagram.

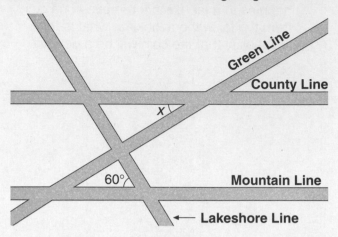

26. Hikers on a nature trail traveled 4 miles west and then *x* miles south. They then walked 5 miles northeast to reach their starting point. What is the distance *x* that the hikers traveled?

(1)   1 mi.
(2)   3 mi.
(3)   4 mi.
(4)   5 mi.
(5)   9 mi.

27. The Mountain Line intersects the Lakeshore Line at a 60° angle as shown. The Green Line is perpendicular to the Lakeshore Line, and the County Line is parallel to the Mountain Line. How many degrees is angle *x*?

(1)   30°
(2)   60°
(3)   90°
(4)   120°
(5)   Not enough information is given.

28. The steepness of a ramp can be notated as the ratio of the rise to the run. What is the steepness of a ramp that has a rise of 5 feet and a run of 30 feet?

(1) $\dfrac{1}{7}$

(2) $\dfrac{1}{6}$

(3) $\dfrac{1}{5}$

(4) 5

(5) 6

END OF EXAMINATION

Answer Key for Practice Test 2

Writing Part 1 Answer Key	Social Studies Answer Key	Science Answer Key	Reading Answer Key	Math Answer Key
1. 2	1. 4	1. 3	1. 3	Part One
2. 3	2. 2	2. 1	2. 4	1. 2
3. 4	3. 5	3. 4	3. 5	2. 1
4. 3	4. 3	4. 1	4. 2	3. 4
5. 5	5. 4	5. 4	5. 4	4. 1
6. 4	6. 2	6. 5	6. 1	5. 4
7. 3	7. 4	7. 2	7. 4	6. 4
8. 1	8. 3	8. 3	8. 5	7. 3
9. 4	9. 3	9. 3	9. 3	8. 5
10. 5	10. 5	10. 1	10. 2	9. 86,000
11. 5	11. 1	11. 3	11. 4	10. 5
12. 4	12. 5	12. 5	12. 4	11. See below
13. 3	13. 4	13. 3	13. 2	12. 4
14. 1	14. 5	14. 4	14. 4	13. 4
15. 5	15. 2	15. 1	15. 2	14. 2
16. 1	16. 5	16. 1	16. 4	
17. 3	17. 3	17. 5	17. 4	Part Two
18. 2	18. 4	18. 2	18. 3	15. 200
19. 2	19. 1	19. 3	19. 5	16. 5
20. 5	20. 1	20. 2	20. 2	17. 4
21. 1	21. 3	21. 3	21. 2	18. 1
22. 1	22. 2	22. 4	22. 1	19. 4
23. 2	23. 1	23. 5		20. 2
24. 4	24. 1	24. 5		21. 3
25. 5	25. 4	25. 1		22. 1/2
26. 4	26. 2	26. 2		23. 3
27. 4	27. 1	27. 2		24. 2
28. 1	28. 5	28. 5		25. 4
	29. 2	29. 3		26. 2
	30. 2	30. 4		27. 1
	31. 4	31. 3		28. 2
	32. 4	32. 4		
		33. 2		

11.

Chapter 30
Practice Test 2:
Answers and
Explanations

Writing—Part I Explanations

1. **2**   This is a sentence fragment. Changing the verb to "can take" fixes the error. The phrase "for example" should be set off by commas, which eliminates (1). "Lots" is less formal than "a lot," so this part does not need to be changed, so get rid of (3). "You're" is the contraction for "you are." The word "time" needs a possessive pronoun before it, so (4) is incorrect.

2. **3**   This sentence is a fragment because the verb "agree" has been put in gerund form as "agreeing." In this case, "agreeing" is a noun, not a verb. In order to correct it, change "agreeing" to "agree." The other corrections listed in the answer choices are not needed.

3. **4**   To break up this run-on sentence, divide it into two after "familiar." Choices (1), (2), and (5) do not fix the run-on. Choice (3) creates a comma splice as well as a verb tense change.

4. **3**   Choice (3) is the only one that provides the subject "puppies" to modify the noun "they" in the dependent clause. The subject must come immediately after the dependent clause so that the sentence makes sense.

5. **5**   The subject of this sentence is a list of three things. Items in a list of three or more things must be separated by commas. Choice (5) is the only option that puts commas after all the listed items.

6. **4**   In this sentence, "whether" should be used instead of the soundalike "weather," which refers to the atmospheric environment. None of the other changes suggested is necessary.

7. **3**   The pronoun "them" should be replaced by "themselves" in order to clarify exactly who is exhausted. "Them" suggests someone other than the babies. "These" would need a noun following it. "These babies" is repetitive. "Them" does not refer to "their crying."

8. **1**   Because the passage is in the present tense, "ignored" should be in the present tense also. Choices (2) and (3) are incorrect because "pleas" refers to the parents' appeals, not to the word referring to the polite request. "There" points to a place, not a possessive pronoun. "Shrieking" is connected to the babies by the possessive pronoun "their." "Parent's" is possessive; the plural "babies" in the passage ignore their plural parents.

9. **4**   To fix the sentence fragments in (1) and (3), turn the gerund "encountering" into the properly conjugated verb "encounter." Choices (2) and (5) would work only if the subject was a singular "baby" rather than plural "babies."

10. **5**   This sentence is fine as written. It does not need a comma, so you can eliminate (1). Since "baby" describes "types," it does not need to be plural, so get rid of (2). Choices (3) and (4) both make "is" plural, just in different tenses. Although "types" is plural, it is not the subject of the sentence. If it were, you could use a plural verb. The subject is singular; it is one "of the baby types." Therefore, the verb is singular.

11. **5**   This sentence does not need any of the suggested changes. Nothing belongs to the houses, so they don't need to be changed into the possessive; you can eliminate (1). The subject and the verb do not need to be separated by a comma , so get rid of (2). The subject of the sentence is "visitors," a plural noun, so the verb should also stay plural, which means you can get rid of (3). "Their" is a possessive and would need to be followed by a noun. "There" is correct because it refers to a location, not ownership of a noun, so (4) in incorrect.

12. **4**   The word "careful" modifies the verbs "speak" and "listen." Therefore, "careful" needs to be written in adverb form with an *-ly* at the end. Without the *-ly*, "careful" is an adjective, and adjectives modify only nouns.

13. **3** The subject is separated from the verb in this sentence. "Composition" is not the subject; if it were, you could use the singular verb "focuses." Because "techniques" is the plural subject, you need the plural verb "focus."

14. **1** In rewriting this sentence, the goal itself should immediately follow its announcement. After "should be," a verb or a gerund should appear. Choice (2) is redundant because "should be" appears twice in a row. Choices (3) and (4) do not fit the criteria either. Although (5) is a gerund, it does not maintain the meaning of the original sentence.

15. **5** This sentence needs no changes. The comma in (1) separates the dependent and independent clauses correctly. If you change "some" to "one," as suggested in (2), the sentence then reads "one young writers"; "writers" is plural and "one" is singular.

16. **1** This sentence works best as written because the infinitive "to express" is needed after the conjugated verb "used." Choice (2) turns the sentence into a fragment. Choices (3), (4), and (5) are all conjugated and thus do not stay in the necessary infinitive form.

17. **3** The correct idiomatic expression is "admired for," not "admired while." "Writers" must remain plural because the verb "are" preceding it is plural. A comma after "admired" will not help to turn this sentence fragment into a complete sentence. "Rich" and "complicated" are the two adjectives describing "language." They need a comma between them, but not after them. In the structure of "to be + verb," the verb must be conjugated as if it were in the past. Therefore, in (5), "admired" is correct.

18. **2** A comma correctly breaks up the two main opposing thoughts in this sentence. Choices (1), (3), and (5) read confusingly without the comma. Choice (4) does not fit after "complexities" unless more words are added.

19. **2** To correct this sentence fragment, add the correctly conjugated verb "is taking place." Choice (1) suggests that the revolution will take place in the future, a claim not supported by the passage. Choices (3) and (4) incorrectly suggest adding commas. The use of the preposition "of" is correct here, so cross off (5).

20. **5** All the parts of this sentence are are properly capitalized, punctuated, and conjugated.

21. **1** The word "since" in this context incorrectly suggests that lack of music control began in this century. Therefore, (3), (4), and (5) are wrong. "Until" means that the lack of control over music ended when this century began, so "until" is the correct word. Choice (2), "after," suggests that the lack of control started when this century ended.

22. **1** Choice (1) is the best combination for two reasons. It sets off the phrase "for a much lower price than hiring an orchestra" with commas on either side. The conjunction "and" nicely joins the two ideas of "made music available" and "expanded the range."

23. **2** This is a common spelling error. "Loose" is an adjective that means "free from attachment." "Lose" is a verb that means "to fail to keep." This part of the sentence requires a verb with the meaning of "to forfeit."

24. **4** The improvements appear in a list of three. Listed items need to be separated by commas, so you need a comma after "quality." None of the other choices addresses this omission.

25. **5** In both the original and the revised sentence, "the listener" is the subject. The subject must immediately follow the dependent clause before the comma, so (5) makes the most sense.

26. 4   The subject of the second clause after the semicolon is "members," a plural noun that requires the plural verb "continue." However, because the subject and verb are separated by many other words, it may incorrectly seem like the singular "industry" is the subject.

27. 4   Because relevant prior experience is more important than hobbies and education, it should be mentioned before them. Hobbies and education are also not more important than the author's discussion of his dream job, so get rid of (3). It is appropriate for the author to state why he is writing the letter before elaborating on his dream job, so the first two paragraphs should not be switched, so eliminate (1). Because the reader needs to know the purpose of the letter first, the first paragraph should remain where it is, so eliminate (2). Paragraph D is essential to the letter because it tells the reader he should be considered for the position, so (5) is correct.

28. 1   Education is more important to a potential employer than hobbies, so education should be first. Choice (2) does not correct this issue. Choices (3) and (4) are inappropriate content for a letter of introduction. Although the items in paragraph C may appear in a resume, the writer should not ask the reader to look at the resume and then immediately restate the resume's contents, so eliminate (5).

Writing—Part II Explanations
ESSAY SCORE: 4

The issue of how generous to be is a controversial one. On one hand, in an ideal world, all of our actions would both benefit ourselves and improve humanity. On the other hand, the people who serve others in the real world, such as charity workers and missionaries, must often sacrifice bettering themselves in order to help humanity. However, in the final analysis, I believe that bettering oneself does better humanity, but only if there is a balance between the two.

At some point in most people's lives, they are idealistic. Like Mother Theresa, their love of helping others fulfills their lives completely. However, Mother Theresa is so well known in part because her lifestyle was so unusual. It's very difficult for most people to maintain that level of selflessness in their lives.

Clearly, the relationship between most people's betterment of humanity and of themselves is more complicated. Another person known for helping humanity is Bill Gates. He donates billions of dollars to different charities through his foundation. However, he is also known for building his computer company using illegal or unethical methods. Generally, people live more like Bill Gates than Mother Theresa. They both give to and take from society, aiming to better both at the same time.

In our own lives, we should do what makes us happy. After all, by bettering ourselves, we are also bettering humanity because we are part of humanity. However, we should also share what we enjoy to help others as well. Journalists could teach struggling kids how to read after school. Doctors could spend vacations healing others in needy countries. Musicians could give free concerts in their hometowns. If everyone shares their personal wealth and abilities, society will benefit as much as the individuals in it.

Reasons the author received a score of 4:

- o The essay is well organized.
  - • The introduction clearly explains what aspects of the prompt the essay will explore.
  - • The body paragraphs flow naturally and with transitions from the introduction.
  - • The conclusion summarizes the author's viewpoint clearly and emphatically.
- o The essay is well supported.
  - • The examples given are realistic and accessible to any reader.
  - • The examples are detailed and thorough.
  - • The examples connect clearly to the main idea.
- o The essay demonstrates a strong grasp of grammar, spelling, and punctuation.
  - • The author varies sentence structure and length.
  - • The essay uses complex vocabulary correctly.

ESSAY SCORE: 2

This isn't true because everyone is selfish for the most part. If every one looks out for themselves because their greedy. Record companies are good examples of this statements being wrong.

When record companies release an album and the artist only gets pennies. The artist is supposed to pay for their own video with that. The record companies get a cut of it all, though cause there bettering themselves economically. But the humanity of the artist isn't bettered so, humanity isn't bettered. Thats why record companies should be more applied to by laws so everythings fairer. LA and NY should watch closer what the record companies do and charge people before when they pay them.

Only in this way will humanity be bettered.

Reasons the author received a score of 2:

- o The essay is poorly organized.
  - • The piece needs a solid introduction and conclusion.
  - • The essay needs several body paragraphs discussing different but related ideas.
  - • Although the point of view is clear, the writing is too scattered, general, and vague.
- o The essay is poorly supported.
  - • The essay's main idea should be clearly described in the introduction.
  - • Opinions should be supported by factual examples.
  - • The essay needs to present both sides. It should mention how record companies help the world by bringing music to the masses before concluding that this deed is not enough to justify their behavior.
- o The essay has numerous grammar and punctuation errors.
  - • There are many comma errors.
  - • There are several sentence fragments.
  - • The essay has many agreement errors and unclear pronouns.
  - • The essay misuses a number of words including possessive nouns.
- o The essay is noticeably shorter than 250 words.

Social Studies Test Explanations

1. **4**   Read *all* the choices before you make up your mind. Although it is possible that the authors of the amendments were legal scholars, this isn't stated in the passage, so (1) doesn't seem likely. Nor is there any mention of the relationship between church and state, so you can safely eliminate (2). (Of course, in the United States, we have always kept church and state separated, but you didn't need to know that to start thinking this isn't the answer—it is enough to know it wasn't mentioned in the passage.) Choice (3) says the writers of the amendments believed in government with ultimate authority—but that seems to go against the idea of granting citizens rights that can't be taken away by the government. Choice (4) basically restates what was in the passage: The writers didn't want to give the government too much power—this seems like it's the answer, but let's just check (5). Choice (5) states an idea from the passage, but takes it too far, saying the federal government should control state governments. The correct answer is (4).

2. **2**   At first glance, *all* of these answer choices seem to be things people wouldn't like—but only one of them doesn't violate the 14th Amendment: Choice (2) requires all citizens to pay taxes, regardless of their beliefs. Choices (1) and (3) deny equal protection under the law. Choices (4) and (5) deny due process of the law.

3. **5**   Amelia Earhart made her historic flights in an earlier era when women were often expected to take a backseat to men. Did her decision to fly alone come from a belief that women are superior to men? That would be going further than the passage does. Choices (2), (3), and (4) raise issues that were not mentioned in the passage and seem irrelevant. The correct answer is (5).

4. **3**   When there is a photo or cartoon, it is important to read the caption very carefully. There were two important clues in this caption: the television is black and white, and the year is 1954. Keep that in mind as you read the answer choices looking for an advertising claim that could NOT have been made back then. The correct answer is (3): Color television sets weren't in use until the 1960s.

5. **4**   Always read the chart first; in this case it shows changes in employment in an number of fields. Now, go through the answer choices. Was there an increase in agricultural jobs? Actually, no there was a decline, so eliminate (1). Was there more growth in administrative support than in any other occupation? No, services had more growth, so eliminate (2). Was there more growth in administrative support than there was in services and technicians and support jobs combined? No, services *alone* had a bigger increase, so eliminate (3). Was there less growth in precision production than in professional specialties? Well, yes, as a matter of fact, there was! This is probably the answer, but let's just check (5). Was there more growth in marketing and sales than in executive, administration, and managerial jobs? Nope. Marketing and Sales rose slightly less than Executive, Administrative, Managerial, according to the chart, so the correct answer is (4).

6. **2**   If high literacy rates go hand-in-hand with industrialization, then there is a link between economic and educational well-being, which is (2). If you were tempted by (4), you were almost right, but just having money for books doesn't necessarily mean that education will be improved. If you didn't know the meaning of *agrarian* (having to do with farming) in (3), you would have had to guess, but you probably know from reading newspapers that there are lots of countries that rely on farming but still have schools.

7. **4**   The author says that because of his inability to control inflation, Jimmy Carter was a bad president. The correct answer, (4), points out that while he may not have been able to control inflation, he accomplished other important things during his presidency that may have been more important in the end. Choices (2) and (3) were irrelevant to the question, because whatever happened before or after Carter's presidency doesn't really matter. While a certain amount of inflation may be good for a country, it doesn't really counter the author's argument that inflation was out of control, so choice (1) bites the dust. And whether or not Carter was weak on foreign policy, the question is asking for a criticism of the passage. Choice (5) seems to agree with the passage, so it can be crossed off.

8. **3** The chart shows the life expectancy rates for men and women in different countries. This question wants to know which group will have the shortest life span. As you look at the chart, you'll notice that women live longer than men in all three countries—which eliminates (1), (2), and (5). Whose life span is shorter: American men or Japanese men? The chart shows the correct answer is (3).

9. **3** Japan's life expectancy is just a bit higher than the other countries. Which of the answer choices accounts for that? Choices (1) and (2) don't supply a reason why Japanese people live longer. Choice (1) discusses Asian men—which could include men from many other Asian countries and doesn't address Japanese women. Choice (2) seems to be a reason why Americans should live longer. Choice (4) is in the right direction at least, but for the most part, natural disasters don't come along that often, and statistically don't change life expectancy much. Actually, there are more earthquakes in Japan than there are in the United States. Choice (5) tells us about birth rates, which don't have that much to do with life expectancy. The correct answer is (3) because it supplies a possible reason why people live longer in Japan: free healthcare.

10. **5** America is a great place, but (1) is unfortunately a little too optimistic. (2) incorrectly says immigrants do not expect to find jobs in the United States. The passage states that they come "in search of new opportunities." The passage makes clear that the United States fosters its reputation as a melting pot by putting up symbols of its openness such as the Statue of Liberty, so we can eliminate (3). The passage makes clear that there is *every* reason for immigrants to believe they can find opportunity in the United States, so we can eliminate (4). The correct answer is (5), which restates what is said in the passage.

11. **1** The answer to this question can be found in the last sentence of the first paragraph: "new opportunities…and an environment free from political unrest and oppression." The correct answer is (1), which simply restates that sentence.

12. **5** Choice (1) can be found in paragraph 2. Choice (2) can be found in paragraph 3. Choices (3) and (4) can be found in the last sentence of paragraph 1. Only choice (5) is not directly supported by the article.

13. **4** This advertisement shows an example of the bigotry shown to new immigrants back in the 1850s. The writer of the advertisement clearly doesn't want any new immigrants coming to the United States or holding office here. So which of the answer choices would this writer disagree with? The correct answer is (4), which proposes a law giving immigrants the right to vote—something the writer clearly would have hated. All the other answer choices were suggestions of ways to keep immigrants or their goods out of the country.

14. **5** You may remember from Chapter 14 of this book that free-market economies set prices based only on supply and demand—which gives you the correct answer to this question: (5). If you didn't know that, you could still have eliminated some answer choices. Emissions standards for cars are set by the government—and the definition in the passage says regulation of industry doesn't happen in a strict free-market economy. Cross off (1). A national health-care system might or might not be able to exist in a free market. The same is true for deposits on bottles to promote recycling. Businesses themselves *could* set up recycling, but it's more likely something the government would do—so cross off (2) and (3). Antitrust laws are created by a government to keep businesses in line—something unlikely to be encouraged in a strict free-market economy, so cross off (4).

15. **2** Which of the answer choices would break up a monopoly (which is when one company becomes the only company to make something, thereby forcing everyone who wants that thing to buy it from the company at whatever price the company sets)? Choices (1), (3), and (4) all actually help a large company to prosper. Choice (5) forces a company to pay taxes, but that doesn't prevent a monopoly. Only (2) does that, by breaking up a big company into smaller companies, none of which could control a market.

16. **5** The graph shows that the least crisis-prone industry is oil refining, which is (5). You may have felt that in this day and age, oil refining is actually pretty crisis-prone. But on the GED, all we have to do is read the graph and write down what it says.

17. **3** You might have been tempted to pick (5) because Speaker E was in favor of community involvement. But the key term in the question was "and support an audit of local education spending." This meant we wanted Speaker C, who believes there is a lot of wasteful spending and wants to examine how the money is spent. Answer (3) is correct.

18. **4** Speaker B wants to abandon public schools completely. He is "out of here." That makes him different from all the other speakers who each may have their own agenda, but who all want to try to fix the system. The correct answer is (4).

19. **1** Speaker A says public schools need money from the government. Speaker C says we need to better spend the money we already get from the government. The correct answer is (1). State funding, religious schooling, and state-run welfare programs are not discussed by either speaker, so we can eliminate (2), (4), and (5). You could argue that Speaker C believes that the community should be the ones to examine how the money is spent—but he/she doesn't say this.

20. **1** Choices (2), (3), (4), and (5) all give opinions that paint a rosy picture of improvements in technology. Only (1) predicts a negative consequence: that new technology will enable companies to cut their workforce, throwing people into unemployment.

21. **3** As we said in Chapter 15, World War II is one of the topics the GED writers cover. Which claim would be most difficult to prove? You might not have known the exact answer to this question, but there were probably some answer choices you could rule out. So far, WWII is the only war in which nuclear weapons have been deployed, so we can eliminate (2). And it is pretty easy to prove that the war resulted in sweeping changes, so we can eliminate (4). Were there more buildings destroyed and more civilian casualties than in any other war? You might not know for sure, but you probably know that it was the largest war in history—so you probably want to cross off (1) and (5). The correct answer is (3), because communist Russia and China emerged victorious from World War II, gaining in territory and influence as a result of their victory.

22. **2** The answer to this question can be found in the second paragraph: "a sense of responsibility for one's fellow man…" Choice (2) restates these thoughts and is the correct answer. The passage doesn't mention disapproval of other religions, choice (3), or the value of hard work, choice (4), or of democracy, choice (5). Choice (1) is an attribute of Buddhist and Hindu religions.

23. **1** The answer to this question comes in the first sentence of the third paragraph: "Buddhists and Hindus, like Jews and Christians, believe that conduct in life determines the quality of what comes afterward." The correct answer is (1). Choices (2) and (4) relate mostly to Buddhism and Hinduism. Choices (3) and (5) relate mostly to the Judeo-Christian religions.

24. **1** The answer to this question comes from the first paragraph: "These beliefs profoundly affect not only how people view death, but how they try to live their lives." Choice (5) is never discussed in the passage, so we can eliminate it. Only some of the religions in the article share a belief in heaven, so eliminate (4). Choice (3) is too broad for it to be completely true. Choice (2) is not discussed in the passage. The correct answer is (1), which restates the first paragraph of the article.

25. 4 Each of the first three answer choices says bad things about the U.S. Constitution, which does not make any of them likely contenders to be correct. Choice (5) says the Constitution can't reflect the goals of its country, which is just silly. So the correct answer must be (4), which says that our interpretations of the Constitution have changed over time. This is illustrated by the example of Congress finally changing its mind about a peacetime draft.

26. 2 This graph shows some statistics about people called to jury duty, broken down by household income. (1) is contradicted by the graph because a greater percentage of higher-income people are called than lower-income people. (3) is contradicted by the graph because only 15 percent of the lower-income people called actually served on juries, a lower percentage than the higher-income people called. Choices (4) and (5) are not in any way supported by the passage.

27. 1 According to the passage, the problem with nuclear power is where to store dangerous by-products. If there was a better way to store these by-products, there might be an increased use of nuclear power. That is exactly what (1) proposes. The other answer choices all propose options that would increase use in non-nuclear sources of energy.

28. 5 All three forms of energy production involve turbines. Erosion is only a problem with hydroelectric power. Waste, smoke, and smog are produced only with fossil fuels and nuclear power.

29. 2 Choices (3) and (4) would make no sense, because a community with large coal or oil reserves would presumably be less likely to use hydroelectric power. A desert community might want to use hydroelectric power, but would have little chance to use one without a source of water. Choice (5) is a good possibility because a community with elevated oil prices might be looking for an alternative, but (2) is the best answer.

30. 2 Some of the answer choices are clearly ridiculous, so the first thing to do is cross off the choices you're sure are wrong. The phonograph, the telephone, and the printing press surely have little to do with popularizing fossil fuel. Gas is a fossil fuel, so you might have thought the gas meter might somehow be important. But we know from the passage that the steam turbine is how fossil fuel is converted to energy. The best answer is (2).

31. 4 Muir was clearly a conservationist. He would have hated (1), (2), and (5) because they are all rationalizations for destroying the environment. Choice (3) was difficult to understand: "Human benefit" could mean almost anything. The best answer is (4).

32. 4 The global map shows four points. From west to east, the four points are D, B, A, and C. The correct answer is (4).

Science Test Explanations

1. 3 The graph shows seismometer waves from two different earthquakes. Unlike some graphs, the left side of this graph is not a scale going from 0 to 100 or from 0 to anything. Instead, it is a scale of amplitude that shows change. At R1 in both Nicaragua and in Fault City, there is essentially no amplitude measurement, as shown by the flat lines. Then, suddenly, the earthquakes hit, as evidenced by the rapid series of waves you can see in each line. Now, let's look at the question. If you picked (1), you thought the Nicaraguan quake was stronger because it was higher on the graph than the Fault City quake. However, as we said, the left side of the graph was not that kind of a scale. The correct answer is (3), as shown by the larger series of waves in the Fault City quake.

2. 1 If you wanted to predict earthquakes, which of the points on the graph would be most critical? If you said R1, you are exactly correct. All the other points are located in moments when the earthquake has already hit—making them useless in terms of foretelling an earthquake.

3. 4   Judd Island, in the middle of the Blue River, has apparently gotten narrower and smaller since 1975, according to the two diagrams. What would account for that? Choice (1) doesn't make sense, because if the water level fell, the island would presumably get bigger. Choice (2) doesn't seem too likely because most rivers don't have tides; oceans do. Choice (3) is also unlikely because continental drift affects entire continents, not small islands in the middle of a river. Choice (4) makes sense for an island in the middle of a river. Choice (5) also seems unlikely given the facts we know. Therefore, the best answer is (4).

4. 1   A dam downriver from the island would make the water level rise, making the island appear smaller. The correct answer is (1). Choice (2) might have seemed tempting because there likely would be less erosion if the river was dammed. However, the water level would be rising too. Choice (3) says the effect of dams is "always" very slight—that seems kind of a sweeping, general assessment, and those are usually wrong.

5. 4   The answer to this question can be found in the last line of the first paragraph: "could not sustain flight." This means the archaeopteryx was incapable of flying. The correct answer is (4). If you picked (2) or (3), you were probably looking at the last lines of the second paragraph. However, the second paragraph gives the viewpoint of ornithologists, not the paleontologists that the question asks about.

6. 5   The first sentence of the second paragraph tells us ornithologists believe the archaeopteryx was a bird. Which answer choice was a kind of bird? There was only one: (5), the parrot.

7. 2   The answer to this question was in the second sentence of the second paragraph: "As evidence, they point to fossil remains…" The correct answer is (2). Choices (1) and (3) are impossible because the animal is now extinct. Choice (4) seems possible, but wasn't mentioned. Choice (5) is also impossible because there were no humans to write about this stuff in the time of the dinosaurs.

8. 3   The volume of solids or liquids cannot easily be halved. Only a gas that has no set volume or shape can be made to fit into a smaller container. The correct answer is (3), C only.

9. 3   Below 32 degrees Fahrenheit, water exists as a solid: ice. From 32 degrees to 212 degrees, it exists as a liquid. From 212 degrees on up, it exists as a gas (water vapor). The correct order is (3).

10. 1   In the passage, only a solid is described as being elastic, which means that after it is struck, it slowly regains its former shape (unless the force was too great). If element Y springs back to its former shape, it can only be a solid. The correct answer is (1).

11. 3   To find out if the church bell is not rung during the winter, the best alternative is comment C: to call someone who lives near the church to see if, in fact, it is being rung. If you picked a choice that involved comments B, D, or E, you had zeroed in on a possible cause of the strange phenomenon—but that wasn't what this question was asking. The correct answer is (3).

12. 5   This question asks for a possible explanation of why the family couldn't hear the bell. B, D, and E provide possible causes, so the correct answer is (5). A directly contradicts the question itself, which says, "If the church bell was, in fact, rung…" C is not an explanation, but a method to find out information.

13. 3   The only comment that is NOT a possible explanation of the phenomenon is comment C, which is instead a possible method to find out information. The correct answer is choice (3).

14. 4   If sound traveled faster than light, then you would *hear* the lightning before you saw it, so we can eliminate (1). Choice (2) sounds vaguely scientific, so if you aren't sure, hold onto this one. Choice (3) just seems to go against common sense: Thunder and lightning *must* be related. If light travels faster than sound, you would see the flash before you heard it—which exactly explains the phenomenon being described in the question. Choice (4) is probably the correct answer, but let's just look at (5): Does thunder cause lightning? Chances are you know it's the other way around. The best answer to this question is (4).

15. 1   When the moon is full, tides are higher along coastlines, so the effects of a hurricane would be worst during a full moon. This means we can eliminate (2), (3), and (4). We are down to (1) and (5). Would a hurricane cause more flooding at high tide or at low tide during a full moon? The correct answer is (1).

16. 1   We are looking for a reason that this flower would bloom only at night. (2) would, if anything, be a reason for it to bloom during the day. Choices (3), (4), and (5) give us information that doesn't have anything to do with why it blooms at night. The fact that the flower has the same pistils and stamens that other flowers do, does not explain its odd behavior. The soil the flower grows in seems to have no bearing, nor does its root structure, which resembles that of a flower we know blooms during the day. The best answer is (1): If the flower can only be pollinated by a particular moth that only flies at night, then there would be no need for the flower to bloom during the daytime.

17. 5   If Pluto is sometimes farther from the Sun than Neptune and sometimes not, that implies that its orbit is elliptical. The passage states that Neptune's "unchanging" orbit is 2.8 billion miles from the Sun, which means that its orbit must be circular. If Neptune is *sometimes* the farther from the Sun and sometimes not, then Pluto's elliptical orbit must sometimes make it the farthest object from the Sun, and sometimes not. So, Neptune's orbit must be circular, and Pluto's orbit must be elliptical. The correct answer is (5). Choice (1) is patently wrong because the passage tells us Pluto is the farthest object from the Sun in our solar system. Choice (2) is exactly contrary to what we are told in the passage, so eliminate it. No moons are ever mentioned in the passage, so we can eliminate (3) as well.

18. 2   Each day on Earth lasts 24 hours because that's how long it takes the earth to make one complete turn on its axis. A day on Jupiter, a planet much larger than the earth, lasts only ten Earth-hours. How does this happen? The correct answer is (2): Jupiter spins faster. If you weren't sure of the answer, were there choices you could eliminate? The number of Jupiter's moons would have no effect on how long its day is, nor would Jupiter's composition, nor the fact that the distance between it and Earth changes throughout the year—so you may have been able to eliminate (1), (3), and (5). If you were a bit confused between what creates days and nights (the spinning of a planet) and what creates seasons and years (the rotation of a planet around a star—in this case, the Sun), then you might have picked (4).

19. 3   To find the right answer, you need to read each of the three statements and figure out whether it is true. Statement A says cheddar cheese has the same amount of fat as whole milk—but the chart says cheddar has 8 grams of fat in 1 ounce, while milk has 8 grams in a cup. Ounces and cups are different amounts of measurement, so statement A isn't true, which means we can eliminate (1), (4), and (5). We are down to B only or C only. Statement B says a cup of sour cream would have more protein than a tablespoon of sour cream. At first glance, that would seem to make sense—but when you read the chart, it turns out there is no protein in sour cream at all, whether a tablespoon OR a cup. This means (2) can be eliminated, and the correct answer must be (3). Checking the chart, a cup of whole milk does contain the same amount of protein as fat.

20. 2   Just do the math. A cup of whole milk is 150 calories. A cup of cheddar is well over 800 calories. An ounce of cream cheese is 100 calories. A tablespoon of sour cream is 25 calories. An ounce of cream cheese plus an ounce of cheddar cheese is 215 calories. The correct answer is (2).

21. **3** In general, the deeper fossils are found in the ground, the older they are. If there are two rock layers, one on top of the other, probably the lower rock layer is older than the one closest to the surface. Whether the layers are composed of shale or came from the 1900s is impossible to tell from the information given—as is whether one layer is heavier than another, so we can eliminate (1), (2), and (4). Choice (5) is possible, because seismic activity will sometimes change the layering of parts of the earth—however, the question asked which conclusion was "most likely." The correct answer is (3).

22. **4** The chart shows you where different forms of energy waves show up on a frequency chart. Extra-low frequencies show up at the low end and X rays and gamma rays show up at the high end of the spectrum. Visible light is actually only a very small portion of the spectrum. Reading the chart, visible light shows up between 10^{14} and 10^{16}. The correct answer is (4).

23. **5** None of the items on this list fits into the infrared light category, so we can eliminate (1). Some of the items on this list (such as AM radios) do not fit into the microwave category, so we can eliminate (2). None of the items on this list fits into the extra-low frequency category, so forget (3). "Ionizing radiation" is a larger category that you will find at the top right of the chart. None of the items on the list fits into that category, so eliminate (4). The correct answer is (5). You will find "Nonionizing radiation" at the top left of the chart.

24. **5** The question says certain bees see energy waves that are only slightly higher in frequency than visible light. Which of the answer choices has a frequency *slightly* higher than visible light? That's right: The correct answer is choice (5), ultraviolet light.

25. **1** When the freezing point of a liquid is lowered, it means that the liquid will stay liquid a bit longer before freezing. Salt prevents water from freezing at 32 degrees Fahrenheit as it normally would. That's why we put salt on roads in the winter—to keep rain from freezing and to melt snow. Another example of this phenomenon is (1), the correct answer. Saltwater, found in oceans, almost never freezes—in part because the salt lowers the freezing point of the ocean. Choice (2) completely reverses what actually happens in real life. Choice (3) is technically true, but has nothing to do with freezing; ditto (4) and (5).

26. **2** Choice (1) gets the information in the passage backward. We see color because that color is reflected back to us, not absorbed. Cross off (1). Choice (2) gets the information right exactly—it is the correct answer. Choices (3) and (4) again maintain that we see colors that are *absorbed* by the object, rather than *reflected* by the object, so cross them off. Choice (5) is confusing because if the apple reflects all three colors, then it should be either multicolored, or some combination of the three colors—a sort of brown—and we know that it is actually red. So (5) can't be the answer either.

27. **2** Using three different drugs at the same time was the method the scientist employed in his experiment. The correct answer is (2).

28. **5** This question is about the scientist's study of one particular virus, so our categories can relate only to that study. The evolution of OTHER species is not specifically related to this study. The easy answers to eliminate are (1) the problem, (2) a method, and (3) a finding. Now, let's tackle choice (4): Is the fact that other species have evolved for thousands of years an assumption? Rereading the definition of an assumption, we are told that an assumption "is not yet proven." Since many scientists agree that evolution has been scientifically proven, we cannot say this is an assumption. The best answer is choice (5).

29. **3** The result, after the three different drugs are used to affect the virus, is that the virus becomes much less dangerous. This is what the scientist discovered. The category for that discovery is called a "finding," choice (3).

30. **4** The first line of the passage states that "viruses may be able to evolve in much the same way that other living species do." This is an assumption, as yet unproven, on which this scientist is pinning his hopes. The correct answer is (4). You may have been tempted to pick (1), "the problem," (which is defined as the major topic being studied), but the problem in this case probably would have been defined as "Can a harmful virus be forced to evolve to the point where it is no longer harmful?"

31. **3** If the virus actually mutated as a result of the three drugs, that would be something the scientist actually discovered, a finding. The correct answer is (3).

32. **4** Because the only part of a coral reef that is alive is its vulnerable outer edge, it can be affected by anything that threatens that outer edge—including a hurricane, global warming, pollution, and a drop in sea level. The only thing that wouldn't affect the *outer* layer would be something that affects only the (already dead) inner layer. The correct answer is (4).

33. **2** When water freezes it gets bigger in volume, but it still weighs exactly the same—although the molecules get stretched, they are still the same molecules. So, if a block of ice is *melted*, it would still weigh the same, but if you measured the water, it would be a bit smaller than it had been when it was frozen. Which answer choice says that? The correct answer is (2). If you picked (1), you probably mixed up volume and mass. Mass is (for the purposes of the GED) basically the same as weight.

Reading Test Explanations

1. **3** To answer this evaluation question, use Process of Elimination. There is no discussion of jealousy, choice (2), or loneliness, choice (4). Although they talk about money and about where to live, both topics are just indicative of the larger problem of incompatibility.

2. **4** To understand Mrs. Mortar's character, quickly read through only her lines. Her anger and frustration with her niece portray her as a very demanding character. There is plenty of evidence to disprove all four other choices. In lines 1–4, she is not supportive, so eliminate choice (1). In lines 35–37, we learn that she is not easygoing or thoughtful, so cross off (2) and (3). Lines 46–50 and 61–62 show how opinionated she is, which is the opposite of indifferent, choice (5).

3. **5** With this stage direction, the playwright shows Martha's discomfort. Instead of engaging in the conversation with her aunt, she tries to distract herself from it by tidying up and hurrying through her words. Earlier in her speech, another relevant stage direction appears: "Rapidly, anxious to end the whole thing." We cannot deduce that Martha is hardworking, neat, wishing to write, or selfish from this direction.

4. **2** Reread the beginning of this excerpt to answer this comprehension passage. Martha suggests a trip to London in lines 5–7 and 10–14. She pushes her idea further in lines 57–60. None of the other choices is mentioned.

5. **4** Martha thinks Mrs. Mortar's accusation that "you're trying to get rid of me" is so ludicrous that she mockingly suggests they will dig up treasure when her aunt departs. Choices (1), (2), and (5) can be eliminated because they have no textual support.

6. 1   In this quotation, "act" does not refer to Mrs. Mortar's occupation, so cross out (2). There is no reason to remind the audience that Mrs. Mortar is leaving since that has been the topic of conversation, so eliminate (3). Martha does not experience jealousy in this passage, so (4) is wrong. Although the audience may feel sorry for Mrs. Mortar, it is unlikely since the playwright has made her as insufferable as possible, so eliminate (5). The audience will side with Martha and her impatience with her aunt, so (1) is the correct answer.

7. 4   The language Mrs. Mortar uses and what we know of her character so far clearly suggest pride. The two women do not discuss the quantity of money available, its source, or bank accounts.

8. 5   Reread the fourth paragraph for grandmother's motivation to keep the badger alive. She says, "I like to have him come out and watch me when I'm at work," which suggests she enjoys his company. There is no support for any of the other choices.

9. 3   This is a synthesis question. Because half the passage is spent describing the girl's quiet time with nature, choice (3) is the best answer. She says she is a little afraid of snakes, so (1) is not correct. There is no proof that she is afraid of her grandmother, wants to feed chickens, or doesn't want to do chores, so you can eliminate (2), (4), and (5).

10. 2   Line 28 describes the girl's "new feeling of lightness and content" when her grandmother leaves, so (2) is the best answer. Although she may have been slightly afraid or worried about snakes, she is more delighted than anything, so eliminate (1) and (3). There is no mention of her feeling hungry or sleepy, so eliminate (4) and (5).

11. 4   Lines 40–50 focus on the details and wonder of the garden, so (4) is the best answer. Natural disasters and urban settings are not mentioned. The girl is not afraid of the animals she is watching, and although the girl knows something about the wildlife, she is not demonstrating it.

12. 4   This is a synthesis question. After reading the whole passage, cross out the least likely answers. Growing vegetables is not described as easy (1). Although dangers may be present in the garden, they are not the focal point (2). As the passage proceeds, the girl's worries dissolve (3). Sleep is used as a metaphor in the last sentence; it is not used to describe the girl. Even though she is lying down, she is not asleep (5).

13. 2   To tackle this evaluation question, use Process of Elimination. The movie cannot be a documentary because the characters are roles played by professional actors, so eliminate (1). Hoffman spent 13 months researching his role, but the filming time added to these months, so eliminate (3). Although the reviewer describes the movie as a masterpiece, he or she does not mention the Academy Awards, so cross off (4). This statement may be true, but is not discussed in the review, so eliminate (5). The reviewer raves about the movie from every angle, so (2) is the best.

14. 4   The sixth paragraph elaborates on the talent and attention to detail Hoffman brought to the role. Lines 56–58 are the transition between the reviewer's analysis of Hoffman and of Cruise. Because the reviewer uses the phrase "equal to the task," it shows that Cruise has the talent to create a complicated and believable character in a "flawless" performance.

15. 2   The review talks about "the bond that develops between the brothers" in lines 33–34. The third sentence clearly states, "their relationship is the heart of the classic 1980s film." This bond is the crux of the story, and, therefore, the presence of Raymond's illness as such a large part of the film must serve to define their relationship. The only answer choice that begins to address their relationship is (2).

16. 4   Lines 50–53 explore how Hoffman prepared for his role. The only answer choice that matches up with the list in the passage is (4). This is a great question on which to practice Process of Elimination!

17. 4 First, think about what "not unpredictable" really means: predictable. Then cross off any answer choices that do not have to do with prediction. Choice (4) is the best answer because it is the only one that ponders the audience's anticipation.

18. 3 Lines 27–30 state, "Raymond cannot survive without constant, protective supervision, which is very wearing on Charlie." The exhaustion factor is most likely to cause tension. Raymond is rich, so the expense of his doctors is not an issue. The review calls the Buick a link between the brothers rather than a source of tension, so get rid of (2). The passage does not mention that Charlie has memorization ability or that Raymond cannot speak, so eliminate (4) and (5).

19. 5 Turn this question into a statement to answer it. Replace "who or what" with each of the answer choices to avoid any pronoun confusion. The messenger is the rose, as stated in lines 1–4.

20. 2 Sarcasm is a type of irony in which the speaker says something that seems positive but is actually very negative. For example, the speaker wonders why no one has sent her a limousine instead of sharing how much the rose touched her. Her feelings at receiving the rose are unexpectedly negative. She masks it in praise by saying "it's always just my luck to get / One perfect rose" in the last two lines.

21. 2 This application question asks you to take the knowledge from the passage and apply it to a real situation. All the answer choices, except (2), describe household objects worn down by use rather than catastrophe. Plan 2 clearly indicates that it will cover only systems broken down by "normal wear." Choice (2) is the correct answer because it describes an appliance destroyed by a hurricane, which is not "normal wear."

22. 1 Lines 36–38 explicitly state that the company would not cover items still under manufacturer's warranty. Choice (2) is a misreading of lines 38–39. The policy specifically states, "It doesn't matter how old your appliances or systems are," so eliminate (3) and (4). The policy specifically will cover items damaged by normal wear and tear, so eliminate (5).

Math Test Explanations

1. 2 This relatively easy math problem simply requires you to read the bar graph. What percent of moviegoers said they preferred mysteries? 22 percent. The correct answer is (2).

2. 1 This setup problem asked you to write an equation. The correct answer is (1). If you picked (3), you switched the price of the first-class and the second-class tickets. If you picked (2), you thought it was okay to add the prices together and then multiply by the total number of tickets; this is incorrect because they sold different numbers of first-class and second-class tickets.

3. 4 To solve this algebraic equation, subtract 3 from both sides (which leaves you with $4x = 16$) and then divide both sides by 4. The correct answer for x is 4.

4. 1 An average is always the total amount divided by the number of things being averaged. This question is asking for the total amount. You can find it by multiplying the number of shoes times the average price (use your calculator!): $45 \times 37.20 = \$1,674.00$.

5. 4 The post office is located halfway between points A and E. Using the diagram, we can calculate that the distance between A and E is 23 miles. Therefore, the post office is located 11.5 miles from A and 11.5 miles from E, right in the middle. Which two points on the diagram is the post office between? The correct answer is (4).

6. 4   Any question about planes, trains, automobiles (or boats) is about the distance formula $R \times T = D$. The sailboat is sailing at a constant rate of 14 miles per hour (which is pretty good for a sailboat). So, how far would it travel in 2 hours? That's right: $2 \times 14 = 28$.

7. 3   Again we'll need the distance formula. The rate (14 mph) × the time (x) = the distance (50 miles), or $14 \times x = 50$. Solve for x, which equals 3.5 hours, the correct answer.

8. 5   In your mind, drive along with the delivery van. It starts off with 962 pounds of newspaper, then gets rid of 345 pounds and then another 218 pounds and then picks up 1,048 pounds. So far, we have $962 - 345 - 218 + 1,048$, which is (5).

9. 86,000   To the nearest thousand, the correct answer is $86,000. If the price had been *less* than $85, 500, the correct answer would have been $85,000.

10. 5   To find the answer to this question, we need the total amount of the check, and then we need to divide by the number of people who are splitting the check. Unfortunately, there's just one problem: We don't know how many people are splitting the check. The correct answer is (5), Not enough information is given.

11. (–5, 1)   If you start at (0, 0) in the middle of the grid on the *x*-axis, count over 5 numbers to the left to negative 5. Then go up one. That is point A. It is in the upper left quadrant of the grid as shown here. If you're having trouble with coordinate grids, you might reread Chapter 26.

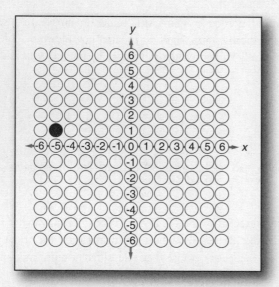

12. 4   Read the information in the chart before you read the question, but don't try to memorize it all—after all, there are only three questions. To answer this question, all you have to do is add up the percentages of the two stain repellents: $1.44 + 0.06$. The correct answer is (4).

13. 4   You could write a complicated equation, or you could backsolve. Let's start with the middle answer choice (3) and assume the sales tax is 7 percent. What is 7 percent of $8.00? Use your calculator, or take away two decimal places from $8.00 to find 1 percent (8 cents) and multiply by 7 to get 56 cents. The answer is supposed to be 64 cents, so we know (3) isn't correct, and we know we need a bigger number. Let's try answer (4), and assume the sales tax is 8 percent. What is 8 percent of $8.00? Use your calculator, or take away two decimal places from $8.00 to find 1 percent (8 cents) and multiply by 8. The answer is 64 cents, which is exactly what it's supposed to be. The correct answer is (4).

14. **2** It is easy to get confused when there are so many different numbers in a problem, some of which aren't even necessary. Try to stay focused on just what you need to answer the question. You need to know the total weight of 8 bags of stain guard. How much does one bag weigh? According to the chart, one bag weighs three-and-a-half pounds or 1.59 kilograms. The answer choices are all in kilograms, so let's use 1.59. Simply multiply 1.59 times 8. The answer is (2). If you picked (3), you found the weight in pounds and didn't notice the answer choices were in kilograms.

15. **200** The classic mistake here is to find 60 percent of $120, or $72. Unfortunately, if you read the question closely, the $120 is 60 percent of Karen's entire paycheck. In other words, what you needed to do was find 60 percent of a number we don't know yet, and *that* equals $120. You can't use your calculator in this section of the test, so let's say this out loud in English and see if we can translate. "$120 is 60 percent of my paycheck." Let's translate that word for word: $120 = $\frac{60}{100}x$. Solving for x, the answer is 200.

16. **5** You might think the answer was (1), which really does equal 3.5 percent of $1,000. However, there's one thing missing here. When does the brother pay back Gary? If he never pays him, Gary will be receiving 3.5 percent every year forever. If he pays Gary back next week, Gary will receive much less than 3.5 percent of $1,000. To know the total amount of interest, we would need to know how long before the loan was paid back. The correct answer is (5).

17. **4** This was another problem where there was more information given than you really needed. After one day, the amount of water in the reservoir had doubled from its original amount. After five days, the amount of water had quadrupled from its original amount. Here's the part you may not have noticed: If all we need to know is how much water there was after *five* days, the fact that it doubled after the *first* day is irrelevant. If x represents the original amount, the correct answer is (4), $4x$.

18. **1** If the wheel turns 2,400 times in an hour, how many times does it turn in one minute? Before we do any math, let's use common sense. In only a minute, there will be a *lot* fewer revolutions, right? So which answer choices are kind of crazy? Certainly (3) and (4) produce numbers that are even more that there were in an entire hour—that can't be right, so we can eliminate them. (2) is a *little* less, but we need a *lot* less. To find the answer, simply divide the number of revolutions in an hour (2,400) by the number of minutes in an hour (60). The correct answer is (1).

19. **4** We need to find the volume of this rectangular space. The formula is on the first page of the GED Math test booklet, as always. Length times width times height. The correct answer is $17 \times 8 \times \frac{1}{2}$, or 68.

20. **2** For this setup problem we need to find the perimeter of the courtyard. Two walls are 130 feet long each, so that's 2(130). One wall is 70 feet long. And then there are the walls on either side of the doorway, which are 2(20). The correct answer is (2). If you picked (3), you forgot about the wall with the doorway in it. If you picked (5), you found the perimeter of the four-sided courtyard as if there had been no doorway.

21. **3** This is another problem that can most easily be backsolved. Start with the middle answer (3). Let's assume that Jar S is the answer. It has a volume of 16 ounces. If we increase it by 25 percent (or one quarter), how big will it be? One quarter of 16 ounces is 4 ounces, so the new jar will hold 20 ounces—and, in fact, that is just what it is supposed to hold. Choice (3) is the correct answer.

22. $\frac{1}{2}$ To find the probability of something happening, add up all the chances of it happening, and put that sum over the total number of possible outcomes. In this case, there are 20 chances that Mark will draw a penny. That becomes our numerator. The total number of possible outcomes is 8 + 12 + 20 or 40, which becomes our denominator. Therefore, the correct answer is $\frac{20}{40}$ or $\frac{1}{2}$.

23. **3** If you are rusty on the distributive property, reread Chapter 23. Most of the answer choices here are much bigger than 18. The correct answer is (3).

24. **2** The angles of a triangle always add up to 180 degrees. In this setup problem, you have to write an expression using the two angles we already know to find the measure of the angle we don't know. The correct answer is (2), which subtracts those two angles from 180 degrees. What's left is the measure of the third angle. If you picked (1), you forgot we were dealing with a triangle and used the measure of a rectangle, which has 360 degrees. If you picked (5), you got confused about the parentheses around 34 – 55. Choice (5) would have been correct had it read "180 – 34 – 35," but 180 – (34 – 35) means something entirely different.

25. **4** The volume of a cube is the length of a side cubed; in this case, 3 × 3 × 3, or 27.

26. **2** There are two ways to solve this problem about a right triangle. First, you might have noticed that this was a 3-4-5 right triangle (which we covered in Chapter 26). Second, you could use the Pythagorean theorem ($a^2 + b^2 = c^2$). If you plug in x for a, 4 for b and 5 for c, you will find that x equals 3. The correct answer is (2).

27. **1** To find the angle x, we need to know the *other* two angles in that triangle. We are told that the Green Line is perpendicular to the Lakeshore Line, which means the lowest angle of that triangle is 90 degrees. Because the County Line and the Mountain Line are parallel to each other, and the small angle formed by the intersection of the Mountain Line and the Lakeshore Line is 60 degrees, we can use Fred's Theorem to show that the angle at the left of the triangle is equal to 60 degrees as well. If the lower angle is 90 degrees and the angle on the left is 60 degrees, then angle x must equal 30 degrees. The answer is (1).

28. **2** You may not have known what a rise and a run were—but you know what a ratio is. In this case, we are told steepness is measured by the ration of the rise to the run. $\frac{rise}{run} = \frac{5}{30} = \frac{1}{6}$. The correct answer is (2).

Scoring Guide for The Princeton Review GED Practice Tests

These half-length practice exams are designed to measure your progress as you prepare for the GED. Use the answer keys to determine the number of correct answers you selected on each section of the exam, and then consult the charts below to determine your scores.

Remember, to pass the GED in most states, no individual score can fall below 410, and the average of the five tests must be 450 or greater.

To calculate your score on the essay, you may want to ask a teacher or friend to read what you wrote and give it a score from 1 to 4 based on the criteria outlined in Part 3 of this book. If you score below a 2 on the real GED, you will be required to take the writing test again.

Language Arts, Writing

Number of Correct Answers on Part 1 (multiple choice)	Estimated GED Score (Part 2 essay score of 2.0)	Estimated GED Score (Part 2 essay score of 2.5)	Estimated GED Score (Part 2 essay score of 3.0)	Estimated GED Score (Part 2 essay score of 3.5)	Estimated GED Score (Part 2 essay score of 4.0)
25	620	660	700	740	800
24	550	590	630	670	730
23	510	550	590	630	690
22	490	530	570	610	670
21	470	510	550	590	650
20	460	500	540	580	640
19	450	490	530	570	630
18	440	480	520	560	620
17	430	470	510	550	610
16	420	460	500	540	600
15	410	450	490	530	590
14	400	440	480	520	580
13	390	430	470	510	570
12	390	430	470	510	570
11	380	420	460	500	560
10	380	420	460	500	560
9	370	410	450	490	550
8	370	410	450	490	550
7	360	400	440	480	540
6	350	390	430	470	530
5	340	380	420	460	520
4	330	370	410	450	510
3	310	350	390	410	460
2	280	320	360	400	410
1	230	270	310	350	400

Social Studies

Number of Correct Answers	Estimated GED Score
25 and up	800
24	700
23	630
22	580
21	550
20	530
19	500
18	490
17	470
16	450
15	440
14	430
13	410
12	400
11	380
10	370
9	350
8	340
7	320
6	300
5	280
4	260
3	230
2	210
1	200

Language Arts, Reading

Number of Correct Answers	Estimated GED Score
20 and up	800
19	650
18	560
17	500
16	470
15	440
14	420
13	410
12	390
11	380
10	370
9	360
8	350
7	340
6	320
5	310
4	280
3	250
2	210
1	200

Mathematics

Number of Correct Answers	Estimated GED Score
25 and up	800
24	690
23	610
22	550
21	520
20	500
19	480
18	470
17	450
16	440
15	440
14	430
13	420
12	410
11	400
10	390
9	380
8	370
7	360
6	340
5	320
4	290
3	250
2	210
1	200

Science

Number of Correct Answers	Estimated GED Score
25 and up	800
24	620
23	550
22	520
21	490
20	470
19	450
18	440
17	430
16	420
15	420
14	410
13	400
12	390
11	380
10	370
9	360
8	350
7	330
6	320
5	300
4	290
3	260
2	240
1	200

Completely darken bubbles with a No. 2 pencil. If you make a mistake, be sure to erase mark completely. Erase all stray marks.

1.

YOUR NAME: _____
(Print)   Last   First   M.I.

SIGNATURE: _____ DATE: ___/___/___

HOME ADDRESS: _____
(Print)   Number and Street

_____
City   State   Zip Code

PHONE NO.: _____
(Print)

IMPORTANT: Please fill in these boxes exactly as shown on the back cover of your test book.

2. TEST FORM

3. TEST CODE

4. REGISTRATION NUMBER

5. YOUR NAME

First 4 letters of last name | FIRST INIT | MID INIT

Name bubbles: A B C D E F G H I J K L M N O P Q R S T U V W X Y Z

6. DATE OF BIRTH

Month	Day	Year
○ JAN		
○ FEB		
○ MAR	0 0	0 0
○ APR	1 1	1 1
○ MAY	2 2	2 2
○ JUN	3 3	3 3
○ JUL		4 4 4
○ AUG		5 5 5
○ SEP		6 6 6
○ OCT		7 7 7
○ NOV		8 8 8
○ DEC		9 9 9

Test Code bubbles: 0-9, A-G, F

7. SEX
○ MALE
○ FEMALE

The Princeton Review.

Form EE Start with number 1 for each new section.
If a section has fewer questions than answer spaces, leave the extra answer spaces blank.

Section 1
1–28. ① ② ③ ④ ⑤

Section 2
1–32. ① ② ③ ④ ⑤

Section 3
1–33. ① ② ③ ④ ⑤

Section 4
1–22. ① ② ③ ④ ⑤

Section 5
1–28. ① ② ③ ④ ⑤

Completely darken bubbles with a No. 2 pencil. If you make a mistake, be sure to erase mark completely. Erase all stray marks.

1.

YOUR NAME: _____
(Print)
Last   First   M.I.

SIGNATURE: _____   DATE: ___ / ___ / ___

HOME ADDRESS: _____
(Print)
Number and Street

_____
City   State   Zip Code

PHONE NO.: _____
(Print)

5. YOUR NAME

First 4 letters of last name | FIRST INIT | MID INIT

A B C D E F G H I J K L M N O P Q R S T U V W X Y Z

IMPORTANT: Please fill in these boxes exactly as shown on the back cover of your test book.

2. TEST FORM

3. TEST CODE

4. REGISTRATION NUMBER

0 1 2 3 4 5 6 7 8 9
A B C D E F G
0 1 2 3 4 5 6 7 8 9

6. DATE OF BIRTH

Month	Day	Year
JAN		
FEB		
MAR	0 0	0 0
APR	1 1	1 1
MAY	2 2	2 2
JUN	3 3	3 3
JUL	4	4 4
AUG	5	5 5
SEP	6	6 6
OCT	7	7 7
NOV	8	8 8
DEC	9	9 9

7. SEX
MALE
FEMALE

The Princeton Review.

Form EE Start with number 1 for each new section.
If a section has fewer questions than answer spaces, leave the extra answer spaces blank.

Section 1
1–28. ① ② ③ ④ ⑤

Section 2
1–32. ① ② ③ ④ ⑤

Section 3
1–33. ① ② ③ ④ ⑤

Section 4
1–22. ① ② ③ ④ ⑤

Section 5
1–28. ① ② ③ ④ ⑤

About the Authors

Geoff Martz attended Dartmouth College and Columbia University before joining The Princeton Review as a teacher and writer. Geoff headed the development team that designed The Princeton Review's GMAT course, now taught in more than 50 cities around the country. He is the author or coauthor of *Cracking the GMAT, Cracking the ACT,* and *Paying for College Without Going Broke.*

Laurice Pearson graduated from Barnard College in 1990 and joined The Princeton Review as a teacher and development person.